KW-361-402

Public Sector Management
Volume I

The International Library of Management
Series Editor: Keith Bradley

Titles in the Series:

Public Sector Management
Volume I

Edited by

Sir John Bourn

Comptroller and Auditor General
National Audit Office, United Kingdom

Dartmouth

Aldershot · Brookfield USA · Singapore · Sydney

© Sir John Bourn 1995. For copyright of individual articles please refer to the Acknowledgements.

All rights reserved. No part of this publication may be reproduced, stored in a retrieval system, or transmitted in any form or by any means, electronic, mechanical, photocopying, recording, or otherwise without the prior permission of Dartmouth Publishing Company Limited.

Published by
Dartmouth Publishing Company Limited
Gower House
Croft Road
Aldershot
Hants GU11 3HR
England

Dartmouth Publishing Company
Old Post Road
Brookfield
Vermont 05036
USA

British Library Cataloguing in Publication Data
Public Sector Management. –
(International Library of Management)
  I. Bourn, John II. Series
  350

Library of Congress Cataloging-in-Publication Data
Public sector management / edited by Sir John Bourn.
        p.   cm. — (The international library of management)
    Includes bibliographical references.
    ISBN 1–85521–517–9
    1. Public administration. I. Bourn, John. II. Series.
JF1351.P842   1995
350—dc20   95–7413
                                                                                    CIP

ISBN 1 85521 517 9

Printed in Great Britain at the University Press, Cambridge

Contents

PART III NEW DIRECTIONS

Acknowledgements

The editor and publishers wish to thank the following for permission to use copyrighted material.

The American Archivist for the essay: Michael A. Lutzker (1982), 'Max Weber and the Analysis of Modern Bureaucratic Organization: Notes Toward a Theory of Appraisal', *American Archivist*, **45**, pp. 119–30.

Association of Government Accountants for the essay: Charles A. Bowsher (1993), 'Budgeting and Accountability in Large Countries: Problems and Opportunities', *Government Accountants Journal*, **42**, pp. 7–20.

Blackwell Publishers UK for the essays: John Storey (1989), 'Human Resource Management in the Public Sector', *Public Money and Management*, **9**, pp. 19–24; Sue Dopson and Rosemary Stewart (1990), 'Public and Private Sector Management: The Case for a Wider Debate', *Public Money and Management*, **10**, pp. 37–40; Barry J. O'Toole (1990), 'T.H. Green and the Ethics of Senior Officials in British Central Government', *Public Administration*, **68**, pp. 337–52; Denise McAlister (1990), 'Option Appraisal: Turning an Art into a Science?', *Public Money and Management*, **10**, pp. 43–50; Neil Carter (1991), 'Learning to Measure Performance: The Use of Indicators in Organizations', *Public Administration*, **69**, pp. 85–101; Terry Banks (1990), 'Performance Measurement: The Needs of Managers and Policy Makers', *Public Money and Management*, **10**, pp. 47–9; Helen Margetts and Leslie Willcocks (1993), 'Information Technology in Public Services: Disaster Faster?', *Public Money and Management*, **13**, pp. 49–56; Christopher Hood (1991), 'A Public Management for all Seasons?', *Public Administration*, **69**, pp. 3–19; D. Harvey (1990), 'Contrast Between Fordism and Flexible Accumulation According to Swynegedouw', Table 2.8 in C. Curson (ed.), *The Condition of Post Modernity*; D. Harvey (1990), 'The Losses in World Stock Markets, October 1987', Table 2.10 in C. Curson (ed.), *The Condition of Post Modernity*; P.M. Jackson (1990), 'Public Choice and Public Sector Management', *Public Money and Management*, **10**, pp. 13–20; Theo A.J. Toonen (1993), 'Analysing Institutional Change and Administrative Transformation: A Comparative View', *Public Administration*, **71**, pp. 151–68.

Blackwell Publishers USA for the essays: Gu Jiaqi (1992), 'Restructuring Government Organization in China and Transforming Government Functions for an Efficient and More Productive Bureaucratic Performance', *Governance: An International Journal of Policy and Administration*, **5**, pp. 391–401; Amelia P. Varela (1992), 'Personnel Management Reform in the Philippines: The Strategy of Professionalization', *Governance: An International Journal of Policy and Administration*, **5**, pp. 402–22.

Conservative Political Centre and William Waldegrave for the essay: William Waldegrave (1993), *Public Service and the Future: Reforming Britain's Bureaucracies*, pp. 5–26.

Brian Cubbon, C.S. Cullerne Bown and Ray Petch (1993), 'New Relations Between Ministers and Civil Servants', *The Times*, p. 15. Published in *The Times* 15 January 1993. Copyright © Sir Brian Cubbon, C.S. Cullerne Bown and Ray Petch.

Elsevier Science Limited for the essay: Nigel Curry and Caroline Pack (1993), 'Planning on Presumption: Strategic Planning for Countryside Recreation in England and Wales', *Land Use Policy*, pp. 140–50.

Her Majesty's Stationery Office for the essay: Robert Armstrong (1985), 'The Duties and Responsibilities of Civil Servants in Relation to Ministers', *HMSO*, **26**, 128–30. Crown copyright ©.

MCB University Press for the essay: David Brookfield (1992), 'Performance Measurement: Focusing on the Key Issue', *Journal of Management in Medicine*, **6**, pp. 39–45.

Gareth Morgan (1989), 'From Bureaucracies to Networks: The Emergence of New Organizational Forms', in his *Creative Organization Theory*, pp. 64–7. Copyright © Gareth Morgan.

Christopher Pollitt (1988), 'Bringing Consumers into Performance Measurement: Concepts, Consequences and Constraints', *Policy and Politics*, **16**, pp. 77–87. Copyright © Christopher Pollitt.

Social Forces for the essay: George Ritzer (1975), 'Professionalization, Bureaucratization and Rationalization: The Views of Max Weber', *Social Forces*, **53**, pp. 627–34.

Stockton Press for the essays: Valerie Belton (1993), 'Project Planning and Prioritization in the Social Services – an OR Contribution', *Journal of the Operational Research Society*, **44**, pp. 115–24. Copyright © 1993 Operational Research Society Ltd. Jonathan Rosenhead (1992), 'Into the Swamp: The Analysis of Social Issues', *Journal of the Operational Research Society*, **43**, pp. 293–305. Copyright © 1992 Operational Research Society Ltd.

Walter de Gruyter & Company for the essay: Robert Cooper (1989), 'Modernism, Post Modernism and Organizational Analysis 3: The Contribution of Jacques Derrida', *Organization Studies*, **10**, pp. 479–502.

Every effort has been made to trace all the copyright holders but if any have been inadvertently overlooked the publishers will be pleased to make the necessary arrangement at the first opportunity.

Series Preface

The International Library of Management brings together in one series the most significant and influential articles from across the whole range of management studies. In compiling the series, the editors have followed a selection policy that is both international and interdisciplinary. The articles that are included are not only of seminal importance today, but are expected to remain of key relevance and influence as management deals with the issues of the next millennium.

The Library was specifically designed to meet a great and growing need in the field of management studies. Few areas have grown as rapidly in recent years, in size, complexity, and importance. There has been an enormous increase in the number of important academic journals publishing in the field, in the amount published, in the diversity and complexity of theory and in the extent of cross-pollination from other disciplines. At the same time, managers themselves must deal with increasingly complex issues in a world growing ever more competitive and interdependent. These remarkable developments have presented all those working in the field, whether they be theorists or practitioners, with a serious challenge. In the absence of a core series bringing together this wide array of new knowledge and thought, it is becoming increasingly difficult to keep abreast of all new important developments and discoveries, while it is becoming ever-more vital to do so.

The International Library of Management aims to meet that need, by bringing the most important articles in management theory and practice together in one core, definitive series. The Library provides management researchers, professors, students, and managers themselves, with an extensive range of key articles which, together, provide a comprehensive basis for understanding the nature and importance of the major theoretical and substantive developments in management science. The Library is the definitive series in management studies.

In making their choice, the editors have drawn especially from the Anglo-American tradition, and have tended to exclude articles which have been widely reprinted and are generally available. Selection is particularly focused on issues most likely to be important to management thought and practice as we move into the next millennium. Editors have also prefaced each volume with a thought-provoking introduction, which provides a stimulating setting for the chosen articles.

The International Library of Management is an essential resource for all those engaged in management development in the future.

KEITH BRADLEY
Series Editor
The International Library of Management

Editor's Note

I am grateful to Dr Keith Bradley who suggested that I should prepare this book of readings and write an introduction to it. I should also like to thank Mr Nicholas Sloan and Professor Christopher Pollitt for their help in compiling the readings and commenting on the introduction. None of them is responsible for any of the views expressed. They are my own.

John Bourn

Introduction

Origins

Public sector management is a product of the Industrial Revolution which, from the middle of the 18th century, greatly increased the output of manufactured goods and associated services in Western Europe and later North America. Its techniques and effects, progressively renewed and extended, have spread and continue to develop throughout the world.

One of the effects of this transformation was the development of the modern state. Many of the ideas encapsulated within the modern state – nationalism, liberty, equality, fraternity, democracy, welfare and progress – may have had distinct intellectual origins divorced from industrialism. But it was the progress of industrialism that provided the resources necessary to try to give them effect, because it is only as societies become richer that they can afford to establish and maintain institutions designed to realize these ideas in law and practice. Again, it is only as societies become more economically complex that they face the problems of providing the physical, educational, political and social infrastructures necessary to support advanced industrial and commercial activities.

This is the context of opportunity and challenge that led to the development of modern public administration in the first two-thirds of the 20th century, with its wide range of duties. These included such measures as the collection of direct and indirect taxes which even in peacetime in many modern states are equivalent to some 40–50 per cent of gross domestic product; the recruitment of mass conscript armies, their provision with advanced technological weapons, and the energizing of whole nations in pursuit of military objectives in two world wars to secure political ideals; the administration of vast schemes of social welfare, including pensions and other forms of financial assistance, as well as health and educational services for all citizens; and the public ownership and management of industries. In some countries in the Communist past, the attempt was made to own and run virtually all industries, while in most countries in Western Europe, significant industries (especially mining, transport, steel, banking and telecommunications) were brought into public control.

The great challenge for public sector management was how to run all these activities in ways that would be seen as honest, lawful and effective by the people, or at least by their legates, the popularly- or self-elected politicians. Behind them stood such stern academic assessors as economists, judging efficiency, and political scientists and philosophers gauging the extent to which public sector management could realize such democratic ideals as responsiveness to the will of the people and public accountability for the actions taken on their behalf.

Bureaucracy – The Principle

The chosen method was bureaucracy, which in this context may be taken to mean the application of late 19th-century industrial methods to public offices and enterprises. In industry, men and women were placed in charge of mechanical and other equipment, material and processes and asked to follow instructions to produce manufactured products. In government offices – perhaps the paradigm case of public sector management (though the same principle applied in banks, insurance companies and other enterprises not in public ownership) – men and women were charged with making decisions in terms of regulations set down – on tax liabilities, on entitlement to financial benefits, on the award of contracts, on the granting of permission to build houses, on the allocation of persons to schools, hospitals and many other institutions.

For this system to work effectively, everyone concerned should behave as required. This does not mean, of course, that all originality and initiative are struck out. Politicians must put forward programmes that capture the public imagination; they will need some help from officials in devising them and certainly a great deal of assistance in carrying them out. Political appointees, policy advisers, private secretaries, ministerial cabinets – all these and other arrangements at the interface between political decision making and public implementation will require men and women with intelligence, imagination, articulacy and flair. Moreover, those attending to professional activities (such as doctors, architects, engineers, teachers and policemen) will need to exercise their skills according to their professional standards and values.

However, all these activities must take place in a controlled setting according to carefully established arrangements so that clear limits may be placed on the scope and scale of officials' work. Max Weber (1864–1920) was the philosopher of bureaucracy. He saw that bureaucracy was more efficient than aristocracy, the system of public management that it largely superseded in Europe. He observed the uniformity of behaviour that can result from what many would see as the partial denial of officials' originality and independence – and hence their humanity. He understood that this uniformity and concentration could be the condition of fair and equal treatment rather than arbitrariness; of predictability rather than uncertainty; of the expertise that comes from experience and repetition; of the ability to replace one official by another in the same post and to know that the same work would be done in the same way. Furthermore, the personnel for bureaucracy were becoming available at the end of the 19th and start of the 20th century as systems of universal education for all and university education for a fair number were turning out many people with what we might now call 'middle class' values and views of life. They seemed only too happy to fit into the worlds of public and private bureaucracy and professional practice and to make a life-time career of so doing. Weber thus saw that the consistency of meaning that public officials normally attach to their actions, and the intentions which they consequently seek to pursue to fulfilment, could become important instruments of what he saw as the progressive rationalization of human life in society.

The problem, of course, was how to bind sufficient human capacities to the bureaucratic last to secure the intended outcomes; or, as it might be put, how to get two-thirds of the genie into the bottle, so that most of its behaviour would be controlled and predictable but that enough initiative should be available to cope successfully with the unexpected.

Bureaucracy – Practice

The answer was taken to lie in such arrangements as the following:

- the separation of tasks into discrete activities to promote specialization and labour division;
- the provision of rules and regulations to show how activities should be conducted, and of supervisors to oversee the process and to attend to difficulties;
- the coordination of activities through hierarchies of command operating through organized structures which were capable of depiction in the well-known 'organizational tree';
- recruitment by objective tests of competence and relevant training and socialization for particular jobs;
- life-time careers, incremental scales of payment and promotion on merit assessed in terms of the quality of the discharge of present duties and likelihood of further development.

These are the same features that many writers and practitioners considered relevant to private sector management as well. They are in fact the staples of the 'scientific' and 'classical' management thinking of the late 19th and first half of the 20th century – of F.W. Taylor, Henri Fayol, Lyndall Urwick, Luther Gulick and many others.

The application of these ideas, well expressed in the metaphor of 'organizations as machines', had great organizational successes to their credit, and the history of the 20th century would have been quite different – for good and ill – without their application. There would have been no world wars, no fascist or communist states, no welfare states and no modern-style democracies since all of these rested on public sector bureaucracies operating very largely according to the principles outlined above.

During the first 60 or so years of the 20th century, these principles were refined in many useful ways which still have continuing significance:

1. Greater attention was paid to personnel management, to understanding and seeking to apply the psychological and sociological factors that secure motivation and commitment, promote leadership and encourage effective teamwork. This was needed because, within the machine-like system of the modern bureaucracy, it was observed that officials too often lost interest in their tasks and sometimes did the very minimum of work. The popular conception of officials who, like the 'fountains in Trafalgar Square ... played from ten to four', became part of 20th-century folklore.
2. Specific concerns were voiced about 'public sector ethics'. Since the mid-19th century, public authorities had placed great emphasis on honesty, on fair dealing and on the stamping out of such activities as bribes, the appointment of relations and friends to public sector jobs and the subversion of contracting processes to determine who should win irrespective of price. All these were forbidden, not only by internal rules and special laws relating to public corruption, but also by the cultivation of the idea that public officials were committed to a special ethos of high standards and fair dealing.
3. Another development in many countries was a strict injunction that public officials should be politically neutral. Thus senior British officials took – and still take – a special pride in the belief that they can serve ministers of any political party with equal loyalty and commitment. This is not echoed in all countries; in the United States, for example, a new President appoints many officials, some with Congressional approval. The question

of whether it is possible for politically uncommitted officials to be completely supportive of ministers and other political officeholders is still a topic of live interest.

4. The idea was broached that, instead of looking at organizations as structures, they could instead be viewed as groups undertaking activities and making decisions in a disciplined and orderly way.

Such decision making was not easy. As Herbert Simon emphasized, there was seldom time, resources or knowledge for decisions to be taken by ideal criteria. Instead, operating with a 'bounded' (rather than a complete) rationality, one usually had to seek to 'satisfice' rather than to 'maximize' in terms of achieving outcomes.[1]

Many lists were proposed to cope with the increasing complexity of the decisions and operations that governments undertook. At one extreme they were short – planning, implementation, review. At the other, they could be long – issue search, issue filtration, issue definition, forecasting, determining objectives and priorities, options generation and analysis, choice of programme options, implementation, monitoring and control, evaluation, policy succession and termination.[2]

Each of these activities bred a specific literature as well as accompanying sets of experts and consultants. For example, decision-making theories and cost-benefit analyses were devised to aid in choosing programme or project options. These involved estimating the costs and benefits of each option over future periods of time; discounting the streams of costs and benefits to their present value in terms of a chosen interest or other discount rate; taking account of the relative probabilities of different outcomes or, where such situations of risk could not be specified, devising strategies for handling uncertainties.

Decision theory drew on the contributions of statisticians, economists, mathematicians and psychologists. While certainly helping managers to be more self-conscious about decision taking and sensitive to a wider range of factors, it also complicated the business of management and encouraged the use of computers and other devices for handling large amounts of data. Indeed, electronic data processing became an important aspect of many bureaucratic activities. Originally promoted as a device to reduce staff and cut costs, it has seldom worked like this in practice. Instead, new kinds of staff have been required to plan and install the systems, which in turn have provided opportunities to do more and increasingly complex work that could not have been envisaged by manual means. Indeed, countries with undeveloped professional and technical infrastructures for compiling, analysing and deploying information in support of administrative action seem likely to fall even further behind the level of economic and other development in Western European, North American and similar societies.

Bureaucracy – Problems

In spite of these new approaches and their successes, there was a marked belief in many countries by, say, 1975 that public sector management had failed and that a new approach was required. Examples of these failures included the following:

1. In nearly every case examined, it was found that the costs of public programmes exceeded their estimates and often their benefits. If the measure was cash, costs almost always

exceeded revenues. If the measure was more complex, say the ability of a weapon system to meet a designated speed, accuracy and success rate, it was seldom achieved. Moreover, programmes involving health and education always seemed to cost more and produce poorer results than planned. These failures were highlighted by the use of the very techniques of planning, analysis and control that had been introduced to make improvements in public programmes. By a strange irony, these techniques seldom seemed to promote the desired results, though they were certainly most useful in demonstrating shortcomings.

2. In many cases, it was found that public sector managers had replaced public objectives with private purposes. In some cases, this took the form of fraud and corruption, but in others it was more subtle. Research programmes designed and funded to investigate one range of phenomena were turned on their heads by the staff concerned who wished to investigate a different range. Astute wording of plans, proposals and progress reports, together with the increasing difficulty outsiders experienced in penetrating specialized programmes, were often adequate defences to enable those concerned to continue doing what most interested them irrespective of their formal remits.

3. As a variant of this fault, many public sector programmes were dominated by producer rather than consumer interests, especially if the producers were the effective monopoly suppliers of the goods and services in question, such as in transport, health and education. Sometimes, but not always, trade unions were the focus of these producer interests, effectively laying down what hours staff should work and what outputs should be produced – the whole focus being the private concerns of producers rather than the interests of consumers.

4. Public programmes often produced unintended consequences – externalities as economists call them. Thus an arms factory might pollute the land on which it tested its products, inflicting costs on future generations. A nuclear facility might endanger the health of its staff right away, as well as that of those who lived close by. The design of a housing estate might provide a ready haven for vandals and criminals, its corridors and staircases ideal for causing trouble and evading arrest. Sometimes these externalities were beyond contemporary knowledge and have only been revealed by hindsight. But often public authorities understood that disregarding externalities offered a 'free good' – the chance to carry out activities at what was, in immediate cost terms, negligible expense.

The extent to which these problems were seen as serious varied between countries. Scandinavia, Germany and France were initially less concerned than the US, the UK and Australia. But even so, by the 1970s – and certainly the 1980s – the cumulative effect of these problems convinced many commentators, politicians and ordinary citizens that public sector management had failed to achieve the promise held out for it at the turn of the century. Vast bureaucracies laboured slowly to produce disappointing results; in Communist countries the failure of the public sector in economic management was increasingly evident, the fall of the Berlin Wall in 1990 presaging the rejection of the Communist system across Europe. In Western Europe, too, nationalized industries were seen as costly and inefficient. Countries like the UK were conscious of a failure to build upon their success in the Second World War; instead, they saw a failure by successive governments to secure their objectives of economic growth and steady prices; to harness developments in science and technology in a fully effective way, or to promote rising standards of health, education and welfare quickly enough. The general judgement was one of disappointment in public sector management.

This does not mean that Western societies were failures in any sense; in most cases they advanced economically to an outstanding degree. Their populations as a whole were richer, better fed, healthier, longer lived and enjoyed more leisure, greater opportunities to travel (with the widespread ownership of cars) and the advantages of television and other aspects of electronic communication than people elsewhere. But of course these benefits were not seen as the results of public sector management.

What were the reasons for this comparative failure? One answer was that public sector management was intrinsically more difficult than private sector management for the following reasons:

- the absence of a clear 'bottom line' of profit;
- the need to balance the many interests of different pressure groups and stakeholders;
- the importance of accountability of officials to elected politicians and legislative bodies, with all that this implies in terms of careful record keeping and a culture of conformity and respect;
- the idea that the role of the public domain was 'the organization of collective purpose, the area in which collective values are pursued';[3]
- the view that public sector management involved an accommodation between three sets of values – Sigma-type values, to keep the organization lean and purposeful; Theta-type values, to keep it honest and fair; and Lambda-type values, to keep the organization robust and resilient, capable of effective response to changes and emergencies.[4]

All these were seen by many as necessary characteristics of public sector management in a modern democracy.

The results of the working of public sector management might sometimes be slow, and lessons could certainly be learned from the private sector and from academics, for instance to focus on costs and timescales and to use modern knowledge from the social and natural sciences. But in pursuing this line of argument, it is important to recognize the fundamental characteristics of good public sector management and to accept its minuses as well as its pluses. This is because, in the last analysis, traditional arrangements for public sector management were argued to be guarantors of democracy and freedom.

Bureaucracy – Paradoxes

Yet such reassurance was not enough, mainly because people felt that public sector management had not guaranteed freedom. Instead, it had propagated a subtle kind of public control so that citizens of most European, North American and other industrialized societies now accepted a degree of authoritarian state control over their lives and fortunes which made a mockery of all the hopes for freedom and self-development proclaimed during the American and French Revolutions of the 18th century and inherent in all subsequent overturnings of monarchical and aristocratic governments.

The criticism of the modern state as promoting alienation and false consciousness among citizens, reconciling them to the distortions of life in capitalist societies, was of course one aspect of the philosophy of Karl Marx. But other writers and philosophers also provided acute condemnations which went to the heart of the problems of public sector management. These were often the more effective – not only because they reached more readers – but because they were couched in the symbolic language of the novelist, the analyst of social and political affairs and the philosopher, rather than in the proclamations of the management specialist.

Franz Kafka's posthumously published novels, *The Trial* (1925) and *The Castle* (1926), portray the ordinary person wrestling with the tentacles of modern bureaucracy, accused, for example, of offences which are never specified and for which he can obtain no explanation. He is always held at bay by a vast and sinister official machine which seems to embody a crazy logic which can never be finally understood, and where all attempts to assert individuality and personal choice are denied by those who, in principle, are servants of the public. Kafka, it should be noted, worked all his life as a civil servant dealing with workers' accident insurance. In his *Animal Farm* (1945) and *1984* (1949), George Orwell shows how bureaucracy can instigate and support manipulative regimes that deny human freedom in subtle ways, as in propagating a new language, 'Newspeak', whose vocabulary is reduced each year to make questioning thoughts literally unthinkable, and as in his aphorism about totalitarian bureaucracies in *Animal Farm*: 'All animals are equal but some animals are more equal than others'.

Michel Foucault describes how various professions, often seen as bulwarks of the modern state and whose members are often valued public servants, may propagate regimes which define and treat those who are 'ill' or 'mad' or 'criminal'. While such categories are represented as the product of objective research and reason and in the interests of the disadvantaged and the deviant, they actually operate to maintain the power, influence, income, authority and prestige of the professional groups concerned, and also of the governmental and other organizational structures within which they work. It may seem harsh to think of modern professional people in this way, yet reflection on methods of treating all the categories of persons mentioned above, in the 18th century and earlier, shows that this possibility should not be ignored.

Finally, this group of critics includes Jacques Derrida who argues that philosophers and other thinkers (including presumably thinkers on management) have been mistaken in believing, from Plato onwards, that a set of essential truths exists that can be discovered by reason and then be used to confirm all kinds of practical activity. Derrida denies that there is 'one best way' either of understanding life or (by extension) of organizing human affairs, either in the management of the public or the private sectors.

Indeed, Derrida argues that all such claims will be found to rest upon or to imply the opposite of the view asserted. Thus in his autobiographical *Confessions*, Rousseau sought to provide a plain statement of his thoughts and actions. Yet to do what he felt was justice to himself, his account was the very reverse of plain and straightforward. And so, by extension, though Derrida has not himself written on management matters, the claims of public management 'to serve the public' can mean the reverse: the public will usually be required to engage in such activities as filling in complicated forms, attending government offices at specified times, appearing as supplicants before officials who are technically their 'servants', and behaving in ways that are the very reverse of what the recipients of a service should expect. Derrida argues that we should 'deconstruct' the utterances of those who put forward bold claims and assertive judgements; it is certainly a useful exercise to apply this technique to many of the statements of public sector managers about their work.

All these writings – of Marx, Kafka, Orwell, Foucault and Derrida – and of others who could be cited may appear to be removed from the everyday world of the public sector manager. Yet they do encapsulate, if in dramatic form, some of the principal reasons why, by the 1960s and 1970s, public sector management was felt to have failed to fulfil expectations and to have disappointed so many of the hopes invested in it.

New Directions – Public Choice and Agile Organizations

At the end of this critical analysis, the reader – and the public sector manager – is left with very little in the way of positive recommendation. What should the way forward therefore be? The answer, increasingly loudly proclaimed from the 1960s, was that public sector management should be turned on its head and adopt the principles and practices of the private sector in a wholehearted way. It would not be enough to pick and choose a few private sector techniques, such as cost accounting and payment by results. Instead of controlling and confining both public officials and the citizency by rules and regulations and enforcing uniform levels and styles of provision, all the freedoms of the private sector entrepreneur should be made available. By putting forward ideas to serve the public in new, imaginative, efficient and effective ways, and by accepting the judgement of experience (whether the citizens liked what was offered or rejected it), the public services would reinforce their successes or, if necessary, liquidate their failures and try again.

In this way, the ordinary person's contribution to democracy would not only be as a citizen, voting at elections for broad principles espoused by different political parties, but also as a customer and consumer, enjoying or rejecting the services on offer by public officials. These officials would henceforth not only respond to broad direction from elected politicians, but also look outside their offices, laboratories, schools, hospitals and other institutions to determine what goods and services people wanted from their public services and to supply them very much as a private sector firm would (or should) – to a high and defined standard, soliciting views on quality achieved, responding to complaints and always seeking improvements within (of course) the limits and expenditures determined by political priorities. The philosophy was the very reverse of deciding upon 'the one best way' of managing affairs; instead, public officials would use imagination, creativity and responsiveness to a much greater degree in their work, while still maintaining high standards of honesty, legality and accountability.

What was the intellectual underpinning of this approach? Put shortly, the answer is 'The New Right'. This intellectual constellation contained several ideas of special significance for management, the first being that of 'public choice'. Public choice applies the methods of economics to the analysis of politics and public sector management. It looks at voters as if they were consumers and at public sector managers as if they were entrepreneurs, seeking to maximize the achievement of their own ambitions by meeting the wishes of consumers as fully as possible. It also seeks the maximum use of economic instruments as tools of government. For example, using taxes and permits can bring the costs of dealing with pollution into the open, instead of leaving them hidden as the use of rules and regulations may well do. In this way, it is possible to combine the contribution of decision-making techniques, noted above, with the promotion of more open government and public debate.

The framework within which these activities take place – the 'political marketplace' so to speak – is set by the elected politicians who form the government of the day. They too act as entrepreneurs, hoping that their framework will successfully appeal to voters at the next election. They therefore decide upon the broad outlines of what the public sector will provide – the product range, in the widest sense – and act as the consumers' immediate proxy in judging the performance of those public sector suppliers of goods and services. The elected government's concern to act in this way is reinforced in democratic countries by the knowledge that the ultimate performance judgement will be made on them as politicians by consumers as voters.

Secondly, and in many ways separately from ideas concerning public choice, there was the development of the idea that change is the condition of all successful organizations. Traditional management theory, as set out above for the public sector, had been very largely concerned to remove uncertainty and to establish settled routines and behaviour. Of course, changes ensued following elections when new policies might be introduced; from time to time changes were also made in the organization and management of departments and in the scope and scale of government activity. Yet many of these changes represented the multi-plication or division of departments and authorities that conducted business in traditional ways – and very often these changes were largely in name only. The essential point was that the bureaucratic culture was one of conformity and continuity. Change was an aberration, to be digested and smoothed away as quickly as reasonably possible.

Yet this approach was increasingly questioned. The idea was propagated, first in the private sector but then in the public sector, that organizations should be agile, constantly searching for improved ways of serving those for whom they provided goods and services. Organizations should be willing to adapt their working methods easily and quickly, be anxious to promote the individual contribution of each member of staff, and incorporate the idea of those at superior levels being the 'facilitators' of their juniors' contributions rather than authoritarian commanders, second-guessing their decisions and multiplying rules and regulations to control their activities. Many books were published which expounded these themes, as their titles testified: Tom Peters wrote *Thriving on Chaos* in 1987; Robert H. Waterman Jr *The Renewal Factor* also in 1987, and Richard Tanner Pascale *Managing on the Edge* in 1990, the last stating an approach to management which was 'predicated on the notion that disequilibrium is a better strategy for adaptation and survival than order and equilibrium'.[5]

An associated approach was set out in Gareth Morgan's *Images of Organisation*: 'The basic premise on which the book builds is that our theories and explanations of organisational life are based on metaphors that lead us to see and understand organisations in distinctive yet partial ways'; 'less effective managers ... seem to interpret everything from a fixed stand-point'.[6] As prisoners of one metaphor, managers 'frequently hit blocks they can't get around; their actions and behaviours are often rigid and inflexible and a source of conflict' (op. cit. p. 12). Instead, the adaptable manager transcends particular metaphors, picking and choosing approaches and insights that are appropriate to the circumstances of the tasks he faces, the technologies he utilizes, and the culture, values and attitudes of staff, customers and politicians with whom he deals. Morgan lists and analyses a wide range of these metaphors. Examples include 'organizations as machines', which arguably is the basic metaphor of traditional scientific, classical and public sector management; 'organizations as cultures'; 'organizations as brains', as the assemblers and processors of information; 'organizations as instruments of domination' over employees and others with whom they deal; and 'organizations as political systems', as centres of conflict and power struggles.

This emphasis upon contingency rather than certainty has also been a feature of writers identifying many of the changes in modern society under the title of 'post modernity'. According to David Harvey, 'fragmentation, indeterminacy, and intense distrust of all universal or "totalizing" discourses' are the 'hallmark of post modernist thought'. This is in contrast to the 'modernist' belief in 'linear progress, absolute truths, the rational planning of ideal social orders and the standardisation of knowledge and production'.[7] 'Modernism' in management was characterized by 'Fordism' – the application by Henry Ford and other pioneers of large-scale enterprise (whether in the private or the public sector) of the ideas of Taylor and Fayol and other writers as described above. Harvey argues that 'Fordism' is being superseded by 'flexible accumulation as I shall tentatively call it',

> marked by a direct confrontation with the rigidities of Fordism. It rests on flexibility with regard to labour processes, labour markets, products and patterns of consumption. It is characterised by ... greatly intensified rates of commercial, technological and organisational innovation ... [and the consequent] time-space compression ... [wherein] the time horizons of both private and public decision making have shrunk, while satellite communication and declining transport costs have made it increasingly possible to spread those decisions immediately over an ever wider and variegated space.[8]

Recent Developments – Privatization

What, in practical terms, has followed from these ideas of public choice and agile organizations in an increasingly flexible 'post modern' society? There are three main approaches. First, there is privatization. This is the appreciation that many of the goods and services provided by public services could be as well or better supplied by private companies. In such cases, the assets and staff previously supplying them should be transferred to the private sector where they would operate as private businesses, subject to the discipline of the market. Thus in the UK, for example, among the public services that have been privatized are the state airline, the telephone and telecommunications service, and the provision of gas, water and electricity. Three basic methods of privatization have been witnessed: turning the public sector organization into a company with limited liability and selling shares on the stock exchange; selling the organization as a going concern to another company; and letting the existing staff organize a 'management buyout' under which they become the owners of the company, often borrowing the money to obtain it. The choice of method and the details of implementation raise many practical issues if the result is to be fair – to the taxpayers as previous owners, to the new owners as purchasers, and to the customers as consumers of the product or service.

Other significant issues arise if the privatized organization is in a monopoly position, with captive customers, as is the case, for example, with the supply of water to domestic consumers. Systems of regulation of prices, profits and standards of quality have been introduced to provide proxies for the pressure of competition. These are clearly important in drawing a difficult balance between the regulator being 'captured' through his close association with the industry he is supposed to be regulating, and, on the other hand, requiring that industry to operate in a straitjacket of controls and price limitations. New investment and product improvement can be deterred if the return on capital is held too low – even allowing for circumstances in which the risks attaching to the activity are relatively modest, as they may well be in monopoly situations.

The impetus for privatization has not only been fuelled by the disappointing performance of industries in public ownership, but also by the realization that it will be increasingly difficult for governments to fund specific innovations out of taxation and sales revenues. Such essential features of developing societies currently include capital intensive telephone and other communication services, including cellular phones, and all the other developments which offer new ways of assembling, storing and communicating information of all kinds. Since governments have often found it hard to provide such services within and without their own organizations, the private sector is seen as a way of providing these services more effectively.

The second area where private sector provision is seen as especially appropriate is in environmental matters, as noted above with the supply and purification of water and the proper treatment of sewage. When in the past governments have both supplied the goods and services and laid down standards, those standards have often been sacrificed to save money or avoid political problems. The idea is that a clearer separation of the role of provider and regulator will work to the public benefit.

Thirdly, there is transport infrastructure, especially roads and railways. Here too vast investment will be required over the next 30 years if modern economies and societies are to grow effectively. And here, too, public investment may be insufficient and oversight inadequate.

Finally, the services now available and required in future to preserve health and sustain people into unprecedentedly old age are hard for the public sector to fund and supply. A private sector contribution through insurance and through the provision of alternative health and welfare services is again one way to ease the problems.

In many countries, these areas are traditionally seen as public sector responsibilities. But the ability of the public sector to fund their rising standards and manage them effectively is increasingly questioned. This is one of the main encouragements to privatization and to other new ways of providing such services.

Many of the public sector responsibilities recently privatized were brought into public ownership just after the Second World War when the nationalization of industry was almost universally popular except in the US. Many of the arguments for nationalization were the opposite of those now urged for privatization: public ownership was supported as enabling the state to compensate for private sector investment deficiencies, whereas the state is now seen as unable to afford the requisite resources. Competition was then seen as 'wasteful', leading to a duplication of provision and the diversion of energies to advertising and promotion that could better be spent on technical improvements. Competition is now seen as releasing energies and initiatives to supply goods and services at lower prices and higher quality than is possible under the 'dead hand' of public ownership.

Recent Developments – Policy and Agency

The second approach concerns the arrangements for policy making and its discharge, the keynotes being the reorganization of structure and change of culture. Details differ between countries, but will usually involve the following:

- drawing a clearer line between the elected politicians in charge of services and the staff who carry them out. In the UK this has taken the form of dividing government departments into small policy-making cores and executive agencies headed by chief executives. Often working on contract, they are presented with a clear set of objectives in a 'framework document' laying down what the agency is to achieve each year, what funds are to be made available to it and the performance standards by which it is to be judged. But within these broad limitations, the idea is that the chief executive and his staff should have the utmost freedom to manage their offices. Similar, though more detailed, arrangements have been introduced in New Zealand, where ministers are responsible for deciding upon and achieving the 'outcomes' of public services, while chief executives are responsible for delivering to time, cost and quality those 'outputs' that ministers have decided upon as relevant;

- a special emphasis is laid on the quality and standards of government work, with the idea that, within the funds allocated by ministers, there should be constant attention to the quality of services provided, their enhancement, and the provision of information to users. Such information includes the standards they can expect, where to complain if these fall short, and opportunities for speedy redress and compensation without recourse to the law or complex appeal arrangements (although the provision of these safeguards is maintained). With organizations this means the promotion of a culture of quality circles, team discussions about improvements and all the other devices featured in the 'agile organization' as discussed above. Outside the organization, it has taken the form in the UK of a 'Citizen's Charter', laying down the standards and other arrangements the consumer may expect from various public services provided by central and local government and public utilities;

- in seeking to promote a new culture among public sector staff, a whole range of devices has been introduced. The objectives of the agency or organization as a whole are broken down so that each member of staff has a clear idea – discussed and agreed with his or her line manager – of what is to be done in the year ahead, of how success is to be measured, and of what training, information and other asistance will be required if the individual is to perform as expected. Advances in pay and promotion will depend upon results achieved, and in many cases there will no longer be careers for life. Instead, contracts will be offered for limited periods, subject perhaps to renewal, but reflecting the idea that people should not expect to make their career within a single organization, but constantly be gaining wider experience in both the public and private sectors;

- so far as structure is concerned, there is the same emphasis as in the 'agile organization' of reducing management layers and, in a word, replacing 'hierarchies' by 'networks' and 'markets' so far as is reasonably possible;

- to oversee this process and to provide a form of accountability appropriate to this innovative approach, new ideas of external audit have been devised since the 1960s. As well as the public sector auditor reporting as usual to the legislature on the extent to which departments and other organizations have spent money on the purposes approved by it and according to the law, attention is now increasingly paid to the following:

(i) economy: the extent to which the organization has purchased its inputs of supplies and staff at the lowest price consistent with required quality;

(ii) efficiency: the extent to which the organization has transformed its inputs into outputs at the most favourable possible ratio; for example, the extent to which a hospital has carried out its treatments at the best possible ratio of input costs to outputs achieved;

(iii) effectiveness: the extent to which outputs achieve the desired outcomes; for instance, in a vocational training programme, the extent to which the output of courses achieves the required levels of skill and knowledge among those attending them.

This is a demanding agenda for change which already has many achievements. But this approach to public sector management has its critics. It is alleged, for example, that the attempt to set objectives in clear and (where possible) quantitative terms is often inappropriate. How, for example, can one specify the work of an Ambassador in such terms; and, if so, is there not a risk that his attention will be directed simply to those things which can be measured at the expense of those which cannot? Furthermore, as public programmes are so often changed as funding resources rise and fall and as politicians alter them in response to immediate political and media pressure (especially mediated through television), it will seldom be possible to say whether performance is in line with intention. Rapid changes create alibis for failures and sometimes give rise to undeserved success.

Again, the idea that the standards of public services should be set out in terms that might be appropriate to a retail business, anxious to please and retain its customers, is held to be inappropriate because of the absence of any effective means of enforcement or redress (short of cumbersome legal action); also because there is no public voice in the establishment of those standards apart from the minister or other elected or nominated politicians in charge. Any political debate about the purposes, standards and quality of public services central to the idea of a working democracy is denied. In any case, it is argued, the idea of public sector agencies as analogues of commercial suppliers of goods and services is often inappropriate. If a service is popular it need not necessarily be expanded; thus health services must in the end be rationed by the size of the public purse. Moreover, a considerable feat of imagination is required to see some of the users of public services as customers and clients – sentenced prisoners would be one example.

Recent Developments – Contractorization

The third approach is contractorization and market testing. This requires public authorities to provide goods and services by hiring contractors rather than by directly employed staff. Contractors have traditionally been utilized by public services: for instance, most ministries of defence use contractors to make many of their weapons systems; many ministries of transport use contractors to build roads, while public services often give individual contracts to medical or other scientific and specialist experts for continuing advice or specific services. But what is new today is the idea that contracts should also be let for what have hitherto been considered core functions, including the financial management of an organization, its internal audit and its personnel management. The idea is that testing what the market has to offer against the specification of the goods or services desired gives a public authority the opportunity to tap into the expertise of specialists, to consider their new ideas and to change suppliers if, at the conclusion of a contract, an alternative supplier offers a more cost-effective service. This approach frees public authorities from the inflexibility inherent in the employment of their own staff. This is not to say, of course, that in-house bids are necessarily ruled out. However, if the in-house team loses, it may have to be disbanded rather than be left 'on ice' against the time of contract renewal.

The organization of the market testing and contracting process requires special skills. These include writing specifications; deciding on whether to let the contract by competition or negotiation; deciding whether 'in-house' bids are to be allowed and on what terms; choosing between a fixed price or a price subject to adjustment against inflation; deciding whether or not to include incentives for beating time and cost targets; evaluating bids; stating whether iterative tendering may take place; specifying plans for payment against progress made; deciding how the quality of deliveries against contract is to be assessed and what arrangements should be made for the settling of any disputes. All these tasks are difficult to carry out successfully.

Problems are also faced in operating an internal market within the public sector. In the UK, for example, free health services are provided for all citizens. But within the health service, district health authorities (and general practitioners if they wish) may use their allocated budgets to bid for services, such as surgical operations, from hospitals and other providers who may set themselves up as self-governing trusts, able to bid for work from public sector purchasers (and the private health sector too). The latter are required to balance costs and revenues and generally to act in a commercial style so far as finance is concerned.

Markets like these employ agents as proxies for direct consumers: doctors and district health authorities (rather than patients) make the relevant decisions on what to buy and how much to pay. The extent to which the operation of such markets replicates the characteristics of a truly competitive market requires careful analysis, as do questions concerning the design and monitoring of such markets. These questions are explored in R. Saltman and D. Otter's *Planned Markets and Public Competition: Strategic Reform in Northern European Health Systems*.[9]

Conclusions

These developments raise the question of whether, as Paul Smith put it, 'civil society is best understood or operated as a species of market, whether private interest can be the mainspring, mechanism or measure of public good, and whether the periodic demand for business government is a distillation of common sense or a crude confusion of categories'.[10] Indeed, market forces do not operate in a social vacuum, but depend for their success upon the support of the wider values, attitudes and common experience that bind together the members of a community. In short, contracts cannot stand alone, but depend upon trust and cooperation in society generally. Undermine that trust, deny that sense of community, and the market will go down with the rest of society and its institutions.

It is clear, therefore, that the new approach to public sector management faces many difficulties and much questioning. But success can be achieved as David Osborne and Ted Gaebler show in *Reinventing Government*.[11] This book catalogues the progress of public sector managers in behaving more like entrepreneurs, adopting the best private sector styles and methods, responsive to 'customers', offering choice among services and managing by a 'mission' rather than rules. Above all, they acknowledge that governments should 'steer not row', seeing their task as enabling services to be provided by purchasing them rather than providing them directly, and measuring success in terms of outcomes rather than the size of the input budget of money and staff.

The authors illustrate their theses with many examples. One concerns a librarian at Oakland (California) who did not just sit back and lend books to those who came to the library, seeing her task as superintending the collection. She had surveys made in the community to discover who used the library which showed that few children or members of ethnic minorities came. So she organized what the library had to offer in new ways – videotapes for the children, collections of books in nine languages and cassettes for Hmong refugees who did not have a written language. Other services were developed on the basis of the staff talking to and surveying the community's needs: a literary project with 800 volunteers, a 'Lawyers in the Library' programme where volunteer lawyers gave free legal advice, and an income-tax form preparation service. All these services flowed from finding out what people wanted from a library and setting out to provide it in ways that met individuals' needs, in the process providing more interesting and fulfilling careers in the library service.

The essays that follow exemplify the developing story of public sector management. They illustrate its traditional approaches; they analyse its strengths and weaknesses; they show the new directions in which it is developing. With the passage of time there will be even more to say, as public sector management tackles its share of the increasingly complex and rapidly changing problems of managing modern societies. These include both individual countries and those brought together in such political groupings as the European Union, as well as by the economic links that increasingly bind regions and countries together through new trading patterns. The task will be to provide frameworks and services of law, order, enterprise and welfare in the spirit of freedom and choice that lies at the heart of the democratic ideal.

Notes

1   H.A. Simon (1947), *Administrative Behaviour*, London: Macmillan, and (1960), *The New Science of Management Decision*, Englewood Cliffs, NJ: Prentice Hall.

2   B.W. Hogwood and L.A. Gunn use this scheme in their (1984) *Policy Analysis for the Real World*, Oxford: Oxford University Press.

3   J. Stewart and S. Ranson (1988), 'Management in the Public Domain', *Public Money and Management*, Spring/Summer, p. 15.

4   On these values, see Chapter 22 by C. Hood in Volume I.

5   R.T. Pascale (1990), *Managing on the Edge*, New York: Simon and Schuster, p. 24.

6   Gareth Morgan (1986), *Images of Organisation*, Newbury Park: Sage Publications.

7   D. Harvey (1990), *The Condition of Post Modernity*, Oxford: Blackwell, p. 9.

8   Ibid, p. 147.

9   R. Saltman and D. Otter (1992), *Planned Markets and Public Competition: Strategic Reform in Northern European Health Systems*, Milton Keynes: Open University Press.

10   *London Review of Books*, 9 September 1993, p. 8.

11   *Reinventing Government*, Reading, MA: Addison-Wesley, 1992.

Part I
Bureaucracy: Origins and Principles

Chapter 1 gives a clear account of Max Weber's views on the development of bureaucracy and of its advantages: 'Precision, speed, unambiguous knowledge of the files, continuity, strict subordination, reduction of friction and of personal and material costs – these are raised to the optimum'. The essay analyses the strengths and weaknesses of this ideal type of bureaucracy from the viewpoint of the archivist (one specific type of modern professional worker whose activities are central to Weber's own scholarly endeavours) in finding the key to a rational future in the records of the past.

Chapter 2 develops the links between the key concepts of professionalism, bureaucracy and rationality, while Chapter 3 shows the darker side of bureaucracy as an instrument of economic and political domination. The latter also identifies the links between Weber and Michel Foucault, who stressed the way in which the concepts and language of professional workers and public servants may serve as instruments of power and oppression.

[1]

American Archivist/Vol. 45, No. 2/Spring 1982   119

Max Weber and the Analysis of Modern Bureaucratic Organization: Notes Toward a Theory of Appraisal

MICHAEL A. LUTZKER

A RECENT ESSAY BY FRANK BURKE decried the lack of a theoretical perspective among archivists.[1] He challenged us to pose some fundamental questions about the nature of society and the records its institutions create. Until we do so, Burke argued, the archival profession will produce no body of theoretical principles, and, as a consequence, those who prepare to enter our profession will continue to receive training but not necessarily education. Using the analogy of the church, Burke suggested that we are turning out priests when we should be preparing theologians.[2] He raised a number of thought-provoking questions; although we are a long way from answering them,

it is appropriate that we explore some of the directions he proposed for us. If we are to administer records as well as process them, we should be developing some theoretical models, and if we are to appraise the multitude of records being created in our time, we will need some general framework of analysis that can be used to guide our judgment.[3]

In attempting to develop archival theory, it is natural that we should draw from the insights of our sister disciplines: sociology, social psychology, public administration, and history. Fortunately, these disciplines offer constructs that can deepen our understanding of how institutions function. It remains for us to scrutinize the

[1]Frank G. Burke, "The Future Course of Archival Theory in the United States," *American Archivist* 44 (Winter 1981): 40-46.

[2]Burke's analogy was apt on more than one count. Given the salaries paid most archivists, a renunciation of all worldly possessions would seem to be in order.

[3]This particular framework is appropriate for archival records rather than manuscript collections. A beginning was made by Francis X. Blouin, Jr. in a thoughtful essay, "A New Perspective on the Appraisal of Business Records: A Review," *American Archivist* 42 (Summer 1979): 312-320. I am grateful to him for guiding my thinking in this direction.

This article is based on a paper given at the 1981 SAA annual meeting. The author is director of the Program in Archival Management and Historical Editing and associate professor of history at New York University. He wishes to thank Francis X. Blouin, Jr., Frank Burke, Hugh Taylor, Eva Moseley, Phyllis Klein, and Sheila Frottier for their helpful comments and suggestions.

literature and apply the insights of these disciplines in order to understand more fully the inner dynamics of the institutions or agencies that create records and the various purposes of records creation.

Let us begin with that dreaded word, "bureaucracy," whose origins are rather innocent. "Bureau" referred to the cloth used to cover the desks of French government officials in the 18th century and became linked with a suffix signifying rule by government.[4] Yet the term has come to signify the multiplication of agencies staffed by narrow-minded and high-handed officials whose work is characterized by innumerable tortuous procedures.

The bureaucrat has been mercilessly satirized in song and story. Charles Dickens complained that, if another Gunpowder Plot had been hatched in his own time and "discovered half an hour before the lighting of the match, nobody would have been justified in saving the parliament until there had been half a score of boards [of inquiry], half a bushel of minutes, several sacks of official memoranda, and a family vault full of ungrammatical correspondence. . . ."[5] And Gilbert and Sullivan's *H.M.S. Pinafore* advised how to get to the top by not making waves: "Stick close to your desks and never go to sea, And you all may be rulers of the Queen's Navee!"[6] Nor can anyone forget Joseph Heller's consummate formulation of bureaucratic rulemaking: *Catch-22*. The terrors of flying many combat missions and having close brushes with death could affect one's mind. But then there was Catch-22:

which specified that a concern for one's own safety in the face of dangers that were real and immediate was the process of a rational mind. Orr, who had flown many such missions, was crazy and could be grounded. All he had to do was ask; and as soon as he did, he would no longer be crazy and would have to fly more missions.[7]

All of us have experienced the frustration of dealing with bureaucracy, and everyone has a favorite horror story. In our more reflective moments we recognize that one does not escape bureaucracy by turning from the public to the private sector. Robert Presthus has called ours the Organizational Society.[8] Our lives, values, and much of our behavior are shaped by interaction with large-scale, relatively impersonal organizations. This is true of all industrialized nations, and as the less developed countries seek to modernize, they, too, will develop more and more complex bureaucratic structures.

It is the contention of this paper that, because archivists must work with the records created by bureaucrats, because the actual operation of the administrative unit is not always reflected in the records, and because the archivist must appraise them for their evidential and informational values—for all these reasons we must examine the most appropriate analytical studies of the administrative process for the light they can shed on the significance of those records.

[4]Reinhard Bendix, "Bureaucracy," *International Encyclopedia of the Social Sciences*, David L. Sills, ed. (New York: Macmillan, 1968), vol. 2, p. 206.

[5]Marc Holzer, Kenneth Morris, and William Ludwin, eds., *Literature in Bureaucracy; Readings in Administrative Fiction* (Wayne, N.J.: Avery Publishing Group, 1979), p. 168.

[6]*Ibid.*, p. 39.

[7]Joseph Heller, *Catch 22* (New York: Simon & Shuster, 1962), p. 46.

[8]Robert Presthus, *The Organizational Society*, rev. ed. (New York: St. Martin's Press, 1978). This work provides a useful introduction to the subject; see particularly its first three chapters.

THE WIZARD OF ID | by Brant parker and Johnny hart

By permission of Johnny Hart and Field Enterprises, Inc.

Max Weber's classic formulation of the bureaucratic concept can serve as the point of departure for archivists seeking to understand the structure or hierarchy within which the process of records creation takes place. The work of administration entails defining and redefining institutional goals, resolving conflict over the exercise of authority, and dealing with the consequences of policy fluctuations. This necessarily calls for the application of rules and precedents in decision making. Despite their different perspectives, most scholars who study administrative processes—whether sociologists, analysts of public administration, political scientists, or historians—acknowledge Weber's work on bureaucracy.[9]

The administrative function has of course been a pervasive element of all societies, ancient, medieval, and modern, but Weber was among the first to recognize the distinctive character of bureaucracy in the modern era. He pioneered in conceptualizing a framework for analyzing administrative systems, and he was prophetic in voicing concern over the psychological consequences to the individual caught in the web of modern large-scale organizations. More than fifty years after his death, Weber's formulations are still valuable in helping us better to understand *all* modern politico-economic systems: capitalist, socialist, and communist. Robert Presthus has called him "perhaps the greatest social scientist of this [the 20th] century."[10]

Weber belonged to a generation (perhaps the last) of universal scholars.[11] Born into a family of moderate wealth and learning in 1864, he had the benefit of the quintessential German university education at a time when that system was the envy of the Western world. He studied successively at the universities of Heidelberg, Berlin, and Göttingen, concentrating on the law. Before completing his studies, however, he had gained professional stature in a broad range of disciplines including economics, history, and philosophy. Appointed Professor of Economics at the University of Freiburg in 1894, he was invited to join the faculty at Heidelberg in 1896.

---

[9]Bendix, "Bureaucracy," pp. 206-208. Every sociology text begins its discussion of bureaucracy with Weber. For examples from other disciplines see Dan Clawson, *Bureaucracy and the Labor Process: The Transformation of U.S. Industry, 1860-1920* (New York: Monthly Review Press, 1980), pp. 16-18; A.M. Williams and W.D.K. Kernaghan, eds., *Public Administration in Canada: Selected Readings* (Toronto: Methuen); and Seymour M. Lipset, *Agrarian Socialism* (Berkeley, Calif.: University of California Press, 1950), pp. 226, 275.

[10]Presthus, *The Organizational Society*, p. 263.

[11]For biographical information I have relied mainly on the lengthy introduction by H.H. Gerth and C. Wright Mills to *From Max Weber: Essays in Sociology* (New York: Oxford University Press, 1946, reprinted 1979), pp. 3-31.

In 1904 Weber came to the United States to deliver a lecture at the St. Louis Exposition and took the occasion to make an extended American tour. Deeply impressed by the energy of the people, he was nevertheless appalled by the vivid contrast of wealth and poverty. He likened Chicago, with its sprawling industry and wretched housing for its teeming population, to a man "whose skin has been peeled off and whose entrails one sees at work."[12] Weber traveled through the Oklahoma territory and visited New Orleans, Booker T. Washington's Tuskegee Institute, and several cities along the east coast. Everywhere he talked with academics, public officials, social reformers, and business and labor leaders.[13]

Weber was particularly interested in the role of bureaucracy in a democracy, and he was quick to recognize the importance of political party machines in managing the electoral process. While aware of their manipulation of the voters and their corrupt practices, he could also understand why the civil service reformers and forces of good government had so much difficulty in dislodging them. It was clear that the egalitarian spirit preferred a set of elected politicians who used the spoils system, yet who could be ousted when too corrupt, to the alternative of a caste of expert civil servants, drawn from the elite, who would despise the voters but would be irremovable. Weber foresaw that, despite this democratic penchant, the increasing complexity of American society would ultimately require better

trained, more professional administrators in government than the political patronage system provided.[14]

A brief sketch cannot possibly do justice to the scope of Weber's interests.[15] Despite frequent periods of physical and mental ill health, by the time of his death in 1920 he had produced remarkable works of scholarship in a number of disciplines. He clearly discerned the powerful forces propelling all of Western society toward the centralized bureaucratic state, and he sought to understand this process by means of an imaginative multicultural analysis. Unlike Karl Marx—by whom he was influenced and whose ideas he challenged—Weber did not produce a holistic world view or political program. No one has erected statues of him, and few, if any, political manifestos invoke his name. But he has also been influential: rather than committed ideologues and activists, his followers are scholars who have used his insights to illuminate many dark corners of human experience, without making excessive claims for his ideas. Archivists should look to him as well.

Weber explained the importance of modern administrative systems by drawing a series of contrasts with those of older societies. In the ancient civilizations there were highly developed bureaucracies but, notes Weber, the keepers of the records were a subservient class:

> The Egyptian officials were slaves of the Pharaoh, if not legally, at least in fact. The Roman latifundia

[12]*Ibid.*, p. 15.

[13]*Ibid.*, pp. 16-17. Weber came away from these discussions with a deep sense of foreboding about the future of racial relations and the ability of the United States to absorb the massive numbers of immigrants coming to its shores.

[14]There are translations of some of Weber's letters detailing his trip in H.W. Brann, "Max Weber and the United States," *Southwestern Social Science Quarterly* (June 1944): 18-30.

[15]The literature on Weber is extensive. For an excellent discussion of the man and his work, see H. Stuart Hughes, *Consciousness and Society* (New York: A.A. Knopf, 1958).

owners liked to commission slaves with the direct management of money matters, because of the possibility of subjecting them to torture. In China, similar results have been sought by the prodigal use of the bamboo as a disciplinary instrument. The chances, however, for such direct means of coercion to function with *steadiness* are extremely unfavorable.[16]

By contrast, the medieval and pre-modern eras were characterized by the leasing or direct sale of administrative office to benefit the royal treasury. The prime aim of the office holder was to turn a profit, so the resultant system of taxation and administration was less than equitable. Another pattern was the honorific appointment of administrators: office was bestowed by a ruler upon court favorites or to reward a subject for military or other services.[17]

These pre-modern administrative systems were characterized by inefficiency, nepotism and other kinds of favoritism, corruption, and coercion; they produced, as a consequence, a decision-making process that was wholly unsystematic, unpredictable, and highly idiosyncratic. It is against this background that one must measure modern systems of administration.

The changes came gradually; one sees a pattern only in retrospect. They paralleled the rise of the European nation-state. In a complex process lasting some 400 years, authority was gradually transferred from numerous local feudal bodies to a central administration. Decision making was removed from local nobles and their agents, who had been influenced by regional customs and loyalties narrowly conceived. Administration came increasingly to be entrusted to distant, more impersonal offices applying a central system of uniform decrees or laws. In time a new type of individual emerged onto the historical stage: the administrator, the civil servant whose task it was to carry out the will of the central authority.[18] The economic theorist Joseph Schumpeter has stated that the development of modern bureaucracy is "a fact no less important than the rise of the business class."[19]

Weber explained the adoption of this system throughout Europe by citing its technical superiority over other forms of organization. The fully developed bureaucratic mechanism compares with alternate administrative structures

> . . .exactly as does the machine with the non-mechanical modes of production.
>
> Precision, speed, unambiguity, knowledge of the files, continuity, discretion, unity, strict subordination, reduction of friction and of material and personal costs—these are raised to the optimum in the strictly bureaucratic administration, and especially in its monocratic form. As compared with all collegiate, honorific and avocational forms of administration, trained bureaucracy is superior on all these points.[20]

[16]Gerth and Mills, *From Max Weber*, p. 208; emphasis in the original.

[17]*Ibid.*, pp. 206-224. It is impossible to do justice to Weber's wide-ranging discussion and complex formulation in so brief a compass.

[18]In a commentary on an earlier version of this essay, Hugh Taylor has called attention to some important differences between England and the European continent in the evolution of the administrative process. This point is well taken. Weber accounts for some of these differences in his discussion of the power of the "great and centrally organized lawyers' guilds" in England as compared to the Continent. See Gerth and Mills, *From Max Weber*, pp. 217-218, 228.

[19]Quoted in Henry Jacoby, *The Bureaucratization of the World*, translated from the German by Eveline L. Kanes (Berkeley, Calif.: University of Californa Press, 1973), p. 27. This is an impressive work on the rise and development of modern bureaucracy.

[20]Gerth and Mills, *From Max Weber*, p. 214.

124   American Archivist/Spring 1982

Weber's concept of modern (as distinct from traditional) bureaucracy is one example of what he called an "ideal type," a method he used to construct a logically precise definition. The word "ideal" did not imply a value judgment. What he sought was a clearly specified set of characteristics that could be tested against historical and current realities.[21] He theorized that modern bureaucracy embodies three groups of characteristics; this formulation, though modeled largely on the German civil service, was intended to apply in general to both private institutions and government departments.[22]

The first group of elements relates to the structure and function of an organization. There exists a hierarchy of offices with fixed areas of jurisdiction specified by laws or administrative regulations; division of labor is acknowledged. Each official's degree of authority and amount of responsibility are clearly set forth, thus promoting specialization and the cultivation of expertise. Decisions are made on the basis of the written regulations. The files documenting these decisions, writes Weber, "are preserved in their original or draught form" and record actions and decisions taken. These records provide a mechanism for monitoring an individual's performance and set precedents for future actions.

A second group of characteristics deals with means of rewarding effort. An official receives a fixed salary, graded by rank. His position should be his sole occupation and is accepted with the understanding that it not be exploited for emoluments or rents (a practice of earlier periods). An official exercises authority by holding office, but he does not own his office and thus cannot designate his successor.

Third, Weber specifies the protections accorded the office-holder. The administrative office constitutes a career, with promotions granted by seniority or achievement. A clearly defined course of training with prescribed examinations is a prerequisite for appointment. The qualification for office is, therefore, ability (presumably ratified by a credential) rather than political or personal connections. In the modern era the administrator is no longer the personal agent of a ruler. As a civil servant, he serves the state and cannot be removed at will by changes in political leadership. He retains his position as long as he satisfactorily discharges his duties.

This Weberian model has already, in a sense, been incorporated into the professional archivist's consciousness. Does not the archivist, during the initial appraisal of records, seek to understand institutional hierarchy and the role of given administrators or agencies in decision making? If we agree that an understanding of the administrative process is essential to assessing the nature of administrative records, how can we selectively apply the extensive Weberian and post-Weberian literature to advance the work of archival appraisal? I will suggest some lines of approach and inquiry while recognizing that these ideas will require testing over time.

---

[21]Another of Weber's great contributions to an understanding of authority systems, and one which bears an important relationship to bureaucracy, was his conceptualization of "charisma." This is not the place to elaborate on such a complex phenomenon, but it is useful to note the linkage Weber made between bureaucracy and charisma. By means of historical accounts Weber demonstrated that virtually all charismatic leaders, whether warriors, religious prophets, monarchs, or revolutionary figures, are impelled to consider how their authority can be passed on to a successor. This involves the creation of some more permanent form of administrative hierarchy, some institutionalization of authority, or, as Weber called it, the "Routinization of Charisma." See S.N. Eisenstadt, ed., *Max Weber on Charisma and Institution Building: Selected Papers* (Chicago: University of Chicago Press, 1968), pp. 48-65.

[22]Gerth and Mills, *From Max Weber*, pp. 196-204.

We have seen that Weber's emphasis was on the rational aspects of bureaucracy: structure, rules, and precedents. Subsequent studies have followed Weber's model, but some have criticized this emphasis on the rational and have concentrated instead on the nonrational factors and informal networks within the formal bureaucratic structure.

Analysis of these elements of human behavior received considerable impetus with the experiments at the Hawthorne Works of the Western Electric Company in the late 1920s and early 1930s. The Hawthorne studies are among the best known in sociological literature.[23] They began, modestly enough, as research on the effects of lighting on worker productivity in the assembling of electrical apparatus. Two groups of workers assembling the same components were separated from the main body of workers in the plant. The test group worked under increased lighting; the other served as a control group. Careful records were kept of the output of each group. To the surprise of the researchers, the productivity of *both* groups rose significantly as compared to that of the rest of the plant. Puzzled, those in charge began to substitute other variables. First the test group was given long periods of rest, then much shorter ones—all this in consultation with the workers involved. The research team was astonished to learn that productivity continued to rise in a steady curve even when the rest periods were substantially shortened.

It was only after many months of continued experimentation that the researchers began to realize that an entirely unanticipated factor was at work. Both the test and control groups had been dealt with differently than the other workers. The original lighting experiment had been discussed with them in advance, and each subsequent change in the conditions of work had been made in consultation with the test group. Both groups had been separated from the rest of the work force and they perceived this treatment as conferring a special status, distinct from the drab day-to-day routine of the other workers in the plant. The additional attention had apparently raised their morale and the resultant esprit de corps had increased productivity. This phenomenon became known in the sociological literature as the "Hawthorne Effect."[24]

Another experiment at Hawthorne, this one with an already established group of production workers known as the Bank Wiring group, produced a quite different set of data. The researchers discovered that these workers maintained among themselves an informal understanding to restrict output and thereby reduce speedup. The group was controlled by a few members, and those who failed to conform were subject to ostracism and intimidation. The researchers also detected an elaborate system of retaliation against those supervisors who showed favoritism, as well as informal devices to cover up for fellow workers even to the point of falsifying records (though to a minor extent as far as management was concerned).

The result of these fascinating studies was an increased respect for empirical research in which the researcher tries to

---

[23]The classic account is by F.J. Roethlisberger and W.J. Dickson, *Management and the Worker* (Cambridge, Mass.: Harvard University Press, 1947); see also the more critical account by Loren Baritz, *The Servants of Power* (Wesport, Conn.: Greenwood Press, 1974).

[24]Frank Burke has suggested that there might be an analogous archival "Hawthorne Effect:" that is, if certain administrators know that their records are destined to come to the archives, that fact may influence the character of the records created.

avoid preconceived notions and follows the data in whatever direction they may lead. Many of these studies, grouped loosely under the heading of the "human relations" model, have been concerned with the effect of organizational structure and authority systems on people at the lower or middle levels of the bureaucracy and have aimed to increase morale and productivity.

"Human relations" studies are of value to the archivist in that they may help to illuminate the informal structures within an organization that never appear on an organizational chart and may not be clear from the records. Indeed, the records will be read differently depending upon the archivist's knowledge of the internal dynamics of the bureaucracy. A generation before Hawthorne, Weber had expressed concern about the psychological consequences of the organizational discipline required by industrialization and bureaucracy. He feared that in the great majority of cases the bureaucrat was becoming "only a single cog in an ever moving mechanism which provides to him an essentially fixed route of march."[25] Now, fifty years later, there is a substantial literature—fiction as well as sociology—testifying to the stresses and frustrations of those involved in large-scale impersonal organizations. How these attitudes affect the records, or are reflected in them, is a question archivists should address.

A quite different direction taken by sociological research emphasizes the structural elements within the bureaucracy and thus remains closer to

Weber's model. It is the established structure and hierarchy that give an organization its stability, its standard operating procedures, and its predictability—as well as its resistance to change. Those who would advance through the ranks soon absorb the cues and behavioral strategies most likely to maximize their chances. More is involved than telling one's superior only what he or she wants to hear. According to Charles Perrow,

> An organization develops a set of concepts influenced by the technical vocabulary and classification schemes; this permits easy communication. Anything that does not fit into these concepts is not easily communicated. For the organization, "the particular categories and schemes of classification it employs are reified, and become, for members of the organization, attributes of the world rather than mere conventions."[26]

Thus even data from outside the boundaries of the organization—for example, scientific papers, reports by consultants, or government studies—may be summarized and assessed according to the institution's own vocabulary and conceptual framework. As a consequence the organization's own archival records may represent misperceptions of the real world, and it might be judicious to preserve the independent studies from which the summaries were derived.

Another model concerns conflict within an organization. The pervasive character of competition is evident not only among individuals but, more important, among groups: departments,

---

[25]Gerth and Mills, *From Max Weber*, p. 228. As if that were not disturbing enough, Weber observed that, as the need for more training and specialization grows in modern administrative work, a high value is placed on the "strictly objective expert" who succeeds in "eliminating from official business love, hatred, and all purely personal, irrational elements which escape calculation." In short, the ultimate irony is that bureaucracy is regarded as most successful when it is, in Weber's word, "dehumanized" (pp. 215-216).

[26]Charles Perrow, *Complex Organizations, A Critical Essay*, 2nd ed., (Glenview, Ill.: Scott, Foresman & Co., 1979), p. 146. In this section Perrow discusses and quotes from James March and Herbert Simon, *Organizations* (New York: John Wiley & Sons, 1958).

agencies, bureaus within the structure. The struggle may concern power, but often involves security, autonomy, discretion, and even survival. Research during the past two decades has lent support to the conflict model. Studies suggest that an organization or institution does not necessarily pursue a single, clearly defined goal. Different groups within a bureaucracy may be in competition even to the extent of pursuing multiple goals. General objectives may be agreed upon—for example, making a satisfactory profit, educating students, or curing the sick—but they are too ambiguous and nonspecific to be readily implemented. Satisfactory profits this year may be made at the expense of profits a few years hence; educating students may involve retrenchment policies to maintain high standards; additional facilities for curing the sick may delay purchase of expensive research equipment. Some goals are less in conflict than others. During periods of expanded resources and growth, even differing goals may be pursued simultaneously or sequentially, while in times of steady state or retrenchment conflict tends to become aggravated.

According to this conflict model, administrators at every level have a more or less articulated file of goals (proposals that imply particular objectives) on hand when the appropriate situation arises: for example, a change in leadership or the coalition of two units in support of a common proposal providing benefits for both. This is hardly a tidy concept. Indeed, its formulators have called it a "garbage can" model, wherein problems are convenient receptacles into which people may toss solutions that happen to advance their in-terests. The resulting accumulation

becomes an opportunity or resource. Depending on the number of . . . proposals around, the mixes of problems in them, and the amount of time people have, they stay with the . . . proposal or leave it for another. The problem then gets detached from those that originally proposed it, may develop a life of its own, or get transformed into quite another problem.[27]

It is clear that theorists who use the conflict model have departed substantially from Weber's framework. Weber assumed a sense of loyalty to the entire structure; in the case of a civil servant it was to the nation-state. Conflict theorists suggest that loyalties operate in a much narrower frame—that is, a department or an even smaller unit within an organization. Yet even the most conflict-ridden institution requires some degree of stability in order to function. Certain normative processes act as rudders, as, for example, preparation of a budget. The conflict theorists are persuasive in showing that the preparation of a budget is something more complex than a rational process the aim of which is to advance the goals of an institution as articulated by its current leader. A notable work characterizes budget making as "an explicit elaboration of previous commitments," among its purposes being the "stabilizing of bargaining and expectations for a year or longer."[28] A second normative element acting as a stabilizing factor in the conflict model is the recourse to precedent, standard procedures, and tradition, evidence of which is usually found in the archivist's records.[29] However, contemporary sociologists testing the conflict

---

[27]Perrow, *Complex Organizations*, pp. 156-158.

[28]Richard M. Cyert and James G. March, *A Behavioral Theory of the Firm* (Englewood Cliffs, N.J.: Prentice-Hall, 1963), p. 33.

[29]*Ibid.*, pp. 105-107.

model in the larger sense have relied very little on historical documentary records but almost entirely on contemporary survey and interview data. Therefore, archivists face substantial problems in applying conflict-oriented studies to the appraisal of noncurrent records.

In spite of these difficulties, if the archivist were to find some elements of the conflict model useful for understanding the way in which the institution functions, would it not markedly affect his or her view of the records? Should this understanding be a factor in the appraisal process? One would think so. A more difficult question is to what extent the archivist should seek to document the bargaining process that conflict theorists have described. Frank Burke urges us to record the actual decision-making process, not merely the decisions themselves.[30] While this may complicate our task of appraisal, will it not bring us a step closer to understanding the realities of policy formation as well as policy implementation? Such records may be of evidential as well as research value. Does this mean retaining far more than we can control? Not necessarily. A clear understanding of the give and take appropriate to the conflict model may lead the archivist to recognize those records that were created essentially to protect the turf of an administrative unit as well as those that represent solutions awaiting problems; both are more suitable for bargaining purposes than for archival retention.

Among the various schools of sociology, one likely to be useful to the archivist is the Institutional School.[31] By focusing

on the case study—that is, the actual operation of an institution—the researcher is more likely to consult the records and, more important, to address the whole issue of records creation.

Results of a study of a California junior college by Burton Clark seem likely to apply to other two-year colleges.[32] Clark found that the original aim of the college was essentially to provide remedial and vocational training to those who could not enter the state's four-year colleges. This institutional goal came into conflict with the aspirations of many students, who, though poorly prepared, sought a more academically oriented program that would prepare them for transfer to the four-year colleges; their ultimate aim was to enter one of the professions. Clark's study shows how the junior college attempted to reconcile these differing visions by a variety of administrative techniques, including academic tracking and extensive counseling. What is noteworthy from our perspective is the combination of sources Clark used. He drew heavily on depth interviews with administrators and faculty, re-interviewing some over a two-year period. But, in order to avoid dependence on hearsay, Clark tells us, "interview information was cross-checked among respondents and especially was checked against information found in documents. . . . Records and memoranda became in this study the primary source of dependable material, as well as a check on interview results." Clark makes the point "because files have had little status in sociology as a re-

---

[30]Frank G. Burke, "The Future of Archival Theory," p. 43.

[31]There is the question of how representative a single institution may be, but an institution studied can be cross-checked against similar agencies to determine how typical it is. A good example is Rosabeth Moss Kanter, *Men and Women of the Corporation* (New York: Basic Books, 1977). While studying a single corporation, and serving as a consultant to other corporations, Kanter found the one she studied to have much in common with others of the same size. See her Appendix I, "Field Study Methodology and Sources of Data," pp. 291-298.

[32]Burton Clark, *The Open Door College* (New York: McGraw-Hill, 1960).

search source. Actually their role in organizational study may be a primary one."[13] This is worth citing not only to argue the case for documentary research but to emphasize that institutional studies, especially those that follow Clark's methodology, may be particularly useful for archivists.[14]

Another institutional study that makes substantial use of the documentary record is one made by Charles Perrow of a hospital; Perrow emphasizes the interrelatedness of goals and power structures.[15] He traces a shift of control over the years from the trustees to the medical staff, to the administrative staff, and then to a system of multiple leadership involving checks and balances. In addition to analyzing the conflicts within the hospital hierarchy, Perrow's study is noteworthy for showing how these conflicts are related to shifting patterns in the medical profession, changes in the community, and new directions in government funding. In other words, the environment in which the institution functions markedly affects its policies and ultimately its power structure.[16] Perrow's work demonstrates how the actual policy-making function may shift from one administrative group to another, and this suggests that the archivist must develop an appraisal method sensitive to such changes.

All working archivists recognize, of course, that the records we receive, no matter how voluminous, contain something less than the full administrative history of our institutions. What the best of the works in sociology and related administrative studies can teach us is how to look at these records in a more perceptive manner. It is useful to be aware of the ways in which nonrational factors affect decision making: to recognize that some records fulfill a purely ritual function; to understand that not all the policy decisions are made at the top of the organization, that conflicting policies can produce records reflecting quite different realities, and that outside forces in the organization's environment affect its records creation. All this makes our task a formidable one. But that is precisely why we need a body of archival theory. The general principles will emerge gradually from the working models we construct while applying the knowledge of our sister disciplines to the process of records creation within a given institution.[17] As we discern the ways in which some administrative layers mesh while others conflict, we will learn to weigh this cooperation–conflict factor in the appraisal process.

The working models we develop may be refined as we discover the informal networks not accounted for in the organizational hierarchy. In some instances a judicious use of the oral history interview will assist us. Rather than trying merely to fill the gaps in the records, we should pose a whole range of new questions that will aid in testing

[13]*Ibid.*, pp. 180-181.

[14]For a contrasting institutional pattern, see Clark's later study, *The Distinctive College: Antioch, Reed, and Swarthmore* (Chicago: Aldine Publishing Co., 1970).

[15]Charles Perrow, "Goals and Power Structures: A Historical Case Study," in Eliot Freidson, ed., *The Hospital in Modern Society* (New York: Free Press of Glencoe, 1963), pp. 112-146. This essay is a distillation of Perrow's dissertation.

[16]For studies of the relationship between organizations and their environments, see Marshall W. Meyer et. al., *Environments and Organizations* (San Francisco: Jossey-Bass Publishers, 1978).

[17]An excellent analytical survey of the sociological literature is Perrow's *Complex Organizations*. It is refreshingly free of sociological jargon. Presthus's *Organizational Society* approaches the subject from the perspective of politics. If one wishes to study bureaucracy through fiction, a good anthology is Holzer, Morris, and Ludwin, *Literature in Bureaucracy*. It contains a useful introduction.

working hypotheses.

Some will question whether one can analyze the organizational structure of which one is a member. Such an internal analysis does require a rigorous intellectual effort, but many archivists would insist that they are sufficiently remote from the power centers of their institutions to be relatively objective.

Enough has been said to suggest that the archivist who is aware of an institution's inner workings is bound to have a clearer insight into its documentary record. In all likelihood this will aid the difficult process of appraisal. But might it mean something more than that? Is it possible that the archivist's role might expand beyond that of keeper of the institutional memory? Could he or she be an appropriate person to suggest how bureaucratic conflict might be mediated, how institutional goals might be clarified, indeed in what ways a dysfunctioning structure might be improved? Is it fantasy to suggest that the archivist might eventually occupy such an enhanced role, one not now incorporated in the training manuals?

In any event, out of our individual searching for the internal dynamics of our own organizations will come the data which, when shared, can produce workable archival theory. Such theory will enrich professional archival training and add another dimension to the expertise of the archivist.

[2]

Professionalization, Bureaucratization and Rationalization: The Views of Max Weber*

GEORGE RITZER, *University of Maryland*

ABSTRACT

Although it has not been recognized, Max Weber had a great deal to say about the professions and the relationship between professionalization, bureaucratization and rationalization. His ideas are very contemporary. He recognized that professionalization, like bureaucratization, is an aspect of the rationalization of society. Unlike some contemporary sociologists, Weber saw that professionalization and bureaucratization are *not* antithetical. Finally, Weber understood that a profession must be viewed from the structural, processual, *and* power perspectives. Weber's rich understanding of the professions is attributed to two factors. First, he saw them as part of the rationalization process. Second, his thinking was not distorted, as was the case with American sociologists, by the aberrant case of the physician in private practice as the prototype of the professions.

This paper deals with the heretofore unrecognized significance of the concept of a profession in the work of Max Weber. My analysis is divided into three sections. First, there is the place of the professions in Weber's general analysis of the rationalization of the Occident and the corresponding failure to develop similar rationality in the rest of the world. Second, I develop Weber's concept of a profession from his widely scattered thoughts on the subject and relate it to current conceptions of a profession. Finally, I take up Weber's ideas on the relationship between professions and bureaucracies. I believe that Weber's thoughts on the professions, and their relationship to the issues of bureaucratization and rationalization are extremely significant for contemporary sociology.

Although Weber's thoughts on the professions have had little effect on the sociology of occupations, it is ironic that his intimately related work on bureaucracies has been the

* This is a revised version of a paper entitled "Max Weber and the Sociological Study of the Professions" presented at the annual meeting of the American Sociological Association, 1974. I would like to thank Kenneth C. W. Kammeyer for his help with this paper.

628 / SOCIAL FORCES / vol. 53:4, june 1975

cornerstone of the sociology of organizations from its inception. The reasons for the disparity between Weber's role in the sociology of organizations and the sociology of occupations are many and can be traced to differences in the history and current status of the two fields. A most important reason, however, lies in the way Weber presented the two concepts. Although bureaucracy appears throughout his work, it is also neatly depicted in the now famous ideal-typical form of bureaucratic organization. This concise description was one of the earliest Weberian concepts to be translated into English and it proved to be seminal for organizational theorists interested in analyzing, testing, and expanding the ideal type. Although the concept of a profession also appears throughout Weber's work, it does not receive the same concise ideal-type treatment. As a result, it must be extrapolated from the body of Weber's work and that task was virtually impossible in America until the translation of *Economy and Society* in 1968. In a sense the Weberian concept of a profession was hidden from American sociologists (except those who read German well enough to read the original) until that time. It is therefore not surprising that the sociological literature on the professions shows comparatively little Weberian influence.[1] The goal of this paper is to rectify this serious omission.

THE PROFESSIONS IN THE OCCIDENT

It is well known that the bulk of Weber's work examines the development of rationality in the Occident and the barriers to that development in the rest of the world. He analyzed a variety of factors that led to the rise of rationality in the West and examined a number of structures that seemed to embody that rationality. Among these structures can be included the market, bureaucracy, *and* professions. I do not mean to imply by this that the concept of the profession is as important as the others in Weber's thinking. But it is clear that a profession *is* an important example of Western rationality.

Calvinism, and the asceticism it produced, played a crucial role in the development of Occidental rationality. The linkage of Calvinism to the spirit and practice of capitalism, to the market, and bureaucracy is very familiar to American sociology. Less well known is the

fact that Weber linked Calvinistic asceticism to the professions: "The clear and uniform goal of this asceticism was the disciplining and methodical organization of conduct. Its typical representative was the 'man of a vocation' or 'professional' (*Berufmensch*), and its unique result was the rational organization of social relationships," (Weber, 1968:556). Although Weber implies here that Calvinism led to the development of the professions, he also attributed a causal influence to professionalism[2] in the Occidental development of rationalism, and in particular capitalism and bureaucracy: "This worldly asceticism as a whole favors the breeding and exaltation of the professionalism needed by capitalism and bureaucracy. Life is focused not on persons but on impersonal rational goals" (Weber, 1968:1200). Here, as in the rest of his work, Weber sees causality as multi-faceted and multi-directional.

In addition to linking professionals to the development of Western rationality, Weber also related them to the development of a variety of specific institutions in the West. The relationship was, of course, two-sided. Professionals contributed to the rationalization of these institutions and, conversely, the rationalizing institutions contributed to the development of the professions. For example, Weber (1968:1164) discussed four factors that characterized the emergence of the more rational church from the medieval hierocracy and first on that list was "the rise of a professional priesthood removed from the 'world,' with salaries, promotions, professional duties, and a distinctive way of life." Conversely, he saw the rise of the modern church contributing to the development of a professional priesthood.

Although Weber linked the professional to a number of institutions, let us examine in some detail his argument on the relationship between professionals and the development of the legal system. On the one hand, Weber (1968:775) asserted that the professional was needed for the development of a rational system of law: "formally elaborated law constituting a complex of maxims consciously applied in decisions has never come into existence without

---

[1] One important exception is the work of Weber's translator, Talcott Parsons, on the professions. See, for example, Parsons (1939).

[2] For convenience, I am using the terms profession, professionalism, and professionalization synonymously in this paper. To the purist, profession refers to the occupational category, professionalism to the process by which individuals become professionals (Ritzer, 1973) and professionalization to the process by which occupations become professions.

the decisive cooperation of trained specialists." On the other hand, the development of rational law led to the need for the professional: "The increased need for specialized legal knowledge created the professional lawyer. This growing demand for experience and specialized knowledge and the consequent stimulus for increasing rationalization of the law have almost always come from increasing significance of commerce and those participating in it. For the solution of the new problems thus created, specialized, i.e., rational, training is an ineluctable requirement."

Weber examined the different forms of legal training and the effects of these diverse forms on the development of law. First, legal training can take the form of a craft occupation with the neophyte learning from established practitioners while on the job. This kind of training tends to produce a craftsman, rather than a professional.[3] In terms of its effects, this type of legal training failed to produce a rational system of law as is the case when lawyers are trained to be professionals. Instead, it produced a formalistic law which "did not aim at all at a rational system but rather at a practically useful sphere of contracts and actions, oriented towards the interests of clients in typically recurrent situations. . . . From such practices and attitudes no rational system of law could emerge" (Weber, 1968:787).

A second possibility in the development of the legal occupation is training by what Weber calls "honoratiores," or notables. Such an elite system of legal training is unlikely to produce a professional lawyer or a rational legal system.

Finally, there is the system of training lawyers that produces both professional lawyers *and* a rational legal system. In this training system "law is taught in special schools, where the emphasis is placed on legal theory and 'science,' that is, where legal phenomena are given rational and systematic treatment" (Weber, 1968:784–785). It is modern legal training in the universities that represents the "purest type" of this brand of legal training. In addition to producing the professional

lawyer, it leads to the development of a rational legal system in which "the legal concepts produced by academic law-teaching bear the character of abstract norms" (Weber, 1968: 789).

It is this last method of producing professional legal experts and the development of a rational legal system that is peculiar to the Occident. Other societies failed to develop a rational legal system because they lacked, at least in part, a system for training professional legal experts. On a general level, Weber (1968: 883) argued that "the stage of law decisively shaped by legal specialists has not been fully reached anywhere outside the Occident."

Weber also turned his attention to specific societies to determine why they lacked a rational legal system. In discussing the legal system in India, he wrote (1968:817) "since no one thus specialized in its study and administration, it escaped . . . rationalization." On China Weber (1968:818) contended that "there also was no stratum of responding jurisconsults and no specialized legal training."

It has been made abundantly clear that the trained legal expert is important for the development of a rational legal system: "formally elaborated law constituting a complex of maxims consciously applied in decisions has never come into existence without the decisive cooperation of trained specialists" (Weber, 1968:775). But, Weber went much further and argued that professional legal training is *the* decisive factor in the development of rational law. Where professionals are in a position to shape the development of law, that law is likely to become rationalized. Such an "intrajuristic" factor is far more important than general economic and social conditions: "The prevailing type of legal education, i.e., the mode of training of the practitioners of the law, has been more important than any other factor" (Weber, 1968:776).[4]

Although I have devoted most of this section to a discussion of the professional legal expert in the Occident, the same argument applies to the development of the professions in general. That is, it is only in the West that we find the wide-scale development of the professional. There were, however, some professionals in other societies just as we do find isolated

---

[3] Unfortunately, Weber is not as clear here as I contend. He uses the term professional to describe the craftsman-lawyer. Such a usage tends to blur the distinctive characteristics of the professional and I have therefore chosen to use the term craftsman to describe the lawyer produced by this type of training program. Weber is not alone in confusing the difference between professionals and craftsmen. More contemporaneously, this confusion can be found in Arthur Stinchcombe (1959).

[4] Here I think Weber is engaging in another of his debates with Marx, or is, at the minimum, seeking to round Marx out by pointing out that in this case specific factors have been far more significant than the economic variable.

630 / SOCIAL FORCES / vol. 53:4, june 1975

bureaucracies outside the Occident. But they were extremely rare and qualitatively different from the Occidential professional. In general, other societies presented barriers to the rise of the professions. Take, for example, Weber's discussion of China: "For the educational achievements, controlled by the examinations, did not impart professional qualifications but rather their exact opposite . . . The Confucian maxim that a refined man was not a tool— the ethical ideal of universal self-perfection, so radically opposed to the Occidental notion of a specific vocation—stood in the way of professional schooling and specialized competencies" (Weber, 1968:1049).

In this section I have sought to demonstrate Weber's concern with the professions and their place in his thinking on the rationalization of the Occident. I now turn to two topics of concern in contemporary sociology, in particular the sociology of occupations. I will first deal with Weber's conception of the professions. I will then turn to Weber's thoughts on the relationship between bureaucracies and professions and their implication for contemporary work on this issue.

DEFINING CHARACTERISTICS OF A PROFESSION

A significant portion of the literature on professions discusses those characteristics that differentiate the professions from all other occupations. There are three sociological approaches to defining the professions; the structural, the processual and the power approaches. The structural approach is ahistorical and points to a series of static characteristics possessed by the professions and lacking in the non-professions. Greenwood (1957) and Goode (1957) offer classic examples of the structural approach to defining professions. In the processual approach, the focus is on a series of historical stages through which an occupation must go enroute to becoming a profession. Representative of this genre is the work of Caplow (1954) and Wilensky (1964). Ritzer (1972) argued that these two approaches can be combined in the idea that there is a professional continuum with occupations at the professional end of the continuum having more of the defining characteristics than those occupations that stand on the non-professional end of the continuum.

The third, and most modern, approach is the power perspective and it is best embodied in the work of Eliot Freidson (1970). The single most important characteristic of the professions is seen as monopoly over their work tasks. A profession achieves such monopoly by convincing the state and the lay public that they need, and deserve, such a right. The power perspective is not, in my view, antithetical to the processual and structural approach and is, to the structuralist, one of the defining characteristics of the profession. We can see power as both the motor force behind drives toward professionalization as well as one of the defining characteristics of the professions.

There is implicit in Weber's work on professions a conception that is very close to the modern perspective that integrates structures, process, and power.

Unlike his ideal-type of bureaucracy, Weber offers no clearly delineated definition of a profession. The defining characteristics of a profession are embedded in discussions of specific occupations to which Weber accords the label of a profession. It is in his discussion of the priest that he outlines most clearly the defining characteristics of a profession. He also accepts the idea of a professional continuum and sees power as a significant dimension of professionalism.

Weber sees the priest as an ideal type that lies on one end of the continuum with another ideal type at the other end which he variously labels sorcerer, magician, or prophet. The priest is the ideal-typical professional and the sorcerer the ideal-typical non-professional. As with all of his ideal types, Weber recognizes that, in reality, there is a continuum and that no neat differentiation exists between priest and sorcerer. The ideal types here, as throughout Weber's work, are heuristic devices, not descriptions of reality. He says of the priest and the sorcerer: "the two contrasted types flow into one another" (Weber, 1968:425). I view such a perspective as compatible with the process approach to the study of professions.

In delineating the characteristics of the priest and the sorcerer, Weber also touches on the dimension of power in the process of professionalization. He sees sorcerers exerting "their influence by virtue of personal gifts (charisma) made manifest in miracle and revelation." (Weber, 1968:425) The power of the sorcerer stems from his charismatic authority. His training "proceeds in part as an 'awakening' using irrational means and aiming at rebirth, and proceeds in part as training in purely empirical lore" (Weber, 1968:425). The sorcerer is a non-rational figure. His source of power is non-rational as is his mode of training. He is powerful in non-rational societies. However, the Occident is moving in the direction of rationality and it is predictable, therefore, that the sorcerer would lose his power to the highly rational priest. The sorcerer simply cannot convince significant others in a rational society that he deserves a series of rights and privileges. In contrast, the priest, who is in tune with the rational society, finds it relatively easy to win a position of significance.

To Weber (1968:425) the priest is distinguished from the sorcerer by "his professional equipment of special knowledge, fixed doctrine, and vocational qualifications." All three of these factors are crucial in distinguishing the priest (and more generally, the professional), but they are subordinated to what is the crucial dimension in Weber's thinking on the professions, the nature of the training program: "the distinction between priest and magician must be established qualitatively with reference to the different nature of learning in the two cases" (Weber, 1968:425). It is the rational and theoretical training of the priest that does the most to distinguish him from the sorcerer and his irrational and empirical training.

Although rational training is crucial to Weber, the question arises as to what professionals (in this case, priests) are being trained in? Contemporaneously, we argue that general, systematic knowledge is a defining characteristic of the professions and the subject of professional training. Although he did not use this terminology, Weber (1968:426) comes close when he says: " 'Doctrine' has already been advanced as one of the fundamental traits of the priesthood. We may assume that the outstanding marks of doctrine are the development of a rational system of religious concepts and (what is of the utmost importance to us here) the development of a systematic and distinctively religious ethic based upon a consistent and stable doctrine which purports to be a 'revelation.' "

I have already delineated several of the defining characteristics of a profession offered by Weber in his discussion of the priest:

1. Power.
2. Doctrine, or general systematic knowledge.
3. Rational training.
4. Vocational qualifications.

Weber offers a number of other characteristics of professions in the course of his discussion of the priesthood:

5. Specialization. "The crucial feature of the priesthood [is] the specialization of a particular group of persons in the operation of a cultic enterprise" (Weber, 1968:426).
6. A full-time occupation. "The full development of both a metaphysical rationalization and a religious ethic requires an independent and professionally trained priesthood, permanently occupied with the cult and with the practical problems involved in the cure of souls" (Weber, 1968:426).
7. The existence of a clientele. At a number of places in his discussion of the priest Weber discusses the need for a laity, or clientele.
8-11. Salaries. Promotions. Professional duties. A distinctive way of life (professional culture): "The rise of a professional priesthood removed from the 'world,' with salaries, promotions, professional duties, and a distinctive way of life" (Weber, 1968:1164).

This list of eleven characteristics, which in Weber's view serve to distinguish professional priests from sorcerers, is remarkably similar to a number of contemporary efforts to enumerate the defining characteristics of professions. Furthermore any effort to enumerate such characteristics is, at least implicitly, an effort to develop an ideal type in the Weberian sense. Finally, many contemporary students of occupations are coming to recognize that professions and occupations form a continuum and that power is a significant factor in the ability of an occupation to move toward the professional end of the continuum. Thus contemporary work in the sociology of occupations has much to gain from Weberian insights. Unfortunately, we have had to rediscover in recent years what Weber had already discovered over half a century ago. However, Weber's major unrecognized contribution to contemporary occupational sociology lies in his thoughts on the relationship between professions and bureaucracies. It is to that topic that I now turn.

PROFESSIONALIZATION AND
BUREAUCRATIZATION

One of the most interesting and hotly debated issues in the sociology of occupations is the

632 / SOCIAL FORCES / vol. 53:4, june 1975

relationship between professionalization and bureaucratization. The most widely held position, at least until recently, is that these two processes (and the resulting structures, professions and bureaucracies) are, at least to some degree, antithetical. This antithesis comes out most clearly in the literature that argues that when a professional is employed in a bureaucracy, he is confronted with conflict because of the basic differences between these two normative systems. (See, for example, Scott, 1966.) But a number of recent studies have tended to cast doubt on the assumption that professionalization and bureaucratization are antithetical (Bucher and Stellings, 1969; Engel, 1969; Hall, 1967; Litwak, 1961; Montagna, 1968; Smigel, 1969).

Weber has a great deal to say on the issue of the relationship between bureaucratization and professionalization. Interestingly, his position is more in line with contemporary research on the question than with the older view that the two processes are opposed. To Weber, bureaucratization and professionalization were complementary processes involved in the rationalization of the Occident. Furthermore, the process of professionalization is viewed by Weber as occurring largely within bureaucracies. The two processes are inseparably intertwined in Weber's thinking. Weber is generally concerned with the "bureaucratic-professional" (Ritzer, 1972:345) that is, with the professional who exists within a bureaucracy and seeks to balance the two systems. To Weber, the priest, and the soldier are, in the Occident, examples of bureaucratic-professionals.

What distinguishes Weber's thinking from that of early American sociology of occupations which saw an inevitable antithesis between professionalization and bureaucratization? One difference is that Weber's thinking was embedded in his broader orientation toward the rationalization of the Occident. When one is examining rationality, it is relatively easy to see that professionalization and bureaucratization are related causes, and consequences, of growing rationality. In contrast, American occupational sociologists tended to look at these processes in isolation and therefore failed to see their linkages.

A second difference between Weber and many American sociologists is the amount of attention they gave to one specific occupation—the physician in private practice. Weber devoted little attention to this occupation while it has occupied the bulk of the attention of those Americans who studied the professions. The focus on this single, in many ways aberrant, occupation served to distort American thinking on the relationship between professionalization and bureaucratization.

Unlike most occupations, the physician existed apart from formal organizations, at least between the late 1800s and the mid 1900s. In those years the physician developed an ethic of autonomy and therefore found himself in conflict with the bureaucracy, when he was employed in one. It is from this single case that occupational sociologists generalized about the antithesis between bureaucratization and professionalization. But most professions never existed outside of bureaucracies, hence never faced the conflict experienced by the physician. In recent years, even the physician finds himself employed in organizations and the occupational sociologist is discovering that the physician can live within a bureaucracy. The concentration on the physician in private practice has distorted the thinking of occupational sociologists on the relationship between bureaucratization and professionalization. Since he ignored this aberrant case, Weber's ideas are far more valid.

Examples of the linking of professionalization and bureaucratization are frequently found in Weber's work. On a general level, he argued that "the bureaucratization of all domination very strongly furthers the development of 'rational-matter-of-factness' and the personality type of the professional expert" (Weber, 1968:998). In addition to such general statements, Weber also linked professionalization and bureaucratization in specific settings:

Military. "Only the bureaucratic army structure allows for the development of the professional standing armies . . ." (Weber, 1968: 981).

Religion. "The rise of a professional priesthood . . . must occur in some kind of compulsory organization" (Weber, 1968:1164). "This worldly asceticism as a whole favors the breeding and exaltation of the professionalism needed by capitalism and bureaucracy" (Weber, 1968:1200).

It is clear from these statements, and the thrust of his work, that Weber saw no antithesis between professionalization and bureaucratization. They are complementary processes involved in the rationalization of the Occident.

Although the bulk of Weber's work stresses the complementarity of professionalism and bureaucratization, there are points where he seems to see a conflict between the two processes. Weber, of course, saw bureaucratization leading to the "iron cage" of mindless routinization. Although he applauded the efficiency of the bureaucracy, he abhorred the mechanization of life it produced. There are points in his work where Weber seems to hold out some hope, although slim, of averting, or at least ameliorating, what was to him a horrid fate. Although specialized, routinized, and rationalized there are some professionals who seem able to resist, to some degree, the bureaucratization of life. The lawyer seems to be one professional who is inclined to resist bureaucratization and call for what Weber calls "judicial creativeness," rather than mindless routine. The opposition of the lawyer to mindless routinization is underscored by Weber (1968:886): "Being confined to the interpretation of statutes and contracts, like a slot machine into which one just drops the facts (plus the fee) in order to have it spew out the decision (plus opinion), appears to the modern lawyer beneath his dignity; and the more universal the codified formal statute law has become, the more unattractive has this notion come to be."

Weber's major hope seems to lie with the professional politician whom he differentiates from the bureaucratic civil servant. Of course, Weber saw that most modern politicians were lawyers, so his views on politicians are intimately related to his views on lawyers. In his famous essay, "Politics as a Vocation" Weber succinctly describes the difference between the politician and the civil servant:

> To take a stand, to be passionate—*ira et studium*—is the politician's element, and above all the element of the political *leader*. His conduct is subject to quite different, indeed, exactly the opposite, principle of responsibility from that of the civil servant. The honor of the civil servant is vested in his ability to execute conscientiously the order of the superior authorities, exactly as if the order agreed with his own conviction. . . . The honor of the political leader, of the leading statesman, however, lies precisely in an exclusive *personal* responsibility for what he does, a responsibility he cannot and must not reject or transfer" (Gerth and Mills, 1958:95).

Weber sees the successful politician in need of heroism and passion and these two characteristics are clearly at odds with the kind of personality produced by the bureaucracy.

Weber, then, sees *some* resistance on the part of *some* professionals to total routinization. But the thrust of his work leads me to believe that Weber felt that they must inevitably fail. The end, for Weber, is clear, unavoidable and horrible. It is a mechanized routinized world in which professionals, bureaucrats, and bureaucratic-professionals are all neat little cogs in a perfectly functioning machine. The events of today seem to support Weber's pessimism as professionals are becoming a part of bureaucracies and indistinguishable from them (Engel and Hall, 1973). It may be, following Weber, that the demise of the professions as a distinctive category spells the end of the last hope of avoiding "the iron cage."

CONCLUSIONS

A major goal of this paper has been to convey some of Max Weber's very rich insights on the nature of professionalization and its relationship to bureaucratization and rationalization. Such an enterprise is necessary since many sociologists either know nothing of Weber's work on the topic, or hold erroneous views. One such error is conveyed in a recent paper where the authors argue "The social organization of both the professions as traditionally conceived and the old crafts results in work situations which are, and were, in the Weberian (1940) sense, irrationally structured" (Engel and Hall, 1973). Quite to the contrary, Weber regarded professionalization as an aspect of the process of rationalization. A similar error is made by Freidson (1973:19) when he argues that professional principles are "logically and substantively in contrast to what might be called the administrative principle, which figures prominently in Max Weber's view of the rationalization of society."

Following Weber, I see *both* bureaucratization and professionalization as aspects of the rationalization of society. As such, they share many more commonalities than is traditionally noted in the literature. There are certainly points of difference, even conflict, between the two processes, but these are subordinated to the enormous number of similarities between them. I think much of the recent literature has tended to support this original Weberian insight. Although we continue to see articles positing an antithesis between bureaucratization and professionalization (Freidson, 1973), the intimate relationship between these processes is fast becoming an accepted sociological tenet.

REFERENCES

Bucher, R., and J. Stellings. 1969. "Characteristics of Professional Organizations." *Journal of Health and Social Behavior:*3–15.

Caplow, Theodore. 1954. *The Sociology of Work.* New York: McGraw-Hill.

Engel, G. 1969. "The Effect of Bureaucracy on the Professional Authority of Physicians." *Journal of Health and Social Behavior:* 30–41.

Engel, G. V., and R. Hall. 1973. "The Growing Industrialization of the Professions." In Eliot Freidson, (ed.), *The Professions and Their Prospects.* Beverly Hills: Sage.

Freidson, Eliot. 1970. *Profession of Medicine: A Study of the Sociology of Applied Knowledge.* New York: Dodd, Mead.

————. 1973. (Ed.). *The Professions and Their Prospects.* Beverly Hills: Sage.

Gerth, Hans, and C. Wright Mills. 1958. *From Max Weber.* New York: Oxford University Press.

Goode, W. 1957. "Community Within a Community: The Professions," *American Sociological Review* 22:194–200.

Greenwood, E. 1957. "Attributes of a Profession." *Social Work* 2:45–55.

Hall, R. 1967. "Some Organizational Considerations in the Professional-Organizational Relationship." *Administrative Science Quarterly:*461–78.

Litwak, E. 1961. "Models of Bureaucracy Which Permit Conflict, *"American Journal of Sociology* 67:177–84.

Montagna, Paul. 1968. "Professionalization and Bureaucratization in Large Professional Organizations." *American Journal of Sociology:*138–46.

Parsons, T. 1939. "The Professions and Social Structure." *Social Forces* 17(May):457–67.

Ritzer, George. 1972. *Man and His Work: Conflict and Change.* New York: Appleton-Century-Crofts.

————. 1973. "Professionalism and the Individual." In Eliot Freidson (ed.), *The Professions and Their Prospects.* Beverly Hills: Sage.

Scott, W. R. 1966. "Professionals in Organizations —Areas of Conflict." In Howard Vollmer and Donald Mills (eds.), *Professionalization.* Englewood Cliffs: Prentice-Hall.

Smigel, Erwin. 1969. *The Wall Street Lawyer: Professional Organization Man.* Bloomington: Indiana University Press.

Stinchcombe, A. 1959. "Bureaucratic and Craft Administration of Production: A Comparative Study." *Administrative Science Quarterly* 4:168–87.

Weber, Max. 1968. *Economy and Society.* Totowa, N.J.: Bedminster.

Wilensky, H. 1964. "The Professionalization of Everyone?" *American Journal of Sociology,* 70:137–58.

[3]

The disciplinary society: from Weber to Foucault*

ABSTRACT

Weber's analysis of bureaucracy is framed in terms of the legal and rational accounting requirements of political and economic organizations. These, in turn, furnish legal domination with its aura of administrative rationality and adequacy. The formal analytic features of bureaucratic discipline are drawn from Weber's studies of the army, church, university, and political party, as well as from the organization of the discovering social sciences. Foucault's studies of the hospital, prison, and school, in addition to accounts of the factory system by Marx and recent social historians, ground Weberian formal analysis in the history of various social techniques for the administration of corporeal, attitidunal and behavioural discipline, i.e., the disciplinary society. Foucault's studies, however controversial, may be seen to extend Weber's concept of rational–legal discipline through studies of the discursive practices that construct a physiology of power/knowledge which deserves the attention of social scientists.

The formidable works of Weber and Foucault may be considered in terms of their convergence upon a single question, namely, *what are the techniques by which man has subjected himself to the rational discipline of the applied human sciences* (law, medicine, economics, education, and administration)? Clearly, it is not possible to pursue this question in the same historical and comparative detail to be found in either the Weberian corpus or in Foucault's recent archaeological studies. Rather, it will be argued that certain developments in Foucault's studies of the disciplinary society (1978; 1979b) may complement Weber's formal analysis of the modern bureaucratic state and economy – despite Foucault's different conception of social rationality. Thus, the formal analytic and historical features of Weber's account of the bureaucratic state and economy may be related to Foucault's analysis of the discursive production of the human sciences of government, economics and social policy and to the concomitant regimentation of *docile bodies* under the disciplines of the prison, the workhouse and the factory. Despite Foucault's critical stance on the Marxist theory of state power, we cannot overlook Marx's attention (as well as that of more recent social historians) to the rise of factory discipline since this is an essential presupposition in the theory of discipline and power espoused both by Foucault and Weber. An historical sketch of the struggle over the work process, labour discipline, Taylorism and the bureaucratization of controls backed ultimately by the State which also guarantees rights to work, health and education, is necessary to understand how labour is rendered docile in the disciplinary culture of the therapeutic state (Miller and Neussus 1979; Hirsch 1979).

I STATE POWER, BUREAUCRACY, AND BIO-POLITICS

It is not far-fetched to consider Weber an archaeologist of the power man exerts over himself, and thus to see him as a precursor of Foucault's conception of the disciplinary society. In each case, history is not ransacked for its rational essence, even though it is only understood as a process of increasing rationalization. Nor is history seen as the story of individual freedom, even though western political history is only intelligible as its invention. What intervenes is the logic of the institutions that bring together rationality, individualism and freedom in the large-scale disciplinary enterprises of capitalism, bureaucracy and the modern therapeutic state. Modern society makes itself rich, knowledgeable and powerful but at the expense of substantive reason and freedom. Yet neither Weber nor Foucault are much beguiled by the socialist diagnosis of these trends. Of course neither thinker is entirely intelligible apart from Marx's analytic concerns. But both are closer to Nietzsche than to Marx in their grasp of the radical finitude of human rationality (Foucault 1970). In this, Weber and Foucault part company with Marx's ultimately romantic rationalism and its sad echoes in the halls of socialist state bureaucracy. Both of them are resolutely separated from any transcendental rationality, although Weber seems at times to have yearned for the desert winds of charisma to blow through the disciplinary society. But Foucault, distinguishing-himself from Weber, shows no such equivocation.

> One isn't assessing things in terms of an absolute against which they could be evaluated as constituting more or less perfect forms of rationality, but rather examining how forms of rationality inscribe themselves in practices or systems of practices, and what role they play within them. Because it's true that 'practices' don't exist

44 *John O'Neill*

without a certain regime of rationality. But rather than measuring this regime against a value-of-reason, I would prefer to analyse it according to two axes: on the one hand, that of codification/pre-scription (how it forms an ensemble of rules, procedures, means to an end, etc.). and on the other, that of true or false formulation (how it determines a domain of objects about which it is possible to articulate true or false positions). (Foucault 1981: 8)

The only possibility of any reversal in the discursive production of the disciplinary sciences and their technologies of administrative control, as Foucault sees it, is that archaeological studies of the knowledge/power complex will simultaneously unearth the *subjugated knowledge* of those groups (not simply identifiable with the proletariat) who have been condemned to historical and political silence (under socialism no less than capitalism). If Weber, on the other hand, saw no relief from his vision of the *bureaucratic production of the state, economy and society*, it is because he regarded science in general, and the social sciences in particular, as 'factions' in the production of the rationalization process they simultaneously discover as a topic and deploy as a resource for their own disciplinary organization (Wilson 1976; 1977). Thus Weber carried out his own vocation as a 'specialist', limited by his reflections upon politics and history itself unable to transcend positive finitude. Weber's commitment to his discipline did not represent a mode of self-alienation or of political bad conscience, so much as the responsible ethic of an individual who had seen the limits of our faith in science as an objective belief. The alternative is a leap into the barbarism of reflection and a utopian invocation of the cycle of history to deliver new men on the back of the old man.

Weber's distillate of the formal features of bureaucratic organization and discipline (1947; 1967) is intended to assist in the study of hospitals, armies, schools, churches, business and political organiz-ations, as well as of the institutions for the production of scientific knowledge of nature and society. Legal order, bureaucracy, compulsory jurisdiction over a territory and monopolization of the legitimate use of force are the essential characteristics of the modern state. This complex of factors emerged only gradually in Europe and is only fully present where legitimacy is located in the body of bureaucratic rules that determine the exercise of political authority. It should be noted that Weber's concept of the legitimacy of the modern legal state is purely formal: laws are legitimate if procedurally correct and any correct procedure is legal. Of course, Weber did not ignore the actual value-contexts of political legitimacy (Schluchter 1981). He saw the historical drift moving from natural law to legal positivism but could not see that the events of the twentieth century would lead to attempts to reinstate natural law in an effort to bridle state barbarism. Foucault's studies of the rise of the modern state apparatus do not

The disciplinary society: from Weber to Foucault   45

alter Weber's conception of the legitimation process but they are
much more graphic. This is meant quite literally. Although Weber
sees the documentary growth of the legal and bureaucratic administrative process, he does not judge its effects upon the *body politic*. By
contrast, like Marx, Foucault never loses sight of the body as the
ultimate text upon which the power of the state and the economy is
inscribed (O'Neill 1972; 1985). By the same token, Foucault is able to
go beyond Weber's legal–rational concept of legitimacy to capture the
medicalization of power and the therapeutic mode of the legitimation
function in the modern state

> In concrete terms, starting in the seventeenth century, this power
> over life evolved in two basic forms; these forms were not
> antithetical however; they constituted rather two poles of develop-
> ment, linked together by a whole intermediary cluster of relations.
> One of these poles – the first to be formed, it seems – centered on
> the body as a machine; its disciplining, the optimization of its
> capabilities, the extortion of its forces, the parallel increase of its
> usefulness and its docility, its integration into systems of efficient
> and economic controls, all this was ensured by the procedures of
> power that characterized the *disciplines*: an *anatomopolitics of the body*.
> The second, formed somewhat later, focused on the species body,
> the body as the basis of the biological processes: propagation and
> longevity, with all the conditions that can cause these to vary.
> Their supervision was effected through an entire series of interven-
> tions and *regulatory controls: a bio-politics of the population*. (Foucault
> 1980: 139)

Weber's discussion of bureaucracy is largely framed in terms of the
legal and rational accounting requirements of political and economic
organization which in turn give to legal domination its administrative
rationality and adequacy. The formal-analytic features of the Weberian
concept of bureaucracy are to be found as constitutive practices in the
operation of the army, church, university, hospital and political
party – not to mention the very organization of the relevant discovering
social sciences. Although Foucault (1975; 1979a) does not study the
bureaucratic process in the Weberian mode, his studies of the prison,
hospital and school go beyond Weber in grounding the legal-rational
accounting process in techniques for the administration of corporeal,
attitudinal and behavioural discipline. Foucault thereby complements
Weber's formal-rational concept of bureaucracy and legal domination
with a *physiology of bureaucracy and power* which is the definitive feature
of the disciplinary society. It is for this reason that, despite the
difficulties in his style, Foucault deserves the attention of social
scientists. There is a tendency in Weber's account of bureaucracy to
identify it with a ruling class, dominating the economy and the

46   *John O'Neill*

bourgeois democratic state. There are a number of overlapping issues here regarding the demarcation of the economy and the polity, of classes and elites, but especially of the distinction between the *state apparatus* and state *power*. Bureaucracy is the dominant mode of operation of the state apparatus, as it tends to be in the economy. But it is neither a class in itself nor is it the state power. Rather, bureaucracy might be treated as a *strategy* for the reproduction of the state's relation to the economy, and for the reproduction of socio-economic relations between individuals in the state. Thus we have to review, however briefly, the history of the separation of labour from the ownership of the means of production. In other words, we have to see how the bourgeois state assigns to the juridical individual his/her legal rights whereby he or she freely contracts into systems of exploitation and discipline (patriarchal, paternalist and bureaucratic) which the state defends even when it corrects its abuses. The ideological function of the state and legal process is to constitute individual agency at the juridical level precisely in order to reproduce the social division of labour and its bureaucratic rationalization independent of 'individuals' and their particularistic attributes (Poulantzas 1973). The sociological codification of this effect is to be found in the Weberian and Parsonian (1951) analysis of the rational–legal accounting process and its pattern variable schematization of required conduct from adequately motivated, i.e., disciplined individuals concerned solely with role-specific functions.

What the ideological isolation of the independent juridical subject achieves is the *inversion* of the economic dependency of the subject who freely contracts into a system of labour dominated by the market. Or rather, precisely because the issue of independence is removed from the level of the economy to the level of the polity, the economy can subject itself to the 'independent' discipline of external laws of the market before which capitalists are as unfree as labourers. These features are preserved when we replace the 'market' with 'bureaucracy' as a gloss upon the isolation of the state and socio-economic processes of capitalist production. By the same token, the bourgeois state limits itself to the integration of the isolated effects of the underlying class system of production and labour discipline but without seeking to radically alter it beyond the defense of individualized rights and duties. But this argument needs to be considered in an historical perspective in order to recapture (however briefly) the movement from which Weber, Marx and Foucault drew their theoretical insights into the stratagems of power that shape the disciplinary society.

II THE RISE OF INDUSTRIAL DISCIPLINE

It may be worthwhile to consider the middle ground between Weber and Foucault by taking even a brief look at the history of *industrial discipline*. This will enable us to weigh the difference between Weber's formal–analytic approach to the rationalization of social and political control and Foucault's approach via the discursive strategies and physiology of *disciplinary power* which were devised in the context of the shift to the factory and its gradual bureaucratization of the work process. By the same token, this will put in perspective Foucault's (1980) critique of the Marxist theory of power by reminding us that industrial and bureaucratic discipline arise from the historical struggle between capital and labour over control of the technical means and social organization of production (Braverman 1974; Burawoy 1984; Pollard 1963; Reid 1976; Thompson 1967). This is necessary since, while Foucault scores nicely against certain Marxist conceptions of state power, his own views are in danger of leaving us the victims of power that is everywhere and nowhere.

Although, as we know from Laslett (1965) and Wall (1983), it is no longer possible to indulge the myth of the family as a natural economy, it is generally agreed that in the mid-eighteenth century the family-based putting-out and domestic system of manufacture came under pressure as the industrial revolution got under way. In the specific case of the cotton industry, the family system had to adjust to a new pace, increasingly independent of the agricultural seasons (Smelser 1959; Edwards and Lloyd-Jones 1973; Anderson 1976). The pull in this direction showed itself in productive bottlenecks, imbalances between spinning and weaving, and the master's increasing dissatisfaction with the independence, self-pacing and casual character of the workers engaged in the putting-out system (Reid 1976). The putting-out system compared unfavourably (Landes 1969) with the factory system of control and discipline and with the Methodist values which serviced the interests of continuous production (Burrell 1984). Thus workers were plagued with charges of idleness, dishonesty, drunkenness and immorality in the courts and the press. The factory masters responded in opposing ways to this perception of wayward labour, namely, with the imposition of harsh and cruel conditions, as a general rule, and with proposals for 'model communities', to transform the old rule. In either case, worker *discipline* was the main ingredient aimed at improving the moral habits of the labouring poor, to make them orderly, punctual, responsible and temperate

In all these ways – by the division of labour; the supervision of labour; fines; bells and clocks; money incentives; preachings and schoolings; the suppression of fairs and sports – new labour habits were formed, and a new time discipline was imposed. (Thompson 1967: 90)

Further stress fell upon the domestic system and the family economy with the differential impact of technological changes in spinning and weaving. The spinning jenny and the water-frame moved spinning into the factory and, by simplifying the labour, at first displaced men with women and children. This, of course, seriously challenged the moral economy of the family, although a modified apprenticeship and family hiring survived in the factory for quite a while. Thus, as Smelser observes

> the water-frame factory of the late eighteenth century moved only 'part way' toward the ideal conditions of economic rationality. Workers were segregated from their means of production, but the remnants of job appropriation by workers remained in the form of a modified apprenticeship system and family hiring. Discipline proved a major problem to the early capitalists, but its enforcement had not differentiated entirely from the more diffuse family ties of the pre-factory social structure. (Smelser 1959: 107)

With the introduction of mule spinning and steam power, the factory system and its discipline became more pronounced. The separation of the workers from the ownership of the means of production increased capital's contol over labour. By the same token, workers lost control over their own pace (Thompson 1967) and became increasingly subject to entrepreneurial discipline. The changes we have observed on the spinning side of the cotton industry could not continue without building pressure for similar changes, differentiation and realignments in the weaving trades. As spinning began to outstrip the weavers, pressure grew to separate weaving from its basis in the domestic putting-out system, moving it into hand-loom factories and eventually power-loom factories. The big difference here is that power-loom weaving, as opposed to mule-spinning, displaced males with women and children. Workers in the cotton industry responded to the changes in their family economy with machine breaking, strikes and riots. They struggled to come to terms with piece rates, child labour, and the ten-hour day, always trying to preserve their skilled status (Penn 1982). The hand-loom weavers turned to pleas for relief, violence, political agitation and were attracted to the utopian movements of Cobbett, Owen and the Chartists. The Acts of 1833 and 1844 combined to reduce child labour and thereby to separate the adult and child working day, putting pressure once again on the family and state agencies to be concerned with child education and family welfare. Thus the workers turned to the organization of unions, friendly societies and savings banks as means of adjusting to circumstances that could no longer be handled by the old poor law relief system.

We cannot pursue these histories. Moreover, the complexity of the issues surrounding the evolution of the working class (Form 1981;

The disciplinary society: from Weber to Foucault   49

1983) and its paths towards reformism or revolution (Burawoy 1984) remains unresolved even by a host of empirical studies. Here it is enough to remark that in most instances worker discipline, even where it involves self-discipline, is always a ruling concern – food riots and strikes, being taken as evidence of the naturally undisciplined nature of workers outside of administrative controls, while the workers struggle to maintain their skills and concomitant social status. The fact remains that industrial discipline has never wholly conquered the working classes. Workers have hung on to many pre-industrial values, they have learned to sabotage, slow down, quit and take off (Palmer 1975; Stark 1980; Littler 1982). Thus labour discipline continues to challenge management and government to this day. It is therefore necessary to avoid a naive economism when thinking of the capitalist control of the means of production. Such control may be more or less efficient when viewed from a strictly technical standpoint and there may even be some competitive push in this direction. But capitalism is a social system concerned to reproduce itself. In other words, any form of social control over the means of production must reproduce the class system of capitalism – and this rule must apply to bureaucracy no less than to technocracy

> all means for the development of production transform themselves into means of domination and exploitation of the producers. (Marx 1906: 709)

Thus capitalists had also to bring themselves into line with the requirements of industrial rationalization (Pollard 1963). It is one thing to be Protestant in outlook and quite another to be so in narrow practice. For this reason, capitalists as entrepreneurs resisted feeding themselves into Taylorism as much as their workers, preferring as Littler (1978; 1982) points out to subcontract worker discipline and management. It fell to the engineers to devise for them the bookkeeping and cost-accountancy functions that increased control over expenses, stocks, overheads, productivity and profitability (Hill 1981). The engineers and middle managers, then, made themselves the servants of capital in this respect. Its prospective control of the work process, craft knowledge and labour solidarity further extended the appeal of scientific management and professional engineers (Rodgers 1979). Here it is vital to see that what was at stake was capitalist hegemony over the primary work process and not some abstract attachment to scientific efficiency. Taylorism was morally alien to the values and dignity of independent labour. Taylor's conception of the labouring man as lazy, bestial and intemperate, working only under the threat of discipline and strict supervision was hostile to self-paced labour. However, Taylorism was gradually adjusted to accommodate unionism, collective bargaining and various paternalistic and welfare concessions to labour, and owners came to terms with working-class struggles against premium systems, piecework, and loss of control of pace and decision in the smallest of tasks. Indeed, the union movement itself incorporated features of scientific management, particularly during World War II. Whenever management fails to negotiate between labour and capital, labour returns to its historical struggle and capital will call upon the police and, if necessary, the army to maintain law and order. It is, however, in the interest of both the state and capital to reserve legal force for exceptional use. This can be achieved so long as the disciplinary society, to which we now turn, can be relied upon to operate with quasi-natural effect, i.e., removed from historical and political consciousness. How this can be uncritically assumed will be seen in some closing remarks upon the liberal conception of bureaucracy (Crozier 1964) and power.

III THE PRISON AND THE FACTORY

The labour history we have briefly sketched needs to be relocated in the original framework of classical political economy and its concerns with 'policing' an impoverished, unhealthy, rebellious and criminal population created by the new industrial economy. The autonomy of modern economics was achieved at the expense of abstracting its concerns from the original disciplinary science of government and morals that occupied classical political economy. Thus it is necessary, in the light of Foucault's studies, to review how industrial discipline arose in relation to prison discipline in the production of a docile labour force suited to the needs of early industrial capitalism. It is then possible to see how the bureaucratic discipline of late capitalism presupposes this early history of bodily discipline which, so to speak, funds society's more superficial attitudinal controls. The formal (contractual) freedom of labour expresses its separation from the ownership of the means of production.

The decline of feudalism, the enclosure movements and the confiscation of monastic property at first released large numbers of former peasants into vagabondage and criminality. Fifteenth and sixteenth century legislation was faced with the task of separating 'the impotent poor' from the anomalous 'able bodied poor'. The former were authorized to beg; the latter were lucky to find their way into the workhouse and forced labour, a slight-step away from prison. In part, the segregation of forced labourers functioned to regulate the supply of free labour; but, in a broader way, it set the model for the discipline and surveillance of former peasants and artisans while they resisted their new freedom. Early capitalists needed not only to depress wages as far as possible; they also needed wage-labour disciplined to accept

The disciplinary society: from Weber to Foucault   51

long hours and harsh conditions of work. They had also to destroy the
popular culture and habits of pre-industrial labour, yet to avoid
entirely destabilizing the social order (Ignatieff 1979: 183–4). Thus
Calvinism was nicely instrumental as a substitute for Catholic
attitudes to charity, holidays and the like. It might be said that if
Protestanism removed religious authority from the community, it
restored it inside the factory. In fact, Protestantism reinvigorated
patriarchy both in the family (Stone 1979: 103–5) and in the
workhouse which it ran on family lines, as it would later the hospital
and prison

> If prison is a model of society – and here one is still concerned with
> metaphor – it will not take many years for the Protestant and above
> all the Calvinist view of society to create a model of the prison of the
> future in the shape of the workhouse. (Melossi and Pavarini 1981:
> 28–9)

In England, despite the challenge to law and order and the
ineffectiveness of its terrible punishments, the propertied classes were
not in a hurry to embrace rationalist and utilitarian penal reforms.
Such reluctance may well have been inspired by a better sense of the
workings of law and authority that enabled the eighteenth century
bourgeoisie to exercise its hegemony without either a large army or a
police force. Between them patronage and pardon seem to have
increased respect for the law in its mercy and through the very
arbitrariness that might strike equally at rich and poor gave rise to a
general sense of justice. A curious balance was attempted between the
law as an instrument of class privilege and the panoply of its
impartiality (Hay 1975).

However, it was inevitable that the increasing demand for labour at
lower wages would destroy the Elizabethan Poor Laws, replacing
charity with forced labour in the workhouse. But the confusion
between the workhouse and the house of correction continued – they
were often parts of the same building. When labour became
increasingly plentiful, unemployed and driven to crime and rebellion,
the houses of correction became even more punitive, while labour in
the houses of correction was limited to intimidating and useless tasks
so that no one would enter them voluntarily. The overall effect was to
teach free labour the discipline of the factory outside and inside the
factory in such a manner that factory discipline in prisons and
workhouses – whatever, and usually due to, the practices of enlightened
penology. Thus the employed and the unemployed learned their
respective disciplines. Thereafter, we might say that in the bourgeois
social order the prison, the factory and the school, like the army, are
places where the system can project its conception of the disciplinary
society in the reformed criminal, the good worker, student, loyal

soldier, and committed citizen. In every case, it is a question of reproducing among the propertyless a sense of commitment to the property system in which they have nothing to sell but their labour and loyalty. The articulation of the disciplinary society in the factory, prison, army, schools and hospitals represented a response to social and moral problems arising from industrial change and conflict

> the new science called political economy arises out of the registering of the new network of constant and multiple relations between population, territory and wealth; and this corresponds to the formation of a type of intervention characteristic of government, namely intervention in the field of economy and population. In other words, the transition from an art of government to a political science, from a regime dominated by structure of sovereignty to one ruled by techniques of government occurs in the 18th century around the theme of population and consequently centres on the birth of political economy . . .
>
> We must consequently see things not in terms of the substitution for a society of sovereignty by a disciplinary society and the subsequent replacement of a disciplinary society by a governmental one; in reality we have a triangle; sovereignty-discipline-government, which has as its primary target the population and its essential mechanism apparatuses of security. (Foucault 1979b: 18–19)

However repressive these disciplinary strategies may look to us, in their own day they were part of the reformist, humane and enlightened discourse that responded to the needs of the times and were often inspired by a pedagogic intention to transform individuals into able bodied citizens. The broad issue here is a complex, shifting relationship between industrialization, law, criminality and the labourers in the town and countryside (Tobias 1967). Thus it is not always easy to decide whether such responses as food riots, poaching, machine breaking, reform movements and trade unionism were popular politics or mob crimes. From the standpoint of the propertied classes, such activities were more likely to be criminalized than politicized, so to speak, since the propertied class had trouble in imagining the kind of political order that might be built upon a propertyless mass. From the standpoint of the peasants and urban labourers faced with immiseration, certain criminal activities were often desperate strategies of maintenance, however colourful they may have made London life. Although the law was used to enact severe and terrible punishments for crimes against rural and urban property, it nevertheless seems to have been employed also to teach lessons of mercy and a universal sense of order. In other words, the bourgeois state tempered the force of law with the ideology of respect for the Law. To the extent that this was achieved, the labouring class also

The disciplinary society: from Weber to Foucault 53

won from the bourgeoisie extensions in the rule of law, freedom of speech and assembly, as well as the right to strike and to organize in the work place. The law, therefore, is not simply the oppressive agency for the bourgeois state. Inasmuch as capitalism must be concerned with its own social reproduction, it will be driven to motivate moral consent as well as sheer physical compliance. Thus the class struggle will propel the law to universalize its prescriptions in the search for solutions on a higher level of control.

In the eighteenth century, the role of the state was at first minimal in the sense that it served to sweep away the feudal order and to institute the necessary discipline of the new industrial labour force. Later, it began to adjust the conditions of labour, passing the factory legislation that to some extent restricted capital while accommodating labour. At this stage, the state's task in softening domination with education is shared by humanitarian, paternal and religious welfare in helping the poor, sick, criminal and ignorant. Foucault (1979a) argues that the disciplinary institutions were conceived to open up a field for the practices of evaluating, recording and observing large populations in order to administer them through the therapeutic institutions of health, education and penality. This is the original matrix of the human and social sciences, rather than any abstractive generalization such as Comte's Law of the Three Stages. Instead, we might speak of the social sciences as *strategies of power* designed to minimize the cost of power, to maximize its coverage and to link 'economic' power with the educational, military, industrial, penal and medical institutions within which the docility and utility of populations can be maximized. In a disciplinary society power works by a sort of capillary action, drawing itself up from individual conduits. Thus, in a certain sense, the operation of power is individualized in order to achieve its maximum concentration

> In a disciplinary regime . . . individualization is 'descending': as power becomes more anonymous and more functional, those on whom it is exercised tend to be more strongly individualized; it is exercised by surveillance rather than ceremonies, by observation rather than commemorative accounts, by comparative measures that have the 'norm' as reference rather than genealogies giving ancestors as points of reference, by 'gaps' rather than deeds.. . . All the sciences, analyses, or practices employing the root 'psycho-' have their origin in this historical reversal of the procedures of individualization. The moment that saw the transition from historico–ritual mechanisms for the formation of individuality to the scientific–disciplinary mechanism, when the normal took over from the ancestral, and measurement from status, thus substituting for the individuality of the memorable man that of the calculable man, that moment when the sciences of man became possible is the

54 *John O'Neill*

moment when a new technology of power and a new political anatomy of the body were implemented. (Foucault 1979a: 193)

IV BEHIND THE STATE: BUREAUCRACY AND THE DISCIPLINARY SOCIETY

When Weber considers the historical roots of bureaucratic discipline, as well as of the factory, he traces them directly to the model of military discipline. 'The discipline of the army gives birth to all discipline' (Weber 1967: 261). This emphasizes the uniformity of obedience and command in an impersonal office. Emotions, status, devotion and charisma are subordinated to a rational calculus of success or profitability from the objective standpoint of the organization. At the same time, Weber concedes that there is no direct link between military discipline and various economic institutions such as the Pharaonic workshops, slave plantations and the factory. He remarks upon the intensification of rational discipline achieved through the American systems of 'scientific management'. But his observations on these topics are not developed and his interest is absorbed by the most general features of formal bureaucratic administration. Thus it may be argued that, while Weber (1950) saw the direct line from monastic discipline through Luther and Calvin to bureaucracy and scientific management, he did not pay sufficient attention to the circuits of the factory, workhouse and prison in the creation of industrial discipline and social control. Discipline in the factory, prison and school involves much more specific strategies of corporeal discipline than is captured by the generalized attitude of Protestant asceticism. In this respect, Weberianism implies a too cognitivist version of capitalist, state and bureaucratic controls. Moreover, it leaves the impression that in late capitalism the state only employs brute force, of a police or military nature, in the last instance. Thus the history we have reviewed makes it possible to see how the Weberian approach can result in Crozier's (1964) portrayal of enlightened bureaucracy produced by taking for granted the *disciplinary society* (family, schools, hospitals and prisons) that underwrites discipline in the workplace and allows the State to reserve its violence on behalf of the property system

> Modern organizations, in contrast to their predecessors, use a much more liberal set of pressures. They deal with people who, through their education, have already internalized a number of basic conformities and a general ability to conform easily to an organization's way . . .. Most important of all, human behaviour is now better understood and therefore more predictable. Because of this, a modern organization does not need the same amount of conformity to get as good results as did earlier organizations. The

modern organization can tolerate more deviance, restrict its requirements to a more specialized field, and demand only temporary commitments. For all these reasons, it can and does rely more on indirect and intellectual means to obtain conformity: communication structure and work flow, the technical setting of jobs, economic incentives, and also, perhaps, rational calculus of a higher sort. The punitive aspect of the conformity achievement process has declined. Direct coercion is still in reserve as a last resort, but it is very rarely used, and people apparently no longer have to see it operate often to retain it in their calculations. (Crozier 1964: 184–5)

Crozier's view of workers' compliance will seem plausible only to the extent that it can presume upon the *natural discipline*, so to speak, of the work place and of the wage system. But this, as we have seen, is always the arena of a struggle with formally free labour to accept its substantive lack of freedom due to the persistent efforts of capitalism to separate labour from control of the work process. Thus the rights of labour to freely contract for wages guaranteed before the law is reproduced in the system of punishment calculated in retribution for crimes against property, against property in persons and ultimately against the crime of propertylessness (Melossi and Pavarini 1981). The legal contract is therefore the sacred fiction of the bourgeois social and political order since it simultaneously reproduces formal freedom and equality with substantive inequality and oppression. The discipline of the factory and the wage system, however much it is bureaucratized, remains the ultimate source of labour's docility. Indeed, it is the work place discipline that funds the apparent organizational effectiveness of state and bureaucratic controls. In fact, these controls also require for their effectiveness that the greater part of the bureaucratic structure be itself subject to the very discipline its middle management employees imagine they are supervising with respect to labour. What is called bureaucratic control must be seen to involve a continuous struggle over

(a) the *technical control* over the work process, and
(b) *disciplinary and punitive control* over the social relations of production.

Whereas in early capitalism paternalist power derived from the personal relationships between the owner and his labourers, technical and bureaucratic control grow out of the formal structure of the firm. The difference is that technical control is embedded in the production process and, as such, may be employed to *naturalize* bureaucratic controls which are embedded in the social organization or power structure of the firm. In practice, paternalistic, technical and

56   *John O'Neill*

bureaucratic discipline will be found to coexist and, while they may be regarded as stages of industrial discipline (Perrot 1979), they have arisen in a pragmatic way as responses to owner/worker struggles for control. Although it is preferable from the standpoint of management to address control issues in terms of a Weberian vocabulary of rational accounting, efficiency and universalistic-achievement requirements – in fact to naturalize the social relations of production to technical relations of production – the reality is that it is relations of power and ideology that are at stake. Where labour freely contracts to meet the wage discipline, it thereby subordinates itself to the conditions of mental and bodily control (Sohn-Rethel 1978) arising from its separation from the ownership of the means, pacing and purpose of production in a substantively rational social enterprise. In detail, this means that workers submit to the direction of their tasks, their nature, method, pace and quality of work (Edwards 1979; Thompson 1961). They thereby simultaneously submit themselves to a system of worker evaluation, punishment and reward. It is, of course, in the interests of bureaucratic management to make worker discipline, punishments and rewards, appear to flow from naturally established organizational rules and procedures. Analytically, there occurs a kind of progression in industrial discipline moving from paternalistic controls to assembly line, machine paced routines and, finally, to bureaucratically imposed discipline. What is involved is a shift from heteronomous paternalist controls to autonomous, internalized discipline, and identification with corporate goals and values. To achieve this, worker evaluation is concerned less with physical productivity than with workers' attitudes to the corporation. In a certain sense, the modern corporation seeks to refamilize the workers while cutting them off from their own class culture. Since such a disciplinary achievement takes time, corporations seek to minimize labour turn-over and to maximize loyalty, ever solicitous of worker attitudes

> What distinguishes bureaucratic control from other control systems is that it contains incentives aimed at evoking the behaviour necessary to make bureaucratic control succeed. It is this *indirect* path to the intensification of work, through the mechanism of rewarding behaviour relevant to the control system, rather than simply to the work itself, that imposes the new behaviour requirements on workers. (Edwards 1979: 148–9)

These considerations suggest further political studies of the internalization of discipline in the enucleated family, in schools, sports and much of modern entertainment. The family has long ceased to be the natural scene of work discipline, while still charged with the production of able-bodied citizens. It has fallen to the schools, social and medical agencies, and the media – inasmuch as the message is

still the ordinary society – to provide the secondary socialization
which Crozier takes for granted in shifting the disciplinary burden
from modern bureaucracy onto an 'educated' citizenry. In short, we
need to re-examine the division between public and private conduct in
terms of historically variable strategies of discipline – even in so-
called leisure – which subserve the social and political imperative of a
disciplined labour force and its current levels of manual, mental and
emotional 'education'. Such a tactic would treat social discipline as a
socio-political strategy whose organizational features are historically
and institutionally variable. Moreover, it would avoid any retrospective
myth of an undisciplined state of nature generated from a Freudian or
a Hobbesian perspective. At the same time, it would not reduce
political discipline to a work place activity, nor indulge prospective
fantasies of an undisciplined society ruled by play and the absence of
the state. By the same token, the approach recommended here might
give social scientists direction in the empirical study of the embodiment
of power as it is achieved in the lives of individuals, families and
educational institutions.

CONCLUSION

It has been argued that Weber's formal theory of bureaucracy needs
to be complemented by the history of factory discipline, the latter
overlapping with prison discipline and eventually overlaid with
bureaucratic discipline. Thus we return to Weber via Foucault and
Marx. The benefit of this approach is that it makes it clear how
Weber's concept of state and bureaucratic discipline alternates
between (i) obedience based upon the observation of rules of technical
efficiency, and (ii) obedience required as a governmental end in itself,
or what Gouldner (1954: 216–17) calls 'punishment centered'
bureaucracy. In reality, the sphere of the technical expert is
subordinate to that of the true bureaucrat whose administration
derives from a presumption of power. For this reason, the disciplinary
tasks of punitive bureaucracy are directed to the industrial control of
minds and bodies, of attitudes and behaviour. Here the studies of
Foucault and the social historians we have cited broaden the
Weberian concept of administrative power into the embodied
strategies of industrial power. Bureaucrats cannot make the Prussian
assumption that their goals are beyond criticism and resistance
(Gouldner 1976). Industrial bureaucracies are less privileged than
government bureaucracies in this respect. For this reason, the two
bureaucracies of state and economy share an interest in depoliticizing
the perception of their power and ideology by subordinating them to
the neutral image of disciplined technology and expertise. With this
strategy, the two bureaucracies seek to manufacture public docility

58 *John O'Neill*

and in this way have citizens support the state which in turn supports them with a modicum of legal force exercised against their occasional disobedience.

John O'Neill
Department of Sociology
York University

NOTES

*Early versions of this article were read in the Department of Sociology at Cornell University, the University of Alberta, Edmonton. and Concordia University, Montreal.

BIBLIOGRAPHY

Anderson. M. 1976. 'Sociological History and the Working Class Family: Smelser Revisited'. *Social History* 3: 317–34.

Braverman. Harry 1974. *Labour and Monopoly Capital. The Degredation of Work in the Twentieth Century*. New York: Monthly Review Press.

Buraway. Michael 1984. 'Karl Marx and the Satanic Mills: Factory Politics Under Early Capitalism in England, the United States and Russia'. *The American Journal of Sociology* 90(2): 247–82.

Burrell. Gibson 1984. 'Sexual Organizational Analysis'. *Organizational Studies* 5(2): 97–118.

Crozier, Michel 1964. *The Bureaucratic Phenomenon*. Chicago: The University of Chicago Press.

Edwards. M., and R. Lloyd-Jones 1973. 'N. J. Smelser and the Cotton Factory Family: A Re-assessment'. N. B. Harte and K. G. Ponting (eds) *Textile History and Economic History*. Manchester: Manchester University Press. 304–19.

Edwards. Richard 1979. *Contested Terrain: The Transformation of the Workplace in the Twentieth Century*. New York: Basic Books.

Form, William 1981. 'Resolving Ideological Issues on the Division of Labour', Hubert M. Blalock. Jr. (ed.) *Theory and Research in Sociology*. New York: The Free Press. 140–61.

Form, William 1983. 'Sociological Research and the American Working Class'. *The Sociological Quarterly* 24 (Spring, 1983): 163–84.

Foucault, Michel 1970. *The Order of Things: An Archaeology of the Human Sciences*. New York: Vintage Books.

Foucault, Michel 1975. *The Birth of the Clinic: An Archaeology of Medical Perception*. Translated by A. M. Sheridan Smith. New York: Vintage Books.

Foucault, Michel 1979a. *Discipline and Punish: The Birth of the Prison*. Translated by Alan Sheridan. New York: Vintage Books.

Foucault, Michel 1979b. 'Governmentality', *Ideology and Consciousness (I and C)*, *Governing the Present*, 6: 5–21.

Foucault, Michel 1980. *The History of Sexuality Volume I: An Introduction*. Translated by Robert Hurley. New York: Vintage Books.

Foucault, Michel 1981. 'Questions of Method', *Ideology and Consciousness (I and C)*, *Power and Desire: Diagrams of the Social*, 8: 3–14.

Gouldner, Alvin W. 1954. *Patterns of Industrial Democracy*. Glencoe, Ill.: The Free Press.

Gouldner, Alvin W. 1976. *The Dialectic of Ideology and Technology: The Origins, Grammar, and Future of Ideology*. New

The disciplinary society: from Weber to Foucault 59

York: The Seabury Press.

Hay, Douglas 1975. 'Property, Authority and the Criminal Law', Douglas Hay, Peter Linebaugh, John G. Rule, E. P. Thompson, Cal Winslow (eds) *Albion's Fatal Tree. Crime and Society in Eighteenth Century England*, London: Allen Lane.

Hill, Stephen 1981. *Competition and Control at Work: The New Industrial Sociology*. Cambridge: The MIT Press.

Hirsch, Joachim 1979. 'The State Apparatus and Social Reproduction: Elements of a Theory of the Bourgeois State'. John Holloway and Sol Picciotto (eds) *State and Capital: A Marxist Debate*, Austin: University of Texas Press, 57–107.

Ignatieff, Michael 1978. *A Just Measure of Pain: The Pentitentiary in the Industrial Revolution 1750–1850*. New York: Pantheon Books.

Landes, David S. 1969. *The Unbound Prometheus: Technological Change and Industrial Development in Western Europe from 1750 to the Present*. Cambridge University Press.

Laslett, Peter 1965. *The World We Have Lost – Further Explored*. London: Methuen and Co. Ltd.

Littler, Craig R. 1978. 'Understanding Taylorism', *British Journal of Sociology* 29 (2): 185–202.

Littler, Craig R. 1982. 'Deskilling and Changing Structures of Control'. Stephen Wood (ed.) *The Degradation of Work? Skill, Deskilling and the Labour Process*. London: Hutchinson, 122–45.

Marx, Karl 1906. *Capital, A Critique of Political Economy*. Chicago: Charles H. Kerr and Company.

Melossi, Dario and M. Pavarini 1981. *The Prison and the Factory*. New York: Macmillan.

Miller, Wolfgang and Christel Neussus 1979. '"The Welfare State Illusion" and the Contradiction Between Wage Labour and Capital', John Holloway and Sol Picciotto (eds) *State and Capital: A Marxist Debate*. Austin: University of Texas Press: 32–9.

O'Neill, John 1972. 'On Body Politics', Hans Peter Dreitzel (ed.) in *Recent Sociology No. 4. Family, Marriage and the Struggle of the Sexes*. New York: Collier-Macmillan, 251–67.

O'Neill, J. 1985. *Five Bodies: The Human Shape of Modern Society*. Ithaca: Cornell University Press.

Palmer, Bryan 1975. 'Class, Conception and Conflict: The Thrust for Efficiency, Managerial Views of Labor and the Working Class Rebellion, 1903–22. *The Review of Radical Political Economics* 7 (2): 31–49.

Parsons, Talcott 1951. *The Social System*. New York: The Free Press of Glencoe.

Penn, Roger 1982. 'Skilled Manual Workers in the Labour Process, 1856–1964'. Stephen Wood (ed.) *The Degradation of Work? Skills, Deskilling and the Labour Process*. London: Hutchinson, 90–108.

Perrot, M. 1979. 'The Three Ages of Industrial Discipline in Nineteenth Century France'. J. Merriman (ed.) *Consciousness and Class Experience in Nineteenth Century Europe*, New York: Holmes and Meier, 149–68.

Pollard, Sydney 1963. 'Factory Discipline in the Industrial Revolution'. *The Economic History Review* XVI, 2: 254–71.

Poulantzas, Nicos 1973. *Political Power and Social Classes*. London: NLB

Reid, Douglas A. 1976. 'The Decline of Saint Monday 1766–1876'. *Past and Present* 71: 76–101.

Rimlinger, Gaston V. 1971. *Welfare Policy and Industrialization in Europe, America and Russia*. New York: John Wiley.

Rodgers, Daniel T. 1979. *The Work Ethic in Industrial America 1850–1920*. Chicago and London: The University of Chicago Press.

Schluchter, Wolfgang 1981. *The Rise of Western Rationalism: Max Weber's Developmental History*, translated by Guenther Roth. Berkeley: University of California Press.

Smelser, Neil J. 1959. *Social Change in the Industrial Revolution: An Application of Theory to the British Cotton Industry*. Chicago: The University of Chicago Press.

Sohn-Rethel, Alfred 1978. *Intellectual and Manual Labour: A Critique of Epistemology*. London: Macmillan.

Stark, David 1980. 'Class Struggle and the Transformation of the Labour Process: A Relational Approach'. *Theory and Society* 9: 89–130.

Stone, Lawrence 1979. *The Family, Sex and Marriage in England 1500–1800*. New York: Harper & Row.

60 *John O'Neill*

Thompson, E. P. 1967. 'Time, Work, Discipline, and Industrial Capitalism'. *Past and Present* 38: 56–97.

Thompson, Victor A. 1961. *Modern Organization*. New York: Alfred A. Knopf.

Tobias, J. J. 1967. *Crime and Industrial Society in the 19th Century*. New York: Schocken Books.

Wall, Richard, Jean Robin and Peter Laslett (eds) 1983. *Family Forms in Historic Europe*. Cambridge University Press.

Weber, Max 1947. *The Theory of Social and Economic Organization*, translated by A. M. Henderson and Talcott Parsons. New York: Oxford University Press.

Weber, Max 1950. *General Economic History*, translated by Frank H. Knight. Glencoe, Ill.: The Free Press.

Weber, Max 1967. *From Max Weber: Essays in Sociology*, translated, edited and with an Introduction by H. H. Gerth and G. Wright Mills. New York: Oxford University Press.

Wilson, H. T. 1976. 'Reading Max Weber: The Limits of Sociology'. *Sociology* 10: 297–315.

Wilson H. T. 1977. *The American Ideology, Science, Technology and Organization as Modes of Rationality in Advanced Industrial Societies*. London: Routledge & Kegan Paul.

Part II
Bureaucracy: Practice, Problems and Paradoxes

Chapter 4 gives an overview of developments in China – a country with one of the earliest bureaucracies – and shows how different circumstances and cultures affect the style and structures of public management. The next three essays look at personnel issues in developed and developing countries, including the links between public and private sector management. Chapters 8 to 11 then examine ethical issues in similar vein, thus rounding off a group of articles on the personnel aspects of bureaucratic systems.

Chapters 12 to 21 consider technical issues in public sector management. These have arisen mainly within bureaucratic settings, though many of the issues and developments also have relevance in a more entrepreneurial culture. The essays cover strategic planning, appraisal and decision techniques, budgeting and performance measurement, evaluation and project management. Together they illustrate some of the developments on a variety of fronts to maintain or improve the science of management in an increasingly complex and uncertain world. By including essays from both theoretical and practical perspectives, an indication may be obtained of the successes and failures of technical processes. The overall lesson would seem to be that more sophisticated analyses help to identify the political and managerial decisions that must be faced, rather than actually offer solutions to problems.

Part II closes with two readings on the general approach to public sector management in the UK, where the concept of the 'New Public Management' is introduced and explored, and on the difference between Canadian and Japanese approaches to management. These readings help to set the following sections in context; they also indicate that the route taken recently by many Governments towards a more business-like management culture is not the only available response to the problems of bureaucracy; nor is it likely in principle to solve all such problems.

[4]

Restructuring Government Organization in China and Transforming Government Functions for an Efficient and More Productive Bureaucratic Performance

GU JIAQI

A sustained, steady economic development and a stable, prosperous society cannot come about by focusing only on the formulation of concrete social and economic policies. Increased attention and priority should be given to the reform of the state apparatus itself, especially of the policymaking and implementation process. Administrative structural reform, particularly China's practice of adjusting organizational structure and transforming government functions and management processes, is an example of the efforts to explore strategies and approaches for the conduct of administrative restructuring and enhancing bureaucratic performance in developing countries.

This article discusses three questions: first, the necessity of adjusting the government organizational structure and rationalizing the administrative policymaking mechanism, as well as some practices in China; second, transforming government management processes towards adapting to the changing social and economic environment in developing countries, e.g., describing what has been done by China in order to change direct and micro-management; and third, concentrating on improving efficiency and productivity.

During the past several decades, developing countries have realized that a sustained, steady economic development and a stable, prosperous society cannot come about by focusing only on the formulation of concrete social and economic policies. Sufficient attention and high priority should be given to reforming the state apparatus itself, especially the policymaking and implementation processes. China is no exception.

By reviewing the history of the past 40 years, particularly that of economic construction and social development, it is commonly recognized that administrative restructuring must go hand in hand with the social and economic development. Remarkable achievements have been recorded in China in terms of economic growth and restructuring in

Governance: An International Journal of Policy and Administration. Vol. 5, No. 4, October 1992 (pp. 391-401), © 1992. Research Committee on the Structure and Organization of Government of the International Political Science Association. ISSN 0952-1895

the 1980s. This, in turn, makes it all the more imperative to conduct large-scale administrative and structural reforms, adjust government organizational structure, and transform government functions and management processes. Administrative reform of this nature is now operational in China and will continue throughout this decade. It constitutes an essential component of the government's general effort to reform its political system, which aims at fitting into and facilitating the social and economic development of the country.

The main purpose of this administrative restructuring is to promote the efficiency of the bureaucracy and to satisfy the public's ever increasing demand for goods and services. The administrative structural reform, particularly China's practice of adjusting the organizational structure and transforming government functions and management processes, is an example of the efforts to explore strategies and approaches for conducting administrative restructuring and enhancing bureaucratic performance in developing countries.

ADJUSTING GOVERNMENT ORGANIZATIONAL STRUCTURE AND RATIONALIZING ADMINISTRATIVE POLICYMAKING MECHANISMS

The government agencies of many developing countries have been expanding under the pressure of ever-increasing social services and the government's deep involvement in economic construction. In the early 1980s, the number of central government agencies in China reached 100 in order to cope with the new social demands and economic development. The civil service was expanding at the same pace. All these resulted in redundant institutions and overstaffing. The fact is, however, that there has been a decrease in productivity. The dilemma is that the more institutions and employees a government has, the more it is preoccupied with miscellaneous businesses, the less it is able to exercise macro-management and ensure the feasibility of its policies. A misleading central government policy produces 100 times more adverse effects than those resulting from a mistake in the process of policy implementation by a lower-level unit. This has been demonstrated throughout our history. Therefore, administrative restructuring is not undertaken solely to streamline government operations characterized by redundant institutions and overstaffing. What is more vital, through the adjustment of governmental institutional structure, is to strengthen and rationalize the government policymaking process.

The governments of developing countries play a special role in making policies and providing guidance for their social and economic development, a point which I sufficiently illustrated in 1989 at the International Workshop on Government Administration and Management.

RESTRUCTURING GOVERNMENT ORGANIZATION IN CHINA 393

Every developing country wishes for an early economic take-off and modernization. Yet, the existing fact is that a high growth rate of economic development is not achieved in many developing countries. In my opinion, there are, among other causes, three major factors.

First, their limited economic strength is due to a not-so-well-organized regulatory mechanism. Operating in such an environment, increased economic growth cannot be achieved through a "laissez-faire" economic policy. Instead, high economic growth depends on governmental involvement in the formulation of rational economic development strategies and rational distribution of resources and funds.

Second, developing countries are facing economic pressures from the industrialized nations as well as fierce and complex international competition. They need their governments to be sensitive and responsive, capable of making the right decisions and missing no opportunities in the ever-changing international situation.

Finally, developing nations also face serious internal social problems and conflicts of interests resulting from economic restructuring. Sustained and steady economic development is dependent on whether these problems can be settled properly and tensions can be eased. In this respect, governments play a unique role. Their power and effective measures have the final say. Therefore, strengthening the government's policymaking ability and rationalizing the administrative policymaking process are of vital importance and should be given first priority in administrative restructuring in developing countries.

There is an old saying in China, "A workman must first sharpen his tools if he is to do his work well." This means that only when the government's policymaking processes have been rationalized and decision-making abilities strengthened will there be effective social and economic development strategies and approaches.

The Chinese government has been attaching great importance to the enhancement of its policymaking ability. Especially in recent years, the central government has been emphasizing that policies must be realistic and feasible so as to avoid drastic fluctuations in economic construction and social development. The administrative structural reform of the State Council in 1988 emphasized the adjustment of the central government's functions, aiming at freeing the central government from daily routines and devoting itself only to macro-management and policymaking. According to this principle, we adjusted the organizational structure of the central government, setting up new institutions for strengthening the capability of the existing agencies in such areas as policy advice and research, national economic planning, statistics and information systems. These institutions provide effective consultancy and service to the State Council for decision-making. We will further deepen the structural reform of the State Council and further rationalize the policymaking process, enabling the government to make realistic policies and provide guidance for social and economic development.

To rationalize the policymaking process and mechanism is of more importance in administrative structural reform at the central government level for, compared with governments at local levels, the central government shoulders a heavier and more comprehensive task in terms of policymaking. China, considering its vast area and huge population, is a typical example of a government preoccupied with daily routines. Furthermore, China is a unitary state. The central government must formulate a series of policies and principles in order to exercise effective leadership over governments at local levels. All these demand a rational, well-established and mature policymaking mechanism.

For developing countries, the following steps need to be taken in order to rationalize the policymaking mechanism of central governments:

A proper separation between policymaking and policy execution
Governments of many developing countries formulate and implement public policies. This dual responsibility forces governments of developing countries to be preoccupied with routines and unable to formulate long-term strategies prudently. In addition, this mixed role of policymaking and execution will lead to lopsided decisions because the governments, as policy executors, will be unavoidably influenced by interests of certain establishments. Therefore, there is a need to set up specialized agencies which are relatively free from influences of different interests and which devote themselves wholly to policymaking.

To rationalize the policymaking process
A rational policy is a product of a rationalized policymaking process. Decisions on important issues have to go through the following procedure: putting forward draft decisions; conducting feasibility studies; extensively enlisting views and comments; and holding discussions and debates in a frank and democratic atmosphere. Of course, it is up to the administrators concerned to make the final decision.

To establish and rationalize policymaking advice and support service
Administrators at various levels, particularly at the central government level, should be assisted by a team of eminent social elite, learned scholars and government practitioners. This brain trust would conduct research and feasibility studies on major issues, provide consultancy and constructive options for administrators during policymaking.

To strengthen governmental abilities

To collect and process information and data, establish an effective information network, provide adequate, accurate and comprehensive information and statistics so as to avoid major mistakes in policy-making resulting from misleading information is essential.

Conducting structure reform in governments and rationalizing the policymaking mechanism should by no means neglect the importance of streamlining and merging redundant institutions and administrative levels, which is also an effective method of improving the efficiency and productivity of governments. Streamlining the size of organizational and personnel establishments, therefore, forms an important component of administrative restructuring in China.

The number of government institutions and administrative levels are in direct proportion to governmental involvement in public affairs. Along with rapid economic progress in developing countries, public affairs bureaus are increasing accordingly. The more public affairs bureaus there are, the bigger the governments are. The more functions a government has, the more institutions it oversees. This vicious cycle will finally lead to redundant institutions, excessive administrative levels and complicated operational procedures. Although certain businesses can be well managed with the establishment of new institutions, the government structure, as a whole, could be jeopardized and its efficiency undermined.

Bearing these ideas in mind, the Chinese government has conducted several administrative reforms to streamline its institutions. Measures include the following: *first*, letting a department handle as much business of similar nature as possible; as to the management of those newly-merged public affairs bureaus, we tend to increase the functions of existing departments instead of setting up new institutions; *second*, reducing the number of administrative levels within a department — it is clearly stipulated that there are only two administrative levels within ministries: commissions and state bureaus under the direct leadership of the State Council, namely the department and the division; *third*, eliminating and merging those departments whose functions have been diminished or eliminated.

TRANSFORMING GOVERNMENT MANAGEMENT PROCESSES TOWARDS ADAPTING TO THE CHANGED SOCIAL AND ECONOMIC ENVIRONMENT

Governments of developing countries not only play an essential role in making policies and providing guidance for their economic construction and social development, but are also substantially involved in direct management of social and economic affairs. In fact, at certain periods of economic and social development, governments of many developing countries need to be directly involved in the running of many welfare projects such as hospitals, schools and so forth and even running state-owned enterprises in areas such as the mining industry, road construction and energy development.

Governments must choose proper ways of managing the ever-growing economic and social affairs. Moreover, rapid social and economic development will definitely result in drastic changes of the economic structure and social environment. This in turn requires governments to adjust their styles of management accordingly. Otherwise, economic growth and social development would be constrained.

Like most developing countries, the Chinese government exercised massive and direct management over its economy in the early 1950s, aiming at recovering from its war-ridden economy and laying a solid foundation for industrializaton.

China pursued a policy of government-planned economy at various levels and exercised micro- and direct management over the operations of enterprises, from production to product marketing, material allocation and consumption. Accordingly, many government agencies in charge of economic development were established. Management of this nature was once effective in utilizing limited resources to produce rapid economic growth and to build a large-scale infrastructure for industrialization because the more the economy develops, the more complex it becomes. The deeper governments get involved in micro-management of the economy, the more they are preoccupied with daily routines of review and approval of numerous economic construction projects which will definitely undermine governmental efficiency and hamper the initiative of enterprises. It is against this background that the Chinese government began its economic restructuring in 1978, separating the ownership and management of state-owned enterprises, reforming the highly centralized system and moving toward a more market-oriented economy. In this situation, the existing government structure and methods of management need to be changed accordingly.

One emphasis of the structural reform of the State Council in 1988 was to transform the government's functions and change its management processes. There is no facile formula for transforming a government's style of management. The outcome of reforms should fit into the changed environment and be conducive to further social and economic development. Under these general principles, there are several directions guiding structural reform and transformation of the government's style of management.

From Exercising Direct and Micro-Management to Indirect and Macro-Management

The fact that the roles and functions of governments of developing countries have grown does not mean that the methods of management have been adjusted and increased accordingly. At the early stages of economic development, society alone was not in a position to organize for economic development. It was necessary for government to exercise both direct and micro-management of the economy in order to achieve a high economic growth rate. After enterprises have established themselves and matured enough to manage their own businesses, governments should shift to macro-management of the economy, help to develop markets, and administer and regulate economic development by formulating macro-economic strategies and policies.

The Chinese government has, proceeding from its own national characteristics, taken three steps to adjust its style of management. First is the gradual separation of the ownership and management of state-owned enterprises. Business operation is managed by the enterprises themselves while government exercises management only in its capacity as owners of the state-owned enterprises. Second is the gradual separation between the government's management of social affairs and that over national properties. The former aims to maintain a good social order and economic environment to provide services to economic entities of different natures. This is a manifestation of the government's regulatory function over economic development through the management of markets and improvement of the economic environment. Third is to maintain an increase in the government's ability to exercise macro-management and regulation of the economy. In fact, transformation of the government's style of management does not simply mean abandoning the old system. There are preconditions for governments to lessen their direct management over enterprises' operations and it is not just a matter of decentralization.

These preconditions include the necessity for strengthening the government's ability for macro-economic management and regulation. Otherwise, the economic order and environment will be out of control. For developing countries, when their economies have evolved to a higher level, governments are required to strengthen their ability to exercise macro-management and regulation of the economy; to shift the management of operations of enterprises to that of the markets; to maintin and create a favorable environment for economic development.

From "Rule of Man" to "Rule of Law"

Owing to various reasons, most developing countries do not have sound and comprehensive legal systems. At the early stages of economic development, economies were underdeveloped and governmental involvement in economic management was limited to relatively smaller, less complex areas. Governments found it was still manageable to use only the experience and intelligence of government employees, along with existing management skills, without applying laws and regulations. Yet, with the development of the economy, governmental involvement expanded to a wider dimension and the complexity of management also increased accordingly. "Rule of law" is called for in economic activities and orders should be defined and regulated by law.

"Rule of Law" means a gradual establishment of a set of legal acts to regulate social and economic activities. Two examples are an "Enterprise Law," defining the rights, operational procedures and scope of an enterprise's business, and a "Law on Industrial and Commercial Administration," legally entrusting to governments the right to define and maintain order for economic activities.

Laws enable enterprises and governments to manage their own business. Governments no longer order enterprises what to produce and what not to. No longer are they responsible for the marketing of products. Instead, enterprises will have to face markets, including bad clients, directly. Enterprises pay taxes, governments collect them and protect the legal rights of enterprises. In addition, governments, in their capacity as owners of state-owned enterprises, supervise the input and output of goods and services and assure the maintenance or rise in the values of national properties.

"Rule of Law" also means disciplining the bureaucracy and the civil service by law, especially the "frontier organizations" and civil servants who deliver goods and services directly to enterprises and the public. In other words, there shall be a linkage between powers and responsibilities. Insofar as the supervision of civil service is concerned, there are two major types in China. One is the supervision over the civil service by corporate bodies and citizens for whom the government is serving on the basis the newly promulgated Administrative Litigation Law; the other is from the government itself, namely from its supervision agencies which have field offices in government at various levels and are responsible for disciplining civil servants.

Improving Efficiency and Productivity

Governments in developing countries face increasing pressures to improve their efficiency and productivity as the economy and society develop to a new dimension and higher level. Governments are being asked (even demanded) to provide not only effective social and economic policies but also their successful implementation and involvement in all social affairs along with achieving satisfactory results. The public demands these results not only in terms of quantity but also in terms of quality. They also demand that governments achieve the best outcomes using fewer inputs. On the other hand, governments themselves feel it imperative to adjust their functions and styles of management because of the development of the economy, the increase in scope of business, the expansion of institutions, administrative levels and the civil service. All of these also require governments to overcome bureaucratic obstacles and improve efficiency and productivity.

The improvement of bureaucratic performance and productivity involves numerous factors. The status of governmental efficiency and productivity and ways to improve them differ from one country to another because of diverse cultures, histories, traditions and various irregular elements in the societies. Yet, for most developing countries, they share many similarities insofar as the improvement of efficiency and productivity is concerned because most of them are underdeveloped economically and culturally, and are attempting to promote a rapid economic growth at the same level in terms of public administration. This article intends to, from the point of structural reform and transforming governmental means of management, elaborate on the following aspects concerning the improvement of efficiency and productivity.

Improving the Validity and Predictability of Government Decisions

An inappropriate government decision will give rise to social disasters. China experienced great suffering as a result of misleading or inappropriate government policies. Social progress and economic development were delayed by these erroneous policies. Therefore, developing countries must establish a scientific policymaking mechanism, rationalize the policymaking process, strengthen policymaking ability and improve the validity and predictability of policymaking on major social and economic issues. These are fundamental objectives of public administration and preconditions for the improvement of bureaucratic efficiency and productivity.

An Effective and Resolute Implementation of Government Policies

For developing countries, effective implementation of government policies in due course is another manifestation of bureaucratic productivity. Sloppy implementation and misinterpretation of government policies are not rare in China. Sometimes, the authority of law and regulations is not firmly upheld and the goals envisaged from appropriate policies are not realized. In developing countries, economy and culture are acutely affected for various reasons where administrative development was at a lower level. With the rapid development of the economy, the bureaucracy is expanding drastically and is increasingly involved in social and economic development. Governments are no longer just responsible for collecting taxes and resolving disputes among different social groups. Instead, governments should, through their well established organizational networks and unified leadership, utilize all available resources to conduct massive economic construction and realize the goal of strengthening national power and improving the living standard of the public. In this context, efficiency and productivity of governments are often the focal point of the public. In fact, the efficiency and productivity of governments in many developing countries are far from satisfactory.

Ironically, military juntas in some countries are more efficient and productive than civilian governments. Unlike industrial countries, developing nations have to concentrate on the drafting of basic administrative "Ia" rather than improving the working conditions and purchasing modern office equipment necessary for greater bureaucratic efficiency and productivity.

To be more specific, there are several elements which are essential to the faithful implementation of government policies. First, the functions and responsibilities of government employees, from top executives to clerical workers, must be clearly defined and a "responsibility system" be established; second, the authority of law, discipline, and stressing the necessity for the governments at lower levels to be subject to their superiors and to a unified command in the process of policy implementation should be upheld. Finally, establishing and perfecting a supervision network within governments in order to check any deviation from and misinterpretation of set policies is necessary.

STANDARDIZING ADMINISTRATIVE BEHAVIOR AND THE ADMINISTRATIVE OPERATING MECHANISM

Many developing countries are facing a dilemma: on the one hand, the public is always complaining that governments have not done what they should have done; on the other hand, governments are so big they have established institutions to handle virtually all public affairs. Under such circumstances, it makes no sense to establish new government agencies and recruit more civil servants. What matters more is the bureaucracy itself, namely, its operating mechanism, the behavior of its staff and their efficiency and productivity. An efficient government relies on its standardized administrative operational mechanism. Procedures, therefore, should not only be limited to adjusting governmental institutions and transforming their functions, but also to be considering how governments and civil service should behave and fulfill their functions. They attach great importance to standardizing civil service behavior and administrative operational mechanisms.

The Chinese government has been emphasizing the importance of reinforcing the mechanism of restriction — thus, keeping the functions and powers of all governments within the bounds of law and regulation and under the supervision of the public. The structural reform of the State Council in 1988 addressed this subject. Efforts were made in the following three areas: first, there has been an attempt to standardize the organizational structure and administrative operational procedure of all departments under the State Council. Specifically, the functions of all central government agencies have been redefined and their interrelations straightened out. The redefined functions, institutional establishment within an organization, the system of leadership and the decision-making process are all consolidated by rules and regulations issued in the name of the State Council. The "Organic Regulation of the State Environmental Protection Agency" is an example. The law has been drafted and survived the close scrutiny of professionals within and outside the government and will be submitted to the State Council for approval and promulgation. Second, the promulgation of the Administrative Litigation Law defines the relationship between the public and administrative behavior. Finally, regulations have been drafted on institutional establishment and management of the State Council defining the standardized procedure for adjusting the organizational structure, the size of organizational and personnel establishment, along with all other functions. This regulation has passed the professional scrutiny and will be subject to State Council approval and promulgation.

The improvement of bureaucratic efficiency and productivity involves a variety of elements. This article, due to limited space, has only touched on a few of them. May our experience and experimentation be of value to all the people concerned.

[5]

Personnel Management Reform in the Philippines: The Strategy of Professionalization

AMELIA P. VARELA

The strategy of professionalization which is a multi-pronged system aimed at efficient, effective, and responsive delivery of government services is the current thrust of the Civil Service Commission (CSC). As such, a package of personnel reform measures is instituted by the Commission which includes the pursuit of merit, competence and performance; development and institutionalization of positive attitudes, ethical conduct and behavior; motivation through an integrated system of rewards and punishments; continuing human resource development; and the encouragement of public sector unionism.

Relevant issues on the professionalization thrust have been raised: (1) since the strategy of professionalization rests more on administrative controls, will the effort bring about increased bureaucratization and routinization instead (or the issue of professionalization vs. bureaucratization)? (2) are the policies coming from diverse sources like the CSC, Department of Budget and Management, Office of the President, and Congress — to mention a few — fully coordinated so as to produce convergent rather than divergent results? (3) is the government really sincere on the issue of public sector unionism since it denies the unions their basic rights to strike and bargain collectively for better pay and working conditions?

There is a need to assess further the current efforts toward professionalization to find out if the Commission is really moving toward its avowed goals of deregulation, decentralization and managerial and professional discretion rather than becoming more routinized or bureaucratic.

This article discusses the personnel management reform of the bureaucracy being undertaken by the Civil Service Commission (CSC) which is intended to professionalize the civil service. The strategy of professionalization is a multi-activity, multipronged systems approach directed at institutionalizing a deep sense of commitment to public service and accountability to the people on the part of government officials and employees. It is aimed at providing prompt and responsive frontline services with utmost dedication and pride as well as with efficiency and effectiveness.

Governance: An International Journal of Policy and Administration. Vol. 5, No. 4, October 1992 (pp. 402-422), © 1992. Research Committee on the Structure and Organization of Government of the International Political Science Association. ISSN 0952-1895

The discussion focuses on the activities adopted by the Commission which include the upholding of merit in entry and personnel movement and progression; value orientation/reorientation and development of positive attitudes and ethical conduct and behavior; a motivational organizational climate that includes a system of rewards and punishments; continuing human resource development to ensure administrative capability; and the activation of a participatory mechanism in decision-making regarding personnel matters through public service unionism.

The article shall not evaluate the policy and action measures presently being implemented toward professionalization, but rather raise issues related to professionalization in general as against that of bureaucratization. Specific issues are directed on the efforts of the Commission to professionalize the civil service. Some suggestions accompany the discussion of the issues being raised and a concluding note ends the article.

LEGAL AUTHORITY AND MANDATE

The Civil Service Commission, a constitutional body, serves as the central personnel agency of the government. As such, the Commission is mandated to: (l) establish a career service; (2) adopt measures promoting morale, efficiency, integrity, responsiveness, progressiveness, and courtesy in the civil service; (3) strengthen the merit and rewards system; (4) integrate all human resource development programs; and (5) institutionalize a management climate conducive to public accountability.[1] In response to its mandate, the Commission seeks to provide the government with competent, well-trained, and motivated personnel, committed to the efficient and effective delivery of public services. In its statement of mission, a priority thrust is the professionalization of the civil service.

The Commission's blueprint for professionalization is a package of personnel reform measures which includes the pursuit of merit, competence and performance; development and institutionalization of positive attitudes and ethical conduct and behavior among civil service personnel; an integrated system of rewards and punishments; a continuing human resource development; and the encouragement of public service unionism.

The concept of professionalization of the civil service can be gleaned from the following objective: "the Commission shall lead in the promotion of government responsiveness to the needs of the people and shall instill a deep sense of responsibility and public service among government workers to achieve professionalization in the civil service" (Civil Service Comm. [CSC, henceforth] 1990b, 3). It is hoped that by

1994, "government workers shall have instilled a deep sense of public service and accountability in themselves. They shall take pride in rendering frontline services to the public with utmost efficiency and effectiveness" (CSC 1990b, 3).

THE STRATEGY OF PROFESSIONALIZATION

The year 1988 was a tumultuous one not only for the Civil Service Commission but for the whole bureaucracy as well. The civil service was reeling from the "most sweeping and unsettling reorganization of the Philippine bureaucracy" (CSC 1989a, 3).

The general feelings of demoralization, anger and frustration over violations of the constitutionally guaranteed principles of security of tenure and of due process and outcries against abuses committed by those in power regarding the placement, separation/retention, and transfer of personnel reverberated all over the bureaucracy.

The clamor for a "professional corps of civil servants who will continue carrying out the business of government despite periodic changes in the nations's leadership" (*The Daily Inquirer* 1990, 4) has long been aired by various sectors, particularly from political scientists and public administrators.

The Pursuit of Merit, Competence and Performance

Tightening Entry Requirements

The Civil Service Commission responded through a statement of goal to professionalize the civil service. Two action measures were immediately undertaken: (l) removal of non-qualified personnel and (2) raising the passing mark in civil service examinations from 70% to 80% (*The Daily Inquirer* 1990, 4). A directive was issued in April 1989 to the effect that starting January 1990, no temporary appointments shall be issued.[2] This means that henceforth all those entering the public service must have the requisite eligibilities (CSC 1989a, 4).

This new passing grade requirement was applied for the first time to the three major national examinations administered by the Commission in 1989. The raised passing mark for the professional and subprofessional career service examinations saw an 8.25% passing rate among the total examinees. Some 40,847 out of 378,170 examinees made it (22,135 for the professional and 18,712 for the subprofessional career service.) A nationwide registration of civil service-eligible people who were desirous of entering government service was undertaken and 11,548 responded. These moves sent clear signals that the Civil Service

Commission was serious in upgrading standards of recruitment into government service (CSC 1989a, 5).

In addition to the career service examinations, there are special laws which grant eligibilities under certain conditions. They are: Presidential Decree No. 907 which grants eligibility to college honor graduates; Presidential Decree No. 1408 to electronic data processing (EDP) specialists; Presidential Decree No. 997 to scientific and technological specialists; and Republic Act No. 1080 which declares bar and board examinations as civil service examinations and passing these examinations would grant civil service eligibility to the persons concerned, among others. The conditions under which these eligibilities are operational are qualifications and experience of individuals and the requirements of public service.

The latest special law is Republic Act 6850 which grants eligibility under certain conditions to government employees under provisional or temporary status with at least seven years of efficient service. There were 17,345 employees who benefitted from this law and who otherwise would have been terminated from service if they could not gain eligibility through appropriate examinations.

As observed by the Civil Service Commission in its corporate plan for 1990–1994, the enactment and implementation of this law has in fact defeated the purpose of professionalizing the bureaucracy. With its emphasis on the length of service rendered in the government, casual and contractual employees may also demand the same privilege extended by the law to temporary employees. In the case of temporary employees, there is the consolation that temporary appointments are extended to persons who are qualified but do not possess the appropriate civil service eligibility. Casual and contractual employees however, are hired based on the exigencies of the service and normally are recruited on the basis of political and/or bureaucratic patronage.

Reaffirming Confidence in the Principle of Tenure and Developing a Culture of Performance

The demoralizing and sweeping reorganization of the bureaucracy in 1988 under the Presidential Commission on Government Reorganization (PCGR) raised important issues on the violations of constitutional and human rights of individual civil servants. The relevant issues raised were those related to the principles of security of tenure and due process of law as guaranteed in the Constitution.

The arbitrariness of the reorganization process engendered distrust of the effort of the new government to trim and professionalize the bureaucracy. This distrust was substantiated by a CSC report on employee accession and separation for the period February 25, 1986 to June 30, 1987 which showed that while 37,885 employees were separated "to trim the bureaucracy," 78,440 were hired to replace them. Thus, for every employee let go, 2.07 were employed (Esleta 1988, 14). The prime focus of the Commission's policies and operations at that time was to reaffirm and strengthen the security of tenure principle and to speedily adjudicate complaint cases filed regarding personnel displacement because of reorganization.

To alleviate the fear of the public personnel that the principle of security of tenure can be wantonly violated via reorganization, Republic Act No. 6656 was passed by Congress on June 9, 1988, signed by the president the following day, and took effect on June 29, 1988 (Lansangan 1988, 4).

The Act declares it a policy of the state to protect the security of tenure of civil service officers and employees in the reorganization of the various agencies of the national and local governments, state colleges and universities expressly authorized by law, including government owned or controlled corporations with original charters, without sacrificing the need to promote morale, efficiency, integrity, responsiveness, progressiveness, and courtesy in the civil service pursuant to Article IX-B. Section 3 of the 1987 Philippine Constitution (Lansangan 1988, 4).

To strengthen its efforts in engendering high performance, the Commission reemphasized that the *sine qua non* of security of tenure is job performance. This stand was upheld by the Supreme Court in 1989 so that throughout that year, the Commission's policies and programs pushed hard the fact that security of tenure is not an absolute right, but should be treated relative to employee performance. Most of the Commission's directives during the year pertained to merit/competence and work performance (CSC 1989a, 5).

The emphasis on performance was also reflected in the Commission's quasi-judicial activities which posted a disposition rate of 82% from 29% of the previous year. The emphasis on performance was also made imperative by a vigilant and politicized workforce, demanding reforms in the administrative system and increased job security and adequate wages. This is likewise enforced by clamor for bureaucratic reforms from a population long impatient for more responsive and efficient delivery of government services (CSC 1989a, 3).

Career Mobility and Merit Promotion

The first two action measures described above were complemented with the institutionalization of agency merit promotion plans throughout the bureaucracy and a system of ranking positions for adoption in all public offices (1989a, 18). Both systems are merit-based and are congruent to agencies' respective performance evaluation schemes.

Promotion also showed a breakaway from the traditional practice of career mobility and promotion based on seniority and next-in-rank principles. Recently, for promotions, the selection process has been done on an organization-wide basis unlike the previous practice wherein the selection was limited to the organizational unit where the vacancy existed. In cases where the specialization/expertise is not available in the organization, deep selection and movements across agencies of government are emphasized.

Promotions from within or "nurturing" had also given way to lateral entry, especially in positions requiring the latest positions technological expertise. This approach discouraged complacency and placed public officers and employees on positive competitive stand, nurtured by a quest for "excellence" through high performance.

The drive for merit and performance however, may be dampened by the passage and implementation of RA 6758 which grants step increments for government workers. Section 13 (c) provides for step increments based on merit and/or length of service effective January 1, 1990. Based on the guidelines for implementation promulgated jointly by the Commission and the Department of Budget and Management,[3] longevity pay shall apply only to officials and employees with permanent status in the career service. Likewise, a one-step increment shall be granted to officials and employees for every three years of continuous satisfactory service in the position. Such increments, however, shall not exceed the maximum step of the salary grade of the position.

At a glance, it seems that the provision of step increases guarantees gradual career progression. However, several dysfunctions which are demotivational to employees would exist as a result. Take the example of a university professor who was not promoted for 21 years because of poor performance, but who got seven step increments within his professorial grade without even sweating it out in terms of teaching excellence nor research outputs. Colleagues of his get only a maximum three steps promotion for meritorious performance in teaching and research. Still another dysfunction that the step increments brought is that in actual practice, the salary increases are based merely on length of service, since the satisfactory performance requirement is completely overlooked. Besides, because of the lack of budgetary allocations for merit promotion, the step increases provided by the longevity provisions remain the only recourse.

The system of merit protection and promotion has been set in place. The combined effects of the higher entry standards, performance-based

tenure and career mobility and promotion system are expected to safeguard the merit principle and system from the intrusion of political
patronage and thus considerably reduce its influence in personnel decisions in the public service.

Development and Institutionalization of Positive Attitudes, Ethical Conduct and Behavior

Code of Conduct and Ethical Standards for Public Officials and Employees (RA 6713)

The passage of Republic Act 6713 or the Code of Conduct and Ethical
Standards for Public Officials and Employees on February 21, 1989 is a
frontal strategy to counteract the perceived and actual behavior in the
bureaucracy as characterized by arrogance, inefficiency, and graft or
corruption. It is directed at strengthening the positive effects that the
policy and action reform measures previously taken can elicit through
similar changes in organizational and personnel conduct and behavior.

The declaration of policy in Section 2 intends that the state promote
a high standard of ethics in public service as exemplified in the following
conduct and behavior: "accountability to the people; discharge of duties
with responsibility, integrity, competence, and loyalty; act with patriotism and justice; lead modest lives; and uphold public interest over
personal interest."

Toward this end, two major programs are underway: (1) value development programs for officers and employees aimed at strengthening
the value of commitment to public service and the promotion of public
interest; and (2) professional, scientific, and technical training programs
aimed at enhancing professionalism, excellence, and skills in the performance of duties and responsibilities.

The organizational system is not spared in the value change effort.
The Code requires every department, office and agency of government
to conduct continuing studies and analysis of their work systems and
procedures to improve delivery of public services.[4] Such studies should
identify factors which contribute to negative bureaucratic behavior, red
tape, and low employee morale. Corresponding measures to correct
negative factors so identified should be pursued to enhance a management climate that is conducive to public accountability (Rule III, Sec. 4,
9).[5]

The state itself is required by the Code to practice the value of transparency of transactions and to provide access to information subject to
reasonable conditions. Openness in government transactions is expected to lessen the opportunities to commit fraud, graft and corrup-

tion, and other acts detrimental to public interests (Rule IV, Sec. 2, 10).[6] The requirement for public access to information is not absolute and is limited whenever the national security, defense, and foreign affairs interests are at stake.

To deter the accumulation of ill-gotten wealth, civil service officers and employees are required to file under oath their statements of assets, liabilities and net worth as well as a disclosure of business interests and financial connections including those of their spouses and unmarried children (Rule VII, Sec. 1, 19).[7]

A corollary provision is for public officials and employees to avoid conflict of interest which occurs whenever their private or business interests are affected or are opposed to their faithful performance of official duties. In case such conflict of interest arises, the official or employee should resign from his position in the private business enterprise and/or divest his interests/shareholdings (Rule IX, Sec. 1-2, 23-24).[8]

Special Programs: "DART" and "Ang Magalang, Bow"

To catalyze the delivery of professionalized, responsive, and effective public services, the Commission launched the following:

(1) **"Do Away With Red Tape" (DART)** — the program launched during the 88th anniversary of the Philippine civil service was a deliberate, organized effort to engage the active participation of all sectors of society to get the bureaucracy to deregulate itself, reduce inefficiency and red tape, and prevent corrupt practices.

Through the mass media, the public was encouraged to report cases of red tape to the DART Action Center which takes care of the complaints. Agencies often complained about are reported to the people via the media, print and radio. This way, the public can fiscalize the bureaucracy and hopefully reduce red tape and its attendant practices of corruption in public agencies.

(2) **"Ang Magalang, Bow"** — started in April 1990.[9] The program was intended to inculcate among government employees the importance of prompt and courteous service and do away with the stereotyped image of arrogant and inefficient bureaucrats. Print and broadcast media were likewise used to popularize the campaign. Selection of the most courteous employees by the clients they serve entitled the winners to raffle tickets for trips to local and foreign destinations. Besides instilling courteous service, the special program also facilitated public service with its 216 public assistance counters.

(3) **Citizen Satisfaction with Government Services** — was also a nationwide campaign designed to complement the two special programs

410   AMELIA P. VARELA

described above. A major component of this campaign is the explicit access of the public to government executives and leaders at specified times during the work-week so their problems can be directly attended to.

(4) "Panibagong Sigla 2000" — seeks to identify areas of reform in the bureaucracy which will ensure improved services as well as a motivated and committed workforce.

(5) "Silang Mahuhusay" — documents the attributes of organizations and managers demonstrating high performance despite the constraints in public governance.

Motivation Through an Integrated System of Rewards and Punishments

Salary Standardization

To give meaning to the professionalization thrust of the government, monetary rewards in terms of salaries and wages were standardized through Republic Act No. 6758 which took effect on July 1, 1989. Formally known as "an act prescribing a revised compensation and position classification system in the government and for other purposes," the law aims to standardize the different pay plans existing in the bureaucracy. The objectives of the law are to achieve equity in pay within government service, and to make the monetary reward system in the government comparable and competitive with those in the private sector.

At the time of its passage, national and local governments enjoyed lower basic salaries and fewer fringe benefit schemes compared to the Office of the President and its agencies; constitutional bodies like the Commissions on Civil Service, Audit and Elections; the government-owned and -controlled corporations and financial institutions.

The salary standardization law had set the minimum wage for the rank and file employees at P2,000. The conduct of a regular review of government compensation and benefits schemes to allow for inflation and other economic factors is similarly provided for. But even with a poverty line income at P5,825 today, government salary scales have not been reviewed to make them realistic. Salary step increments are moreover granted to officials and employees based on merit/length of service. A one-step increment based on length of service is granted for every three years of continuous satisfactory service in a particular position.

To alleviate the economic plight of government employees due to inflation, and since the government cannot afford salary increases, cost-of-living allowances are being given temporarily. Another measure provided the government employees is the monetization of a maximum of ten days of the accumulated leave credits, tax-free.

The standardization law, in addition to compensation, provided for a new position classification system. Positions are categorized into four main categories, namely: professional supervisory, professional non-supervisory, sub-professional supervisory, and sub-professional non-supervisory. In the implementation of the law, the classification failed to capture the existing substantial differences in professional competence, satisfactory work experience, and performance and potential. A case in point is academia where positions are based on rank classification.

In state colleges and universities, the categorization collapsed dissimilarly-ranked positions under the same salary grades, e.g., associate professor positions at higher salary steps and full professor positions at lower salary steps which totally ignored rank. The consequence was demoralization among the full professors whose entire academic lives were evaluated and reviewed before they were granted the full professor rank. The collapse of academic ranks disregarded this highly valued system in academia.

The allocation of positions to certain salary grades outside of Grades 33 to 30 (these are assigned to the president, vice-president, Supreme Court justices, Senate president, Speaker of the House, and others on down to secretary and undersecretary levels), is the task of the Department of the Budget and Management. The placement of all other positions below these grades into salary grades of "equivalent ranks" was seen to have been done arbitrarily so that bureaucracy-wide complaints and appeals arose. At present, many such complaints and appeals have remained unresolved.

Incentive Awards Scheme

To meet the need of the workforce for recognition, and to develop their esteem and high value for merit and exemplary performance, several intrinsic incentive awards are given to deserving civil service officials and employees. These are:

(1) **"Lingkod Bayan" Presidential Award** — given to an individual or group who/which has made an extraordinary contribution that has benefitted the country;

(2) **"Silangan" Presidential Award** — given to an individual or group of persons 30 years old or younger who has shown exemplary performance in their duties;

(3) **"Dangal ng Bayan" Award** — conferred to employees or employee associations as provided for in the Code of Conduct and Ethical Stan-

dards for demonstrating exemplary ethical behavior in the following norms of conduct: *1) commitment to public interest; 2) professionalism; 3) political neutrality; 4) responsiveness to the needs of the public; 5) nationalism and patriotism; 6) commitment to democracy; and 7) simple living.*

(4) Special Presidential Award — conferred to agencies for institutional excellence in service to the public.

(5) "Pag-asa Award" — presented by the Civil Service Commission to individuals and groups for dedication to service, innovativeness, and efficient performance. These awards are conferred to deserving winners during the annual civil service week celebration after a year-long nation-wide search.

Runners-up to these awards are cited by their respective nominating agencies in simple rites during the week-long celebration. These non-material incentives are expected to push forward the civil service quest for professionalism and exemplary performance as well as provide the recognition for government officials and employees and institutions for having demonstrated examples of professionalized and committed service to the public.

Continuing Human Resource Development

Pursuant to the constitutional mandate for human development (HRD), the Civil Service Commission had set in a four-pronged strategy of HRD consisting of manpower planning; training and other HRD interventions; performance appraisal system/contract; and research in aid of an improved HRD.

Manpower planning, a component of HRD, is a critical aspect of personnel management since it provides the information necessary for rational and responsive decision-making regarding personnel matters. Although a previously neglected aspect of personnel administration, the commission has established a pilot program of manpower planning for itself. Its experience, policies and guidelines will soon be implemented by other government agencies.

Human resource development has been traditionally met in the civil service through training directed at improvement of knowledge, skills, and attitudes of personnel at different hierarchical levels, functions/tasks being performed, and technologies being utilized. Government functionaries are provided with opportunities for professional growth and readied for alternative use in higher positions in the future. There are seven broad categories of training programs in the bureaucracy: professional/technical/scientific; executive development; employee development; supervisory development; middle management; pre-retirement; and orientation/reorientation. Value internalization training is presently available to comply with the code of conduct and ethics and the president's thrust to develop honesty and integrity in government.

In order to dovetail training activities to feed into agency needs, the commission decentralized the training functions and gave agencies the autonomy and flexibility in their training and developmental activities. With decentralization, direct training activities by the commission had been deemphasized. Instead, priority is now redirected toward policy formulation and the monitoring and controlling of HRD activities of individual agencies.

The need for better personnel management despite the constricting budgetary allocations makes it imperative for the commission to find alternative approaches to HRD. Thus, job counselling/coaching; distance education; job enrichment through job rotation, cross-posting, secondments, and productivity circles are now in the pipeline.

Public Sector Unionism

The constitutional call for public sector unionism as a positive force in nation-building and in promoting harmonious labor-management relations offered an expanded role for the commission. It launched its program for the promotion of unionism in the public sector. For starters, seminars and symposia on the subject were conducted across the bureaucracy. From the output of these seminars, the commission had set in place the grievance machinery as a preventive mechanism against strikes and walkouts. The basic groundrules in the exercise of union rights were likewise laid down. The commission also declared that the right to self-organization shall always be protected, but that strikes and work stoppages shall be dealt with accordingly.

Through the encouragement and assistance offered by the commission, 190 unions in the public sector were registered in 1990. Of this number, 51 were certified to act as agents of the employees in collective negotiations. The commission also issued the policy guidelines in conciliation/mediation and the policy directions on the right to collective negotiations in the public sector.

To ensure that government employees and the general public get equal treatment in government irrespective of gender, religion, ethnic origin, or political belief, the equality advocates program (EQUADS) had been set up so that any victim of discrimination could get redress. This measure also acts as a safeguard against inequality of treatment due to the reasons cited above.

414   AMELIA P. VARELA

ISSUES ON PROFESSIONALIZATION

General Issues: Professionalization vs. Bureaucratization

Professionalization is pursued today as a valued goal in organizations. There is a strong trend away from routinization and toward increased professionalization in the private sector. Likewise, professionalization is also taking place in the public sector. There is considerable talk about problem-solving and adaptability; about achieving excellence and maintaining high standards in recruitment, performance, and conduct/behavior — but routinization, characteristic of the bureaucracy, continues unabated. There is a less visible shift toward professionalization (Benveniste 1987, 3-4).

Professionalization and bureaucratization go hand in hand in a bureaucracy. Knowing the professions can help in understanding how to maximize the use of professionals in bureaucratic organizations as well as of the professionalization efforts underway in the Philippine bureaucracy.

A profession has structural and attitudinal characteristics. The structural elements are: 1) application of skills based on special knowledge; 2) requirements for advanced education and training; 3) formal testing of competence control on admission to profession; 4) existence of professional associations; 5) existence of codes of conduct or ethics; and 6) existence of an accepted commitment or calling, a responsibility for service to the public and humanity beyond monetary rewards or career progression in an organization (Hickson and Thomas 1969, 33).

The professional attitudes and values are as follow: 1) the belief that the profession is a significant reference group and the source of major ideas and judgments; 2) the belief in service to the public; 3) the desire for autonomy in work situations; 4) preference for self-regulation, particularly for peer control review; and 5) the notion of a calling, of a devotion to work even if fewer extrinsic rewards are provided (Hall 1968, 44).

The civilian bureaucracy employs 620,815 professionals (or 49.37% of the workforce) in the second level of its three-tiered personnel system. They are hired because of their special skills, competencies and knowledge. The application and utilization of their expertise is however regulated by the bureaucratic organization.

By training and professional specialization, the professionals behave predictably in uncertain and complex situations. Engineers remain calm and collected during power plant breakdowns; medical doctors respond almost intuitively to save lives in cases of emergencies, accidents, or natural calamities; social workers reach out to the victims of calamities

PERSONNEL MANAGEMENT REFORM IN THE PHILIPPINES   415

with compassion; teachers zealously mold the youth; while human rights lawyers stand ready to defend victims of injustice and human rights violations despite real threats to their lives.

The civil service today confronts situations where task variability and complexity prevail, and where the environment is not only uncertain but even hostile. Problem-solving and flexibility are essential characteristics required of the civil service. Thus, it needs to be action-oriented. But the civil service has not shed its bureaucratic qualities: there is routinization through rules and regulations and standard operating procedures. There is a hierarchy of authority and responsibility, and a system of control from top management to rank and file passing through different hierarchical levels.

The issue of organization of work is critical to the efforts to professionalize the civil service. What alternative structural arrangements can maximize the participation of professionals in the bureaucracy? The conventional bureaucratic form of organization reduces the effectiveness of professionals to contribute to the attainment of goals. Hierarchy, rules and regulations, procedures are control mechanisms which contribute to the narrowing of the area of discretion that professionals expect. The bureaucratic treatment of professionals is contrary to their expectation of autonomy in the work situation. The authority issue of what constitutes managerial authority compared to professional authority is another constraint to professional participation in public organizations. In service, there is an overlap between managerial and professional authority. When professional knowledge is needed in management decisions, professional participation or delegation of management authority takes place (Benveniste 1987, 67). This means sharing managerial tasks where professional values, knowledge, and skills are relevant and necessary. The goal or mission of the organization, its environment and technology, and the relevance of professional tasks within the organization determine the extent to which management allows professional-managerial participation. But in a bureaucracy like the civil service, management controls professionals and routinizes participation. *Ad hoc* routines are established to elicit limited and routinized professional participation by the staff. If ever professionals are allowed to participate in decision-making, management determines the scope of such professional participation.

To increase professionalization of the civil service *vis a vis* bureaucratization, it is important to know which tasks are predictive and repetitive and thus could be routinized. More complex tasks that require adaptation and problem-solving as well as taking on responsibility on the spot are not easily routinized. These tasks are more appropriate to professionals who expect more discretion in their work.

Assigning complex and non-predictive tasks to professionals can also contribute to their utilization by management more as problem-solvers and risk/action takers instead of being paper shufflers and pen-pushers. Coordination and teamwork between managers and professionals can also be enhanced by such a participatory arrangement.

Another issue is the domination of professionals by the bureaucracy and the dependence of professionals on the bureaucracy. Professionals in public organizations depend very much on their organizations to provide them with the equipment, technology, personnel, and rewards. Nuclear scientists, medical doctors, science researchers, university professors, to mention a few, are provided by their organizations with the nuclear facility, hospital, laboratory, and academic space to enable them to function professionally. They are also rewarded (intrinsically and extrinsically) by their own organizations which oblige professionals to accept excessive bureaucratization. This situation is in direct contrast with professionals who are private practitioners (e.g., medical doctors and lawyers) and who therefore can operate independently of bureaucratic organizations. Thus, the domination of the professionals by the bureaucracy continues. Most professionals are in scientific, technical, and professional support functions and are often subordinate to management/managers. The extent to which the professions are dominated by bureaucracy had been documented before.[10]

Professionals in the civil service are also required to be accountable to the public and are expected to conduct themselves with utmost consideration of public interest first before personal interest. The public accountability required of professionals tends to make them protect themselves from legal suits and administrative charges by hiding behind regulations and procedures, thereby resulting in more bureaucratization.

A corollary issue is the encouragement by the organization for the professionals to innovate, be creative, and take risks. However, the rules and regulations governing their activities, together with the requirements of public accountability do not allow them to make mistakes.

Punishments abound in case of errors: medical doctors can lose their licenses, lawyers can be disbarred, accountants and engineers can be expelled from professional organizations, as can the academicians. Organizational rewards can also be used to punish: promotion, status, or career can be denied, while others may take the form of transfers or dismissal/termination from service. The bureaucracy does not reward risk-takers. Only *successful* risk-takers get rewarded. But risk-taking implies the uncertainty of success or failure. This is why risk avoidance is the common bureaucratic norm. Avoiding risk deters organizational learning which is quite necessary in seeking alternatives and in implementing change (Benveniste 1987, 195).

Thus, any effort to professionalize the bureaucracy requires the provision of allowances for errors and a visible reward system for risk-takers. This way, professionals may be encouraged to exercise a wider latitude of discretion that may later result in acceptable debureaucratization in the civil service.

The bottom line issue is how can professionalization reduce excessive bureaucratization? Increasing professionalization of the civil service implies the substitution of discretionary roles for routinized roles. Professional roles rely on a knowledge basis and discretion within the limited domain of that base. Professional roles also provide an ethical stance and assume a commitment that goes beyond organizational boundaries and economic rewards. Some basic attitudes and values of the professions which are internalized by the professionals are significant inputs to change conduct and behavior from one of arrogance and inefficiency to one of commitment and performance.

The alternative to bureaucracy is a profession-oriented organization characterized by professionalized personnel involved in the core activities of the organization; structure that permits management to have access to professional know-how and vice-versa; and a control system based not on regulations, but on professional discretion, professional restraint, and professional regulation. This is assuming that the professions demonstrate exemplary self-regulation (Benveniste 1987, 257).

Professionalization of the civil service goes beyond bureaucracy. The management of professionalized civil service must rely more on sharing between professionals and managers in meeting organizational tasks; less control but more discretion; more emphasis on intrinsic motivation, trust, and ethics; and improved personnel utilization through enhancing professional participation in core activities where their professional expertise can fine-tune policies and programs of public governance (Benveniste 1987, 259-265).

Specific Issues: On Efforts to Professionalize the Philippine Civil Service

The Civil Service Commission has been on the fast-track toward professionalization. The commission and its leadership should be congratulated for having accomplished so much in a short period of time — about three years. It had set in motion the administrative machinery and value goals required in its serious efforts to give the Filipino people the dedicated and responsive public service that they deserved.

At a glance, the policy and action reform measures appear to move in a unified direction toward professionalization. A closer and longer look however shows some pitfalls and constraints. The whole strategy of professionalization seems to rest on controls: from recruitment of personnel to their utilization. The strict requirements for appointments at entry levels; the tightening of standards for permanency and tenure; the emphasis on high performance and excellence; and the requirements for ethical conduct and behavior, including public accountability have attendant rules and regulations and procedures which could lead to increased bureaucratization and routinization in the long run. Despite various reorganization attempts to improve the bureaucracy, changes in the structural arrangements have not resulted in providing for more space which allows for professional participation in policymaking nor in the sharing with management in making decisions regarding core programs and similar activities. For the Aquino government, the only visible structural changes were the bloating of the bureaucracy at the undersecretary and assistant secretary levels and the increased size of the bureaucracy by the creation of *ad hoc* task forces, committees, and commissions whose functions can be assigned to regular line agencies. New policies had been passed during the process of professionalization. Unfortunately, the sources of such policies are diverse: Congress, Office of the President, Civil Service Commission, Department of Budget and Management, among others, such that the policies are divergent rather than convergent as far as results are concerned.

For example, the Civil Service Commission tightened the entry and tenure requirements while Congress relaxed the tenure requirements by allowing the grant of eligibility and permanency based on the criterion of length of service. For another, Congress had passed a salary standardization law by which the government envisioned to promote productivity and performance as well as attract the best qualified people to government service. In passing the law, Congress aimed toward pay equalization for similar work within the government and pay comparability with the private sector.

However, the Department of Budget and Management, in operationalizing the law, failed to conduct exhaustive consultations with the affected sectors. This therefore led to complaints and objections to its implementation because the resulting salaries and classification of positions did not reflect actual work/functional responsibilities, work experience and qualifications, competence and performance. Besides, the salary scheme did not compensate for the rising costs of living because of inflation and other economic factors. The law provided for a regular review of the compensation scheme in order that it remains competitive and able to meet employees' needs. But since its implementation on July 1, 1989, no such review has been made despite the very much decreased purchasing power of the peso.

Another component of the salary standardization law is the grant of step increments to government workers which weakened the thrust for merit and high performance, since the increments in practice were granted based on length of service alone. In addition, it remained temporarily the only way for employees to advance — but only in terms of salary increases allowable within each grade. Its effect had been to substitute merit promotion (which has achievement and rank components) with step increments (mostly monetary based on length of service regardless of rank).

As a reward system, therefore, it has very limited impact since step increments for the majority of the government employees (mostly rank and file) means a few pesos, while for managers and professionals, the step increments mean not only inadequate extrinsic rewards but no intrinsic rewards — which they value more. The step increments in real terms do not spur the quest for excellence and performance but rather encourage the maintenance of "acceptable" performance. Step increases also feed on bureaucratic behavior and not on professionalism since as a career progression tool, increments create rank stagnation.

The discussions above raise the issue of policy coordination among the governmental agencies making the policies and those implementing them. The professionalization effort should be moving in one direction rather than in diverse directions in order to avoid policy results canceling each other out. The various measures for professionalization undertaken by government led by the Civil Service Commission appear on the surface to be very good measures. But underneath are the accompanying rules, regulations, controls and routinized roles for personnel. The more controls there are to elicit professional behavior, the less professional discretion remains for the professionals. The result would be increasing bureaucratization. A case in point is the code of conduct and ethical standards.

Under Rule VI, Sections 1 to 8, the detailed provisions on what the officials and employees can do and cannot do leave them no opportunity for an alternative behavior arising from exercise of professional and managerial discretion. The rules of conduct added more to the innumerable mandated responses and routinized rules already in force.

Rules VII and IX on public disclosure of assets and liabilities and on conflict of interest and divestment respectively, can be loosely interpreted as a lack of trust of the government regarding the inherent honesty of officials and employees in the civil service.

The effect of these regulations on government employees is one of disgust since the majority are occupying positions which do not give them undue advantages for personal economic gains nor for opportunities for graft and corruption. If the intent of the code is to elicit exemplary and ethical behavior in the bureaucracy, the government should think again. Compliance with the rules are made for the sake

420 AMELIA P. VARELA

of compliance, so that the information contained in the statements of assets and liabilities may be half-truths. The same can be said when there is conflict of interest and of divestment.

Assuming that the statements are filled honestly and truthfully, the agencies do not analyze the filed statements for accuracy nor checked them out with the record of indebtedness or losses as claimed in the statements. Thus, they are not effective instruments to detect ill-gotten wealth.

As to the issue of public sector unionism, there seems to be a double standard in the treatment of the rights of government workers. While the workforce in better paying government offices like public enterprises and financial institutions can go on strike and bargain collectively, the same rights are denied to workers in agencies performing governmental functions.

The ban on strikes for public sector *unions* makes them *pseudo* labor unions and are thus weak mechanisms to promote smooth labor/management relations because employees will always negotiate from positions of weakness and inequality. The value of labor unions to the professionalization efforts is for them to function as professional organizations which could enhance competence, integrity, ethics, and professional conduct and behavior in the civil service.

CONCLUSION

The Civil Service Commission had undertaken forward steps toward professionalization. Even if professionalization is interpreted to mean less bureaucratization, the Commission's best efforts can only lead to *more* routinization, rules and regulations, bureaucratic procedures, and fewer professionalized roles based on discretion rather than strict compliance.

What is needed at this point is for the leadership, political and bureaucratic/administrative to review and assess its program of professionalization to find out initial results. It can also determine whether the program direction is moving toward deregulation, decentralization, and managerial and professional discretion.

The bureaucratic organization obtaining in the Philippine civil service which brings about the tendency to routinize governmental activities should be relaxed to make room for more discretion and power/authority sharing among critical actors. A professional-oriented organization, strengthened by joint management which ensures the participation of managers and professionals, is a first step toward professionalization. The development of an organizational climate and culture where the values of excellence and achievement, honesty and integrity, ethics and morality, and intrinsic rewards are basic, could be the Philippine model and answer to the existing bureaupathology. Policies and action measures, properly calibrated to avoid and deflect the pitfalls of excessive bureaucratization, must be found if the program thrust toward professionalization is to be successfully achieved.

Notes

1. Constitution of 1987; Executive Order No. 67, Sec. 4 (1986 Reorganization Act of the Civil Service Commission [CSC]; 1987 Administrative Code.
2. Memorandum Circular No. 29, Series 1989, Civil Service Commission [CSC], Quezon City, Philippines, 19 July 1989.
3. Guidelines in the Implementation of Joint CSC-DBM, Circular No. 1, Series 1990.
4. Rule 111, Sec. 4, *Rules Implementing the Code of Conduct and Ethical Standards for Public Officials and Employees*, p. 8.
5. ———, p. 9.
6. ———, Rule IV, Sec. 2, p. 10.
7. ———, Rule VII, Sec. 1, p. 19.
8. ———, Rule IX, Sections 1 and 2, p. 23-24.
9. Literally means *"the courteous one, take a bow."*
10. Mosher F. C. and R. Stillman, Jr. 1977. A Symposium: The Professions in Government, *Public Administration Review* 37:631-685; also Mosher, F. C. and R. Stillman, Jr. 1978. A Symposium: The Professions in Government *Public Administration Review* 38:105-130.

References

Abbott, Andrew. 1988. *The System of Professions: An Essay on the Division of Expert Labor.* Chicago: University of Chicago Press.

Abrahamson, Mark. 1967. *The Professional in the Organization.* Chicago: Rand McNally and Co.

Benveniste, Guy. 1987. *Professionalzing the Organization: Reducing Bureaucracy to Enhance Effectiveness.* San Francisco: Jossey-Bass Publishers.

Civil Service Commission (CSC). 1988. *Civil Service Reporter: July-December.* Quezon City: CSC.

———. 1989a. *Annual Report.* Quezon City: CSC.

———. 1989b. *Memorandum Circular No. 29, Series 1989.* Quezon City: CSC.

———. 1990a. *Annual Report.* Quezon City: CSC.

———. 1990b. *Five-Year Corporate Plan (1990-1994).* Quezon City: CSC.

———. 1991. *Memorandum Circulars, Series 1990.* Quezon City: Personnel Officers Association of the Philippines, Inc.

——— and Department of Budget and Management. 1990. Guidelines in the Implementation of Joint CSC-DBM Circular No. 1, Series 1990. Quezon City: CSC.

Editorial. 1990. *Philippine Daily Inquirer.* 9 January:4.

Esleta, Asucena. 1988. Report on Employee Accession and Separation. *Civil Service Reporter* July-Dec:14.

422 AMELIA P. VARELA

Hall, R. H. 1968. Professionalization and Bureaucratization. *American Sociological Review* 33:92-104.

Hickson, J. D. and M. W. Thomas. 1969. Professionalization in Britain: A Preliminary Measurement. *Sociology* 3:38-59.

Lansangan, Amelia Mendoza. 1988. Security of Tenure vis-a-vis Reorganization. *Civil Service Reporter* July-Dec:4.

Mosher F. C. and R. Stillman, Jr. 1977. A Symposium: The Professions in Government. *Public Administration Review* 37:631-678.

——. 1978. A Symposium: The Profesisons in government II. *Public Administration Review* 38:105-144.

Republic of the Philippines. 1986a. Section 4. *Reorganization of the Civil Service Commission.* Quezon City: CSC.

——. 1986b. Executive Order No. 67 (21 Nov.). *Reorganizing the Civil Service Commission.* Quezon City: CSC.

——. 1987a. Administrative Code (25 July).

——. 1987b. Constitution of the Republic of the Philippines (11 Feb.).

Republic Act No. 6656. 1988. *An Act to Protect the Security of Tenure of Civil Service Officers and Employees in the Implementation of Government Reorganization,* June 9, 1988.

Republic Act No. 6713. 1989a. *An Act Establishing a Code of Conduct and Ethical Standards for Public Officials and Employees,* 20 February 1989.

Republic Act No. 6758. 1989b. *An Act Prescribing a Revised Compensation and Position Classification System in the Government and for Other Purposes,* 21 August 1989.

[6]

Human Resource Management in the Public Sector

John Storey

It is said that the practice of industrial relations in the private sector has been transformed over the past decade. An approach to people management that seeks commitment from employees, and not merely their compliance, has been created. How far can this analysis be applied to the public sector?

The basic underlying debate in industrial relations throughout most of this decade has turned on the nature and extent of change in the practice of contemporary industrial relations. At first sight, the facts seem fairly obvious: strike incidence has been reduced; union membership has declined; management appears to be in the ascendant and labour productivity has increased significantly. All of these changes to the 'system' of industrial relations are, moreover, equally evidently embedded in a markedly different 'environment'. Most notably, the legal framework has been altered, the winds of competition (domestic and global) have been felt more keenly, and the political climate under 'Thatcherism' has been radically transformed.

Against such a backcloth, conventional wisdom would seem to dictate that the main, if not the only point of interest, from a public sector standpoint would be the extent to which the revised managerial practices, honed, it is believed, in the private sector, have 'spilled over' into the public sector. However, the situation is far less straightforward than this depiction would imply.

The first difficulty to be encountered is that the issue is far from being a simple factual one: on the contrary, it is clouded with ideological overtones and so is highly charged politically. Thus, for example, it has to be noted that it is undoubtedly part of the Government's intention to 'tell the story' in the way implied above. The party-line is that overmighty trade unions were confronted unflinchingly, that, following legislation and the 'taking' of major strikes, in steel and coal for example, the unions were vanquished. Moreover, the story continues, the promised rolling back of the State' has progressed and the laggardly and cosseted public sector has been subject, and will be further subject, to the disciplines customarily experienced by the more efficient private sector.

A second difficulty is the extent to which, even in the private sector, there has been the kind of transformation implied above. This has been a hotly contested issue. Third, while the preferred 'official' view of management practice may depict the relationship of the private and public sectors as 'leader' and 'lagger' respectively, this assumption should not go unquestioned. The underlying logic of requiring a more 'commercial' orientation within the public sector in itself tends to suggest the inherent superiority of such an approach and

also again implies that the public sector is following the private sector and has much to learn from it.

The analysis which follows will question these common assumptions through an examination of the nature and extent of change in employment management across the private and public sectors – but with primary attention directed towards the latter. The article is divided into four sections. First, the meaning and nature of 'human resource management' is discussed; in the second and third sections, evidence of transition towards human resource management in both sectors is examined; finally, we explore the factors which may constrain the adoption of the full-blown model in the public sector. Much of the data upon which this article draws was collected from 15 large organisations in both sectors between Spring 1986 and Autumn 1987.

Definitions and Key Features

Human resource management is commonly used in both a generic sense simply as a loose synonym for 'personnel management', and in a more specific way when it is intended to denote the adoption of a particular kind of approach to managing labour. It is when this second usage is adopted or implied that the label becomes interesting. Current fascination with the term stems from the idea that it may be used as the signifier for the (possibly interconnected) web of recent managerial initiatives with regard to employee relations and indeed the whole management of the 'human side of enterprise' which are frequently reported as 'leading edge' cases in the management journals and, from time to time, in the national press.

So what are the hallmarks of this 'particular approach' and, furthermore, is it 'better' than those which have preceded it? There is, in fact, no agreed definition of human resource management but a constellation of elements can be constructed which, in broad terms, reflects what many commentators seem to want to signal by their use of the phrase. Perhaps the key point is that, whatever the finer details, it suggests a decisive break with the emergent conventional wisdom of post-Donovan proceduralism (Donovan, 1968), that is, the prescription to 'formalise' rules, agreements and relationships which had erstwhile been 'informal', and, in the case of the

John Storey is a principal research fellow in the Industrial Relations Research Unit at the University of Warwick

US, a break with the long-standing 'New Deal' forged in the Roosevelt years (Kochan et al., 1986).

As an ideal type it may be suggested that the main pillars of the 'new approach' are fourfold. First, that the sense of direction for the way in which the human resource is to be managed stems, quite explicitly, from the corporate strategy. In other words, human resource management is supposed to be better 'integrated' – both internally in the sense that selection, appraisal, reward systems and so on are in greater alignment than was typically the case under conventional personnel and industrial relations management, and 'externally' in the sense that the whole philosophy or approach is in turn emergent from the business plan.

A second feature is that the objective is to elicit the commitment of employees and not merely secure their compliance. Third, that the means of so doing are seen as attainable through a more systematic and careful approach to recruitment, selection, appraisal, training, reward and communication. That is, managerial attention is fundamentally shifted from reliance on 'collective' forms of accommodation with labour to more 'individualistic' ones.

Finally, unlike personnel management and industrial relations, human resource management is 'owned' by line managers and not by personnel specialists. This, in itself, might be presumed to foster the integration referred to above.

Taken together, these four features might be expected to bring about a more strategic and long-term approach to labour management in contrast to the short-term, ad hoc, pragmatic approach which has been noted as characteristic of most personnel and industrial relations management in the British context (Purcell and Sisson, 1983; Thurley, 1981). The classic complaint about the *ancien regime* was that it was marked by 'fire-fighting' – that is, it was too reactive; the new order is supposedly quintessentially pro-active. In so far as management in recent years would appear to have been not only in a position to, but in actuality to have, 'taken the initiative' then to this extent at least there would be some grounds for believing that there has been some measure of change.

Nonetheless, there is considerable scepticism surrounding human resource management. At one level, this merely arises out of ill-informed comment. Human resource management is thought to be merely 'about quality circles' and other 'flavour of the month' initiatives (though, incidentally, it would be wrong to think that all quality circles are of this ilk). On a more serious plane, there is ample scope for doubt when the prescriptive, idealised statements concerning human resource management are set alongside similar earnest statements that have frequently been made about personnel management. Legge (1989) has undertaken just such an exercise and having systematically compared sets of prescriptions finds little cause to declare a new dawn. Legge constructs what is undoubtedly the most convincing critique of the celebratory tone often found surrounding this concept and the

associated 'excellence' literature (Peters and Waterman, 1982; Goldsmith and Clutterbuck, 1984). What surely matters most, however, is what is happening, in practice, rather than what may or may not have been espoused.

The evidence which has so far been published concerning change in industrial relations and personnel management in the 1980s in Britain, tends, on the whole, to give little support to the notion that a 'new industrial relations' has dawned (Batstone, 1984; MacInnes, 1987; WIRS 2; Marginson et al., 1988). But much of the survey work has been directed towards detecting any major abandonment of or departures from prevailing collective procedures. This is precisely the site of a major ambiguity in the pattern of change which our 15-case research project revealed. Even in those cases where extensive initiatives by management on selection, individual communication, the establishment of problem-solving groups and the like had been established, management had, in the main, kept their high profile human resource management policies institutionally separate from 'old fashioned industrial relations'. Thus, unions have typically not been de-recognised, collective bargaining machinery was still 'maintained', but the centre of gravity had shifted. The time, energy and other resources given by management was undoubtedly directed in favour of the former set of approaches to 'people management' and not to the latter. It is one thing to 'maintain' negotiation machinery; using it in the same way as before may be quite a different matter.

This brings us to the other question which was raised earlier; is human resource management 'better' than traditional personnel and industrial relations? David Guest (1987) expressed the conventional academic view on such matters when he argued that no one approach can be recommended as 'best practice' in all circumstances. What is 'best' is contingent upon the particular circumstances: for example, the objectives of the key players, the prevailing labour and product market conditions, and so on. Even so, there has been a persistent undercurrent to a considerable amount of recent comment, which, in lamenting British managers' failure to invest in human resource development, to take a long-term strategic view, to communicate effectively with employees, systematically to select, appraise, and reward in an integrated way, in effect, is tantamount to recommending large parts of the human resource management programme. Indeed, Guest (1989: 55) has explicitly stated that for British industry to catch up further with its international competitors will require 'a shift in emphasis away from the industrial relations system towards human resource management policies as the main path to improved performance'.

Private Sector Model

Arguably, the fullest expressions of what the human resource management model looks like in practice are to be found in certain cases of Japanese and US companies operating in Britain

21

– for example, Nissan (Wickens, 1987) and companies such as IBM and Hewlett Packard. The main British instances of human resource management which are usually cited, such as Marks and Spencer, tend to be non-union. Moreover, whether unionised or not, there has always been a perception of 'exceptional' cases – exceptions that is, to the perceived pragmatic mainstream of British employment practice. Hence, it may be asked, what is new?

Evidence would suggest that a number of far-reaching changes are in process. There is space here only to give a flavour of some of the more important indicators. For this purpose it is appropriate to select companies within an industry sector which has been especially notorious for its traditional and entrenched industrial relations practices. Hence, the illustrations given here are drawn from the British motor industry.

In Austin Rover, Ford, Jaguar, and Peugeot alike, managerial energy has been poured into 'alternative' initiatives such as direct communication with employees, joint problem-solving groups, flexible working, more systematic selection (including the use of psychometric tests for manual recruits), the introduction or re-introduction of appraisal and evaluation systems; an increased attention to training; and a move towards linking reward to performance.

Each of these companies has consciously sought to project line managers into a higher profile role with regard to labour management. This new assertiveness for the line manager is evident at all levels: from supervision and first line management, through the much neglected middle management levels and right up to the now familiar emphasis on the strategic responsibilities of the chief executive.

At the previously neglected middle level the newly-created general 'area', 'zone' or 'manufacturing' managers have increasingly become responsible not only for the production function but for the total range of activities such as quality assurance, maintenance, cleaning, and supply of materials. Crucial to each and every one of these it should be noted, is the assumed responsibility and capability to manage the human resource. Thus, steps have been taken to 'free-up' the line manager so that he or she will take personal responsibility for the deployment of labour, its reward, its upgrading through training, its motivation and the provison of a sense of direction through direct and effective communications. This emphasis on the re-invigoration of the line or core operation manager turned out to be a key theme in nearly all of the case studies across a range of different industries, including those in the service sectors as well as manufacturing.

Before turning to consider developments in the public sector there is one other important point that must be borne in mind. The most crucial developments in the way the human resource is managed are frequently neither designed nor presented as specifically human resource mangement initiatives. The thrust of change may come, for example, in the form of a 'total quality management' programme. Alternatively, it may derive from a perceived need to enhance the organisation's image in the area of customer care. Such a push is likely to entail 'people issues' in respect of training, in appraisal, selection and reward – and in the mode of supervision or even teamworking.

Public Sector Trends

There are a range of ways in which tendencies in the public sector seem to have echoed the developments towards human resource management in the private sector. Indeed, at first sight at least, what is most striking is the degree of commonality. In order to explore these we will again make use of our four-part conceptual framework.

Integration: As in the private sector, attempts have been made to derive the direction for the management of people from 'corporate objectives' rather than from some 'professional' tenets. The shift towards a view of local authorities as 'corporate entities' stems, in no small measure, from the work of the Bains Committee. The idea from the start was to have these new bodies headed by a chief executive, mirroring the position in private sector companies. (The same notion is reflected in the transmogrification of polytechnic directors into chief executives.) At the same time, the integrative concept of 'general management' was being pressed by Stewart (1973). This would facilitate integrative strategic planning at corporate rather than departmental level.

An influential catalyst on this front has been the Audit Commission. Its insistent message is that bureaucracy is no longer an appropriate organisational mode for today's environment. What is currently required, it suggests, is flexibility and responsiveness. An example of its thinking is its publication 'Good Management in Local Government' (Audit Commission, 1985). The emphasis is on the management of change 'rather than administering standstill or growth'. It talks of developing a 'vision' and deriving from this strategies, plans and budgets. These are to be followed up with systems for performance review.

Bradford, under its last Labour administration, is a good example of a large metropolitan council which sought to transform its people management approach by taking the lead from an elaborated corporate strategy. This, which the Council labelled its 'Social Strategy', was a policy document which aimed to orientate the whole range of Council activities in what was claimed to be a 'customer-led way'. The Personnel Directorate re-assessed its total approach so as to engineer compatibility with this corporate plan. The plan stated, in true mission statement style, that 'Bradford Council is committed to putting people first'. But it added an unusual rider: namely, 'particularly those who are most in need'. This later priority indicates the kind of *adaptation* of currently fashionable ideas which deserves further exploration.

In line with the private sector practice of high profile, direct communication with the workforce, the council leader, Phil Beeley, issued a series of letters and documents with his by-line and photograph. This was a way of firmly establishing a sense of corporate identity and central leadership which also characterised the approach by Len Peach as chairman of the NHS Management Board. Indeed, the parallels with the initiatives in the health service go much further as a reading of the NHS Training Authority report, *Better Management: Better Health* (1986), clearly demonstrates.

Commitment and responsiveness: These aims find expression through devolved management and flexibilty. The key to these has been identified as that rather elusive phenomenon: sustained commitment. 'Committed' employee behaviour rather than 'mere' observance of formal procedure is, in many ways, at the heart of human resource management. For organisations which, in the recent past, have often had the greatest difficulty in gaining 'disciplined' behaviour (attendance rather than absence, punctuality rather than lateness, application rather than dilatory behaviour) this may seem an overly-ambitious objective. But conditions of heightened competitiveness and straitened budgetary circumstances have led many managers to believe that, however unlikely, it simply has to be the adopted objective. Expectations have certainly been raised.

The methods adopted in both the private and public sectors have been similar. Any self-regarding top team has long since forged its mission statement. Chief executives and key line managers have accepted responsibility for communicating the 'message'. Videos abound with chief executives spelling out targets and progress towards those targets. Newsletters have been launched and noticeboards tidied. Meanwhile, commitment has also been sought by 'involving' staff. A key device here has been the quality circle. Even when this term is not used for local political reasons, similar methods such as problem-solving teams have been in wide evidence. It is notable that health authority units and districts make up one of the largest client groups of the National Society of Quality Circles.

Relatedly, few health authorities can have avoided some programme or other directed towards treating patients as 'customers'. This has implied quality initiatives which, in turn, put the spotlight on the need for staff training and the need for a committed workforce rather than one which merely follows the rules and acts according to procedure. A key example is Trent Regional Health Authority's 'personal service' initiative and its associated training programmes.

In each case, whether the method has been unit-based customer-service initiatives or devolved budgeting (in education and local government) the underlying idea has been to mark a departure from overt centralised control through formal rules to a more localised form of control involving flexible response, self-control and commitment. It has been realised that in order to effect such a shift a host of human resource levers would also have to be activated.

Collectivism to individualism: In the 1960s and 1970s following the Royal Commission on Trades Unions & Employers' Associations (the Donovan Commission) the conventional wisdom dictated a greater formalisation of relations with employees on a collective basis. The personnel function was to become more established and specialised and this led to a growth of personnel departments. Workplace trade union representatives (shop stewards) were to be formally recognised and provided with facilities – including time off for trade union duties. Most importantly, domestic agreements were to be formalised. In total, relations with workers generally were put on a more proceduralised footing. The rapidly expanding personnel departments set about producing written procedures to cover every eventuality. This 'proceduralisation' was nowhere so marked as in the NHS and in local government.

In the 1980s the emphasis has shifted radically. While outright de-recognition may not have widely occurred nor the outright abandonment of agreements and procedures, the emphasis lent to them has been significantly reduced. To the fore instead have come a raft of devices which reach out to the employee on an individual basis. Key among these has been a far more systematic approach to selection so that organisational entry is more effectively controlled.

Similarly, there has been widespread use of individual performance appraisal. This is frequently wedded to individual goal setting and the more systematic measurement of performance. From here it is a short step to performance-related pay – again on an individual basis. British Rail offers just one apposite example of an organisation which is cascading this constellation of measures from senior managers steadily through the rest of the organisation. Indeed, in the case of British Rail and the NHS we have seen the further development of the movement of senior managers onto individualised contracts. One consequence in British Rail is that the union which represents managerial grades (the TSSA) has declared that it is, in effect, no longer engaged in the collective negotiation of terms and conditions.

Line managers: In the NHS the rise of the general managers following the Griffiths report has been quite marked. Len Peach as the first chief executive of the NHS Management Board and Sir Roy Griffiths as a member of that Board have both emphasised the importance of clear and definite 'leadership' from managers in the new health service. Down through the organisation at regional, district and unit management levels, many have interpreted the central theme of change in the past four years to have been precisely this: to secure general management and line management control over an organisation which was previously built around a federal-like structure of loosely coordinated self-governing professions and semi-professions. Together, they reached some modicum of order via consensus-seeking. Under the new regime human resource management was to mean a more managerially-directed utilisation of staff and other resources. First, clinical-budgeting was tried and then 'resource management'. Line managers began to study their accountancy texts and began to regard their accountant as the key member of their management team.

The premier part played by line and general managers in human resource management is particularly evident in the market-trading parts of the public sector. Top management in Austin Rover (before it was sold to British Aerospace) and in British Rail made it clear that the direction for people-management would be set not by industrial relations and personnel specialists but by the key operational managers. This found expression both in terms of devising and driving the new forms of management and in the delivery at local level via, for example, team briefings. In the market-trading parts of the public sector just as in the private sector the emphasis has been placed on the concept of 'managerial leadership'.

A common element across the sectors has been the seizing of the initiative by line managers on the issue of how human resources should be utilised. In British Rail not only have they 'contracted' for a certain level of service for a certain price but they are also intruding into the details of precisely how the personnel specialist function goes about its business. It is perhaps not surprising therefore that traditional assumptions about how people management should be conducted are coming under radical reappraisal.

Constraining Factors

While re-appraisal and experimentation are proceeding apace, this does not necessarily translate into a systemic transformation. Here we examine some of the main factors which would seem to be constraining a more widespread adoption of human resource management in Britain – particularly in the public sector.

A major consideration arises out of the distinctive nature of management in the public sector. As Stewart and Ranson (1988: 17) have cogently argued:

> *One reason why models drawn from other sectors distort the nature of management is that they assume the dilemmas (which characterise management in the public domain) do not exist or do not have the depth implied, because they do not do so in other sectors.*

These dilemmas derive from the unbounded demands within the public domain; they derive also from the inherently political nature of the values and objectives which must inescapably govern the direction taken by public sector managers. Bureaucracy in public service is not easily discarded. While it undoubtedly impedes responsiveness of service, it none the less offers a way to achieve consistency, equity and impartiality of service – all of which rightly command high priority in public service organisations. Whether they are compatible with the full-blown human resource management approach is more questionable.

Another factor turns on the interplay between 'strategic human resource management' and the political nature of strategic objectives in the public sector. As we noted earlier, a defining feature of human resource management is the idea that it takes its cue from the corporate plan. Now, it might be argued that public sector organisations such as local authorities also have their own corporate plans but, as Stewart and Ranson (1988: 17) argue, 'strategic planning' in the public domain is of a subtly different character from its private sector counterpart. While it is possible to devise human resource plans in, for example, a local authority, these will always be contingent not upon an accurate reading of the market but upon political programmes and the retention of power.

Hence, successful human resource management in the public sector requires not only top management support but also political support from elected politicians. The adversarial nature of the party political system puts the continuity of support into jeopardy. The massive reversal of Bradford Council's social strategy and its attendant human resource management approach is a case in point. In recent years the force of this point has, if anything, been strengthened by the 'politicisation' of local government administration – a feature recorded, for example, in the research for the Widdicombe Enquiry (Leach et al., 1986). And in their analysis of the role of performance indicators in central government, Flynn et al. (1988) show how the use of these in the public domain are inevitably shaped by political constraints.

Another brake on the widespread adoption of a fully-fledged human resource management approach in Britain arises from the comparatively poor education and training of managers. A range of recent reports (Mangham and Silver, 1986; Mumford et al., 1987; Constable and McCormick, 1987; Handy et al., 1988) have accumulated a substantial body of evidence which demonstrates that, in comparison with major advanced competitor countries, British managers are grossly under-trained – especially in management. In consequence, relatively few managers have had sufficient exposure to the formal processes of planning: to many, planning is associated, at best, with financial planning or budgeting. This is likely to be an obstacle in the private and public sectors alike.

Although the private sector model has been influential – not least in its powerful impact on 'marketing' and 'customer care' – there are limits to the validity of this model in public sector organisations. While British Rail managers may (enthusiastically) attend 'aggressive marketing' seminars and while the concept of the 'customer' has suffused the NHS, recipients and employees of public service organisations are, in truth, enveloped in a much more complex web of relationships than simple customer-provider. A further problem is that decisions about human resource utilisation and levels of reward cannot be governed solely by market factors. The comparability principle has, at least for the time-being, effectively been discarded. None the less, the problem it was designed to solve has not gone away.

The high level of unionisation in the public sector also needs to be taken into account. British trade unions have, in the main, failed to formulate a thought-through response to human resource management initiatives. One consequence has been that initiatives are often taken without union involvement of any kind; an associated factor is the inchoate character of the resulting package of employment policies. Restructuring has not been halted but it has been slowed. In the public sector with, for the foreseeable future, its continued high union density, the implied 'dualism' of an ongoing industrial relations system and a separate set of human resource policies and practices, all this suggests a problematical path for human resource management.

A final consideration which ought to counsel caution in the way in which techniques are 'borrowed' from the private sector derives from the diverse composition of the human resource in organisations such as the NHS. Clinical staff and para-medics maintain a professional orientation and frequently a deep-seated personal commitment to patient care. In addition, they have been used to a collegiate approach to problem analysis. In such a setting the unadapted paraphernalia of 'customer-care' lapel badges, comic videos and the like have been known to strike a counterproductive chord among such staff.

This final point of caution carries a wider implication for the analysis presented here. The constraints upon a widespread adoption of human resource management in the public sector should not necessarily be seen as insurmountable barriers. Rather, they should be seen for what they are: indicators that principles and approaches, refined originally within large, and exceptional private sector organisations, such as IBM, should not be expected to translate easily into organisations in very different settings. This being so, it is perhaps not surprising that the overall verdict on the state of play for human resource management in the public sector at the present time has to be one which declares: extensive discussion and diverse experimentation but as yet, with a somewhat limited impact upon staff attitudes and behaviour.   ∎

References

Audit Commission (1985), *Good Management in Local Government*, London: HMSO.

Batstone, E. (1984), *Working Order: Workplace Industrial Relations Over Two Decades*, Blackwell, Oxford.

Constable, J. and McCormick, R. (1987), *The Making of British Managers: A Report for the BIM and CBI into Management Training, Education and Development*, London: BIM.

Donovan (1968), Royal Commission on Trade Unions and Employers' Associations (1968) Report, Cmnd no 3623. HMSO, London.

Flynn, A. et al. (1988), 'Making Indicators Perform', *Public Money & Management*, Winter.

Goldsmith, W. and Clutterbuck, D. (1985), *The Winning Streak*, Penguin.

Guest, D. (1987), 'Human Resource Management and Industrial Relations', *Journal of Management Studies*, 24: 5.

Guest, D. (1989), 'Human Resource Management: its implications for industrial relations and trade unions', in J. Storey (ed.), *New Perspectives on Human Resource Management*, Routledge, London.

Handy, C. (1987), *The Making of Managers: A Report on Management Education, Training and Development in*

the *United States, West Germany, France, Japan and the UK*, London: NEDO.

INLOGOV (1988), *The Challenge of Change in Local Government: A Survey of Organisational and Management Innovation in the 1980s*, University of Birmingham: Institute of Local Government Studies.

Kochan, T. A., Katz, H. C. and McKersie, R. B. (1986), *The Transformation of American Industrial Relations*, New York: Basic Books.

Leach, S. et al. (1986), *The Political Organisation of Local Authorities*, Report of the Committee of Enquiry into the Conduct of Local Authority Business, Chairman: D. Widdicombe, Q.C., Cmnd 9798, London: HMSO.

Legge, K. (1989), 'Human Resource Management: A Critical Analysis', in J. Storey (ed.), *New Perspectives on Human Resource Management*, Routledge, London.

McInnes, J. (1987), *Thatcherism at Work*, Milton Keynes: Open University Press.

Mangham, I. and Silver, M. S. (1986), *Management Training: Context and Process*, ESRC, London.

Marginson, P., Sisson, K., Martin, R. and Edwards, P. (1988), *Beyond the Workplace*, Oxford: Blackwell.

Mumford,, A. Robinson, G. and Stradling, D. (1987), *Developing Directors: The Learning Processes*, Sheffield: MSC.

Peters, T. J. and Waterman, R. H. (1983), *In Search of Excellence: Lessons from America's Best Run Companies*, Harper and Row, New York.

Purcell, J. and Sisson, K. (1983), 'Strategies and practice in the management of Industrial Relations', in Bain, G. (ed.), *Industrial Relations in Britain*, Blackwell, Oxford.

Stewart, J. D. (1973), *New Approaches to Management in Local Government*, London: Local Government Chronicle pamphlet.

Stewart, J. and Ranson, S. (1988), 'Management in the Public Domain', *Public Money & Management*, Spring/Summer.

Stokes, G., Oppenheim, F. W. and Davies, M. (1988), *The Challenge of Change in Local Government: A Survey of Organisational and Management Innovation in the 1980s*, INLOGOV, University of Birmingham.

Storey, J. (ed.) (1989), *New Perspectives on Human Resource Management*, Routledge, London.

Storey, J. (forthcoming), *Developments in Human Resource Management*, Oxford: Blackwell.

Thurley, K. (1981), 'Personnel Management in the UK: a case for urgent treatment?', *Personnel Management*, August, 24–30.

Wickens, P. (1987), *The Road to Nissan*, London: Macmillan.

WIRS 2 (1986), *British Workplace Industrial Relations*, by Millward, N. and Stevens, M., The DE/ESRC/ACAS Survey, Aldershot: Gower.

[7]

Public Management

Public and Private Sector Management: the case for a wider debate

Sue Dopson and Rosemary Stewart

There is much theoretical debate about the differences between management in the public and private sectors. But what of differences between the two sets of managers? Research has shown that public managers are less positive when faced with change that their private sector counterparts. There are, however, good reasons for this.

Over the past decade, managers in the public sector have been responding to politically driven initiatives designed to improve the efficiency and effectiveness of public services. Many of the changes have involved the transfer of private sector managerial practices. Up to now, the debate surrounding the application of private sector management practices to the public sector has primarily concentrated on differences in function and environment.

Recent research suggests that there are three areas in which the debate needs to develop: improving our understanding of the attitudes of public sector managers to change; recognising the complexity of the private sector, and identifying the differences within the public sector relevant to considering the appropriateness of adopting private sector practices. This article will concentrate on the first of these, drawing on evidence from a research study taking place in six western European countries into the attitudes of middle managers to change.

The study, initiated and partially funded by the European Foundation for the Improvement of Living and Working Conditions, and later by the Leverhulme Trust, defined middle management broadly as those below the very top management and above supervisor level. In the first year of the United Kingdom study, two out of eight case studies were drawn from the public sector: district inspectors in the Inland Revenue and managers in the national health service. The second year involved three, more detailed, studies: a traditional manufacturing company; a new public sector agency, Her Majesty's Stationery Office; and a distributor of automobile parts.

Reactions to Change

Managers from both sectors were in agreement on a number of issues. For example, most middle managers saw themselves as playing a more generalist role in their organisations. As a result, many were required to change their attitudes and to become more flexible and adapt-

able. They were also required to acquire new managerial skills, including more financial knowledge, a greater ability to manage staff of different backgrounds, a wider understanding of what was happening in other departments and a greater awareness of marketing and strategic issues.

A majority of managers in both sectors reported that their jobs were now more stressful. Managers in the Inland Revenue attributed this stress to the increasing complexity of the tax law; the hardened attitude to investigation which meant that the work was more confrontational; the declining calibre of staff (particularly in districts in the south east); a demoralised work force and the sheer number of management initiatives tagged onto their case work, which was being done with a reduced staff. The main source of stress for middle managers in the national health service was the feeling that their health district could not give as good a service as was possible because of limited resources. In Her Majesty's Stationery Office, managers were experiencing greater stress because of the need to achieve profits, as well as because of tensions between the wealth generating and service divisions. Managers in the private sector attributed their increased stress to the need to ensure greater productivity and performance, as well as to the general tightening of standards of performance measurement.

Managers in both sectors felt that they were more demanding of their staff, reflecting the increased demands on them as managers and, sometimes, because of a reduced staff. For some managers in Her Majesty's Stationery Office this was perceived as a positive factor because it represented a distinct break from the past. As one manager put it:

> *It didn't matter if the job was half a job. People were public servants and that justified their existence. It didn't matter that the time was not filled up.*

The majority of both public and private sector managers we interviewed saw that the broader changes had created a more challenging

Sue Dopson is a research fellow and Rosemary Stewart a fellow in organisational behaviour at Templeton College, Oxford

environment in which to work. Most of the public sector managers, with the exception of the district inspectors, said they enjoyed their work more because they were more accountable; jobs were also viewed as more interesting, both because of the increased responsibility and because of the new management systems that had clarified objectives.

Overall, however, managers in the public sector appeared to be less enthusiastic than their counterparts in the private sector about both the possibility and the desirability of change. For example, some managers in Her Majesty's Stationery Office found a more commercial approach within the constraints of the Civil Service a source of frustration. For those managers, Treasury control, coupled with tight manpower targets, was seen to militate against the entrepreneurial spirit advocated by central government. Indeed, many public sector managers commented on the paradoxical nature of the demands being placed on them by government. There was a feeling that managers were given the responsibility, but not the power, to meet specified targets.

This more negative and cautious attitude among public servants has been noted by other commentators. For example, in their study of public managers in the US, Whorton and Worthley (1981) elicited comments such as 'the rules tie our hands'; 'politics undermines the intent of the project'; 'if only the unions were not so powerful'. According to Whorton and Worthley, responses such as these may help managers to rationalise the paradoxes and competing values in their environment. They go on to argue, however, that managers' responses may cloak managerial attitudes and excuses for non-management that are reinforced and maintained by the prevailing culture:

> In this culture, restraints on individual behaviour take on important symbolic and methodological meaning by being elevated to an institutional status. Where these controls are institutionalized, they cease being negative statements about self worth and become, instead, devices easily viewed by managers as limiting their ability to manage.

Another consequence of this culture is that, not only do public administrators tend to use 'if onlys' to lessen their responsibility for action, they also use them to discount their own managerial accomplishments.

Pak (1980) suggests that the political system itself offers an explanation for the cautiousness of public managers. He argues that it is unfriendly and unforgiving. Accomplishments often go unrecognised and the mistakes tend to be widely publicised and ridiculed, therefore cautiousness may well be viewed as an asset by public sector managers.

In this country, there has been a debate over whether private sector management concepts can be transferred to the public sector. Commentators who argue that such a transfer is inappropriate draw on well-rehearsed arguments central to the public administration tradition (for a summary of the arguments, which have been discussed in this journal before, see the Public Administration Tradition). Others challenge the view that the differences between the two sectors make for insurmountable difficulties in transferring managerial concepts to the public sector (see Public Management Perspective).

Widening the Debate

One small-scale study cannot permit us to make any firm generalisations about the differences in attitude to change among public and private sector managers. However, the research does raise a number of important questions: are such negative or cautious reactions desirable in a public sector manager or, if not desirable, can they be changed? A necessary first step is to try and understand the reasons for these attitudes.

Other commentators, as well as our own research, suggest that a more cautious attitude may be the result of a tendency, both at the organisational and the individual level, to criticise mistakes, rather than to recognise accomplishments. Another reason may be a feeling amongst public servants of having an excessive number of constraints on the job. This may indeed be the case, or it may be because managers perceive it to be so, and do not recognise the areas of freedoms that they do possess.

So far as recent managerial reforms are concerned, a distinction must be made between policy changes which affect the public, and which civil servants expect to implement for their political masters, and initiatives which are concerned with their own methods of working. The managers we interviewed viewed recent reforms as politically imposed rather than necessary and inevitable, as they would be seen in a private company which faced a strong competitive threat. Some managers saw commercially oriented working practices as inimical to public services because they undermined traditional values and the distinctive sense of professional identity and ethos.

Indeed, the importance attached by those in some occupations to professional identity and to the practice of their specialist skills can lead to resentment at the amount of time spent on managerial activities. Such resentment was expressed during the course of our research by doctors in the health service and by district tax inspectors. Occupational groups who see themselves as professionals – of whom there are more in the public than the private sector – will have a stronger identification with their role and may oppose reform which they perceive as a threat to that role.

Another explanation for the less positive attitude to change among public sector managers may be the fact that their expectation tends to be one of organisational and role stability. By contrast, managers in the private sector are accustomed to frequent initiatives, which become part of their managerial lives.

Finally, a series of specific factors appear to influence managers' reactions to the introduction of private sector practices:

● length of time since the first more commercial changes were introduced;

- degree of exposure of the organisation to political debate;
- degree of exposure of the organisation to public and media debate;
- power of the consumer to influence the managers' priorities;
- proportion of professionals employed in the organisation and how powerful they are in influencing policy;
- difficulties of attracting and retaining staff;
- extent to which the work can be contracted out to the private sector;
- strength of the public service culture;
- managers' age profile: older managers may be less enthusiastic about change.

Fostering Positive Attitudes

Realities such as reduced public spending, central government demands for economies, increased consumer demands and relatively low pay all suggest that managers in the public sector are likely to be less positive about new managerial practices than their counterparts in the private sector. However, much more could be done by government and by public sector managers themselves – at all levels – to foster more positive attitudes.

First, accomplishments need to be recognised and rewarded. For example, it is often forgotten by its critics that the national health service achieves remarkably well when one considers the relatively small proportion of the national income which goes into the service. The public sector and its critics alike need to keep such achievements in mind as laudable efforts are made to make the sector more efficient and effective.

Second, greater care needs to be taken when using terminology from the private sector. Words such as 'consumer', 'marketing', 'quality assurance' and 'competition' may be seen as undermining the very values of public service which may have been a major reason for individuals joining the public sector in the first place. It is necessary to explain to managers how such concepts can be used to provide a better service to the public and that they need not undermine public sector values. This is particularly necessary when dealing with professionals, many of whom receive little training in management or organisational skills until relatively late in their careers.

Third, managers need to be given greater control over resources. The private sector managers whom we interviewed felt more in control of the resources which they needed to achieve their objectives. They now often controlled resources for which previously they had to rely on service departments to provide. Even within the necessary constraints of the public sector, its managers could be given a greater sense of ownership, as the example of some hospitals has shown.

Finally, there is a greater need for positive leadership. The variety and the extent of changes affecting organisations mean that much more is expected from most managers than in the past. There is no indication that the rate of change will

Public Administration Tradition

Critical Factors in the Environment
- *The public sector is thought to have less market exposure resulting in less incentive to reduce cost or to operate efficiently.*
- *The public sector, it is argued, has a wider stakeholder interest than the private sector, most notably politicians, taxpayers and voters. Pressure group influences are particularly significant in the public sector because the resources are both finite and limited and are distributed as an act of political will. As Potter (1988) points out, this creates an immediate dilemma for the pure application of consumer principles.*
- *The private sector is thought to work with a clearer conception of its customers. In the public sector the existence of customers, clients, consumers and citizens makes it difficult to define exactly who the customer is.*
- *Flynn et al (1988) argue that environmental scanning is more difficult for public sector managers because of the perennial uncertainty as to which specific issue will in practice become politically significant.*

Organisational Constraints
Many of the organisational constraints arise from the overt and direct political input into the public sector. Flynn et al (1988) argue that this is: 'one of the most significant differences between management in the private and the public sector.'

Ring & Perry (1985) put forward five key constraints on public managers at the organisational level:
- *policy directives tend to be more ill-defined for public than for private organisations;*
- *the relative openness of decision-making creates greater constraints;*
- *public sector policy makers are generally subject to more direct and sustained influence from interest groups;*
- *public sector management must cope with time constraints that are more artificial than those that confront private sector management;*
- *policy legitimisation coalitions are less stable in the public sector and are more prone to disintegrate during policy implementation.*

Another constraint often cited is the existence of professional structures within the public sector that often conflict with bureaucratic processes of accountability. Such factors, it is suggested, can lead to further constraints such as a lack of clarity in organisational design and a lack of strategic direction.

Joubert (1988) argues that strategic management has been a little used concept in the non-traded public sector, particularly the Civil Service. He notes:

'. . . the way in which strategy has traditionally manifested itself in the public sector has been in terms of inputs (such as external financing limits, the public expenditure survey and manpower ceilings) rather than outputs.'

He goes on to argue that this situation is exacerbated by the lack of political framework and uncertain definitions of the roles of ministers, civil servants and the relationship between them.

The nature of payment systems is another area of difference in organisational constraints. Wright and Williams (1988) point out that the significantly different culture and values of the public sector make it difficult for employees to accept elements of private sector practice into their pay arrangements. High levels of unionisation and unclear performance measures have inhibited radical restructurings of payment systems seen in some private sector firms.

Managers' Responsibility and Influence
- *The nature of accountability:* This is thought to be more complex for the public manager and includes: traditional accountability to parliament and external watchdog bodie, managerial accountability within the department hierarchy for the results achieved, value for money accountability, professional peer group accountability and accountability to the community, client or end user.
- *Inability to influence input:* Gunn (1988) points out that whilst at the operational level in the public sector managers are increasingly asked to take responsibility for output they have, unlike their counterparts in business, little scope for negotiation of relevant inputs, for example, the picking or sacking of members of their team.
- *The problems of measuring outcomes:* Defining and measuring outcomes across a broad range of service delivery is a complex and difficult task, not only because of the nature of those objectives, but because of politicians' fears of bad news. Flynn et al (1988) put forward this argument to explain why evaluation of outcome has remained subservient to economic policy. One implication of this is that political interests are placed above those of good management.

diminish. For the public sector, change is likely to increase as government policies are implemented and the effects of such policies become clearer. Traditionally, public sector managers have not been expected to be leaders but administrators.

40

Public Management Perspective

Gunn (1988) believes that the public/private distinction is often overstated, arguing that the 'grey zone' of QUAGO *'s (quasi-governmental organisations) and* QUANGOS *(quasi-non-governmental or quasi private organisations) has long been recognised. He also points out that, in future, the public sector will become more congested and complex, with the co-existence of services that have been contracted out to private firms, or that are provided by public agencies.*

Gunn is critical of the over-simplistic view held by public administration that little, if anything, can be learned across the sectional divide. He is equally critical of the business management approach that argues that the public sector has everything to learn from efficient business practices in the private sector. He suggests that a third approach is necessary – public management, and cites Perry and Kramer (1983) as providing the clearest exposition of this approach when they argue that 'Public management is a merger of the normative orientation of traditional public administration (a concern with issues of equity, consistency and equality) and the instrumental orientation of generic management.'

For Gunn, public management is an attempt to combine much that is still relevant in the classical view that public administration is different from the private sector, with the insights of a generic management approach which holds that there are common problems that managers in both sectors face and common managerial processes.

Stewart and Ranson (1988) suggest that one way of examining the argument that management in the public sector is unique, is to examine the ways in which public sector organisations differ from their private sector counterparts. They produce a public domain model which they claim captures the public sector's distinctive rationale. This, they argue, is no easy task because the public domain is in principle unbounded, therefore any interest or individual can make claims on it. This leads to dilemmas that are inherent in its nature: 'We look to the public domain to reconcile interests that may be unreconcilable and to meet aspirations that may not be capable of attainment.' The private sector organisation resolves such dilemmas by defining them 'out of its area of organisational concern'.

Now, they are expected to learn to be managers. In times of rapid change leadership is also required if people are to be encouraged to respond positively to change. Stewart (1989) argues that the public sector now needs leaders at all levels who will think positively about what they can do to improve public service, not merely about how they can survive within limited resources. A good leader should both show the way and make others feel enthusiastic about following it. Change can then become positive, exciting and challenging. ■

References/Further Reading

Brotrick, O. and Paton, R. 'Constraints to Management in the Public Sector', *Optimum* (Canada), Vol. 15 – 1, 1984.

Flynn, A., Gray, A., Jenkins, W., Rutherford, B. and Plowden, W., 'Accountable Management in British Central Government: Some Reflections on the Official Record'. *Financial Accountability in Management*, 4(3), autumn 1988.

Flynn, N., 'Consumer Oriented Culture', *Public Money & Management*, spring/summer 1988.

Fry, G., Flynn, A., Gray, A., Jenkins, W. and Rutherford, B., 'Symposium on Improving Management in Government'. *Public Administration*, Vol. 66, winter 1988.

Gunn, L., 'Public Management: a third approach?', *Public Money & Management*, spring/summer 1988.

Johnson, N., 'Change in the Civil Service: Retrospect and Prospects', *Public Administration*, Vol. 63, winter 1985.

Joubert, C., 'Strategy in the Public Sector', *Public Money & Management*, autumn 1988.

Knapp, M., 'The Mixed Economy of Welfare: a Stopgap Solution?', *Public Money*, September 1986.

Pak, C. M., 'Public Executive Can't', *Bureaucrat*, Vol. 13, Pt. 2, 1984.

Perry, J. L. and Kramer, K. L., 'Public Management, Private and Public Perspectives', 1983, California, Mayfield Press.

Pollitt, C., 1987, 'Performance Measurement and the consumer: hijacking a bandwagon?', *Performance Measurement and the Consumer*, National Consumer Council, London.

Potter, J., 'Consumerism and the Public Sector: How Well Does the Coat Fit?', *Public Administration*, Vol. 66, summer 1988.

Robertson, K., 'Employee Involvement in the Public Sector: a Better Bet', *Public Money*, June 1985.

Smith, Ring, P. and Perry, J. L., 'Strategic Management in Public and Private Organizations: Implications of Distinctive Context and Constraints', *Academy of Management Review*, 1985, Vol. 10, no. 2.

Stewart, J. and Clark, M., 'The Public Service Orientation: Issues and Dilemmas', *Public Administration*, Vol. 66, summer 1977.

Stewart, J. and Ranson, S., 'Management in the Public Domain', *Public Money & Management*, spring/summer 1988.

Stewart, R., 'Leading in the NHS: A Practical Guide', Macmillan, 1989.

Whorton, J. W. and Worthley, J. A., 'A Perspective on the Challenge of Public Management: Environmental Paradox and Organizational Culture', *Academy of Management Review*, 1981, Vol. 6, no. 3.

Wright, V. and Williams, R., 'Public Sector Pay: from experiment to permanent change', *Public Money & Management*, spring/summer 1988.

[8]

THE DUTIES AND RESPONSIBILITIES OF CIVIL SERVANTS IN RELATION TO MINISTERS

Note by the Head of the Home Civil Service

During the last few months a number of my colleagues have suggested to me that it would be timely to restate the general duties and responsibilities of civil servants in relation to Ministers. Recent events, and the public discussion to which they have given rise, have led me to conclude that the time has come when it would be right for me, as Head of the Home Civil Service, to respond to these suggestions. I am accordingly putting out the guidance in this note. It is issued after consultation with Permanent Secretaries in charge of Departments, and with their agreement.

2. Civil servants are servants of the Crown. For all practical purposes the Crown in this context means and is represented by

the Government of the day. There are special cases in which certain functions are conferred by law upon particular members or groups of members of the public service; but in general the executive powers of the Crown are exercised by and on the advice of Her Majesty's Ministers, who are in turn answerable to Parliament. The civil service as such has no constitutional personality or responsibility separate from the duly elected Government of the day. It is there to provide the Government of the day with advice on the formulation of the policies of the Government, to assist in carrying out the decisions of the Government, and to manage and deliver the services for which the Government is responsible. Some civil servants are also involved, as a proper part of their duties, in the processes of presentation of Government policies and decisions.

3. The civil service serves the Government of the day as a whole, that is to say Her Majesty's Ministers collectively, and the Prime Minister is the Minister for the Civil Service. The duty of the individual civil servant is first and foremost to the Minister of the Crown who is in charge of the Department in which he or she is serving. It is the Minister who is responsible, and answerable in Parliament, for the conduct of the Department's affairs and the management of its business. It is the duty of civil servants to serve their Ministers with integrity and to the best of their ability.

4. The British civil service is a non-political and disciplined career service. Civil servants are required to serve the duly elected Government of the day, of whatever political complexion. It is of the first importance that civil servants should conduct themselves in such a way as to deserve and retain the confidence of Ministers, and as to be able to establish the same relationship with those whom they may be required to serve in some future Administration. That confidence is the indispensable foundation of a good relationship between Ministers and civil servants. The conduct of civil servants should at all times be such that Ministers and potential future Ministers can be sure that that confidence can be freely given, and that the civil service will at all times conscientiously fulfil its duties and obligations to, and impartially assist, advise and carry out the policies of, the duly elected Government of the day.

5. The determination of policy is the responsibility of the Minister (within the convention of collective responsibility of the whole Government for the decisions and actions of every member of it). In the determination of policy the civil servant has no constitutional responsibility or role, distinct from that of the Minister. Subject to the conventions limiting the access of Ministers to papers of previous administrations, it is the duty of the civil servant to make available to the Minister all the information and experience at his or her disposal which may have a bearing on the policy decisions to which the Minister is committed or which he is preparing to make, and to give to the Minister honest and impartial advice, without fear or favour, and whether the advice accords with the Minister's view or not. Civil servants are in breach of their duty, and damage their integrity as servants of the Crown, if they deliberately withhold relevant information from their Minister, or if they give their Minister other advice than the best they believe they can give, or if they seek to obstruct or delay a decision simply because they do not agree with it. When, having been given all the relevant information and advice, the Minister has taken a decision, it is the duty of civil servants loyally to carry out that decision with precisely.the same energy and good will, whether they agree with it or not.

6. Civil servants are under an obligation to keep the confidences to which they become privy in the course of their official duties; not only the maintenance of trust between Ministers and civil servants but also the efficiency of government depend on their doing so. There is and must be a general duty upon every civil servant, serving or retired, not to disclose, in breach of that obligation, any document or information or detail about the course of business, which has come his or her way in the course of duty as a civil servant. Whether such disclosure is done from political or personal motives, or for pecuniary gain, and quite apart from liability to prosecution under the Official Secrets Acts, the civil servant concerned forfeits the trust that is put in him or her as a servant of the Crown, and may well forfeit the right to continue in the service. He or she also undermines the confidence that ought to subsist between Ministers and civil servants and thus damages colleagues and the Service as well as him or herself.

7. The previous paragraphs have set out the basic principles which govern civil servants' relations with Ministers. The rest of this note deals with particular aspects of conduct which derive from them, where is may be felt that more detailed guidance would be helpful.

8. A civil servant should not be required to do anything unlawful. In the very unlikely event of a civil servant being asked to do something which he or she believes would put him or her in clear breach of the law, the matter should be reported to a superior officer or to the Principal Establishment Officer, who should if necessary seek the advice of the Legal Adviser to the department. If legal advice confirms that the action would be likely to be held to be unlawful, the matter shoul be reported in writing to the Permanent Head of the department.

9. Civil servants often find themselves in situations where they are required or expected to give information to a Parliamentary Select Committee, to the media, or to individuals. In doing so they should be guided by the general policy of the Government on evidence to Select Committees and on the disclosure of information, by any specifically departmental policies in relation to departmental information, and by the requirements of security and confidentiality. In this respect, however, as in other respects, the civil servant's first duty is to his or her Minister. Ultimately the responsibility lies with Ministers, and not with civil servants, to decide what information should be made available, and how and when it should be released, whether it is to Parliament, to Select Committees, to the media or to individuals. It is not acceptable for a serving or former civil servant to seek to frustrate policies or decisions of Ministers by the disclosure outside the Government, in breach of confidence, of information to which he or she has had access as a civil servant.

10. It is Ministers and not civil servants who bear political responsibility. Civil servants should not decline to take, or abstain from taking, an action merely because to do so would conflict with their personal opinions on matters of political choice or judgment between alternative or competing objectives and benefits; they should consider the possibility of declining only if taking or abstaining from the action in question is felt to be directly contrary to deeply held personal conviction on a fundamental issue of conscience.

11. A civil servant who feels that to act or to abstain from acting in a particular way, or to acquiesce in a particular decision or course of action, would raise for him or her a fundamental issue of conscience, or is so profoundly opposed to a policy as to feel unable consientiously to administer it in accordance with the standards described in this note, should consult a superior officer, or in the last resort the Permanent Head of the department, who can and should if necessary consult the Head of the Home Civil Service. If that does not enable the matter to be resolved on a basis which the civil servant concerned is able to accept, he or she must either carry out his or her instructions or resign from the public service — though even after resignation he or she will still be bound to keep the confidences to which he or she has become privy as a civil servant.

ROBERT ARMSTRONG

[9]

The Times
15th January 1993
Page: 15

New relations between ministers and civil servants

From Sir Brian Cubbon

Sir, The letter (January 7) from Robert Armstrong and Frank Cooper about relations between ministers and civil servants is correct as far as it goes. I first became a permanent secretary when Lord Wilson of Rievaulx was prime minister. When I retired, Lady Thatcher had been prime minister for nearly nine years. I never felt for one moment that I was regarded by her or anyone else as different from the permanent secretaries she appointed.

But the relations between ministers and civil servants *are* changing, along with our system of government. Senior civil servants are deeply involved in the political problems and style of their ministers. Detachment and objectivity are more difficult.

You, Sir, in your leader on January 9, rightly say that "the way in which ministers and civil servants go about forming policy" should be examined.

For good reasons, government is now more open and accountable. Ministers are under enormous daily pressure to justify publicly what they are doing and not doing. Their political future depends on their handling of issues, incidents and appointments. They are political executives, more than just policy-makers.

For this role they often depend on the abilities of their senior civil servants. They want help from them, rather than the impartial advice required by civil service doctrine. It is not surprising that ministers want to influence appointments and promotions in their departments.

Senior civil servants spend a great deal of time helping ministers to win acceptance for their decisions, and sometimes acting for them in this. In Brussels, and with outside interests and with local services like the police, civil servants are in practice advocates of the ministerial line, and you are a better negotiator if you believe in the merits of the line you are taking.

Civil servants appearing before select committees speak on behalf of their ministers and while they can deflect the direct question about the merits of the key policy, they are expected to put that policy in a good light in their answers about its detailed execution. This emphasis on presentation and advocacy can brainwash away objectivity and inhibit the rethinking of policy.

The doctrine is that officials should at all times conduct themselves so as to retain the confidence of ministers. Is this the same as earning the gratitude of ministers? Gratitude for help with their political problems? How much is left of the notion of the senior civil servant as the impartial adviser of ministers on policy?

In all areas civil servants will continue to do their best to discharge their professional duty, but changing circumstances mean that there is now a hole in the simple Victorian doctrines about these matters. Filling it is not a matter for another batch of executive agencies, or some new contracts for civil servants, or a bland code of practice, or indeed anything from the civil service alone.

The first step, as you suggest, is some hard thinking, about the present roles of both ministers and the top ranks of the civil service.

Yours etc,
BRIAN CUBBON,
c/o Oxford and Cambridge Club,
Pall Mall, SW1.
January 11.

From Mr C. S. Cullerne Bown

Sir, The present danger is not that Whitehall is "turning Tory" (article, December 22) but that the stronger the minister, the more likely he or she is to receive the advice wished for.

There are many reasons for this decline: the diminishing power and quality of the House of Commons and its select committees; the increasing arrogance of governments and the executive and the often absurd polarity between the political parties; the growth in numbers and power of ministers' special advisers, who are responsible to no one except the minister (in effect though not in theory); and the relatively recent perception by politicians that with a big enough majority they can achieve almost anything.

Will present and future generations of civil servants be as vigilant as Lord Armstrong and Sir Frank now suggest they should be? Will governments wish to preserve rather than dismantle those institutions which help to guarantee our traditional freedoms and way of life?

Yours etc,
C. S. CULLERNE BOWN
(Chief Press Officer,
Home Office, 1966-74),
11 Reeds Place, NW1.

From Mr Ray Petch

Sir, Lord Armstrong and Sir Frank Cooper rush to defend Whitehall from relatively innocuous charges. But much more serious and, in my view, largely justified disquiet is that the mandarinate has over the past 30 years or so become increasingly self-serving.

The system is now dedicated to the avoidance of true personal accountability. In my experience the public interest is hardly ever mentioned in policy discussions; and even ministers' expressed wishes are often ignored.

Yours faithfully,
RAY PETCH (Assistant Secretary, Home Civil Service, 1973-86),
3 Laureate Gardens,
Newmarket, Suffolk.

[10]

T. H. GREEN AND THE ETHICS OF SENIOR OFFICIALS IN BRITISH CENTRAL GOVERNMENT

BARRY J. O'TOOLE

This article is an attempt to move away from microeconomics in the study of administration and to concentrate on British administrative ethics from a philosophical perspective. Thus, ethics is used here not in the sense of the ethics of managers dealing with accounts but as the 'science' of ranking moral values. The intention of the article is to examine how political theory can be used to help illustrate the dilemmas of public servants working in a climate which is distinctly hostile to disinterested ideals. The ideas of T. H. Green, the English Idealist philosopher who contributed so much to our understanding of public service, form the basis of the theoretical discussion, and the work of senior officials in Whitehall is the material used for illustrative purposes. Where do the loyalties of civil servants lie? What are their duties and responsibilities to ministers? To whom, for what, and how are civil servants accountable?

The aim of this article is not to present a definitive account of the ideas of Thomas Hill Green. Such accounts already exist (see, for example, Milne 1962; Richter 1964; Chapman 1965, 1966; Vincent and Plant 1984). Nor is the aim to undertake a comprehensive review of all the literature on ethics from a comparative public sector management perspective. That task would be huge and almost certainly of little value. It would be of little value because, although there are similarities between one administrative system and another, there are also wide differences, especially in administrative culture. Such differences would make the quest for generalizations applicable in all circumstances almost impossible. The aim instead is to raise questions and stimulate debate about British administrative practice in central government from a particular perspective: to examine current practice in the light of observations made by T. H. Green. In the words of Melvin Richter, 'few, if any, other philosophers exerted a greater influence upon public thought and policy than did T. H. Green'. He 'converted Philosophical Idealism...into something close to a practical programme for the left wing of the Liberal Party'. His tutelage led to a 'stream of serious young men dedicated to reform in politics, social work and the Civil Service' (Richter 1964, p. 13). In his references Richter gives long lists of people directly influenced by Green, including Bernard Bosanquet, A. C. Bradley, Edward Caird, H. S. Holland, R. L. Nettleship, D. G. Ritchie and

Barry J. O'Toole is Lecturer in Public Sector Management at Loughborough University of Technology.

Public Administration Vol. 68 Autumn 1990 (337–352)
© 1990 Royal Institute of Public Administration ISSN 0033–3298 $3.00

338　BARRY J. O'TOOLE

Arnold Toynbee. These people in turn influenced others and Richter lists Lord Haldane and Sir Ernest Barker as being among these. Many others could be included in such lists and many occupied senior positions in the civil service in the first part of the present century (see also Vincent and Plant 1984, pp. 1–5).

Whether or not Green still exerts an influence in the senior ranks of the British civil service is not the question here. What can be said in passing is that just as Northcote and Trevelyan may be seen as having laid the foundations for the structure of the present civil service so Green may be seen as being responsible (in a more indirect sense) for part at least of the philosophical and ethical outlook of the people in the service, at least in the first part of this century. If that is accepted, then it can be further argued that, through the process of socialization, so often referred to by students of the British civil service, Green still exerted an influence *at least* until the recent onset of managerialism inspired by the present government.

Be that as it may, this article seeks to raise questions about whether Green's philosophy, in particular his ideas about ethics and about the 'common good', *ought* to guide public servants in the present administrative climate. In other words, just as questions should be raised about the potentially revolutionary changes in the structure of the civil service, so this article seeks to raise questions about the ethics of civil servants. The two are linked because the attempts at inculcating so-called 'managerialism', in line with structural changes, will almost certainly have an effect on administrative ethics. Few people seem to be addressing themselves adequately to the implications of any of these changes for our system of government.

Ethics are concerned with the application of moral standards. They are, it could be argued, concerned with ranking moral values. T. H. Green suggested that morality is 'the disinterested performance of self-imposed duties' (Green 1931, pp. 39–40). For Green the end of the institutions of civil life, namely government, was that of enabling the individual 'to give reality to the capacity [of] will: they enable him to realise his reason, i.e. his idea of self-perfection, by acting as a member of a social organisation' (Green 1931, pp. 32–33). In other words there is a 'common good' in social organization without which an individual would not be able to realize himself. The practical question then arises as to what is this 'common good'? Further, who is to be judge and what are the sanctions of the transgressions of the 'common good'?

Green's argument is as follows. Man is conscious of himself as an end in himself. He constantly seeks personal satisfaction, in the sense of moral fulfilment or 'self-realization'. However, 'self-realization' is dependent upon relations with other members of society. Green argued that man 'cannot contemplate himself as in a better state or on the way to the best, without contemplating others, not merely as a means to that better state, but as sharing it with him' (Green 1969, p. 210). Thus:

> Having found his pleasures and pains dependent upon the pleasures and pains of others, he must be able, in the contemplation of a possible satisfaction of himself, to include the satisfaction of those others, and. . .a satisfaction of them as ends in themselves and not as means to his pleasure. He must, in short, be capable of conceiving and seeking a permanent well-being in which the permanent well-being of others is included (Green 1969, p. 212; see also Richter 1964, pp. 191–221, especially 212–15).

SENIOR OFFICIALS IN BRITISH CENTRAL GOVERNMENT 339

In other words, man's nature is to be part of society, and anything which contributes to the creation, well-being or harmony of society is to be encouraged.

The 'common good' then is the mutual harmony of all in society, brought about by each seeking his own 'self-realization' which includes the self-realization of others. Such a notion may be contrasted with Utilitarian ideas about the relationship of the individual to society.

In the Utilitarian scheme of things:

> It is in vain to talk of the interest of the community without understanding what is the interest of the individual. A thing is said to promote the interest, or to be *for* the interest, of an individual, when it tends to add to the sum total of his pleasures: or, what comes to the same things, to diminish the sum total of his pains (Bentham 1948, p. 3).

Moreover, the principle of utility, 'to promote or to oppose...happiness', (Bentham 1948, p. 2) applies only to the individual, and to the community insofar as the community is the sum of the individuals who make it up. Thus, for Bentham: 'The community is a fictitious *body*, composed of the individual persons who are considered as constituting as it were its *members*. The interest of the community then is, what? – the sum of the interests of the several members who make it up' (Bentham 1948, p. 3). Nothing could be more anathema to Green. For him, personal good, properly understood, is *part of* the 'common good', and does not take into account personal considerations. (Milne 1962, p. 100–106) In other words, the community comes first; and the common good is the mutual harmony of all in society seeking their own self-realization through the self-realization of others.

Moreover, Green recognized that this meant that the function of government was to create the conditions in which this mutual harmony could come about. Of course, the currently prevailing climate is not Idealist, it is Utilitarian both in government, including increasingly the civil service, and in society more widely. The 'public interest' has become nothing more than the sum of the interests of the public (expressed specifically as the interests of the duly elected government). The question is should not the public interest be interpreted as the Idealist 'common good'? And could not the public official, both politician and civil servant, usefully look to Green as an inspiration in this respect?

In order that these questions can be dealt with more clearly, the nature of morality needs further investigation. Two questions need to be raised about this concept of morality as the 'disinterested performance of self-imposed duties'. First, what are the sources of these duties? Are they divined internally, that is are there immutable and natural laws which govern human impulse? Or are they perceived as a result of human experience, that is are they conceived as a result of observing what is *actually* good and then perceiving what the real good is? The answer to this question probably lies in the nature of morality and its inseparability from the 'common good'. If morality requires this social dimension then it can be argued that duties imposed are duties inspired by the need to seek the good of society.

The second question is this: what are the rewards and what are the sanctions for the performance or non-performance of these self-imposed duties? Green would

340   BARRY J. O'TOOLE

hold that the reward or sanction would be one of conscience: that is to say that to do good, to perform a moral duty, is reward in itself. The sanction would be the danger of living in a society that would hinder the individual's self-realization.

The argument so far is as follows: first, morality is the disinterested performance of self-imposed duties. These duties are performed with the intention of self-realization. Self-realization involves not just the satisfaction of self, but satisfaction of self in a society which includes others who are also concerned with their own self-realization. Thus, the ultimate end of morality is the mutual harmony of all in society, or to use Green's phrase the 'common good'. An act is moral insofar as it contributes to this 'common good', though it must have as its motive the 'common good' to be counted as being a moral act. That is, motive is important in determining the morality or otherwise of an act. Government exists to promote the 'common good' by maintaining the conditions in which morality shall be possible: it does this by removing the hindrances to the achievement of self-realization, which is the realization of self in a society which includes others.

Although all people are called upon to lead a moral life, there is one group of people upon which it is particularly incumbent to act with these moral principles in mind: the governors, both politicians and officials. Government is, after all, called upon to create the conditions in which morality shall be possible. However, it has already been noted that the prevailing moral climate, a moral climate set in particular by politicians, is Utilitarian in nature. It may even be argued that politicians, no matter what their political party, are quite incapable of acting in any other way than with Utilitarian principles in mind. This then leaves officials as being the keepers of the 'common good', or to use a phrase they might be more at home with, the 'public interest'. Or does it? The questions now become, why should we see officials as the keepers of the public interest? What indeed is the public interest from the perspective of the world as the official might *actually* perceive it? And might a code of ethics, that is to say a means of ranking moral values, help these keepers of the public interest (if indeed they can be regarded as such) in the performance of their duties?

The first problem is that it must be borne in mind that civil servants are precisely that: they are the servants of the civil institutions of society. More particularly they are the servants of ministers. Ministers it should be remembered, are the representatives of the public in the departments of government. They are, moreover, the political heads of their respective departments and as such are accountable to Parliament, in particular to the directly elected House of Commons. Although not directly elected to their high offices as ministers, nevertheless they do have the legitimacy derived, first from (usually) having been elected to represent a particular parliamentary constituency, and secondly, of having the sanction of Parliament, in particular the House of Commons, in the performance of these duties as ministers. The constitutional convention which governs the performance of these duties as ministers is known as ministerial responsibility, of which there are two aspects: first, that the ministers collectively accept responsibility for *all* of the acts of the government as a whole, thus enabling the House of Commons, if it so wishes, to dismiss the government as a whole in a vote of censure; secondly, and more importantly, that ministers are individually responsible to Parliament for *all* the official acts of all civil servants within their particular individual departments. That is to say that it is ministers, and only ministers, as politicians and representatives of the public in departments, who are responsible and answerable for all the activities of their departments and who can face the sanction of dismissal from their office if Parliament does not approve of the actions of any of the officials within departments. Thus, no civil servant when acting on the behalf of his department, has a constitutional personality of his own. He is always acting in the minister's name. This doctrine, the doctrine of individual ministerial responsibility to Parliament, must surely raise the question of whether it is ministers, both individually and collectively, who should be seen as the keepers of the public interest.

The problem is complicated by the fact that the convention of ministerial responsibility is derived from two higher constitutional doctrines: these are what the famous constitutional lawyer A. V. Dicey referred to as 'the twin pillars of the Constitution' – the sovereignty of Parliament and the rule of law. For present purposes the rule of law means simply this, that nobody, including ministers of the Crown, is above the law. The law has two main sources, the common law, which is essentially a system of precedents built up over the centuries by the judges, and the statute law, which is the accumulation of Acts of Parliament. The sovereignty of Parliament means essentially that no body or institution has precedence over the constitutional entity known as the Queen in Parliament. That is to say that Parliament can make and unmake any law – including codifying the common law – and that the laws that it makes are binding upon the judges and take precedence over common law.

For civil servants this constitutional position raises numerous dilemmas, most notably, where there is conflict between Parliament and the government, the question as to where the civil servant's primary loyalty must lie. Is it to the Queen's ministers? Or is it to the Queen's Parliament? Or is it to neither? Should the civil servant's loyalty be solely to the 'public interest'? This is the point at which civil servants, managers in British central government, might be called upon to make judgements about the 'public interest', and in so doing to make moral judgements in line with Green's definition of morality as 'the disinterested performance of self-imposed duties'. The duty is to the public interest. It is disinterested in the sense that personal considerations, perhaps the possibility of being dismissed or even of prosecution, ought not to play a part in the decisions made. Indeed, the personal good, which properly understood is part of the common good in Idealist philosophy, does not take into account personal considerations (Milne 1962 p. 105–6).

The Clive Ponting and Westland affairs illustrate this point admirably (Ponting 1986; Fry 1985; Drewry 1987; Hennessy 1986; Oliver and Austen 1986; Chapman 1986), as do the recent débâcles over the government's handling of water privatization and the Lockerbie air disaster. These episodes, and others, indicate that ministers behave politically: that is to say that their judgements are affected by party political or parliamentary advantage considerations. Although not universally true, it is fair to say that such considerations are essentially selfish, or on the behalf of particular interests, and although they may on occasion coincide with 'the public

342   BARRY J. O'TOOLE

interest', they are not primarily concerned with 'the public interest'. In Green's philosophy, a moral act is one which not only enhances the 'common good' but also has as its intention that enhancement. It is motivation which makes a good act a moral act. Moreover, any act must be considered to be a good act in itself before it can be considered a moral act, in the sense of enhancing the common good. From this it can be argued that ministers often behave in ways which make them quite unfit to be the keepers of the public interest.

If ministers are often unfit, and leaving aside civil servants for the time being, what about Parliament? Dealing first with the House of Commons it is true that in a strictly constitutional sense Members of Parliament are the representatives of their constituents. That is to say, following Edmund Burke, that they exercise their judgement on behalf of their constituents bearing no other factor in mind except the merits of the issues before them. This, of course, is a fallacy. MPs belong to political parties. They are chosen in a majority of cases not by their local electorates but by their local constituency parties. This stems from the type of electoral system we have in this country, the so-called 'first-past-the-post' system of simple plurality which allows political parties to amass concentrations of votes making the majority of constituencies 'safe' for one party or another. If the conscience of MPs somehow survives this problem, the second problem is one of ambition and advancement once in Parliament. Most MPs seek ministerial office, and this means supporting the current leadership of their particular party in the hope of being visited by the patronage held in the hands of that leadership. Even if this is an unfair characterization it is nonetheless true that the vast majority of MPs belong to a political party. Whether or not an MP genuinely regards those beliefs and values as being in the national or public interest, the fact remains that such is not necessarily the case.

Turning from the Commons to the Lords. Can their noble lordships be regarded as the keepers of the public interest? They are, after all, dependent on nobody for their positions, and it is true that their deliberations are often far more sensible and reflective than those of the lower house. However, the question must be raised here as to the legitimacy of that august body the House of Lords. Many peers are hereditary: they take part in the legislative process merely because of the privilege of their birth. Of the rest, most are there because of services rendered, many because of party political services rendered. Thus, while the House of Lords may aspire to act as the only effective opposition to the present government, this lack of political legitimacy renders it incapable of acting as the keeper of the public interest.

This, then, leaves the civil service, in particular those grades which have senior and middle management roles, from Permanent Secretary to Principal. The first objection which might be raised to thinking of civil servants as keepers of the public interest is the fact of their own lack of legitimacy. In the sense that civil servants are not elected this observation cannot be refuted. However, legitimacy may have other sources than election and may be other than party political in character.

The classic source of ideas on this matter are the writings of Max Weber, on bureaucracy, authority and legitimacy, (Gerth and Wright Mills 1948, Introduction

SENIOR OFFICIALS IN BRITISH CENTRAL GOVERNMENT   343

and pp. 77–128 and 196–244). Authority for Weber was the legitimate exercise of power. Legitimacy had three possible sources, what he referred to as the Charismatic, Traditional and Legal-Rational types of authority. Granted that these are ideas and that sources of authority can be multiple, the House of Commons is primarily based on a Charismatic form of authority (expressed through the electoral process), the House of Lords on a Traditional form of authority and the civil service on a Legal-Rational form of authority. The Legal-Rational form of authority was, for Weber, the basis upon which bureaucracy, which was the 'technically superior' means of administering large and complex organizations, was built and from which it derived its legitimacy. Essentially such legitimacy depended upon knowledge and ability and strict impartiality or objectivity. And since the British civil service must be acknowledged as something approaching the extreme and delimiting case of Weber's 'Ideal Type' bureaucracy, it is in the light of these ideas that the legitimacy of the civil service can be discussed. In the first place, all civil servants are appointed according to publicly known criteria. The basis of appointment to 'apprentice' positions for senior management, the grade of Administration Trainee (AT), is first of all the possession of at least a good honours degree, supplemented by rigorous examination according to criteria designed by the Civil Service Commission. The commission was set up as a body independent of both ministers and the civil service which is charged with the responsibility of certifying that candidates have the necessary pre-requisites for employment in the civil service and that they are capable of carrying out whatever duties may be assigned to them. Promotion within the service is based on merit, and only at the very top of the service, the grades of Under Secretary, Deputy Secretary and Permanent Secretary, is there any ministerial involvement in appointments. By the time aspiring Permanent Secretaries have reached the grade of Assistant Secretary, they have proven themselves in the arts of administration. Moreover, in the process of acquiring these arts, and partly deriving from their backgrounds and educations, they have lost (probably never even had) any vestiges of party political bias. The civil service has always prided itself on its party political neutrality and thus on the acceptability of its work on the part of all governments of whichever political party. All civil servants become 'socialized' into this atmosphere of party political neutrality and were recruited in the knowledge that they could succumb to such 'socialization'. In other words, people who have strong party political views would not normally be appointed. Indeed it is unlikely that people with strong party political views would present themselves for consideration for appointment in the civil service (Chapman 1968).

In essence, the British civil service possesses many of the pre-requisites for assuming the legitimacy deriving from Legal-Rational authority: it is recruited according to publicly known stringent criteria; promotion within it is based on merit, that is on acknowledged ability within, and specialist knowledge of, the 'political environment'; and it is strictly impartial, both as between political parties and in dealing with the public.

The question now is, does it also possess some of the possible dysfunctions of bureaucracy, most notably the insularity and self-serving tendencies identified with

344   BARRY J. O'TOOLE

bureaucratic organizations? If it does, then it cannot act as the keeper of the public interest, as which, by default of other institutions of civil life, it might be called upon to act. If morality consists in the performance of acts from the motive of enhancing the 'common good' through the process of self-realization, and must also be compatible with the self-realization of others in society, then any civil servant who acts in such a way that it is the bureaucracy's interests which are being served cannot be considered to be acting for the 'common good', or more practically, 'the public interest'.

This raises the question of codes of ethics, because, as noted earlier, codes of ethics are concerned with the application of moral standards and may thus have the effect of reducing the tendencies towards the bureaucratic dysfunctions mentioned: that is to say they may have the effect of helping senior managers in the public service perform acts from the motive of the 'common good'.

The practical question of a code of ethics for managers in British government has become vitally important in recent years, fuelled in particular by the plight of Clive Ponting and the behaviour of certain ministers over the Westland Helicopter company. Where do the loyalties of civil servants lie? What are their duties and responsibilities to ministers? To whom, for what, and how are civil servants accountable?

Traditionally, the civil service has eschewed codes of conduct. *The Civil Service Pay and Conditions of Service Code*, formerly *Estacode*, puts it like this:

> It has never been thought necessary to lay down a precise code of conduct because civil servants jealously maintain their professional standards. In practice the distinctive character of the British Civil Service depends largely on the existence of a general code of conduct which, although to some extent intangible and unwritten, is of very real importance.

However, as early as 1970, the First Division Association felt that: 'The existence of a comprehensive but intangible and unwritten code would be hard to verify and runs counter to many people's experience. We believe reliance on it leads to a dangerous complacency' (FDA 1970, para. 7).

The FDA's concern with professional codes of conduct first emerged seriously in the late 1960s because the Fulton report had offended many Administrative Class civil servants by criticizing them for their 'amateurism'. This concern was reflected in the following motion passed by the 1969 Annual General Meeting of the association:

> To call attention to the need to define the professional standards expected from public servants in the light of their constitutional role and developments in government administration, and to ask the Executive Committee to play its part in stimulating discussion of this question within the public service and more widely (FDA 1970, para. 1).

The resolution was moved by Mr D. H. Morrell of the Home Office in a speech which is regarded by many as one of the most moving ever given at an FDA Annual General Meeting. In it he argued fiercely that civil servants were not amateurs:

SENIOR OFFICIALS IN BRITISH CENTRAL GOVERNMENT   345

We are professionls. Ever since the great reforms of the last century we have exhibited the two primary characteristics of a true profession. We profess an ethic regulating our work: and we possess knowledge and knowhow specific to that work.

Our ethic is simply stated. We stand committed to neutrality of process. We profess that public power is not to be used to further the private purposes of those to whom it is entrusted. It is to be used solely for the furtherance of public purposes as defined by constitutional process.

The difficulty lay in the practical application of this 'principle of universal validity.' In particular Mr Morrell recognized the difficulties inherent in evolving a set of procedural rules such that officials who were applying them, people who were 'not in themselves value-neutral – because they are human beings with needs and aspirations' – could, by accepting them, contribute to the process of determining and administering public policies. He argued:

We still do not accept the reality of our individual humanity; we have not therefore evolved rules of procedure such that we can contribute all that we are to a process having public not private outcomes. And the price which we and the public pay for pursuing a myth is heavy.

Speaking personally, I find it yearly more difficult to reconcile personal integrity with a view of my role which requires the deliberate suppression of part of what I am...

But the price which the public has to pay is even heavier. For the part of ourselves we are asked to suppress is the creative part.

In the light of these observations Mr Morrell suggested:

that our professional commitment to neutrality of process needs to be worked out afresh in rules of procedure which will liberate, and make available for the public good, the immense store of human sensitivity and creativity which I believe to be imprisoned by an outmoded myth of personal objectivity.

His immediate plea was:

that the Executive Committee should consider whether circumstances could be created in which our representatives could sit down, on neutral ground but with the blessing of the political and permanent heads of the Service, to thrash out in company with politicians, representatives of other professions and of the community at large, freely and openly, the issues which I have tried to raise (FDA 1969).

The response of the Executive Committee was to set up a Sub-Committee on Professional Standards in the Public Service.

There was, 'of course...no question of the FDA committing itself to a specific point of view' (FDA 1971); but it is interesting to note some of the views being expressed by members of the association on professional standards in their own occupation. It is also interesting to note that the membership of the sub-committee included Miss (now Dame) Anne Mueller (formerly Second Permanent Secretary in

346   BARRY J. O'TOOLE

the Cabinet Office in charge of personnel management in the civil service) and Mr (now Sir) Peter Middleton (now First Permanent Secretary at the Treasury).

The starting point of the sub-committee was where the Fulton committee had left off. The Fulton committee:

> did not consider [some] organisational problems, such as relations between departments with overlapping or conflicting interests. Nor did they explore the difficult boundary of what Ministers have a right to expect and civil servants a duty to provide. And they left completely untouched the question of ethical standards which determine how civil servants perform their work in relation to the loyalties they observe and the conflicts they perceive. . .(FDA 1970, para. 4).

Moreover, academics and other interested outsiders had not made serious comment on such matters (FDA 1970, paras. 5 and 6), and in official quarters within the civil service itself there had not been any thought about professional matters since 1928.

What then were the issues this sub-committee considered? First of all it seemed sensible to state what responsibilities a civil servant had. His primary duty was to his minister and to the ministerial office which he (the civil servant) was concerned to maintain (FDA 1970, para. 9). Secondly, he had a *de facto* duty towards his official superiors (FDA 1970, para. 10). Thirdly, he arguably had a duty to the administration as a whole – however, 'with executive powers vested in individual Ministers, and the power to reward and punish individual civil servants vested in their official head, the system is biased in favour of the interests of the part where they may conflict with the interests of the whole' (FDA 1970, para. 11). More debatable than these three duties was whether civil servants had still wider responsibilities, to Parliament and to the democratic system (FDA 1970, para. 12); and whether they 'should be conscious of [the democratic process] and of the rights and desires of the individuals who make up the community' (FDA 1970, para. 13).

The views that the sub-committee had on these matters were not unanimous. One view, *not* shared by the majority, was that:

> any discussion of professional standards for civil servants must be based on the proposition that civil servants have a duty only towards the government whom they serve and that this duty is fully discharged by loyal, truthful and objective service to Ministers. . .Ministers would be answerable for their policies to Parliament and the electorate and civil servants would be debarred from altering, applying or presenting government policy so as to take account of anything other than the wishes of the government (FDA 1970, para. 30).

This was a 'restricted view' and might lead civil servants 'in certain circumstances [to] find it difficult to act in a manner which was honourable, truthful and in accordance with their conscience.' For example:

> they might believe the government's policy to be against the public interest, unfair, or simply irrelevant to the real facts. They might be reluctant to defend government policy when, in their opinion, the arguments against it were stronger and more in accordance with the facts than the arguments for it. They might find it hard, in presenting government policy, to present all the facts in perspective (FDA 1970, para. 31).

SENIOR OFFICIALS IN BRITISH CENTRAL GOVERNMENT 347

Within this restricted view it would be a mistake to seek to solve conflicts by widening the duties of civil servants. Such a move 'would introduce the notion that officials become in some sense the trustees of the interests of Parliament and the public when Ministerial policies fail adequately to take these interests into account.' That would be contrary to the constitutional position (FDA 1970, para. 32). Efforts should instead be made to make the opposition, pressure groups and the Press more concerned to obtain the facts from government; there should be a move towards leaving ministers to present public policies; and:

> above all efforts should be directed towards maintaining and developing, but only as part of the internal dialogue between Ministers and civil servants and among civil servants themselves, the wide freedom of expression, and the right to disagree constructively, which have traditionally been tolerated in many parts of the higher Civil Service (FDA 1970, para. 33).

However, a majority of the sub-committee took a wider view of civil servants' duties. They did not believe that the duty to the minister and duty to wider institutions were mutually exclusive or that in all conceivable circumstances the primacy of the duty to the minister was beyond all dispute: to suppose that was to oversimplify the civil servant's position (FDA 1970, para. 34). 'The majority of us feel', read the sub-committee's report, 'that the possibility of conflict between Ministers' wishes and professional standards must be faced, and that making the departmental Minister the final judge in all circumstances does not provide a sufficient practical guide to solving such problems' (FDA 1970, para. 37).

Within this majority there were several strands of opinion. One was that the civil servant had a duty to the 'public interest'. Despite the many problems in defining what the public interest was, some of the sub-committee felt that the civil service:

> should recognise a professional task of ascertaining objectively what is the public interest in a particular context. Individual responsibility would be an important component and formative element in this ethic: the erosion of anonymity should be accepted as one consequence, and management by objectives adopted widely so as to ensure that responsibility was not diffused. New methods of consultation on policy such as Green Papers would lead to a wider agreement on the aims of departments, and thus provide more objective criteria of the public interest (FDA 1970, para. 39).

Another view was that action should be taken to preserve the integrity of the service against threats arising from 'tendentious briefing, the corruption of power, and the inattention to the true interests of the people'. This action would involve a new charter or 'contract of service to the people', laying down a code of conduct which neither senior officials nor ministers might overrule (FDA 1970, para. 41). It would forbid censorship of facts and opinions, insist on merit rather than conformity as the criterion for promotion, and institute machinery in which there was staff participation to deal with discipline and grievances.

These were radical views indeed, though never seriously acted upon by the FDA. Nevertheless, they do indicate that there was some concern amongst senior members

348   BARRY J. O'TOOLE

of the civil service about the nature of their obligations. However, despite the ever increasing demoralization of senior civil servants (O'Toole 1989; Chapman 1988b), and the episodes mentioned above which have reopened the debate about professional standards and the role of codes of ethics, the FDA have not really lived up to their radicalism of the 1960s and 1970s. Their response, for example, to the so-called Armstrong memorandum was tame in comparison.

In his memorandum, the 'Note of Guidance on the Duties and Responsibilities of Civil Servants', Sir Robert essentially restated a famous statement made in 1928 by Sir Warren Fisher, the first officially recognized Head of the Civil Service, that: The first and most important duty of a civil servant is to give his undivided allegiance to the state on all occasions and at all times when the state calls upon his services...A civil servant is not to subordinate his duty to his private interests' (Fisher 1928, para. 56).

Armstrong expanded on this statement thus:

> Civil servants are servants of the Crown. For all practical purposes the Crown in this context means, and is represented by, the Government of the day. There are special cases in which certain functions are conferred by law upon particular members or groups of members of the public service; but in general the executive powers of the Crown are exercised by and on the advice of Her Majesty's Ministers, who in turn are answerable to Parliament. The civil service as such has no constitutional personality or responsibility separate from the duly elected Government of the day...The civil service serves the Government of the day as a whole, that is to say Her Majesty's Ministers collectively, and the Prime Minister is the Minister for the Civil Service. The duty of the individual civil servant is first and foremost to the Minister of the Crown who is in charge of the Department in which he or she is serving. It is the Minister who is responsible, and answerable in Parliament, for the conduct of the Department's affairs and the management of its business. It is the duty of civil servants to serve their Ministers with integrity and to the best of their ability.

He went on:

> The British Civil Service is a non-political and disciplined career service. Civil servants are required to serve the duly elected Government of the day, of whatever political complexion. It is of the first importance that civil servants should conduct themselves in such a way as to deserve and retain the confidence of Ministers, and as to be able to establish the same relationship with those whom they may be required to serve in some future Administration. That confidence is the indispensable foundation of a good relationship between Ministers and civil servants. The conduct of civil servants should at all times be such that Ministers and potential future Ministers can be sure that confidence can be freely given and that the civil service will at all times conscientiously fulfil its duties and obligations to, and impartially assist, advise and carry out the policies of, the duly elected Government of the day (Armstrong 1985, paras. 2–4).

This statement is an impeccable statement of constitutional theory; it is however, a parody of political practice. It uses the words 'integrity' and 'conscientiously'

SENIOR OFFICIALS IN BRITISH CENTRAL GOVERNMENT   349

without thinking of those words in the context of the people to whom it specifically applies, that is civil servants, and it certainly ignores the 'integrity' and 'conscience' of ministers. To some extent, that deficiency was remedied in a new edition of the statement which included a new paragraph which quoted from the government's response to the Seventh Report of the Treasury and Civil Service Committee, thus: 'The Government believes that Ministers are well aware of the principles that should govern their duties and responsibilities in relation to Parliament and in relation to civil servants. It goes without saying that these include the obligations of integrity' (Armstrong 1987, para. 2).

In its evidence to the Treasury and Civil Service Committee and its investigation into the duties and responsibilities of civil servants, which was specifically concerned with the so-called 'Armstrong Memorandum', the First Division Association was extremely critical of Sir Robert's statement. It was 'a narrow statement of existing conventions with heavy emphasis on a civil servant's duty and little about resolving ethical dilemmas' (FDA 1986, pp. 59–60).

To remedy this deficiency the FDA made suggestions of its own about a code of ethics for civil servants. But even this seems somewhat traditional and its general statements of principle read as follows:

> Civil Servants in the United Kingdom are servants of the Queen in Parliament. The civil service is politically neutral and individual civil servants may be expected to serve a succession of administrations. Their conduct should be such that a new administration need have no reason to suppose that they are unable or unwilling to implement its policies or serve it loyally; this implies that in their official duties they should avoid personal identification with the political philosophy of any particular administration. Civil servants have a professional duty to provide Ministers with honest and impartial advice whether or not this accords with the Minister's or Government's views; advice which in any way departs from this is in breach of civil servants' duty and damages their integrity as servants of the Crown.

> Civil servants are also servants of the executive, which is a function of the Crown carried out by Ministers who are accountable to Parliament. It follows that civil servants should diligently pursue the implementation of government policies unless they are in posts where statutory duties or professional responsibilities require them to act independently. They should not seek to obstruct these policies by delay, by witholding relevant information or by misusing delegated powers in a manner contrary to the spirit or letter of government policy. It also follows that civil servants should preserve the confidences of Ministers and should not divulge them without authorisation (FDA 1985, preamble).

This seems to be more or less what Sir Robert Armstrong had in mind. It begins promisingly with civil servants as being 'servants of the Queen in Parliament', but this turns out to mean, essentially, the Crown, and, in Sir Robert's phrase: 'For all practical purposes the Crown in this context means and is represented by the Government of the day'. This does not seem to be any different from the FDA's statement. True, it should, as the FDA pointed out, be read in the context of their desire to see the repeal of Section 2 of the Official Secrets Act and its replacement

350   BARRY J. O'TOOLE

by a Freedom of Information Act. True also that the code goes on to lay down procedures to resolve difficulties which arise where a civil servant's conscience renders him incapable of serving the minister in the manner expected or where he is asked to perform an illegal act. However, so too does Sir Robert's memorandum – and although the FDA's procedures may be more formal and may involve the Chairman of the relevant Parliamentary Select Committee, the gap between the two does not seem so large as to be unbridgeable.

Unlike the FDA's earlier efforts in this area, neither the FDA's 1985 document nor the Armstrong Memorandum deal with the 'public interest' or the 'common good'. Perhaps it is unrealistic to expect that they should, and certainly the difficulties inherent in the Idealist view of the 'common good' would make it an almost impossible task. For example, if the 'common good' is 'the mutual harmony of all in society', what exactly is meant by harmony? The same is true of statements about the functions of government, for example Green's assertion that they are 'to maintain the conditions in which morality shall be possible', and that they should remove hindrances to 'self-realization'? What are the criteria for the 'conditions' of morality? What are the hindrances to 'self realization'? What exactly is 'self-realization'?

Perhaps most importantly of all, however, is the inability in any society, but especially in a democratic society, to get away from politics. Green does not really address himself to this question; but it is a question which needs at least to be raised here. For, as noted above, civil servants *are* servants; it is politicians as ministers who are the masters: and this is as it should be in a democratic society. However, politicians by definition, behave politically, and political acts are not necessarily acts geared towards the 'common good' or the 'public interest'. Perhaps the question could be settled simply by asserting that there is an *acceptable* area of political controversy and political debate bounded by a perimeter of *propriety* labelled the 'public interest' or the 'common good'. When that perimeter is breached then it is the duty of *all* concerned, not just civil servants, but other politicians and citizens more widely, to act to defend that breach. But when is this perimeter to be set up? Who is to guard it or to judge whether it has been breached?

The answer to this question lies in the nature of the system of government. In most societies the system of government is established and controlled by a single, sovereign document, the constitution. In this society however, no such document exists. And, as Richard Chapman points out in his sharp and provocative inaugural lecture, it is the highly regarded traditions of public sector management which provide one of the bases for the stability of the state (Chapman 1988b, pp. 16–17). Or at least *provided*. Those traditions are under threat from developments apparently aimed at cutting the cost of government. As Chapman states:

> These developments seem to represent such a significant change of emphasis and ultimately of direction, that even if welcomed on the grounds of cost cutting and rolling back the frontiers of the state, they seem out of character with the highly regarded traditions, standards and expectations of public sector management in this country. It may seem premature to issue dire warnings of the dangers of corruption, but if the sorts of safeguards that worked so well in the past

SENIOR OFFICIALS IN BRITISH CENTRAL GOVERNMENT 351

are removed - safeguards involving regular posting of staff, recruitment on the basis of open competitions with the objective assessment of applicants, and socialisation which encourages the highest standards of integrity and public service as the most desirable qualities in public sector management - if these safeguards no longer exist, then it may be necessary to ask if alternative measures should be introduced to ensure that high standards of public sector management are still achievable (Chapman 1988b, pp. 16-17).

In other cultures, Chapman writes, there are different safeguards against the dangers he outlines: ombudsmen, *droit administratif*, written constitutions and enforceable codes of ethics. And it is at this point that the question raised earlier may be raised again. The question is whether in the circumstances outlined a 'code of ethics' is of any practical use. Will a code of ethics help civil servants determine when the perimeter of propriety has been overstepped and give an indication of what action to take in consequence? True, in this current context it can state what the constitutional position is; it can lay down where, for most practical purposes, a civil servant's everyday duty should lie; it can establish procedures of appeal against the unfair treatment of civil servants. What it cannot do is lay down the criteria, except in the most general terms, of what it is to be 'good', or what the word 'ought' means in its ethical sense. That is to say it cannot lay down what morality is or what a moral act is in any given circumstances. This, in the end, is for the personal judgement of all individuals who must make their decisions in the light of all the evidence available to them. That is to say that ethical theory has simply this as its basis: it can lay down the criteria for what *sort* of questions an individual should raise with himself over particular situations; but it cannot lay down the questions themselves. Nor does it provide any of the answers.

And this is where T. H. Green may once again be considered. For Green, as Milne points out, a theory of morality can be of help only to the man who is trying to be moral (Milne 1962, p. 110–20). The question is: what are the sources of the ideas which govern that man's actions, and, of course, their morality or otherwise? For civil servants it is those very traditions which Chapman sees as being under threat from the current developments in public sector management. In the past civil servants would have had as one of their primary considerations in carrying out their work the 'public interest', in the sense of the community coming before the individual (Chapman 1988a, pp. 313–14; 1968 and 1970; O'Toole 1989). However, the prevailing moral climate is Utilitarian, and has been for at least a decade, and probably longer. Civil servants have, almost inevitably, become increasingly concerned with their own interests (O'Toole 1989; Chapman 1988a, pp. 312–14 and 1988b, pp. 15–16). The traditions of public service, of disinterestedness and of impartiality are under threat. What really is needed now is a thoroughgoing review of the position of the civil service in government and society, perhaps a royal commission, which can raise some of the questions raised here; and provide some answers. And perhaps such a review could look to T. H. Green and his concern with the 'common good' as its inspiration. What can be said is that in the past, civil servants could have been regarded as keepers of the 'public interest'. Today, such a proposition would be questionable. Where, then, does society turn?

352   BARRY J. O'TOOLE

REFERENCES
Armstrong, Sir Robert. 1985. *Note by the Head of the Home Civil Service, The duties and responsi-bilities of civil servants in relation to ministers*, 25 February. London: Cabinet Office.
——. 1987. *Note by the Head of the Home Civil Service, The duties and responsibilities of civil servants in relation to ministers*, 2 December. London: Cabinet Office.
Bentham, J., 1789, 1948. *The principles of morals and legislation*. New York: Haffner.
Chapman, Richard A. 1965. 'Thomas Hill Green, 1836–1882', *Review of Politics* vol. 27, pp. 516–31.
——. 1966. 'The basis of T. H. Green's philosophy', *International Review of History and Political Science* vol. 3, pp. 72–88.
——. 1968. 'Profile of a profession', memorandum 2 in vol. 3, No. 2 of *The Civil Service*. Fulton Committee. Cmnd. 3638. London: HMSO.
——. 1986. 'Whitehall and Westminster: issues for education and public debate', *Parliamentary Affairs* vol. 40, pp. 133–5.
——. 1988a. *Ethics in the British civil service*. London: Routledge.
——. 1988b. *The art of darkness*. University of Durham.
Civil Service Commission. 1988. *Annual report*. Basingstoke: CSC.
Drewry, Gavin. 1987. 'The Defence Committee on Westland', *Political Quarterly* vol. 58, pp. 82–7.
First Division Association. 1969. *Minutes* of the Annual General Meeting held on 10 May, Speech of Mr D. H. Morrell, FDA file reference 180 367.
——. 1970. *Report of the Sub-Committee on Professional Standards in the Public Service*, FDA File reference A00082.
——. 1971. *Monthly notes*. April.
——. 1986. Memorandum submitted to the Treasury and Civil Service Committee, 'Civil servants: duties and responsibilities', *Seventh Report from the Treasury and Civil Service Committee, Session 1985–86, Civil servants and ministers: duties and responsibilities Volume II*, pp. 59–64, HC 92–II, 1986.
Fisher, Sir Warren et al. 1928. *Report of the Board of Enquiry appointed by the Prime Minister to investigate certain statements affecting civil servants*. Cmd. 3037. London: HMSO.
Fry, Geoffrey K. 1985. 'Government and the civil service: a review of recent developments', *Parliamentary Affairs* vol. 39, pp. 267–83.
Gerth, H. H., and C. Wright Mills. (eds.) 1948. *From Max Weber*, London: Routledge and Kegan Paul.
Green, T. H. 1879, 1931. *Lectures on the principles of political obligation*. Longmans Green and Co.
——. 1883, 1969. *Prologemena to ethics*. New York: Thomas Y. Cromwell.
Hennessy, Peter. 1986. 'Michael Hesseltine, Mottram's Law and the efficiency of cabinet government', *Political Quarterly* vol. 57, pp. 137–43.
Milne, A. J. M. 1962. *The social philosophy of English idealism*. London: George Allen and Unwin.
O'Toole, Barry J. 1989. *Private gain and public service: the Association of First Division Civil Servants*. London: Routledge.
Ponting, Clive. 1985. *The right to know: the inside story of the Belgrano affair*. London: Sphere Books.
Richter, Melvin. 1964. *The politics of conscience: T. H. Green and his age*. London: Weidenfeld and Nicolson.
Vincent, Andrew, and Raymond Plant. 1984. *Philosophy, politics and citizenship: the life and thought of the British idealists*. Oxford: Basil Blackwell.

[11]

By KEITH C. SIMMONDS

The Politicization of Bureaucracies in Developing Countries: St. Kitts-Nevis, A Case Study

ON SEPTEMBER 19, 1983, St. Kitts-Nevis obtained political independence and became the 163rd member of the United Nations, after having been a colony of Great Britain for over three hundred years. Ironically, St. Kitts, which earned the historical distinction of being the "mother colony" of the West Indies, was almost the last island to become independent.

St. Kitts-Nevis is a twin island state with a federal form of government. The national government is in St. Kitts, situated in the capital town of Basseterre. Together the islands are approximately 128 square miles with a population of about 52,000, over 90 percent of which are of African descent. Geographically, St. Kitts-Nevis is a part of a southeastern chain of islands in the Caribbean Sea located relatively close to Cuba and Jamaica to the north and Venezuela to the south. Economically, the main industry is sugar, but persistent efforts have led to growing diversification of light industries, including textile manufacturing and electronics assembly plants. Regionally, St. Kitts-Nevis is a member of the Caribbean Economic Common Market (CARICOM) and also of the sub-regional organization, the Organization of Eastern Caribbean States (OECS). St. Kitts-Nevis shares much of the political history of the other English speaking island-states of the Commonwealth Caribbean.

Like most of the newly independent states of the English speaking Caribbean, St. Kitts-Nevis experienced three main phases of political evolution prior to political independence. Slavery and plantation domination characterized the first period, which lasted from the early 1600s to about 1850. Formal political authority was shared between the British Crown and the landed gentry through the form of the Old Representative System.[1] The period ended with the arrival of emancipation, subsequent mass protests and elite conflict.

The second phase, known as the Crown Colony period, lasted for about one hundred years, approximately between 1850 and 1950. There was no substantive change in the power relationship between the imperial authorities and the plantocracy. Essentially, the shared power relationship that existed during the Old Representative System was maintained throughout much of this phase. As a means of appeasing elite demands for elected assemblies, however, the imperial power partially acceded to these demands by settling for formal domination of both legislative and executive powers.

After the 1940s, the Crown Colony phase evolved into a political/administrative system which is sometimes referred to as the ministerial system. The administrative arm of the colonial government was developed to implement

---

[1] For a more detailed discussion on the Old Representative System and the overall political evolution of the former British territories see Morley Ayearst, *The British West Indies: The Search for Self-Government* (New York, 1960), esp. Chapter 2.

some of the "enlightened" social policies of the imperial power. By this time of political development, St. Kitts-Nevis like most of the other former colonies had experienced labor unrest and other types of mass protests, the intent being to obtain an improvement in the quality of life in such areas as working conditions, health care, and education. Gradually the state assumed greater responsibility for the provision of social services and maintenance of law and order.

Satisfied that the indigenous elite showed potential in managing the internal affairs of the islands, recognizing that diminishing returns had set in on the economic advantages once gained from the colonies and, finally, realizing that it would be universally unpopular to hold on to the colonies, Britain set the final stage for eventual political independence. For St. Kitts-Nevis in particular, it was the adoption of the Associated Statehood status which essentially meant that St. Kitts-Nevis had full responsibility for internal affairs while Britain retained responsibility for external affairs and defense. The grooming for political independence lasted for eleven years, after which St. Kitts-Nevis sought and obtained its independence.

One can conclude from this discussion of the political history of St. Kitts-Nevis that the state has inherited many British political values and institutions and currently possesses the appropriate administrative machinery to facilitate established social, economic and political values. St. Kitts-Nevis is not unlike most of the other former colonies in the Caribbean and elsewhere where transplanted colonial values and institutions have impacted significantly on the body politic of the now politically independent countries. What is certain to develop in the future is a clash (or at a minimum, an uneasy coexistence) between established institutions and new ideas about doing things in post-independence St. Kitts-Nevis.

One institution and its attendant values that is certain to be affected by the winds of change is the bureaucracy, the administrative arm of government. British bureaucratic practice rests upon a fundamental theory universally known as "political neutrality." It implies that the bureaucracy is above politics; it is simply the servant of the administration in power; it implements, not dictates, policy. Political neutrality has been a traditional characteristic of the St. Kitts-Nevis bureaucracy although, admittedly, it is problematic to precisely define the degree of historical adherence to the theory. But the theory nevertheless runs in the veins of the traditional bureaucracy of the state.

It is the contention of this paper, however, that political neutrality as a concept and practice will be seriously challenged by a new approach to bureaucratic activity, which here shall be called bureaucratic activism. Additionally, the paper argues that given the very nature and composition of the post-independence bureaucracy, as well as the government's goals of social change, it seems certain that the value of political neutrality will give way significantly to the force of an action-oriented bureaucracy. There is a certain logic to this contention: that is, there is a high degree of consistency between social change and bureaucratic activism. This shall become more clear as the paper develops.

60   PHYLON

Bureaucratic activism almost invariably results in the politicization of the state's bureaucracy. Many developing countries in their attempt to accomplish social change have found it convenient to merge political leadership with administrative function and activity. The results are not always happy and in fact are even counterproductive at times. A central concern of this paper therefore, is to discuss the process of politicization itself and to examine the role of politicized bureaucracies in St. Kitts-Nevis in particular and third world countries as a whole.

In this essay, politicization implies that the administrative machinery of government is not clearly distinct from the political machinery, but that the former, given its monopoly on expertise, acts as the centerpiece for societal change. The principal objective, therefore, of a politicized bureaucracy is to effect social change and development. This approach to the study of bureaucracy in third world countries breaks with the traditional view of bureaucracy, and it is the author's intention to identify with those students of bureaucracy who argue that, given the imperatives of developing countries, the bureaucracies in less developed states (LDCs) are left with no choice but to play an active role in accomplishing change. The St. Kitts-Nevis bureaucracy is one such example that has developmental responsibilities, and in the pursuit of them its politicization is probable.

It is necessary first to establish a frame of reference for the discussion if the posture of politicized bureaucracies is to be clearly understood. This requires that the features of politicized bureaucracies be contrasted with those of "non-politicized" bureaucracies. Max Weber, perhaps the most respected writer on bureaucracy, almost a hundred years ago theorized that the role of public bureaucracy is to implement policy.[2] Bureaucracy if it is to be efficient must serve the values of the political machinery, not usurp it. The political leadership leads, the bureaucracy follows. Weber theorized that a rational, efficient, and achievement-oriented bureaucracy must emphasize:[3]

1. Political neutrality. Bureaucracy must be instrumental in nature. The legal duties of the civil service are restricted to policy implementation.
2. Hierarchy. That is, a pattern of authority which clearly defines superior-subordinate relationships. Hierarchy establishes a chain of command, facilitates span of control and other mechanisms of control and coordination.
3. Specialization of tasks and knowledge, facilitated by staff and line responsibilities.
4. Formal communication and record management.
5. Objective standards and impersonal rules which would ensure organizational reliability and predictability.

---

[2] For a general treatment of Max Weber's "ideal" bureaucracy, see Robert K. Merton et al., eds., _Reader in Bureaucracy_ (New York, 1956); Alfred Diamant, "The Bureaucratic Model: Max Weber Rejected, Rediscovered, Reformed," in Ferrel Heady and Sybil L. Stokes, _Papers in Comparative Public Administration_ (Ann Arbor, 1962).
[3] Adapted from a more detailed summary of Weber's "ideal" Model in Robbert Simmons and Eugene P. Dvorin, _Public Administration: Values, Policy, and Change_ (New York, 1977) pp. 192-94.

ST. KITTS-NEVIS, A CASE STUDY   61

6. Recruitment of personnel on the basis of merit; promotion based on performance.
7. Discipline and loyalty to the organization.

For most of this century, public administration scholars have codified Weber's characteristics of public bureaucracy and have presented them as the "ideal" model. Consequently, the characteristics are used. to measure the maturity of bureaucracies in Western democracies as well as in developing countries.[4] Guided by Weber's concept, students of comparative administration have developed two broad typologies of bureaucracy: (1) Developed or representative bureaucracies, and (2) Developing bureaucracies.[5] Western democracies are typically viewed as well developed bureaucracies or as exemplifying a high degree of Weberian features while developing bureaucracies are said to be at various points from the other end of the continuum.

Typology of Developing Bureaucracies

Ferrel Heady suggests that there are three broad types of developing bureaucracies. These are (1) ruling, (2) party-state, and (3) military-dominated bureaucracies.[6]

Ruling Bureaucracies: Traditionally, these have been colonial bureaucracies which have exercised local political authority in the colonies on behalf of the imperial power. These bureaucracies facilitated a patron-client relationship in their efforts to implement imperial laws and to protect the economic interests of the Crown. Once the colonial country became politically independent, the functional role of these bureaucracies also tended to decline. Examples of ruling bureaucracies include English Caribbean territories of the Pre-World War II period.

Party-State Bureaucracy: Since the advent of political independence for nonwhite peoples everywhere, many new states have adopted a form of government which emphasizes the dominance of the party, e.g., Tanzania in East Africa and Guyana in the West Indies. In these countries which have opted for this form of government, ultimate political authority rests with the party and thus the government is subordinate to the dictates of the ruling party. Generally, political direction, mass mobilization and political education are principal functional roles of a state bureaucracy. The party sets the tone for the country.

Military-Dominated: While some new states adopted party-state systems, others, perhaps due to peculiar circumstances, became military-dominated ones. Most of these are non-ideological, authoritarian systems, which have experienced periods of political instability. Military regimes, according to some scholars, have a stabilizing influence on the political order of some

---

[4] As part of the ethnocentrism which exists in the political/bureaucratic development literature most Western scholars have tended to regard anything that is characteristic of and often peculiar to Western political/bureaucratic system as a universally applicable normative standard. Regarding bureaucratic development, Western scholars have traditionally viewed bureaucratic change and development as characterized by a progressive rationalization, i.e., a unilinear movement from traditional bases of legitimizing authority to the rational-legal authority type.
[5] Ferrel Heady, *Public Administration: A Comparative Perspective* (2nd ed.; New York, 1979), pp. 167-282.
[6] Ibid.

62 PHYLON

countries. Examples of military regimes are those in Latin America and West Africa.

While Heady limited his types of bureaucracies to these three, this paper suggests a more complete picture by offering a fourth, known as semi-representative bureaucracies, many of which would include the Commonwealth Caribbean states.

Semi-representative Bureaucracies (SRBs): These are the most developed bureaucracies of LDCs. SRBs have adopted a significant amount of Weberian features and, in a vague sense at least, seek to accomplish the traditional goals of efficiency and economy. SRBs are one step away from fully representative bureaucracies of developed countries. Like developed countries, SRBs recognize that ultimate authority rests with the people and that it is vital for bureaucracy to be responsive to the public. However, these bureaucracies can be expected to adopt features of bureaucratic activism or to exhibit evidence of politicization since many of these states are undergoing a period of social change.

Common Traits

There exist far more differences in public administrative systems among less developed countries than among the relatively few developed countries of Western Europe, Canada and Japan. In the less developed countries there exists a greater cultural diversity whereas in the developed states most countries are European or are closely tied to Europe. Notwithstanding the array of peculiarities in structures and processes in individual LDCs, there are certain common traits:[7]

1. Emphasis on development. This includes governmental efforts to increase agricultural or industrial production; improvement in the standard of living of individuals within the country; improved public health care, education and pension services, housing facilities, etc.
2. Heavy reliance on the public sector for leadership and the provision of above-mentioned services.
3. Preoccupation with political dogma which is often used as a vehicle for mass mobilization purposes.
4. Political instability, often manifested in political/military coups.
5. Formalism, that is, a marked discrepancy between the forms and realities of administrative features. Often, one finds that existing institutions, practices and procedures are intended to be modeled on the former colonial power or based on prescriptions given by visiting consultants from the United States, Canada or Europe.
6. Administratively, the bureaucracy is less instrumental; it is more action-oriented.
7. Public Administration is less functionally specific.

[7] Common traits Nos. 1 through 3, adopted from Ira Sharkansky, *Public Administration: Agencies, Policies and Politics* (Chicago, 1982), pp. 275-76. The other traits cited are viewed by the author as additional common traits which are relevant to his essay.

8. Many LDC bureaucracies are less concerned with the preservation of the status quo; they are more preoccupied with the accomplishment of nation-building objectives.

It is not intended in this paper to suggest, however, that public administrative structures and processes in LDCs are significantly different from those in developed countries; they are not. The differences, at best, are a matter of degree. The comparative administration literature clearly attests to this as, for example, a study of Fred Riggs' "Prismatic" and "Sala" models,[8] or a study of politics and bureaucratic behavior in the Southern states of the United States would reveal.[9] The differences in emphasis and orientation which tend to distinguish politicized from non-politicized bureaucracies may be further understood by citing a characteristic of Weber's bureaucracy which has received greater stress in Western states with non-politicized bureaucracies: That is, in politicized bureaucracies there is less emphasis on political neutrality and, consequently, one sees continually in LDCs the emergence of a politically charged environment in which administrative activities such as management, planning, budgeting and decision-making are influenced significantly by political considerations.

THE CASE OF ST. KITTS-NEVIS

Ecological Factors

Fred Riggs and others have contended that it is important to understand the ecological context of a state bureaucracy if one is to obtain meaningful insights into that bureaucratic system.[10] Ecological factors are conditions or circumstances which influence or shape institutions and the way they function. They are the essence of political life in a given country, and the St. Kitts-Nevis bureaucracy is no exception. A few ecological influences will be mentioned below.

Social-cultural: Historically, the St. Kitts-Nevis bureaucracy is a colonial invention. Its principal purposes were to (1) coordinate the political and economic relationships between the colonies and the colonial power (i.e., Great Britain); (2) act as an instrument of the law and order — again, in the interest of the colonial power. Clearly such functions would qualify the St. Kitts-Nevis colonial bureaucracy prior to the 1950s as a ruling bureaucracy which then operated on the sole basis of a patron-client relationship. The functions and patterns of behavior just described are now part of St. Kitts-Nevis' heritage of slavery and colonial domination which today exhibit some influence on contemporary bureaucratic behavior.

For instance, the inherited bureaucratic pattern of behavior has created and perpetuated a feeling of domination and subordination in a cultural system of hierarchy in which whites once occupied the dominant position, "brown" and light skin individuals were in the middle, and blacks mostly clustered at the bottom. It is useful to recall here that this social stratification characterized

[8] Fred Riggs, "An Ecological Approach: The Sala Model, in Ferrel Heady and Sybil L. Stokes, *Papers in Comparative Public Administration* (Ann Arbor, Mich., 1962.)
[9] See Sharkansky, op. cit.
[10] Fred Riggs, *The Ecology of Public Administration*, (New Dehli: Asia Pub. House, 1961.)

64   PHYLON

the civil service hierarchy throughout the colonial period. To be sure, changes in this rigid social stratification have occurred in recent years because of the income and educational achievements of blacks; yet there is still a residue of that colonial pattern existing in the St. Kitts-Nevis (and other Caribbean) bureaucracies.

Economy

Because of the plantation system which once formed the basis of life in the colonies, today the St. Kitts-Nevis economy has been relegated to severe dependency and persistent poverty. The economy is locked into a dependency relationship between itself on one hand and the former imperial power on the other. (It is also significant to note that new imperial powers are entering into this relationship — the United States the most prominent example.)

Every conceivable form of economic dependence characterizes and underscores the existing dependency relationship. Some examples: dependence through (1) foreign ownership and control of key sectors of the economy, (2) foreign aid, (3) reliance on foreign human resources, (4) foreign capital (money and physical hardware), and (5) imported consumption and production patterns.[11]

Eager to develop economically, St. Kitts-Nevis has adopted the economic strategy of "industrialization by invitation" which, as has been experienced elsewhere, involves granting lucrative tax holidays and the indiscriminate lease or puchase of land. The main objective of course is to induce quick, substantial private capital investment which, ultimately, would lead to medium or large scale industrialization. These economic arrangements have led this writer to surmise that while the St. Kitts-Nevis political leadership is relieving itself of one form of colonialism, economically it may be embracing another.

Constitutional Change

Change of any kind brings tension and conflict to the changing environment. This has been evident in the St. Kitts-Nevis bureaucracy where the introduction of the ministerial system and new opportunities for indigenous elites to manage the political machine themselves have resulted in personnel changes and rearrangement of political and administrative roles.

Historically, conflict has occurred between ministers and appointed officials.[12] The transfer of power and responsibility from the Colonial Office and governors to indigenous elected department heads brought friction, tension and mutual suspicion between ministers and career officials. Prior to the

---

[11] William Demas, "Situation and Change," in *Caribbean Economy*, George L. Beckford, ed., (Institute of Economic Studies, U.W.I., 1974), p. 64 regards these as the five forms of economic dependence. They are of relevance to this discussion since the State of St. Kitts-Nevis as a newly independent country will seek new or wider economic relationships with metropolitan countries. These economic ties can result in these characteristics of economic dependence.
[12] G. E. Mills, "Public Administration in The Commonwealth Caribbean: Evolution, Conflicts and Challenges," *Social and Economic Studies*, Vol. 19, No. 1 (March 1970): 13.

ministerial system, career officials were accustomed to be a part of the legislative and executive policy-making process and took no orders from government department heads. But the arrival of the ministerial system shifted the importance and role of career officials, who became subordinates to political authority which was (and still is) exercised by the minister of the government department concerned.

Relations between administrator and technical personnel are also affected by these constitutional changes. Many administrative personnel acquired their positions without obtaining any specialized or extensive training. The professional/technical staff, generally younger, more qualified and eager "to get things done," often exhibited impatience and a lack of respect for their administrative superiors.[13]

Perhaps I can summarize by suggesting that ecological influences, coupled with the trend among third-world countries to pursue political and economic development, have generated enthusiasm among the political elite in St. Kitts-Nevis (and other Commonwealth Caribbean states) to establish a bureaucratic environment to facilitate the goals of social change and development. It is clear that the political leadership there expects the bureaucracy to play a vital role in shifting the country away from its undeveloped, colonial past to a developed and independent future. Consequently, the bureaucracy increasingly will become politicized, the manifestation of which will be (a) in decisions regarding who gets recruited and to what position, and (b) with respect to the governing party's increasing role in administrative functions. It is even conceivable that, in due time, the bureaucracy might actively aid the party in its political socialization and mobilization functions. Involvememt overtly or covertly in such activities will clearly highlight the politicized posture of the bureaucracy and the deemphasis of orthodox bureaucratic practices.

Functional Role of the St. Kitts-Nevis Bureaucracy

Prior to 1953, St. Kitts-Nevis was governed by a ruling bureaucracy which for the most part carried out the colonial designs of the "mother country," Great Britain. The election to office of the St. Kitts-Nevis Labor Party in 1953 began a genuine first step to indigenous political rule. The Labor government, then led by Chief Minister[14] Robert Llewelyn Bradshaw (machinist by trade), governed the state from 1953 to 1980. Bradshaw died in 1978 of cancer and his Deputy Premier, Lee Moore (attorney), became Premier from that year to March 13, 1980. The Labor party was defeated in the 1980 general elections by the People's Action Movement (PAM). Kennedy Simmonds (medical doctor) became Premier after his party (PAM) joined with the Nevis Reformation Party (NRP) to form a coalition government.

---

[13] Ibid., p. 16.

[14] From 1953 to 1979, the political head of the St. Kitts-Nevis government was officially designated as *Chief Minister*. This title indicated that under the ministerial system which was introduced in 1953 in St. Kitts-Nevis, the political heads of cabinet departments were (and still are) called *ministers*. The government leader, therefore, was called *Chief Minister*. A change in title occurred in 1967 after St. Kitts-Nevis obtained Associated Statehood status. The official name of the political head of government was *Premier*. The head of the independent state is officially referred to as *Prime Minister*.

The coalition government, like the former labor government, has adopted nation-building[15] as its principal mission and, substantially, is implementing similar policies toward that goal. Whatever apparent changes in policies there might be, they are mostly a matter of style rather than emphasis. One would expect this since the need to develop the state's infrastructure is as great today as it was under the former government. Thus, the expansion of public works programs continues to be a major governmental activity. Education, health, pension, housing and other social programs, likewise, remain major areas of governmental expenditure and commitment. Economic growth and development, notably in the agricultural sector where there is a need for continual expansion in the production of fruits, vegetables and livestock for purposes of domestic consumption and export, remain a primary concern of the coalition government.

These areas of needed development require the expertise of well trained engineers, economists, public administrators, geographers, to name a few. Invariably, these qualified personnel make up the technical and administrative core of a public bureaucracy. These experts assist in the formulation of engineering, economic, educational, and other policies and participate in their implementation. In St. Kitts-Nevis technicians and administrators have traditionally functioned as policy implementors, but as the problems of national development increase, one can expect influential bureaucrats to play a more significant role in the policy-making process. Therefore, the imperatives of nation-building and the reality that the bureaucracy monopolizes the state's expertise have rendered political neutrality only as an ideal to be ultimately achieved.

The differences in the educational backgrounds of elected and appointed officials (where the former have been less formally educated than the latter officials during the 1950s and 1960s) would also indicate why the bureaucrats have played a significant role in the initiation and implementation of national development policies. Now that the state of St. Kitts-Nevis has entered into its historic era of independence, the role of the state bureaucracy will be further enhanced by the quest for social, economic, cultural and political development. The bureaucracy will be the centerpiece of all developmental activities. Thus, instead of increased efforts to achieve political neutrality in St. Kitts-Nevis, this writer anticipates increasing politicization of the St. Kitts-Nevis bureaucracy.

Key Functions

It is my contention that there is a corresponding relationship between the rate of nation-building and the rate of bureaucratic activism. Simply, as the

---

[15] The term *nation-building* implies a unidimensional process of social, cultural, political, economic and administrative development. Generally speaking, the newly independent countries of Africa, Asia, Latin America and the Caribbean have adopted various developmental strategies with a view to improve the socioeconomic conditions of their respective peoples and institutions. These strategies are intended to lift the post-war independent states from their underdeveloped conditions to developed conditions. Governmental efforts to develop the St. Kitts-Nevis economy and its bureaucratic institutions would be appropriate examples of aspects of nation-building.

ST. KITTS-NEVIS, A CASE STUDY

former increases, so does the latter. When nation-building slows down, politicization or bureaucratic activism will likely slow down as well.

It is beyond the scope of this paper to examine the numerous aspects of nation-building; however, in an attempt to acquaint the reader with some of the responsibilities of a government that is pursuing economic development as an aspect of nation-building, below is a listing of these responsibilities or functions. Once development is accepted as the focal point of political activity in a country, the functions of a government will grow in size and importance since many undertakings and issues relating to development can be handled only by the government or with its support.[16] Some key examples include:

1. Economic planning or central guidance of the general direction in which the economy must move. In St. Kitts-Nevis, as in most other developing countries, only the government has the capacity to effectively accumulate data necessary for overall economic planning and development. The government is best equipped to carry out the distribution function, i.e., allocating scarce resources "for accelerating development or the financial, monetary and other means to influence economic trends, social welfare and the like."

2. Institutional reforms involving dislocation of institutions which have outlived their usefulness and establishment of new ones; also, the revitalization of institutions which have in the past and can, in the future, serve the needs of the people.

3. In St. Kitts-Nevis, as in other developing states, government is often the only major source of capital necessary for economic development. Government acts as a provider of the financial resources that can attract foreign investment.

4. Public ownership of essential services in order to assure continuous availability of such services and, where necessary, establish laws that will ensure quality and fair distribution of services. Also, public ownership or control over natural resources or the "commanding heights" of the economy; establishment of laws which are intended to increase the quality and quantity of the nation's resources.[17]

These responsibilites have become an important characteristic of governments in both large and small developing countries. These socioeconomic roles, understandably, will shake the nation's fundamental political value of political supremacy given the very nature of the administrative functions that are to be performed by the bureaucracy. An expansion of "politics" in the administration of developmental activities, therefore, seems inevitable.

The inevitability of an expansion of politics in the nation's administrative fabric does not imply, however, ultimate emergence of an uncontrollable political octopus. St. Kitts-Nevis does not have a military dominated or party-dominated type of political bureaucracy. The political culture of St. Kitts-Nevis still looks very unkindly on any political supremacy. This, then, is the

[16] United Nations, *Current Approaches and Trends in Public Administration for National Development* (Department of Administration, United Nations, 1975), p. 9.
[17] Ibid.

contradiction in the St. Kitts-Nevis political culture: there is that desire to retain (at least) a superficial separation of politics and administration, yet there is that conscious attempt to entertwine politics and administration as a means to accomplish socioeconomic development. The bureaucratic politicization process, therefore, will have to be a very delicate balancing act, the success of which will be very much open to question. The risks will be many (e.g., political instability), but the benefits will also be many. If St. Kitts-Nevis is to continue along the path of nation-building, if the state is to thrive with creativity, imagination and innovation, if the bureaucracy is to play a pivotal role as an agent of change, then the politicization risks must be faced. It is imperative, however, that both political and administrative leaders take the time to study and observe the experience of other countries whose bureaucracies became or have become very politicized during the process of social, political and economic development.

The Grenadian Experience: Some Lessons

While the abortive Grenadian socialist experiment did not focus exclusively on the transformation of the state bureaucracy, but more on the total restructuring of society itself, it is clear that the bureaucracy would have had to play a pivotal role in the implementation of social change. The Bishop government inherited a state bureaucracy that was content largely to maintain the status quo and therefore could not have been relied upon to implement social change. Indeed, many of the senior level bureaucrats showed no particular affinity for Bishop's socialist endeavors and therefore sought in various ways to retard the government's socialist program. Recognizing the centrality of the bureaucracy in the ruling party's revolutionary efforts, Bishop targeted it for ideological and administrative change so that it could actively assist in the accomplishment of developmental goals.

Bishop clearly wished to politicize the bureaucracy, to give it a mind-set consistent with his regime's policies of social change. He was not prepared to have such an important part of the government machinery creating stalls, backfiring or just limping along. Grenada, as then perceived by the Bishop government was well on the way to a successful national democratic revolution with several new state structures already taken root. To ensure the strengthening of these structures, Bishop was prepared to transform the civil service by:

> recruiting ideologically developed personnel, the retirement of some traditional service bourgeoisie, often hostile to socialism, and [to implement] some organized efforts at the reorientation of civil servants in general.[18]

---

[18] Patrick Emanuel, "Revolutionary Theory and Political Reality in the Eastern Caribbean," *Journal of Inter-American Studies and World Affairs*, 25, No. 2 (May 1983): 220.

ST. KITTS-NEVIS, A CASE STUDY   69

Admittedly, the lessons cannot be stated conclusively because the socialist experiment died in infancy, due to several causes, including externally generated destabilization efforts and internal intraparty conflicts, perhaps a consequence of the destabilization efforts. However, enough has been observed in order to make even cautious statements about the likely consequences of bureaucratic politicization in the Commonwealth Caribbean in general, and St. Kitts-Nevis, in particular.

First, a developing country wishing to divest itself of colonial values, practices and structures will have to rely heavily on the bureaucracy to accomplish deep rooted social change. As stated earlier, the bureaucracy, like a magnet, attracts the nation's best expertise in virtually every aspect of the state's socioeconomic life.

Second, the bureaucracy itself will have to be ideologically consistent with the governing party and other important institutions similarly supportive of the goals of social change. This will require personnel changes and ideological reorientation consistent with the policy objectives of the ruling party.

Third, one and two above will result in systemic conflict, particularly centered within the bureaucracy. The nature of the conflict will be a contest between traditional values of bureaucratic role and behavior on the one hand, and the action-oriented bureaucratic style of management on the other. Who wins (and thus the fourth lesson) will depend on (a) the political base of the leadership, (b) its mobilization capability, (c) the degree of loyalty to the ruling party within and outside the bureaucracy, and (d) the perception of the military as the internal and external consequences of existing systemic conflict.

Fifth, bureaucratic politicization and bureaucratic activism seemingly couched in non-capitalist ideology will very likely meet with active disapproval from the United States.

The Grenadian abortive socialist experiment, which clearly sought to reorient both the political consciousness of the people and to "retrofit" the major institutions accordingly as a means of ensuring broad-based social change, is an ugly reminder of a Caribbean reality, that the geographic size of the Caribbean ministates has rendered them insignificant in the eyes of the U.S. but that their proximity to the giant of the north makes them strategically significant. Unfortunately, their economic dependence on the U.S. only worsens an already harsh reality.

CONCLUSION

Several studies of political order in LDCs, particularly since the 1960s to the present, indicate that a major reason for continuing instability is the lack of balance between policy-making institutions and bureaucratic policy-implementing structures. Clearly, in states that have military-dominated bureaucracies, the relative weakness of political institutions often results in the appropriation of political functions by the military bureaucrats. This is a danger to be avoided in the future by the State of St. Kitts-Nevis. While currently a military-dominated bureaucracy may be alien to the political values of Kittians and Nevisians, the development of such a phenomenon is not impossible. A military-dominated bureaucracy can emerge if both political and bureaucratic leaders lose their respective sense of purpose and become embroiled in protracted political conflicts. Then the military, acting as the ultimate force and authority, may step in.

The greatest challenge to the State of St. Kitts-Nevis in the future lies in the critical task of maintaining political neutrality while experimenting pragmatically with bureaucratic dynamism during the process of nation-building. This will create an uncomfortable fit between a traditional notion and a modern bureaucratic imperative. The challenge may even, figurately, engender a sense of gravel in one's shoes, as one journeys down an unpaved, dusty road. How willing are the leadership and people of St. Kitts-Nevis to rise to this challenge is a question that cannot be answered here. However, if the past is any guide, when one observes the state's history of relative political stability, the people's respect for tradition and their simultaneous willingness to effect change, it is reasonable to conclude that the people of St. Kitts-Nevis will accept the challenges of tomorrow and, with a cooperative political/ bureaucratic leadership, will step into the future and unlock new frontiers that will benefit not only Kittians and Nevisians but others beyond the nation's shores.

[12]

Planning on presumption

Strategic planning for countryside recreation in England and Wales

Nigel Curry and Caroline Pack

Strategic policies for countryside recreation are founded on a very poor empirical basis. This has led to a confusion between recreation demands and needs and a presumption, through both forecasting and the charting of influences over demand, of an enduring growth in recreation consumption. As a result, there have been presumptions about recreation damage, and recreation policies that are almost universally restrictive. The questionable nature of presumptions about growth, and the lack of evidence relating to long-term recreation damage, suggest that the restrictive nature of strategic policies for countryside recreation is not justified.

Nigel Curry is Professor of Countryside Planning, and Caroline Pack is Research Associate, both at the Centre for the Study of Rural Environments, Faculty of Environment and Leisure, Cheltenham and Gloucester College of Higher Education, Francis Close Hall, Swindon Road, Cheltenham, GL50 4AZ, UK.

[1]Countryside strategies are discussed more fully in N.R. Curry, 'Nature conservation, countryside strategies and strategic planning', *Journal of Environmental Planning and Management*, Vol 35, No 1, 1992.
[2]Ministry of Housing and Local Government, *Development Plans, a Manual of Form and Content*, HMSO, London, 1970.
[3]*The Town and Country Planning Act, Part III, Section 6*, HMSO, London, 1971.
[4]J.E. Palmer, 'Recreation structure planning', *Planning Outlook, Special Issue: Planning for Recreation*, summer 1975; M. Fitton, 'Countryside recreation: the problems of opportunity', *Local Government Studies*, July/August 1979.

Strategic planning for countryside recreation at the local authority level has two principal forms. Within the development plan process, all structure plans in England and Wales contain policies on countryside recreation, though their form and content vary considerably. Since 1988 a series of countryside strategies or countryside recreation strategies has also been produced at the country level, in response to a number of stimuli such as agricultural change and the Countryside Commission's 'Enjoying the Countryside' policies. These provide an informal strategic planning counterpart to development plans and allow the consideration of non-land-use issues.[1] This paper explores the extent to which both these strategic planning forms for countryside recreation base policies on a clear empirical understanding of participation patterns of the population for which policies are promulgated. It offers some of the consequences of basing policies on presumptions about these participation patterns for countryside recreation without collecting empirical information.

Until 1988, when Planning Policy Guidance Notes (PPGs) were introduced, guidance on the production of structure plans came principally from the Development Plans Manual (and subsequent circulars), outlining the 'scope of material that the Minister would normally expect to see in association with the plan, in order to satisfy himself that the plans are soundly based'.[2] In the case of countryside recreation, this 'scope of material' required surveys to establish recreation 'demands' and current usage, future changes in demand and consumption and future 'needs', and to provide an analysis of the likely influences on changes in demand for countryside recreation over time.

The 1971 Town and Country Planning Act, however, in defining countryside recreation not as a 'principal issue' but as an 'other matter' for consideration in structure plans, gave local authorities discretion over whether surveys were conducted or not.[3] This led, as Palmer and Fitton have both noted, to the vast majority of counties failing to carry out any survey work at all in the formulation of countryside recreation policies during the 1970s.[4]

0264-8377/93/020140-11 © 1993 Butterworth-Heinemann Ltd

This failure was attributed both to a lack of staff time available for the consideration of recreation subjects, and to an expertise among planning staff that 'often left much to be desired' in terms of experience of countryside recreation.[5]

Since 1988 guidance on the empirical requirements for recreation policy formulation in structure plans has been less specific. PPG 12 no longer distinguishes principal issues from other matters, but defines leisure and recreation as one of the nine relevant topics for consideration in structure plans.[6] For these topics, surveys are still to be conducted, and made readily available to the public. For countryside recreation in particular, PPG 17 states:

in the context of an anticipated growth in pressure on the countryside, the planning system should ensure the adequate provision of land and water resources for informal recreation. This should be done by assessing recreational needs against current provision to provide opportunities for all.[7]

Strategic planning for countryside recreation: evidence of survey work

Given this enduring requirement to produce survey work in structure plan policy formulation for countryside recreation, has empirical data collection for this purpose improved since the 1970s? A survey of all 80 extant structure plans in 1985 shows that only five structure planning authorities (Durham, 1981; Avon, 1985; Cheshire, 1979; Greater Manchester, 1981; and Greater London, 1976) provided any direct evidence of having undertaken comprehensive recreation participation surveys in structure plan formulation.[8] A further four authorities made use of a number of individual site surveys to inform plans, but for the remainder assertions about recreation behaviour were based on informal observations and broad national trends. It was commonly recognized that, in plans up to this time, the paucity of empirical work limited plan formulation, and that surveys should become a priority in structure plan reviews.

A re-survey, by the authors, of this article of all 62 structure plans current in the summer of 1992 indicates that this situation has not improved. Only 11 of these plans make any reference at all to empirical surveys of the population, and of these only four refer to local surveys. The remaining seven again cite national statistics on participation, principally the Countryside Commission's 1984 National Survey of Countryside Recreation.[9] In one instance, summary statistics from the Sports Council are also included.[10] A number of plans restate their intention to undertake surveys in the future.

There is no formal requirement on countryside strategies with recreation components, or on countryside recreation strategies, to produce empirical data in policy formulation, since they are not statutory planning documents. Despite this, their approach to survey work is more reverential and more fully considered than in structure plans. Over one-third of the 15 countryside strategies with recreation components produced by mid-1992 make reference to local site studies or other local studies to provide background information for countryside recreation proposals. Two-thirds of these strategies also cite the 1984 National Survey of Countryside Recreation, and one strategy refers to Regional Council for Sport and Recreation data. However, where such information is used, it is extrapolated directly to the county level.

[5]M. Fitton, *op cit*, Ref 4; A.J. Veal and A.S. Travis, *Local Authority Leisure Services: The State of Play*, Centre for Urban and Regional Studies, University of Birmingham, Birmingham, UK, July/August 1979.
[6]Department of the Environment, *Development Plans and Regional Guidance*, Planning Policy Guidance Note PPG 12, HMSO, London, 1992.
[7]Department of the Environment, *Sport and Recreation*, Planning Policy Guidance Note PPG 17, HMSO, London, 1991.
[8]N.R. Curry and A. Comley, 'Recreation policies in structure plans', unpublished report to the Countryside Commission, Cheltenham, UK, 1985.
[9]Countryside Commission, *National Survey of Countryside Recreation: 1984*, CCP 201, the Commission, Cheltenham, UK, 1985.
[10]Sports Council, *Sport in the Community: The Next Ten Years*, Sports Council, London, 1992.

Most strategies acknowledge their shortage of empirical information as an aid to planning. Derbyshire (1990), for example, admits a lack of recent material – their latest site survey was conducted in 1982 – and recognizes the need to update information. Kent's strategy (1990) includes as one of its objectives 'to improve information on the public's needs for countryside recreation', and intends to fulfil this by carrying out market research on consumer preferences. Some strategies simply confess a lack of data. For example, Shropshire (1991) states 'precise figures do not exist for measuring the scale of recreational use in the countryside'. Others argue that such data are not informative in policy making: 'the numerical quantification of demand for organised sport and leisure needs in the countryside is an inadequate guide for provision' (Leicestershire, 1989).

Countryside recreation strategies pay closest attention to the importance of empirical data. Of the 11 such strategies produced to mid-1992, two undertook specific local household surveys, and a further two refer to existing site surveys. Frequent reference is made to the 1977 and 1984 National Surveys of Countryside Recreation, and the 1986 General Household Survey is also cited. Nearly all strategies contain a summary of whatever surveys have been used, including the principal characteristics of both participants and non-participants in countryside recreation.

In addition, three strategies discuss the problems of the lack of knowledge of demand and participation at the local level, and the difficulties of applying national statistics to the county and sub-county level. They register their intention (and the need) to carry out some form of monitoring or survey work to provide more accurate information at the local level.

Strategic planning for countryside recreation is thus characterized by a shortage of empirical information on recreation participation with which to help formulate a plan. Evidence from the 1985 and 1992 surveys of structure plans suggests that, in more recent plans, empirical surveys are carried out even less often than before. This information deficiency is recognized more overtly in informal plans than in structure plans, and it is through these informal channels that empirical databases seem most likely to improve. Given this paucity of information, what, then, are the principal presumptions about recreation behaviour in strategic plans that form the basis of such planning?

Trends and forecasting

Structure plans set the context for countryside recreation policies, with some form of forecasting procedures to establish trends in participation. However, forecasting recreation behaviour has so far proved highly speculative, since nearly all the work of identifying factors that affect participation is based on statistical association, rather than direct cause and effect. The problem of unreliability becomes more acute at the county level because of inaccuracies in extrapolating national data sets to apply to the much smaller areas. These problems are recognized by many county councils. In the 1985 survey, for example, forecasting recreation behaviour was considered difficult and unreliable in several plans.[11] A majority of plans made use of Countryside Commission estimates of the growth of recreation. One county, Gloucestershire (1982), had made forecasts simply on the basis of historical patterns, while another, Devon (1981), had made forecasts based on anticipated

[11]Curry and Comley, *op cit*, Ref 8.

changes in the factors presumed to influence demand, especially age and gender profiles.

As a result of these processes, all counties formulated countryside recreation policies based on a presumed increase in recreation participation. Some (for example, North Yorkshire, 1980) considered this growth to be accelerating, but others (Northumberland, 1980) considered it to be slowing down.

In 1992, extant structure plans still contain information on forecasting. One in 10 plans again explicitly discusses difficulties in forecasting, recognizing in the main that simply projecting past participation patterns is no guide to future consumption. It is changes in the factors influencing demand that are a more reliable guide. Because of the difficulties in quantifying these, a number of plans revert to considering growth in recreation pressures rather than recreation consumption, allowing them to focus policies on particular 'pressured' areas.

Despite these difficulties, all plans assert a continuing growth in countryside recreation participation in the future, usually based on some notion of its inherent importance, rather than any formal projections. Examples include statements such as 'visiting the countryside is the most popular leisure activity in Great Britain' (Clwyd, 1991) and 'informal countryside recreation is the most popular outdoor pursuit in Great Britain' (Kent, 1990).

In contrast to structure plans, both countryside strategies and countryside recreation strategies pay little attention to forecasting either the influences over demand, or participation patterns. Those that do mention trends assume a continuing increase in participation. Despite admitted difficulties in forecasting, and evidence that it is used less often in more recent plans, the underlying ethos for all countryside recreation strategic planning, both formal and informal, is one of a continuing growth in participation.

Influences on countryside recreation demand

Most structure plans produced during the 1970s asserted some general influences on demand. These mainly comprised mobility, incomes, leisure time, attitudes and fashion. Some plans produced into the 1980s (for example, Wiltshire, 1983; Surrey, 1980; and Hampshire, 1983) and some plan reviews (Northamptonshire, 1985), however, stressed a changing set of demand influences focused on unemployment, new technology, early retirement and an ageing society. Some plans also offered local influences over demand, and others, such as Devon (1981), articulated different demand influences for different activities. However, no plans distinguished the different demand influences of different social groups.

In terms of the structure plan's own ability to influence demand, a number of authorities (for example, Central and North Lancashire, 1983) considered that this was limited because of the supply-based nature of structure plan policies. On the other hand, some authorities felt that policies would have a direct influence over demand, since supply itself influences demand.

The 1992 re-survey of structure plans indicates that many plans are very detailed in suggesting the factors influencing changes in countryside recreation demand. A third of plans mention an increase in leisure time, and a further third an increase in real incomes or affluence (though one or two acknowledge this is not for all sectors of society). Increases in leisure time are further attributed in about half the plans to changing work patterns such as early retirement, a shorter working week and more holidays. Time and money are therefore seen as the two biggest influences over demand.

Beyond these factors, a growth in car ownership and personal mobility are mentioned in a fifth of the plans (some cite the availability of better roads) while eight plans suggest that changing attitudes to sport and recreation also have a significant influence. (Reference is made here to Sports Council campaigns, and to recognition of the importance of exercise to health and well-being.)

Further factors mentioned include an ageing population structure and increasing environmental or 'green' awareness. Four plans include unemployment as a demand factor, increasing time but not money. A growth in tourism is also cited as having an influence on recreation demand more generally, and greater links with Europe are seen as a possible future influence over demand especially in the South-East.

A number of plans in the 1992 survey also list local influences on demand. Most important in this respect is accessibility from large population centres, but possessing large areas of attractive countryside, local population growth and the impacts of local tourism policies are also considered significant.

In some plans, provision of better recreation facilities, and greater awareness of and improved access to those that exist, are seen as factors influencing demand. In four plans 'latent demand' is explicitly mentioned, whereby the provision of new facilities to some extent creates its own demand: 'much existing demand is latent, and only expresses itself when new facilities become available' (Devon, 1989); 'to a significant extent, the supply of countryside recreation facilities tends to create additional demand' (Shropshire, 1987). All countryside and countryside recreation strategies mention influences over recreation demand. These are similar to, and as diverse as, those articulated in structure plans.

There are three principal shortcomings in these analyses of influences over recreation demand in strategic plans. Firstly, such a large range of them is articulated that even if they were empirically verifiable, any precise notion of their influence would be difficult to discern. In this respect, the advantage of citing them as an aid to policy formulation is questionable. Secondly, they are, of course, only assertions, and no evidence is presented in plans in respect of any causal relationships. Thirdly, and perhaps more importantly, nearly all of the influences articulated are those that might be expected to trigger increased consumption in the future. Little attention is given to those factors related to economic recessive cycles or declining real incomes that might lead to reduced participation. For the 1970s, for example, Stoakes was able to show a relationship between increases in petrol prices and reduced recreation participation.[12] The principal purpose, therefore, of itemizing these influences over demand seems to be to reinforce the assertion of a continued growth in countryside recreation participation.

Participation, demands and needs

[12]R. Stoakes, *Oil Prices and Countryside Recreation Travel*, Working Paper 20, Countryside Commission, Cheltenham, UK, 1979.

In addition to statements on forecasting and presumed influences over demand, many structure plans provide information about current and anticipated participation patterns, again with the intention of informing policy formulation. In this respect, terminology is imprecise and ambiguous: notions of participation (current consumption levels), demand (an expression of a willingness and ability to incur expenditure) and need (a desire not matched by ability to pay) are used interchangeably.

In the 1992 survey, 17 of the 60 extant structure plans make no mention at all of current levels of participation, demand or need. Of those that do (as they did in the 1985 survey) most suggest that the purpose of recreation provision is to cater for anticipated increases in levels of participation. This often is couched either in terms of demands, for example, 'informal countryside recreation is becoming increasingly popular, and these new demands should be catered for' (Cleveland, 1990); or needs, 'greater numbers of people will have a greater amount of leisure time in the future to devote to leisure activity and . . . these needs must be met wherever possible' (Avon, 1990); or it is seen simply as being incontrovertible, 'recreation is an increasingly essential ingredient to modern life . . . and a failure to make adequate provision in suitable locations will cause it either to take place in locations where it conflicts with other countryside interests, or to be suppressed with undesirable consequences' (Kent, 1990).

Although the consideration of needs is less common than either participation or demand in both the 1985 and 1992 structure plan surveys, the use of the term is particularly ambiguous. Teeside (1977) and Staffordshire (1984), for example, both claim a need for more golf-courses because Sports Council standards have not been met (need here equates to the failure to meet a prescribed level of provision). In Cambridgeshire (1980) the need for a country park is considered to be greatest around Cambridge (need here equates to unsatisfied demand). In Avon (1985), by contrast, it is considered that the bulk of the need for informal recreation arises from urban areas (here, need could equate either to unsatisfied demand, or to some form of deprivation).

In the 1992 survey, more than a third of plans contain some reference to meeting the recreation needs of certain groups in society, more overtly in the context of some form of deprivation. These references are more common in more recent plans. Although some plans mention simply the need to provide for all groups in society, 10 of the 60 plans refer specifically to the disabled and to non-car owners. Other named groups include the elderly, those deterred for whatever reason from visiting the countryside, and 'disadvantaged' groups generally. Some plans even target specific types of recreation facility, particularly public rights of way, to disadvantaged groups.

Countryside strategies and countryside recreation strategies are more systematic in their consideration of needs in the context of deprivation. A high proportion of all strategies comment on the importance of catering to the needs of those social groups that, traditionally, visit the countryside only rarely. The elderly, the disabled, ethnic minorities and the car-less are a particular focus here and it is commonly proposed that public transport be improved, and greater publicity be given to developing of their needs. Two strategies, Durham (1989) and Hereford and Worcester (1991), depart from this view somewhat, claiming that efforts are better targeted at 'occasional' users, such as white-collar workers and skilled manual workers, than those who go to the countryside rarely, if participation rates are to be increased to greater effect.

From both structure plan surveys assertions are also made about the changing structure of participation patterns for particular countryside recreation activities. East and West Cleveland (1977), Gwent (1981) and North Yorkshire (1980), for example, anticipate a move away from team and group activities towards more informal, or as one plan terms it 'simple' (Shropshire, 1991), pursuits such as walking. Thirteen plans in the 1992 survey focus specifically on the increasing demand for golf and the shortage of provision to meet this demand. Agricultural diversification provides an opportunity to develop more courses, but these 'still need to be targeted to the main areas of demand' (Devon, 1991).

The increasing demand for water recreation (specifically mentioned as a priority in 12 plans in the 1992 survey) is also emphasized, and in many areas concern is expressed that facility provision cannot match demand. In countryside strategies, golf and water recreation are noted as growth areas, but a number of them also focus on a growth in active and 'noisy' sports. For example, the Suffolk (1992) strategy considers that in the case of sports that cause visual or noise intrusion 'the demand for some of these facilities seems almost limitless'.

Without clear empirical evidence, these statements exhibit a confusion about whether strategic policies for countryside recreation are intended to cater for market demands or social needs or both. This is exemplified in the Kent (1990) countryside strategy cited above which 'seeks to improve information on the public's needs' by carrying out 'market research'. A clearer understanding is required of the actual nature of demands, and particularly of social needs. There is some evidence to suggest, for example, that non-participation in countryside recreation may be due more to a lack of interest than to any material deprivation.[13] If this is so, needs policies are likely to be less than successful, and in extreme cases might even be socially regressive – subsidized provision for the disadvantaged might lead to more use by the affluent.

Proposals for improved public recreation transport to benefit the disadvantaged, again on the assumption that they will use it, may be particularly misguided. Groome and Tarrant's review of experiments in public recreation transport showed that they attracted few customers, and those that did use them tended to be the more affluent who chose not to use the car.[14]

In the context of the promulgation of social needs policies, too, it may well be that for structure plans these simply are not legitimate. PPG 12 reasserts the fact that structure plans are land use plans and any social considerations are beyond their remit.[15] This is unfortunate, since the structure plan surveys show, during the same time that there has been a reduction in the number of empirical surveys, an increasing interest in social issues. Such social considerations may more appropriately be restricted to a place in non-statutory countryside strategies, which are not subject to such government advice.

Presumptions, too, about the shifting structure of participation away from organized activities and towards more informal pursuits may be ill-founded. The Sports Council's championing of sports in the countryside is perceptibly more promotional than that of the Countryside Commission for informal recreation, and its effectiveness may increase further with the formation of the new English Sports Council in 1993, specifically created to increase mass participation in sport.[16]

Again, all assumptions about participation, demands and needs are predicated on a ubiquitous notion that they will all increase into the future.

[13]N.R. Curry, 'Countryside recreation sites policy: a review', *Town Planning Review*, Vol 56, No 1, 1985.
[14]D. Groome and C. Tarrant, 'Countryside recreation: providing access for all?', *Countryside Planning Yearbook, 1985*, Geo Publications, Norwich, UK, 1985.
[15]DoE, *op cit*, Ref 6.
[16]Sports Council, *Sport in the Community: Into the 1990s*, Sports Council, London, 1988, and *A Countryside for Sport: A Policy for Sport and Recreation*, Sports Council, London, 1992; N.R. Curry and C. Pack, 'Government advice for rural leisure planning', *Landscape Issues*, Vol 9, Nos 1 and 2, 1992.

Consequences of planning on presumption

The sparse use of empirical information as an aid to the formulation of strategic plans for countryside recreation places a great burden on presumptions about recreation behaviour. For this reason alone, resultant policies can be questioned on the basis of whether the presumptions are justified. But even where empirical information is used, serious questions may also arise about its legitimacy. The vast majority of empirical inputs to the formulation of both structure plans and countryside strategies include inferences from either site surveys or national data. Both are flawed for use at the county level.

Site surveys, of course, provide information about participation patterns only at individual sites. They say nothing about behaviour elsewhere in the county. More importantly, they say nothing at all about non-participation in the wider population whom the plans and strategies are designed to serve. Thus their observations about recreation behaviour are biased towards those already active in recreation, who are, by definition, atypical of the wider population in this respect.

National data, too, may only be of tangential relevance at the county level. The Countryside Commission's 1977 National Survey of Countryside Recreation, for example, showed regional variations in participation patterns in excess of 30%.[17] This result severely reduces the value of national data extrapolated to the regional, let alone county, level.

Further, the most comprehensive source of national data on recreation behaviour in mid-1992 was the 1984 National Survey of Countryside Recreation, which is still being cited in plans some eight years after it was carried out. It is quite possible that recreation participation patterns have experienced a degree of structural shift since that time.

The presumption behind all plans relating both to trends and to influences over demands and needs is that participation will increase. This fundamental presumption defines the ethos of a vast majority of structure plans. However, it is questionable. Between the 1977 and 1980 National Surveys of Countryside Recreation, the number of visits to the countryside nationally declined from 101 to 81 million; day-trips from home declined by 5%, and day-trips taken on holiday fell by nearly a third.[18] Moreover, the average number of trips to the countryside taken in a month by participating households certainly did not increase in the 1980s, but if anything it declined slightly, as Figure 1 indicates.[19]

These trends are not substantially contradicted by data from the 1986 General Household Survey (GHS).[20] This reveals that the proportion of the population making visits to the countryside declined from 1977 to 1983, and had shown no signs of increase by 1986. GHS data for 1990 also show that, in terms of specific activities, participation rates in outdoor sports apart from walking showed only a modest increase through the 1980s.[21] In tourism, too, statistics published by the British Tourist Authority indicate that, between 1972 and 1988, holiday tourism by British residents declined from 83 to 73 million trips.[22]

In considering trends in recreation, it is difficult from statistical information to distinguish between local or indigenous recreationists, migrant recreationists and tourists (from home or overseas) in rural areas, all of whom may be influenced by different factors and exhibit different patterns of participation. However, although all these figures are limited by being national and are a tenuous indicator of overall levels of participation, taken together they do cast doubt over the presumption of its continued growth.

[17]Countryside Commission, *Leisure and the Countryside*, CCP 124, Countryside Commission, Cheltenham, UK, August 1979.
[18]J. Blunden and N.R. Curry, *The Changing Countryside*, Croom Helm, Berkhampstead, UK, 1985.
[19]G. Broom, 'The context', in *Our Priceless Countryside: Should it be Priced?*, Countryside Recreation Research Advisory Group Annual Conference, University of Manchester Institute of Science and Technology, Manchester, UK, September 1991.
[20]Office of Population Censuses and Surveys, *General Household Survey 1986*, HMSO, London, 1988.
[21]Office of Population Censuses and Surveys, *General Household Survey 1990*, HMSO, London, 1992.
[22]British Tourist Authority, *Digest of Tourist Statistics, No 14*, British Tourist Authority, London, 1990.

Strategic planning for countryside recreation in England and Wales

Figure 1. Trends in countryside recreation participation.

Source: G. Broom, 'The context', in *Our Priceless Countryside: Should it be Priced?*, Countryside Recreation Research Advisory Group Annual Conference, University of Manchester Institute of Science and Technology, Manchester, UK, September 1991, citing Countryside Commission National Surveys of countryside recreation.

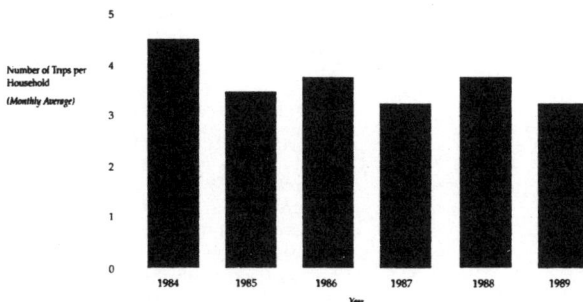

In addition, the principal factor explaining these differences in consumption at any time is none of the socioeconomic parameters considered by strategic planners to influence demand, but the weather.[23] This is simply not considered as a demand influence in strategic plans, which is unfortunate since it has a significant impact on short-term participation patterns, even though in longer-term trends the influence of the weather may be ameliorated.

The questionable presumption of an incessant growth in consumption is perhaps a legacy from Michael Dower's 'Fourth Wave'.[24] It has led strategic plans to take an unduly restrictive stance in promulgating countryside recreation policies. For the 1970s, Fitton has argued that such presumptions were often the cause of 'moral panic' and a preservationist concern for the countryside that was popular with the public at large.[25] This concern, he suggests, arose from the common misconception that recreation was a problem – that people and their activities had a negative effect on the ecological and aesthetic balance of the environment and on other land users.

Such misconceptions often led to policies being more restraint-orientated than development orientated in the 1970s. According to Fitton, phrases such as 'over-visitation' and 'people pollution' led to structure plan policies that were designed to provide alternative facilities such as country parks and picnic sites close to major urban centres in order to stop the 'unnecessary' use of more vulnerable areas. Fitton also notes instances of policies that were even more negative than these policies of containment: 'At the extreme in some local planning authority documents (notably of shire counties adjacent to conurbations), policies are clearly for exclusion.' He goes on to discuss the types of words that were used at that time in some structure plans in relation to countryside recreation – 'destroy', 'explode', 'intercept', 'filter' and 'containment' – and parallels them with 'activity at some set-piece battle rather than a description of people seeking to enjoy themselves'.

Writing in the 1970s, Shoard also cites the unjustifiable presumption of a growth in participation, and the fear of the damage that people might do to the countryside, as the underlying cause of the negative nature of recreation policies in structure plans, particularly in respect of agricultural land.[26] In the 1970s, too, there was evidence that these restrictive policies did not necessarily accord with the views of the public at the public participation stage of structure plan formulation.[27] For example, in West Yorkshire, consultation with public agencies, council members and quangos revealed that, in their opinion, the local economy

[23]Broom, *op cit*, Ref 19.
[24]M. Dower, *The Fourth Wave: The Challenge of Leisure, A Civic Trust Survey*, Architect's Journal, London, 1965.
[25]Fitton, *op cit*, Ref 4.
[26]M. Shoard, 'Access: can present opportunities be widened?', in *Countryside for All?*, Countryside Recreation Research Advisory Group Annual Conference, CCP 17, Countryside Commission, Cheltenham, UK, 1978.
[27]S. Law, 'Leisure and recreation: problems and prospects', *Planning Outlook, Special Issue: Planning for Recreation*, summer 1975.

was the most important issue for the structure plan, whereas public surveys placed countryside recreation above this.[28] In Greater Manchester, Fenton notes that recreation policies originally were given scant attention, but public participation was directly responsible for elevating the importance of recreation in the plan.[29]

Into the 1980s and 1990s, the presumption of recreation growth has led to similarly restrictive countryside recreation policies in structure plans. In both the 1985 and 1992 structure plan surveys, by far the most common areas in which recreation is discouraged are those of landscape conservation value and nature conservation value. Principal areas of encouragement, however, are considered to be areas of derelict land, and sites that will absorb capacity. Where encouragement is given at all, almost universally it is to informal passive, rather than formal active, recreation.

These types of policy may be less than appropriate for two principal reasons. Firstly, steering people away from high-value landscapes will not maximize consumer satisfactions from the recreation experience. Secondly, there is increasing evidence to suggest that areas of derelict land, if not aesthetically pleasing, are rich in habitat diversity, and are in their own way every bit as valuable as more commonly recognized sites, such as Sites of Special Scientific Interest, because of their lack of human disturbance.[30] In these areas, recreation is as likely to damage habitats as in more traditionally valued areas.

From the two structure plan surveys, there is a perceptible change in motivations for such restrictive policies. During the 1980s they were driven principally by the questionable 'fear of a recreation explosion'. Into the 1990s, however, particularly after the government White Paper *This Common Inheritance*, restrictive policies have been justified more on the grounds of elevating environmental objectives in all government decision making.[31]

Yet, as in the 1970s, there is still little evidence that recreation, even in the context of presumed growth, does have any significant widespread and long-term impact on the environment, either visually or ecologically. Lack of objective data is still a substantial problem. As the Sports Council comments, this, together with misleading interpretation of existing data, 'has led to a sometimes inappropriate, over-restrictive approach towards the use of a resource by an activity'.[32]

The Sports Council also draws an important distinction between short-term disturbance and long-term damage.[33] Linked to this is the necessary distinction between localized and more widespread impacts. There is ample evidence from the literature of localized damage to vegetation through trampling, but such problems, although acute in places, in general carry no threat to long-term species survival. In a review of ecosystem loss published in 1984, the (then) Nature Conservancy Council cited recreation as a contributory factor in only two cases, coastal dunes and higher mountains with alpine/arctic flora, both of which are particularly fragile systems and may experience intense recreational pressure.[34]

Similarly, research into the impact of water recreation on birds suggests that it can cause local disturbance and redistribution but has little effect on national bird populations.[35] More generally, in the (then) Nature Conservancy Council review of decline in breeding bird populations, only one case (that of the little tern) was related to recreation through the loss of coastal shingle nesting habitats.[36] Some concern has

[28] West Yorkshire Metropolitan County Council, *A Report of Survey of Public Attitudes in Connection with the Preparation of the Structure Plan*, Opinion Research Centre for West Yorkshire, Directorate of Planning, Engineering and Transporation, Wakefield, UK.

[29] H.M. Fenton, 'Structure planning in the metropolitan context: Greater Manchester', in D.T. Cross and M.R. Bristow, eds, *English Structure Planning: A Commentary on Procedure and Practice in the 1970s*, Pion, London, 1983.

[30] M. Spray, 'Keeping some of it a bit rough', *Town and Country Planning*, Vol 53, No 1, 1984.

[31] Department of the Environment, *This Common Inheritance*, White Paper, cm 1200, HMSO, London, 1990.

[32] Sports Council (1992), *op cit*, Ref 16.

[33] Sports Council, *opera cit*, Ref 16.

[34] Nature Conservancy Council, *Nature Conservation in Great Britain*, Nature Conservancy Council, Peterborough, UK, 1984.

[35] M. Owen, 'The impact on waterbirds of recreation on lowland wetlands', in *Recreation and Wildlife*, Countryside Recreation Research Group Annual Conference Report, York University, York, UK, September 1987.

[36] Nature Conservancy Council, *op cit*, Ref 34.

also been expressed at the effects of recreation on some moorland bird species.[37] Overall, however, after a comprehensive survey of the impact of countryside recreation on nature conservation, Sidaway is able to assert that, 'overviews of ecosystems and species groupings have concluded that recreational disturbance and damage are relatively insignificant to the survival of species'.[38]

Moreover most recent reviews of the topic conclude that the impact of recreation needs to be seen in the context of the much greater environmental effects of, for example, agriculture and pollution, and that, 'with appropriate research, sympathetic management, and modest investment, most conflicts between recreation and nature conservation can be resolved'.[39] In that spirit, the Sports Council, for isolated sensitive areas, puts forward the notion of 'sustainable management' as part of a package that is much more promotional than any to be found in strategic plans.[40]

Conclusions

Strategic planning policies for countryside recreation have been promulgated on a very poor empirical understanding of participation patterns. This stems from the 1971 Town and Country Planning Act, where the identification of recreation as an 'other matter' made survey work discretionary. Where empirical data are cited in plans, they invariably draw on site surveys and national data, both of which are of limited value at the county level.

Presumptions about forecasting influences on demand and participation have led to a confusion over the distinction between demands and needs, and universally lead to the assertion that recreation participation will continue to grow into the future. This assertion leads, in turn, to the presumption that increasing participation will cause increasing damage in the countryside, and thence to policies in both structure plans and countryside strategies that are almost universally restrictive. Yet the presumption of growth is, at the very least, questionable, and the assertion about long-term damage simply unproven.

Undoubtedly, a fuller empirical understanding of both participation patterns and recreation damage would provide a sounder basis on which to build strategic policies for countryside recreation, and would quite possibly lead to policies based more clearly on promotion for both market demands and social needs, with 'sustainable management' being developed along the lines offered by the Sports Council.

But the legacy of countryside recreation as an 'other matter', despite its apparent elevation on the structure planning agenda in PPG 12, and the cumbersome organizational structure for countryside recreation within local authorities, has ensured that it is of residual importance in structure plan formulation.[41] Even the growth in countryside strategies and countryside recreation strategies from the late 1980s has, at the admission of many of them, had more to do with securing grant aid than with any increased importance of recreation on the local authority agenda.[42] Until countryside recreation matters are accorded greater importance, it is unlikely that strategic policies for them will be founded on anything other than a somewhat questionable presumption.

[37]National Parks Review Panel, *Fit for the Future*, Countryside Commission, Cheltenham, UK, 1991.
[38]R. Sidaway, *Sport, Recreation and Nature Conservation*, Study Number 32, Sports Council, London, UK, 1988.
[39]B. Goldsmith, 'The wildlife perspective', in *Recreation and Wildlife*, Countryside Recreation Research Group Annual Conference Report, York University, York, UK, September 1987.
[40]Sports Council (1992), *op cit*, Ref 16.
[41]Centre for Leisure Research, *Access to the Countryside for Recreation and Sport*, CCP 217, Countryside Commission, Cheltenham, UK, and Sports Council, London, 1986.
[42]Curry and Pack, *op cit*, Ref 16.

[13]

J. Opt. Res. Soc. Vol 44, No. 2, pp. 115-124

Printed in Great Britain. All rights reserved

0160-5682/93 $8.00+0.00
Copyright © 1993 Operational Research Society Ltd.

Project Planning and Prioritization in the Social Services—an OR Contribution

VALERIE BELTON

Department of Management Science, University of Strathclyde

This paper describes a study carried out for the Social Services Department of a UK County Council towards the development of a system for the evaluation and prioritization of project-based work. There are three major components of the study: an activity analysis to investigate how managers in the department spend their time, with a view to establishing a time budget for the project work; a pilot study to introduce a simple system for project planning and workload balancing with a specialist team; and the development of a multiple criteria model for the evaluation and prioritization of projects. We envisaged a Decision Support System which integrated all of these elements; however, this was never developed; instead, the resultant benefits were of a very different nature. We reflect on the reasons for this and the implications for the success of the study.

Key words: local government, project planning, activity analysis, multiple criteria analysis

INTRODUCTION

This paper describes work carried out over a period of 18 months with the Social Services Department of Kent County Council (KSS). The project was initiated by the deputy director of Social Services who initially perceived the problem as one of project management which may be resolvable by the use of tools such as critical path analysis. The problem faced by the department was a fairly typical situation of managers faced with an ever-increasing workload and insufficient resources to handle it. Consequently, the managers themselves were under pressure to work excessively long hours, projects were not being completed on schedule, new deadlines were not established and often the status of a project was unknown. The problem was seen to be caused by an increasing number of new development initiatives, prompted by changes in the management culture, changes in the organization's environment and new legislation.

The structure of the paper is as follows: the following section describes the nature of the organization and its work in more detail, we then go on to discuss the nature of the problem and outline the work undertaken—this has three major strands to it, a longitudinal study of how managers actually spent their time, a pilot workload planning study, and the development of a project prioritization model—each of these sub-studies will be described in more detail, and finally we reflect on the benefits to the organization.

BACKGROUND

The Social Services departments of England's County and Metropolitan Borough Councils have a responsibility which encompasses work with the elderly, mentally handicapped, mentally ill, physically handicapped and children and families. Figure 1 gives more information on the nature of the work. KSS employs around 6500 staff and has an annual revenue budget of around £75m (1986–87). In 1986 a new Chief Executive was appointed to the County Council with a specific brief to 'change the culture'. Shortly afterwards a new Director of Social Services was appointed. Under this new leadership the County committed itself publicly to a cultural revolution characterized by a move from a traditional bureaucratic model enlivened by personal style towards rational management based on comprehensive information systems (see Jeffrey[1]). This was accompanied

Correspondence: V. Belton, Department of Management Science, University of Strathclyde Business School, Livingstone Tower, 26 Richmond Street, Glasgow GV 1XH. UK

Journal of the Operational Research Society Vol. 44, No. 2

by pressures at national level — highlighted by the Audit Commission's '3 E's' — Economy. Efficiency and Effectiveness[2] — which implied a need for increased measurement, accountability and customer-responsiveness. Thus, it was a time of substantial internal change. The external environment was also undergoing substantial change resulting in increased pressures on Social Services Departments; rising expectations fuelled demand as resources became more constrained; demographic changes meant a shift in emphasis from children to the elderly; the move from residential to community care necessitated a retraining of staff, a need for substantially different facilities, and a rethinking of professional attitudes; additional pressures resulted from, for example, increased reporting of child abuse, increased violence to staff and a general climate of media hostility.

The Elderly
Residential Homes
Day Care
Community Care
Home Care/Meals on Wheels

Children and Families
Preventative Work
Adoption
Foster Parents
Residential Care
Child Protection Work

Mental Health
Care in the Community Programme
Day Care — Hostels — Sheltered Housing
Rehabilitation of Drug Users

Learning Difficulties
Day and Residential Care
Training

Physical Handicap
Day Centres
Appliances and Adaptations

FIG. 1. *The work of Social Services Departments.*

The nature of the problem faced by the management of KSS is described briefly in the introduction. A major impact of the cultural revolution was an increasing emphasis on strategic thinking and, as a consequence, an increasing workload associated with the development of new initiatives. An initiative may be internally driven, for example, the development of a management information system, or a review of the assessment of people with learning difficulties, or it may be in response to legislation, for example, putting in place a system which allows client access to records. In all cases the process of developing a working system based on such an initiative is one which requires management. The burden of this work has fallen principally on the Area Managers — middle managers, as can be seen from the organizational structure shown in Figure 2. already carrying a heavy operational workload. The rapid growth of this project-based component of the workload was initially handled in a very *ad hoc* manner, which was proving to be inadequate. Jeffrey[1] writes '. . . middle managers tasked with a project often do not have full, written terms of reference; the resource implications of the task are not properly examined; and no systematic review and evaluation of work takes place. . . . (they) complain forcefully of resource log-jams, random-seeming displacement of previously understood priorities, foreshortened deadlines, and an overall sense of overload and chaos.' As a result, relationships between senior and middle mangers were becoming strained. There was an overwhelming feeling that 'something has to be done'.

It was against this backcloth that the Department of Management Science at The University of Kent (UKC) became involved, with the initial belief that knowledge of project management techniques could be of help. Initial discussions of the problem took place with the Senior Assistant

Valerie Belton – Project Planning and Prioritization in the Social Services

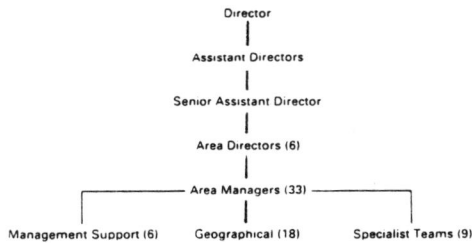

Director
|
Assistant Directors
|
Senior Assistant Director
|
Area Directors (6)
|
Area Managers (33)
|
Management Support (6)   Geographical (18)   Specialist Teams (9)

FIG. 2. *Managerial structure.*

Director, and a project steering group was set up comprising the Senior Assistant Director, two Area Directors and Dr Belton from UKC. The programme of work outlined in Figure 3 was agreed upon. It was envisaged that this would fall into distinct stages, as discussed below; the first stage being principally undertaken by Kate Amos and Julia Iredale, third year students in Management Science at UKC, working with KSS staff, under the direction of the steering group. This work was undertaken as the project which formed 25% of the third year of their degree. The aim of this programme of work was to provide a basis for a structured approach to the planning, prioritization and management of the work on development initiatives, with a view towards the provision of an integrated decision support system.

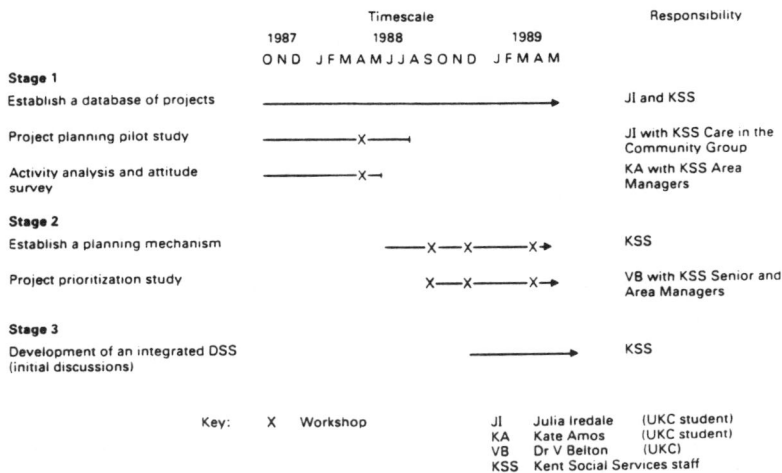

	Timescale			Responsibility
	1987	1988	1989	
	O N D	J F M A M J J A S O N D	J F M A M	
Stage 1				
Establish a database of projects		—————————————————→		JI and KSS
Project planning pilot study		————X———⊢		JI with KSS Care in the Community Group
Activity analysis and attitude survey		————X⊣		KA with KSS Area Managers
Stage 2				
Establish a planning mechanism		——X—X————X→		KSS
Project prioritization study		X—X————X→		VB with KSS Senior and Area Managers
Stage 3				
Development of an integrated DSS (initial discussions)		————————→		KSS

Key: X   Workshop   JI   Julia Iredale   (UKC student)
                                KA   Kate Amos   (UKC student)
                                VB   Dr V Belton   (UKC)
                                KSS   Kent Social Services staff

FIG. 3. *Work programme.*

The first stage of the work was to establish the fundamental building blocks of such a project management system. These were considered to be as follows:

A database of current projects
    This is essential for monitoring the ongoing workload, but also provides the context in which newly proposed initiatives are evaluated and considered for addition to the portfolio.
A resource planning mechanism
    To be able to plan the allocation of resources to projects it is necessary to have a forecast of the workload implications of a project. The provision of this was one of the objectives of the project planning pilot study.

Journal of the Operational Research Society Vol. 44, No. 2

A measure of the resources available

In allocating resources some knowledge of the availability is essential. The activity analysis was to provide information on current utilization of resources, as a basis for future planning.

The second stage of the work was to develop a process for the evaluation and prioritization of initiatives, and a mechanism whereby this could become a routine part of management. This would enable new initiatives to be considered against the portfolio of current initiatives and their resource implications. Informed decisions could then be taken about whether or not work should begin on a new initiative, when it should begin, whether it should be at the expense of ongoing projects, and if so, which project(s) to delay.

A third stage would be the development of an integrated decision support system.

Each aspect of the work is described in more detail in the following sections.

THE DATABASE OF PROJECTS

It was envisaged that this would constitute a record of ongoing projects, and a skills database drawing on current and completed projects. Eventually it would also hold information derived from the prioritization exercise which would provide the basis for comparison of new project proposals against the existing portfolio and inform the process of deciding which proposals should be incorporated in the portfolio. The existing records were paper-based and often consisted of no more than the project heading, the origin of the project and an indication of where the work was being carried out. Information for planning, namely target dates, key milestones and resource implications, if it existed, was sketchy and often out of date. The development of the database was done by KSS staff.

THE RESOURCE PLANNING MECHANISM

The development of a planning mechanism was the project task of Julia Iredale. As a project brief it was a broad and challenging one, particularly as two previous attempts had fallen on stony ground. Initial groundwork confirming the problems described by Jeffrey (see above), revealed that despite an awareness of, and in some cases, training in project management techniques (a finding of the survey to be described in the following section) there was little attempt to use these, and it attributed the failure of the two previous attempts to long-winded and excessively wordy guidelines which were difficult and time-consuming to implement. Jeffrey[1] also cites the lack of commitment to, and coordination of, implementation as a reason for the failure to achieve this.

Iredale[3] concluded that the essence of an appropriate system should be simplicity; it should be easy to understand and make minimal demands on time. A system based on visual presentation of information was chosen with a view to promoting ease and speed of understanding. A trial study was conducted with staff of the Care in the Community group. This covered the development of an appropriate system with the staff of this group and a practical assessment of the system. The key elements of the proposed mechanism were; a flow chart for each project, highlighting key milestones and enabling individuals to see clearly when and how they were required to contribute to the project; a formalized procedure for registering acceptance of the project plan by all those required to contribute to it; and a series of loading charts which displayed and planned workload, either for a selected project or for individuals, or aggregated to departmental level. The first two elements are feasible as paper-based exercises, but the loading charts are only practically feasible using a computerized system. We had clear visions of an appropriate visual interactive model, but the available technology precluded this and a demonstration system was implemented in a spreadsheet. Subsequent work has been done to develop a prototype visual interactive system in the Department of Management Science at Strathclyde University, which is currently being refined with Lothian Regional Council. Iredale's work was well received by the Care in the Community group and was presented to the Area Managers and Area Directors at a workshop held at UKC in April 1988; to be discussed in a later section.

Valerie Belton — Project Planning and Prioritization in the Social Services

AN INVESTIGATION OF THE RESOURCES AVAILABLE

This aspect of the study was the main focus of Kate Amos' project work. Although the senior managers were aware of the increasing level of involvement of Area Managers in work on development initiatives, they were unable to quantify the level of involvement and did not know if some were more affected than others. It was felt that in order to establish a resource budget, it was necessary first of all to establish the current level of resource utilization. A classic study of how managers spend their time is that by Stewart[4], in which she evaluated how 140 managers in the UK spent their time over a four week period. She describes three ways of investigating the allocation of management time; self-estimation, diary and observation. In this study the primary approach was that of a longitudinal activity survey (diary). This involved 33 Area Managers who recorded how they spent their work time activities on a day-to-day basis over a period of four weeks on pre-prepared activity sheets. The results are shown in Table 1. The initial design was piloted with three of the managers and up-dated accordingly.

TABLE 1. *Activity sheet showing the recorded breakdown of work*

Activity	Day to day running		New initiatives		Total	
Area Management Team meetings	2.5h	(6.1%)	1h	(1.8%)	3.5h	(7.9%)
Meetings involving Social Services Department staff only	3.5h	(8.0%)	1.5h	(3.6%)	5h	(11.6%)
Meetings involving other organizations	2.5h	(5.4%)	1h	(2.5%)	3.5h	(7.9%)
Consultations with peers and/or line managers	1.5h	(4.0%)	0.5h	(1.0%)	2.5h	(5.0%)
Training subordinates	0.5h	(0.8%)	10mins	(0.4%)	0.5h	(1.1%)
Recruitment	1h	(2.5%)	5mins	(0.2%)	1h	(2.7%)
Disciplinary matters	0.5h	(1.5%)	negligible		0.5h	(1.5%)
Processing complaints/enquiries	1h	(2.0%)	negligible		1h	(2.0%)
Supervision of subordinates	3.5h	(7.7%)	0.5h	(0.8%)	4h	(8.5%)
Planning	1h	(2.0%)	1.5h	(3.0%)	2.5h	(5.0%)
Financial work	1h	(2.8%)	1.5h	(3.7%)	3.0h	(6.5%)
Paperwork/phonecalls	8.5h	(19.3%)	0.5h	(1.3%)	9h	(20.6%)
Duty system work	0.5h	(1.6%)	negligible		0.5h	(1.6%)
Travelling	2.5h	(5.5%)	12mins	(0.4%)	2.5h	(5.9%)
Case Conferences	0.5h	(0.9%)	nothing		0.5h	(0.9%)
Sick leave	1h	(2.1%)	nothing		1h	(2.1%)
Annual leave	1.75h	(4.0%)	nothing		1.75h	(4.0%)
Time spent on training courses	1h	(1.9%)	nothing		1h	(1.9%)
Other activities	1.5h	(2.9%)	7mins	(0.3%)	1.5h	(3.2%)
Total	35.5h	(81%)	8h	(19%)	43.5h	(100%)

Note: Figures are the mean time per week (based on 33 four-week diaries) spent on each activity. Times are rounded to the nearest 30 minutes, unless 15 minutes or less. Percentages are based on the unrounded times.

Prior to the activity analysis an attitude survey was conducted. The aims of this were to ascertain: the extent to which managers felt overworked and suffered from stress; how much time they thought they spent working on development initiatives; their opinions on the Department's approach to managing to new initiatives; suggestions for improving efficiency and effectiveness; and their approach to planning. A copy of the questionnaire can be found in Jeffrey[1] and Amos[5].

It is not possible to report the results of the study in full here; refer to Jeffrey[1] or Amos[5] for a more detailed presentation. The key findings of the activity analysis are presented in Tables 1, 2 and 3.

Table 1 shows the breakdown of work into the identified categories for day-to-day running and new initiatives for all managers, Tables 2 and 3 display an analysis of time spent on initiatives by type of manager and by area.

The responses to the attitude survey were in line with expectations. They reinforced the picture of an overworked and under-resourced group of managers. Additional clerical or secretarial support was frequently cited as an urgent need. The need for improved consultation and availability of information in planning new initiatives was highlighted. The average estimate of time spent on initiatives was 42%, much higher then revealed by the activity analysis.

Journal of the Operational Research Society Vol. 44, No. 2

TABLE 2. *Average working week and time spent on initiatives by type of manager*

Type of manager	Average hours worked per week	Percentage of time spent on initiatives	
		Recorded	Estimated
Management support	42	29	51
Geographical	43	14	40
Specialist service	46	21	43

TABLE 3. *Average working week and time spent on initiatives by area*

Area	Average hours worked per week	Percentage of time spent on initiatives	
		Recorded	Estimated
Canterbury and Thanet	41.5	22	34
Dartford and Gravesham	41	12	46
Maidstone	42	29	43
Medway/Swale	47	16	36
South East Kent	45	19	46
West Kent	43	18	49

In conclusion, the activity survey showed that the managers worked on average a 43.5 hour (effectively a six day) week and that on average 19% of their time (higher for Management Support managers) was spent on new initiatives. Many managers commented that they worked longer in total than expected, but actually spent less time than anticipated on new initiatives. This may be attributable to the general lack of coordination and planning associated with new initiatives which leads to feelings of pressure and a heightened awareness of this element of the work. The feelings of inadequate clerical/secretarial support is borne out by the fact that on average almost 20% of a manager's time is spent on administrative tasks (paperwork and phone-calls).

The results of both surveys were presented to the group of managers involved at the previously mentioned workshop.

INITIAL WORKSHOP

In April 1988 the Area Managers and Area Directors were invited to a workshop at UKC at which the findings from the studies to date would be presented and at which broader issues of project planning would be discussed. After presentation and discussion of the findings of the studies the participants were divided into small working groups to address the specific issue of 'institutionalizing a more systematic approach to project prioritization, planning and management'. A number of concrete proposals were put forward, largely influenced by the studies which had taken place. These included the specification of an annual programme of initiatives consistent with an agreed allocation of time (tentatively proposed as 20% of senior and middle management time), the need for a database of projects, the need for simple project management techniques on a universal basis, the introduction of a system of formalizing the acceptance of planned contributions to projects and their associated timescale, a critical examination of the 80% of time spent on day-to-day running of the Department with a view to identifying possible efficiency savings, particularly with respect to the provision of clerical and secretarial support, support for an extended trial of the use of the workload planning procedures piloted in the Care in the Community group.

All in all, the participants in the workshop welcomed the efforts to introduce a more explicit and rational procedure for initiating and managing projects and voiced enthusiastic support for further work. This had three major strands.
(1) Iredale was invited to continue work with the Department during the summer to progress the proposals for project planning.
(2) Attention was to be given within KSS to the establishment of a mechanism to institutionalize the planning process.
(3) Consideration was to be given to establishing a system for prioritizing projects. The work in this area is described in the following section.

Valerie Belton — Project Planning and Prioritization in the Social Services

A SYSTEM FOR THE EVALUATION AND PRIORITIZATION OF PROJECTS

KSS was looking for a framework which would enable them to evaluate and prioritize projects in a manner which was systematic and applicable to the wide range of projects undertaken. The problem is one to which multiple criteria analysis (see Belton[1]) is well suited and it was decided to use this approach, initially to help clarify the factors which influenced current practice, and from there to develop a model to support future decision making. We felt it was important that as many as possible of those who had attended the initial workshop continued to be closely involved in the process. With this in mind a series of workshops was chosen as the forum for model development. Each workshop involved 12-15 of the KSS managers and two facilitators, one principally concerned with guiding the process of developing the model and one providing technical support. Analysis was carried out using V·I·S·A, software for interactive multiple criteria analysis using a hierarchical multi-attribute value function model (see Belton and Vickers[2]). The process of model development and the nature of the workshops is described in chronological sequence.

First workshop — August

At this workshop a first attempt was made at structuring an evaluation model. The first stage simply sought to identify criteria which were relevant in identifying successful, and unsuccessful, projects. This was done in small groups using brainstorming and a plus/minus/interesting analysis (De Bono[8]) of a number of current and completed projects. Each group was assigned a set of projects which they were asked to consider, first individually and then as a group. For each project, they were asked to note positive, negative and interesting features which they felt were relevant in evaluating it. Each feature was noted on a piece of A5 card and stuck to a large whiteboard. By the end of this process the whiteboard was adorned with pieces of card. An initial attempt was made to structure this information by grouping the cards relating to similar issues and from this exercise a hierarchy of criteria began to emerge. No attempt was made to refine this structure at this stage, rather, we went on to use it in the evaluation of four current projects. This led to much discussion about the meaning of criteria; some criteria were aggregated with others; new criteria were added; and many criteria were regrouped. The evaluation of the four projects was not completed in any sense; indeed, it was not intended that this should be the case. The principal outcomes of this first workshop were a shared language which would facilitate further discussions of the issue, and a preliminary model structure.

Follow up meeting — September

Subsequent to the workshop we had worked on the model to refine and simplify it. This was further refined at a meeting of the steering group in preparation for a follow up workshop to pilot and further validate the model. The structure of the model at this stage is illustrated in Figure 4. To someone seeing the model for the first time at this stage it appears very simple and it may be difficult to imagine that it captures the complexity of an evaluation of this kind. However, it is important to remember that the model is the distilled knowledge of those involved in the evaluation, thus it captures *their* perception of the problem, and that it has emerged from the initial, far messier, picture of the problem.

Second workshop — November

This workshop, which involved about the same number of managers but included two or three different individuals, worked on the detail of the model. This was achieved by constant reference to ongoing projects — thus anchoring the model in the real world and tying it in with the knowledge of the managers concerned. A scale was defined for each of the bottom-level criteria in the model by relating the extremes (0 and 100 points) to current projects. Each of three groups of four managers used the model, which had been input to V·I·S·A, to evaluate four current projects. This required the groups first to evaluate each of the projects against the scale defined for each bottom-level criterion in the model and then to specify criteria weights which reflected their priorities. The

Journal of the Operational Research Society Vol. 44, No. 2

Project evaluation

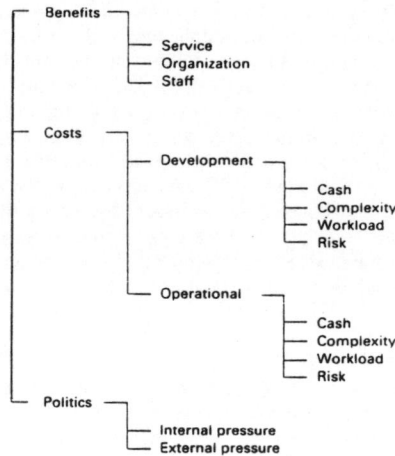

FIG. 4. *Project prioritization model.*

criteria weights were not elicited directly; instead, the groups made use of the facilities for visual interactive sensitivity analysis provided by V·I·S·A (see Belton[6]) to arrive at a set of criteria weights with which they felt comfortable and which, incorporated in the model, reflected their intuitive feelings about the overall assessment of the four projects. This exercise was valuable in validating the model for, as the groups experimented with the visual interactive analysis, they were able to see immediately that as they increased the weight given to 'Benefit to the service', those projects which had the most beneficial impact on the service performed relatively better. When the model did not behave in a manner consistent with their expectations it caused them to think harder about the way in which they had scored projects, or about the criteria. This stimulated some further discussion about the structure of the hierarchy of criteria and the possibility of adding criteria. Having three groups working independently on the same task made it possible to gauge the consistency with which the model could be applied. The workshop identified additional work which needed to be done in specifying the detail of the model in order to clarify points of potential misunderstanding. The responsibility for this work was left with the managers themselves.

Two progress meetings were held with a small group of managers during February and March.

Third workshop — April

An expanded group of 20 managers carried out a final test of the model, again working in small groups to evaluate a number of projects, using the more detailed guidelines that had been prepared since the previous workshop. This confirmed that much of the scope for inconsistency identified at the second workshop had been ironed out. The group now spoke as if they 'owned' the model and were anxious to progress to using it in practice.

ESTABLISHMENT OF A PLANNING MECHANISM

In parallel with the development of a model for evaluation and prioritization of projects, work was being done within KSS to establish a mechanism for planning. This took the shape of a sub-committee of the District Managers Group, with a remit to monitor the current portfolio of projects and to evalute new proposals. Guidelines were established for the initiation of new proposals.

Valerie Belton — Project Planning and Prioritization in the Social Services

REVIEW OF THE SITUATION

It was now about 18 months since this work began, eight months since the work on developing the model for evaluation and prioritization began. The general climate at the time was one of enthusiasm and impatience to make progress. We were restrained from progressing to a full implementation of the envisaged integrated decision support system as the Department was awaiting the arrival of a new computer system. This was to be the home of the Management Information Systems, to which the proposed database of projects would be linked.

The study appeared to have already yielded significant benefits to the organization. These were not necessarily in the form of any tangible outcomes — it was not the findings of the surveys, nor the prototype database and planning systems, nor the model for evaluation and prioritization, that were the most significant benefits, although these were interesting and useful — it was the consequences of the involvement in developing these that were of far greater relevance. A problem which had been a fermenting source of unrest had been brought to the surface, openly accepted to be a problem and shared. Potential means of managing the problem had been explored in a manner which involved all the key personnel, the undercurrent of discontent which had characterized the initial workshop had been replaced by an enthusiasm for action.

WHAT HAPPENED NEXT — SUCCESS OF FAILURE?

If I were able to report that when the new computer system was installed and over its teething problems we went ahead according to our initial expectations, developed and installed an integrated decision support system which is now in regular use for the monitoring and evaluation of ongoing projects and new proposals, we could all reflect on a successful project, although no doubt others would have done it differently. However, that did not happen!

Something which had influenced the development of the planning mechanism briefly described above was the observation of the need for a project champion; our project champion, the deputy director, moved to a post in another authority, resulting in some internal reorganization. Responsibility for the further development of the envisaged DSS fell to the manager of Information Technology. Nothing else happened. One is less likely to conclude that the project was an outright success, I have to express some personal disappointment that it did not continue, but is that right? Should we conclude that the project failed? More importantly, what issues does the experience raise and can we learn from them?

The first observation I would like to make is that the perceived lack of success is relative to the goals which were stated at the beginning of this paper. These goals were never stated at the beginning of the project, they emerged as the work progressed. It is not clear even to what extent they were our, the analysts, goals, imposed on the clients, and to what extent they reflected the clients' own goals.

The second observation is that neither I, nor the members of the steering group, nor most of the managers involved in the workshops, considered any of the work done to be a waste of anyone's time.

As I wrote above, the fact that the work was carried out at all was significant in helping to resolve the organizational frustration which was building up in relation to the problem. A large number of issues were made explicit as a result of the three studies. A consequence of this is that one is forced to acknowledge the problems and to try deal with them, or live with them. The impetus may only be short term and may lose strength as other pressing issues emerge. It certainly seemed that a significant momentum had been generated by the close of the final workshop described, and it is possible that this enabled the organization to resolve its difficulties in its own way, in a manner which was more consistent with the style of the new senior management group than the DSS which we had envisaged. If this was the case, it would be my view that the exercise had fulfilled its enabling, or facilitating role. Unfortunately, I am unable to judge; it would be interesting to return to the organization now, two years later, to try to assess the impact of the exercise on those who took part. However, all three members of the steering group have moved on, two to directorships of other local authorities, where they have introduced some of the approaches to planning described

Journal of the Operational Research Society Vol. 44, No. 2

in this paper. I am currently investigating the feasibility of carrying out a follow-up study with those remaining in KSS who participated in this work.

Social Services Departments are now actively being encouraged to view themselves as 'Learning Organizations'[9] or 'Learning Companies'[10]. Although these ideas have only recently been popularized in the UK, it is interesting to reflect on the experiences described in this paper in the light of the concept of a learning organization. Senge[9] nominates five elements as the key to the learning organization. These are: systems thinking; personal mastery; mental models; a shared vision; and team learning. Pedler *et al.*[10] list the following, slightly more concrete, features of the learning company: a learning approach to strategy; participative policy making; informating; formative accounting and control; internal exchange; reward flexibility; enabling structures; boundary workers as environmental scanners; inter-company learning; a learning climate; and self-development for all. Central to both of these views is the need to provide a learning climate, in which members of the company can develop both as individuals and as a team, providing the opportunity to explore and experiment with their own and others' ideas, values, and mental models. Senge[9] puts forward microworlds, computer simulations based on systems dynamics, as the technology of the learning organization. Elsewhere, Belton and Elder[11] have suggested that a principal benefit of the use of visual interactive modelling is the way in which it promotes learning, citing the work described in this paper as an example. Although it was not a stated objective at the start of the work, nor indeed an objective of which any of the participants were consciously aware, it would appear, on reflection, that we were effectively providing the learning climate which can help promote a learning organization.

Acknowledgements — Many individuals contributed to the work which is described in this paper, in particular, I would like to acknowledge the following.
Kate Amos and Julia Iredale, whose work forms a large part of the study.
Mike Lauerman, Jean Jeffrey and Don Brand, who formed the Steering Group which directed the study.
The KSS managers who participated in various aspects of the study.
Stephen Vickers for software development and assistance with workshops.

REFERENCES

1. J. JEFFREY (1988) Managing projects in social services: making better use of time, techniques and people. MA Thesis, Leicester Polytechnic.
2. AUDIT COMMISSION (1986) *Performance Review in Local Government—Social Services*. HMSO, London.
3. J. IREDALE (1988) Workload management and project planning for Kent Social Services. University of Kent at Canterbury, Project in Management Science.
4. R. STEWART (1967) *Managers and their Jobs*. Macmillan, Basingstoke.
5. K. E. AMOS (1988) An analysis of how managers spend their time in Kent Social Services. University of Kent at Canterbury, Project in Management Science.
6. V. BELTON (1990) Multiple criteria analysis—practically the only way to choose. In *Operational Research Tutorial Papers* 1990 (L. C. HENDRY and R. W. EGLESE, Eds) pp. 53–101. Operational Research Society, Birmingham.
7. V. BELTON and S. P. VICKERS (1989) V·I·S·A—VIM for MCDA. In *Improving Decision Making in Organisations* (A. G. LOCKETT and G. ISLEI, Eds) pp. 287–304. Springer-Verlag, Berlin.
8. E. DE BONO (1985) *De Bono's Thinking Course*. Ariel Books, BBC, London.
9. P. M. SENGE (1992) *The Fifth Discipline. The Art and Practice of the Learning Organisation*. Century Business, London.
10. M. PEDLER, J. BURGOYNE and T. BOYDELL (1991) *The Learning Company: A Strategy for Sustainable Development*. McGraw-Hill, Maidenhead.
11. V. BELTON and M. D. ELDER (1993) Decision support systems: learning from visual interactive modelling. To Be published in *Decision Support Systems*.

[14]

J.Opt. Res. Soc. Vol 43, No. 4, pp. 293-305
Printed in Great Britain. All rights reserved

0160-5682/92 $3.50+0.00
Copyright © 1992 Operational Research Society Ltd.

Into the Swamp: The Analysis of Social Issues*

JONATHAN ROSENHEAD

London School of Economics

Prior analysis of the implications of public policy initiatives is commonly quite inadequate, and spectacularly so in recent government history. There has been a retreat from reason in public affairs. Until now Operational Research has largely failed to address or be applied to issues in the public policy domain. However, the new generation of problem structuring methods offers forms of analysis well suited to the environment in which public policy is formed. The quality of public debate would be much enhanced by a wider dissemination of analytic support. Cabinets, Parliamentary Committees, political parties, and a wide range of community-based groups could benefit in this way. A network of think-tanks and research institutes, whose inter-disciplinary basis would incorporate operational research, is proposed to provide the requisite analytic capability.

Key words: policy analysis, think-tanks, community OR

INTRODUCTION

The subject matter of this paper is the overlap between the domain of politics, and the sort of analysis which operational research (OR) — and other kindred approaches — can offer. This is a topic which has not been much addressed, and for complementary reasons. Many, perhaps most, of its practitioners have seen operational research as apolitical in nature, or even positively technocratic — with a mission to substitute technical expertise for 'irrational' political decision making processes[1]. Equally, and at least partially in consequence, operational research has made little contribution to those processes; its visibility to those active in public-policy making has been low. Its tools and techniques, methodology and approach have been applied elsewhere.

The dichotomy of problem types, and methods for engaging with them, has been vividly evoked by Schon[2]:

In the swampy lowland, messy, confusing problems defy technical solution. The irony of this situation is that the problems of the high ground tend to be relatively unimportant to individuals or society at large, however great their technical interest may be, while in the swamp lie the problems of greatest human concern.

The practitioner must choose. Shall he remain on the high ground where he can solve relatively unimportant problems according to prevailing standards of rigor, or shall he descend to the swamp of important problems and non-rigorous inquiry.

The swamp metaphor neatly encapsulates the most significant debate in contemporary operational research, which also has far wider implications. This paper will address in turn the restriction of OR (and related approaches) to problems of the high ground; the consequent impoverishment of the analysis of social issues: the nature of the relevant contribution which OR can make to the analysis of policies: and the need for an institutional framework through which analytic capability could be deployed to improve the quality of political debate.

PROBLEMS OF THE HIGH GROUND

Although I am the first holder of the established Chair in Operational Research at the London School of Economics (LSE), the School's commitment to the subject is of long standing. Ailsa Land

*Extended text of an inaugural lecture delivered on 15 November 1990

Correspondence: J. Rosenhead, London School of Economics, Houghton Street, London WC2A 2AE, UK.

Journal of the Operational Research Society Vol. 43, No. 4

was the first holder of the title of Professor of Operational Research, and graduate teaching in the subject has been carried out for more than 30 years.

Indeed, the historical connection between LSE and OR precedes not only the inception of our masters degree, but also the origins of the subject itself, for one of the pioneers of war-time operational research, Cecil Gordon, was, in the early 1930s, a PhD student at the School, under Lancelot Hogben in the Department of Social Biology. Operational Research itself, as an activity with an explicit and continuous identity, dates only from about 1937.

Some consideration of the historical origins and development of operational research will prove useful for an understanding of the subsequent restriction of operational research's range of application. A fuller account of operational research's history up to the early post-war period is given by Rosenhead[3,4]. OR emerged initially from work associated with the development of radar in the late 1930s. While much effort went into extending the range and accuracy of the equipment, other scientific and technical resources were devoted to ensuring that effective use was made of radar's information in operational conditions. To distinguish it from the more conventional activity known as weapons research, this second strand was designated as 'operational research'.

The work relating to radar was a great success, and rapidly led to the spread of the approach from its starting point with Fighter Command to the many other commands where radar was deployed. Soon the scope of work extended beyond radar, to a wide variety of issues in which the critical and quantitative approach of operational research's scientifically-trained practitioners could clarify the likely consequences of alternative policies. Cecil Gordon, for example, was a member of Coastal Command Operational Research Section. This group carried out, among others, classic studies of the optimum convoy size, and the best fuse-setting for anti-U-boat depth charges.

Gordon's own work was concerned with maintenance policies for Coastal Command aircraft. By treating flying and maintenance as component phases of a single cycle, conclusions were derived which dealt not only with the organization of the maintenance workshops, but also with doctrine on the need for a minimum 'serviceability percentage' of aircraft. When the recommendations were implemented, it proved possible to achieve a doubling of the number of sorties flown with the same number of aircraft and personnel. 'Planned Flying, Planned Maintenance', as it was called, made a crucial contribution to winning the Battle of the Atlantic against the German U-boat fleet. Gordon was given the job of transferring the approach throughout the RAF, and beyond.

Cecil Gordon's work can serve as an example of the war-time achievements of OR; we will also encounter, below, his post-war activities. However, as a person he also exemplifies a significant aspect of the early make-up of operational research, for he shared one characteristic with other better known leaders in the field (for example, Bernal and Blackett), as well as many also who were less senior — he was a committed socialist. Others still, like Watson-Watt and Waddington, were touched to a greater or lesser extent by socialist ideas.

That socialist scientists were active and prominent in operational research was no accident. The dominant intellectual influence in the strong radical science movement of the 1930s was that of Bernal. Following Bernal (see in particular his *The Social Function of Science*, published in 1939), they held that capitalism could not make use of science's benevolent potential, and pressed for science to be used in the pursuit of public, not sectional interests. The campaign met with little substantive success in peace-time. When the war-time emergency opened doors, it is not surprising that socialist scientists of this persuasion disproportionately made and seized opportunities to work in the government service and in the national interest.

It is at the end of the war that Cecil Gordon became, for a short period, the central figure in the attempted transfer of operational research to civilian Government. Most of the more established scientists returned rapidly to their former disciplines. Cecil Gordon, in particular, tried to pursue the operational research project, as the crystallization of radical science's pre-war programme, into the period of post-war reconstruction. He was appointed in 1946 to the key government operational research post, as head of the Special Research Unit at the Board of Trade. In that position he attempted to devise and implement quantitatively-based methods for improving the efficiency of British industry. The underlying assumption was of an interventionist government committed to the regulation of important economic activities in accordance with priorities. Gordon lasted at the Board of Trade only two years, and the Unit was closed down behind him.

Jonathan Rosenhead — Into the Swamp: The Analysis of Social Issues

The Board of Trade's successor ministry is the Department of Trade and Industry. Writing in the context of the Central Policy Review Staff's work on industrial policy in 1976, Blackstone and Plowden[5] characterized the DTI as 'short on what might be called "analytic propensity".' Shortness of analytic propensity was also in evidence in 1946. However, by 1948 there were added factors militating against the Special Research Unit's success.

The Attlee administration had shifted decisively against physical, non-market controls; and the Cold War had started, carrying with it an intellectual climate in which central planning was tarred with the brush of Stalinist totalitarianism. On all these grounds operational research was unacceptable. It was virtually evicted from government, with other high profile OR activities suffering the same fate as the Board of Trade unit. Curiously, operational research went on to find acceptance, instead, in industry, where operational methods for strengthening central control proved quite welcome.

There were significant consequences for the development of OR in this change of direction. Operational research went on to develop analytic tools for handling decision-making under uncertainty and especially complexity. The tools, however, were developed in and for the conditions of industry, and of business more generally. (In the United States, to which operational research had diffused during the war, a military influence remained significant.) The even more complex, turbulent and interactive world in which public policy in peace-time is formulated did not appreciably shape the subsequent growth of OR, or its methods.

In the 1950s and 60s, operational research developed approaches for finding technical solutions to complex but well-defined problems. These were, at base, efficiency problems within large, unitary organizations. The specialized techniques were developed to find the best way of pursuing an objective already agreed, with implementation through the organization's chain-of-command. Uncertainties were handled, typically, by reducing them to the form of mathematical probabilities (see, for example, Rosenhead[6]).

These are the problems of the *high ground*. The problems of the swamp are quite different:

- how to agree what subset of all the inter-acting factors constitutes, at least for the time being, the problem;
- how to negotiate a way forward in situations beset with uncertainties;
- how to find a policy which takes account of both technical feasibility and the existence of diverse interest groups.

For problems such as these, common in the public policy domain (and also at strategic levels in unitary organizations), OR's optimizing techniques offered, and offer, no appropriate handle.

For a brief period in the late 1960s and early 1970s, nevertheless, it was attempted. That is, it was thought that it might be possible simply to expand the scope of those optimizing techniques. Throw in more variables! Solve the whole social problem! The phrase 'moon-ghetto metaphor' was coined to characterize this approach[7]. It was expressed in many variants, but that of Hubert Humphrey while Vice-President of the United States in 1968 is representative: 'The techniques that are going to put a man on the moon are going to be exactly the techniques that we are going to need to clean up our cities' (cited by Quade[1]).

The (mostly US) proponents of this approach called it 'policy analysis'. (See, for example, Dror[8] and Nagel[9]). Their hopelessly over-ambitious claims gave those words a bad name (which is why they do not feature in the title of this paper). The outcome of the resulting collapse of policy analysis under the weight of its own pretentions has been bad for operational research — but worse for society.

ANALYSIS DEPRIVATION

The absence of a methodology capable of providing analytic contributions consistent with the complex, interactive process of public policy formation has been a significant deprivation. Important social issues have been left without appropriate analytic structuring; in some cases this vacuum has permitted the over-structured and one-sided formulations of economists to achieve near hegemony.

Journal of the Operational Research Society Vol. 43, No. 4

The complexity of public policy decisions has a number of dimensions. The most obvious is that a large number of factors may need to be handled simultaneously. At the governmental level 'decisions on even apparently isolated issues can have repercussions for the programmes and policies of other departments', as well as on the standing of the government as a whole[5]. Porter[10] makes a similar point on the difficulty facing the US President, and others in positions of comparable authority:

> they are expected to make a large number of decisions about issues on which they themselves are not expert, and therefore they are going to rely on the other people for information, for analysis, for structuring alternatives and for an assessment of the advantages and disadvantages associated with the alternatives. Many of the issues coming at them, and on which they are expected to decide, are interrelated, in the sense that what they decide on issue A today will affect the choices, and the relative attractiveness of those choices, on issue B, C and D that they are going to be considering two weeks, three months or a year from now.

Furthermore, many of the factors with a bearing on the situation will be shrouded in uncertainties — from the reliability of a forecast, through the possible future actions of parties capable of affecting the outcome, to the priorities which should be applied (see Friend and Hickling[11]). To such complexity must be added that of the multiplicity of groups with related interests, whose purposes and perceptions of any intervention will condition their responses.

Indeed, these groups will be intent not merely on responding, but also on trying to set the terms of public debate selectively to give emphasis to those aspects of the issue which support their positions. Arguments will be advanced and rebutted not just in terms of how well they fit objective features of the situation, but also for their ability to build consensus, assist in coalition formation, mobilize support. There may well be hidden agendas and Machiavellian calculations. As an example, consider the policy towards public services of a government with little commitment to them. The government may nevertheless be persuaded that radical and risky restructuring should be undertaken. The (private) argument might run that success (should it materialize) can be claimed as a government triumph, while failure (it is hoped) will only serve to discredit the service organization and make its dismemberment more politically feasible.

Situations such as these do not lend themselves to structuring by simplistic quantitative models, which purport to identify optimum solutions. But neither do they lend themselves to intuitive decision-making. Their complexities will, in many cases, overwhelm cognitive capacities. The result is that actors may, individually and collectively, overlook strategies which are mutually preferable, or fail unnecessarily to guard against plausible threats. Outcomes may be worse than they need be across a range of participants, or be reached only after undue delay and costly friction.

Lindblom and Cohen[12], in their critique of 'professional social inquiry', have argued that analysis, to be useful in social problem solving, should be both competitive with, and complementary to, partisan interaction. Professional social inquiry, they say, should not attempt authoritative pronouncements. It should, rather, restrict its ambition to helping participants who are interacting in the policy arena by providing them with analysis and information suited to their particular roles. Such a refocusing could clearly have a considerable impact on the process of public debate between contrasting policies. It is precisely here that the current inadequacy of public policy analysis contributes to an impoverishment of political discourse. All too often the cases for particular policies based on their possible consequences (including their interactions with other policies and interests) have been neither clearly advanced nor effectively rebutted. The language and tradition are not there.

SOURCES OF POLICY GUIDANCE

This general diagnosis is exemplified by the disarray of British public policy making in the years since 1979. Of course, the shambles has by no means been all the fault of operational research's sins of omission. Larger forces have been at work.

One straw in the wind was the demise of the Central Policy Review Staff (CPRS). Set up by Edward Heath when Prime Minister in 1971, it was a pioneering attempt to provide enhanced analytic capability at the centre of government. The CPRS was abolished by Mrs Thatcher in 1983.

Jonathan Rosenhead – Into the Swamp: The Analysis of Social Issues

The CPRS's particular mix of virtues and shortcomings will not be explored here; they have been extensively analysed elsewhere (Ashworth[13]: Plowden[14]: Blackstone and Plowden[5]).

However, before proceeding to examine the implications of the abolition of the British 'think tank', a brief historical detour will serve to link it to some of the earlier aspirations of operational research. (A fuller account is given in Rosenhead[3,4].)

In 1948 Cecil Gordon was the principal author of a report advocating a body quite similar to the CPRS. The purpose of this Report, called 'Principles and Practices of Operational Research', was to encourage wide dissemination of OR throughout industry and government. It was adopted by the Panel on Technology and Operational Research of a short-lived government body called the Committee on Industrial Productivity. The Report was killed off by a combination of traditional civil servants and anti-interventionist Ministries, and it was never formally published.

It is just one of the Report's recommendations which concerns us here. This was that 'an Operational Research Unit should be established as part of the central machinery of government to undertake the study of broad national problems and to be available to the Central Economic Planners'. This ambitious proposal was lost with 'Principles and Practices of Operational Research'. It did not happen. CPRS, set up a generation later, is clearly recognizable as a relative of what Cecil Gordon and his colleagues were proposing. However, though established to fulfil a quite similar role, the CPRS was no Operational Research Unit. One of its members, indeed, was recruited from a government operational research group; at least a further three had some OR experience, but had moved on to other functions before joining CPRS. Nevertheless, the CPRS carried out no studies whose character was perceptibly influenced by operational research.

The fate of CPRS, then, had no direct implication for operational research. However, its abolition in 1983 certainly was indicative of a negative attitude by the government of the day (which at the time of writing is still the government of *our* day) to policy choice based on evidence and argument rather than on principles and gut reaction. What analysis has been conducted in the environs of Downing Street since 1983 has been carried out in the Prime Minister's Policy Unit.

An illuminating account of how the Policy Unit worked during the Thatcher administrations has been provided by a former member David Willets[15]. Unlike the CPRS, it did not undertake long-term, large-scale studies. Rather, it offered policy advice on matters of current concern, with deadlines from an hour to a few days away. More importantly, the advice did not go to Cabinet where it could be rebutted by Departmental Ministers, and debated. It was for her eyes and ears only. This gave the Policy Unit an extraordinary freedom. According to Willets 'the Policy Unit, because it is directly subordinated to the most senior and astute politician of the lot, is not afraid of putting forward what might initially appear to be politically far-fetched.' As an unfriendly observer put it to me off the record, this is a channel for the delivery of untreated sewage. (Perhaps significantly, excremental metaphors flow both ways. One was employed also by John Biffen to describe his treatment at the hands of the then Prime Minister's Press Secretary, Bernard Ingham, which prepared the ground for his dismissal from the Cabinet. Ingham, he said, was 'the sewer, not the sewage.')

Why should any Prime Minister want this stuff in her back yard? It does not take a very jaundiced eye to see it as a component of a stratagem, used repetitively and to great effect, for securing implementation of a favoured policy without debate which might derail it. Blackstone and Plowden describe a tactic, called 'the bounce', employed by seasoned civil servants. This consists of the presentation to Cabinet of a Departmental paper urging a particular course of action – at the last minute, on a topic on which delay will be highly damaging. The intention, and often the result, is to secure instant and unreflective action, which can only be commitment to the proffered strategy. Assessment of the downside effects, and awareness of possible alternative policies, may be effectively excluded.

The Thatcher administration perfected, if that is not too strong a word, a variant of this device. In the light of its consequence it could appropriately be designated 'the boomerang'.

The use of the boomerang has not been confined to the Prime Minister of the day; there have also been tactical variations in how it has been employed. Nevertheless, it will simplify exposition to present it here in its canonical form. In this, the Policy Unit supplies the Prime Minister with a radically new policy consistent with her principles and instincts. She announces this policy in a glare of publicity, thereby establishing a political *fait accompli*. The debate having thus been

Journal of the Operational Research Society Vol. 43, No. 4

finessed and forestalled, the relevant Department is left with the job of trying to make the innovation work. As the policy is commonly only in outline form and has not been subject to the filter of critical scrutiny, this task has been known to present some difficulties.

For those who care about good government it would be reassuring to believe that the 'boomerang' was merely an expression of one politician's style and can now safely be confined to the history books. This is, however, an over-optimistic reading. The practice of launching measures without consultation on unsuspecting institutions and interest groups has continued under her successor. One classic example is the January 1992 transfer of funding for teacher education from training colleges to schools. The announcement was sprung under conditions of high security, with implementation to follow at maximum speed. This continuity of style and method is supported by ample other evidence that the influence of the New Right revolution extends further than one prime minister (and, wider, indeed, than a single party).

Only a sub-set of the innovatory ingredients of Conservative government policy after 1979 was devised at the 10 Downing Street Policy Unit. Right-wing think-tanks, and in particular, the Centre for Policy Studies, the Institute of Economic Affairs, and the Adam Smith Institute, have had a very significant impact. Part of this has been achieved through the drip-effect of their insistent promotion of market-based policies, which has secured palpable shifts in what is perceived as the accepted wisdom. There are also many areas in which the think-tanks' influence on policy has been more direct, as the first or last advocate of policies subsequently adopted by the Government.

The typical method of arriving at or justifying policies promoted by these think-tanks has a robust simplicity. It starts with strong value assertions and then proceeds directly to detailed prescriptions. Argumentation is intuitive (with a 'public choice' flavour), and proposals are not costed or quantified. There is appeal, at most, to anecdotal evidence, but certainly not to research.

The list of policies traceable to such influence is formidable:

> the poll tax;
> enterprise zones;
> privatization of public enterprises;
> competitive tendering;
> the right to buy council houses;
> opting out — housing estates;
> opting out — schools;
> opting out — hospitals;
> NHS internal market;
> student loans;
> the National Curriculum and compulsory testing;
> GCSE English syllabus;
> privatization of the schools inspection service.

Many have produced administrative or political chaos (or both), or have failed even in terms of their own objectives. This record is not surprising in view of the poverty of preceding analysis implicit both in the think-tanks' methodology and the government's approach to the policy process.

SOME WORKED EXAMPLES OF AN IMPOVERISHED POLICY PROCESS

This general picture of an abbreviated policy process with slip-shod or absent analysis, and its consequences, can be enriched by a few examples.

Opting out of schools

The Educational Reform Act of 1988 contained a clutch of measures affecting many aspects of the education system. Government proposals were given limited circulation in duplicated form in August 1987 with comments required by that October. The legislation — unaffectionately labelled GERBIL, for Great Educational Reform Bill — was published the same autumn and passed into law at top speed.

Jonathan Rosenhead — Into the Swamp: The Analysis of Social Issues

Among the measures in the bill were arrangements for ballots on the opting-out of schools from local authority control. No research appears to have been conducted as to the attitudes of parents to local authority control, which would affect the response to the scheme. One possible interpretation of this lack is that the government was in the grip of an ideologically-based certainty — that parents would be falling over themselves to escape from local tyranny. If so, the assumption was incorrect; the take-up of opted-out status, despite significant financial inducements, proved so small as to be politically embarrassing. There is an alternative interpretation of the shedding of research or effective consultation in the breakneck rush to commitment — that it was motivated by the view that such proposals were unlikely to survive debate informed by analytic scrutiny.

Student loans

One of the companion measures to the school opt-out provision was the establishment of a student loan scheme. Grants were to be frozen, leaving students with the option of supplementing them with loans or suffering the privations of a growing inflationary gap. The proposal can be seen as part of a game plan (with other components) aimed at doubling the UK age participation rate in higher education without a matching increase in government expenditure.

Colleagues at LSE made major contributions to discussion on the student loan question. Their alternative proposals, and criticisms of the Government scheme, led to meetings with Ministers, economic advisors and other senior civil servants from both the Department of Education and Science and the Treasury. A loan scheme of this kind depends crucially for its workability on a range of very practical implications — the take-up rate, the accumulating size of debt, the administrative costs of repayments over the pay-back period, the default rate. It became clear at these meetings that it was LSE, not the Government, which had done its homework on such issues. In particular, the LSE group told the Government that their proposals could not be acceptable to the banks — who were supposed to administer it but, typically, had not been consulted. When, within a year, the banks — despite government pressure — withdrew, the Government was forced to establish its own independent student loan company, at still greater expense. At the time of writing there are still considerable doubts about the medium-term viability of the scheme.

A lack of prior analysis was only one dimension of the government's mishandling of the student loan question. It has been cited[16] as an 'extraordinary example' of an issue around which the basis for a policy consensus had already developed 'but which when translated into concrete proposals met with widespread, vociferous opposition.'

National Health Service reforms

By late 1987 the Government was under intense pressure over the National Health Service. Public opinion was aroused over under-funding and hospital bed closures; the Presidents of the Royal Colleges were even moved to sign an unprecedented joint warning about the state of the health service. It was in this atmosphere that Mrs Thatcher launched a 'boomerang'. In a television interview (with Jonathan Dimbleby) in early 1988 she announced that there would be a fundamental review of the NHS. When asked if this would be carried out by a Royal Commission, her response was negative. This was a thrusting government, and the review would be over within a year. The initiative was one of which the entire NHS and Department of Health, even to their top echelons, had no advance notice.

Within a year the Review was to achieve the complete redesign of an organization which, depending on the measures employed, could be classed as the third largest in the world. The avoidance of the Royal Commission format certainly permitted a faster pace, but at a cost. The Review was carried out in private by a Ministerial Committee with highly selected advisors. There was no Green Paper setting out first government thoughts, no general call for evidence, no background papers of analysis open to criticism. Discussions were of the principles of grandiose change, without detail or staff work.

The result of this was the White Paper *Working for Patients*[17] of February 1989. Its content emerged from a welter of discussion rather in the manner of a game of musical chairs — the outcome

Journal of the Operational Research Society Vol. 43, No. 4

depended on the state of play when the music stopped. Thus, only two weeks before the publication of *Working for Patients* the question of whether the main proposal, for an internal market between health purchaser and provider agencies, should be limited to hospital and primary care, or also embrace community care had still not been settled. Only two *days* before publication, an independent management expert was telephoned from the Policy Unit at 10 Downing Street. Advice was requested — on whether the National Health Service should have separate Management and Policy Boards, or a single board responsible for both functions. An idiosyncratic policy process, to say the least. Yet the scheme which emerged was legislated virtually unchanged, and pressured into operation by April 1991.

The Poll Tax

The last of these case studies of policy process without policy analysis concerns the introduction of the poll tax (the so-called 'Community Charge') as the mechanism for local taxation.

The background to this major convulsion, the key factor in the ejection of Margaret Thatcher as Conservative Leader and Prime Minister, was the continuing unpopularity of the existing rating system, a property-based tax, and a long-standing Conservative commitment to abolish it. For the first five years of the Thatcher administration this pledge was not acted on. Indeed a well-argued government Green Paper[18] concluded that none of the alternatives to domestic rates was acceptable.

There the matter might have rested, had it not been for the periodic revaluation of the rates which became necessary in Scotland in 1985. This resulted in a massive redistribution of the local tax burden with attendant political furore. At a public meeting held in Scotland, Mrs Thatcher cut the Gordian knot by throwing a boomerang from the hip. The rating system would be abolished in Scotland. In a flurry of improvised post-edict clarification, it was established that the change would, subsequently, apply to the rest of the country.

Hurried internal governmental studies eventually led to the selection of the poll tax as the new system. The selection process consisted of eliminating the other alternatives (local sales tax, local income tax etc) — on either administrative or ideological grounds.

As far as can be determined no significant studies were conducted of the wider economic consequences of the poll tax — its redistributive impact, its effect on inflation or pay-bargaining. Perhaps more seriously for the government, there was no adequate analysis of its differential impact on different sectors of the electorate before the decision was taken to go ahead. Indeed there seems not to have been an awareness that this was a researchable question.

A range of independent studies conducted between 1987 and 1990 (see Gibson[19]) revealed a pattern of winners and losers whose grim implications for the Government were only slowly appreciated. The redistribution of the tax burden resulting from the change favoured the very rich in large houses, but penalized multiple adult families in (for example) flats purchased from local authorities under the Government's own 'right-to-buy' legislation. The former group were committed Conservative voters; the latter were in many cases marginal voters on whom the Thatcher coalition crucially depended.

Despite this accumulation of evidence the Government persisted. As poll tax related violence spread in early 1990 even to the smaller towns of the comfortable South East, Conservative MPs without large majorities grew deeply apprehensive about their prospects. The scene was set for the Heseltine challenge for the Conservative leadership, the ousting of Margaret Thatcher, and the prompt ditching of the poll tax.

The various possible explanations of why the Government engaged in an attempt to 'tough it out' over the poll tax, even after both political reaction and analytic critiques had demonstrated its flaws even in terms of governmental self-interest, do not concern us here. The focus of this account has been on that earlier process which generated the Government's predicament. Margaret Thatcher's *ex cathedra* pronouncement broke the political log-jam over local taxation by creating new political 'facts'. But in the absence of effective analysis open to effective criticism, the outcome, of her 'flagship' legislation was quite different from the intention.

Jonathan Rosenhead — Into the Swamp: The Analysis of Social Issues

RETREAT FROM REASON

The purpose of recalling and recording these four case studies is not to assert that operational research-based analysis was in each case the vital missing ingredient — though in several cases it might have been instrumental in avoiding unintended effects and side-effects. Nor is it my view that all governmental policies under the recent administration were as badly prepared as these. Nor would I suggest that those policies which *did* have the benefit of analysis were appreciably more socially desirable than those which did not. Indeed, in terms of their divisiveness, inequity, philistinism, illiberality and short-sightedness all of these policies have much in common. The thrust of the present exposition, rather, is to draw attention to a different feature — the catastrophic retreat from reason in public affairs.

Such a feature is especially serious in a radically interventionist government. A key argument was well put 200 years ago:

An ignorant man, who is not fool enough to meddle with his clock, is, however, sufficiently confident to think he can safely take to pieces and put together, at his pleasure, a moral machine of another guise, importance and complexity, composed of far other wheels and springs and balances and counteracting and cooperating powers. Men little think how immorally they act in rashly meddling with what they do not understand.

Perhaps this quotation raises the knotty problem of whether Edmund Burke[20] can really be considered 'one of us'. Certainly it is capable of more than one interpretation. It can be read as an anthem to inaction — though one which is necessarily futile in turbulent times. However, it also makes a convincing call for better analysis.

Morality, then, as well as common-sense, suggests that governments should do their best to anticipate the consequences of significant reforms. This 'best' should include, where appropriate and by no means exclusively, the quantitative analysis of interaction between relevant factors.

If this holds for a radical right government, then it is still more true for a radical government of the left. Such a government can confidently expect a less supine and compliant media and would not wish, one hopes, to adopt the recent administration's bully-girl tactics to the press and broadcasting. It would therefore be more unmercifully exposed in any policy bungling through inadequate analysis. It follows that a radical left government would stand to gain from an active informed debate about policies ahead of commitment. (How this might be fostered will be considered shortly.) This would serve both to identify and eliminate proposals lacking cogency, and to generate the popular support which would be its principal bulwark in the tilted arena in which controversies are played out.

There is a second reason why a radical government of the left would have more reason to rely on reasoned analysis. This is that it would be less committed to the market as motor and arbiter of social choices.

This line of argument leads us back to the intellectual underpinnings of the recent government's extraordinary analytic record. For poverty of analysis does not spring from one person or personality, however powerful. There is now a widespread, almost hegemonic ideology which incorporates a semi-mystical belief in the beneficial properties of market forces. The underlying assertions are

(i) that through market forces individual preferences can find untramelled expression;
(ii) that the market handles the equilibration of supply and demand better than bureaucracy can; and,
(iii) that free competition provides an automatic mechanism for achieving efficiency improvements.

These assumptions underlie both the Conservative government programmes of the late 70s to early 90s, and the 'Public Choice' school of political analysis practised by right-wing think-tanks. The market is viewed as correcting Government failures (rather than vice versa). No matter that, as in so many instances of privatization (electricity, for example) the most intricate socio-economic engineering can only produce a market which is artificial, rigged, imperfect and imperfectable. Nevertheless, the market is seen, uncritically, as a pseudo-natural phenomenon which substitutes for the exercise of collectively rational choice. The down-grading of rational choice based on

Journal of the Operational Research Society Vol. 43, No. 4

analysis, then, is by no means an accidental, isolated phenomenon. It stems, rather, from the elevation of the market to almost divine, omnipotent, omniscient status.

The dominant position which this ideology holds is relatively new, and might yet prove to be short-lived. However, it has been prepared for and supported by a persistent current of thought associated with such names as Popper, Hayek and Lindblom. These are intellectuals who stress the weakness of predictive theory, and the limitations of cognitive capacity. They express deep pessimism about the rational solubility of social problems. Out of this matrix of ideas has developed a critique of 'hyper-rationalism', identified by Lindblom and Cohen,[12] and defined by Elster[21] as 'the irrational belief in the omnipotence of reason.'

There can be no doubt that hyper-rationalism was indeed both common and a problem in the boom days of the systems approach (which reached their peak in the middle 1960s). It is no longer a widespread phenomenon. On the contrary we now more commonly encounter a deformation of thinking about social organization which might be called 'hyper-irrationalism.' This I would define as 'a willful failure to concede a significant role to reason in the practice of collective decision-making.'

Hyper-irrationalism in an advanced society with large-scale enterprises and dense interconnectedness of policy issues is a recipe for disaster – for both market failure and government failure.

METHODS FOR COLLECTIVE RATIONALITY

There is a need, therefore, to rescue the concept of 'rationality' from those who a generation and more ago gave it a narrow, calculative and predictive interpretation as the elimination of the need for judgement. The meaning needs to be extended to include systemic approaches to the partial structuring of complexity and uncertainty to enrich and inform collective judgement, and so enable it to be employed with due confidence.

Methods for doing just this have recently emerged in some number from the discipline of operational research. Paradoxically, or perhaps not, they have grown from a trickle into a stream during the past dozen years of societal retreat from reason. These 'problem structuring methods', in distinction from the techniques which were developed in the 1950s and 1960s, do not have the aim of finding optimal solutions to well-formulated problems. Their function, rather, is of helping a group with disparate perspectives to agree nevertheless on a common problem focus and a shared commitment to action. Examples of these methods, and discussion of their applicability, can be found in Rosenhead.[22]

Problem structuring methods, like more conventional OR techniques, provide analytic help through the formal structuring of complexity. However, unlike their predecessors, problem structuring methods are transparent and participative, enabling rather than controlling. This increase in accessibility (and in the range of problem situations to which they can be applied) is bought at a price. This price is an abandonment of much of the mathematical formalism (continuous variables, algorithms, probabilities, trend extrapolation) which has, until recently, been the principal stock-in-trade of operational research. It is a bargain.

It is worth recalling the advice to those receiving advice, offered by someone with high level experience of policy analysis (and who took the chair at the delivery of this lecture): 'do not despise formal methodologies.' 'Rulers' are distrustful of them, but used knowledgeably and appropriately they can illuminate policy options[13]. Problem structuring methods reinforce that conclusion. For they provide forms of guidance particularly appropriate to the testing conditions of swamp navigation.

These methods are still relatively new. They have been developed disproportionately in Britain, and over a period in which, as we have seen, the British government was not over-concerned as to the quality of its advice. It is not therefore surprising that they have been little used so far in public policy analysis. Their application has been particularly evident at higher levels in private corporations, and in work for grass-roots community groups. (Some possible reasons for this jarring conjunction of clienteles is suggested in Rosenhead.[23])

There is ample scope for these methods in, and in relation to, government decision making.

Jonathan Rosenhead — Into the Swamp: The Analysis of Social Issues

(Indeed the rather different potentials of OR's more traditional methods have also been far from fully exploited.) There is scope:
- where complexities and inter-connectedness abound
- where uncertainties are high
- where issues cross departmental boundaries
- where diverse interests need to be taken into account
- where there are alternative versions of the nature of the problem
- where there are contending priorities for urgent action.

It would be superfluous to cite examples. These features are the rule rather than the exception in the public policy arena. They are also indicators for the potential relevance of problem structuring methods.

THE DISTRIBUTION OF ANALYSIS

It is not only government which suffers from a lack of appropriate analytic support. The case has been made above for greater government utilization of the methods of operational research, and particularly of problem structuring methods, in the preparation of policy. But just as we may not wish the devil to have all the best tunes, we can ask whether government should have all the best analysis.

Consider the effect of the abolition of the Central Policy Review Staff. This led to the centralization of policy advice on the Prime Minister rather than the Cabinet. The impact on the process of debate and criticism from which viable policy can emerge, and on the possibility of effective Cabinet responsibility, was negative. Multiple advocacy, one of the bases of sound policy making[24], was undermined.

The arguments for multiple advocacy, however, are not confined by Cabinet walls. Policy on important issues is not the product of a delimited group assembled at one place and time. Policy formation is, or should be, a more extensive process, which could benefit through enhanced multiple advocacy if analytic capability were more widely disseminated.

One example of such a scheme is proposed by Bennett and Pullinger[25]. They recommend the establishment of 'policy research and information units' for all Parliamentary Select Committees. Their purpose would be to make the committees' scrutiny of government policy more effective, but access to the units would also be available to individual MPs.

The principle can be extended also beyond Parliamentary boundaries. In many areas political parties would be better able to devise strategies and policies if they were to have the means of sifting through the multiple alternatives in a coherent way. One illustrative example is the Plant Committee[26], set up by the Labour Party in 1990 to explore the merits of alternative electoral systems. The Committee proceeded without access to staff support with an OR component. Yet the issue almost cries out for an operational research input (see Dunleavy *et al.*[27]) There is a range of alternative electoral arrangements which could be applied in various combinations to local, regional, national and European elective bodies; there are at least five, and perhaps as many as 13, major relevant criteria, and a wide variety of possible voting patterns to consider. There is, of course, no objectively 'best' electoral system. That is a matter of judgement, and one on which different individuals and interests will differ. However, there are a number of OR methods which would be of considerable value to any particular grouping in finding its way through the complexity — in the identification of a problem focus, the elimination of dominated options, the elicitation of requisite preference information, the structuring of short-lists etc.

So we have a developing picture of problem-structuring assistance to Prime Ministers, Cabinet, Parliamentarians, parties. But there is no need to regard analytic advice as a privilege for those active in formal politics. Advanced societies are thickly populated with organized groups each pursuing or defending the particular interest which unites its members, whether at national or local level. These organizations include:
- community centres
- Community Health Councils
- housing cooperatives

Journal of the Operational Research Society Vol. 43, No. 4

- parent-teacher associations
- pressure groups
- production cooperatives
- tenants associations
- trade union branches

Many could never afford full-time analytic support, but are nevertheless involved from time to time as participants (or victims) in problematic engagements whose resolution is significant both to their members and to other sections of society. Analytic assistance, including that of an OR-nature, can help them to clarify unresolvable uncertainties which reveal the need for flexibility. It can help them to appreciate the positions of other groups in relation to their own, and so identify possible coalitions and negotiating strategies. It can help them to prepare a case which will carry credibility in the public arena.

The quality of the political process at all levels will be greatly improved when its participants and potential participants can prepare and present their cases more adequately, and position themselves more effectively in the policy space. Active citizenry will become a reality when we have institutions to support informed debate.

There are a number of models already available for how such support might be provided. In the Netherlands there are 'science shops', offering scientific and technological information and advice in the high street. In Stockholm there is Arbetslivcentrum (the Swedish Centre for Working Life), an independent institute for practical interdisciplinary research on work-life issues, funded by a wage tax paid by all employers.

There are also examples in Britain. The Royal Town Planning Institute established 'Planning Aid' to help individuals and groups otherwise disadvantaged by lack of professional advice. In the context of this paper the Community Operational Research initiative of the Operational Research Society is particularly relevant[28, 29]. The Society has set up (with support from a number of charitable foundations) a Community Operational Research Unit at Northern College outside Barnsley, in association with Sheffield City Polytechnic. The purpose of the Unit is to carry out OR studies for community groups. In parallel, a network of several hundred volunteers has sprung up around the country, for information exchange and the execution of community operational research projects. This movement is still developing.

The question of how to provide disseminated analytic support would repay further study. It is likely that a multiplicity of forms and channels should be adopted for this provision. As yet the necessary units to carry out this work do not exist in sufficient numbers, and would need to be brought into being. We will need a substantial and continuing growth in the number of think-tanks and research institutes with a pragmatic commitment to applied policy analysis. This necessary development will probably require a matching programme of funding both for analytic provider agencies as well as for classes of user organizations. Direct funding of the applied policy analysis units should be one component: it will provide scope for pursuing and developing self-generated topics which might not initially be perceived as a priority by any individual potential client. Particular think-tanks will no doubt specialize in particular application areas. However, the characteristic orientation should be towards interdisciplinary studies, within which operational research would be one component.

Provision of this capability will not be cheap, but it will be cheap at the price. What we buy with such a package is the opening-up and enrichment of policy debate, with the consequent sharpening of the critical process out of which policies emerge.

In an increasingly information-rich society, the ability to analyse that information as it affects one's own interests is a pre-requisite for effective involvement in the democratic process. The 'Right to Information', although fundamental, may be of limited use by itself. Indeed, bureaucrats can as well hide the facts by 'swamping' people in information as by withholding it. There should also be, in an Information Society, the Right to Analysis. 'Liberty! Fraternity' Analytic Capability!' has an unfamiliar ring to it. But then, no doubt so did the original rallying cry of 200 years ago.

Acknowledgements—In preparing this paper I had the advantage of discussion, advice and information from John Ashworth, Gordon Best, James Cornford, Iain Crawford, Pat Dunleavy, Richard Gibbs, Howard Glennerster, Christopher

Jonathan Rosenhead — Into the Swamp: The Analysis of Social Issues

Hood, Brendan O'Leary, Colin Thunhurst and Tony Travers. I could not have written it without them; though they have, of course, no responsibility for the use which I have made of their material.

REFERENCES

1. E. S. QUADE (1975) *Analysis for Public Decisions*. American Elsevier, New York.
2. D. A. SCHON (1987) *Educating the Reflective Practitioner: Towards a New design for Teaching and Learning in the Professions*. Jossey-Bass, San Francisco.
3. J. ROSENHEAD (1989) Operational research at the crossroads: Cecil Gordon and the development of post-war OR. *J. Opl Res. Soc.* **40**, 3–28.
4. J. ROSENHEAD (1991) Swords into ploughshares: Cecil Gordon's role in the post-war transition of operational research to civilian uses. *Public Administration* **69**, 481–501.
5. T. BLACKSTONE and W. PLOWDEN (1988) *Into the Think Tank: Advising the Cabinet 1971–1983*. Heinemann, London.
6. J. ROSENHEAD (1989) Introduction: old and new paradigms of analysis. In *Rational Analysis for a Problematic World: Problem Structuring Methods for Complexity, Uncertainty and Conflict* (J. ROSENHEAD, Ed.) pp. 1–20. Wiley, Chichester.
7. R. R. NELSON (1974) Intellectualizing about the moon-ghetto metaphor: a study of the current malaise of rational analysis of social problems. *Policy Sci.* **5**, 375–414.
8. Y. DROR (1971) *Ventures in Policy Sciences*. American Elsevier, New York.
9. S. S. NAGEL (1984) *Contemporary Public Policy Analysis*. University of Alabama Press, University, Alabama.
10. R. PORTER (1987) The United States. In *Advising the Rulers* (W. PLOWDEN, Ed.) pp. 86–91. Blackwell, Oxford.
11. J. K. FRIEND and A. HICKLING (1987) *Planning Under Pressure*. Pergamon, Oxford.
12. C. E. LINDBLOM and D. K. COHEN (1979) *Usable Knowledge: Social Science and Social Problem Solving*. Yale University Press, New Haven, Connecticut.
13. J. M. ASHWORTH (1982) On the giving and receiving of advice (in Whitehall and Salford). Presented at Manchester Statistical Society, 16 November, 1982.
14. W. PLOWDEN (Ed.) (1987) *Advising the Rulers*. Blackwell, Oxford.
15. D. WILLETS (1987) The role of the Prime Minister's Policy Unit. *Public Administration* **65**, 443–454.
16. S. FARRELL and E. TAPPER (1991) *Student Loans: the Failure to Consolidate an Emerging Political Consensus*. School of English and American Studies, University of Sussex, Brighton (mimeo).
17. Department of Health (1989), *Working for Patients*. HMSO (Cmnd. 555), London.
18. Department of the Environment (1981) *Alternatives to Domestic Rates*. HMSO (Cmnd. 8449), London.
19. J. GIBSON (1990) *The Politics and Economics of the Poll Tax: Mrs. Thatcher's Downfall*. EMAS, Warley.
20. E. BURKE (1791). Quoted by E. S. QUADE (1975) *Analysis for Public Decisions*. American Elsevier, New York.
21. J. ELSTER (1989) *Solomonic Judgements: Studies in the Limitations of Rationality*. Cambridge University Press, Cambridge.
22. J. ROSENHEAD (Ed.) (1989) *Rational Analysis for a Problematic World: Problem Structuring Methods for Complexity, Uncertainty and Conflict*. Wiley, Chichester.
23. J. ROSENHEAD (1986) Custom and Practice. *J. Opl Res. Soc.* 37, 335–343.
24. Y. DROR (1984) Policy analysis for advising rulers. In *Rethinking the Process of Operational Research and Systems Analysis* (R. TOMLINSON and I. KISS, Eds.) pp. 79–123. Pergamon, Oxford.
25. P. BENNETT and S. PULLINGER (1991) *Making the Commons Work: Information, Analysis and Accountability*. Institute for Public Policy Research, London.
26. Working Party on Electoral Systems (1991) *Interim Report*. Labour Party, London.
27. P. DUNLEAVY, H. MARGETTS and others (1991) *Alternative Electoral Systems for the UK*. United Kingdom Political Studies Association, Salford.
28. C. THUNHURST (1991) Community Operational Research: thinking globally whilst acting locally. In *Operational Research '90* (H. E. BRADLEY, Ed.) pp. 23–35. Pergamon, Oxford.
29. R. PARRY and J. MINGERS (1991) Community operational research: its content and its future. *Omega* 19, 577–586.

Option Appraisal: Turning an Art into a Science?

Denise McAlister

This paper discusses the role of option appraisal in the decision-making processes of government departments. The paper divides into three main parts. First, the background to the introduction of option appraisal is discussed briefly. Second, the current state of the art of option appraisal is examined. Finally, the paper reflects on the organizational constraints and political pressures which are likely to affect the impact that the technique will have on the way in which service developments are conceived and evaluated.

Introduction

Since the 1960s there has been an increasing awareness of the need in all sectors of the British economy to improve efficiency and to introduce economic policies which would help upgrade performance across both public and private sectors. As Sir Robert Armstrong (1985) stated:

> *The economic recession of the late seventies and very early eighties forced industrial and commercial concerns, for the sake of sheer survival, to make themselves as efficient and as productive as they could. The public service is not exposed to the disciplines of the market place. Nonetheless, it is spending the taxpayers' money, and there is no less need for it than for the private sector to be as efficient and productive as possible and for the introduction of disciplines and systems that will bring that about.*

The economic recession thus gave an impetus to the assessment and development of various rational techniques that might be used within a planning framework. One could catalogue a number of activities, for example PAR, MINIS, Rayner Scrutinies (Likierman, 1982; Gray and Jenkins, 1982, 1983), which were directed specifically at the civil service during this period. The process of improved internal financial management was given even greater impetus with the launch, in May 1982, of the Financial Management Initiative (Cmnd 8616). And there were a number of other initiatives across much of the rest of the public sector (Flynn, 1990; Taylor and Popham, 1989).

Yet it might be argued that is only during the past eight years that the pursuit of efficiency has become really evident, to such an extent that efficiency may now be said to be a dominant theme in current political and economic thinking in government departments and other public sector bodies. These various initiatives should not be regarded as being independent of each other, but are, perhaps, better regarded as parts of the one process, the pursuit of an efficiency

strategy for the public sector. Such a strategy reflects the beliefs of the Conservative Government in the superiority of the private sector management model and the presumed transportability of private sector managerial acumen and techniques into the public sector.

Against this background of restraint in the public sector, and a renewed emphasis on the need to ensure that limited resources are used in the most efficient and effective way, the Treasury published guidelines (Treasury, 1982, 1983, 1984) on the use of investment appraisal (also referred to as option/project appraisal) techniques in the public sector. The approach is intended to aid departments determine priorities, a short-hand term for criteria which help to allocate limited resources between competing uses in the absence of market mechanisms. It is but one of a range of quantitative approaches to the problems of resource allocation within government. It merits specific attention since it is a necessary but not sufficient prerequisite for obtaining Treasury and/or departmental approval for capital funding.

Definition of Option Appraisal

Mooney & Henderson (1986) define option appraisal as:

> *a systematic examination of all the advantages and disadvantages of each practicable alternative way of solving some problem or ameliorating some deficiency, with the purpose of promoting efficiency through informing rather than determining decisions.*

It can best be thought of as that part of economic appraisal which is concerned with comparing alternative strategies from the perspective of economic efficiency.

To an economist the term 'efficiency' has two aspects. The first, *allocative efficiency*, is concerned with whether society's scarce resources have been allocated in accordance with the preferences and constraints of the consumers of the final products.

Denise McAlister is Senior Lecturer in Public Finance and Economics at the University of Ulster.

More simply, allocative efficiency seeks to ensure that the best level and mix of goods and services is provided from available resources. The second dimension is *technical-* or *X-efficiency*, which refers to the supply side. Here the concern is to ensure that, regardless of the optimum level or mix of goods and services decided upon, i.e. allocative efficency, those goods and services are produced at the lowest possible cost.

Efficiency is a relevant perspective since, given scarcity, there are not and never will be sufficient resources to undertake all the worthwhile objectives that can be identified. The problem is, therefore, how to decide which projects should be undertaken. Choice implies the notion of sacrifice or benefits foregone. That is why economists often refer to the notion of *opportunity cost*, that is, the cost of a resource is equal to the benefits that it would have generated in its best alternative use. Efficiency implies that projects should be compared not only in terms of their relative benefits, or effectiveness, but also in terms of their relative costs, i.e. the benefits foregone. In other words, it is not enough to provide benefits, but to ensure that the benefits provided outweigh any alternative use to which the resources involved could be put. The goal of efficiency is to maximize the excess of benefits over costs. The purpose of appraisal is to promote efficiency by providing a 'vehicle for structuring questions about policy and lending these an arithmetic cast' (Colvin, 1985).

At its heart the approach is inherently rational. Rational, that is, in the economic sense. The flavour of this perspective on rationality is neatly summarized by Colvin (1985) as follows:

> *An important facet of rationality, and one that is of great significance ... is the practice of resolving all economic questions into problems of counterpoint ... Rational behaviour in the Neoclassical sense is centered upon given ends and given means. It is this pair of concepts, this counterpoint, that is fundamental to the structure of micro-economic theory, so much so that economics is replete with pairs of concepts that in varying degrees reproduce the symmetry of the ends-means dyad: demand and supply, needs and satisfactions, outputs and inputs, benefits and costs.*

Rationality, in other words, is about relating means to determined objectives or goals and it is this juxtaposition that has had important consequences for the economic methodology. Option appraisal provides a framework which is based on a very broad notion of what constitutes a rational decision. Rational analysis involves the evaluation of alternatives using a consistent set of criteria. Proponents of individual options are usually strongly placed to argue the merits and demerits of their particular project and will frequently use non-comparable criteria to denegrate or promote particular alternatives. However, comparative analysis often involves weighting conflicting criteria against one another

rather than weighting different options using the same set of consistent criteria. Hence, in this important sense, as Laver (1986) argues, actual debate is explicitly non-rational. Nevertheless, trading-off and weighting different criteria is frequently necessary in order to arrive at a decision. Even in a simplified example where the choice concerns a decision to purchase outright or lease an identical piece of equipment, differential criteria may apply. Not purchasing the equipment outright may confer a degree of flexibility which may be valuable especially if there is a high risk of obsolescence. Outright purchase, on the other hand, may avoid the problems associated with unfavourable conditions being written in to the leasing agreement.

Herein lies one of the purported strengths of this approach since, in theory, option appraisal aims to provide a framework whereby differing choices can be evaluated by reference to a common set of criteria. The practice is, however, more difficult to achieve since it implies some common unit of measurement and there is no generally accepted common denominator. So evaluation will inevitably entail comparing the non-comparable. How do we compare, for example, the benefits of a more varied curriculum made possible by the rationalization of schools with the greater costs to some staff and students of reduced accessibility? Yet in making difficult choices we have to do this anyway, and we do it using value-ridden criteria which may be explicit or implicit. The advantage of option appraisal is that it enables such assumptions to be made more explicit.

Stages in the Option Appraisal Process

The stages involved in carrying out an option appraisal are as follows:

Stage 1
• Define the problem.
• Set the associated objective.
• Identify and consider the options.

Stage 2
• Identify the costs, benefits, timing and uncertainties of each option.
• Discount costs and benefits.
• Weigh up uncertainties by sensitivity analysis.
• Assess intangibles.
• Presentation of results.

Stage 3
• Monitoring and ex post appraisal.

There are essentially three main stages to the appraisal process. This apparently logical sequence is frequently not observed in practice for some of the reasons discussed below and is complicated by problems and constraints which need to be dealt with at each stage. These include, *inter alia*, ill-defined objectives, unclear or conflicting criteria, imperfect knowledge and uncertainty about future scenarios.

Stage 1: Defining the Problem

The process begins with a definition, or outline, of the problem to be addressed. Often what is defined as a problem is really a combination of problems and the various strands need to be separated and identified. Public sector organizations sometimes suffer from the mistaken belief that what they do is so self-evidently beneficial so that the more of it that they do, the better. Questioning the rationale for the activities proposed is frequently noticeably absent. The need for action can be identified as emanating from a reactive situation or a proactive initiative. A government department, for instance, may be reacting to a perceived problem (for example overcrowded accommodation), or may be initiating a scheme on the basis of a current or future deficiency against prescribed standards of service (for example unfit dwellings), or as an integrated part of a service strategy (for example computerization of benefit payments).

Recognition and identification of the need for something to be done will entail at least a description, and wherever possible, quantification of the problem, making reference where appropriate to statutory responsibilities and highlighting any significant political, social or environmental factors. The likely consequences, both present and future, of not tackling the problem should be outlined.

A local educational authority, for example, may wish to make a case for improved accommodation in one of its secondary schools. It cites a General Inspection report which highlighted a number of educational problems; a number of existing rooms are undersized, some of the practical subjects lack purpose-built accommodation, storage facilities are inadequate, and a large number of temporary classrooms and the sprawling development of the permanent accommodation results in tortuous and partially uncovered circulation routes. Here the perceived problems need to be explored in more detail. To what extent are rooms undersized? How inadequate are the facilities? To what courses do they relate? These questions can be given some quantitative measurement.

Setting the Associated Objective

The objective of the appraisal is simply a question or statement that indicates what it is that undertaking the appraisal is designed to achieve. Henderson (1984) stated that normally the objective will take one of the following forms:

(1) What, or how much, is it worth doing about the problem?
(2) What is the least costly way of doing a specified amount to solve or ameliorate the problem?
(3) What is the best way of spending a specified amount of resources on solving or ameliorating the problem?

These statements really clarify if the appraisal to be carried out is a Cost Benefit Analysis (CBA) or a Cost Effectiveness Analysis (CEA). If the question or objective is framed as in (1) above, a CBA is being carried out. CBA attempts to assess the worthwhileness, absolute and/or relative, of an expenditure proposal. The efficiency criterion here is based on an assessment of the relative benefits and the relative costs of programmes. The range of benefits and costs to be considered should be comprehensive and will be necessarily heterogeneous. Some common measure of value is therefore required if a wide range of disparate costs and benefits are to be compared. One approach is to use monetary values as the measuring rod, although in principle anything would do. Analyses which attempt to value the beneficial consequences of a programme in money terms so as to make them commensurate with the costs are usually referred to as cost-benefit analyses. In practice, however, few cost-benefit appraisals provide estimates of all the costs and benefits in money terms and often omit intangible items.

Questions (2) and (3) refer to the more limited technique of CEA. CEA is appropriate when comparing two or more ways of meeting the same objective.

If, for example, two alternative proposals meet an objective equally well, then the less costly would be chosen on efficiency or cost-effectiveness grounds. CEA is useful in comparing programmes whose effects or outcomes are measured in the same physical units. No attempt is made to value the effects, so the approach cannot therefore be used to compare disparate projects or projects that have multiple effects, nor does it say anything about whether the objective is worth attaining.

A further type of appraisal, known as cost-utility analysis, is useful where projects have more than one dimension of output associated with them. In this approach utilities are used as a measure of the value of programme effects and can be assessed directly or indirectly by reference to the preferences of individuals or members of the general public. Different outputs or effects have to be converted into a composite index before the effectiveness of the project can be determined.

One such index, which is sometimes used in the evaluation of health-care programmes, is the Quality Adjusted Life Year (or QALY), which is a weighted composite index of a number of different dimensions of health effects.

QALYs provide a quantified index of people's judgements of the quality of life associated with different states of health. This facilitates comparison of benefits between radically different types of therapies using a common unit of value which can then be linked to the costs of the therapies. For example, if a typical patient has an

46

additional life expectancy of five years after undergoing therapy X, and the quality of life scores for each of those five years are 0.6, 0.6, 0.4, 0.3, and 0.2, the benefit from that procedure will typically equal 2.1 QALYs. By contrast, therapy Y yields an additional life expectancy of three years, with quality of life scores for each of those three years of 0.7, 0.6, and 0.4 i.e. 1.7 QALYs in total. We can conclude, therefore, that therapy X is more effective than therapy Y, but whether it is more cost-effective will also depend on the relative costs of the two therapies. Suppose, for example, that X costs £6300 and therapy Y costs £3400, then the cost of producing one QALY under X is £3000 as opposed to £2000 under Y. Since the cost per QALY for X is dearer than for Y we can conclude that therapy X is less cost-effective than therapy Y.

It should be stressed that these clear distinctions between the various types of analyses are made for purely pedagogic reasons. In real life the distinctions are frequently blurred with many appraisals taking the form of modified cost-effectiveness analyses.

It is particularly important to ensure that the problem and objective should not be defined in such a way as to unduly restrict or bias the identification of relevant options. Wherever possible published statements about objectives should be referred to. A government health department, for example, that has a stated objective to reduce deaths from cardiovascular disease should not simply confine its attention to primary care methods of intervention for example health education or the taxation and regulation of disease-inducing products but should also consider tertiary prevention and treatment, for example coronary care ambulances or care units in hospitals. This is to ensure that the definition does not, at this stage, take the form of a proposal to spend or commit resources to a specific programme or item. The wider the scope of the appraisal the more confident it is possible to be that witting and unwitting biases will be avoided and the most appropriate strategy chosen.

Identify and Consider the Options

A greater understanding of the process by which options are identified and generated for consideration is still one of the crucial missing links in the appraisal process, as many writers, for example Gunn and Hogwood (1984), evaluating the importance of the technique in the field of public policy stress. It is suggested that while there may be techniques available to assist the individual to appraise options, insufficient attention is paid to where these options come from. Are many options considered or just a few? Who decides what options are to be considered and by what means?

Prescriptively it might be considered wasteful to concentrate limited analytical resources on the technical appraisal of specific proposals, if the options have been identified and selected by arbitrary or biased procedures, because, in the final analysis, the potential usefulness of an option appraisal depends less on the quality of the subsequent underlying technical appraisal, although that is important, than on the ability to find good options or solutions to the problems under investigation. In practice insufficient time is sometimes spent on considering whether all reasonable alternatives have been explored, and how any particular proposal might be improved. The inevitable consequence of this is that there is a tendency for the appraisal process to begin when the options have been identified, rather than letting the process of appraisal contribute, as it should, in helping to justify, refine, question or change the objectives. Such oversight will lead, at best, to failure to identify some good options, and at worst misjudgement of the true nature of the problem.

In summary, then, the fundamentals of project justification can be brought out through explicit consideration of the following questions:

• Why is the project necessary?
• What is it designed to achieve?
• What are the various alternative ways of achieving it and to what degree?

Stage 2: Identify the Costs, Benefits, Timing and Uncertainties of Each Option

The second stage of the process entails an assessment of the costs and benefits of the options under consideration. This process can itself be broken down into the distinct stages of:

• Enumeration.
• Measurement.
• Explicit valuation.
• Allowance for differential timing and uncertainty.

Enumeration involves the identification of all the relevant changes brought about by the alternatives being appraised. Most of these changes are in the direction of extra resource use (costs). The range of costs and benefits to be considered poses a number of measurement problems, not least the fact that appraisals of the efficiency of choices requires evidence of their effectiveness. In fact, of course, it is not benefits that are difficult, and costs that are easy, to measure.

When market *valuations* are available they are often accepted and are broadly acceptable as indicators of the value of benefits or costs if the prices reflect society's valuations of the final services and resources involved. Problems arise, however, if market prices are not deemed to truly reflect value or if they are non-existent. In the former case, prices taken from uncompetitive markets may have to be adjusted, whilst in the latter, indirect evidence is sought regarding the values which individuals place on such benefits or costs. For example, travel time is often valued by reference to the different choices travellers make between modes of transport and different fare structures, and time spent travelling. Nevertheless whilst economists have made progress in assigning monetary values to a diverse range of programme outcomes, the underlying assumptions necessary to make these estimates often render the analysis vulnerable to criticism in public debate. In health care and urban road appraisal, for example, it is frequently necessary to attempt to place monetary values on pain and grief suffered as a result of death or personal injury, not to mention loss of life itself. In such instances, if a measure is suggested, the appraiser is accused of attempting to measure the immeasurable. If no measure is suggested, then the accusation is made that the approach has failed to produce answers which are any better than those which would have been achieved by a simple political or planning decision.

One useful and pragmatic approach to the problem of unquantifiables in benefit estimation is the weighting and scoring approach, also known as multi-attribute or multi-criterion evaluation. Its purpose is to attach numeric values to people's judgements. Its advantage is that it forces appraisers to consider carefully and explicitly the relative benefits that would be achieved by the respective options. It is thus important that those carrying out the exercise are knowledgeable in the area that is being assessed and that the process does not simply reflect the views of a single person or group. The results of such exercises also need careful interpretation. This is because of the subjective nature of the process. Nevertheless, the approach can assist in drawing attention to important factors which have not been quantified and help identify significant differences between options in regard to these factors.

The money values of costs and benefits should normally be expressed in 'real', as opposed to 'nominal', terms, that is the future streams of benefits and costs should exclude any element of future general inflation. Only if changes are expected to be significantly greater or less than the general rate of inflation do price changes need to be taken into account. Whilst the use of real values in the UK reflects the particular preferences of HM Treasury, the use of nominal values is also legitimate. Whichever method is adopted, the essential point is consistency of approach.

Discount the Costs and Benefits

One further problem faced in estimating the benefits and costs of any measure or policy is that they normally will not accrue at the one point in time but will be spread over a number of years. In general, individuals are not indifferent to the timing of costs and benefits. They normally prefer to receive goods, i.e. benefits, sooner rather than later and to postpone costs for as long as possible. In the economist's jargon they are said to have *positive time preference*. The relevance of the existence of time preference is that it means that we cannot treat each unit of benefit or cost as being of equal value regardless of when it occurs. Since preferences count, we must somehow downgrade or discount a benefit, or cost, in the future compared to a benefit, or cost, now. The normal way of reflecting this time preference is through discounting which allows a future stream of benefits or costs to be equated with a certain sum now, the present value. Feldstein (1964) defines the discount rate calculation as:

> *a functional relationship that makes output at different points in time commensurable with each other by assigning them equivalent present values.*

But why should we assume that the discount rate will be positive? Firstly, expected future consumption is subject to risk and uncertainty and people generally require compensation for risk-bearing. Secondly, it is rationally implied by the inevitability of death. Thirdly, as the level of real consumption per head of a community increases, each absolute addition to it will yield successively smaller increases in economic welfare. In economist's jargon, the marginal utility of consumption decreases through time. Fourthly, society simply prefers the present to the future: there is 'pure myopia'.

Whilst it is accepted that future real benefits and costs need to be discounted at some percentage rate so that they can be compared with benefits and costs now, disagreement arises among many economists as to the percentage rate which should apply, particularly in relation to the public sector. The literature devoted to this issue is vast. Yet, in practice, the foundation for the discount rate to be used in the public sector is clear. The rate, known as the *test discount rate*, reflecting the average rate of return on private investment, is determined by the Treasury and is currently fixed at a real or inflation-adjusted rate of 6%.

Weigh-up Uncertainties through Sensitivity Analysis

Often, measures of costs and benefits have to rely upon estimates or assumptions that may be unreliable. This unreliability arises mainly from two sources. First, perfectly accurate information is rarely available. Second, the future is inevitably uncertain. Clearly, estimates of costs and benefits become increasingly difficult with the remoteness of the period in which they occur. Many strategies for dealing with uncertainty have been suggested, none wholly satisfactory. One suggestion is to assign a higher discount rate than would otherwise be appropriate. The argument here is that, as a rough guide, uncertainty increases exponentially with time, and, in the absence of a corrective, there is a consistent bias to overestimate certain magnitudes.

In practice, a reasonably eclectic and

frequently satisfactory resolution is to do a sensitivity analysis on particular elements of benefit and cost estimation. This procedure involves assigning alternative values to some of these estimates with a view to assessing, what impact, if any, such a change will have on the final outcome or recommendation. Many uncertain magnitudes do not matter; those that do can be looked at more carefully to see if the estimation can be made more precise. Assumptions which remain especially uncertain should be highlighted as such in the final presentation of the results. Notwithstanding the usefulness of sensitivity analysis in dealing with the problem of uncertainty in appraisals, there is still considerable scope for improvements in how studies deal with uncertainty especially in appraisals concerning technology assessment. Use of techniques such as robustness analysis (Rosenhead, 1984), and other approaches to decision-making under uncertainty (Fischhoff, Lichenstein, Slovic, Derby and Keeney, 1981), need to be developed in this area.

Presentation of Results

The objective of appraisal is to provide managers with the best information available to reach a decision on the choice of option. It follows then that summarizing the findings and presenting them in a clear and concise manner is an important part of the appraisal process.

Although the final choice clearly rests with management rather than with the appraisal team, the option appraisal should attempt to highlight the significant issues, including key assumptions and major uncertainties that are felt to be relevant to the final decision.

Stage 3: Monitoring and Ex Post Appraisal

The final stage of the process of appraisal should involve monitoring and ex post evaluation. Once the project has been implemented this will necessitate reviewing the original assumptions, estimates and forecasts of costs and benefits to discover which ones have been borne out in practice and, even more importantly, which have not and why they have not. The purpose of this is not to apportion blame, but, rather, to improve future planning by providing useful feedback into the project appraisal process.

Distinct from monitoring is the retrospective appraisal. Such appraisals may be carried out :

• To help with the development of new policy, by comparing the results of past policies with the results of possible alternatives.
• As part of a pre-planned review.
• To check the success of past policy-making or management procedures.
• To meet the requirements of public accountability.

Option Appraisal and the Policy Process

The realistic use of economic appraisal must be based on an awareness of the tentative and value-laden nature of its results. Although the approach can assist in establishing matters of fact and narrow areas of disagreement, different value judgements will lead to different conclusions. Too much emphasis therefore on the consensus-generating role would be misguided. Value diversity is a basic ingredient in organizations and economic appraisal cannot impose a common mould. The technique frequently assists more in helping to clarify the important dimensions of a problem and to identify differing stakeholders than it does in specifying optimum choices. By enhancing the debate surrounding policy and programme choices, appraisal seeks to raise the quality of that debate which typically mirrors prejudice rather than reasoned argument.

The desirability of the information provided by the approach is undeniable. Nevertheless, there are conceptual and practical difficulties to be overcome in providing the information, particularly in political settings, characterized as they are by conflicting values and perspectives. Value judgements in option appraisal are unavoidable. What matters is that they should be made explicit. The reason why this is important is that in a prescriptive discipline, such as economic appraisal, it is conceivable that applying a different set of value judgements may lead to a different conclusion or recommendation. Appraisals tend to be sensitive to the value judgements underpinning them. It is therefore important to know what value judgements are being applied, what alternative ones might be used and their effect, if any, on the result.

Effective appraisal will require sensitivity and responsiveness to its users and those likely to be affected by its use: policy-makers, employees, clients. The information on costs and benefits which is generated in the course of an appraisal needs to be considered in decision-making contexts by the affected parties. Awareness of the political, organizational, social and psychological contexts in which decisions are taken is therefore as important as the application of technical skills. Of course, within these constraints there are still opportunities to improve decision-making through the use of systematic analysis. Whilst the outcome will certainly depend on the resolution of the different value judgements which might apply, the appraisal process helps to clarify and inform but not resolve such judgements. Appraisal does have a useful contribution to make, but it is necessarily a partial one. It must be complemented by other sources of feedback including political evaluation which may itself be an appropriate form of analysis. It is, nevertheless, a useful supplement and corrective, to traditional selection criteria, which, because they lack explicit ways of evaluating choices, allow personality to dominate discussions - with enthusiasts wanting to rush in where sceptics fear to tread.

Analysts, especially economists, also encounter challenges to their way of thinking from other professionals. The economists' emphasis on economic rationality can come into conflict with codes which apply in professions such as medicine, social work and policing. The contentious point relates to an attempt by the professional to affirm their professional rights and ethical codes as against the economist's desire to impose rational criteria. In addition, many professionals in the public sector feel threatened by appraisal. Greater effort must be directed to encourage professionals in the belief that appraisal does not seek to ursurp their influence as professionals, but to enable this expert opinion, or, more cynically, collective ignorance, to be displayed more systematically, and if necessary questioned, by facilitating the aggregation of knowledge from a variety of professional areas.

The organizational environment in which appraisal takes place is very important. Some view appraisal as just another move in a game to be played between the different management tiers. They regard it as an additional obstacle to be surmounted before funds will be approved for specific proposals. Frequently it is seen as a delaying mechanism with otherwise comprehensive appraisals being returned to organizations or departments for minor adjustments which, whilst they might perfect on the mathematics of the exercise, will not affect the relative rankings of projects nor reverse their absolute worthwhileness. Such tactics only frustrate and in some cases undermine what practical appraisal is supposed to be about. A recent example involves cases were appraisals were returned to organizations for revision of calculations following the change in the Treasury test discount rate. Others regard formal evaluation as being irrelevant anyway if success at securing political support locally supersedes the results of appraisals.

This latter point lends support to the accusation that appraisals are frequently used for political purposes to advance a case or protect an organization from outside interference, rather than for purely evaluative reasons. The impact of decisions taken on political grounds cannot be overlooked, and will seek to undermine the impact which formal appraisal will have. As Ludbrook and Mooney (1984) rightly point out, no matter now strong the arguments for the technique, decision-making also encompasses the political dimension. However, this should not be viewed as a defeatist or negative approach, as economic appraisal may affect political judgements and not merely be the recipient of them.

Managers often comment that the risks of abuse of appraisal outweigh the benefits of its proper use. But proponents of abolishing the use of option appraisal should beware. The problems the approach was designed to address will remain.

Option appraisal is a tool, an evaluative tool. Like all tools it can be used badly. It can also be used well.

What is clear from an examination of the use of option appraisal techniques in public sector organizations is that the practice is very piecemeal and heterogeneous. Some service areas, for example health and housing, seem more advanced overall in their level of sophistication in applying the technique than other areas like education and economic development. Nevertheless there is still considerable variation in practice within the more advanced areas. Examples of good and bad appraisals can be identified since standardization of practice and quality assurance in appraisals is still rather poor. Furthermore, what are considered by some to be acceptable appraisals are in practice often less than comprehensive, and perhaps not surprisingly, their contribution to the decision-making process is questionable.

When questioned about the poor quality or lack of appraisals being undertaken, managers will point to staff shortages and the dearth of personnel equipped to undertake such evaluation. Appraisal is seen as a process which is both time-consuming and technical. The idea of appraisal being essentially a way of thinking is noticeably absent.

Perhaps it is not surprising that in the early stages of the introduction of the technique more attention is devoted to the technical and numerical parts of the technique rather than to its underlying process. There is recent evidence however, that some organizations are attempting to standardize procedures for dealing with problems of recurrent spending - for example urban renewal schemes, housing action areas etc.

Considerable time has been spent in describing traps for the unwary. However, the mere existence of such traps would be a poor reason for not advancing. As suggested, excellent progress has already been made in some parts of the public sector. Further practical experimentation is the best way to spot the traps and avoid them.

It does seem, however, that certain sets of conditions are likely to enhance the chances of an option appraisal being perceived as a useful adjunct to the usual decision-making processes. These include:

• A prevailing attitude that value for money is important.
• A predilection of Ministers and key personnel to evaluation.
• Narrow and reasonably well-defined objectives.
• Clear profiles of projected costs and benefits clear and fall within administrative jurisdictions of spending departments.
• The availability and effective use of specialist advice.
• A multi-disciplinary approach to appraisal.
• Clear procedural and technical guidance.
• Integration with the consultative process.

50

• A healthy recognition of the inherent limitations of appraisal.
• Effective incentives for good appraisal.

Conclusion

Option appraisal as a criterion for policy choice is appealing. There is a temptation to believe 'that benefit-cost analysis is a mechanical substitute for common sense'. However, as Gramlich (1981) continues, 'nothing could be further from the truth. Benefit-cost analysis is really a framework for organizing thoughts...'.

Such a modest approach to economic appraisal will avoid exaggerated claims for what appraisal could reveal. Stakeholders using economic appraisal err if they assume the technique provides an objective and comprehensive guide to making choices. As indicated appraisal is largely a reflection of values. Whilst it may appear to provide a quantitative balance sheet about the value of a particular scheme or expenditure proposal, qualitatively it provides a framework for identifying the relevant economic factors involved. The importance, if any, to be attached to these factors in the decision-making context are quite rightly in the domain of the decision-maker. Given such a perspective, blanket approval or condemnation of the methodology would be foolhardy.   ■

References

Armstrong, Sir Robert(1985), Opening address to the CIPFA Centenary Conference, reprinted in *Public Expenditure and Management: Public Finance Foundation Discussion Paper No.5.*
Cmnd 8616 (1982), *Efficiency and Effectiveness in the Civil Service.* HMSO, London.
Cmnd 9058 (1983), *Financial Management in Government Departments.* HMSO, London.
Colvin, P. (1985), *The Economic Ideal in British Government.* Manchester University Press, Manchester.
Feldstein, M.S. (1964), The social time preference discount rate in cost benefit analysis. *Economic Journal,* Vol.74, pp. 360-79.
Fischhoff, B., Lichenstein, S., Slovic, P., Derby, S.L. and Keeney, R.L. (1981), *Acceptable Risk.* Cambridge University Press, Cambridge.
Flynn, N. (1990), *Public Sector Management.* Harvester, Hemel Hempstead, UK.
Gramlich, E.M. (1981), *Benefit-Cost Analysis of Government Programs.* Prentice-Hall, Englewood Cliffs, New Jersey.
Gray, A. and Jenkins, B. (1982), Efficiency and the self-evaluating organization: the central government experience. *Local Government Studies,* pp. 47-54.
Gray, A. and Jenkins, B. (1983), *Policy Analysis and Evaluation in British Government.* Royal Institute of Public Administration.
Gunn, L. and Hogwood, B.(1984), *Policy Analysis for the Real World.* Oxford University Press, Oxford.
Henderson, J. (1984), Appraising Options, SOAP 2. HERU Series of Option Appraisal Papers, University of Aberdeen.
Laver, M. (1986), *Social Choice and Public Policy.* Basil Blackwell, Oxford.
Likierman, A. (1982), Management information for ministers: the MINIS system in the Department of the Environment. *Public Administration,* Vol. 60, No.2, pp.127-142.
Ludbrook, A. and Mooney, G. (1984), Economic appraisal in the NHS: problems and challenges. *Northern Health Economics.* HERU, University of Aberdeen.
Mooney, G. and Henderson, J. (1986), Option appraisal in the UK National Health Service. *Financial Accountability & Management,* Vol. 2, No. 3, pp. 187-202
Rosenhead, J. (1984), An education in robustness. *Journal of the Operational Research Society,* Vol. 29, No. 2, pp.105-111.
Treasury, H.M. (1982), *Investment Appraisal in the Public Sector.* HMSO, London.
Treasury, H.M. (1983), *Investment Appraisal in the Public sector: A Management Guide for Government Departments.* HMSO, London.
Treasury, H.M. (1984), *Investment Appraisal in the Public sector: A Technical Guide for Government Departments.* HMSO, London.

[16]

Charles A. Bowsher

Mr. Bowsher is Comptroller General of the United States.

Budgeting and Accountability in Large Countries: Problems and Opportunities

Editor's Note: *The author also submitted this article as a technical paper, to be included in the proceedings for the XIV World Congress of Accountants, Washington, D.C., October 11-14, 1992. The event is held every five years and has been held at several different cities around the world.*

One of the fundamental principles of democracy is that a government is accountable to the citizens of the nation. In the final analysis, this accountability is implemented through the ballot box. All democratic governments must, from time to time, present themselves to an electorate which has the power to continue that government in office or to select another.

A Model of Accountability

Accountability, however, means much more than just the requirement to face an electorate. For the electorate to exercise its choices responsibly, the citizenry must understand its choices and know what its government is doing. This requires that voters be informed of the government's activities in at least two important respects.

First, an accountable government owes the citizen a clear explanation of the policies that the government has chosen to pursue and of the anticipated consequences of those policies.

Second, an accountable government owes the citizen an assessment of the actual consequences of its policies. If reality turned out to be different from the plan, as will inevitably happen from time to time, an accountable government owes the citizen an explanation of what caused the variances and the corrective actions, if any, that are deemed appropriate.

Governmental structures and institutional relationships differ vastly from one nation to another and particularly between parliamentary systems and presidential systems of government. Nevertheless, there is a certain conceptual commonality in the mechanisms by which these two forms of accountability are satisfied.

All governments of developed nations prepare budgets and, in all democratic governments, the budget is one of the primary means by which the government publicly announces the policies it has chosen to pursue. At their heart, all budgets are financial plans for the government, describing the revenues that are to be raised and the amounts that are to be spent for various purposes and the way in which the difference, if any, is to be financed.

For a budget to serve its accountability function, however, it must be more than a financial plan. In the modern era, the budgets of most developed countries have also become program policy plans, management plans and, to varying degrees, national economic plans.

To say that budgets should be all these things - policy plan, management plan, financial plan and economic plan - is not to say that contemporary budgets serve all of these objectives well. In one part of this paper we will be discussing a number of ways in which budgets, particularly those of the United States, fall far short of the ideal and we will suggest steps that might be taken to correct those failings. Before turning to that issue, however, we should first introduce the other piece of our accountability model, government's responsibility for reporting after the fact what happened to its plans and why.

It is commonly recognized that one aspect of accountability for any entity is to report on its financial performance. Publicly held corporations, for example, provide periodic financial reports to their shareholders. Similarly, governments usually make some form of public report of the financial results at the end of each fiscal period. In the United States, for example, Article I, section 9 of the Constitution requires that *"a regular statement and account of the receipts and expenditures of all public money shall be published from time to time."*

However, just as accountability for policies requires a budget that goes beyond a financial plan for the government, accountability after the fact should encompass more than just reporting how much public money was collected and spent. Democratic governments must also be held accountable for how well the approved plans were executed, how efficiently the available resources were used and the actual consequences of the policies adopted by the government. Finally, governments must be accountable for the assets they acquire and the liabilities they incur in the normal course of carrying out their responsibilities.

As with the front end of the ac-

countability model (planning and budgeting), our ability to describe the things for which government should be accountable after the fact does not imply that the present forms of accountability are adequate. We will be turning to those issues later in this paper. Meanwhile, let us return to the budget and discuss some of the problems in accountability at the front end of the policy process and ways in which those problems might be overcome.

Accountability for Planning and Budgeting

A budget is a financial plan for the government. But a meaningful financial plan must reflect accurately the programs and policies that the government intends to pursue. Almost any change in government policy will cause the numbers in the budget to change. Thus, a comprehensive budget must reflect the government's policies and an accountable budget must include an explanation of those policies, how they impinge on the components of the budget and the budget totals and what effect they are likely to have.

A budget is also a management plan for the government. By allocating resources for the payment of government employee salaries, for the purchase of land, buildings, computers and other equipment, the budget becomes a primary mechanism by which the government decides and announces changes in its management strategies and policies. As part of an accountability system, the budget should articulate the government's management priorities and explain how these will affect the efficiency and effectiveness with which government carries out its operating responsibilities.

Finally, government financial activities, (taxes, spending and the creation or liquidation of government debt), affect the economy and vice versa. In some nations the government itself is a sizable portion of the total economy. Even where this is not the case, the effect of the government on the economy is well recognized.

Since the Great Depression of the 1930s, a country's government has been seen as responsible for the management of its economy, with fiscal policy (governmental taxation and spending policies) being one of the primary means (along with monetary policy) by which that responsibility is implemented.

Thus the anticipated effect of the budget policies on the level of economic activity is usually an important issue in the budget. Because of this inescapable link, the budget is in an important sense, an economic plan for the country, as well as a financial plan for the government. An accountable budget, therefore, should seek to explain how the government expects the economy to perform and how it expects the policies proposed in the budget to affect that level of economic performance.

In most countries, budgeting procedures have evolved idiosyncratically, with current practices reflecting the accumulation of customs and traditions that developed out of decades - or even centuries - of experience unique to that country. Despite each country's unique budgetary practices, however, some features are found in almost all of them. For purposes of this discussion, two of those features are of particular importance, the cash basis of budgeting and the annual period of budgeting.[1]

Both are reasonable. After all, it is the cash-deficit in the budget that must be financed and the annual cycle is so prevalent in human affairs that its adoption for budgeting would seem almost inevitable. However, these features of budgeting contain the seeds of some of the problems in

"front-end" accountability.

Problem: An Excessively Short Term Focus for Budget Policy

In the United States, at least, there is a firm pattern of looking at each year's budget in isolation. Since the mid-1970s, each year's budget has contained projections and estimates for several years into the future, but only rarely are these the subject of serious analysis and debate. (The most recent exception to this occurred in 1990, when Congress and the President negotiated a five-year agreement on budget policy). Most commonly, the debate centers on how much money is being provided for particular programs and activities in the immediately ensuing fiscal year, not on where current policy choices are likely to leave the country, five, ten or more years in the future.

There are at least two adverse consequences of this concentration on the short term. One flows from the fact that budget policy is inherently sluggish. It often takes several years to enact a change in policy and for it to yield perceptible change in the financial results. If the financial consequences of politically difficult policy action, such as reducing benefits or increasing taxes, are not evident for several years, the one-year-at-a-time focus of budgeting makes it much easier not to act. The political costs are visible immediately; the economic or other benefits may lie outside the time horizon of the debate.

A second adverse consequence of the short time horizon of budgeting flows from the increasingly evident fact that the national economic consequences of fiscal policy choices can be very long term in nature, at least in a country as large as the United States. In a smaller country that is more completely integrated into the world economy, fiscal policy "errors" are likely to be reflected rather promptly in its external accounts - weakening exchange rates, inability to finance external debt at acceptable interest rates, etc.

The United States is a different case. Despite the growing internationalization of the U.S. economy, it remains relatively insensitive to changes in its international trading and financial relationships (at least as compared to most other countries). This is partly because of the size of its internal market and partly because, at least for the time being, it remains relatively attractive to foreign capital.

In combination, this has meant that huge U.S. budget deficits over the past decade, which might produce rapid and intolerable economic effects in another country, have been largely shrugged off and ignored. But the deficits have had effects, nevertheless. They have caused a dearth of national savings and of domestically financed capital investment, leading to slow growth in the economy and a rising share of U.S. income flowing to foreign investors.

These, however, are only statistics and most citizens are largely unaware of their meaning. The real effects, in the form of a lower standard of living, will only appear in the future, when the government that made the errors has long passed from the scene.[2] Thus, the very short term focus of budgeting may permit a government to avoid accountability for the long term economic consequences of its actions.

The lack of accountability for long term economic effects is probably most severe in a country such as the United States, with its huge internal market for goods and services and its highly developed capital markets. But the issue probably exists in any large country and might well emerge as a matter of concern in the European community, for example, if current efforts toward economic and political integration prove successful, yielding a single integrated economy equal to or larger in size than that of the United States.

The solution to the problem of short term political effects combined with medium term financial consequences and long term economic effects is a greatly extended time horizon of budgeting. This is not to suggest that we should all be developing detailed operating budgets for 10 or 15 years into the future. That would be neither realistic nor meaningful. Rather, we should be developing detailed budgets for one or two years ahead, as is the current practice. But those budgets should be developed within an agreed plan for how budget policy is intended to behave over the next five years or so. And that five year budget plan should be analyzed and explained in terms of its anticipated effect on the economy over the ensuing 20 or 25 years.

If this approach were pursued conscientiously, it might have several salutary effects on the policy process. First, by constraining annual budgets to conform to an agreed five year budget plan, it would be easier to explain the necessity of politically difficult budgetary choices. Programs that appear cheap in the short run, but will grow in the future, will be more easily revealed for the budget threats that they are. Second, by routinely analyzing the medium term budget plan's long term economic effects, the terms of the political debate may gradually change.

As the public and the press become accustomed to reading analyses of how the budget will affect the economy 25 or 30 years. into the future, they can begin holding governments accountable for the choices they make between current consumption and investment for future economic growth and development.

Problem: *Credibility of Estimates*

The future cannot be known with certainty. Predicting the future, therefore, requires the exercise of judgment. This is as true of budgeting and economic forecasting as in any other profession. But some judgments are better than others and, if budgeting is to be meaningful (particularly the sophisticated, future-oriented budgeting suggested in the previous section), those making the budgetary decisions need a certain degree of confidence that the judgements on which they are basing their decisions are reasonable. Unfortunately, governments do not have a terribly good record in this regard.

The reason is simple. There are never enough budgetary resources to do all the things that governments want to do. There is a natural tendency to look for ways to stretch those resources and two such ways are readily apparent. Faster economic growth generates greater tax revenues than slower growth. Thus there is an incentive to be optimistic about the future behavior of the economy. The lower the cost of a program, the easier it is to find room for it (and for competing claims on resources) in the budget. This creates an incentive to underestimate program costs.

This is not to say that governments always overestimate economic growth and underestimate costs. In the United States in recent years, the reality is more complicated than this; sometimes the economy outperforms the Administration forecast and occasionally a program costs less than estimated in the President's Budget. Of course, no forecaster - public or private - has proven consistently reliable at predicting major turning points in the economy such as the onset or ending of a recession.

With this caveat, the recent pattern seems to be that the official short run economic forecasts (for the next 18 months or so) are generally fairly reliable and are usually reasonably consistent with the consensus of private forecasters. Beyond this point, however, the credibility of the official forecasts begins to evaporate. In the later years of a five year forecast, it is common to see economic growth rates that are somewhat above, and interest rates and inflation rates that are significantly below those considered likely to private economics. This implies, of course, that projected budget deficits for those years may be materially understated.

With respect to cost estimating, examples abound of programs and projects that entail costs far in excess of those originally estimated. Defense weapons systems are among the most notorious cases, but similar estimating errors are found in the development of major computer systems such as those for the Internal Revenue Service, the Federal Aviation Administration's air traffic control system modernization and in projections for the rapidly escalating health care financing programs.

The solution to the lack of credibility of forecasts and estimates is conceptually simple. The first step is to establish that estimating and forecasting errors will not be ignored. This requires someone routinely to compare the actual results to the estimates (a matter discussed further in a later section of this paper) and to analyze significant variances.

With respect to program costs, for example, errors can come from any of three sources. The estimating methodology may be flawed, the data underlying the estimate may be in error, or external events may have impinged on the program in unanticipated ways. Sometimes the source of error and means of correcting it are readily apparent. In other cases, it will take a great deal of effort to find and overcome the root cause of the problem.

Developing credible economic forecasts presents a somewhat different problem. No one is entitled to expect a precisely accurate forecast of the performance of the economy of a large country. Econometricians have made great strides in the past few decades, but the economy is much too complex for its internal workings to be fully replicated in a finite number of econometric equations.

Short of an unattainable perfection, what decision makers should expect is an economic forecast that is plausible in the sense that most economists would judge it to have a relatively high probability of being approximately correct, given the policy assumptions on which it is based.

In the present U.S. fiscal environment, decision makers should also expect a conservative forecast, one in which the errors are more likely to be pleasant than unpleasant. Faced with the prospect of deficits rising toward half a trillion dollars or more by the end of this decade, it is much easier to accommodate the effects of an economy that outperforms expectations than the opposite.

This suggests a forecasting process that is built around a consensus of economists, with somewhat greater weight being accorded to the moderately pessimistic end of the forecast range. The primary obstacles to adopting such a forecasting process are political, not technical.

Problem: Integrity of Data

Another problem affecting budgetary decision making is that the data used in the budget process may simply be wrong. As noted earlier, this can contribute to estimating errors but it also can be a much more pervasive problem. In our experience, the cause of the problem can usually be found in one of three weaknesses. One is the inability of an agency's accounting system to produce reliable data in a timely manner that conforms to the requirements of the budget process.

The result is that those preparing the budget must rely on informal records that have usually not been subjected to the discipline of audit, and in which errors may lie undetected for extended periods of time.

A second source of error may be the accounting systems themselves. If the accounting system has not been fully audited, data in that system may be erroneously classified, potentially misleading whoever may be using accounting reports in the development of budget estimates.

Finally, a matter of growing concern to us at the General Accounting Office is that the accounting concepts and principles used in either budgeting or accounting (or both) may be seriously flawed. At the center of this problem is the cash basis of accounting that dominates most governmental budgeting at the national level. As noted earlier, cash is important because, among other things, it is the cash deficit that must be financed. But cash data alone can be highly misleading.

The accumulation of unfunded liabilities has become a serious problem for the U.S. government. If those preparing budgets focus exclusively on the cash numbers, they run the risk of suddenly encountering an enormous demand for cash to finance the liquidation of obligations they cannot ignore, and for which they have not prepared themselves in their budget planning. The budgetary consequences of the collapse of the U.S. thrift industry, and the resultant insolvency of the Federal Savings and Loan Insurance Corporation provide a particularly vivid example of such a situation.[3]

Solving the problem of data integrity in the budget process will require a lot of hard work, but the strategy can be quite straightforward. Conceptually, the first step is to define the accounting principles and standards that will be used in both budgeting and accounting. This effort should start with a clear understanding of who needs the information and for what purpose. Existing accounting standards should be used where they meet these users' needs, but the needs of government are different from the needs of publicly held corporations, so we should expect some of the standards to be unique to government.

In the United States, this effort is going forward under the leadership of the Federal Accounting Standards Advisory Board, sponsored jointly by the General Accounting Office, the President's Office of Management and Budget and the Treasury Department. The issues being examined by this group of experts will be discussed in greater detail in a later section of this paper.

The second step is the modernization of the accounting systems themselves, so that they are capable of producing reliable data in the format and on the schedule required by those developing the budget. Building modern accounting systems can be an expensive, time consuming process, but the costs are minuscule compared to the costs associated with flawed decisions based on erroneous data. This issue, too, will be discussed later in the paper. The third step is regular audit of the accounting system and of the data it produces, to assure that the data used in the budget process is reliable and is being used properly.

This is by no means an exhaustive list of the problems in budgeting in large countries. But if we, at least in the United States, can overcome the problems of an excessively short planning horizon, estimates and forecasts that lack credibility and erroneous data based on flawed concepts and antiquated accounting systems, we will have taken a very large step toward producing a budget system that provides a basis for holding the government accountable for its policy choices.

Accountability for Results

As was noted at the outset, it seems axiomatic that governments owe their citizens an accounting of financial results. But a simple tabulation of money taken in and money spent is a far cry from true accountability.

Two additional areas of accountability are reasonably apparent. In the budget process, financial resources were provided in specific amounts to achieve specific purposes. The first question to which government owes its citizens an answer is whether or not the resources were actually collected as planned and used as intended. How do the financial results compare with the approved budget? Variances are inevitable, but the public is entitled to an explanation of what caused the variance and what implications it may have for policy.

The differences between the plan and reality often reflect changes in the performance of the economy, so adequate accountability in the financial area should encompass a discussion of how the economy behaved and what caused it to depart from what was anticipated when the budget was prepared. But variances from plan will also reflect changes in program policy or in the ability of management to carry out policies. An accountable government also owes an explanation of these.

A second accountability question relates to performance. The financial resources specified in the budget were provided with the expectation that certain results would be forthcoming. To what extent were they achieved? If policies changed, why and with what effect? At the center of the performance question is the issue of what the taxpayers got for the money they turned over to the government?

Two other areas of after-the-fact accountability have assumed growing importance in recent years, at least in the United States. These relate not to government's income and expense, but to its balance sheet. Each year, resources are provided for the acquisition of assets, such as land, buildings, equipment and inventories of supplies and spare parts. Once these assets are acquired, governments must be accountable for managing and protecting them and for using them wisely. Are they still needed? Is the government planning adequately for renovation or replacement of items as they wear out or become obsolete?

Similarly, governments routinely accumulate actual and contingent liabilities and must be accountable for controlling and financing them. In the United States these can be illustrated by our experience with the collapse of many federally-insured deposit institutions, with a large portion of the resulting liabilities being borne by the taxpayer.

In other countries the source of the liabilities will be different. In some, the greatest risks may lie in large state-owned corporations that find themselves in severe financial difficulty. They may present the government with the choice of politically destabilizing closures of factories or budgetarily intolerable levels of subsidy. This is one of many painful dilemmas facing the governments of the formerly communist countries of eastern Europe and central Eurasia as they struggle toward the development of market economies. But the risk is not limited to those countries; it has been a problem elsewhere, as well.

Whatever the source of the liabilities, however, governments should be accountable for anticipating them, keeping them under control, recognizing them when they appear and providing an appropriate means for funding them.

Problem: Lack of Systematic Reporting

In the United States today, there are serious weaknesses in accountability for results on the part of the national government. Financial reports are unreliable at any level beyond the actual reporting of cash transactions; little attention is paid to huge variances from the budget estimates for revenues and mandatory spending;[4] performance reports are largely unavailable and where they exist they are usually developed from administrative records of dubious reliability and completeness; and balance sheet audits routinely reveal enormous discrepancies, grossly inflated asset values and the failure to record large and growing liabilities.

This condition reflects an atmosphere of concern only for the moment. Once the budget for a fiscal year has been approved, it disappears from the area of concern of the political leadership, the press and the public. Attention immediately turns to the ensuing fiscal year and the controversy that is certain to arise when the budget for that year is published a few months hence. Thus the myopic, excessively short term perspective that characterizes the budget process blinds us to events that have just transpired. As we find ourselves unable to consider the longer term implications of the choices prepared promptly at the end of each fiscal period.

In the U.S. system of government, these reports should be prepared by each operating department or agency and addressed to the President and to that agency's oversight committees in the Congress. In a parliamentary system, the official recipients might be different, depending on the structure of the parliament and the relationships between operating agencies, ministries, Cabinet and parliament. Regardless of the official recipients, however, the reports should be public documents, available to the press and to any citizen interested in reviewing them.

In addition to the individual agency reports, there should be a summary report prepared by the government (the President in the U.S. system, the Prime Minister or the Cabinet collectively in a parliamentary system) and submitted to the legislative body and the public.

The purpose of this system of reports would be to provide a public accounting of the government's stewardship of the public resources with which it was entrusted during that year. As suggested by the earlier discussion, the reports should, at a minimum, cover these areas:

Budget Execution. How did the actual collection and use of financial resources compare to the plans represented by the budget? Where there were variances, why did they occur? What was done about them? The summary report from the government should also discuss the performance of the overall economy, how that departed from expectations and how the government responded or plans to respond in the future.

Operating Performance. This part of the individual agency reports should be based on carefully constructed performance measurement systems that would allow the reader to gage the efficiency and effectiveness of that agency's operations, and to assess what the citizen received for the resources entrusted to that agency. The government's summary report should focus on significant issues revealed in the individual agency reports, with special attention to major

or systematic problems and the steps that may be needed to deal with them.

Management of Assets. If an agency is responsible for significant amounts of assets, such as inventories, buildings, weapons systems, etc. its annual accountability report should include a section revealing its stewardship of those assets. Which of those assets are still needed and for what purpose? What is the status of depreciation of assets? Is there a backlog of maintenance or replacement? Which assets are no longer needed? How does the agency intend to dispose of them? The government's summary report should examine these issues from a global perspective. Is the government as a whole managing its assets wisely? Does the existence of unneeded assets reveal opportunities to reduce resource allocations in the future? Does a pattern of progressive obsolescence or deterioration reveal the need for additional resources for modernization, overhaul, or replacement?

Control over Liabilities. Any agency whose responsibilities entail the potential accumulation of government liabilities, whether actual or contingent, should include a section in its accountability report discussing those liabilities. What is their status? What is the likelihood of known or suspected contingent liabilities becoming financial claims on the government? Have reasonable arrangements been made to fund the liabilities? Have they been recognized in financial reports and budget plans? What steps have been taken to control the growth of liabilities? The government's summary report should assess the overall pattern of actual and contingent liabilities. Do the trends portend a significant increase in the financial resources needed to liquidate current and anticipated liabilities? If so, what does this imply for future budgets and for the policies giving rise to the liabilities?

The creation of a system of annual accountability reports of this sort would represent a major step forward in our ability to understand what was happening in government operations and in holding government accountable for its performance and for its stewardship of public resources. In the U.S. system, we anticipate that these reports would provide the basis for systematic annual oversight of agency management by the responsible committees of the Congress. In other systems, different ways would no doubt be found for accomplishing the same accountability objective.

To have its greatest value, however, such a system of reports should be based on more complete and reliable data than currently exists, at least in the United States. The gaps lie in two areas, measurement of performance and the quality of financial data.

Problem: Lack of Performance Measures

Systematic measurement and reporting of program and service accomplishments is a cornerstone of accountability. No system of accountability reporting can be complete without it. Yet, no country, to our knowledge, has a fully operating system. That is changing. Performance measurement is an element of management reform being pursued in many industrialized democracies.

Australia, New Zealand and the United Kingdom, for example, are undertaking public sector management reforms in which professional managers of operating agencies are held accountable for achieving performance objectives in return for a reduction in the level and complexity of traditional public sector management controls.

This experience, and the "natural experiment" created by the markedly different ways in which the three countries are approaching the task, is worthy of observation by other nations for the lessons it may hold with respect to both performance measurement and the potential for increased efficiency in public sector operations.

At the federal level in the United States we are just getting started. Some states and local governments have been measuring performance for several years with varying degrees of success.

Over the years, democratic governments have assumed responsibility for a huge array of services. A growing part of the U.S. budget is devoted to service delivery and especially to financing services delivered by others (state and local governments, nonprofit organizations and the private sector). Universally, government budgets set forth the amounts to be spent for these programs and services. But few, if any, have a systematic process for measuring what those programs and services actually accomplish and for linking those results to budget estimates.

There are certain steps that should be taken to improve accountability for program and service results.

Specify Goals. Government agencies and the legislature need to clearly articulate the goals and citizen expectations for each program and service. These goals should address the pertinent aspects of performance and be written in terms that can be used to judge progress toward achieving them.

Measure Performance. Agencies need to develop specific measures for assessing progress toward achieving their goals. While measures must be tailor made for each program and service, there are six aspects of performance that should generally be considered for measurement - costs, quality, timeliness, efficiency, effectiveness and customer satisfaction.

Report Results. Agencies need to report regularly on their progress to the government, the legislature and the public. In a separation-of-powers systems such as we have in the United States, it is essential that the legislature be actively involved in overseeing agency performance. If the legislature does not take performance results seriously, neither will the agencies. In parliamentary systems, that role may better be assigned to the responsible ministry or the Cabinet.

Developing a framework for measuring performance will not be easy. In the United States, the process of defining the measures and establishing the reporting arrangements will be an especially complex task. Not only must the legislative and executive branches come into agreement, there is the additional complexity of programs that are partially financed at the federal level but operated by other units of government and non-governmental entities. For performance measurement to work, all involved parties must be part of the system and be committed to it.

As with many useful endeavors, the development of effective performance measurement systems will be a formidable challenge; but it is essential. Not only is it a vital element of accountability, it also induces a focus on results that can improve government operations. We do not need to start with complete coverage, but we do need to get started. In this age, it is important that citizens know what their government is accomplishing.

Problem: Lack of Comprehensive Financial Reporting Using Appropriate Accounting Principles

As indispensable as program and service accomplishment reporting is, no system of accountability reporting is complete that does not provide information on financial results. To support accountability for financial results, governmental entities must have reports and statements that are comprehensive and reliable, based on appropriate accounting principles. Financial report users need information they understand and believe.

Financial reporting of this nature is not now available, at least not in the United States. The traditional vehicles for providing information on financial results - the budget and financial statements - do not do the job. The budget is predominantly on a cash basis and is not comprehensive.

Federal financial statements are built on models designed for profit making entities which are not well suited to government. In the United States we now recognize that we need a new set of financial statements and related accounting principles that are relevant to the federal government.

By law, the Comptroller General of the United States publishes accounting standards for federal agencies, in consultation with Treasury and the Office of Management and Budget. To help in the development of new accounting standards meeting the unique needs of the federal government, we created a joint legislative and executive branch group, the Federal Accounting Standards Advisory Board, in early 1991 to make recommendations for federal accounting principles. The Board's objective is to ensure consistency and suitability of accounting principles used for federal financial operations.

The Board is made up of nine members from the federal government and private sector. It is "advisory" in that the members recommend proposed standards to be adopted by Treasury, OMB and GAO. The Board is now developing a body of accounting standards centered on a family of financial statements covering budget execution, operating performance of programs and services, management of assets and status of liabilities.

Our view at GAO, which was general agreement of the Board members, is that the budget has been and will be the principal vehicle for making policy and management decisions in the federal government, at least those decisions having material financial consequences. Therefore, in setting accounting principles we must try to achieve as much consistency as possible between accounting and budgetary principles.

When consistency is not possible, ,,or for good reasons based on user needs, it is not desirable, then we need simple reconciliations that make the accounting information acceptable for use by programs managers, budgeteers and Congress.

One such case is the recognized need to have cost information on the operation of programs and services. Here, we will need an easily understandable way of reconciling cost figures on an accrual basis with budget amounts on a cash basis. If we do this right, not only will we have additional financial management tools available from accounting, but we will make budgeting a more effective decision process.

The Board's procedures give a broad range of affected parties an opportunity to express their views before an accounting standard is recommended. Public comment has already been received on an exposure draft containing nine accounting standards involving financial resources and funded liabilities. Future exposure drafts will cover other areas, including inventories and other material held by government entities, loans and loan guarantees, unfunded liabilities, revenue recognition and physical assets.

It is too early yet to predict the outcome. But if we are able to clear our minds of traditional thinking, we will develop innovative accounting principles and financial statements that are uniquely suited to the needs of our government.

Problem: Lack   of   Modern Accounting Systems

However, before financial reports based on appropriate accounting standards can be a reality, modern financial systems must be put in place. In the United States, many federal financial systems are weak, outdated and inefficient, and cannot routinely produce relevant, timely and comprehensive information. The basic structure of many of the present systems are World War II vintage.

The financial reports flowing from these systems provide a flood of information but little of the reliable operations and cost data that are essential to monitor programs, ancitipate overruns and provide a basis for program and budget planning. Many federal agency systems cannot provide basic accountability and control. Billions of dollars have been spent on uncoordinated efforts to upgrade these systems. Despite improvement over the years, they are still second or third rate compared to what is possible.

In Australia, for example, the national government has had a modern, integrated accounting system for a number of years. This system yields reliable data that is available to all users on a timely basis and permits audited financial statements to be published within four months of the close of the fiscal year. Some state governments in the United States also have accounting systems that are substantially more efficient and effective than those of the federal government.

In 1985, we issued a tow volume report, Managing the Cost of Government,[5] the culmination of a major study of the government's financial management practices. The report identified significant problems affecting the federal financial management structure, proposed a conceptual framework to guide improvement efforts and outlined and implementing strategy. Since then, we have seen a growing consensus on the need to reform our financial management systems and on what needs to be done to accomplish meaningful and lasting improvements.

Yet, agencies continue to identify financial management systems problems in annual reports to the Congress under the Federal Managers' Financial Integrity Act. The Office of Management and Budget has designated a number of agency financial management operations as "high risk" and is closely watching actions the agencies take to correct those problems.

In 1990, Congress enacted the Chief Financial Officer's Act, potentially the most far-reaching financial management legislation this country has seen in over 40 years. Among the important provisions is a requirement that agencies maintain financial systems that comply with applicable accounting internal control standards. Further, agency financial systems are to integrate accounting and budget information, report cost information and provide for the systematic measurement of performance.

These requirements provide the underpinning for top-notch financial systems. But, much remains to be done to modernize federal financial management systems which the Director of the Office of Management and Budget described as being "essentially a primitive cash budgeting system - without satisfactory controls or audits; without accruals; without balance sheets; without a clear picture of assets, liabilities, returns on investment, or risks." The Director likened the system to one associated with a 20-person restaurant rather than the government of a superpower.

Conclusion

In an ideal system, a democratic government would be accountable before the fact for clearly articulating its policy choices and their expected effects, and after the fact for explaining what actually happened and why. Both elements of accountability are vital and they need to be closely linked.

Today, in the United States - and we suspect in many large countries - we are far from the ideal. Our budget, which is the principal vehicle for explaining policy choices being proposed or adopted by the government, is severely deficient in that regard, obscuring some of the most critical issues more frequently that it informs the public about them. Accountability after the fact is notable primarily for its absence.

If we are to expect democratic governments to behave in an accountable fashion, we must begin holding them accountable for their actions. We must start by insisting that governments supply the information - both before and after the fact - that must be the basis of accountability.

Endnotes

1. One national government, New Zealand, has shifted to an accrual basis of budgeting. New Zealand's experience is worthy of close observation by other nations for the lessons it may teach.

2. For a more extensive discussion of these issues, see Budget Policy: Prompt Action Necessary to Avert Long-Term Damage to the Economy, GAO/OCG-92-2, June 1992.

3. As noted earlier, New Zealand has shifted to an accrual basis of budgeting. The United States has introduced some aspects of accruals in its budget process, most notably with respect to military retirement benefits and credit programs (direct loans and loan guarantees) and has begun discussing an accrual approach to some large contingent liabilities (deposit

insurance) but without resolution at this time.

4. See, for example, Budget Issues: 1991 Budget Estimates: What Went Wrong, GAO/OCG-92-1, January, 1992.

5. GAO/AFMD-85-35 and 85-35A, February 1985.

[17]

LEARNING TO MEASURE PERFORMANCE: THE USE OF INDICATORS IN ORGANIZATIONS

NEIL CARTER

Performance indicators (PIs) are central to the Thatcher Administration's strategy for reforming the management of government. This paper reports on research into the development and use of PIs in government departments, public agencies and private businesses in the 1980s. This comparative approach shows that the problems of performance assessment and the methods adopted for the design of PI systems, cut across the public/private divide but are related to the specific characteristics of organizations and their environment. The paper further analyses various dimensions of PI systems – notably, the measurement of quality and consumer satisfaction – and examines their implementation and evolution. The life-cycle of PIs suggests a possible prescriptive theory: the 'mature' PI model seems to be characterized by being designer-built, parsimonious and timely. The drive towards the development of PI systems, it is concluded, is likely to intensify in the 1990s, in response to the Next Steps initiative and as instruments for the regulation of privatized monopolies.

Performance indicators were very much the fashion of the 1980s: they were embraced at the highest levels of government and promulgated throughout the public sector. The Prime Minister offered active, sustained support for managerial reform throughout government, central to which was the wider use of PIs. Although the government was breathing new life into old ideas – ideas previously popular in the 1960s (Carter, Klein and Day 1991) – the enthusiasm was unprecedented, and infectious. The shift of interest from the traditional focus on inputs to outputs was partly because the government needed to find out what departments were actually doing and partly because of the overriding concern of the Thatcher Administration to control public expenditure. Hence the obvious attraction of a system that emphasized outputs rather than defining all improvements in terms of inputs. The government was also anxious to improve managerial competence. The ascendancy of the 'three Es', economy, efficiency and effectiveness, was intended to increase central control over service delivery as

Neil Carter is a Lecturer in Politics at the University of York. This article is a product of research carried out jointly with Rudolf Klein and Patricia Day. It was funded by the Economic and Social Research Council and titled 'An evaluation of performance in the public sector: a comparative, cross-sector study' (award number E 09250013). The author would like to thank Rudolf Klein and Patricia Day for reading and commenting on this paper. For a full analysis of this research see Carter, N., R. Klein and P. Day. 1991. *How organizations measure success.* London: Routledge.

Public Administration Vol. 69 Spring 1991 (85–101)
© 1991 Royal Institute of Public Administration ISSN 0033-3298 $3.00

86   NEIL CARTER

much as it was to cut costs, although the two were inextricably linked (Carter 1989). Pressure came from other sources too; in particular, parliamentary committees had repeatedly demanded a currency of evaluation that would increase ministerial accountability (Public Accounts Committee 1981; Treasury and Civil Service Committee 1982). Significantly, this new political interest in PIs came at a time when information technology could play a critical facilitating role in the development of the information systems necessary to support PIs.

This build up of interest resulted in the Financial Management Initiative (FMI) which emphasized that managers at all levels in government should have a 'clear view of their objectives; and assess, and wherever possible measure, outputs or performance in relation to these objectives'; a principle that made it essential to develop 'performance indicators and output measures which can be used to assess success in achieving objectives' (Prime Minister and the Chancellor of the Exchequer 1983). The most obvious manifestation of this clarion call was an epidemic of PIs in the Public Expenditure White Paper: multiplying from 500 in 1985 to over 2000 by 1988 (Carter 1988). Whether this impressive productivity record had any more substance than a Soviet Five Year Plan is a more open question; it may simply be evidence of the skill of civil servants in relabelling existing statistics as PIs in order to conform to the latest Whitehall fashion. If so, then the ebbing of enthusiasm for the FMI at the end of the decade may have rung the death knell for PIs; conceivably, they could just join the litany of failed and forgotten managerial reforms that includes PPB (Planning, Programming, Budgeting) and PAR (Programme Analysis and Review).

However, it is our thesis that the quest to develop PIs will be pursued in the 1990s with ever more vigour. Two developments in the latter part of the 1980s explain this assertion. First, PIs seem likely to play an increasing role in the regulation of monopolies, whether public or private. During the 1980s, most nationalized industries developed an array of PIs in response to pressure from the government (Treasury 1978) and numerous critical reports from parliamentary committees and the Monopolies and Mergers Commission. Thus far the government has been mostly interested in financial indicators (Carter 1990), but it seems likely that the changing climate of growing concern about consumer satisfaction and quality of service, particularly if it finds sufficient voice through Parliament and consumer pressure groups, will encourage the greater use of such PIs. This will be true not just in the remaining nationalized industries, but also in privatized monopolies such as the water and gas industries, where the various regulatory authorities will need to use PIs to measure, for example, river pollution or the time that a customer has to wait for gas fitters to call.

This regulatory role overlaps with the second factor, the implementation of the 'Next Steps' initiative to break up threequarters of the civil service into separate executive agencies (Jenkins, Caines and Jackson 1988). Despite being burdened with the claim that it represents 'the most ambitious attempt at Civil Service reform in the twentieth century' (Treasury and Civil Services Committee 1990, para. 1), early results are impressive: by the summer of 1991 there should be 50 agencies with around 200,000 civil servants working in them, about half the civil service (para. 9). The unanimous support of the Treasury and Civil Service Committee also suggests that 'Next Steps' – in Hennessy's phrase, 'a piece of transferable technology operable by governments of any political persuasion' (para. 82) – may well survive political change. Sustaining the entire agency exercise is the use of performance measures as instruments of hands-off managerial control and democratic accountability: central departments, particularly the Treasury, need PIs to exercise control without breathing down the necks of the new chief executives; Parliament and the public need PIs to ensure that agencies are delivering the desired services efficiently and effectively. Specifically, each agency is required to publish performance targets in its Framework Agreement which will be the subject of a quarterly review by its sponsoring department and the scrutiny of parliamentary committees and individual politicians. To this end, the Treasury is co-ordinating 'extensive work on assisting parent departments and agencies to develop a suitable "portfolio" of output and performance measures' (para. 21). In short, the pressure to develop PIs is unabated.

Hence the relevance of this paper reporting on research into the development of PIs during the 1980s across a variety of government departments and public agencies, as well as a number of private businesses (reported fully in Carter *et al*. 1991). The research explores the conceptual and technical problems involved in designing new tools of government; one of the reasons why the experience of the 1980s is still highly relevant for the 1990s is that the design task is far from complete. Moreover, to study the evolution and implementation of PIs in British government is to gain an insight into organizational politics and values, and the power of different organizational actors such as judges, prison officers and the police.

In this paper, we address some of the lessons from this experience. First, the different dimensions of performance and the currencies of evaluation embodied in PI systems are examined, with particular reference to the emerging issues of consumer attitudes and quality assessment. Second, the possibility of moving towards some form of prescriptive theory of PIs is explored; in other words, are there characteristics common to all 'good' PI systems? Finally, the patterns of implementation of PI systems are analysed and a number of important organizational and environmental constraints are identified. However, before reporting on our findings, it is necessary to outline the rationale of the research and the selection of organizational case studies.

ORGANIZATIONAL LEARNING

The literature on comparative organizational analysis is a notorious conceptual minefield; note, for example, the critical debate surrounding the Aston programme of studies (Pugh and Hickson 1976; Clegg and Dunkerley 1980 *inter alia*), or the complexity of the bureaumetric approach to public sector comparative analysis (Hood and Dunsire 1981; Dunleavy 1989). So, we attempted no more than to identify selectively some of the key dimensions along which organizations differ and which might be relevant to the shaping of performance indicators. Seven dimensions were isolated that might account for variations in performance assessment between organizations. First, *ownership*, simply whether an organization is in the public or private sector. Second, *trading status*, whether it is a trading or non-trading organization. Third, the degree of *competition* between organizations providing similar products or services. Fourth, the extent to which an organization is politically *accountable*. Fifth, the *heterogeneity* of an organization refers to the number of different products or services it provides. Sixth, the degree of *complexity* is the extent to which an organization has to mobilize a number of different skills in order to deliver its services or produce its goods. Lastly, organizations vary in the *uncertainty* about the objectives and between the means and ends of achieving those objectives (see Carter *et al.* 1991 for a full discussion). These dimensions were intended to form a set of benchmarks for analysing variation in the problems of performance measurement. We were not developing yet another typology for explaining differences in performance or structure between organizations.

In adopting a comparative strategy of inquiry, we wanted to test the conventional wisdom that there is some particular quality about the public sector – some Platonic essence of 'publicness' – which makes transplanting techniques from the private sector inappropriate or difficult. Indeed, when interviewing civil servants engaged in implementing the FMI, we found a near-unanimity that the assessment of performance in the private sector was different (and unquestionably easier). Two explanations were commonly used to explain this difference in public/private performance measurement. The first assumes that because private firms possess the famous bottom-line – profit – then performance measurement is a straightforward, incontestable technical procedure; the second focuses on the particular social and political pressures operating on public sector organizations. These factors clearly have some significance, but we question whether they are all-important.

The example of profit illustrates this point. Even at the level of the firm in the market sector, the common belief that profit is a satisfactory PI presents a misleading picture. The accounts raise questions but do not answer them (Vickers 1965). To imagine that profit figures are a mechanical product is to ignore the fact that accountancy is one of the creative arts; often more art than science (Hopwood 1984). This is well illustrated during takeover battles when accountants are apt to manipulate the figures in order to send up the price of shares. To assess the meaning of profits (or of alternative key indicators such as market share or return on capital) involves forming a judgment on the performance not just of the firm in question but of its competitors, as well as strategic judgements about the long-term effects of current pricing and investment decisions. In short, the 'bottom line' turns out, on closer inspection, to be a plasticine concept, both malleable and movable across time. Furthermore, within the firm, it is essential to have immediate output and outcome measures that assess likely performance against the long-term objective of profit maximization. This is particularly important in industries like banks or building societies where it is difficult to construct a simple profit-and-loss account for individual branches. Thus it is necessary to appreciate the limitations of profit as a measure of performance of either the units within organizations or of the organizations themselves.

LEARNING TO MEASURE PERFORMANCE   89

TABLE 1   Organizational dimensions

Organizations	Ownership	Trading/Non-trading	Competition	Accountability	Heterogeneity	Complexity	Uncertainty
Police	public	NT	low	yes	medium	low	high
Courts	public	NT	low	yes	low	med/high	low
Prisons	public	NT	low	yes	med/low	low	low
Social Security	public	NT	low	yes	low	low	low
NHS	public	NT	low	yes	high	high	high
Supermarket	private	T	high	no	med	med/low	low
High Street Retailer	private	T	high	no	med	med/low	low
Bank	private	T	med→high	no	low	low	low
Building Society (two)	private	T	med→high	no	low	low	low
Jupiter (TVHire)	private	T	high	no	low	low	low
British Rail	public	T	medium	yes	low	low	medium
Water (2)	public	T	low	yes	med/low	medium	low
BAA	private	T	low	no	low	low	low

Notes: The arrows indicate where an organization is in the process of change
(1) This refers to formal, public accountability, not actual accountability
(2) This refers to the pre-privatization water industry

So we started from the assumption that the problems of introducing and developing PIs might also reflect specific organizational characteristics cutting across the public-private divide. Accordingly our 14 case studies were chosen in order to study the evolution of PI systems in contrasting organizations which, however, all had a large number of branches or units (except BAA) and consequential problems of internal control over the performance of those branches (see table 1). So, we explored, for example, whether social security might have more in common with a bank than with the national health service or a supermarket. For if there is to be cross-sector learning, if there are to be successful transplants of ideas and techniques, it is essential that the donor should be matched accurately to the recipient.

Therefore, in each case, we sought to explore the natural history of PI systems over time: i.e. to present an evolutionary picture. Given the number of organizations in our comparative study it was impossible to undertake an in-depth study of each one. However, in every organization managers were interviewed at each level: central headquarters, regional/district offices and the individual unit. Where possible the operational researchers responsible for designing the system were also interviewed. Findings were supplemented by documentary evidence including evaluation reports and performance reviews.

THE DIMENSIONS OF PERFORMANCE

Performance is currently one of those buzzwords that seem to permeate all discussions about public sector management. It is widely used by politicians and managers alike perhaps because, in Pollitt's words, performance 'exudes an aroma of action, dynamism and purposeful effort. It suggests a sorting out of the good from the bad' (1986, p. 160). Part of its attraction is that performance is a very broad, and vague, concept: it has various meanings for different audiences in

90   NEIL CARTER

different contexts. For example, the Treasury tends to focus on financial performance whereas Parliament may be more interested in the effectiveness of policy, while consumers are anxious about the quality of service delivery. This adds to the difficulties of designing PIs because the same set of PIs may need to be used to answer questions about all the different dimensions of performance.

In the 1980s, the debate about PIs was dominated by the 'three Es': economy, efficiency and effectiveness, a model couched in the language of private sector financial management. The three Es were promulgated in the FMI, and in numerous official reports emanating from the Treasury, the Efficiency Unit, the Audit Commission, parliamentary committees, and, at the coalface, by the plethora of management consultants who invaded the corridors of Whitehall and the municipalities. The precise definition of economy, efficiency and effectiveness became an industry in itself (Beeton 1988; Flynn *et al.* 1988; Levitt and Joyce 1987; Pollitt 1986 *inter alia*). The hegemony of the 'three Es' model was generally criticized in the academic literature. For many commentators it was bad enough that performance was defined purely in terms of the three Es but, worse still, it seemed that in this era of retrenchment the government was only really interested in economy and efficiency, or, as many saw it, in cutting costs, shedding labour and increasing productivity (Pollitt 1986). The new PI schemes springing up in nearly every government department (Treasury 1986) were therefore widely condemned for ignoring not just effectiveness, but several additional dimensions of performance, such as efficacy and equity (Flynn *et al.* 1988), quality (Pollitt 1987) and consumer voice (Pollitt 1988). But the continuing lack of consensus on the fundamentals – both the definitions and the dimensions of performance – suggests that this literature, like the targets of its criticisms, was stronger on outputs than outcomes.

Much of the criticism underestimates the conceptual and technical complexity of measuring effectiveness – the extent to which policy impacts meet policy aims, or outputs achieve outcomes. In short, the existence of effectiveness indicators presumes the ability to measure outcomes. But the problems of measuring the impact of, say, police patrols on crime rates or of health care on longevity, are virtually insurmountable because of the various mediating organizational and environmental factors. Not surprisingly, whilst our research confirmed that there was an overall paucity of effectiveness measures in the annual Public Expenditure White Paper (Carter 1988), it was also apparent that this was explained more by technical incapacity rather than by political bias. This is illustrated by the way in which an organization like the NHS, which has now progressed to its third package of PIs, has gradually managed to develop a broader range of measures at each stage. To be sure, the hostile criticisms it received from within the health service (North East Thames Health Authority 1984) as well as from academics, may have encouraged these changes, but it would appear that the will to do so was there, even if the capacity was (and is) often lacking.

Moreover, in many caseload departments throughput measures are widely used as a reasonable proxy for effectiveness. These include the Lord Chancellor's Department which seeks primarily to ensure the quick, efficient passage of cases through the judicial system, and money-shuffling departments like social security which aims to pay benefits speedily and accurately: where, in effect, process *is* the outcome. Thus PIs here are the length of time a defendant has to await trial or the number of days between claiming and receiving benefit. Indeed, in these departments, far from there being a preponderance of efficiency PIs, it has actually proven very difficult to produce efficiency measures based on unit costs. The one sector where there does seem to have been significant political pressure to concentrate on financial measures, even though there were perfectly acceptable and long established quality of service indicators, was in the nationalized industries. It is clear that British Rail, labouring under tight external financing limits and forced to pursue stringent financial and productivity performance targets (British Rail 1990), operates a hierarchy of PIs in which quality of service comes a poor third.

If the analysis of PIs in the 1980s was very much in terms of the three Es, it is likely that there will be a greater demand for indicators of consumer satisfaction and quality in the 1990s. Despite criticisms about the lack of consumer-oriented PIs in the public sector, the experience of private sector firms and public utilities demonstrates the feasibility of developing such indicators. In particular, their PI systems often include indicators that seek to measure consumer satisfaction as an *output*, quite distinct from the sales figures: so, for example, complaints appear to be seen and used as a positive tool of management in a way which does not normally happen in the public sector. Similarly, consumer surveys are frequently used as tools of performance appraisal: both supermarket and high street retailer routinely use them to monitor consumer reactions to the way in which their branches are being run. The finding would seem fairly predictable. Private sector firms, particularly in competitive markets, have good reasons to seek feed-back about their consumers: here again the famous 'bottom line' is a very inadequate indicator – if a very good incentive – since waiting for profits to dip as a signal of consumer discontent may be courting the risk of bankruptcy. In contrast, monopoly public utilities – like water and BAA – do not. But here the explanation for the design of their PI systems is that consumer sensitivity (or at least the appearance of it) is the political price paid for their monopoly position. In effect, they are being required to demonstrate that they are not exploiting their captive consumers: in this respect, the way they assess their own performance has to be seen in the context of the wider regulatory systems within which they operate.

However, most public sector services face two specific problems in assessing consumer views. The first is conceptual: multiple objectives reflect the existence of multiple and disparate consumers. The second is practical: how best to devise indicators of consumer reactions. The first point is simply illustrated. Who are the consumers of police services? Is it those who have to call on their help, or have others dealing with them, or those who look to them to maintain an environment in which their help is not required? Who, similarly, are the consumers of prisons? Is it those who are in gaol or those who see prisons as the bastions protecting society against crime? Who are the consumers of the NHS? Is it those who actually use hospital and general practitioner services or those who see them as insurance against the day they have a heart attack? And sometimes, of course, the service providers see themselves as the main consumers. Clearly, these different audiences may have requirements from PIs that are mutually exclusive.

The last example from the NHS identifies the further problem that there is a fundamental ambiguity in the concept of consumerism when applied to public services. In the private market place, consumerism means the ability to signal demands for specific types of goods. If the consumers want more cars, and if they have the money to pay for them, they will get them. This concept creates problems in the case of public services operating with fixed budgets like the NHS, where consumer groups are effectively in competition with each other for scarce resources: improving services for the acutely ill may be at the expense of services for the chronically ill. It is therefore possible to argue (Klein 1984) that a certain degree of insensitivity to consumer demands is positively desirable in order to protect the interests of those consumers with the least resources for either exit or voice – that is, the most vulnerable.

Just as there has been criticism of the lack of consumer-oriented PIs, so there have been frequent complaints in the literature about the paucity of quality PIs. In particular, there is a yearning for quality PIs seen in terms of outcomes: i.e. the nature of the final product. And there were indeed some quality PIs in the systems that we studied which conformed to this model: for example, in the water industry it is possible to test various aspects of quality in this sense, such as purity and taste. The difficulties begin in organizations where the process of service delivery is the product. In these cases, 'quality' is not something identifiable in its own right, rather it is the by-product of activities that are being carried out. Quality, in this sense, can best be seen as the result of competence in the routine activities of the organization: something, in short which permeates all activity and is integral to everything that happens as distinct from being an add-on-extra. This was particularly clear in the case of private sector firms which used PIs to measure whether the process of providing goods or services is running smoothly and is tuned to consumer requirements. How often do the automatic pay-out points break down? How swiftly does the TV repairer call? Such indicators, as we have seen, may be either positive or negative. It may still be possible to have negative outcome indicators which signal that competence has not been achieved: if there is an excess of mortality or morbidity following NHS operations in a given hospital this may well be a signal that the quality of medical care is deficient. But, more often, the real indicators of quality will be that the ordinary, routine things are being done properly and on time: so, for example, the PI measuring the proportion of emergency ambulance calls which meet response time standards can be seen as a quality indicator in this larger sense. Similarly, social security has managed to use consumer surveys to help generate quality indicators and targets, such as the length of time that claimants have to wait in offices, the standard of the interview, and the quality of correspondence.

To summarize our findings, the task of designing and using PI systems would be made much easier if both quality and consumer satisfaction are regarded primarily as aspects of process – the way in which a service is delivered – rather than *what* is being delivered; that is if we see quality as a by-product of other activities rather than as a separate entity. To a large extent the quest for separate distinctive quality measures is illusory. Quality is actually part of the concept of efficiency, rather than its antithesis.

IDEAL INDICATORS?

In this section we consider whether it is possible to move towards a prescriptive theory of PIs (setting aside for now all reservations about the desirability of PIs *per se*). In other words, what makes a good PI? What are the characteristics and requisites of an acceptable PI system? It would be foolish, as others have acknowledged (Cave *et al.* 1988; Jackson 1988), to suggest that there are any definitive answers to such questions; indeed, our approach is premised on the assumption that the form a PI system takes will be contingent on the needs of different organizations. However, our findings do suggest that there tends to be an evolutionary pattern of convergence between PI systems. So, in addressing these questions, we use a mixture of a priori reasoning combined with what, broadly speaking, appear to be the 'best practices' adopted in the case studies.

Self-evidently, PIs should be relevant to the needs and objectives of the organization; in other words they should measure aspects of performance that are central to the efficient and effective delivery of quality services. They should not be susceptible to manipulation by the person or unit to be assessed, such as the citation level which, although gaining popularity as an indicator of academic research quality, is open to misuse by academics forming 'citation circles' to boost one another's rating (Cave *et al.* 1988). PIs should be reliable, being based on data produced by accurate information systems. And PIs need to be, as far as possible, unambiguous: i.e. not open to challenge by staff. They have to be a means of 'stopping up excuses', in the words of one manager.

But, as practical organizational tools, it is essential that PIs should be both comprehensible and usable. The satisfaction of this apparently modest a priori requirement seems to depend on three features of a PI system: volume, timeliness and data design. For a system to be comprehensible, it needs to be parsimonious. There is little point in the NHS (with some 2,000 PIs) or the police (over 400) possessing enormous numbers of PIs if the primary intended users – regional, district and unit managers – are confused by the sheer volume of statistics. Contrast this with social security or bank, the Lord Chancellor's department or supermarket, where a small core of no more than twenty (and usually less) PIs, provide an easily accessible, comprehensible picture of performance. Big systems are unwieldy, so parsimony also helps make PIs usable: managers find it easier to monitor progress against a handful of measures. However, to be usable, PIs must also be timely; in other words, they must record information quickly enough for it still to be meaningful as a guide to action. Hence NHS PIs which report information several months old are of little use for spotting and remedying immediate problems unlike supermarket, where the managing directors have information about shelf-fill in individual stores by mid-morning each day, or even the prison service where the Governor's Monitoring System provides detailed information about activity on a weekly basis. Lastly, PIs are both more comprehensible and usable if the system is custom-built. Thus the initial NHS package of PIs, hastily constructed in the wake of a Public Accounts Committee (1981) report that condemned the NHS for its poor management control systems, was primarily an exercise in relabelling existing statistics; a feature common to many departments after the subsequent introduction of the FMI. If, however, a PI system is *designed* with specific objectives and a clear vision of how it will be used, then its purpose is more likely to be comprehensible and its product usable.

These three characteristics also help to discriminate among organizational attitudes towards the design of PI systems. So we would expect an organizaton designing its PI system as part of a deliberate management strategy – as distinct from following the prevailing Whitehall fashion – to design its own data set, to want to have information quickly, and to concentrate on a handful of indicators linked to organizational objectives. Conversely, we would expect a conscript organization to have a system driven by existing data, to be leisurely in its time requirements, and to hope that the sheer quantity of information would fudge the need for precise managerial decisions.

However, organizational attitudes and, indeed, the development of comprehensible and usable PIs, will be influenced by the ability to overcome various conceptual design problems; in particular that of *performance ownership*. In short, who can be held responsible for which dimension or element of performance? The responsibility for performance within the organization may depend on central decisions over which the branch or unit manager has little control. Or, drawing on one of the organizational characteristics, the degree of complexity – the interdependence of different units, services or activities – will constrain the capacity of individual managers to act autonomously; for example, the throughput of a case through the court system will depend on the actions of judges, solicitors, barristers, court listings officers and, crucially, the nature of the defendant's plea. Environmental factors may also shape the impact of organizational actions. The uncertainty of the cause and effect relationship, illustrated by the difficulty of measuring effectiveness, therefore makes the construction of PIs very difficult.

The nature of these design problems will inevitably influence the way that PIs are used. They can be employed either as dials or as tin-openers (Carter 1989). 'Performance' can be read off the dials: that is, there is a set of norms or standards against which achievement can be assessed, as in measuring the quality of water. These norms or standards may be either positive or negative; prescriptive or postscriptive. Tin-openers are simply descriptive. They do not speak for themselves. They may signal that a particular unit, be it a crown court, prison or bank, is a statistical outlier, but no conclusions can be drawn from this fact in itself. It is simply an invitation to investigate, to probe and to ask questions. Thus where performance ownership is relatively straightforward, it is easier to construct dials; where it is ambiguous, then PIs are generally used as tin-openers. It should, however, be noted that PIs can be used as dials, or signals, even where there is no full understanding of cause and effect.

Underlying all of these factors is that of the acceptability of PIs to the staff and management within the organization: it is no good having an ideal system if it engenders serious, insurmountable resistance. But here we are moving into the issue of implementation.

IMPLEMENTING PERFORMANCE INDICATORS

In this section we outline the main patterns of implementation observed in our case studies and show how various organizational and political factors shaped these developments.

TABLE 2   Characteristics of performance indicators in the case studies

Organizations	Design Off-the-peg/Bespoke		Timeliness Slow/Quick		Volume Promiscuity/Parsimony	
Police	X		X		X	
Courts	X →			X		X
Prisons		X		XX		X
Social Security		X		X		X
NHS	X		XX		X	
Supermarket		X		XXX		X
High Street Retailer		X		X		X
Bank	X →		X			X
Building Societies (2)	X →			X		X
Jupiter (TVHire)		X		X		X
British Rail	X →			X	X →	
Water		X		X		X
BAA	X →			X		X

Notes:
  i) The arrows indicate where an organization is in the process of change
 ii) Timeliness: Quick – XXX – daily to weekly reporting; XX = weekly; X = monthly
         Slow – XX = half-yearly; X = quarterly
iii) Volume: promiscuity = over 100 performance indicators
        parsimony = a maximum of 30 performance indicators

The most significant conclusion to be drawn from our study is that differences between organizations do not follow neatly the public/private divide, and that there are differences within each group. The first column of table 2 shows that there is an almost even split between those organizations where the PI systems are based on data that pre-dated their invention (off-the-peg) and those where they developed their own data base (bespoke). A majority of private sector organizations, but not all, fall into the bespoke category while the public sector divides down the middle. The second shows the speed of production, with only two organizations – both in the public sector – in the historical category, i.e. relying on year-old data. The third shows the quantity of PIs generated, on a scale from parsimony (numbering, at most, thirty PIs) to promiscuity (over a hundred PIs), with these same two organizations – the NHS and the police – in the 'promiscuous' column; British Rail which was in the same category when our study started had already begun to move towards 'parsimony'. So it would seem that the second conclusion that can be drawn from the evidence is that the NHS and the police are somehow different from the other organizations studied.

Both conclusions are confirmed by the way in which organizations use PIs. While our studies showed that nearly all the organizations were at least beginning to move, if only tentatively, towards the prescriptive use of indicators – i.e. setting objectives or targets against which performance can be measured – the NHS and the police remain behind the pack. In this respect, however, they were joined by the prison service which, as table 2 shows, has a bespoke, parsimonious and quick PI system. All three continue to use PIs as tin-openers rather than as dials (the NHS uses targets in the annual review cycle between the Department of Health and the regional health authorities but these have not been incorporated in the PI package). Again, the differences between organizations do not follow the public/private distinction.

If the public/private dichotomy does not help us much in explaining the way in which organizations set about assessing their own performances, what does? The famous bottom line may be the driving force behind the development of PIs in private firms but it does not dictate convergence between them any more than its equivalent in the public sector, prime ministerial enthusiasm, brings about convergence among the departments and agencies examined. For a more elaborate explanation of this complex pattern, other organizational characteristics are more helpful.

Two organizations, the NHS and the police, stand out from the rest. In the NHS, just about all the factors liable to make the definition and measurement of performance difficult are present. It is characterized by heterogeneity, complexity and uncertainty. That is, it is a multi-product organization, which has to mobilize a large cast with a high degree of interdependence between the different actors and where the relationship between activity and impact is often uncertain. It is not always clear who 'owns' the performance; the activities of the NHS are only one of many factors influencing the health of the population. The overall objectives, even when defined, tend to be at a high level of generality. In addition, the principal actors involved – notably but not exclusively the medical profession – enjoy a high degree of autonomy. The structure of authority is complex. The line of accountability from periphery to centre is clear in theory but often blurred in practice: indeed the introduction of PIs can be seen as part of a strategy to centralize knowledge about local performance while decentralizing responsibility for the execution of government policies – centralizing in order to decentralize (Perrow 1977). All in all, despite some recent evidence of change (for example, PIs may soon be available on a monthly rather than yearly basis), the NHS thus stands out as the paradigmatic example of the organizational characteristics likely to produce a data-driven, slow and promiscuous set of PIs, which are then used descriptively rather than prescriptively.

The police display many, though not all, of the organizational characteristics of our paradigmatic case. The service is low on complexity, but high on heterogeneity and uncertainty. The ownership of performance is often uncertain; the principal actors, though lacking professional status, enjoy a high degree of autonomy; authority is divided between central and local government and accountability is fuzzy. So the fact that the NHS and the police have a similar record when it comes to the design and use of PIs seems to vindicate our emphasis on organizational characteristics as decisive factors influencing the assessment of performance across and within the conventional public/private groupings. The point is further reinforced if we look at the other three 'service' agencies – social security, the courts and the prison service – within the public sector. The profile of social security – low on heterogeneity, complexity and uncertainty, with clear lines of accountability and a labour force that works within a set of very precise rules – is reflected in its bespoke, parsimonious system, relatively timely PIs, and the recent development of targets or norms against which performance can be 'read off'. The prison service has, if anything, a more streamlined system but uses its PIs descriptively rather than prescriptively while, conversely, the courts have a less bespoke system but do have some dials. The last two examples may provide a mixed picture, of course, precisely because their organizational characteristics are less clear-cut than the other public sector agencies so far discussed.

Clearly, one implementation constraint underlying developments in all of these public sector organizations relates to the autonomy and power of service providers. The acceptability of PIs to staff will depend not just on the technical design of the system but also on the broader implications it has for the distribution of power within the organization. The imposition of a top-down system designed by and for managers, generates considerable suspicion; like the dreaded factory time-and-motion study the introduction of PIs may be seen as an instrument of management control.

Professional opposition is not confined to managerial initiatives, it may also resist consumer power. Although it appears self-evident that consumers of public sector monopolies offering no means of exit should have the opportunity to exercise voice, in practice there are a number of important interests who may be reluctant to listen: these include politicians, managers and, most important, agenda-setting professional service providers fearful of any incursion by the consumer on their autonomy.

Successful implementation therefore may depend on the willingness to fight the political battle against service providers as well as on the ability of managers to negotiate change. Significantly, trade unions were able to resist management by objectives and other performance measurement schemes in the early 1970s (Garrett 1980). But by the 1980s, the diminution of union influence coupled with the absence of any autonomous professional grouping, help explain the differences between social security and the other public sector organizations systems where there is strong opposition from service providers – doctors, police, judges, prison officers. In this context, it is worth noting that the Treasury and Civil Service Committee (1990) recommended that each agency be assessed on 'how well it delivers the goods and the extent to which it meets the needs of the customers' (para. 23), that 'performance bonuses should be linked to customer service targets as well as other financial and non-financial targets' (para. 53) and noted approvingly the wide number of quality performance targets already in use. It will be interesting to observe whether this can substitute for the competitive market which brings its own pressures to provide what consumers want.

98   NEIL CARTER

All the public services so far considered are non-trading organizations. How important is this factor, as distinct from the 'publicness' of the organizations concerned? To answer this question, we can turn to the public utilities (one of which, water, was on the point of moving into private ownership at the time of our field work). These are all services which sell their products or services. Like firms in the private sector they therefore have a 'bottom line': at the end of the year they have to account for their financial performance. They are quite a homogeneous group: very much closer to the social security than the NHS model – with bespoke, relatively quick and parsimonious PI systems, and sets of standards or norms against which performance can be 'read off'. But there are problems about interpreting this finding since it could be attributable to a variety of factors. Obviously, it could reflect the fact that they are in tradable sectors. But there may be other explanations as well. It could reflect the fact that the organizational characteristics of the utilities are much closer to social security than to the NHS: i.e. they tend to be low on heterogeneity, complexity and uncertainty. It could reflect the fact that they have hierarchical authority structures and do not depend on professionals or others who have successfully asserted their autonomy. It could reflect the monopoly position of two out of the three utilities – water and BAA – which has created the demand for a system of PIs designed to protect consumers against exploitation by giving visibility to the achievement of specific standards; and while the third, British Rail, is not quite a monopoly it does have captive consumers on some commuter lines.

To disentangle these alternative – or possible complementary – explanations, let us turn to the private sector firms. If the decisive factor were the 'bottom line', i.e. the fact these firms sell their goods or services, then we would again expect to find a homogeneous group. But, in practice, there are considerable variations within it; for example, the contrast between supermarket – the paradigmatic case at the opposite end of the scale to the NHS – and bank is as great as that, say, between social security and the police in the public sector. But heterogeneity, complexity and uncertainty are not the decisive factors here. Rather, the degree of competition appears to be critical. Thus supermarket operates in a highly competitive environment, with everyone in the organization aware of the struggle for market shares, while bank was operating in what had, until recently, been a somewhat sleepy market, with customers inherited rather than won over. Indeed during the course of our study, bank was in the process of smartening up its PI system: a clear response to the increasingly competitive environment in which it found itself.

This also underlines a more general point: the time dimension (Pollitt 1990). Most of the systems covered by our case studies were evolving and developing during the period of our inquiry (and no doubt are continuing to do so). Overall, the evidence suggests certain regularities in this pattern of organizational learning: an innovation cycle. First, the pressure to introduce performance measurement leads to perfunctory compliance, expressed in the production (often over-production) of PIs – perhaps, as in the case of the NHS, through the mass baptism of existing statistics as PIs. Next the production of PIs leads to resistance, notably attempts to discredit them by questioning their validity, timeliness and appropriateness. There appears to be a standard repertory of denigration common to almost all the organizations studied. In response, refinements follow, leading to the discovery that PIs may, after all, be useful – although not necessarily always in the ways intended by their designers (so, for example, the organization may 'capture' the PI system in the sense that indicators are used to justify bottom-up claims for resources rather than as top-down instruments of control). Similarly, over time and with experience, indicators initially used as tin-openers may become dials. We do not wish to suggest that this cycle is inevitable in any deterministic sense or that all organizations will necessarily follow it, let alone that it is a normative or prescriptive model. Rather, it illustrates the intricate organizational processes and negotiations that will inevitably accompany the implementation of a PI system.

Our evidence therefore underlines the complexity of trying to understand the way in which different organizations set about assessing their own performance. No one explanation will do the trick. We can certainly dismiss the conventional view that the decisive factor is the presence or absence of a bottom-line or the difference between organizations in the public and private sectors. We can, tentatively, suggest that organizational characteristics tend to shape PI strategies in the public sector (although the initial catalyst was external political pressure), while it is the degree of competition which is the chief driving force in the private sector. But our findings are a warning, if anything, about adopting any mono-causal explanation: the way in which PI systems will be shaped and used is contingent on a constantly changing environment, where new demands will create the need for adaptive organizational responses. This can be illustrated by reconsidering one of the 'ideal' features of a PI system – parsimony. The heterogeneity and complexity of the NHS mean that a small set of PIs would fall hopelessly short of providing any sort of credible, comprehensive coverage of organizational performance. Indeed, as we have seen, the NHS has responded to criticisms of its earlier systems from politicians, managers, providers and consumers by multiplying the number of PIs. This suggests a further observation: the more audiences with conflicting interests that an organization has to satisfy, the more likely it is to offend against parsimony.

CONCLUSION

Performance is a complex and contestable concept. This statement holds whether or not an organization has the benefit of a bottom-line. For it is a central finding of our research that the problems of performance measurement transcend the public/private divide, and that cross-cutting organizational characteristics are most helpful in explaining variation in the nature and use of PIs. Even within the public sector there are many dimensions of performance and currencies of evaluation in circulation. The academic literature, in concentrating on the domination of the 'three Es' model and berating the cost-cutting objectives of the government during the 1980s has, on the one hand, underplayed the conceptual and technical difficulties of measuring performance and, on the other hand, underestimated the extent to which organizations are using measures of effectiveness. It is therefore possible to speculate that

100   NEIL CARTER

the large number of 'caseload' services among the new 'Next Steps' agencies implies that throughput will be a core effectiveness indicator in the 1990s. Already the Treasury and Civil Service Committee cites examples, such as Companies House aims to reduce the time taken to process documents by 20 per cent and the Driving Standards Agency to decrease the waiting time for driving tests to an average of eight weeks (1990, para. 49). Moreover, both PIs are examples of quality PIs, illustrating our finding that public sector organizations can measure quality (and consumer satisfaction), particularly if quality is regarded as a by-product of doing the basic tasks well. However, technical capacity may not be enough to guarantee the emergence of the consumer PI; our findings show that the constraints on measuring consumer satisfaction frequently arise from organizational politics rather than any inability to solve conceptual puzzles.

A crucial factor determining the evolution of PI systems in the 1990s may, therefore, turn out to be whether or not the politics of design and implementation change. As we have seen, in the 1980s PI systems in the public sector evolved largely in response to a variety of governmental initiatives, reflecting a preoccupation with *internal* or managerial accountability (Day and Klein 1987): i.e. a concern with making government agencies answerable for their use of resources. The market or audience for PIs was accordingly restricted; the number of policy actors was limited. The question for the 1990s is whether or not the market and the actors will expand. Will PI systems become recognized as instruments of *democratic* accountability and come to be seen as a way of making government answerable to Parliament and others? If so, the nature as well as the size of the market will change, and PI systems in turn will inevitably be adapted to respond to different sets of interests and values.

REFERENCES
Beeton, D. (ed.) 1988. *Performance measurement: getting the concepts right*. London: Public Finance Foundation.
British Railways Board. 1990. *Annual report and accounts 1989/90*. London: BRB.
Carter, N. 1988. 'Measuring government performance', *Political Quarterly* 59, 3, 369–75.
——. 1989. 'Performance indicators: "backseat driving" or "hands-off" control', *Policy and Politics* 17, 2, 131–8.
——. 1990. 'Britain' in R. Wettenhall and C. O'Nuallain (eds.), *Public enterprise performance evaluation: seven country studies*. Brussels: IIAS.
Carter, N., R. Klein and P. Day. 1991. *How organizations measure success*. London: Routledge.
Cave, M., S. Hanney, M. Kogan and G. Trevitt. 1988. *The use of performance indicators in higher education*. London: Jessica Kingsley.
Clegg, S. and D. Dunkerley. 1980. *Organization, class and control*. London: Routledge Kegan Paul.
Day, P. and R. Klein. 1987. *Accountabilities*. London: Tavistock.
Dunleavy, P. 1989. 'The architecture of the British central state', *Public Administration* 67, 3, 249–75.
Flynn, A., A. Gray, W. Jenkins and B. Rutherford. 1988. 'Making indicators perform', *Public Money and Management* (winter): 35–41.
Garrett, J. 1980. *Managing the civil service*. London: Heinemann.
Hood, C. and A. Dunsire. 1981. *Bureaumetrics*. Aldershot: Gower.
Hopwood, A. 1984. 'Accounting and the pursuit of efficiency' in A. Hopwood and C. Tomkins (eds.), *Issues in public sector accounting*. Oxford: Philip Allan.
Jackson, P. 1988. 'The management of performance in the public sector', *Public Money and Management* (winter), 11–16.
Jenkins, K., K. Caines, and A. Jackson. 1988. *Improving management in government: the next steps*. London: HMSO.

LEARNING TO MEASURE PERFORMANCE 101

Klein, R. 1984. 'The politics of participation' in R. Maxwell and N. Weaver (eds.) *Public participation in health*. London: King Edward's Hospital Fund.

Levitt, M. and M. Joyce. 1987. *The growth and efficiency of public spending*. Cambridge: Cambridge University Press.

North East Thames Regional Health Authority. 1984. *Responses to DHSS 1985 package of performance indicators*. Mimeo.

Perrow, C. 1977. 'The bureaucratic paradox: the efficient organisation centralizes in order to decentralize' *Organizational Dynamics* Spring, 3–14.

Pollitt, C. 1986. 'Beyond the managerial model: the case for broadening performance assessment in government and the public services', *Financial Accountability and Management* 2, 3, 155–70.

——. 1987. 'Capturing quality? The quality issue in British and American health care policies', *Journal of Public Policy* 7, 1, 71–92.

——. 1988. 'Bringing consumers into performance measurement: concepts, consequences and constraints', *Policy and Politics* 16, 2, 77–87.

——. 1990. 'Performance indicators: root and branch' in M. Cave, M. Kogan and R. Smith (eds.), *Output and performance measurement in government*. London: Jessica Kingsley.

Prime Minister and Chancellor of the Exchequer. 1983. *Financial management in government departments*. Cmnd. 4506. London: HMSO.

Public Accounts Committee. 1981. *Financial control and accountability in the National Health Service*. 17th report, Session 1980–81. London: HMSO.

Pugh, D. and D. Hickson. 1976. *Organizational structure in its context: the Aston Programme 1*. Aldershot: Gower.

Treasury. 1978. *The nationalised industries*. Cmnd. 7131. London: HMSO.

——. 1986. *Output and performance measurement in central government: progress in departments*. (ed. S. Lewis) Treasury Working Paper No. 38.

Treasury and Civil Service Committee. 1982. *Efficiency and effectiveness in the civil service*. 3rd report, Session 1981–82. London: HMSO.

——. 1990. *Progress in the next steps initiative*. 8th report, Session 1989–90. London: HMSO.

Vickers, G. 1965. *The art of judgement*. London: Chapman Hall.

Performance Measurement: Focusing on the Key Issue

David Brookfield
University of Liverpool, UK

Background

Budgeting and the control of costs, in one form or another, has been an issue of major focus in the NHS for over 20 years. An excellent summary exists[1] of the different initiatives over that period: management budgeting, the Griffiths Report, resource management, and so on. In one respect, their common denominator has been failure from the point of view of there being little evidence that clinicians have accepted managerial responsibility for their medical decisions[2]. One possible reason for this lack of success is simply stated, as Wildavsky[3] observed: every "budget" or resource-constraint *implies* conflict. To put it another way, the word "budget" implies the negative "no". This is not merely semantics, because if funds are resource-constrained then a decision to use resources on the treatment of one condition means that those same resources cannot then be used to treat another condition. A real opportunity cost exists in that the cost of treating one condition is the pain and discomfort another patient must endure while their condition awaits treatment. This seems almost too obvious to require stating, yet the fact has been frequently ignored in attempting to gain acceptance of budgetary responsibility by those whose decisions use up resources. No amount of meetings to educate and no amount of tinkering with different financial systems will alter or address the basic conflict that budgetary responsibility impinges on clinical judgement: the decision whom to treat in the light of a resource constraint. Inevitably, clinicians view new budgeting schemes as another way of altering this decision which, they would argue, should only be medically based.

But has the focus on budget responsibility been correct? Do clinicians really exert a great deal of influence over the amount of money spent within a unit? And are the existing financial systems an accurate reflection of unit performance? The objective of this article is to indicate how some of these issues may be seen differently in the light of new research into performance measurement.

Budget Focus and Performance Measurement

The main criticism of existing budgetary practices is that they are of little interest to clinicians[1]. This exposes a deeper problem assuming the objectives of clinicians are congruous with those of patient care: that is, for budgetary systems to be acceptable to clinicians they must/should accord with the primary objective of a public health service which might be expressed in terms of promoting health care and curing/treating conditions of all types.

Journal of Management in
Medicine, VOL. 6 No. 2, 1992,
pp.39-45. © MCB University Press
0268-9235

Journal of
Management
in Medicine
6,2

40

Clinicians' objectives are then assumed to be goal-congruent with the stated objective of a public health service. One way clinicians may work to maximize public benefit in the NHS is to achieve the greatest level of patient throughput consistent with best medical practice/suitable outcomes[4]. This is a straightforward and easily identifiable measure of performance. However, carried too far, high throughput rates inevitably lead to budget deficits in a resource-constrained environment. This does not imply that budget deficits are only caused by high throughput rates, but that the focus on budget deficits being the result, say, of mismanagement of units cannot be entirely correct since there is much evidence that throughput rates have risen dramatically over recent years: average length of in-patient stay in England has fallen from 9.4 days in 1979 to 6.4 days in 1989/90 while available beds fell from 361,670 to 220,334 over the same period[5]. In this sense, budget deficits and throughput rates (clinicians' efficiency) are directly related. The reason why budget deficits do not principally reflect on mismanagement is that much of NHS expenditure is fixed on a within-year basis (upwards of 80 per cent of annual budget)[6, p. 29], the main item of expenditure in the NHS being manpower (upwards of 75 per cent)[6, p. 65], which is only variable *at the margin* because unit managers do not and cannot rigorously operate a hire and fire policy. The remaining 25 per cent of costs (drugs, food, etc.) are not all variable: although the clinician can alter the mix of treatment, there will always be an element of cost whatever mix is chosen since bed occupancy rates are of the order of 80 per cent (average daily available beds as a proportion of average daily occupied beds for the 1980s)[5]. What little room for manoeuvre exists in admitting patients at the margin will have associated costs which are truly variable (or marginal) and hence it is these patients who give rise to expenditure greater than anticipated when throughput rates increase.

Thus, if the budget allocation to a unit was variable in accordance with throughput rates then budget deficits would have their usual accounting interpretation: a greater utilization of resources, or excess efficiency; not an excess of expenditure. This view is supported in the context of reducing waiting lists. If budget allocations to units reflect the desire to achieve the objective of a public health service then why does the existence of a budget deficit, which leads to financial stringency, increase waiting lists and, more importantly, waiting time? If clinicians and managers are asked to be more efficient then why is efficiency penalized when the consequences of a budget deficit have to be faced? It is because efficiency measured in relation to budget allocations and effectiveness measured in terms of medical care are contradictory. That is, the existing focus of budgetary responsibility is essentially in conflict with a desirable public health service objective.

An Alternative Measure of Performance
Questions as to whether financial and performance reporting are in conflict with the basic objective of an organization are being addressed in the business world with some interesting results. Instead of financial reporting acting as a constraint on the activities of a business, new performance measures encourage greater

expenditure but only if it is consistent with the basic objective of a business: making a profit. The fact that the business's objective is to make a profit does not mean these new accounting measures are irrelevant to a public health service; what does make the new procedures relevant is that they are consistent with the basic objective, whatever it is.

The new techniques are described in terms of throughput analysis (hereafter referred to as throughput accounting)[7], which recognizes the fact that operational decisions are taken within the context of an environment where most expenditure is fixed, or the decision-making process should recognize that only relatively few inputs are truly variable in the short term: these inputs may give rise to a high proportion of cost in some business situations, but they are relatively few in number and hence easy to identify and control. Clearly, this is a short-term analysis since in the long term all costs are variable. But that is the arena of strategic policy and has only general impact on short-term operational decisions. For the NHS, the amount of expenditure which is variable (the true marginal cost) in the short term is a small proportion of the total: logically then, accounting systems which measure unit performance should reflect this fact.

41

The identification of truly marginal costs has a number of benefits. First, the recognition by clinicians that those with financial responsibility (typically not the clinicians) are focusing resources on those areas which meet the public health/benefit objective is likely to encourage a greater financial interest by clinicians: they would be foolish to ignore it. Second, the identification of truly marginal costs (a joint clinician/manager process) which support the main objective ensures that resources are allocated to those areas which need them in terms of maximizing throughput since maximizing throughput is consistent with the main objective: in terms of existing performance indicators there is evidence that "in combating premature mortality, morbidity, pain and distress it is better to maximize patient throughput"[4]. Third, this process must inevitably lead to an improvement in the quality of communication between clinicians and managers; not because it is forced on clinicians, but because it is in their interest (goal congruence).

The success of this type of operational policy may be measured by what is known as the Primary Ratio[8].

$$\text{Primary Ratio (PM)} = \frac{\text{Throughput}}{\text{Total cost} - \text{Marginal cost}}$$

The figure adopted for throughput will typically be deaths and discharges, although this does not preclude an alternative which offers an indication of outcome in relation to discharges only (this will be dealt with in greater detail later). Total cost less marginal cost would ordinarily be referred to as some measure of fixed cost (marginal costs in this sense are the costs relating to those activities which could be redeployed if unused[9].) However, in terms of throughput accounting it is only valid to call this fixed cost in relation to those costs that are invariant with throughput in the short term.

Journal of
Management
in Medicine
6,2

42

In another context, some of these costs may be variable (in the long term, for example). Thus, as throughput increases the efficiency of the unit increases in terms of stretching a greater amount of utilization of resources over fixed costs. Since costs are, in the majority, fixed then any measure which promotes greater throughput obtains greater benefit from those activities which consume most of the hospital budget. The effectiveness measured by the Primary Ratio is critically dependent on the choice of throughput measure. In other words, it is dependent on the measure of efficiency identified by clinicians and management which, when maximized, leads to greater public benefit. This has been expressed in terms of using a set of "management coefficients"[10]. This should indeed be the case, since the measure is not merely a financial one but is based on a considered view of how best to deliver patient care based on collective experience.

In this way, account is taken of priorities and capacities at a unit level where operational, short-term decisions are made. Moreover, the Primary Ratio is not a global measure which, when applied, automatically allocates resources over competing demands since, in order to do this, it would have to be calculated over each of the clinical and/or other procedures which give rise to a competing demand. It is capable of doing this because it is precisely at this point where the use of management coefficients have a role to play in determining how best to maximize patient benefit and to establish what opportunity costs arise in a fixed-resource environment. Although "management coefficients" imply commercial judgement it is not the case in this context. The coefficients referred to would represent a clinically determined workload. Once set, performance will then be measured against the utilization of fixed resources.

Implications

The adoption of throughput accounting performance measures which recognize the Primary Ratio as reflecting the objective and purpose of a public health service leads to some rather difficult policy implications.

First, as currently measured budget deficits are seen as "bad" but in terms of the Primary Ratio are perceived as "good" since they are directly related to throughput which is to be maximized if the public health service goal is to be achieved. It is inevitable that hospitals operate in a resource-constrained environment and hence the question of the adoption of the Primary Measure to assess units has funding implications beyond the scope of this article. What is being highlighted is the inconsistency of existing measures as reflected in budget deficits.

Second, if it is desirable to integrate the two pillars of activity within a unit (medical and administrative) then goal congruence is undeniable[11]. If it is accepted that better public health is a desirable objective and that greater throughput is consistent with this, then an accounting measure which conflicts with greater throughput conflicts with the (assumed) objectives of clinicians and hence dysfunctional behaviour is unavoidable.

Third, throughput accounting cannot, in the form presented, provide an answer to all medical decisions which have an impact on unit throughput; but that does not mean it is inconsistent with them. This is particularly the case with respect to *which* patients are treated. This decision is rightly made by clinicians on medical grounds, but consider the following example: patients A and B are to be considered by the surgeon for in-patient treatment. Patient A will occupy twice as much theatre time as patient B. Patient C has the same medical condition as patient B and is similar in all respects in terms of using the same unit resources as patient B. The choice facing the surgeon is whether to treat patient A or patients B and C for the same use of resources. Throughput accounting would suggest that patients B and C are treated. But if patient A's condition was such that it rated greater urgency then the surgeon would, explicitly or implicitly, attach greater weight to patient A's condition (explicitly by a factor greater than 2, in this case, since that would then generate greater throughput) and hence patient A would be treated at this moment. The attachment of a weight to the treatment of patient A is undertaken all the time and is done implicitly when clinicians categorize their waiting lists into "urgent", "soon" and "routine". If the Primary Measure is to be fully consistent with better medical care then this weighting scheme needs to be specifically addressed. This is not extra work, but explicit identification of existing practice.

Fourth, empty beds are "good". If it is the case that the following week's schedule of in-patient admissions give rise to particularly lengthy, per-patient theatre use and correspondingly there is no need to admit in-patients until theatre time is available, then performance measures which are based on bed utilization provide inconsistent measures of better medical care. In other words, performance measures which recommend a course of action which have no bearing on the ultimate objective, at a particular period of time (the short term) cannot affect or contribute to the ultimate objective. This does not mean to say that the hospital is being negligent in its duty in having empty beds, but that medical decisions have been made which have prioritized such a schedule (given that it is assumed that medical decisions are consistent with the ultimate goal). Alternatively, if it is the case that the following week's schedule of admissions requires full utilization of available beds as a result, say, of long post-operative care, then this may give rise to unused theatre time. In this case, empty theatres are "good" since throughput is being maximized by the highly-weighted patients who currently occupy bed space (compare with recent criticism of empty theatres by the Public Accounts Committee[12]). What all this highlights are not the inefficiencies of clinicians and managers in being able to utilize all resources simultaneously, but the bottlenecks in patient care. If it is good to have empty beds then the bottleneck may be theatre time. If it is good to have unused theatre time then the bottleneck may be bed availability. This process therefore suggests where resources be directed in accordance with the main objectives.

Fifth, administration of the hospital budget becomes a simpler task. Beyond the constraint on the budget itself, the complexities of cost allocation can be ignored. Although it is appreciated that any cost allocation scheme is arbitrary, the key point to recognize is that, for example, the treatment of one extra patient does not give rise to extra administrative costs, support staff costs or any costs

Performance
Measurement

43

Journal of
Management
in Medicine
6,2

44

which are typically derived from service centres. The reason is that, although personnel working in providing such services are essential to the overall operational capability of the unit, their associated costs are fixed in the short to medium term and will therefore not vary at the margin where important operational decisions are made.

Sixth, the throughput accounting approach overcomes the criticism that all accounting systems are solely motivated by economy. Economy and operating within a budget are important issues in a resource-constrained environment, but throughput accounting can operate to a budget, and not lead to the penalization of efficiency and hence to dysfunctional behaviour, because it promotes efficiency in accordance with the ultimate objective within the confines of a budget. In this sense, throughput accounting is a different and more correct way of measuring success within or outwith the confines of a budget. Throughput accounting has implications for the introduction of Diagnostic Related Groups (DRG) and the costing of a "package of treatment" (speciality, clinical or patient costing and other allocation or recharging methods are relevant here). In terms of charging a patient for resources used, a DRG calculation is appropriate since cost recovery is essential in a profit-making institution. This does not apply to the NHS since it is not profit-making and DRGs are only appropriate for information purposes. They cannot form the basis of decision making regarding treatment since they include an element of cost which is unrelated to any one individual patient treatment and are therefore irrelevant to the achievement of the main objective.

Conclusion

This article does not ignore the fact that health authorities are cash-constrained or that units are required to work in such an environment. What is suggested is that performance measures should not lead to the penalization of hospitals which are effective in delivering patient care. As seen, this is not necessarily indicated by budget surpluses, high bed occupancy and a high level of theatre utilization. Any performance measure must be seen in the context of delivering patient care by the identification of those costs which arise at the level of the individual patient: one way of measuring this is to use the (weighted) Primary Ratio. This is consistent with the ultimate objective. In addition, it promotes greater throughput activity without necessarily compromising medical care and, in so doing, maximizes the benefits to be derived from existing resources. This, too, is consistent with reducing waiting lists and, more importantly, waiting time.

References
1. Pollitt, C., Harrison, S., Hunter, D. and Marnoch, G., "The Reluctant Managers: Clinicians and Budgets in the NHS", *Financial Accountability and Management*, Vol. 4, Autumn, 1988, pp. 213-33.
2. Wickens, I., Coles, J.M., Flux, R. and Howard, M., "Review of Clinical Budgeting and Costing Experiments", *British Medical Journal*, Vol. 286, 1983, pp. 575-86.
3. Wildavsky, A., *Budgeting: A Comparative Theory of Budgetary Processes*, Little Brown, Boston, MA, 1975.
4. Bourn, M. and Ezzamel, M., "Costing and Budgeting in the National Health Service", *Financial Accountability and Management*, Vol. 2, 1986, pp. 53-71.

5. HMSO, *Health and Personal Social Service Statistics for England*, Department of Health, 1991.

6. Perrin, J., "Resource Management in the NHS", Van Nostrand Reinhold (UK), in association with Health Services Management Centre, 1988.

7. Goldratt, E. and Cox, J., *The Goal*, Gower Press, Aldershot, 1984.

8. White, K., "Making it Flow", *Accountancy Age*, October 1991, pp. 37-9.

9. Drummond, M.F., Ludbrook, A., Lowson, K. and Steel, A., *Studies in Economic Appraisal in Health Care*, Vol. 2, 1986, Oxford University Press, Oxford.

10. Aggarwal, S.C., "MRP, JIT, OPT, FMS?", *Harvard Business Review*, September-October, 1985, pp. 8-16.

11. Eskin, F., "Hospital Clinicians and Managers: Adversaries or Partners", *Journal of Management in Medicine*, Vol. 2, 1987-88, pp. 233-42.

12. Public Accounts Committee, *Fourth Report of the Committee of Public Accounts, Progress on NHS Operating Theatres and Waiting Lists in England*, HMSO, 1991.

(All communications in respect of this article should be made to Dr D. Brookfield, Department of Economics & Accounting, PO Box 147, University of Liverpool, Liverpool L69 3BX.)

Performance
Measurement

45

[19]

1

BRINGING CONSUMERS INTO PERFORMANCE MEASUREMENT:
concepts, consequences and constraints

Christopher Pollitt

As the practice of formal measurement of the performance of public services spreads attempts are beginning to be made to combine this measurement with the even more recent fashion for a 'consumer approach'. This paper argues that there are a range of sometimes incompatible ideas at play behind the popular label of 'consumerism'. The consequences of combining performance measurement with a consumer approach will depend very much on *which* concept of the consumer is being invoked. In conclusion it is pointed out that, while current conceptions of the public service consumer are often stultifyingly apolitical and narrow, the bolder versions of consumerism also face apparently considerable but largely unexplored constraints.

Background

During the last decade, and especially the last five years, most public services have taken on board formal performance measurement, (Pollitt, 1986a). The NHS has evolved an elaborate system of 'performance indicators', and the universities are now, laboriously, following them. Local authorities are obliged to include certain performance information in their annual reports. Under the Financial Management Initiative Whitehall departments have developed a very wide range of performance measures. The police, the prison service, social service departments, libraries — all these and more have become caught up with the trend to formalize, quantify and publish under the 'performance' label information concerning salient aspects of their activities (see, for example, Audit Commission, 1985; CIPFA, 1984; Cullen, 1986; Elton, 1987; James, 1987; Lewis, 1986; Pollitt, 1985 and 1986b; Schuller, 1987; Turney, 1987; Yates, 1983).

In most cases consideration of the use service *consumers* might make of the data thus generated

was fairly low down the list of priorities of those hurrying to put performance measurement systems in place. On the contrary, the majority of performance measurement schemes appear to have been 'top-down' affairs, propelled by the interests of politicians and senior officials in controlling both expenditure and the range and types of activities engaged in by lower level officials, particularly the 'street level' service deliverers — counter staff, schoolteachers, social workers and so on (Pollitt, 1986a). Consumers were to be involved, if at all, only in the most indirect manner — as eventual beneficiaries of the enhanced efficiency which performance indicators were supposed to identify and encourage. Two examples will help to illustrate this. The second set of NHS performance indicators, circulated in the late Spring of 1985, were supposed to incorporate several improvements over the first (1983) package, not least by a special emphasis on the 'acceptability' of clinical services. Yet not a single patient was to be asked a single question in order to establish this 'acceptability' — the concept was to be realised through a set of indirect measures invented by a national working party of clinicians and senior administrators. The second example comes from higher education. At a 1986 OECD conference in Paris a senior DES official presented a fascinating paper reviewing progress with P.I.s for UK universities and polytechnics (Cullen, 1986). The paper knowledgeably discussed a number of technical and methodological problems with P.I.s in higher education. Nowhere, however, were the desirability or practicability of devising and disseminating performance data for students and/or their parents even broached. Reading on and between the lines of this and other recent government documents it is clear that P.I.s are being pressed on our institutions of higher education by central government. The performance dialogue remains one between the government and the profession (Turney, 1987). In the continuing struggle for control/autonomy between Vice Chancellors, Polytechnic Directors and the DES the consumer has no place at the table.

During the last two or three years, however, 'consumerism' has appeared on the public service scene, not for the first time (there was an earlier flicker of fashion in the late 1960s and early '70s), but now with the vigour of an idea whose time has officially come. 'Consumer choice', of course, is one of the more popular slogans of the neo-liberal 'new right', and it has recently begun to receive regular ministerial approbation in (most obviously) the fields of public health care and education. It was probably only a matter of time before someone started to link consumerism with performance measurement. One early sign came, appropriately enough, from the National Consumer Council. In 1986 the Council published the first results of a substantial initiative to develop consumer-oriented measures of local authority services, (NCC, 1986) and then in September 1987 mounted a major conference, *Measuring up: performance measures in the local government and health sectors.*[1] On the surface this would appear to be a stylish union. The pro-active, performance-conscious public service professionals of the late '80s open a dialogue with their consumers, sharing information and constantly striving to get closer to expressed consumer wishes. This is the vision of the future held out in the Griffiths Report (1983), Kenneth Baker's 1987 education bill, the FMI white papers and a host of other official statements and documents. To the political theorist, however, all this enthusiasm bypasses some important prior questions. These concern the whole character of 'consumerism' in the public services.

'Consumerism' and the public services
Any diligent survey of the recent literature soon reveals that rival conceptions are at work here, ranging all the way from cosmetic, 'charm school' approaches through improved provision of information to direct consumer participation and power-sharing. In hospitals, schools, housing schemes, libraries and elsewhere managers are being exhorted to pay more attention to consumer wishes, and to develop techniques for 'marketing' their particular service. But if we ask which brands of consumerism are actually being implemented, what do we find? The picture is far from clear, but there are at least *prima facie* grounds for the suspicion that many initiatives cluster at the charm-school-and-better-wallpaper end of the spectrum.

As one Community Health Council official wrote of the NHS:

'Consumerism in 1985 is about customer relations, not patients' rights ... this model is a "harmless" version of consumerism — it requires little serious change but much public visibility' (Winkler, 1987, p. 1).

This may be an unduly harsh, or geographically specific, or quickly-dating judgement (but see NHS, 1986). Yet it is a concern that has been echoed many times, in both NHS and local authority contexts, (e.g. Stewart and Clarke, 1987, pp. 169–170; Rhodes, 1987). On the other hand there are cases where recent policy shifts have gone beyond improved presentation and information-giving, and have clearly enhanced consumer rights or otherwise empowered the customer or client for a public service. The right-to-buy legislation in public housing was one such example, the extension, through the 1980 Education Act, of parental participation in school governing bodies another. Tenant self-management schemes, at least in some varieties, are a third. Overall, therefore, it is difficult to generalise: the consumer emphasis in housing, health, education and welfare services is even newer than performance measurement. It is still embryonic, fragile, diverse in its forms. 'Improving consumer information', for example, *could* mean offering consumers performance data which they could use to make real choices. Far more often, however, it *actually* means giving consumers times and names and maps and signposts, lists of available services and details of how to complain or appeal. These are all laudable activities, of course, but they do not amount to the empowerment which comes with the possession of information about effectiveness, quality, cost and the availability of alternatives.

Perhaps it is naive to expect more than a handful of public services managers to be self-starting in the provision to consumers of this kind of data. After all, it may easily make their already difficult jobs still more pressurised. They will remain just as short of resources, just as constrained by professional, geographic and institutional demarcation lines. So to ask them to volunteer highly sensitive performance information — which often they do not even have — to an unpredictable, 'unprofessional' and highly self-interested public may appear a less than overwhelmingly attractive course of action. Better customer relations is one thing, but performance indicators are another and partnership or power-sharing something else again.

Behind these immediate issues of current practices and motivations there stand deeper conceptual problems with 'consumerist' approaches. Foremost among these are those of the *identity* of the consumer, and the particular characteristics of *public* services which limit the usefulness of private sector analogies. Both have a bearing on defining the 'performance' that is to be measured, and on the 'how' and 'when' of the measurement process.

Who is the consumer?
The easy answer — and the one which is frequently taken in current consumer initiatives — is that the consumer is the person currently actually using the service in question. Thus consumer relations managers distribute their questionnaires to the patients presently in the hospital, the parents of the children currently attending the school, the tenants occupying the existing council housing stock. For some purposes this may be sensible and administratively convenient. But for others matters are not so straightforward. For example, Williams asks for whom is the GP responsible, and offers four possible answers;

1. those under active treatment by the practice at the time
2. those currently known to be waiting for treatment
3. those believed to need treatment but not currently seeking it
4. anyone who might ever need treatment.

He then goes on to point out that 'A doctor as clinician may assert that only the patient in front of him at some point in time is relevant, but the same doctor as practice manager has to consider how that patient got there and why others did not' (Williams, 1985, pp. 4–6). The relative weights given to these different conceptions of 'the consumer' in the minds of policy makers and service providers can have very concrete consequences. If, for example, the medical or teaching professions wish to place importance on their capacity to serve future generations, then the amount of time devoted to research and the development of new services and techniques will increase and the amount spent on dealing with today's customer correspondingly diminish. If those believed to need treatment, or a college course, or public housing or family planning advice but not currently seeking it are held to be of great significance then the emphasis will shift from maximising throughput with existing consumers in existing settings to more effective publicity and outreach programmes. No-one is seriously proposing to address the AIDS epidemic solely by responding to each victim as he or she presents him or herself.

Value-laden judgements concerning the identification and prioritising of different groups of consumers can only, in our liberal-democratic political culture, be regarded as fully legitimate if taken openly by accountable public representatives. Yet this is sometimes an extremely painful exercise, especially for the ambitious politician. Orthodox democratic theory therefore sees the reciprocal task of citizens as being to ensure, by pressure and probing, that priorities are kept clear, and that accountability is not fudged or unduly delegated. And in practice it is the citizen-as-immediate-consumer who is perhaps most highly motivated to be active in this respect.

These difficult problems of weighting the needs of different groups of service users, potential users and future users do not exhaust the complexity of defining the consumer. For there are other members of the community who are affected by the provision of public services. Most obviously, friends and relatives may derive considerable benefits — or disbenefits — from the effects of the service on the user. The parents of a severely handicapped child; the relatives of a sufferer from Alzheimer's disease; the friends of a homeless person: all may find great relief from hard work, inconvenience and anxiety through the provision of public services. Do these outcomes register on existing performance indicators? No — and yet it is hard to justify restricting our purview even to these effects on these immediate kin — husbands, wives and parents. Ours is a society where a significant fraction of households consist of unmarried partners or single persons or some other combination that does not fit our now seriously dated stereotypes of nuclear families.

A further layer of complexity enters when the taxpayer is brought into the picture. Analogies with consumers of marketed, private sector services frequently fail to take sufficient account of the fact that the consumer of public services usually does not pay anything like the full cost of those services. Even where charges for service are made at a level where the cost *is* covered, the shop or supermarket analogy still misses a great deal of what is distinctive about our public services. If we are fully to explore the possibilities for developing appropriate, consumer-oriented performance measures then it is necessary to analyse this distinctiveness in some depth.

What is distinctive about public services?
Our British debates about privatisation and about improving the efficiency of the public sector have

had many consequences. One of these (unforeseen, perhaps, by the privatising zealots of the 'new right') has been to remind us that many of our public services are not just bundles of activities which happen, by some historical or ideological whim, to have taken up temporary residence outside the private sector. Similar reminders have been heard with increasing urgency in many other countries — for example Sweden, Denmark, New Zealand and the United States (see, e.g. Boston, 1987; Gustafsson, 1987).

Broadly speaking there are two quite different approaches to the identification of these distinctive properties of public services. One is through welfare economics, the other through normative political theory. In welfare economics there may be a number of reasons for providing certain goods and services by political/bureaucratic allocation and administration rather than through the market. First, there are goods which, when once provided for one group cannot in practice be denied to others. Defence is one classic case, street lighting another. In economic terms these *public goods* produce additional marginal benefits for zero marginal cost. The street lights of Birmingham may be paid for by the city's residents, but it is impractical to exclude the visitor from Harrogate from their benefits, her enjoyment of which is procured at no extra cost to the providers. Charging consumers directly for such services is not impossible, but it tends to lead to too little being supplied, and to an inefficient distribution of resources. 'Public goods demand some form of intervention in the market — typically in the form of public provision' (Charles and Webb, 1986, p. 68).

The non-excludability of public goods does, therefore, create unusual relationships between consumer and consumer and between consumers, on the one hand, a provider on the other. For our present purposes, however, the significance of this may be quite limited. This is because most public services are *not* (economically speaking) pure public goods, or anything like. In health care, education and social work, for example, it is clearly possible to exclude would-be consumers, and adding new ones seldom leaves the marginal costs wholly unchanged.

More significant, probably, is the problem of *externalities*. We have bumped into these already, though in non-economic language, in the discussion in the previous section of the benefits public services frequently afford to friends and relatives of consumers, as well as to the consumers themselves. [Notice, incidentally, that there is also a gender issue here. As the unpaid carers in our

society are overwhelmingly women they will be the ones most helped by improvements or expansions in many of our public services.] More generally, the major public services generate very considerable benefits (and occasionally some costs) *for society as a whole*. These are additional to those costs and benefits directly connected with the immediate providing organisations and its individual pupils/clients/patients/customers. The benefits of a literate, healthy, well-educated, low-crime society are extremely pervasive — life is made easier for government, employers, friends and relatives — everyone. Yet a narrow 'accountancy' approach focused on the immediate provider-customer transaction, whilst it might capture much of the significance of the purchase of a car or a holiday, fails to embrace those important 'external' effects of basic (usually public) services. Here, then, is a reason for caution over taking analogies with supermarkets or ICI too far. Most public services do generate large externalities, and performance measures for them need to be designed in such a way as to register this.

At a more mundane level the public service consumer/provider transaction also frequently displays immediate features which have little or no parallel in over-the-counter 'customer relations'. These include

1. The public service consumer does not necessarily buy the service.
2. The consumer may have the statutory *right* to receive the service.
3. The consumer may even be *compelled* to receive the service.
4. On the other hand other consumers, though wanting the service and even willing to pay for it, may be refused on the grounds that they do not meet criteria for need of the service determined by a mixture of political and professional judgement.
   (For 1 to 4 see Stewart and Clarke, 1987, p 170).
5. Very often the disappointed public service consumer, or the one who believes the service received has actually done harm, has little or no opportunity to sue the provider (Winkler, 1987, p 1).

If economists see public services as 'different' — at least in degree — from private sector economic transactions, most liberal democratic political theorists most certainly do so. From political perspectives these differences arise mainly because consumers of public services are not merely consumers, they are also, simultaneously and unavoidably, *citizens*. In a stimulating review of the movement for a 'public service orientation' in local government Rhodes argues that, following the new American management bible, *In search of excellence*, local authorities must not merely endeavour to be 'close to the consumer', they must also be 'value driven' (Peters and Waterman, 1982; Rhodes, 1987). Rhodes suggests that the value orientation most distinctive of the public sector should be that of encouragement of active citizenship. Every public service consumer is also a citizen, and the mode and manner of provision needs to recognise that:

'the twin values of caring and citizenship provide the rationale for consumerism. The latter can be defended on the grounds that it increases the efficiency and effectiveness of service delivery. Without minimizing the relevance of these considerations, a rationale grounded in political theory has the distinct advantage that it provides an ethic for local government which both enhances the standing of that institution and contains the potential to motivate all those who participate in it' (Rhodes, 1987, pp 68–69).

This approach broadens the scope for discussion beyond 'customer relations' to include aspects of performance which rarely seem problematic in the supermarket or even the private hospital, but which are intimately linked to the concept of citizenship. These specific aspects of citizenship, as opposed to consumerdom include, for example, assigning high values to *equity, equal opportunities, representation* and *participation*. These values are *additional* to those of efficiency and service which are supposed to characterise market-driven processes. 'The efficient production and distribution of goods is one valued goal, but so is the creation of rewarding and reassuring relationships based on other-regarding — rather than self-regarding — motivations (Charles and Webb, 1986, p. 71)'. Citizenship is a status which, historically, has been defined and won through a series of struggles emphasising these non-market values. And they are values which have immediate implications for performance measurement.

A concern for equity, for example, might make us want a performance indicator to show whether waiting lists for citizens with similar medical conditions are of roughly equal length in different parts of the country. [Now — thanks first to John Yates at the University of Birmingham and to the College of Health and only later to the DHSS or NHS — we know they are not.] It would also alert us to the significance of evidence that working class consumers found it harder to use a particular public service configured in a particular way than

their middle class counterparts. There would be concern, too, that occupational classes IIIB, IV and V seem under-represented in consumer organisations. Similarly, a citizen's interest in equal opportunities would lead to requests for data on the employment practices of health and local authorities, both over time and in comparison with one another. A heightened consciousness of our citizens' rights of representation and duties of participation could lead in several directions. For example, should citizen and consumer groups be directly represented when decisions are taken about what kinds of performance indicators are to be included in local authority annual reports or might be given to NHS patients contemplating major surgery? Again, these features imply a need for particular performance measures, e.g. to monitor trends in the use of radical statutory powers such as child care orders, or in the percentage of claims or applications turned down.

The consequences of expanding the concept of public services consumerism

The tendency of this paper has been to argue that consumerism in the public services needs new and distinctively *public* models. The model of the private sector consumer, though sometimes a useful beginning, is frequently inadequate. Instead, perhaps, developments might be guided by a normative model of a (potentially) active, participating citizen-consumer, concerned with a range of values, of which efficiency, important though it is, is only one. Furthermore the model should incorporate definitions of the costs and benefits of public services that recognise the substantial externalities associated with many of them. It also needs to take account of the 'compulsoriness' or at least absence of alternatives (e.g. for social security) which sometimes structure consumer/ provider relationships.

But what are the consequences of such an approach, and how far can one envisage these consequences being accommodated within the practical realities of everyday politics and administration? In this section an attempt will be made to draw out some of the possible consequences. This will be done, first, by a conceptual exploration then by a brief, illustrative examination of some actual current developments, speculating on how they might be amended to incorporate a specifically public service brand of 'consumerism'. In the following, and final section I will turn to the issue of constraints — the power structures, uncertainties and technical problems which stand in the way of a practical implementation of the model outlined above.

The literature on *how* to measure — on the methodology of performance measurement — vastly exceeds that on *why* or *for whom* we should measure. It would be impossible to summarise it here. It seems more appropriate to concentrate on identifying just a few key *desiderata* for a consumer-oriented scheme. First, there is the argument over 'objective' vs. 'subjective' measures, with some purists insisting that only the former (usually quantified) type of measure carries legitimacy. From a consumer perspective there are considerable dangers in this 'objectivist' position. The situation is not one of a polarized choice between white ('objective') measures and black ('subjective') ones. Rather *every* set of performance indicators, however 'hard' the measures, is thoroughly suffused with values and judgemental uncertainties. At the outset, for example, there is always the judgement as to what to measure and what to leave out. That can never be entirely 'objective', so in a consumer-oriented scheme one would expect there to be direct consumer representation in the process of selection. Then there is the practical problem that many, if not most, of the statistics that go into our performance indicators are tainted with problems of inaccurate recording, ambiguous coding and so on. Thus several researchers have found uncomfortably high error rates in some of the data that goes into the NHS Hospital Activity Analysis. If there is a refusal to work, provisionally at least, with partial and sometimes inaccurate data large areas of the *status quo* will be effectively sealed off from scrutiny and debate.

Furthermore, for consumers it is particularly important that 'subjective' measures should not be excluded or regarded as somehow belonging to an inferior class. To do so would be to exclude or downgrade attempts directly to consult consumers themselves. There is actually nothing inherently inferior in measures of 'feelings' or perceptions or judgements. Commercial companies use surveys of consumer wants and consumer satisfaction to inform their investment decisions. Academics working in the field of cognitive psychology encounter a vast and frequently extremely rigorous literature on psychometrics. Both would be surprised to have their labours dismissed as 'soft' or 'unreliable' (Pollitt, 1986b). Indeed if consumers — and public service managers — are really going to take an interest in 'value for money' then they have no alternative but to become involved with relatively 'subjective' measures. This is because, while 'cost' may be measured in the apparently objective currency of money, 'value'

cannot. The value of a service will vary from one consumer to another and even vary for individual consumers over time, depending on their circumstances. What is more we have ample and reliable evidence to show that even well-meaning professional service providers are not always accurate surrogates in second-guessing the values and priorities of those who consume their services (e.g. McNeil et al, 1978; Ehrenreich and English, 1979).

Second, there is a need to reappraise the debate over the relative merits and practicability of input, process, output and outcome measures. Elsewhere, I have argued for greater attention to be devoted to the development of outcome measures and have warned against the seductions of the more easily and cheaply collected input and process measures (Pollitt 1986a). This battle has yet to be won, and it is a particularly important one from the consumer's viewpoint. Yet the argument in favour of putting more energy into the development of outcome measures should not be interpreted as a call for the abandonment of other kinds of measure. Input costs remain relevant because they provide one leg of the value for money ratio. Even relatively crude indicators of staffing input can provide invaluable warning signs. Most of the overlong list of tragedies at NHS mental illness and mental handicap hospitals *could* have been anticipated by sensible interpretation of quite a crude set of resource input indicators (Yates, 1983). Process measures can also be extremely useful. This is especially the case where the public service in question involves prolonged personal contact between consumers and service providers. Health care, education and the personal social services obviously fall within this category. In these cases it is not only the eventual outcome that matters to the consumer but the way he or she has been treated on the way to getting there. This is one reason why the renewed recent research interest in complaints procedures is welcome (Seneviratne and Cracknell, forthcoming). Especially in compulsory or 'no-alternative' services simple and prominent complaints systems are not only required in the interests of natural justice, they are also a fertile potential source of consumer-sensitive performance indicators. Naturally, public authorities should *not* wait for complaints. They need to be proactive. Thus Brighton Health Authority's action plans for reducing outpatient waiting, ensuring privacy, making public telephones available and so on deserve the praise they have received (Brighton Health Authority, 1986). Also the patient satisfaction surveys now being carried out by a number of health authorities are potentially very useful. Whether this potential is realised, however, depends on what is done with the findings (Raphael, 1974). Recent complaints of the shameful conditions at an old people's home in London trailed back to 1979 but it was not until 1986 that serious action got underway (Perera, 1987). This returns the discussion to the question of participation.

What has been conspicuously absent from most of the performance measurement schemes thus far embarked on in our public services has been direct consumer-citizen participation in the design and operation of these schemes. In a sense this kind of participation is a more fundamental requirement than those identified in the preceding discussions of objectivity and input, process and outcome measures. For while it is often relatively easy to add a new indicator to a system or otherwise make running improvements, it is far more difficult to alter the overall design of a performance measurement system, doubly so if one is not directly represented in the deliberations concerning that system. There is a long way to go here — and that is one reason why it seems essential for consumer organisations to continue to develop performance measurement schemes of their own, as well as lobbying for change in the schemes run by governmental and other public service bodies.

Where consumer representation is achieved, there will still be much to be done. The development of satisfactory outcome measures will not be achieved overnight. The idea that a direct input of consumer perceptions is not only legitimate, but something that should be used and acted upon in policy formulation will need to be advanced and defended. But perhaps as important as either of these there will be the issues of presentation and dissemination. How can performance data be presented in such a way as to make it intelligible to the wide range of people who consume most of our major public services? Even if it can be made intelligible, how can it best be communicated to this audience? For example, what is the best *time* to give them the information? In general terms the answer would appear to be that they need the information at that point in their affairs when they are about to take consequential decisions about using or not using the service in question. Yet even this generalisation has its exceptions. Immediately before major surgery may not be the best moment at which to present an individual patient with a hospital league table or information about alternative therapies. There are a myriad of problems and considerations here. The question of *when* to provide information has only recently begun to be

addressed in a systematic way, and there is clearly much to learn.

There has already been occasion to make several references to consumer 'participation'. To conclude this conceptual exploration, it is worth noting that the term has the useful property of allowing individuals of rather different underlying political perspectives to work together for limited practical objectives. Those with an essentially *instrumentalist* conception and politics, who regard the political process as principally a means of satisfying individuals' wants, see participation as a device for increasing provider sensitivity to consumer preferences. Others, however, regard the *developmental* aspects of participation as its paramount value. Participation is held to develop civic consciousness and enhance individual and group autonomy (Held, 1987, pp. 267–299). Despite different aims and beliefs, thinkers from these two positions can both assent to the general idea that 'If we wish to enhance liberal democracy, and lighten the 'dark side' of bureaucratisation, then greater direct participation should be our direction of travel' (Pollitt, 1986c, p. 189).

It may help put some flesh on the bones of the foregoing if brief examination is made of a selection of concrete possibilities for the future. These will be examples of current work in developing performance measures, chosen for the opportunities they appear to present for deeper and more influential consumer involvement than has been usual in the past. This is certainly *not* to say that such consumer involvement is currently planned or intended: rather that there are opportunities here to be seized upon and worked for.

One area where there will surely be both an opportunity and a need for a major consumer effort is in our schools. Whatever one may think of the government's current proposals for reorganising education, it seems highly probable that, in the near future, schools and school teachers will be assessed more often and more rigorously than ever before. Consumers — both parents and, in suitable cases, students — need to barge their way into this process. In some local authorities they will find that doors are already open; in others a good shove will be needed (Ranson et al, 1986). Already, of course, schools are obliged to publish their examination results. Whilst these are no doubt one important measure, used in isolation they can become 'a method which fragments and destroys the public as community' (*ibid*). One shudders to think of, say, debates about possible opting out from LEA control being conducted solely on the basis of raw examination scores. Greater consumer participation could enrich the process of assessing schools and build a stronger basis of community support for an agreed educational process.

The dangers of QALYs (Quality Adjusted Life Years) becoming yet another device by which the 'experts' (in this case economists) actually *exclude* lay understandings has recently been developed at some length (Mulkay *et al*, 1987). Yet, sensitively handled, the QALY approach holds out the possibility of a considerable opening-up of at least some aspects of the resource allocation process in the NHS. There has always been de facto rationing in the NHS; QALYs could give us a clearer picture of the outcomes of that rationing.

Moving into the community, there are a variety of interesting schemes. One, based on the World Health Organization's Healthy Cities initiative, has involved Sheffield Health Authority and City Council in a large scale consultation exercise. The basic idea is to allow the citizens of Sheffield to set their own health targets, or at least to adapt the basic set of targets suggested by WHO. It would be an interesting piece of long term research to track this initiative and see how far consumer interest in the setting and subsequent progress towards these health targets can be sustained.

Another key area is primary health care. If GPs are henceforth to be required to provide more information about the services they provide (Hildrew, 1987) what information will this be, how will it be disseminated, and to whom? Are consumers content to rest with the GPs' own view: 'The second working party did in fact seriously consider soliciting opinion of the practice's patients but concluded that this was not feasible. Furthermore, it would have detracted from the status of the assessment as a peer review conducted by fellow professionals ...'? (Royal College of General Practitioners, 1985). It would appear from the December 1987 White Paper on primary care that the government is content to go along with this. Patients are to have more choice, but the information they will be given to choose with will concern the *range* of services provided, not their *quality*.

My penultimate example comes from the personal social services sector. A set of key indicators is currently being developed from the DHSS personal social services data base. It is hoped that these will become operational during 1988 and will help the social services inspectorate to decide where to concentrate most of their energies. The first signs are that this may be a typical, top-down scheme concentrating on financial inputs and staffing levels and making little or no attempt to assess outcomes. Here, then, is a challenge for social and community workers and their clients alike. Is there no way in which this scheme can be adapted or added to so as to accommodate measures based on the perceptions of those who receive these services?

Finally, the whole rapidly-developing field of information technology is one where the consumer voice has thus far been notable mainly for its absence. Major new IT systems are being installed in supplementary benefit offices, GPs' surgeries, public libraries, housing departments and elsewhere. Intensive attention has been focused on the kinds of information these systems will present to senior and middle management and, in some cases, to 'grass roots' officials (Land et al, 1987). But how much energy has been invested in the question of what kind of information these systems could display for the consumers of these services? The possibilities are extensive — how many public waiting rooms are there where VDUs could be installed with performance data available at the touch of a user-friendly key (Pollitt, 1986c, pp. 135–9)? Yet somehow our computerised information systems have been allowed to become another feature which divides the service providers from their consumers rather than a shared resource which might be used in the promotion of shared understandings.

Constraints

Initiatives of the kinds described above *could* be taken, but will they? Three types of constraint are likely to operate. First, there are considerable technical and cost problems in developing the appropriate measurement systems. Processing the quantities of data involved usually requires computers and computer operators. Designing questionnaires or consumer information guides also requires considerable skill. Output and outcome indicators are hard to devise, and chasing 'outcomes' (which are usually, literally, 'out there', in the community) is frequently an expensive as well as an elusive business. Yet, given the effort that has already been put into non-consumer-oriented performance measurement systems, one might feel reasonably optimistic if it were *only* technical and cost barriers that lay ahead.

There is, however, a second and more tenacious type of constraint. The existing patterns of power relationships in the public services do not favour consumers or consumer groups. If consumers are going to influence the further development of performance measurement in the public services they will need resources, resourcefulness, organisation and allies. Even then the task will be difficult and the effort will have to be sustained over a period of time. An eventually favourable outcome may be worth trying for, but it is far from certain.

The challenge is twofold. First, consumer organisations need to develop their own ways of measuring the performance of public services, and then successfully disseminate the data thereby assembled to their members. Second, consumer organisations need to seek to influence the design and operation of the performance measurement systems used by governmental and public institutions themselves. Both these tasks require the accumulation of a certain expertise, a familiarity with the field which it is normally impossible for the individual consumer to acquire. Hence the need for organisation and collective representation. Hence also the need for resources.

Consumer organisations are seldom lavishly resourced. Nor do they often wield the political clout of major service providers. So they need all the trustworthy allies they can find. Friendly academics can be useful of course, but better still are persons on the *inside* of public service policy-making and delivery organisations. For there are both elected and appointed officials who recognise that greater consumer representation in performance measurement holds promise as well as threat. Those local authorities which co-operated with the National Consumer Council's *Measuring Up* initiative obviously contained such individuals (National Consumer Council, 1986). So did the health authorities which were willing to experiment with consumer-based quality of life assessments as a guide to resource allocation (Drummond, 1987; Gudex, 1987) and with the maternity guides produced by the City and Hackney Community Health Council (City and Hackney CHC, 1983). So do those social service departments which believe that 'consumer views should be sought as an integral part of the planning process' (James, 1987, p. 14). So, finally do those schools where it is understood that, as one headteacher said:

'We have to negotiate [with the community]. We have to reach agreement about what we are to do. In the absence of agreement, criteria are not helpful. With agreement there are some reasonable expectations of the purpose of education — what we should be teaching. Without this agreement any judgements about a school's performance are arbitrary' (quoted in Ranson et al, 1986).

Finally, there are almost certainly lessons to be learned from the experience of consumer groups in other countries. Budgetting and performance measurement techniques are now an international currency and — with suitable allowances for different political and institutional contexts — British consumer groups may sometimes be able to borrow ideas, or avoid pitfalls and dead ends, by communicating with, say, their American or Swedish counterparts. In Sweden, for example, new standards for the accessibility of public services are being developed by systematic consultation with consumers (Gustafsson, 1987, p. 188). In the US the National Association of Health Data Organizations, financed by business consumers of health care, is working hard to identify and disseminate reliable indicators of the clinical quality of hospital services. The release, during 1986, of hospital-by-hospital medicare mortality rates certainly showed, however crude the figures, that there was no shortage of consumer or media interest in this kind of information (Pollitt, 1987a).

The final category of constraint might be termed 'conceptual'. Is it, perhaps, the case that the whole language of 'performance measurement' is actually alien and unintelligible to most citizens, a construct being forced upon them by other interests? Mulkay *et al* (1987) pose three disturbing questions. These were asked of the QALY approach already referred to, but could be applied, in varying degrees, to many other performance measurement systems, actual and proposed. First, do the categories used by the [measurement system] capture the evaluations service consumers make in the course of ordinary, everyday life? Second, do most people 'carry around a set of internal preferences or evaluations which are relatively stable?' (Mulkay *et al,* 1987, p. 556). If not — and there is some evidence of high variability in preferences from situation to situation — then our measures of consumer opinion may have very low portability in either time or space. Third, the *quantification* involved in some measurement processes may also distort 'real' consumer feelings. Of QALYs Mulkay says that 'it seems likely that the smooth distribution of scores produced in these attempts to measure quality of life is a result of respondents' recognition of a quantification already implicit in the analyst's pre-arranged categories' (op. cit, p. 556).

However, Mulkay *et al* conspicuously, indeed resolutely, refuse to offer any alternatives. Meanwhile the problem of the consumer-responsiveness (or lack of it) of public services remains. The sociological critique will therefore be interpreted here as a warning. Ethically, the categories and procedures of measurement should indeed be constrained by the 'cognitive styles' of citizen-consumers themselves. The measurements must not become unrecognisable to their users.

Conclusions

The argument here, then, is not merely that existing performance measurement systems should be more accessible to the citizen-consumer, or even that consumer organisations need to continue to develop performance measurement schemes of their own. Whilst progress on these fronts would be important, a central contention of this paper is that there is a case for rethinking the *context* in which performance measurement systems are used. The rethinking has begun, but it has not gone very far. The index of *The international yearbook of organizational democracy* does not even contain an entry for 'consumers', and the substance of the book does not discuss them (Stern and McCarthy, 1986). In this paper the case has been made for ways of using performance measurement that are essentially participative and which are negotiated between service providers, service consumers and the wider community. Such a development would entail the use of performance indicators for educative purposes as well as aids to decision making. It would be bound to be a long term project, though not necessarily a 'gradualist' one. It could constitute a significant enrichment of the political process, and an enhancement of our currently often narrow and passive conceptualisation of 'the citizen'. It is a long way from the charm school or even the efficient supermarket. The aim is not merely to *please* the recipients of public services (difficult and worthy though that may be) but to *empower* them.

NOTE

1. This article was developed from an earlier paper presented at that conference. The author would like to thank Glen Bramley and Rod Rhodes for their improving suggestions and comments.

REFERENCES

Audit Commission (1985) *Managing social services for the elderly more effectively*, London: HMSO.

Boston, J. (1987) 'Transforming the public sector in New Zealand: Labour's quest for improved efficiency and accountability', *Public Administration*, 65:4, Winter (forthcoming).

Brighton Health Authority (1986) *A better deal for outpatients* (mimeo).

Charles, S. and Webb, A. (1986) *The economic approach to social policy*, Brighton: Wheatsheaf.

CIPFA (1984) *Performance indicators in the education service: a consultative document*, London: Chartered Institute of Public Finance and Accountancy.

City and Hackney Community Health Council (1983) *Pregnancy and birth in Hackney and the City of London. How to make the maternity service work for you in City and Hackney Health District.*

Cullen, B. (1986) 'Performance indicators in UK higher education: progress and prospects', OECD Conference paper, Paris.

Drummond, M. (1987) *Research allocation decisions in health care: a role for quality of life assessments*, University of Birmingham Health Services Management Centre Discussion Paper No 21.

Ehrenreich, B. and English, D. (1979) *For her own good: 150 years of experts' advice to women*, London: Pluto.

Elton, L. (1987) *Teaching in higher education: appraisal and training*, London: Kogan Page.

Fairhall, J. (1987) 'The silenced majority', p. 11, *Guardian*, 1st September.

Griffiths Report (1983) *NHS management inquiry*, London: Department of Health and Social Security.

Gudex, C. (1987) *QALYs and their use by the health service*, Discussion Paper 20, Centre for Health Economics, University of York.

Gustafsson, L. (1987) 'Renewal of the public sector in Sweden', pp. 179–191, *Public Administration*, 65:2, Summer.

Held, D. (1987) *Models of democracy*, Cambridge: Polity Press.

Hildrew, P. (1987) 'Moore faces row over new health charges', p. 4, *Guardian*, 16th November.

James, A. (1987) 'Performance and the planning process', pp 12–14, *Social Services Insight*, 2:10, 6th March.

Land, F. F., Conford, A., Pichaud, D., Farbey, B. and Avgerou, C. (1987) *Work process, service quality and information technology in social welfare institutions: national report review'*, London School of Economics and Political Science (mimeo).

Lewis, S. (1986) *Output and performance measurement in central government: progress in departments*, Treasury Working Paper No. 28, London, HMSO.

McNeil, B., Weichselbaum, R. and Pauker, D. G. (1978) 'Fallacy of the five year survival in lung cancer', pp. 1397–1401, *New England Journal of Medicine*, 229:25.

Mobbs, T. (1985) *Public opinion and local democracy: beliefs and practice in County Cleveland*, Birmingham, Institute of Local Government Studies (4 Vols).

Mulkay, M., Ashmore, M. and Pinch, T. (1987) 'Measuring the quality of life: a sociological intervention concerning the application of economics to health care', pp. 541–564, *Sociology*, 21:4, November.

National Consumer Council (1986) *Measuring up: consumer assessment of local authority services: a guideline study*, London: NCC.

NHS (1986) 'Improving customer relations in the NHS' p. 3, *NHS Management Bulletin*, 3rd November.

Perera, S. (1987) 'Two inquiries failed to reveal home's catalogue of cruelty', p. 3, *The Guardian*, 22nd July.

Peters, T. J. and Waterman, R. H. (1982) *In search of excellence: lessons from America's best-run companies,* New York: Harper and Row.

Pollitt, C. (1985) 'Measuring performance: a new system for the National Health Service', pp. 1–15, *Policy and Politics,* 13:1.

Pollitt, C. (1986a) 'Beyond the managerial model: the case for broadening performance assessment in government and the public services', pp. 155–170, *Financial Accountability and Management,* 2:3, Autumn.

Pollitt, C. (1986b) 'Soft measures for tough policies?', pp. 59–65 in *Policy management and policy assessment: developments in central government,* London: Peat Marwick/Royal Institute of Public Administration.

Pollitt, C. (1986c) 'Democracy and bureaucracy', pp. 158–191 in David Held and Christopher Pollitt (eds), *New forms of democracy,* London: Sage.

Pollitt, C. (1987a) 'Capturing quality? The quality issue in British and American health policies', pp 71–92, *Journal of Public Policy,* 7:1 Autumn.

Pollitt, C. (1987b) 'The politics of performance assessment: lessons for higher education?', pp. 87–98, *Studies in Higher Education,* 12:1.

Ranson, S., Hannon, V. and Gray, J. (1986) 'Citizens or consumers? Policies for school accountability' in Barton, L. and Walker, S. (eds) *Policy, teachers and education,* Milton Keynes, Open University Press.

Raphael, W. (1974) *Survey of patient opinion surveys in hospitals,* London: Kings Fund.

Rhodes, R. A. W. (1987) 'Developing the public service orientation — or lets add a soupcon of political theory', pp. 63–73, *Local Government Studies,* May/June.

Royal College of General Practitioners (1985) *What sort of doctor? Assessing quality of care in general practice,* Reports from general practice 23.

Schuller, T. (1987) *Performance and the practice of continuing education,* Paper presented to the annual conference of the Standing Conference of University Teaching and Research into the Education of Adults.

Seneviratne, M. and Cracknell, S. (forthcoming) 'Consumer complaints in public sector services' *Public Administration.*

Stern, R. N. and McCarthy, S. (eds) (1986) *International Yearbook of Organizational Democracy,* Chichester: Wiley.

Stewart, J. and Clarke, M. (1987) 'The public service orientation: issues and dilemmas', pp. 161–178, *Public Administration,* 65:2, Summer.

Turney, J. (1987) 'Trouble in the ranks' p. 8, *Times Higher Education Supplement,* 13th November.

Williams, A. (1985) *Medical ethics: health service efficiency and clinical freedom,* Nuffield/York Portfolios, No. 2.

Winkler, F. (1987) 'Consumerism in health care: beyond the supermarket model', pp. 1–8, *Policy and Politics,* 15:1.

Yates, J. (1983) 'When will the players get involved?' p. 1111–1112, *Health and Social Service Journal.*

Christopher Pollitt
Senior Lecturer in Government
Faculty of Social Sciences
The Open University

Performance Measurement: the needs of managers and policy makers

Terry Banks

In the rush to create a 'can-do' Civil Service, which adopts a more managerial organisational culture, it is important not to forget the importance of policy analysis. Unless policy options are well developed and robust, the emphasis on management may simply lead us more efficiently and more effectively into the mire of policy failure.

The Financial Management Initiative stresses the need – both for management and policy evaluation purposes – to measure performance by measuring outputs. There is a huge difference, however, between management and policy analysis. This article argues that, by tacking the second on to the first, the overall performance of the public sector could be damaged in ways that no amount of good management will repair. With its emphasis on intermediate outputs, the Initiative goes a long way towards motivating individuals and convincing them that they are contributing to the worthwhile output of their organisations. Crucial to all this, however, are good policies which analysis shows to be effective.

Conceptual Framework

We use money to buy resources, to produce goods and services (intermediate outputs), to satisfy customers with better health, defence and so on (final outputs). In the public sector, intermediate outputs can include regulations which impose costs on others, in order to produce final outputs such as a better environment. Management is concerned with buying resources economically and using them efficiently to produce intermediate outputs: cars, hip replacements. Policy analysis, including appraisal before implementation and evaluation afterwards, is concerned with deciding what intermediate outputs will be effective in achieving final outputs – the ultimate goals (see Management *v* Policy Analysis). It uses such techniques as market research in the private sector, cost-benefit analysis in the public sector.

The interplay between these two aspects of performance measurement has a long and fascinating history. In the 1960s in the US, the 'Planning programming and budgeting system', which clearly belongs to the intermediate output side, ran into trouble partly because it tried to take over the final output side as well: to collect, record, analyse and output the information needed to assess effectiveness. The result was an unusable mass of computer print-out under which the system sank without trace. In the UK, we confined PPBS strictly to intermediate outputs, e.g. in the health and education fields. In the early 1970s this approach was complemented by PAR, policy analysis and review. One of the features which probably undermined PAR was an attempt to hitch it to the Public Expenditure Survey cycle, turning it into a bureaucratic treadmill. Another was secrecy. But it did produce some very valuable analyses, such as the Department of Health & Social Security's 1976 consultative document on Priorities for Health and Personal Social Services in England, which had a beneficial impact on service development for many years.

During the 1980s the emphasis was, of course, all back on the efficiency side. The Financial Management Initiative requires a concrete, measurable output plan, with a measurable (and compatible) budget to carry it out, which is rolled forward annually, and against which performance is monitored at least annually and probably in year. All this implies working with intermediate outputs. No one should be ashamed of this – in the private sector, routine planning and monitoring is about producing cars, not happy motorists. This is familiar territory, but I would emphasise three points which are not always fully recognised.

First, forward planning needs to ensure that resources are geared feasibly and coherently to produce the required intermediate output: obvious, you might think, but a revelation of the

Mrs Banks is Director of the Carnegie Inquiry into the Third Age (working in close association with the Public Finance Foundation) and lately Registrar General.

Management *v* Policy Analysis

Management	Policy analysis
● Concerned with intermediate outputs, efficiency & economy	● Concerned with final outputs. effectiveness
● Relatively easy to measure: quantity, quality, time, cost throughput or milestones ratios e.g. unit costs weighted output and resource volume indices compatible objectives	● Difficult to measure: values including time preference causal relationships externalities conflicting objectives
● Annual planning and monitoring	● Occasional in-depth research: models, sensitivity analysis
● Home in on particular policy. course of action	● Look at wide range of alternatives
● Look up to five years ahead	● Look long term
● 100% routine information	● Specially collected information e.g. sample surveys, random controlled trials

earlv health programme budgets was that the allocation of money, development of manpower and capital investment programmes were all inconsistent with avowed policies on service delivery and location (and incidentally, with each other). Without a feasible and consistent plan, and the funding to support it, the Financial Management Initiative approach cannot begin.

Second, having made a plan, it is essential that local managers and their staff are left to do the job within their budgets, and to hold them accountable for intermediate outputs. This may seem an obvious point: however, the then Department of Health & Social Security took many years in the mid-1980s to persuade, first, the National Audit Office and then the Public Accounts Committee that health authorities should be held accountable for the services they provided, and not the mixture of inputs (nurses and other staff, beds etc) which they used.

Third, the emphasis on accountability for intermediate outputs does not mean losing sight of inputs. There should always be the further objective of improving efficiency. Usually, there are two components in improved efficiency: cash savings and higher output from existing resources. Government departments are required to make total efficiency improvements of at least 1.5 per cent a year. As with service delivery, it should be for the local managers to decide how to achieve this. The top management of the Office of Population Censuses & Surveys knows best the order in which to tackle things so as to get a good return out of the many options available; better information technology, financial management systems, training, work organisation, staff inspection, accommodation, location, procurement, energy savings and so on. The role of Ministers and the Treasury is to hold departments to account for overall improvement, not to try to tell them how to do it.

Individuals and Motivation

The emphasis which the Financial Management Initiative places on intermediate outputs and efficiency (as opposed to inputs and process), as well as giving better direction to managers, also motivates staff. First, the plan, provided it is communicated to staff, means that individuals have a sense of direction, see how their contribution fits into a wider picture, and are not asked to do the impossible. I have been very struck how, in the Office of Population Censuses & Surveys, staff are not usually hostile to change, but do desperately want to see what it will mean to them, how they fit in to a wider picture, and the path by which goals will be reached.

Second, the delegation gives room for individual freedom and initiative; after the initial shock, most people love holding budgets provided the limits to their freedom and the information to support them are clear.

Third, performance is measured and recognised in terms of throughput or milestones achieved, which, in turn, visibly contribute to the output of the organisation, at least at an intermediate level. Social survey staff are much more

excited to see MPs using one of our surveys in a debate than to learn that the cost per million weighted key depressions has fallen 5 per cent.

But what about individual performance? It is usually the intention that performance should, to a large extent, be measured in the same terms as the perfomance of that part of the organisation. Where someone is carrying out a repetitive task, this can be done. However, other theory says that breaking work down into small repetitive tasks is demotivating. Certainly, the move from production line to a whole job approach at the NHS central register increased throughput by 20 per cent and is liked by most staff. The 'whole job' teams have two advantages:

● each team organises the work to suit its own members; it provides everyone with variety and feels in control;
● the team as a whole is responsible for a higher level (though still not final) output: the provision of a service to a group of family practitioner committees, whom they visit and get to know.

However, because the work is organised in this way, the NHS central reigster can only measure performance – throughput and accuracy – at the level of the team. The contribution of each individual has to be assessed by the team leader. The twin objectives of directing performance measurement to the real purposes of the organisation, and of motivating staff to achieve them, are both served by moving the measurement of performance away from low level tasks towards the services provided, and by moving the level at which work is measured away from individuals and towards higher levels of the organisation. But the implication is that assessment of individual performance will depend on the judgment of supervisory staff, and that means we must ensure that they are trained and able to carry out this function effectively.

Policy Analysis

Moving on to final outputs, a recent seminar used the jingle 'leadership is about doing the right thing; management is about doing the thing right'. Leadership is paramount because the cost of doing the wrong thing (however efficiently) is usually much greater than that of doing the right thing badly, and in some cases doing a bad thing inefficiently can actually limit the damage. So how does 'the leader' know what is the right thing?

In the private sector, profitability is a clear. high-level goal and leadership does have to consider, for example, what will make future motorists happy. This forces a discipline of product development and market research. and. in the longer term, consideration of what business to be in. In the public sector leadership is, of course, primarily political. with the discipline of getting re-elected. There is also strong professional leadership, e.g. from doctors in the health service. However, the democratic process and professional training and experience do not necessarily provide a guide to what is 'the right thing'. Government activities are mainly in those areas where the market does not work; where resource allocation is not optimised by individuals buying what they want and producers seeking their custom. Politicians and the professions need information to assist their decisions which direct market experience cannot supply: they need policy analysis.

However, there are several areas of difficulty associated with cost–benefit analysis in the public sector – values, causal relationships, externalities and conflicting objectives.

Values: Professionals such as doctors, teachers, architects and engineers may have objectives which differ from those of their customers. However, good research can reveal the relative values which people attach e.g. to freedom from pain and longevity, or to using a private car and having a good urban environment. Those deciding policy can, if they wish, use such information to impose a discipline on the public sector akin to consumer choice in the market.

Causal relationships: These are often quite different from what people assume. For instance, might road building in cities in certain circumstances actually increase road congestion? Again good research can illuminate cause and effect.

Externalities: These are not always obvious, and even where they are, the extent, the causal relationships and the value to be placed on them need to be properly assessed. Environmental issues are fraught with these difficulties.

Conflicting objectives: All possible courses of action may have some unwanted effects, and there has to be a trade-off. This is ultimately a matter of judgment, but at least the conflicts can be made explicit and resolved as a matter of policy; otherwise those executing policies may be forced to act in a context of unresolved conflicts, which is bad for performance and morale. For instance, in the social security field there is an inherent conflict between economical administration and safeguarding individual rights, but the cost of reducing error rates by given amounts can often be quantified, the most cost-effective methods chosen, and the cut-off point explicitly decided.

The Treasury is concerned that the Financial Management Initiative should not neglect policy analysis, hence its 1988 document 'Policy Evaluation: a guide for managers'. The guide does distinguish evaluation from monitoring and mentions the need to keep an eye on causal relationships between intermediate outputs and the desired ultimate objectives. However, the whole model is based on planning and monitoring; it highlights evaluation of the chosen policy against a base case (whilst referring to the possibility of looking at alternatives); it proposes making assumptions about causal relationships (whilst testing them where possible); and there is no hint that so-called 'ultimate objectives' might require systematic research. The Treasury's shorter, 1988, guide 'Output and Performance Measurement in Central Government' talks about all levels of management being involved in 'monitoring effectiveness' and 'policy evaluation'. All this is to be done through 'output and performance measurement systems' which are to be linked with 'departmental budgeting systems' and the Public Expenditure Survey.

Such an approach could burden managers with tasks they do not have the skills to undertake, and burden routine monitoring systems with misleading and unusable information. Worse, policies themselves could go unchallenged, and if assumptions about causal relations are wrong, a misconceived policy could lead to adverse effects and still more of the same perverse policy.

Looking Ahead

Looking to a future Civil Service with far more executive agencies, three points may be made. First, the new agencies are excellently designed for management, for doing the thing right. But it is the parent departments who will need to take responsibility for policy analysis, for advising Ministers on doing the right thing. Second, it is, therefore, essential that those civil servants who remain in central government should show real professionalism in policy analysis. Thid, there is also a need for informed public debate based on external policy analysis. Britain has many institutions which are concerned with policy analysis, however none has the resources or expertise of, for example, the Brookings Institute.

Finally, what of motivation? So far as the executive agencies are concerned, if they are asked to carry out misconceived policies, no amount of good management will motivate staff; whereas if policies are well conceived and their basis properly explained, staff motivation and performance may be strong enough to survive much bad management. For instance, health service efficiency started to improve from 1976 onwards, long before the 1980s' management reforms. This happened because staff of all kinds strove to keep pace with growing demands and to improve services, within much tighter financial constraints than previously, because they cared about the service delivered.

The 'policy' Civil Service will also need to have its performance measured and to be properly motivated. Proper policy analysis carried out with professionals in various fields, including economics, should be a major element in this. This is not a passing fad, any more than recent management initiatives; it is a continuing need. The 1918 Haldane Report on the machinery of Government is still as relevant today:

Turning next to the formulation of policy, we have come to the conclusion after surveying what came before us, that in the sphere of civil government the duty of investigation and thought, as preliminary to action, might with great advantage be more definitely recognised. It appears to us that adequate provision has not been made in the past for the organised acquisition of facts and information, and for the systematic application of thought, as preliminary to the settlement of policy and its subsequent administration. This is no new notion. . . . ∎

Information Technology in Public Services: Disaster Faster?

Helen Margetts and Leslie Willcocks

Introducing Information Technology (IT) into organizations is a high-risk, hidden-cost process. Two government departments are used in this article to provide examples of common risk issues being played out in public services contexts in the 1990s. It is argued that some major trends in public administration leave the sector particularly vulnerable to risks introduced by IT.

In the analysis, design and building of information systems, at the levels of managerial attitude and actual practice, issues of risk in public services are commonly treated as peripheral. Risk is most often regarded as added to the system when it is in operation, and as most usually relating to systems security, the need for back-up in the event of technical failure, issues relating to data protection legislation and/or the prevention of fraud. However, the processes involved in designing and introducing large-scale databanks and computer networks into organizations bring new hazards of which those in positions of responsibility are often unaware. This is especially true when these people are unfamiliar with, suspicious, or even frightened, of the technology itself. In addition, in the public sector context, the prospect of information systems being managed badly, going wrong or introducing new risks, is not a favoured subject for academic study. Certainly it is not a subject favoured by IT consultants, many of whom have a strong presence in the UK public sector.

UK Government expenditure on IT is rising rapidly, now representing 1.7% of central government expenditure. Tony Newton, Secretary of State for Social Security has stated, correctly, that in his department, 'the future is beginning to arrive courtesy of IT' (Newton, 1989). But what kind of future? Is the traditional, cautious resistance to innovation in the public sector being eroded by the perceived necessity for enormous financial investment in large-scale computer systems? Is this an intentional desire to bring public administration into the 1990s, or are politicians and public sector managers unaware of the risks and hazards involved? What are the new risks generated by IT, and are there any which are likely to be increased when it is being introduced into a public sector organization? This article looks at these questions with reference to examples of public sector computerization projects.

The Public Sector

A range of factors commonly regarded as distinguishing the public sector from the private sector would seem to impinge on processes of adopting IT in public sector environments. These include:

• Projects are large scale (usually endeavouring to deal with a national, or a regional, population).
• Inclination to move into unproven technologies (because they are underwritten by the State).
• Non-interactive decision-making (there is no customer comeback).
• No 'bottom-line' decision-making: new resources can always be raised rather than admitting mistakes; no bankruptcy fear; no fear of management takeover.
• Separation of policy-making and administration.
• Statutory and parliamentary regulation.
• Responsiveness to political masters and short political time-horizons.

A quick glance at these factors suggests that there may be additional risks that are specific to or exacerbated by virtue of the organization implementing the technology being in the public sector. Arguably also, the listed factors themselves may have been changing over the last decade as government has sought radical redefinition of the parameters and processes constituting the public sector. As one example, privatization of IT services in some local boroughs and some regions in the National Health Service (NHS) may have made fear of management or external takeover more real. Furthermore stricter financial disciplines may introduce more 'bottom-line thinking' in public sector IT projects. Equally, central government initiatives in 1991 would suggest greater attention will need to be given to customer service issues, whether or not IT-related, in public sector organizations. A later argument will be developed that suggests that such 'new public management' initiatives, particularly where (as they frequently are) underpinned by developments in public sector use of IT, themselves constitute considerable risk. However, before this set of issues is addressed, and to provide some concrete examples, risk issues are first analysed in the context of two public sector computerization projects, one in the Foreign and Commonwealth Office (FCO), and the other in the Department of Social Security (DSS).

Helen Margetts is currently researching the US Budget with Professor Patrick Dunleavy in the Department of Government, London School of Economics. Leslie Willcocks is Fellow in Information Management, Templeton College, University of Oxford. He is also Executive Editor of the 'Journal of Information Technology'.

© Public Finance Foundation, 1993
Published by Blackwell Publishers, 108 Cowley Road, Oxford OX4 1JF and 238 Main Street, Cambridge, MA 02142, USA.

The FCO

During 1989 the FCO introduced a new computerized accounting system to make payments, record transactions and produce their four annual appropriation accounts. However, it did not work properly, and final accounts, which should have been signed in August 1989, were not produced until the end of November 1989. These accounts were based on ledgers which did not balance. The Comptroller and Auditor General qualified all four accounts; this was the most serious qualification of an appropriation account which the present Comptroller and Auditor General had ever made. The accounts eventually produced in November showed a net imbalance of £5.3M, and included £26.4M which the FCO has posted to 'dump accounts' in an attempt to resolve the discrepancies.

In February 1988, the FCO appointed Price Waterhouse to study their book-keeping requirements and to identify and evaluate a suitable software package to replace their six-year-old system. Price Waterhouse identified seven possible packages and after these had been evaluated against various criteria, including their financial backgrounds, it was agreed that Memory Computers Ltd should be selected.

The FCO's aim was to run the old and new systems in parallel from Autumn 1988. However, because of delayed deliveries by Memory, extensive parallel running did not start until November 1989. Although most of the necessary software was in operation, it was not possible to reconcile the output from the two systems. In February 1990 Memory delivered the final parts of the software, but shortly afterwards the company went into liquidation. In the same month the old accounting system broke down irreparably: the hard disk shattered. There was no back-up in case of system failure. After questioning at the Public Accounts Committee (PAC), it appeared that the old system had been without back up in the eight years in which it had been in operation.

Payments made to consultants were calculated by the National Audit Office (NAO) at £937 000, including £285 000 paid to Price Waterhouse to deal with the problems caused by Memory, the company they had recommended. The implications from the problems caused were considerable; all accounting information had to be reconstructed from raw data. At one stage there was a difference of £485M between the Parliamentary Grants recorded as drawn and the sum shown in records as released from the Consolidated Fund.

This example illustrates one of the most obvious risks in computerization projects: if information and systems are not backed up, large amounts of resources have to be devoted to restoring them if the hardware fails. It also illustrates one of the risks of senior managers leaving technology entirely in the hands of technical experts. Questioning by the PAC in March 1991 to discuss the qualification of the FCO accounts reveals a worrying lack of involvement of senior civil servants in either the choice or implementation of the new computer system or the disaster that resulted. The Permanent Under Secretary of State was unable to state who had been responsible for the original decision to employ Memory, going against the advice of the Central Computer and Telecommunications Agency (CCTA) (the government agency with the remit to advise agencies on their use of IT). Furthermore, he had never met Price Waterhouse to discuss the problems with them, although problems with Memory had first started to materialize in 1989. The reliance on consultants was such that the PAC suggested that the FCO was almost ancillary to Price Waterhouse rather than a prime mover in the project.

Computerization of the DSS: the Operational Strategy

The Operational Strategy, the project to automate fully the DSS, provides an example of computerization on a much greater scale. The DSS is one of the largest government departments, consuming 30% of public spending and employing around 10% of central government staff. The Operational Strategy was a plan involving the construction of large-scale computer systems and the installation of 40 000 terminals in 1000 local offices and unemployment offices. It is claimed to be the largest programme of computerization ever undertaken in Europe. Full national coverage was expected in 1991.

Work carried out on the strategy falls into three stages. The planning and design phase lasted from 1982 until June 1985, designated by Dyerson and Roper (1990), as 'the endless planning years'. At the PAC in 1984, concern was raised at the apparent lack of control by department managers over the programme's progress. In 1985, the Government announced its plans for the reform of social security in a two-volume green paper. This had far-reaching implications for the systems in the strategy and new plans had to be made to account for the subsequent restructuring of benefits. The third stage started in 1987 when it became clear that many of the projects had slipped behind their original target dates. The speed of implementation after 1987 was fast and furious, and subsequent target dates for individual projects were largely met. More detailed descriptions of the history of the Operational Strategy have been given in Willcocks and Mason (1987) and Margetts and Willcocks (1991). In the present context what is more interesting is: how far and which objectives have been achieved by the beginning of 1992?

Economy

The costs of the project have risen from the proposed £700 to £2600M (and are still rising). Between 1982, when the first broad estimates were made and 1988, the estimated costs of the Strategy rose from £713M to £1749M in real terms (an increase of 145%) (NAO, 1989). The net savings fell from £915M to £414M in real terms (a fall of 55%). The achievement of the net 1989 value of £175M depends crucially on the level of staff savings to be achieved. A 17% shortfall in the estimate could reduce that value to nil and put the financial viability of the Strategy at risk (NAO, 1989). Since then the estimates of costs have risen to £2.6 billion. The ratio of work received to work processed for Income Support has remained fairly constant; 'manpower requirements for assessment have not decreased to any noticeable degree as compared with clerical methods' (DSS, 1989).

The NAO found that 'from the outset the Department aimed to avoid compulsory redundancies and to absorb savings through natural wastage' (NAO, 1989). However, by early 1988 it became clear that, because of increases in necessary projected savings and regional variations in wastage rates, other options such as transferring staff voluntarily to offices with staff shortages or transferring work to areas with likely staff surpluses would have to be considered. Eventually a policy of no compulsory redundancies was proposed provided that 'the unions co-operate fully with the delivery of the strategy' (PAC, 1989). More recently, the line between compulsory and voluntary redundancies has become more blurred, with the DSS considering compulsory transfers to other DSS offices and government departments (Dyerson and Roper, 1990). The cost of such actions is estimated at between £12 and £35M which the DSS made no allowance for in its estimates (PAC, 1989).

Job Satisfaction

Dyerson and Roper (1990) suggest that 'job satisfaction in the short run has increased because new skills are being acquired and the refurbishment of the offices has improved the work environment', but long-term effects look more problematic. A 1988 DSS report on job design concluded that a wider, flatter hierarchy would result from implementation, with most duties transferred to the clerical officer (LOII) level. It is now widely perceived that this and other assumptions made in the report were mistaken. Furthermore, the tasks undertaken by LOIIs appear to have become more rather than less routine: 'Rather than being liberated from calculation in order to spend more time with clients, LOIIs felt that they had become mere text inputters' (Dyerson and Roper, 1990). The DSS Pilot Evaluation Report (DSS, 1989) states that: 'as far as job design and organization is concerned, it is still early days', but, given that increased job satisfaction for Local Office staff was one of the primary objectives of the strategy, this might have been considered a major priority before this stage in implementation.

Quality

The quality of service has improved in some ways. For example claimants do not have to wait while case-papers are found. However, most of the smaller projects that have disappeared from the plans were those that were to enhance the service to claimants, for example VDU screens for claimants to work out their own entitlement before official assessment.

The 'whole person concept' was always open to a wide number of interpretations, ranging from an objective of computer systems design (DHSS, 1982) to that of a key plank in policy formulation. Adler and Sainsbury (1990b) point out that 'in spite of numerous rhetorical references to the "whole person concept" the Operational Strategy document contained little evidence that much thought had been given to what this might mean'. Adler and Sainsbury (1990a) have produced a two-volume report funded by the DSS on the whole person concept but this takes the form of a survey of opinions as to what the most desirable organization of local offices would be, and there is little sign that the DSS are able or willing to invest what would be needed to implement the recommendations. It is clear that the main elements of LOP, the Income Support System (ISCS) and the Pension System (PSCS) have been developed and implemented independently and there are few links between them. The claimant is treated as a 'whole person' on arrival at a local office, where initial information is given (sometimes from a VDU) at a single reception point, but processing is still carried out in separate areas depending on the benefit being claimed. Staff within local offices still deal with one particular benefit and there are no plans to train general benefit advisers in local offices.

The accuracy of the new systems has been cause for public concern. Problems with software handling the social fund caused the Comptroller and Auditor General to qualify the 1988-1989 account. One problem included a £200 000 shortfall in the system's £1.6M calculation. In October 1990, the accounts for the 1989-1990 financial year were again questioned after the head of the National Audit Office estimated that one in seven income support claims, and one in five claims for family credit, were miscalculated (*Independent*, 27 October 1990).

Robustness

Although unstated, that the system should work was presumably an implicit objective of the plans for computerization. The speed of implementation after 1987 undoubtedly caused numerous and major errors in the early stages. In February 1990 the weekly average number of faults officially reported averaged 80 per week. One office had logged 1860 faults up to 5 March 1990 (NUCPS, 1990). However, such errors can be expected to decrease as the system becomes more stable.

According to the DSS, the system is running at 98% availability, but these figures do not include down-time agreed by the department to allow work on the system by technical divisions, or unavailability affecting one or more staff within an office and unless a problem affects all offices it is not recorded (NUCPS, 1990). When the full complement of local offices are online it seems possible that such failures could become more frequent.

Common Risks in IT Projects

Risk is involved in all IT projects. In research across a range of government departments Willcocks and Margetts (1991) found a range of critical variables influencing levels of risk. As one generalization the higher the level of 'innovativeness' the IT represents to the organization, the higher the risks being undergone. Other significant factors encountered include:

• Organizational readiness for change.
• IT experience and history.
• The 'strategic maturity' (ability of the organization to operate strategically).
• Number of functions/departments being computerized.
• Size of IT project.
• Industrial relations context.

Another way of assessing risk is through utilizing innovation theory. Thus Harrow and Willcocks (1992) adopt from Rogers and Kim (1985) five attributes of innovations that affect adoption rates in public sector contexts. In terms of IT projects, innovations with the following features are more readily and rapidly adoptable than others:

• Greater relative advantage (over preceding practices).
• More compatibility (with potential adopters' needs and values).
• Less complexity.
• More 'trialability' (testing possible on a limited basis).
• More observability (results visible to others).

All these factors can be quite easily read back into the histories of the FCO and DSS to indicate risk levels in the respective iT projects. Willcocks and Mark (1989) have also shown them coming strikingly together in the rush to implement IT designed to provide management information crucially supporting the NHS general managers appointed following the Griffiths proposals. A further finding by Willcocks and Margetts (1991) is that even situations diagnosed as low risk (that is where many of these factors tend to support IT adoption), risk can be reintroduced by financial and time constraints imposed by central government that do not reflect the realities of project managing robust usable systems into the organization. To build on the argument so far, the following represent some of the most common risks, as illustrated by the above examples.

Risk of Costs Rising out of Control

In the case of the DSS Operational Strategy, the original proposal, published in 1980 but on which

work had started under the previous Labour Government in 1977, appeared to assume that reductions in cost and increases in service and staff satisfaction could all be achieved without acknowledging possible tension between them. A foreword by Patrick Jenkin, however, warns that:

we shall, as time goes on, have to make choices, trading off objectives like improved service to the public and greater job satisfaction for the staff against each other and against resource costs. (DHSS, 1980.)

It appears that such choices were indeed made. Since 1987 one objective has been given priority; that the Strategy should be implemented as quickly as possible to achieve the planned staff savings. However, given the improbability of such savings ever being achieved, what was the point in finishing on time? The spiralling costs of the project mean that DSS management have failed to achieve the objective to which they gave the highest priority.

Risk that the System will not Reflect User Requirements

In 1989 the NAO considered that 'there must be some risk that projects shortly to be implemented may not adequately reflect the requirements of users'. Bearing in mind the NAO's predilection to phrase criticisms euphemistically, this must be seen as a reasonably serious problem. For example the lack of a notepad facility; case-papers contain a form on which all details of telephone calls or visits from the claimant are kept and which is regularly referred to; there was no equivalent method of recording such information on the new computer system. Although senior users were recruited to a plethora of user committees and project steering groups involved in planning the Strategy, users below higher executive officer level were not involved until implementation began in 1987. The discrepancies between user requirements and the system itself have narrowed since then, partly due to the efforts of regional implementation teams (Dyerson and Roper, 1990). However, the functionality of a computer system depends crucially on the extent to which the systems *design* involved understanding the work processes involved, and it was at this stage that low-level user involvement was at a minimum.

Risk that the Organization will not Possess Sufficient IT Expertise

The Operational Strategy has struggled with staff turnover rates of 45% (*Computer Weekly*, 22 March 1990). The NAO have identified shortage of IT staff as the reason for slippages in several computerization projects in the Ministry of Defence (MoD), the NHS and the Inland Revenue. Shortage of information technology staff is not only a problem for governmental organizations. It has been described as 'the most important single issue inhibiting the UK IT industry'. The situation in the future will be acutely aggravated by the demographic pattern.

© Public Finance Foundation, 1993

The Trade and Industry Committee in 1989 stated that 'the best solution to the worsening IT skill shortage is increased service training'. One witness spoke of the 'terrible legacy of apathy' about training in the IT user sector in the UK. In the civil service unions' response to the Trade and Industry Committee's first report on IT, a series of recommendations were made for the recruitment, training and retention of IT staff within the Civil Service. These include a recommendation that there should be ring-fenced training budgets which are planned in advance to be adequate and cannot be cashed or traded in for consultants, as at present. These proposals, along with most of the 52 recommendations made by the Trade and Industry Committee in the First Report on Information Technology were largely ignored by the Government.

In fact, the DSS dealt with the problems of skills shortages almost exclusively via the use of consultants. At the outset, the DSS planned on the basis that their own staff would undertake most of the computer development work and that outside consultants would supplement this as required. However, consultants were involved right from the start; these were principally Arthur Anderson, CAP and Computer Sciences Corporation (CSC). In April 1984 the major tender for the development of the system software went to a consortium made up of ICL, Logica and three universities: Imperial College, Lancaster and Surrey. In November 1984 the Government rejected a plan proposed by the PAC to overcome data-processing skill shortages through special treatment for computer staff (*Computing*, 29 November 1984). In 1986-1987, the DSS employed around 150 consultants at a cost of £12.1M.

After 1987 when Eric Caines took over as Director of Operational Strategy, the number of consultants used on the project increased significantly. Half the internal programmers working on the project were moved to other areas because they were seen as a strike risk. This eroded the skills base that had started to build up at the development centre in Lytham. CSC were dismissed and Arthur Anderson became the principal consultants used. Price Waterhouse were employed to recalculate the projected savings of the project. In 1989 the entire Livingstone Computer Centre was contracted out to Electronic Data Systems (a company owned by Ross Perot), a non-unionized firm, for a preliminary period of five years, after three firms had been invited to tender. A memorandum from John Moore, then Secretary of State, said the decision was part of his programme for 'making my department's computer installations less vulnerable to disruption from industrial action' (*Guardian*, 20 November 1989). The price of the EDS bid was £15M, less than those of the other firms but half a million pounds more than an in-house bid. There are similar plans for Norcross, the area computer centre in North Fylde, although in this case the tender was awarded without competition. The number of consultants employed

in 1987-1988 was 235, at a cost of £22M, nearly five times the cost of equivalent in-house staff (NAO, 1989). This is in line with a wider trend in government computing; in 1987-1988, approximately one-third of the Government's IT staff costs was spent on external support (Trade & Industry Committee, 1989).

Risk of Consultant Bankruptcy

The use of consultants in the DSS undoubtedly contributed to the spiralling costs of the project. However, there is another risk involved in the use of consultants; that of the consultants who designed or wrote the system going into liquidation. This was illustrated by the FCO and also recently in the NHS (PAC, 1991). The only safeguard against this is to investigate the financial soundness of the organization before placing contracts: this is very difficult because of the unpredictability of the computer consultancy market. In fact, this was the function that Price Waterhouse performed, unsuccessfully, for the FCO; even such an experienced and well-established organization was unable to safeguard against this risk.

The Separation of Policy-Making and IT

To some extent there is an unavoidable split between policy and administrative decisions. It is neither politically acceptable for technology to dictate policy, nor financially feasible for policy to be made independent of the administrative apparatus available. The Trade and Industry Committee concluded in 1989 that 'the most effective users of Information Technology are those where the board has a strategy for the company and an IT strategy which flows from that'. They also recorded a comment from DTI officials:

> *the commitment of senior management and by that one does not mean senior data-processing managers but the top managers of an organization – is crucial to the effective implementation of Information Technology.*
> (Trade and Industry Committee, 1989.)

Obviously these preconditions for success will always be difficult to achieve in a government organization where policy is decided by elected representatives and administration carried out by appointed officials. Yet during the Operational Strategy the policy and management domains seemed in some ways to be unnecessarily divided. The social security reforms of 1985-1988 had far-reaching effects on the project. Little development work had taken place on the main projects at the time the reforms were introduced, but the changes meant that project plans had to be altered within a relatively brief period of two years up to April 1988. According to many sources those involved in planning the Operational Strategy were not consulted until the green paper was published. Eric Caines indicated at the PAC in 1989 that the urgency of modifying supplementary benefit software to income support software in time for the introduction of the new benefit was the cause of many of the problems experienced. Many of the smaller projects, largely those designed to improve quality of service, were dropped from the plans. It appears that a rules-based benefit such as income support was easier to computerize than supplementary benefit, which is discretionary. However, the lack of consultation gives cause for concern.

While those in charge of administration appear unconcerned with policy issues, it also seems that politicians are reluctant to equip themselves with an understanding of IT. As the Trade and Industry Committee pointed out in 1989, most government departments now have an IT strategy committee. Ministers do not attend these meetings. The Trade and Industry Committee (1989) suggested that, although these committees could be classified as Civil Service rather than Ministerial: 'the absence of Ministers from their meetings shows either that ministers are not as closely involved in running their departments as might be expected or that they do not attach high priority to the use of Information Technology'.

The separation of policy-making and the use of IT means that public sector organizations may be particularly vulnerable to risk of the requirements of information systems changing abruptly when policy changes are made. In The Netherlands this is dealt with by compelling legislators to produce reports on the implications for technology whenever legislation is changed; there is no equivalent system in the UK. Furthermore, flexibility in policy-making may be lost when those implementing technology are unaware of the kind of policy changes that might be planned or desired in the future. For example, the possibility of merging the income tax and social security systems after computerization was included in the plans for the Strategy. It has been mentioned as a possibility since then by, for example, Nigel Lawson in his budget speech in March 1985. It appears that policy-makers think that because both systems are computerized the problems of merging them cannot be insurmountable. However, John Kenworthy, Head of the Information Technology Services Agency (ITSA), has been quoted as saying it would in fact be impossible; there are technical, physical and conceptual barriers (Civil Service College Seminar, June 1991).

Risk of Crash or Failure

Crash or failure can lead to loss of information but also loss of resources in recovering the damage. This is demonstrated by the FCO and potentially illustrated by the DSS. There is little evidence to suggest that public sector organizations like the DSS are investing in the disaster-recovery systems which banks and other large companies in the private sector know from bitter experience are necessary if large-scale computer networks are to be implemented and relied upon with confidence. In a recent CCTA survey reported to the PAC on

the contingency plans of government departments for standby hardware and software systems in case of disaster, the DSS were one of the 10% of government departments that failed to reply (PAC, 1989). It appears that their contingency plan is based on the ability to switch work between area computer centres, a facility originally introduced to reduce the risk of stoppage due to industrial disputes. It is unlikely that this contingency has ever been tested and given that the DSS, like most implementors of any technology from computer systems to the M25, have underestimated transaction loads perhaps they need a disaster in order to learn how to have one.

Isolation of IT

The Operational Strategy was the first attempt to introduce computers into the heart of the DSS, by incorporating their use in all aspects of the department's work. All the problems encountered seem to point to one major feature of the DSS's use of IT. While succeeding in bringing the computers themselves into the heart of the organization, all expertise in IT has been kept firmly on the periphery. While much of the design and specification of the system has been carried out by consultants, those with experience of actually using the DSS administrative systems were largely excluded. The politicians and policy-makers have made little effort to understand the implications of the technology. Senior managers appear to regard it as a cost-cutting tool, which can be administered as far as possible in isolation from the rest of the organization. The resistance of DSS management to the training of in-house staff means that integration of IT into management, improvement of IT project management skills and the overcoming of shortages in IT specialist staff may never happen.

The isolation of IT could be increased by the introduction of the agency structure to the UK civil service. Further marginalization of computer expertise in the DSS has seemed likely after April 1990 when all the DSS's information technology staff were moved to ITSA, deepening the division between IT and clerical staff. The annual budget of ITSA is around £400M. April 1991 also saw the birth of the Benefits Agency, consisting of all staff who worked on NI contributions. The management of ITSA are proud that in the future their worth can be measured by the competitiveness of the computer consultancy market; if the Contributions Agency or the Benefits Agency are dissatisfied with the service they get then they can go elsewhere. However, it is far easier for users of computer services to define what they want when they possess an understanding of what is possible. If all technological expertize has been moved to the periphery of the organization, it seems unlikely that the DSS will know whether they are dissatisfied or not.

The Future of IT in Public Administration

This final section investigates whether larger trends in public administration are laying the future public

© Public Finance Foundation, 1993

55

sector especially open to the risks introduced by IT. Hood (1990) has identified five 'megatrends' in public administration today. These are:

• Attempts to check the growth of government.
• The internationalization of public administration.
• Automation in public administration.
• The privatization of public sector provision.
• The rise of the 'new public management'.

As Hood has pointed out, these trends are neither jointly exhaustive nor mutually exclusive. All might be facilitated by, or exacerbated by, the widespread introduction of IT. For example, the Operational Strategy appears to demonstrate all of the trends.

The objective given the highest priority, to cut costs, was to be achieved by the reduction in staff facilitated by the new system. It makes possible John Kenworthy's (ITSA) aim that UK social security systems should link up with others in Europe. Germany and Austria already share data. It has automated the local offices. It was achieved by the employment of large numbers of private consultants and contract staff in preference to the training of in-house staff. And the management techniques used satisfy the criteria of what Hood terms 'the new public management', a term that he (and others) have used to indicate a shift away from issues of policy to issues of management involving a strong emphasis on cost-cutting and efficiency criteria. The term also involves a disaggregated approach to the management of the public sector, involving the break up of traditional public bureaucratic structures and attempts to increase 'contestability' and competition in public services provision.

Hood has highlighted three problem areas likely to arise from these trends. All three can be illustrated by examples from computerization projects in the public sector.

Waste: Avoidable incompetence and inefficiency
The new public management places great emphasis on reduction of waste. The Operational Strategy appears to provide further evidence for Hood's thesis that 'it is capable of creating waste too. Its tendency to denigrate most kinds of technical expertize other than economics or accounting can leave it vulnerable to implementation fiascoes'. Its focus on the short term and the measurable can leave it vulnerable to the pattern of achieving transient success followed by collapse.

The Operational Strategy also illustrates the different types of waste to which the public sector is vulnerable. IT can be used as an 'instrument of policy', to facilitate policy-making hitherto impossible and to make the implementation of existing policies easier.

However, this means taking a more strategic approach to the purchase and use of technology, rather than viewing it narrowly as a cost-cutting tool. The failure of policy-makers and politicians to familiarize themselves with such approaches has actually narrowed the possibilities for social security

policies in the future; for example it would now be prohibitively expensive to implement a system based on means tested benefits.

Malversation: Problems which lie in abuse or potential for abuse of public office rather than in excess costs or incompetence, paid for in terms of loss of trust and effective political rights for citizens
This is illustrated by the extensive private sector participation in public management, which has helped to give it the characteristics of a 'policy boom' (Dunleavy, 1989), and the increased use of consultancy, franchising and contracting making the area of overlap between the public and private sectors far larger than before. As demonstrated above, the continued use of private sector consultants has meant many government departments becoming involved in expensive long-term relationships with specific firms that are virtually impossible to break.

The potential for invasion of privacy by the existence of the DSS central index also opens up possibilities for 'malversation'. It has been used as a strong argument against the privatization of ITSA: as John Kenworthy pointed out at a Civil Service College Seminar in 1991 - 'You are all on my computer now!'. Certainly it raises questions of democracy, especially with the departmental exchange of data via the Government Data Network. The possibility of Europe-wide social security systems indicates the need for a European directive on data protection at the very least.

Catastrophe: Socially created disasters, the capacity of government or other human action to create physical damage on a large scale as a result of system failure
In a discussion of the risk involved in large-scale computerization, Angel and Smithson (1989) show how the failure of prediction (more difficult with information technology than other large-scale projects) grows when 'what should be a wide-ranging investigation of the implications of the new system turns out to be a much narrower cost analysis', entailing a number of critical assumptions that cannot be justified without a far deeper examination. Ironically, by being presented with IT as a mechanism primarily for reducing costs rather than a potential disaster area, public sector managers are being encouraged to undertake enormous financial risks.

Furthermore, Hood suggests that the resilience of the public sector may be endangered by a break up of the public sector into a fragmented structure of separate managerial units. Recent reorganization of the DSS is a good example of how IT can form part of a rethinking of overall organizational design. In 1989 the 'Moodie report' (DSS, 1988b) proposed the relocation of administrative functions in Glasgow, Belfast and Wigan for 21 offices that were deemed to be delivering an unsatisfactory service. These local offices will remain as reception points with terminals for viewing only while the assessing of claims will be carried out in the social security centres. Further reorganization will divide the 500

© Public Finance Foundation, 1993

local offices into 200 clusters consisting of two or three branch offices which will be service delivery points linked to a main administrative office. The Moodie Report has initiated a move towards customer serving local offices supported across the wires by locationally separate back offices.

This illustrates how fragmentation is facilitated by, and would perhaps be impossible without, the introduction of large-scale computer networks. In addition it shows how the break up can lead to contradictions between organizational and technological forms. While the public sector is being broken up into non-integrated units, the managers of these units are being provided with centralized, standardized systems over which they have no control.; This becomes a particularly dangerous situation when units who are supposed to share information via such systems are actually set up in competition with each other, as is happening with hospitals who are opting out of the NHS under the current UK health service reforms.

Conclusion

By making economy the primary objective of computerization, to some extent ignoring the human factors and losing the wider benefits that IT can bring, the DSS experienced problems that were costly and, ironically, took them further from their aim. Computing is not in itself a powerful and influential force within organizations. Rather, it is the actions (or lack of action) of senior management that have a vital effect on the style of computing that emerges. The development and implementation of the Operational Strategy appears to illustrate many of the trends observable in the management of public bureaucracy in the 1990s. At the same time, it highlights the dangers. IT as an instrument of policy is not an uncontentious or unproblematic issue. It cannot be used as a straightforward cost-cutting tool in isolation from the rest of the administration. If it is viewed as such by 'new' public managers, then the public sector will become increasingly vulnerable to risk.   ∎

References

Adler, M. and Sainsbury, R. (1990a), Putting the whole person concept into practice – Final report: Parts 1 and 2. (Report to the DSS).

Adler, M. and Sainsbury, R. (1990b), The social shaping of information technology: computerization and the administration of social security. Paper at the Social Security Workshop at the London School of Economics.

Angel, I. and Smithson, S. (1989), *Managing Information Technology: A Crisis of Confidence*. LSE Department of Information Technology, Working Paper No. 20. London School of Economics, London.

DHSS (1980), *A Strategy for Social Security Operations*. Working paper. HMSO, London.

DHSS (1982), *Social Security Operational Strategy: A Framework for the Future*. HMSO, London.

DSS (1989a), *Operational Strategy Pilot Evaluation Report; Management Summary and Main Report*. HMSO, London.

DSS (1988b), The business of service. The report of the regional organisation ocrutiny. Internal document, DSS.

Dunleavy, P. (1989), The architecture of the British central state, parts I and II. *Public Administration* (Winter).

Dyerson, R. and Roper, M. (1990), *Computerization at the DSS 1977-89: The Operational Strategy*. LBS Technology Project Papers Number 4. London Business School, London.

Harrow, J. and Willcocks, L. (1992), Management, innovation and organizational learning. In Willcocks, L. and Harrow, J. (Eds.), *Rediscovering Public Services Management*. McGraw Hill, London.

Hood, C. (1990), Beyond the public bureaucracy state. Extended text of Inaugural lecture, London School of Economics, London.

Margetts, H. and Willcocks, L. (1991), Information technology as policy instrument? Trends and prospects in the UK social security system. Paper given to the EGPA Conference: Information in the Public Sector. The Hague, the Netherlands.

NAO (1989), *Department of Social Security, Operational Strategy*. Report by the Comptroller and Auditor General. HMSO, London.

Newton, T. (1989), Keynote address at Investing in Quality: Managing the Technological Change of the 90s. RIPA/Hoskyns Joint Symposium, London.

NUCPS (1990), DSS Local Office Computerization and Administration. Briefing Document prepared by NUCPS, London.

PAC (1989), Foreign and Commonwealth Office: Qualification of Accounts. House of Commons paper 275i, Session 1990/91.

Rogers, E. and Kim, J. (1985), Diffusion of innovations in public organizations. In Merritt, R. and Merritt, A. (Eds.), *Innovation in the Public Sector*. Sage, Beverly Hills.

Trade and Industry Committee (1989), *First Report on Information Technology; and Minutes of Evidence, Session 1988/9*. HMSO, London.

Willcocks, L. and Margetts, H. (1991), Informatization in UK public services: from implementation, through strategy to management. Paper at the EGFPA Conference: Informatization in the Public Sector. The Hague, the Netherlands.

Willcocks, L. and Mark, A. (1989), IT systems implementation: research findings from the public sector. *Journal of Information Technology*, 4, 2.

Willcocks, L. and Mason, D. (1987), *The DHSS Operational Strategy, 1975-1986. Business Case File in Information Technology*. Van Nostrand Reinhold, London.

© Public Finance Foundation, 1993

[22]

A PUBLIC MANAGEMENT FOR ALL SEASONS?

CHRISTOPHER HOOD

This article discusses: the doctrinal content of the group of ideas known as 'new public management' (NPM); the intellectual provenance of those ideas; explanations for their apparent persuasiveness in the 1980s; and criticisms which have been made of the new doctrines. Particular attention is paid to the claim that NPM offers an all-purpose key to better provision of public services. This article argues that NPM has been most commonly criticized in terms of a claimed contradiction between 'equity' and 'efficiency' values, but that any critique which is to survive NPM's claim to 'infinite reprogrammability' must be couched in terms of possible conflicts between *administrative* values. The conclusion is that the ESRC's 'Management in Government' research initiative has been more valuable in helping to identify rather than to definitively answer, the key conceptual questions raised by NPM.

THE RISE OF NEW PUBLIC MANAGEMENT (NPM)

The rise of 'new public management' (hereafter NPM) over the past 15 years is one of the most striking international trends in public administration. Though the research reported in the other papers in this issue refers mainly to UK experience, NPM is emphatically not a uniquely British development. NPM's rise seems to be linked with four other administrative 'megatrends', namely:

(i) attempts to *slow down or reverse government growth* in terms of overt public spending and staffing (Dunsire and Hood 1989);

(ii) the shift toward *privatization and quasi-privatization* and away from core government institutions, with renewed emphasis on 'subsidiarity' in service provision (cf. Hood and Schuppert 1988; Dunleavy 1989).

(iii) the development of *automation*, particularly in information technology, in the production and distribution of public services; and

(iv) the development of a more *international* agenda, increasingly focused on general issues of public management, policy design, decision styles and inter-governmental cooperation, on top of the older tradition of individual country specialisms in public administration.

(These trends are discussed further in Hood 1990b).

NPM, like most administrative labels, is a loose term. Its usefulness lies in its convenience as a shorthand name for the set of broadly similar administrative doctrines which dominated the bureaucratic reform agenda in many of the OECD

Christopher Hood is Professor of Public Administration and Public Policy in the University of London.

Public Administration Vol. 69 Spring 1991 (3–19)
© 1991 Royal Institute of Public Administration ISSN 0033–3298 $3.00

4 CHRISTOPHER HOOD

group of countries from the late 1970s (see Aucoin 1990; Hood 1990b; Pollitt 1990).

Although ill-defined, NPM aroused strong and varied emotions among bureaucrats. At one extreme were those who held that NPM was the only way to correct for the irretrievable failures and even moral bankruptcy in the 'old' public management (cf. Keating 1989). At the other were those who dismissed much of the thrust of NPM as a gratuitous and philistine destruction of more than a century's work in developing a distinctive public service ethic and culture (cf. Martin 1988; Nethercote 1989b).

NPM's rise also sparked off debate as to how the movement was to be labelled, interpreted and explained. What exactly was the public management Emperor now wearing? Where did the design come from, and did its novelty lie mainly in presentation or in content? Why did it find favour? Was it an all-purpose and all-weather garment? This article attempts to discuss these questions, with particular attention to the last one.

WHAT THE EMPEROR WAS WEARING: THE DOCTRINES OF NPM

Different commentators and advocates of NPM have stressed different aspects of doctrine. But the seven overlapping precepts summarized in table 1 below appear in most discussions of NPM. Over the last decade, a 'typical' public sector policy delivery unit in the UK, Australia, New Zealand and many other OECD countries would be likely to have had some exposure to most of these doctrines. But not all of the seven elements were equally present in all cases; nor are they necessarily fully consistent, partly because they do not have a single intellectual provenance.

TABLE 1 Doctrinal components of new public management

No.	Doctrine	Meaning	Typical justification
1	'Hands-on professional management' in the public sector	Active, visible, discretionary control of organizations from named persons at the top, 'free to manage'	Accountability requires clear assignment of responsibility for action, not diffusion of power
2	Explicit standards and measures of performance	Definition of goals, targets, indicators of success, preferably expressed in quantitative terms, especially for professional services (cf. Day and Klein 1987; Carter 1989)	Accountability requires clear statement of goals; efficiency requires 'hard look' at objectives
3	Greater emphasis on output controls	Resource allocation and rewards linked to measured performance; breakup of centralized bureaucracy-wide personnel management	Need to stress results rather than procedures

A PUBLIC MANAGEMENT FOR ALL SEASONS?   5

Table 1 continued

No.	Doctrine	Meaning	Typical justification
4	Shift to *disaggregation* of units in the public sector	Break up of formerly 'monolithic' units, unbundling of U-form management systems into corporatized units around products, operating on decentralized 'one-line' budgets and dealing with one another on an 'arms-length' basis	Need to create 'manageable' units, separate *provision* and *production* interests, gain efficiency advantages of use of contract or franchise arrangements *inside* as well as outside the public sector
5	Shift to greater *competition* in public sector	Move to term contracts and public tendering procedures	*Rivalry* as the key to lower costs and better standards
6	*Stress on private-sector styles of management practice*	Move away from military-style 'public service ethic', greater flexibility in hiring and rewards; greater use of PR techniques	Need to use 'proven' private sector management tools in the public sector
7	Stress on greater *discipline* and *parsimony* in resource use	Cutting direct costs, raising labour discipline, resisting union demands, limiting 'compliance costs' to business	Need to check resource demands of public sector and 'do more with less'

WHERE THE DESIGN CAME FROM: NPM AS A MARRIAGE OF OPPOSITES

One way of interpreting NPM's origins is as a marriage of two different streams of ideas. One partner was the 'new institutional economics'. It was built on the now very familiar story of the post-World War II development of public choice, transactions cost theory and principal-agent theory – from the early work of Black (1958) and Arrow (1963) to Niskanen's (1971) landmark theory of bureaucracy and the spate of later work which built on it.

The new institutional economics movement helped to generate a set of administrative reform doctrines built on ideas of *contestability*, *user choice*, *transparency* and close concentration on *incentive structures*. Such doctrines were very different from traditional military-bureaucratic ideas of 'good administration', with their emphasis on orderly hierarchies and elimination of duplication or overlap (cf. Ostrom 1974).

The other partner in the 'marriage' was the latest of a set of successive waves of business-type 'managerialism' in the public sector, in the tradition of the international

6   CHRISTOPHER HOOD

scientific management movement (Merkle 1980; Hume 1981; Pollitt 1990). This movement helped to generate a set of administrative reform doctrines based on the ideas of *'professional management'* expertise as *portable* (Martin 1983), *paramount* over technical expertise, requiring high *discretionary power* to achieve results ('free to manage') and *central* and *indispensable* to better organizational performance, through the development of appropriate cultures (Peters and Waterman 1982) and the active measurement and adjustment of organizational outputs.

Whether the partners in this union were fully compatible remains to be seen. 'Free to manage' is a rather different slogan from 'free to choose'. The two can conflict, particularly where the NPM revolution is led from above (as it was in the UK) rather than from below. The relative dominance of the two partners varied in different countries even within the 'Westminster model' tradition (cf. Hood 1990c). For example, in the unique circumstances of New Zealand, the synthesis of public choice, transactions cost theory and principal-agent theory was predominant, producing an analytically driven NPM movement of unusual coherence. But in the UK and Australia business-type managerialism was much more salient, producing a more pragmatic and less intellectually elegant strain of NPM or 'neo-Taylorism' (Pollitt 1990, p. 56). Potential frictions between these partners were not resolved by any single coherent or definitive exposition of the joint philosophy. Indeed, the New Zealand Treasury's *Government Management* (1987) comes closest to a coherent NPM 'manifesto', given that much of the academic literature on the subject either lacks full-scale elaboration or enthusiastic commitment to NPM.

WHY NPM FOUND FAVOUR: THE ACCEPTANCE FACTOR

There is no single accepted explanation or interpretation of why NPM coalesced and why it 'caught on' (cf. Hood 1990b; Hood and Jackson 1991 forthcoming, ch. 8). Many academic commentators associate it with the political rise of the 'New Right'. But that on its own does not explain why these particular doctrines found favour, nor why NPM was so strongly endorsed by Labour governments ostensibly opposed to the 'New Right', notably in Australia and New Zealand. Among the possible explanations are the following four.

First, for those who take a sceptical view of administrative reform as a series of evanescent fads and fashions, NPM's rise might be interpreted as a sudden and unpredictable product of 'loquocentric' success (Minogue 1986). (Spann (1981) offers a classic statement of the 'fashion' interpretation of administrative reform.) 'Cheap, superficial and popular', like the industrial 'rationalization' doctrines of the 1930s (Hannah 1976, p. 38, fn. p. 34), NPM had many of the necessary qualities for a period of pop management stardom. A 'whim of fashion' interpretation has some attractions, and can cope with the cycles and reversals that took place within NPM – for instance, the radical shift in the UK, from the 'Heseltine creed' of *Ministers* as the hands-on public managers to the 'Next Steps' corporatization creed of professional managers at the top, with ministers in a strictly 'hands-off' role (cf. also Sturgess 1989). But equally, the weakness of a simple 'whim of fashion' explanation is that it does not account for the relative *endurance* of many of the seven precepts identified in table 1 over more than a decade.

A PUBLIC MANAGEMENT FOR ALL SEASONS? 7

An equally sceptical explanation, but one which better accommodates the recurring or enduring features of many aspects of NPM, is the view of NPM as a 'cargo cult' phenomenon – the endless rebirth, in spite of repeated failures, of the idea that substantive success ('cargo') can be gained by the practice of particular kinds of (managerial) ritual. Downs and Larkey (1986) describe a recurring cycle of euphoria and disillusion in the promulgation of simplistic and stereotyped recipes for better public management in the USA, which shows striking similarities with the well-documented cargo cults of Melanesia (Lawrence 1964; Worsley 1968). However, this explanation cannot tell us why the NPM variant of the recurring public management 'cargo cult' appeared at the time that it did, rather than at any other.

A third, less sceptical, approach might be to view the rise of NPM through Hegelian spectacles and interpret it as an epoch-making attraction of opposites. The opposites in this case are two historically distinct approaches to public administration which are in a sense fused in NPM. One is the German tradition of state-led economic development (*Volkswirtschaft*) by professional public managers, with its roots in cameralism (Small 1909). The other is the Anglo-Saxon tradition of liberal economics, allied with a concern for matching self-interest with duty in administration, that has its roots in utilitarianism (Hume 1981). But, like the 'cargo cult' interpretation, the 'synthesis of opposites' interpretation on its own does not help us to understand why those two distinct public administration traditions should have united *at this particular time* rather than at any other.

A fourth and perhaps more promising interpretation of the emergence of NPM is as a response to a set of special social conditions developing in the long peace in the developed countries since World War II, and the unique period of economic growth which accompanied it (see Hood 1990b and 1991 forthcoming). Conditions which may have helped to precipitate NPM include:

— changes in income level and distribution serving to weaken the 'Tocqueville coalition' for government growth in the electorate, and laying the conditions for a new tax-conscious winning electoral coalition (Tocqueville 1946, p. 152; Peacock 1979; Meltzer and Richard 1981);
— changes in the socio-technical system associated with the development of the lead technologies of the late twentieth-century Kondratiev cycle ('post-industrialism', 'post-Fordism'), serving to remove the traditional barriers between 'public sector work' and 'private sector work' (cf. Bell 1973; Piore and Sabel 1984; Jessop 1988).
— A shift towards 'new machine politics', the advent of a new campaign technology geared towards making public policy by intensive opinion polling of key groups in the electorate, such that professional party strategists have greater clout in policy-making relative to the voice of experience from the bureaucracy (cf. Mills 1986; Hood 1990c, p. 206).
— a shift to a more white-collar, socially heterogeneous population less tolerant of 'statist' and uniform approaches in public policy (cf. Hood and Schuppert 1988, p. 250–2).

8   CHRISTOPHER HOOD

The fourth explanation is somewhat 'overdetermined', but it seems more promising than the other three in that it has the power to explain what none of the others can do, namely why NPM should have emerged in the particular time and place that it did and under a variety of different auspices.

AN ALL-PURPOSE GARMENT? NPM's CLAIM TO UNIVERSALITY

Like many previous administrative philosophies, NPM was presented as a framework of general applicability, a 'public management for all seasons'. The claim to universality was laid in two main ways.

Portability and diffusion. First, much the same set of received doctrines was advanced as the means to solve 'management ills' in many different contexts – different organizations, policy fields, levels of government, countries. From Denmark to New Zealand, from education to health care, from central to local government and quangos, from rich North to poor South, similar remedies were prescribed along the lines of the seven themes sketched out in table 1. Universalism was not complete in practice; for instance, NPM seems to have had much less impact on international bureaucracies than on national ones, and less on controlling departments than on front-line delivery units. Moreover, much was made of the need for local variation in management styles – so long as such variations did not challenge the basic framework of NPM (Pollitt 1990, pp. 55–6). For critics, however, much of the 'freedom to manage' under NPM was that brand of freedom in which whatever is not forbidden tends to be compulsory (Larsen 1980, p. 54); and the tendencies to uniformity and 'cloning' under FMI points to possible reasons for the decline of FMI and its supersession by the corporatization creed of Next Steps.'

Political neutrality. Second, NPM was claimed to be an 'apolitical' framework within which many different values could be pursued effectively. The claim was that different political priorities and circumstances could be accommodated by altering the 'settings' of the management system, without the need to rewrite the basic programme of NPM. That framework was not, according to NPM's advocates, a machine exclusively tunable to respond to the demands of the New Right or to any one political party or programme (see, for example, Scott Bushnell and Sallee 1990, p. 162; Treasury and Civil Service Committee 1990, pp. ix, 22, 61). In this respect, NPM followed the claims to universality of traditional Public Administration, which also purported to offer a neutral and all-purpose instrument for realizing whatever goals elected representatives might set (Ostrom 1974; Thomas 1978; Hood 1987).

COUNTER-CLAIMS: CRITICS OF NPM

If NPM has lacked a single definitive 'manifesto', the ideas of its critics are equally scattered among a variety of often ephemeral sources. Most of the criticisms of NPM have come in terms of four main counter-claims, none of which have been definitively tested, in spite of the ESRC's 'Management in Government' initiative.

A PUBLIC MANAGEMENT FOR ALL SEASONS? 9

The first is the assertion that NPM is like the Emperor's New Clothes in the well-known Hans Andersen story – all hype and no substance, and in that sense a true product of the style-conscious 1980s. From this viewpoint, the advent of new managerialism has changed little, apart from the language in which senior public 'managers' speak in public. Underneath, all the old problems and weaknesses remain. Implicitly, from this viewpoint, the remedy lies in giving NPM some real substance in order to move from 'smoke and mirrors' to reality – for example, in making output contracts between ministers and chief executives legally binding or in breaking up the public service employment structure, as has happened in New Zealand (cf. Hood and Jones in Treasury and Civil Service Committee 1989–90).

The second is the assertion that NPM has damaged the public service while being ineffective in its ability to deliver on its central claim to lower costs per (constant) unit of service. Critics of this type suggest that the main result of NPM in many cases has been an 'aggrandizement of management' (Martin 1983) and a rapid middle-level bureaucratization of new reporting systems (as in the remarkable growth of the 'performance indicator industry'). Budgetary and control framework changes such as 'top-slicing' and 'creative accounting' serve to destabilize the bureaucracy and to weaken or destroy elementary but essential competences at the front line (see, for instance, Nethercote 1989b, p. 17; Nethercote 1989c). From this viewpoint, the remedy lies in applying to the NPM *system* the disciplines that it urges upon service-delivery bureaucracies but so signally fails to impose on itself – particularly in strict resource control and the imposition of a battery of published and measurable performance indicators to determine the overall costs and benefits of the system.

The third common criticism is the assertion that NPM, in spite of its professed claims to promote the 'public good' (of cheaper and better public services for all), is actually a vehicle for *particularistic* advantage. The claim is that NPM is a self-serving movement designed to promote the career interests of an élite group of 'new managerialists' (top managers and officials in central controlling departments, management consultants and business schools) rather than the mass of public service customers or low-level staff (Dunleavy 1985; Yeatman 1987; Kelleher 1988; Pollitt 1990, pp. 134–7). Implicitly, the remedy suggested by these criticisms is to have disproportionate cutbacks on 'managerial' rather than on 'operational' staff (cf. Martin 1983), and measures to 'empower' consumers, for instance by new systems of direct democracy (cf. Pollitt 1990, pp. 183–4).

The fourth line of criticism, to which most attention will be paid in the remainder of this paper, is directed towards NPM's claim of *universality*. Contrary to NPM's claim to be a public management for all seasons, these critics argue that different administrative values have different implications for fundamental aspects of administrative design – implications which go beyond altering the 'settings' of the systems.

In order for their counter-claim to have any significance, it must be able to survive obvious objections. First, it must be able to show that the objection is more than a semantic quibble about where the line comes between a different programme

10   CHRISTOPHER HOOD

and a change of 'settings'. For that, it must be able to show that the incompatibility problem lies in NPM's 'hard core' research programme rather than in its 'elaborative belts' (Lakatos 1970). Second, it must be able to show that it is more than a trivial and obvious proposition. In order to survive this objection, it needs to show that there are different management-system implications of different *mainstream*, relatively orthodox values, without reference to values at the extremes of the orthodox belief spectrum (since it needs no elaborate treatise to show that different 'fundamentalist' values have different implications for public management). Third, the 'incompatibility' argument needs to rest on a plausible case that an 'all-purpose culture' either does not exist or cannot be engineered into existence. Unless it can do so, it risks being dismissed for mechanically assuming that there is a particular set of administrative design-characteristics which goes with the ability to achieve a particular set of values. Finally, it needs to show that the debate relates to *administrative* values – values that relate to conventional and relatively narrow ideas about 'good administration' rather than to broader ideas about the proper role of the state in society. Unless the critique of the 'all seasons' quality of NPM relates to administrative values in this sense, it risks being dismissed simply as an undercover way of advocating different *political values* from those currently held by elected governments. A case built on such a basis would not essentially be an administrative design argument, and would neither demonstrate that NPM is incapable of being adapted to promote alternative political values nor that NPM is a false recipe for achieving the narrow 'efficiency' values of the current orthodox agenda.

Most of the orthodox criticisms of NPM in this vein are vulnerable to counter-attack from this last objection. Most academic attacks on NPM have questioned NPM's universality by focusing on the equity costs of a preoccupation with cost-cutting and a focus on 'bottom line ethics' (Jackson 1989, p. 173). For instance, a focus on outputs allied with heavy 'hands-on' demands on managers is often claimed to downgrade equity considerations, particularly in its implications for the ability of female managers to reach top positions in the public service (cf. Bryson 1987; Pollitt 1990, pp. 141–2). A focus on disaggregation and a private-sector PR style is likewise often claimed to reduce the accessibility of public services by increasing the complexity and opacity of government (Nethercote 1990c), and increasing the scope for buck-passing and denial of responsibility, especially for disadvantaged consumers. However, any simple dichotomy between 'efficiency' and 'equity' can be countered by NPM's advocates on the grounds that 'efficiency' can be conceived in ways which do not fundamentally conflict with equity (cf. Wilenski 1986), and that equity values could perfectly well be programmed in to the target-setting and performance indication process, if there was strong enough political pressure to do so.

THREE CLUSTERS OF ADMINISTRATIVE VALUES

In administrative argument in the narrow sense, the rival values in play typically do not fall into a neat dichotomy. At least three different 'families' of values commonly appear in debates about administrative design, and these are summarized in table 2 below (cf. Hood and Jackson 1991 forthcoming). Broadly, the 'sigma' family of values relates to *economy* and *parsimony*, the 'theta' family relates to *honesty* and *fairness*, and the 'lambda' family relates to *security* and *resilience*.

TABLE 2   Three sets of core values in public management

	Sigma-type values	*Theta-type values*	*Lambda-type values*
	KEEP IT LEAN AND PURPOSEFUL	KEEP IT HONEST AND FAIR	KEEP IT ROBUST AND RESILIENT
STANDARD OF SUCCESS	*Frugality* (matching of resources to tasks for given goals)	*Rectitude* (achievement of fairness, mutuality, the proper discharge of duties)	*Resilience* (achievement of reliability, adaptivity, robustness)
STANDARD OF FAILURE	*Waste* (muddle, confusion, inefficiency)	*Malversation* (unfairness, bias, abuse of office)	*Catastrophe* (risk, breakdown, collapse)
CURRENCY OF SUCCESS AND FAILURE	*Money and time* (resource costs of producers and consumers)	*Trust and entitlements* (consent, legitimacy, due process, political entitlements)	*Security and survival* (confidence, life and limb)
CONTROL EMPHASIS	*Output*	*Process*	*Input/Process*
SLACK	*Low*	*Medium*	*High*
GOALS	*Fixed/Single*	*Incompatible 'Double bind'*	*Emergent/Multiple*
INFORMATION	Costed, segmented (commercial assets)	Structured	Rich exchange, collective asset
COUPLING	*Tight*	*Medium*	*Loose*

The trio corresponds roughly to the management values used by Susan Strange (1988, pp. 1–6) in her account of the evolution of different regimes in the international sphere; and at least two of the three correspond to the groups of values given by Harmon and Mayer (1986, pp. 34–53) in their well-known account of the normative context of public sector organization. It cannot be claimed that these values are esoteric or extreme, or that they are not 'administrative' values.

12   CHRISTOPHER HOOD

Sigma-type values: match resources to defined tasks. In the 'sigma' family come administrative values connected with the matching of resources to narrowly defined tasks and circumstances in a competent and sparing fashion. Such values are central, mainstream and traditional in public management. From this viewpoint, frugality of resource use in relation to given goals is the criterion of success, while failure is counted in terms of instances of avoidable waste and incompetence. If sigma-type values are emphasized, the central concern is to 'trim fat' and avoid 'slack'.

Classic expressions of sigma-type values include:

  (i) 'just-in-time' inventory control systems (which avoid tying up resources in storing what is not currently needed, pushing the onus of accessible storage and rapid delivery on to suppliers);
 (ii) payment-by-results reward systems (which avoid paying for what is not being delivered); and
(iii) administrative 'cost engineering' (using resources sparingly to provide public services of no greater cost, durability or quality than is absolutely necessary for a defined task, without excessive concern for 'externalities').

The principal 'coin' in which success or failure to realize sigma-type values is measured is time and money, in resource costs of consumers and producers.

It can be argued that an orthodox design for realizing sigma-type values would closely parallel the 'mechanistic' structures which have frequently been identified in contingency theory as applicable to defined and stable environmental conditions (cf. Burns and Stalker 1961; Lawrence and Lorsch 1967). Since the 'sigma' group of values stresses the matching of resources to defined objectives, the setting of fixed and 'checkable' goals must be central to any design for realizing such values. The fewer incompatible objectives are included, the more readily can unnecessary fat be identified and removed. Equally, the more that the control emphasis is on output rather than on process or input, the more unambiguous the waste-finding process can be. To make output control a reality, two features are necessary. One is a heavy emphasis on output databases. Such an emphasis in turn requires a technological infrastructure of reporting which will tend to make each managerial unit 'tightly coupled' in informational terms. The other is the sharp definition of responsibilities, involving separation of 'thinking' and 'executing' activities and the breakup of organizations into separate, non-overlapping parts, to come as close as possible to the ideal of single-objective, trackable and manageable units. It follows that information in such a control system will be highly segmented and valuable, so that it will be guarded with extreme care and traded rather than given away. These design characteristics map closely on to the recipes offered by the corporate management strain of NPM.

Theta-type values: honesty, fairness, mutuality. 'Theta-type' connotes values broadly relating to the pursuit of honesty, fairness and mutuality through the prevention of distortion, inequity, bias, and abuse of office. Such values are also central and traditional in public management, and they are institutionalized in appeal mechanisms, public reporting requirements, adversary bureaucracies, independent scrutiny systems, attempts to socialize public servants in something more than 'bottom line ethics' or a high 'grovel count' (Self 1989). From this viewpoint, success is counted in terms of 'rectitude', the proper discharge of duties in procedural and substantive terms, while failure is measured in terms of 'malversation' in a formal or substantive sense. If theta-type values are placed at centre stage, the central concern is to ensure honesty, prevent 'capture' of public bodies by unrepresentative groups, and avoid all arbitrary proceedings.

Classic expressions of theta-type values include:

(i) recall systems for removing public officials from office by popular vote;
(ii) 'notice and comment' and 'hard look' requirements in administrative law (Birkinshaw, Harden and Lewis 1990, p. 260);
(iii) independent anti-corruption investigatory bodies such as the 1987–9 Fitzgerald Inquiry which effectively brought down the Queensland government in 1989 (cf. Prasser, Wear and Nethercote 1990).

The 'coin' in which success or failure is measured according to theta-type values may be partly related to 'balance sheet' items (insofar as dishonesty and abuse of office is often linked with palpable waste of resources), but also involves less tangible stakes, notably public trust and confidence and the ability to exercise citizenship effectively.

Putting theta-type values at the centre of the stage has implications for organizational design which are different from an emphasis on 'sigma-type' values. Where honesty and fairness is a primary goal, the design-focus is likely to be on process-controls rather than output controls. Goals, too, are less likely to be single in nature. 'Getting the job done' in terms of aggregate quantities is likely to be supplemented by concerns about *how* the job is done (cf. March and Olsen 1989, pp. 47–52).

Hence 'double bind' elements (Hennestad 1990) may be central to goal setting, with line management under complex cross-pressures and with control operating through a shifting-balances style (Dunsire 1978). The cross pressures and 'double bind' process may operate through the activities of independent adversary bureau-cracies, rather than with corporate objectives settled in a single place – for example, in the Hong Kong style of independent anti-corruption bodies. Similarly, concern with process may cause the emphasis to go on the achievement of maximum *transparency* in public operations – for example, extensive public reporting requirements, 'angels' advocates' (the practice of incorporating representatives of 'public interest' groups on corporate boards), freedom of information laws, 'notice and comment' procedures, rather than simple 'bottom line ethics'.

Indeed, the logical conclusion of putting theta-type values first in designing public management would be to minimize the ability of those in high office to sell or distort public decisions as a result of 'capture' by particular groups – for example, by the entrenchment of adversarial processes within the bureaucracy or by greater use of direct democracy in public decision-making (Walker 1986; Pollitt 1990, pp. 183–4).

Lambda-type values: reliability, robustness, adaptivity. 'Lambda-type' values relate to resilience, endurance, robustness, survival and adaptivity – the capacity to

14   CHRISTOPHER HOOD

withstand and learn from the blows of fate, to avoid 'competency traps' in adaptation processes (Levitt and March 1988; Liebowitz and Margolis 1990), to keep operating even in adverse 'worst case' conditions and to adapt rapidly in a crisis.

Expectations of security and reliability are central to traditional public administration values, and have often been associated with the choice of public rather than private organization for the provision of a hazard-related task. Perhaps the classic historical case is of the Venetian arsenal and *Tana* as instruments for ensuring the security of Venice's maritime power by direct state production of ropes and vessels (cf. Lane 1966).

From the viewpoint of lambda-type values, success is counted in terms of resilience and reliability, while failure is measured in terms of catastrophe, breakdown and learning failure. If lambda-type values are placed at centre stage, the central concern is to avoid system failure, 'down time', paralysis in the face of threat or challenge.

Classic expressions of lambda-type values include:

 (i) *redundancy*, the maintenance of back-up systems to duplicate normal capacity;
 (ii) *diversity*, the maintenance of quite separate, self-standing units (to avoid 'common mode failure', whether in technical terms or in terms of 'groupthink'); and
 (iii) *robustness*, use of greater amounts of materials than would ordinarily be necessary for the job (cf. Health and Safety Executive 1988, p. 11).

The 'coin' in which success or failure is measured in lambda-type values includes security, survival and the robustness of basic assumptions about social defence mechanisms.

Orthodox discussions of learning problems and catastrophes tend to focus on specific failings of individuals rather than systemic or structural factors in organizational design (Turner *et al.* 1989, p. 3). But some tentative pointers to the administrative design implications of putting lambda-type values at centre stage can be gleaned from three closely related literatures: 'contingency theory' ideas about structural factors related to highly uncertain environments (cf. Lawrence and Lorsch 1967); the literature on the organization of socially created disasters (Dixon 1976; Turner 1976 and 1978; Perrow 1984); and the developing and related literature on 'safety culture' (Westrum 1987; Turner *et al.* 1989).

Some of the ideas to be found in this literature about the engineering of adaptivity and error-avoidance are contradictory. A case in point is the debate about 'anticipation' versus 'resilience' (Wildavsky 1988). Moreover, Perrow (1984) claims that for some technologies, administrative design for error-avoidance is impossible, even if safety is highly valued. However, much of this literature tends to relate error-generation, capacity for resilience and learning failures to three elements of institutional structure

 (i) degree of *integration* – the extent to which interdependent parts of the system are linked in decision and information terms rather than isolated into separate compartments, each trying to insulate itself independently against system failure;

A PUBLIC MANAGEMENT FOR ALL SEASONS?   15

(ii) degree of *openness* in the culture or management system, avoiding authoritarian barriers to lateral or systemic thinking and feedback or learning processes; and

(iii) the extent to which there are systemic pressures for *misinformation*, rather than sharing of information, built in to the organizational process.

From the perspective of this literature, an organizational design which maximized lambda-type values would need to involve: multiple-objective rather than single-objective organization (van Gunsteren 1976, p. 61); a relatively high degree of 'slack' to provide spare capacity for learning or deployment in crisis; a control framework which focused on input or process rather than measured output in order to avoid building up pressures for misinformation; a personnel management structure which promoted cohesion without punishing unorthodox ideas; a task division structure organized for systemic thinking rather than narrow compartmentalization; and a responsibility structure which made mistakes and errors admissible. Relatively loose coupling and an emphasis on information as a collective asset within the organization would be features of such a design structure.

Compatibility. From this discussion, as summarized in table 2, one fundamental implication is that these three sets of mainstream administrative values overlap over some of their range, like intersecting circles in a Venn diagram. For example, dishonesty frequently creates waste and sometimes leads to catastrophe. Frugality, rectitude and resilience may all be satisfied by a particular set of institutional arrangements in some contexts.

However, the discussion also suggests the hypothesis that any two out of the three broad value sets may often be satisfied by the same organizing principle for a set of basic administrative design dimensions; but that it is hard to satisfy *all three* value sets equally for any of those dimensions, and probably impossible to do so for all of them. Put simply, a central concern with *honesty* and the avoidance of policy distortion in public administration may have different design implications from a central concern with *frugality*; and a central concern with *resilience* may also have different design implications. If NPM is a design for putting frugality at centre stage, it may at the limit be less capable of ensuring honesty and resilience in public administration.

IMPLICATIONS FOR NEW PUBLIC MANAGEMENT

The work of the ESRC's Management in Government Initiative has helped us to identify the specific forms that NPM took in the UK and to trace its history. But, like many research initiatives, it has perhaps been more successful in prompting the critical questions rather than in answering them definitively. Two key questions in particular seem to deserve more examination, in order to 'put NPM in its place' intellectually.

First, NPM can be understood as primarily an expression of sigma-type values. Its claims have lain mainly in the direction of cutting costs and doing more for less as a result of better-quality management and different structural design. Accordingly, one of the key tests of NPM's 'success' is whether and how it has delivered on that claim, in addition to succeeding in terms of rhetorical acceptance. We still have remarkably little independent evidence on this point, and work by Dunsire *et al*. (1988) has some path-breaking qualities in that it is a serious attempt to develop indicators of organizational structure and control systems in a way that helps us to understand how privatization and corporatization works. It offers tentative evidence for the proposition that a shift in management structures towards decreased command-orientation and increased 'results-orientation' is associated with improvements in productivity. But the results obtained so far are only indicative: the study does not test fully for 'Hawthorne effects' or secular trends, and it has no control groups. We need much more work in this vein.

However, the critics' questioning of NPM's universality also offers a way of putting NPM in its place and involves crucial claims that need proper testing. Even if further research established that NPM was clearly associated with the pursuit of frugality, it remains to be fully investigated whether such successes are bought at the expense of guarantees of honesty and fair dealing and of security and resilience.

Broadly, NPM assumes a culture of public service honesty as given. Its recipes to some degree removed devices instituted to ensure honesty and neutrality in the public service in the past (fixed salaries, rules of procedure, permanence of tenure, restraints on the power of line management, clear lines of division between public and private sectors). The extent to which NPM is likely to induce corrosion in terms of such traditional values remains to be tested. The effects of NPM 'clones' diffused by public management 'consultocrats' and others into contexts where there is little 'capital base' of ingrained public service culture (as in many Third World countries and perhaps in Eastern Europe too) will be particularly interesting to observe. The consequences for 'theta-type' values are likely to be most visible, since the effects are likely to be quicker and more dramatic there than in countries like Australia and the UK which are still living off 'public service ethic' capital.[1]

Equally, the extent to which NPM's precepts are compatible with 'safety engineering' in terms of 'safety cultures' deserves more analysis. NPM broadly assumes that public services can be divided into self-contained 'products', and that good public management requires de-emphasis of overarching externalities and emphasis on running services within given parameters. Whether the emphasis on cost-cutting, contracting-out, compartmentalizing and top-slicing is compatible with safety culture at the front line needs to be tested. The new breed of organizationally created disasters over the past fifteen years or so, of which some dramatic examples have occurred in the UK, suggest that the issue at least needs investigation.

Only when we can test the limits of NPM in terms of relatively narrow *administrative* values can we start to establish its proper scope and put it in its historical place.

NOTE

1. I owe this idea to a suggestion by Dr. John Baker of John Baker and Associates.

A PUBLIC MANAGEMENT FOR ALL SEASONS? 17

REFERENCES
Arrow, K. J. 1963. *Social choice and individual values*. New Haven: Yale University Press.
Aucoin, P. 1990. 'Administrative reform in public management: paradigms, principles, paradoxes and pendulums', *Governance* 3, 115–37.
Bell, D. 1973. *The coming of post-industrial society*. New York: Basic.
Birkinshaw, P., I. Harden and N. Lewis. 1990. *Government by moonlight: the hidden parts of the state*. London: Unwin Hyman.
Bogdanor, V. (ed.). 1987. *The Blackwell encyclopaedia of political institutions*. Oxford: Blackwell.
Bryson, L. 1987. 'Women and management in the public sector', *Australian Journal of Public Administration* 46, 259–72.
Burns, T. and G. M. Stalker. 1961. *The management of innovation*. London: Tavistock.
Carey, B. and P. Ryan. (eds.) 1989. *In transition: NSW and the corporatisation agenda*. Sydney: Macquarie Public Sector Studies Program/Association for Management Education and Research.
Carter, N. 1988. 'Performance indicators: "Backseat Driving" or "Hands Off" Control?' *Policy and Politics* 17.
Castles, F. G. (ed.) 1989. *The comparative history of public policy*. Cambridge: Polity.
Day, P. and R. Klein. 1987. *'Accountabilities'*. London: Tavistock.
Dixon, N. F. 1979. *On the psychology of military incompetence*. London: Futura.
Downs, G. W. and P. D. Larkey. 1986. *The search for government efficiency: from hubris to helplessness*. Philadelphia: Temple University Press.
Dunleavy, P. J. 1985. 'Bureaucrats, budgets and the growth of the state', *British Journal of Political Science* 15, 299–328.
——. 1989. The United Kingdom: paradoxes of an ungrounded statism', pp. 242–91 in F. G. Castles (ed.) *The comparative history of public policy*. Cambridge: Polity.
Dunsire, A. 1978. *Control in a bureaucracy*, vol. 2 of *The execution process*. London: Martin Robertson.
Dunsire A., K. Hartley, D. Parker and B. Dimitriou. 1988. 'Organizational status and performance; a conceptual framework for testing public choice theories', *Public Administration* 66, 4 (Winter), 363–88.
Dunsire, A. and C. C. Hood. 1989. *Cutback management in public bureaucracies*. Cambridge: Cambridge University Press.
Gustafsson, B. (ed.) 1979. *Post-industrial society*. London: Croom Helm.
Hannah, L. 1976. *The rise of the corporate economy*. London: Methuen.
Harmon, M. and R. Mayer. 1986. *Organization theory for public administration*. Boston: Little, Brown.
Health and Safety Executive. 1988. *The tolerability of risk from nuclear power stations*. London: HMSO.
Hennestad, B. W. 1990. 'The symbolic impact of double bind leadership: double bind and the dynamics of organizational culture', *Journal of Management Studies* 27, 265–80.
Hood, C. C. 1976. *The limits of administration*. London: Wiley.
——. 1987. 'Public administration' in V. Bogdanor (ed.) *The Blackwell encyclopaedia of political institutions*. Oxford: Blackwell.
——. 1990a. 'Public administration: lost an empire, not yet found a role' in A. Leftwich (ed.) *New directions in political science*. Aldershot: Elgar.
——. 1990b. 'Beyond the public bureaucracy state? Public administration in the 1990s', inaugural lecture, London School of Economics, 16 January 1990.
——. 1990c. 'De-Sir-Humphrey-fying the Westminster model of governance' *Governance* 3, 205–14.
——. 1991 (forthcoming). 'Stabilization and cutbacks: a catastrophe for government growth theory?' *Journal of Theoretical Politics*.
Hood, C. C. and G. W. Jones 1990. 'Progress in the government's Next Steps initiative'. Appendix 6 in HC 481, 1989–90, 78–83.
Hood, C. C. and M. W. Jackson. 1991 (forthcoming). *Administrative argument*. Aldershot: Dartmouth.
Jackson, M. W. 1989. 'Immorality may lead to greatness: ethics in government' pp. 160–77 in S. Prasser, R. Wear and J. Nethercote (eds.) *Corruption and reform: the Fitzgerald vision*. St. Lucia: Queensland University Press.
Jessop, B. 1988. 'Conservative regimes and the transition to post-Fordism', *Essex Papers in Politics and Government* No. 47, Department of Government, University of Essex.
Kast, F. E. and Rosenzweig, J. E. 1973. *Contingency Views of Organization and Management*. New York: Science Research Associates.
Keating, M. 1989. 'Quo vadis: challenges of public administration', address to Royal Australian Institute of Public Administration, Perth, 12 April 1989.

18   CHRISTOPHER HOOD

Kelleher, S. R. 1988. 'The apotheosis of the Department of the Prime Minister and Cabinet', *Canberra Bulletin of Public Administration* 54, 9–12.

Lakatos, I. 1970. 'Falsification and the methodology of scientific research programmes' pp. 91–196 in I. Lakatos and A. Musgrave *Criticism and the growth of knowledge*. Cambridge: Cambridge University Press.

Lakatos, I. and A. Musgrave. 1970. *Criticism and the growth of knowledge*. Cambridge: Cambridge University Press.

Lane, F. C. 1966. *Venice and history*. Baltimore: Johns Hopkins University Press.

Larson, E. 1980. *Wit as a weapon: the political joke in history*. London: Muller.

Lawrence, P. 1964. *Road belong cargo*. Manchester: Manchester University Press.

Lawrence, P. R. and J. W. Lorsch. 1967. *Organization and environment*. Boston: Harvard University Press.

Leftwich, A. (ed.) 1990. *New directions in political science*. Aldershot: Elgar.

Levitt, B. and J. G. March. 1988. 'Organizational learning'. *Annual Review of Sociology* 14, 319–40.

Liebowitz, S. J. and S. E. Margolis. 1990. 'The fable of the keys', *The Journal of Law and Economics* 33, 1–26.

March, J. G. and J. P. Olsen. 1989. *Rediscovering institutions: the organizational basis of politics*. New York: Free Press.

Martin, J. 1988. *A profession of statecraft? Three essays on some current issues in the New Zealand public service*. Wellington: Victoria University Press.

Martin, S. 1983. *Managing without managers*. Beverly Hills: Sage.

Meltzer, A. H. and S. F. Richard. 1981. 'A rational theory of the size of government'. *Journal of Political Economy* 89, 914–27.

Merkle, J. 1980. *Management and ideology: the legacy of the international scientific management movement*. Berkeley: California University Press.

Mills, S. 1986. *The new machine men*. Ringwood: Penguin.

Minogue, K. 1986. 'Loquocentric society and its critics', *Government and Opposition* 21, 338–61.

Nethercote, J. R. 1989a. 'The rhetorical tactics of managerialism: reflections on Michael Keating's apologia, "Quo Vadis"', *Australian Journal of Public Administration* 48, 363–7.

——. 1989b. 'Public service reform: Commonwealth experience', paper presented to the Academy of Social Sciences of Australia, 25 February 1989, University House, Australian National University.

——. 1989c. 'Revitalising public service personnel management', *The Canberra Times* 11 June.

Niskanen, W. A. 1971. *Bureaucracy and representative government*. Chicago: Aldine Atherton.

Ostrom, V. 1974. *The intellectual crisis in American Public Administration*. Alabama: University of Alabama Press.

Peacock, A. 1979. 'Public expenditure growth in post-industrial society', pp. 80–95 in B. Gustafsson (ed.) *Post-industrial society*. London: Croom Helm.

Perrow, C. 1984. *Normal accident: living with high-risk technologies*. New York: Basic.

Peters, T. and R. Waterman. 1982. *In search of excellence*. New York: Harper and Row.

Piore, M. J. and C. F. Sabel. 1984. *The second industrial divide*. New York: Basic.

Pollitt, C. 1990. *Managerialism and the public services: the Anglo-American experience*. Oxford: Blackwell.

Prasser, S., R. Wear and J. Nethercote (eds.). 1990. *Corruption and reform: the Fitzgerald vision*. St. Lucia: Queensland University Press.

Scott, G., P. Bushnell and N. Sallee. 1990. 'Reform of the core public sector: New Zealand experience', *Governance* 3, 138–67.

Self, P. 1989. 'Is the grovel count rising in the bureaucracy?' *The Canberra Times* 14 April, p. 11.

Spann, R. N. 1981. 'Fashions and fantasies in public administration', *Australian Journal of Public Administration* 40, 12–25.

Strange, S. 1988. *States and markets: an introduction to international political economy*. London: Pinter.

Sturgess, G. 1989. 'First keynote address' pp. 4–10 in B. Carey and P. Ryan (eds.), *In transition: NSW and the corporatisation agenda*. Sydney: Macquarie Public Sector Studies Program.

Thomas, R. 1978. *The British philosophy of administration*. London: Longmans.

Tocqueville, A. de 1946. *Democracy in America*. London: Oxford University Press.

Turner, B. A. 1976. 'How to organize disaster', *Management Today* March 56–7 and 105.

——. 1978. *Man-made disasters*. London: Wykeham.

——. 1989. 'How can we design a safe organization?' paper presented at the Second International Conference on Industrial and Organizational Crisis Management, Leonard N. Stern School of Business, New York University, November 3–4.

Turner, B. A., N. Pidgeon, D. Blockley and B. Toft. 1989. 'Safety culture: its importance in future risk management', position paper for the Second World Bank Workshop on Safety Control and Risk Management, Karlstad, Sweden, 6–9 November.

Treasury and Civil Service Committee. 1990. Eighth report of Session 1989–90 *Progress in the Next Steps initiative*, HC 481, London: HMSO.

van Gunsteren, H. R. 1976. *The quest for control: a critique of the rational-central-rule approach in public affairs*. London: Wiley.

Walker, G. de Q. 1986. *Initiative and referendum: the people's law*. Sydney: Centre for Independent Studies.

Westrum, R. 1987. 'Management Strategies and Information Failure' pp. 109–27 in J. A. Wise and A. Debons (eds.) *Information systems failure analysis. NATO ASI Series F Computer and Systems Science, Vol. 3*. Berlin: Springer.

Wildavsky, A. 1985. 'Trial without error: anticipation vs. resilience as strategies for risk reduction' *CIS Occasional Papers* 13. Sydney: Centre for Independent Studies.

Wilenski, P. 1986. *Public power and public administration*. Sydney: RAIPA/Hale and Iremonger.

Wise, J. A. and Debons, A. (eds.) 1987. *Information systems failure analysis. NATO ASI Series F. Computer and Systems Science, vol. 3*. Berlin: Springer.

Worsley, P. 1968. *The trumpet shall sound*. 2nd. ed. London: MacGibbon and Kee.

Yeatman, A. 1987. 'The concept of public management and the Australian state in the 1980s', *Australian Journal of Public Administration* 46, 339–53.

[23]

Sandford F. Borins

Management of the public sector in Japan: Are there lessons to be learned?

Abstract: The objective of this article is to determine whether there are any Japanese *public* management practices that the government of Canada might emulate. The article discusses the career paths of Japanese senior public servants and the functions of Japanese central agencies. Recruitment of the "best and brightest" by competitive examinations, lifetime employment within one department, a variety of "organizational learning" assignments for younger senior public servants, and bottom-up decision-making all combine to produce a senior public service of the highest calibre. The Japanese have controlled the growth of government by committing themselves to strict limits on the growth of spending, bureaucratic personnel and new organizational units. A central agency program evaluation unit and ongoing administrative reform commissions are evidence of a serious commitment to program evaluation. It is suggested that we attempt to emulate the Japanese by rotating senior officials less frequently so they can develop greater expertise within specific departments, by adopting firmer limits on bureaucratic growth and by strengthening our central agencies' program evaluation capabilities.

Sommaire : Cet article a pour but de déterminer s'il existe des pratiques de gestion *publique* au Japon que le gouvernement du Canada aurait intérêt à adopter. L'article examine le cheminement de carrière des fonctionnaires japonais ainsi que les fonctions des organismes centraux au Japon. Le recrutement des meilleurs éléments par l'intermédiaire de concours, l'emploi à vie dans le cadre d'un même ministère, l'affectation des hauts fonctionnaires plus jeunes à une variété de postes d'apprentissage organisationnel, ainsi qu'une chaîne décisionnelle ascendante sont autant d'éléments dont la combinaison finit par produire des hauts fonctionnaires de très grande qualité. Les Japonais ont enrayé l'expansion du gouvernement en adoptant des limites très strictes pour l'augmentation des dépenses et du personnel bureaucratique et pour l'établissement de nouvelles unités organisationnelles. Une section centrale d'évaluation des programmes des organismes ainsi que des commissions permanentes de réforme administrative illustrent bien le sérieux de l'évaluation des programmes. L'article suggère qu'il faudrait essayer d'imiter les Japonais en mutant les hauts fonction-

The author is associate professor of Business and Public Policy, Faculty of Administrative Studies, York University. The comments of Donald D. Gordon, T.J. Pempel, Ezra Vogel, and three anonymous referees, and the financial support of the Faculty of Administrative Studies, York University, and the Social Sciences and Humanities Research Council are gratefully acknowledged.

SANDFORD F. BORINS

naires moins souvent, afin qu'ils acquièrent de meilleures connaissances dans le cadre d'un ministère donné, en adoptant des limites plus strictes à notre croissance bureaucratique, et en améliorant la capacité de nos organismes centraux à évaluer les programmes.

As the Trudeau years came to an end, many commentators, both academic and media observers, and civil servants speaking anonymously, expressed the concern that the federal civil service was being mismanaged. Colin Campbell and James Gillies claimed that the central agencies had become too powerful and the line departments too weak. They both argued that there were too many central agencies and that procedures for interdepartmental coordination were too cumbersome, thereby slowing the government's decisions and making it difficult for individual departments to take policy initiatives.[1] Campbell felt that individual public servants in the central agencies exercised an undue influence over policy outcomes, though they lacked any clear sense of public accountability. Furthermore, their career orientations were much more attuned to personal advancement than the ideal of public service.[2]

The inability of the government to control its spending was also a concern, and the Lambert Commission gave as one reason for this the fact that the Trudeau government promoted very young people to senior positions on the basis of their conceptual skills as policy advisers, rather than on the basis of any proven experience as departmental managers.[3] Campbell, attributing these promotions to Trudeau, Pitfield and their inner circle, claimed that they undermined morale throughout the bureaucracy. In summary, it was felt that the distinction between bureaucrats and politicians became muddied because the cabinet decision-making process was bureaucratized and the senior ranks of the bureaucracy were politicized.

The two months of Turner and the first year of Mulroney government have seen some reforms which are consistent with these critiques, such as the disbanding of MSERD and MSSD, the simplification of the PEMS machinery, the depoliticization of the PCO, and the increase in the size and importance of ministerial staffs. Mulroney has also expanded the size and scope of the PMO. Nevertheless, concerns are being expressed that this new structure has its own problems; the PMO lacks expertise, and the dismantling of much of the

1 See Colin Campbell, *Governments under Stress: Political Executives and Key Bureaucrats in Washington, London, and Ottawa* (Toronto: University of Toronto Press, 1983), pp. 77-99, 147-63, 221-27, 351-55; and James Gillies, *Where Business Fails* (Montreal: Institute for Research on Public Policy, 1981), pp. 81-101.

2 Campbell, *Governments under Stress*, pp. 89-90, 251-54, 331-34. A more popular version of this analysis can be found in Christina McCall-Newman, *Grits: An Intimate Portrait of the Liberal Party* (Toronto: Macmillan of Canada, 1982), pp. 175-238.

3 Royal Commission on Financial Management and Accountability, *Report* (Ottawa: Supply and Services Canada, 1979).

MANAGEMENT OF THE PUBLIC SECTOR IN JAPAN

coordination mechanism built up in the Trudeau years means that too many decisions are being taken in the Priorities and Planning Committee, which is becoming overburdened.[4]

The objective of this article is to advance this discussion by bringing to bear on it a new perspective, namely that of the management of the public sector in Japan. Hitherto, most discussions of the Canadian public management in international perspective have gone no farther afield than our closest geographic and intellectual neighbours, the Americans and the British. Yet the Japanese do have a governmental system that is in many ways similar to our own, with a Parliament (Diet), cabinet and a strong and expert bureaucracy. Like the federal government and many of the provinces, the Japanese political system has been dominated by one party, the Liberal Democratic Party, which has held power for the last thirty years.

Our academic cousins in business management, impressed by the success of Japanese business, have already created a large literature on Japanese business management practices and the lessons North American managers can learn from them.[5] We in public sector management have not yet followed their lead, even though we would recognize that the public sector played a role in converting a strong popular will for economic progress into policies that supported Japan's growth-oriented economy. Furthermore, the Japanese public sector can claim some credit for such public management successes as the bullet trains, the low crime rate, the dramatic clean-up of environmental pollution in the 1970s and the high educational attainments of Japanese students. This article, then, can also be seen as an attempt to initiate a comparable line of research in public management.

The basis for this research is both a reading of the literature on Japanese public management and approximately forty interviews with Japanese public servants, politicians, and academics and western academic and Canadian embassy observers, conducted on two visits to Japan in recent months. Given the time and cost constraints of this study, the inquiry was limited to those topics which would be most relevant to drawing lessons on how the Canadian federal government might cope with the problems discussed above. Thus, for instance, the study avoided the whole area of business-government relations, in particular the role of the Ministry of International Trade and Industry (MITI), which has already been studied by western economists and political scientists.[6] Because the problems in the Canadian government primarily concern the functions of the central agen-

4 Jeffrey Simpson, "Problems of the PMO," *Globe and Mail*, July 4, 1985, p. 6; Jeffrey Simpson, "The Missing System," ibid., July 5, 1985, p. 6.
5 A good review and analysis of the literature can be found in Charles J. McMillan, *The Japanese Industrial System* (Berlin: de Gruyter, 1984).
6 Chalmers Johnson, *MITI and the Japanese Miracle* (Stanford: Stanford University Press, 1982).

SANDFORD F. BORINS

cies (of which a major one is the handling of the careers of senior officials), the interviews were conducted in the following Japanese central agencies: the Prime Minister's Office; the Management and Coordination Agency, which has some of the coordinating functions of the Privy Council Office and organizational management functions of the Treasury Board Secretariat; the Economic Planning Agency, which does the macroeconomic forecasting and management of our Department of Finance; the Ministry of Finance, whose Budget Bureau is comparable to our Treasury Board Secretariat; the National Personnel Authority, which is comparable to the Public Service Commission of Canada; and the Foreign Affairs Ministry. The primary objective of these interviews was to learn about the structure and functions of these agenices (to which, incidentally, western observers have paid far less attention than to MITI.) Given the diverse set of interviewees, the interview evidence that emerged is presented impressionistically, rather than as a statistical sample.

The specific fields which will be discussed in this article are the selection, work environment and career paths of Japanese senior public servants; public sector labour relations; control over public sector spending and bureaucratic expansion; and interdepartmental coordination. The timing of the interviews (spring 1985) turned out to be particularly opportune for the last topic, because the Japanese government was then involved in a major, and difficult, interdepartmental exercise in opening the Japanese market to more imports. After discussing each of these areas, the article will then conclude with the question the title asks, namely whether there are some management practices in the Japanese government which we in Canada might adopt.

Life in the fast track

Japanese senior public servants are recruited directly from school by means of competitive examinations designed to pick the best and the brightest. The fact that the national bureaucracy has great prestige ensures that the best and the brightest will, in fact, apply. Once a year, the National Personnel Authority administers an examination, taken by approximately thirty-five thousand college seniors and post-graduate students, which consists of written general knowledge and specialized knowledge sessions, and, for those who have done well in the written section, an interview. Only fifteen hundred – less than 5 per cent – pass the exam.[7] The successful candidates tend to be graduates of the most prestigious national (state-supported) universities, in particular the law school at Tokyo University, five hundred of whose students usually pass. The fact that so many of the senior bureaucrats who conduct the interviews are Tokyo law graduates probably gives Tokyo law candidates something of an advantage.

7   National Personnel Authority, *Annual Report, Fiscal 1985* (Tokyo, 1985), pp. 2-5.

MANAGEMENT OF THE PUBLIC SECTOR IN JAPAN

The Japanese government has no affirmative action programs, so that "merit" alone, as defined by the ability to succeed in the examination, determines who will be hired. The result, due also to the fact that Japan is a very male-dominated society, is that women are very poorly represented in the senior public service; for example, of the 1,589 people in the "designated service," which includes deputy ministers,[8] agency heads, chiefs of government laboratories and hospitals, and presidents of national universities, only two (.1 per cent) are women.[9]

The successful candidates then have interviews with various government ministries and agencies, and each ministry or agency independently makes offers to a number of candidates. The offer represents a lifetime career with that particular department or agency; only about one thousand of the successful candidates accept the offers, the rest presumably having received better lifetime employment offers in the private sector. There are also entrance examinations for middle-level and junior positions, taken by people with more modest academic credentials. Here the success rates are somewhat higher, approaching 10 per cent.

The system of entrance by examination clearly stratifies the public service. Those who have passed the senior entrance exam are assured in the course of their careers of positions comparable to those in the SX group in Ottawa; conversely, it is most unusual for someone who took the intermediate entrance exam to rise even to the lower rungs of the executive group. However, in recent years, more egalitarian values among Japanese bureaucrats have led to some resentment by members of the intermediate groups towards those who were marked out for high office at the tender age of twenty-two by virtue of their success on an examination. In response, the National Personnel Authority has instituted a special training course to prepare promising members of the intermediate group for the lower executive positions; nevertheless, only fifty people take this course each year, a small number in comparison to the thousand who enter the senior executive class through the examination.[10]

The first few years of work for the Japanese bureaucratic elite consist mainly of on-the-job education. Several years are spent in assignments of several months' duration in the various bureaus of a department. The next step is to spend a year or two overseas, possibly studying for a graduate degree, or perhaps serving as an attaché at a Japanese embassy or the Japanese External Trade Organization. After that, the young senior public servant may be loaned to another department, the common practice being

8   The Canadian equivalents of Japanese public service ranks (e.g., deputy minister) will be used, rather than either the usual English translations of the ranks (e.g., administrative vice-minister) or the Japanese terminology (e.g., jimu jikan).

9   National Personnel Authority, *Annual Report, Fiscal 1985*, p. 13.

10   Interview, Hisaki Kurita, Director of the Research Division, Bureau of Compensation, National Personnel Authority, Tokyo, May 13, 1985.

SANDFORD F. BORINS

for those in central agencies to work in line departments, and vice versa. Or, if the ministry has regional offices outside Tokyo, he may spend some time in a senior position there.[11] By that point, in his early thirties, the senior public servant has acquired a good deal of experience in his environment inside and outside the government, and is ready to begin the serious competition for the highest posts in his own ministry.

What is the pace and style of work like for senior public servants in the Japanese government? The first thing that impresses the western visitor is the crowdedness and openness of Japanese government offices. Officers work in large rooms without any partitions, and desks are placed back-to-back. There are meeting rooms on the periphery, but it is clear that most bureaucratic life takes place in the open office area. Only the most senior bureaucrats receive private offices, and this will probably not happen until they have been with the government for twenty years. Thus, it is very common to see someone comparable in rank to a federal government director or director-general sitting in the corner, in full view of the unit he is supervising. Clearly, the objective of this open office space is to promote communication within the unit, which is an important basis for the consensual style of Japanese decision-making.

The Japanese government, like Japanese business, usually operates on a consensual style of bottom-up decision-making. Regularly before cabinet meetings there is a meeting of deputy ministers to set the agenda.[12] This meeting is a last opportunity to ascertain that all departments are in agreement with the recommendations that will go before cabinet. Cabinet meetings, therefore are a formality. (Indeed, Japanese newspapers commonly report on the outcome of cabinet meetings *before* they are held.) This is not to say that there is no political input into decisions, as will be discussed below; rather it has occurred long before the cabinet meeting. The implication of bottom-up decision-making is that the younger public servants have substantial opportunities to propose policies or, when politicians and deputy ministers identify a need for a new policy, to do the policy development and write what are equivalent to our memoranda to cabinet. This environment encourages initiative and creativity on the part of the younger senior public servants. The fact that younger and older members of the senior group often work closely together on key issues means that strong vertical ties, or mentor-protégé relationships, are often developed. These, of course, will become important to the protégé's later advancement. As in Japanese

11 Johnson, *MITI and the Japanese Miracle*, p. 62; Albert M. Craig, "Functional and Dysfunctional Aspects of Government Bureaucracy," in Ezra Vogel, *Modern Japanese Organization and Decision-Making* (Los Angeles: University of California Press, 1975), p. 6; T.J. Pempel, "Organizing for Efficiency: the Higher Civil Service in Japan," in Ezra N. Suleiman, ed., *Bureaucrats and Policy-Making* (New York: Holmes and Meier, 1984), pp. 89-93.
12 Isao Sato, "The Cabinet and Administrative Organization," in Kiyoaki Tsuji, ed., *Public Administration in Japan* (Tokyo: University of Tokyo Press, 1984), p. 25.

MANAGEMENT OF THE PUBLIC SECTOR IN JAPAN

business, it is common that everyone who has been consulted in the development of a policy affixes his seal (*ringi*) to the ultimate document.

This consensual form of policy-making means that policy analysis in a Japanese context is very different from Canadian policy analysis, at least in theory. Ideally, we maintain that bureaucrats should lay out for politicians a set of options, assess the consequences and implications of the various options, and then the politicians should pick their desired policy. In a setting where only one option will be recommended, the procedure is different. The Japanese public servants described a process in which many bureaucratic and political players go back and forth between determining both what the state of the world is and what the government's objectives ought to be; the more one understands of one, the more one can understand of the other. Ultimately, when both the facts and objectives are well understood by all the players, then the desired policy should become clear, and there will only be one option. One of the interviewees suggested that members of the senior executive group all learn to think like the prime minister; that is, they feel it is part of their responsibility to understand the politicians so they can be effective policy analysts in this setting.[13] Probably, Canadian policy analysis approximates the Japanese model more often than we imagine; it is due to the influence of the Westminster model on our thinking that we do not recognize this.

The young Japanese senior public servants become accustomed to careers of hard work. As we will discuss in terms of budgetary control, there is tight control on the size of the public service at all levels, including the senior, so that the workloads are quite onerous. It is common to see cots folded up in the corners of meeting rooms, available for evenings when senior public servants must work too late to catch the last train home.

What is the relationship between senior officials and their intermediate-level subordinates? While the intermediate-level civil servants occupy most of the department's line offices, some of them are also present in the central offices in which the senior officials work. Ideally, the intermediate-level officers will stay in a branch for their entire careers, becoming virtual "walking dictionaries" in terms of the branch's functions. Thus, the older, experienced branch officers will provide support for the younger members of the executive group who will be their supervisors for a relatively short time before moving on to something else.[14]

As their careers progress, the members of a given class of senior officials (defined in terms of the year when they entered the department) initially all advance at the same pace. However, this cannot continue indefinitely because the organization is, after all, hierarchical. Thus classmates become

13 Interview, Hisao Tsukamoto, Assistant Director for Research, Administrative Management Bureau, Management and Coordination Agency, Tokyo, May 14, 1985.
14 Johnson, *MITI and the Japanese Miracle*, p. 63.

SANDFORD F. BORINS

involved in relationships with one another that are both competitive and cooperative; they have now known each other for many years and must work together to develop policy consensually, but, on the other hand, they are competing for a limited number of posts higher up the ladder. Within any department, the senior group determines promotions within its ranks internally, though there is some input from the minister. There is strict seniority in the senior ranks of the Japanese public service so that it is unusual for a younger person to be supervising someone older. The pressure of advancing classes of senior officials combined with the seniority rule means that individuals hold senior positions for relatively short periods of time; for instance, deputy ministers will hold their positions for two years at the longest. The practice that people should be supervised only by their seniors means that when one member of a class becomes deputy minister, all his classmates in the department (and any remaining members of classes which entered the department earlier) must resign. This generally happens at about age fifty-five. The common practice is for an incoming deputy minister to provide for his colleagues by finding them employment in either a government corporation or agency or in a private sector firm in a related area which could use the individual's expertise. This is known as *amakudari*, or descent from heaven. [15] Of course, it tends to facilitate business-government relations.

What individual traits characterize those who have made it to the top of the public service? Given that they are drawn from a rather homogeneous body of intelligent people, it is rarely sheer brilliance or conceptual ability. Generally, the winners tend to be those who have both strength and stamina to put up with the heavy workload, and who are adept chairmen of meetings, skilled at framing compromises, rather than brilliant conceptualizers or tough, bold leaders. [16] The ideal Japanese deputy minister would therefore be more comparable to a Lester Pearson than a Michael Pitfield or a Simon Reisman.

Finally, mention must be made of the very close ties between the bureaucracy and the ruling Liberal Democratic Party. Approximately 30 per cent of the party's representatives in the Diet are former bureaucrats. The party has a strong policy development unit, known as the Policy Affairs Research Council, through which its Diet members can influence the bureaucracy's bottom-up policy development process. For example, it is quite common for bureaucrats to meet with the party during the early phases of policy development. Finally, many bureaucrats belong to informal study groups which discuss policy problems of common interest with journalists, academics, businessmen and politicians. [17]

15   Ibid., pp. 54-55, 65; Yoshihisa Ojimi, "A Government Ministry: the Case of the Ministry of International Trade and Industry," in Vogel, ed., *Modern Japanese Organization and Decision-Making*, p. 110.
16   Tsukamoto interview.
17   Johnson, *MITI and the Japanese Miracle*, pp. 52-53; Inoguchi Takashi and Iwai Tomoaki,

MANAGEMENT OF THE PUBLIC SECTOR IN JAPAN

Interestingly, the relationship between a minister and his deputy assumes far less importance for the Japanese than it does for us. Cabinet ministers in Japan serve for only a year or so, the main reason being that the party attempts to spread positions of responsibility around the various factions of which it is composed. Thus, individual ministers are rarely in power long enough to assert control over their departments; the exceptions are politicians who have public service backgrounds who spend a term in charge of their former department. The closeness between politicians and bureaucrats is thus more subtle, due to the fact that they have shared power for so long that they have learned each others' way of thinking. Were the Liberal Democratic Party to be defeated, one wonders whether the bureaucracy would be able to work equally closely with its successor.

Public sector labour relations

Public sector labour relations in Japan are very different from those in Canada. A series of strikes by government railroad workers in 1948 seriously disrupted the postwar economy, which led General MacArthur, the commander of the Allied Occupation Army, to order the Japanese government to ban strikes by public sector employees. This practice has been retained to the present time. Public servants are allowed to organize but not to strike or even to bargain collectively. Employees of government corporations, such as the Japan National Railroad or the Post Office are allowed to bargain collectively, but not to strike. Japan has nothing like the Rand formula, so that the payment of union dues is purely voluntary. Even though union dues are relatively low (on average, $150 Canadian per annum), the membership rate in the public service is only 63 per cent. [18]

In the absence of collective bargaining, public sector salaries are determined by surveys conducted by the National Personnel Agency. Compensation packages for administrative workers in the public service are surveyed and compared to a large sample of private sector employees who perform similar tasks. The National Personnel Agency then recommends that the cabinet grant compensation increases that will ensure comparability between the public and private sectors. Generally, the cabinet goes along with these recommendations, but in 1982 and 1983, due to the government's weak budgetary situation, the cabinet granted much smaller wage increases. As a result, by the end of 1983, the compensation of public sector employees had fallen 6 per cent below that of their private sector counterparts. [19]

"The Growth of Zoku: LDP Politicians in Committees, 1964-1984," paper presented at the annual meeting of the Association for Asian Studies, Washington, D.C., March 25, 1984; T.J. Pempel, "Organizing for Efficiency," pp. 83-89; Atsushi Odawara, "The Union of the LDP and the Bureaucracy," *Japan Echo* 4, no. 4 (Winter 1984), pp. 68-75.

18   National Personnel Authority, *Annual Report*, pp. 46-47.

19   Ibid., pp. 9-21.

SANDFORD F. BORINS

Control over public sector growth and spending

In the postwar era, there has generally been a consensus in Japan that the national government should be as small and efficient as possible. While government spending has grown from 20 per cent of GNP in the late 1960s to approximately one-third of GNP at the current time, it is still a smaller proportion than in any of the other major OECD countries.[20] This section discusses Japanese budgeting, administrative inspection and controls on bureaucratic expansion, three practices which give meaning to the Japanese desire for small and efficient government. One very concrete piece of evidence concerning the emphasis the Japanese place on the parsimonious management of government is that, in a capital containing what by our standards are very spartan government accommodations, the shabbiest building of all houses the powerful Ministry of Finance, the guardian of the budget.

The budgetary process

The Japanese budgetary process consists primarily of negotiations between spending departments and the Budget Bureau of the Ministry of Finance, conducted from August to December every year. The Ministry of Finance begins by announcing a ceiling for all departmental spending requests for the next fiscal year; it has decreased from 25 per cent (in current dollars) in the rapid-growth 1960s to zero since 1983. The negotiations are incremental, in that they deal only with the next year's budget. The Ministry of Finance has recently begun to publish five-year forecasts of government spending, based on the assumption of no policy change and economic growth forecasts developed by the Economic Planning Agency; the main reason for the production of such forecasts appears to be that Finance is attempting to stimulate public concern over the size of the deficit. The forecasts play no role comparable to the British Public Expenditure Survey or the Canadian long-range envelope forecasts.[21]

The emphasis in budgetary negotiations is on the maintenance of balance among competing programs. This is a subtle concept, and can mean a number of things, such as "fair treatment" of programs in an environment of cutback management, or the need to ensure that budget changes are comparable in interrelated programs. John Campbell, author of *Contemporary Japanese Budgetary Politics*, the definitive study in this area, has shown that the growth of spending in different budgetary areas has been very stable

---

20   Department of Finance, *Economic Review, April 1984* (Ottawa: Supply and Services Canada, 1984), p. 179.
21   Ministry of Finance, "The Budgetary System," in Tsuji, ed., *Public Administration in Japan*, pp. 153-71; Masahiro Horie, Budget Examiner, Science and Technology area, Budget Bureau, Ministry of Finance, May 17, 1985.

MANAGEMENT OF THE PUBLIC SECTOR IN JAPAN

over time, much more so than in the United States.[22] This indeed is in keeping with the emphasis placed by Japanese culture on the maintenance of harmony and consensus.

The political input in Japanese budgeting comes at two stages: first, in determining the overall budgetary stance, when the minister of finance and prime minister are the key players, and second, towards the end of the process, in accommodating demands for budgetary support for the various interest groups which support the Liberal Democratic Party. The latter stages involve negotiations between Ministry of Finance bureaucrats and LDP politicians for the allocation of an extra 1 to 3 per cent of "slush money" that the Finance Ministry generally makes available for projects of political priority.[23]

There is little room in the Japanese budget for supplementary expenditures; these are generally restricted to spending which results form unpredicted external factors, such as changes in interest rates or natural disasters. The Japanese provide for linkage between policy and expenditure by doing their budgeting at only one time of the year. The Ministry of Finance has the clout to defer the consideration of major spending department proposals to budget season. Departments have some freedom to reallocate smaller sums.[24]

The Japanese are well aware of the western interest in rationalizing the budgetary process through such techniques as PPBS, ZBB, PESC or PEMS, and they are, very frankly, not impressed. They feel that the high quality of the Ministry of Finance senior officials, incrementalism and a strong will to hold the line on public expenditures are sufficient.[25]

The Administrative Inspection Bureau

In addition to the incremental review of the normal budgetary process discussed above, there is a mechanism for more comprehensive program review. The Japanese Management and Coordination Agency (which will be discussed in the section of this paper dealing with interdepartmental coordination) combines the non-budgetary components of our Treasury Board Secretariat with some of the coordination functions of the PCO. In addition, it has a branch, called the Administrative Inspection Bureau (AIB), headed by an assistant deputy minister, with approximately one hundred and fifty staff in Tokyo and eleven hundred in regional offices throughout the country, and an annual budget of about $40 million.[26]

22 John C. Campbell, *Contemporary Japanese Budgetary Politics* (Berkeley: University of California Press, 1977), pp. 1-11.
23 Ibid., pp. 115-43.
24 Horie interview.
25 Campbell, *Contemporary Japanese Budgetary Politics*, pp. 107-9; Horie interview.
26 Administrative Management Agency, "Administrative Inspection," in Tsuji, ed., *Public Administration in Japan*, pp. 173-83.

SANDFORD F. BORINS

The AIB was first established in 1948 as an organizational ombudsman, with a mandate to receive and investigate public grievances about government corruption and inefficiency. Since then its mandate has grown to include program evaluation for all government departments and agencies, including public corporations. The AIB is organized by program area, with nine directors dividing up the range of government activities. Its priorities for study include: programs of priority to the government, programs with the potential for substantial improvements in efficiency, areas of overlap or duplication, programs that appear to be obsolete, problem areas identified by the local offices or the media, and new programs that have been in operation for several years. The AIB's legal mandate requires government departments to cooperate with AIB studies and investigations. In addition to participating in studies chosen by the Tokyo office, the regional AIB offices will launch inspections of their own. AIB studies are usually published. The department(s) whose programs are being investigated must respond to the AIB's recommendations publicly within six months. If the AIB is not satisfied with a department's response, it can launch another investigation. In addition, the AIB maintains close ties with the Budget Bureau of the Ministry of Finance, and its studies are often used by Finance in the next year's budgetary review and negotiations.[27]

The AIB appears to be effective for a number of reasons:

- it has a strong legal and institutional mandate, and a great deal of independence;
- its administrative counselling service, which hears approximately 200,000 citizen complaints each year, is an independent source of information;
- its local offices are also an independent source of information, and provide information about program delivery and implementation at the local level;
- it limits the number of its investigations, thus concentrating on the most significant problem areas;
- its mandate to publish studies creates public pressure for departmental action to implement its recommendations; and
- the Budget Bureau of the Ministry of Finance is a powerful client for its studies.

Controls on bureaucratic expansion

In addition to strict budgetary control, there is even stricter control over the size of the public service. In 1969 the Diet passed a law limiting the total personnel in the government's departments and agencies to the level in

27   Interview, Koji Shioji, Director, Coordination Division, Administrative Inspection Bureau, May 9, 1985; interview, Yuichi Seki, Administrative Inspection Bureau, May 9, 1985.

MANAGEMENT OF THE PUBLIC SECTOR IN JAPAN

1967, which was 506,571. This law has not been amended since then. The Administrative Management Bureau, another section of the Management and Coordination Agency, is in charge of reviewing organizational structure and reallocating staff among departments. Between 1969 and 1982 a total of 152,000 positions were abolished and 141,000 created, for a net reduction of 11,000 in the size of the public service. The areas with the largest staff gains are national universities and hospitals, whose staff are counted as public servants.

The Administrative Management Agency enforced the staffing cuts by requiring all ministries, including central agencies, to make similar reductions, usually 5 per cent of staff, over a three-year period. The gradual nature of the cuts meant that they could be achieved by attrition, rather than firings (as has been the case with some more drastic recent cuts in Canada). Departments were responsible for implementing the cuts, which forced them to establish priorities for their own programs.[28] The Japanese government employs very few consultants, so this policy is not being subverted by a massive use of "contracting out." However, the reduction in the size of the federal public service has entailed a devolution of power to local governments; as a consequence, the number of local government officials grew from 2.5 million in 1970 to 3.2 million in 1980, an increase of 28 per cent. Despite this, the proportion of the labour force engaged in public administration in Japan is smaller than in the other OECD countries.[29]

28 Administrative Management Agency, "Staff Number Control," in Tsuji, ed., *Public Administration in Japan*, pp. 71-86; T.J. Pempel, "Organizing for Efficiency," pp. 98-99.
29 Table 1, "Number of Public Employees in Five Industrial Nations," p. 73 in Administrative Management Agency, "Staff Number Control," finds that the percentages of the population employed by all levels of the government (including national defence and government enterprises) in 1980 were 4.5% in Japan, 10.9% in the U.K., 8.3% in France, 8.2% in the U.S. and 7.6% in Germany. Excluding national defence, the percentages were 4.2% in Japan, 10% in the U.K., 7.5% in France, 6.9% in the U.S., and 5.6% in Germany.
Comparing Japan to Canada, the percentages of the population employed by all levels of the government for 1980 were: including national defence and government corporations, 4.5% in Japan and 5.5% in Canada; excluding national defence and including government corporations, 4.2% in Japan and 5.0% in Canada; including national defence and excluding government corporations, 3.7% in Japan and 4.5.% in Canada; and excluding both national defence and government corporations, 3.4% in Japan and 4.0% in Canada. (Sources: Table 1, "Number of Public Employees in Five Industrial Nations" for Japan and Statistics Canada cats. 72-009 [local government employment], 72-004 [federal government employment], and 72-007 [provincial government employment] for June 1980.) These statistics bias the estimates of Japanese public sector employment upward, because the totals include workers in hospitals and universities, who are not considered government workers in Canada. In comparing the Canadian data and those for the U.S., U.K., France and Germany, the percentage of Canadians working in the public service is lower than in each of the other countries because it appears that the Japanese, in comparing their public sector to the other four countries, added educational and hospital workers, which I have not done for Canada.

SANDFORD F. BORINS

There are also structural limits on the expansion of government. The law governing the cabinet limits its size to twenty members.[30] The Diet has much more control over the government's organization than does our Parliament; for example, legislation is required to add, amalgamate or abolish a department's bureaus, that is, its largest sub-units, each of which is headed by an assistant deputy minister. In 1968, in order to restrain bureaucratic expansion, the government required every ministry and agency to abolish one bureau. Since then, ministries and agencies must follow the policy of "scrap and build," namely, they are allowed to add a bureau only if they abolish another.[31]

Finally, since 1962 Japan has had a series of commissions on administrative reform, composed of former public servants, academics and business leaders. The commissions have continuously recommended ways to streamline government and improve efficiency, and many of these recommendations have been implemented. The commissions have helped form a public consensus in support of small and efficient government. The most recent such commission also called for the termination, privatization or restructuring of many government corporations, including the major ones: Japanese National Railways, Japan Tobacco and Salt Public Corporation, and Nippon Telegram and Telephone. The latter two were privatized earlier this year, while changes in the railway are still being studied.[32]

Interdepartmental coordination

Interdepartmental coordination is a problem in the Japanese government, just as it is in Canada. Difficulty in interdepartmental coordination is the obverse of the strong departmental loyalties and high morale that characterizes the Japanese government. Individual ministries fight tenaciously for bureaucratic turf and attempt to define problems in ways which are favourable to the enlargement of their own responsibilities. Furthermore, the importance the Japanese place on consultation and achieving consensus militates against individual departments simply ignoring other departments which have a legitimate interest in the spillover effects of their policies. As a consequence, there is a tendency for departments to consult endlessly and, if consensus cannot be achieved, to be unable to depart from the status quo.[33]

30 The Cabinet Law (Law No. 5 of 1947). See Tsuji, ed., *Public Administration in Japan*, p. 254.
31 A good history of policies to reduce bureaucratic expansion in the postwar period up to 1981 can be found in T.J. Pempel, *Policy and Politics in Japan: Creative Conservatism* (Philadelphia: Temple University Press, 1982), pp. 255-95.
32 Genrokuro Furuhashi, "Postwar Administrative Reform Efforts in Japan," paper presented to an International Symposium on Administrative Reform, Tokyo, September 14, 1982; Provisional Commission on Administrative Reform, *Fifth (Final) Report on Administrative Reform* (Tokyo: Institute of Administrative Management, 1984).
33 Johnson, *MITI and the Japanese Miracle*, pp. 73-74, 78; Craig, "Functional and Dysfunc-

MANAGEMENT OF THE PUBLIC SECTOR IN JAPAN

It appears that the need for interdepartmental coordination in the Japanese government has increased in recent years. In the past, each department concerned itself with its traditional mandate, which was that of promoting growth in some specific area of the economy. The simpler economic structure, combined with the rapid growth of the economy as a whole, meant that there was little need for interdepartmental coordination. Today's more sophisticated economic structure has raised new issues which are not clearly within any one ministry's mandate. Furthermore, the challenges of a more hostile international economic environment, slower growth and foreign pressure to open up the Japanese market force harsher tradeoffs to be made among the preferences of the various departments.[34] In some sense, the current Japanese experience is comparable to that of the Canadian government in the late 1960s and early 1970s; increasing social and economic complexity required the development of organizational structures to handle the increased burden of interdepartmental coordination.

This section will discuss a number of different coordination mechanisms that have developed in recent years: the Management and Coordination Agency, the role of the Prime Minister's Secretariat, and the use of cabinet committees and joint LDP-cabinet committees.

The Management and Coordination Agency (MCA) was established in 1984, by reorganizing a number of elements of the Prime Minister's Office. (The Japanese Prime Minister's Office looks very much like the Executive Office of the President in the United States, which is composed of rather disparate elements, many of which are special interest offices with little direct contact with the president.) The MCA united a number of bureaus concerned with the overall management of the government, such as the Personnel Policy Bureau, the Administrative Management Bureau, the Administrative Inspection Bureau, the Pension Bureau and the Statistical Policy Bureau. Thus it performs similar functions to the "management" units in the Treasury Board Secretariat or the American Office of Management and Budget.

In addition, the MCA has a number of offices concerned with interdepartmental coordination: the Traffic Safety Policy Office, the Policy Office for the Aged, the Youth Affairs Administration and the Policy Office for Regional Improvement. These offices are composed of up to thirty public servants, mostly seconded from the departments whose mandates overlap in these policy areas. For instance, the Youth Affairs Administration is respon-

---

tional Aspects of Government Bureaucracy," pp. 16-17; Chalmers Johnson, "Japan: Who Governs? An Essay on Official Bureaucracy," *Journal of Japanese Studies* 2, no. 1 (January 1978), pp. 1-28.

34 Interview, Shuji Shimokoji, Deputy Director, Economic Affairs Bureau, Ministry of Foreign Affairs, Tokyo, May 28, 1985; interview, Takashi Omori, Deputy Director, Coordination Division, Coordination Bureau, Economic Planning Agency, Tokyo, May 30, 1985.

SANDFORD F. BORINS

sible for handling Japan's participation in the International Year of Youth and international youth exchange programs; as well, it provides a forum whereby the Department of Justice and the National Police Agency can coordinate their approach to the problem of juvenile delinquency.[35] In addition, the Youth Affairs Administration identifies policy problems in this area for further study by the Administrative Inspection Bureau. A recent example is a make-or-buy study of the production of school lunches.[36] To summarize, the policy coordination offices in the MCA were formed to facilitate interdepartmental coordination on a number of ongoing problems. Conceivably, more such units could be established within the MCA in the future.

A second mechanism for interdepartmental coordination is the Cabinet Secretariat. The Cabinet Secretariat has a section, composed of forty-six staff members, who act as trouble-shooters. They concern themselves with the policy spillovers that occur when departments take the initiative in making policy, becoming involved when the departments are unable to achieve consensus by their own efforts. Three common modalitites of interdepartmental conflict they deal with are: the effects of one department's proposals on other departments, jurisdictional fights among departments for an attractive new policy area (e.g., conflict between the Ministry of Posts and Telecommunications and the Ministry of International Trade and Industry over regulation of the telecommunications industry), and troublesome policy problems which all departments wish to avoid (such as the Indo-Chinese boat people). This section is responsible for organizing ad hoc interdepartmental committees to reach some kind of consensus; it appears to function most effectively when it has some sort of deadline that can be used to force the departments to reach an agreement. Once agreements are reached, these issues can proceed to the cabinet for formal approval.[37]

The third method of interdepartmental coordination is through the use of cabinet committees. The Japanese tend to use a mix of standing and ad hoc cabinet committees, somewhat closer to the practice in the Mulroney government than under the Trudeau administration, which tended to assign most issues to standing committees. At present there are twenty cabinet committees, some of which deal with: external and domestic economic affairs, national security, consumer and wholesale prices, privatization of the Japanese National Railway, compensation for national government employees, public pension programs, the construction of a new international airport for Osaka/Kobe and cancer research. The titles of the cabinet committees give a sense of the issues that are of interest to the politicians. The prime minister has the responsibility of forming the cabinet com-

---

35 Interview, Masahiro Ando, Counsellor, Personnel Bureau, Management and Coordination Agency, Tokyo, May 29, 1985.
36 Seki interview.
37 Interview, Mr. Taniguchi, Councillor, Cabinet Secretariat, May 28, 1985.

MANAGEMENT OF THE PUBLIC SECTOR IN JAPAN

mittees and designating which department or agency will have a mandate to do its staff support work. Given the Japanese practice of developing policy from the bottom up, the identity of the lead agency can have considerable impact on the ultimate outcome.

The Japanese use of ad hoc cabinet committees may strike Canadian readers as being organizationally sloppy. However, it should be realized that a Japanese prime minister has much less power than his Canadian counterpart. His personal staff is very small, and the Liberal Democratic Party's constitution prevents anyone from serving as party leader (and hence prime minister) for more than four years. Furthermore, the society's emphasis on consensus and harmony undercuts the possibility of charismatic leadership.[38] As a consequence, one of the few ways a Japanese prime minister can influence the policy process is by his choice of which ministers and departments will be the key players on particular issues. It is unlikely he would wish to reduce his limited personal influence still further by allowing such decisions to be made by default in a more "rational" committee structure.

In addition to the use of cabinet committees, a Japanese prime minister will occasionally establish a joint LDP-cabinet headquarters to deal with a policy problem. This mechanism gets the party involved earlier in the resolution of the problem, and thus build support for the eventual outcome. In this case as well, a department will be chosen to provide the staff work.

The most interesting recent policy problem requiring a great deal of interdepartmental coordination is the Japanese government's attempt to open its domestic market to increased imports. Such a policy became necessary because of increasing foreign concern over Japan's huge balance-of-trade surplus and threats, particularly from the United States, to reciprocate by restricting Japanese access to their markets.

In November 1984 Prime Minister Nakasone gave Toshio Komoto, the leader of a small LDP faction and a minister without portfolio, the special responsibility for external economic relations. The most likely reason Nakasone chose Komoto was because he is a well-respected senior leader in the LDP whose assistance would be useful in building a consensus to support a market-opening initiative. Komoto's mandate was to examine Japanese policies affecting the level of imports (such as tariffs, procurement rules, standards and certification rules) and to recommend changes. Staff were seconded to a task force from the departments whose interests were most af-

38 For example, while Prime Minister Nakasone enjoys the highest popularity of any Japanese prime minister in recent years and a strong international image, it seemed clear by the spring of 1985 that the LDP would not amend its constitution to permit him to serve another two-year term; therefore, leaders of LDP factions began jockeying to replace him when his term expired in October 1986. (Interview, Mitsuo Kimura, President, House of Councillors, National Diet of Japan, Tokyo, May 17, 1985.)

SANDFORD F. BORINS

fected: the Foreign Ministry, the Economic Planning Agency, Finance, MITI, Posts and Telecommunications, Health and Welfare, and Agriculture, Forestry and Fisheries. The role of secretariat to the task force went to the Foreign Ministry and the Economic Planning Agency, the two ministries that had the strongest "open market" orientations in the group.

Numerous task force meetings were held during the winter; the Economic Planning Agency participants found them to be interminable, often lasting on into the early morning hours, and immensely frustrating.[39] There were endless arguments over the wording of draft policy proposals, and a consensus was not being reached. The departments which saw their mandates in terms of the health of certain industries did not want too much foreign competition too soon, nor did Health and Welfare wish its regulations of product quality and safety dismantled. In addition, the group had no deadline to force closure.

Prime Minister Nakasone's televised speech to the nation on April 9, 1985 a most unusual act for a Japanese leader, was an attempt to mobilize public opinion to support greater market opening. The speech was drafted by the officials of the Economic Planning Agency who were serving as the secretariat to the Komoto task force.[40] Nakasone also established a deadline of June 20 for departments to report to the task force on what they would be doing to support the initiative and another deadline of late July to announce the policy changes to the world. Throughout the spring, opponents of these policies, in particular Japan's heavily subsidized and sheltered farmers (a group who are electorally over-represented and strong supporters of the LDP) continued to lobby against changes in the status quo.

On July 30, as promised, the Japanese government announced a program consisting of tariff cuts, particularly on food from South-East Asia and automobile parts, a simplification of safety and quality standards for goods produced abroad, and more purchases of foreign goods by the government. Foreign governments still see these steps as insufficient and the task force's work is continuing.[41] The emphasis on the bureaucracy's work has now shifted to macroeconomic policy measures, such as tax cuts to reduce savings and stimulate demand. However, Prime Minister Nakasone has maintained his interest in market opening, and is even bypassing the bureaucracy; on October 15, he announced the establishment of a study group, directly responsible to him, to look at "structural economic adjustments for the sake

---

39 Omori interview.
40 Omori and Shimokoji interviews.
41 Government of Japan, "Establishment of the Government-Ruling Parties Joint Headquarters for the Promotion of External Economic Measures," April 19, 1985; Susan Chira, "Japanese prepare plan to increase buying of imports," *New York Times*, July 29, 1985, pp. A1, D5; "Japan set to open its markets, but U.S. reaction remains cool," *Globe and Mail*, July 31, 1985, p. B3.

MANAGEMENT OF THE PUBLIC SECTOR IN JAPAN

of international cooperation." The group, composed of business executives, heads of private research institutions and former bureaucrats, is to report in March 1986. It can also be viewed as another way to create public support for his policy. [42]

This case is instructive in that it shows a strong prime minister using unorthodox methods (a televised speech, public deadlines, every available interdepartmental coordination mechanism, and the creation of a special advisory group outside the government) to move the bureaucracy; the less-than-immediate and limited reaction is clear evidence of the limitations of a Japanese prime minister's power.

Conclusion: Can (or should) we emulate the Japanese?

The picture of the Japanese public bureaucracy that emerges has two dominant themes. The first is that it reflects key characteristics of Japanese culture, such as the achievement of consensus through consultation, the bottom-up decision-making process, and the practice of lifetime employment for the best and the brightest. The second theme is the importance placed on keeping government as small, efficient and uncomplicated as possible. The aspects of Japanese government that are so rooted in Japanese culture are those which would be the hardest for us to adopt, given how profoundly our culture differs from theirs.

On the other hand, the institutional simplicity of Japanese government is something with which we should not be entirely unfamiliar, even in terms of our relatively recent history. During the Thirties, Forties and Fifties, the "golden age of the Ottawa mandarins," our major departments probably functioned similarly to Japanese departments today. Consider the two central agencies then regarded as the centres of excellence in the government, namely External Affairs and Finance. In both cases, there was meritocratic recruitment of the best and the brightest, External Affairs by its examinations, and Finance by hiring the best Canadian economics graduates of prestigious foreign universities. Perhaps because of the specialization of these departments' roles, many staff members stayed for most of their careers. Junior officers were given a great deal of responsibility for the department's analytical work, and most observers agreed that it was of very high calibre. While only a few made it to the pinnacle, most of the elite had respectable careers, and some undoubtedly "descended from heaven" into responsible, and more lucrative, private sector positions. [43]

---

42 Bruce Roscoe, "Getting round bureaucracy to the 'expert' committees," *Far Eastern Economic Review*, November 7, 1985, pp. 58-60.
43 J.L. Granatstein, *The Ottawa Men: The Civil Service Mandarins 1935-1957* (Toronto: Oxford, 1982).

SANDFORD F. BORINS

It is sadly ironic that External and Finance are the two departments whose stature has fallen most in the last fifteen years. From a Japanese perspective, what has happened to the Canadian bureaucracy in recent years, in particular the Trudeau era?

The trends that are most in evidence are the decline of the strong departments, the rise of the central agencies and the increased mobility of senior public servants. The first two have been discussed at length by Campbell and Gillies. However, consider the origins and implications of the third. The Glassco Commission was among the first to promote the idea that there is a science of public management, which one can exercise in many different organizational contexts. Rapid mobility of senior public servants began a few years later. To some extent, the Trudeau government felt that the power of ministers could be increased if long-time deputies no longer ruled their departments. In addition, the notion grew that it is important to achieve a good personal chemistry between a minister and his deputy, so that ministers could ask for a shuffle of deputies in order to find the right match. With deputies moving rapidly, the phenomenon spread to lower levels. Many deputies developed an entourage of protégés, who followed them on their moves, of course receiving promotions as they went. In addition, we have had constant departmental reorganizations. In this world, it seems clear that a rational self-interested bureaucrat will attempt to continuously move around town to where the action is (most likely the central agencies). If he or she develops any expertise, it is on how to move policy proposals through the ever-changing machinery of government, rather than on the actual merits of the proposals. [44]

From a Japanese point of view, the consequences of all this organizational churning and shifting are obvious: the ability of the Canadian government to formulate intelligent policies is limited because expertise and trust, based on long years of experience with a policy area and with one's colleagues, are sadly lacking. The advice we would get from the Japanese is to go back, if at all possible, to stronger, more stable departments, in which senior officials have longer tours of duty to develop more expertise and trust in one another.

A second lesson that emerges from the Japanese experience is the importance of limits – limits on spending, limits on the number of bureaucrats and their salaries, and limits on the growth of government organizations. The Japanese again seem to be much more effective than we are in this area. The Trudeau government's major effort to control spending, the envelope system,

---

44   In his survey of Canadian central agency bureaucrats, Colin Campbell asked them what they considered their main area of expertise. Sixty-nine per cent could be considered generalists (citing such skills as administration or management, administrative policy, political, legal, analytical, interpersonal, and economics, generally) while only 30 per cent considered themselves specialists (citing a specific policy sector or sector of economics). See Campbell, *Governments under Stress*, p. 312.

MANAGEMENT OF THE PUBLIC SECTOR IN JAPAN

was dramatically weakened by the success individual ministers had in going to the Priorities and Planning Committee to make exceptions to fund special programs.[45] Initiatives to reduce the size of the civil service have often been nullified by the use of consultants or quasi-governmental organizations.[46]

Perhaps in this regard Mancur Olson is correct in his Hegelian argument that the highly developed economies of the western world bear within themselves the seeds of their own destruction in terms of their equally highly developed interest groups, of which the bureaucracy is one, which often succeed in obtaining favourable policies at the expense of the country's overall economic performance.[47] Conversely, Japan appears to have been more successful than other nations in exerting discipline over its interest groups and bureaucracy, thus facilitating more rapid economic growth. One wonders if in Canada there is either a public consensus or the political will to follow a course even approaching that of the Japanese.

A third observation is that the Japanese government continues to show a great willingness to evaluate its policies, as evidenced by the important roles played by the Administrative Inspection Bureau and the ongoing commissions on administrative reform. Our performance, once again, is less commendable. Since the abolition of the Treasury Board's Planning Branch in the late 1970s, there has been a gap in the area of ongoing policy and program review at the central level. The Office of the Comptroller General has attempted to do this, but it had great difficulty getting off the ground, and still lacks the political clout to evaluate major programs.[48] In the early 1980s, MSSD and MSERD functioned mainly as staff to their respective cabinet committees, and their analyses were primarily "quick and dirty" assessments rather than thorough reviews. The auditor general's mandate for program review is still uncertain; while he can always get headlines, his adversarial relationship with the government reduces his access to information and limits the impact of his recommendations. The current task forces operating under the aegis of the deputy prime minister are a step in the right direction, but their work to a great degree involves the classification rather than the analysis of programs, and is quick and dirty, rather than thorough, and their mandate may be of limited duration, rather than ongoing.

We still have not succeeded in institutionalizing some central agency organ to undertake policy and program review, focusing on key problem areas, with good access to information as input, and with direct access to

---

45   Richard Van Loon, "The Policy and Expenditure Management System in the Federal Government: the First Three Years," CANADIAN PUBLIC ADMINISTRATION 26, no. 2 (Summer 1983), pp. 255-85.

46   John L. Langford, "The Question of Quangos: Quasi-public Service Agencies in British Columbia," CANADIAN PUBLIC ADMINISTRATION 26, no. 4 (Winter 1983), pp. 563-76.

47   Mancur Olson, *The Rise and Decline of Nations* (New Haven: Yale University Press, 1982).

48   Colin Campbell, *Governments under Stress*, pp. 224-25.

SANDFORD F. BORINS

both cabinet and public opinion, so that its recommendations will stand some chance of being implemented.

One final area in which the conclusions are not quite so clear is the role played by central agencies in coordinating policy development. The Japanese have a cultural imperative that requires interdepartmental consultation, but delays the taking of a decision until a consensus is reached. Coordinating mechanisms tend to be fairly ad hoc, designed at getting interested parties to talk until consensus is reached. Outcomes can be affected by deadlines, by structuring the discussions to give one side or another the stronger voice, or by public or political pressure. However, the growing complexity of the Japanese economy is increasing the need for more sophisticated coordinating mechanisms, throwing into question the ability of the current system to cope.

In the Canadian case, we have experimented with large and complicated central coordinating mechanisms, indeed larger and more complicated than those of other governments.[49] Nevertheless, we have also seen key policies made by small, tight groups, operating under the direct supervision of the prime minister and the clerk of the Privy Council (for example, the National Energy Policy). Our continual experimentation, from the elaborate system of the Trudeau years to the simplifications introduced by Mulroney, suggest we still have not got it right. The Japanese are also experimenting, trying to develop systems that allow for the more rapid achievement of consensus in these more difficult times. Neither of us have a conclusive answer yet, and perhaps our ongoing experiments will be mutually instructive.

On balance, I found my study of Japanese public management as sobering as our private sector counterparts have found their studies of Japanese business management. In the public sector, we see a nation that organizes its departments to operate with great expertise and high morale, that sets limits on the expansion of bureaucracy, and that makes serious efforts to undertake central agency review of key programs. I am afraid that our performance in all of these areas is no match for theirs, and I am not optimistic that we will be able to summon up the will to improve it very much in the near future.

49　Ibid., pp. 77-79.

Part III
New Directions

Derrida denied that there was 'one best way' of understanding human activities, arguing that we all too easily tend to provide accounts of our activities that rest upon contradictions and confusions of various kinds. These can be revealed by the 'deconstruction' of these accounts into their underlying ideas and conceptions. Chapter 24 shows how attempts to apply organizational theories often become commentaries on the theories themselves rather than analyses of the organizations under review. In this way, traditional accounts of how organizations work can often be misleading.

The table from E. Swyngedouw (Chapter 25) and the table from C. Curson (Chapter 26) draw out contrasts in the labour market, production arrangements and government activity between the 'Fordist' era of mass production by rigid controls and the 'flexible accumulation' era of contingencies and opportunities exploited by 'agile organizations'. Chapter 27 by Morgan illustrates the nature of such flexible organizations and how they function.

There then follow three essays exploring the political and economic ideas behind recent reforms, and the implications for public servants. They reflect United Kingdom and Canadian experience but, as later sections show, are common to many other countries. A summary of developments in Eastern Europe in Chapter 31 concludes the section. Toonen shows that, although many themes are common to both Western and Eastern European thought and practice, the need to create new constitutions, administrative structures and cultures, as well as systems to supply the necessary human resources, all give a different twist to the nature and pace of reform.

Modernism, Post Modernism and Organizational Analysis 3: The Contribution of Jacques Derrida

Robert Cooper

Abstract

Robert Cooper
Department of
Behaviour in
Organizations,
University of
Lancaster, U.K.

This paper, the third in a series on the relevance of the modernist-post modernist debate to organizational analysis (Cooper and Burrell 1988; Burrell 1988), examines the work of Jacques Derrida. Specifically, Derrida's work is viewed as a contribution to the analysis of *process* (as opposed to *structure*) in social systems. In this context, three interrelated themes of his work — deconstruction, writing, 'difference' — are described in some detail and their implications explored for social and organizational analysis. Derrida's account of the logic of writing shows it to be fundamental to the division of labour and therefore to significant dimensions (complexity, formalization) of formal organization. Since 'organization theories' are themselves products of writing and the division of labour, their essential function is to explain and justify the structures they represent; they are therefore more concerned with maintaining their own consistency and the stability of the organized world they describe rather than critical understanding. This point is illustrated by a detailed deconstruction of two major approaches to the study of bureaucracy (the 'formalist' and 'expertise' models) in organization theory. Finally, it is suggested that the affinity between the logic of writing and the division of labour underlies Michel Foucault's concept of *knowledge–power* and the development of areas of professionalized knowledge such as accountancy.

Introduction

The recent 'symbolic turn' in organizational studies provides an appropriate context for understanding the relevance of Jacques Derrida's work to organizational analysis. In a programmatic introduction to the symbolic approach, Pondy and Mitroff (1979) argue that the chief feature of human organization is the use of language and symbolism (including the attribution of meaning to things and making sense of the world). They claim that traditional approaches to the study of organizations have completely neglected language. Specifically, they cite Thompson's (1967) 'open system' model as the dominant way of thinking about organization. This is essentially an input–output model which emphasizes the control of environmental uncertainty. Among various criticisms, Pondy and Mitroff argue that Thompson's model has forgotten that it is dealing with *human* organizations, so that the characteristically human capacities of symbolism and language are not addressed as components of the organizing process.

Organization Studies
1989, 10/4: 479–502
© 1989 EGOS
0170–8406/89
0010–23 $1.00

In their emphasis on language, Pondy and Mitroff begin to approach Derrida's concern with discourse, text and writing as the bases of human institutions. But it is not difficult to show that the way in which they understand language and symbolism is light years away from Derrida's thought, and that their work is still contextualized by the input–output logic they criticize in Thompson's work. For example, they say that 'language is a technology for processing both information and meanings just as production technologies process material inputs into outputs' (p. 25). Despite the apparent critical intent of their analysis, Pondy and Mitroff remain caught up in the thought-world they wish to overturn.

For them, language appears as a mere carrier of information and meaning. For Derrida, in contrast, language is a structure of material marks or sounds which are in themselves 'undecidable' and *upon which meaning has to be imposed*. Derrida thus goes beyond Pondy and Mitroff's position that language (somehow) reveals the organizational world to us and shows especially that it is a process that reflexively includes its own antithesis. Applied to organizational analysis, this means that organization always harbours within itself that which transgresses it, namely, disorganization. Whereas traditional organization theories presuppose, and therefore give priority to, the notion of organization, Derrida's strategy is to show how the supposedly rational and stable aspects of organization are constantly under threat by their devious and insidious countermovements. He also shows that the task of understanding organization from the perspective of disorganization demands an appropriately reflexive logic and intellectual practice from the analyst. For these reasons, Derrida's work holds much promise for the further development of the 'symbolic turn' in organization theory.

His work addresses a central problem of social analysis: the logics of *structure* and *process* and their interaction. He starts from the position that our traditional ways of thinking are structure-biased and are therefore incapable of revealing the nomadic and often paradoxical character of process. So deep does structure run in our mental habits that when we actually try to analyse process we turn it into structure. Derrida's task has been to reverse this predilection and show that process is primary to structure.

Although occupationally a philosopher — until recently he occupied a chair in philosophy at the École Normale Supérieure in Paris — Derrida resists attempts to 'place' him in the academic division of labour, arguing that this is a lazy accommodation to the institutionalized demands of structure which, by definition, must preclude the serious pursuit of process. To subvert this tendency, he employs an intellectual strategy that is 'outside' traditional philosophy, being less concerned with the 'content' or 'meaning' of philosophical arguments and more concerned with the 'rhetorical' tactics that philosophers use to privilege their positions. Philosophy thus becomes just like any other form of human exchange in which actors vie with each other for status, honour or the place of 'truth'. But underlying this covert social struggle is the more fundamental problem of discourse itself which is subject to the turbulence of displacement, condensation and elision. The philosopher (like any other professional academic) seeks to structure his or her discourse so as to eliminate the wildness intrinsic to it. Derrida's project is therefore not so much 'philosophical' in the institutionalized sense but has more to do with the new logics of information and communication that characterize postmodern science (Lyotard 1984) and which disclose the essential uncertainty of human discourse. It is this feature of Derrida's work that makes it so relevant to the field of the social sciences whose own subject matter is distinguished by such communicational concepts as 'interaction' and 'relation'.

In this brief introduction to Derrida's thought, I hope to bring out the major themes of his work and show their general significance for the analysis of social systems and, more especially, organizations. One difficulty in attempting this is the problem of translating Derrida's intricate and multi-levelled style of thinking and writing (often like a difficult crossword puzzle) into an intellectual tradition (here, that of social science) which puts a prime value on clarity and coherence of communication. In fact, Derrida assumes that such a demand may actually work against the genuine understanding of process since it is implicitly grounded in the idea that knowledge is somehow already clearly structured for us in the 'external' world, if only we can apply the 'correct' methodology to 'reveal' it. Nothing could be farther from Derrida's project which instead rests on the idea that knowledge and discourse have to be 'constructed' out of a continuously chameleonic, and indeed ultimately phantasmic, world. To think in terms of 'process' requires a radical transformation of the structural cast of mind that prevails in the social sciences — in short, nothing less than its unconditional 'deconstruction'.

Deconstruction

Derrida starts from the position that human experience is pervaded by an existential 'ambivalence' which in turn serves as the drive to organize. In itself, this is hardly news since common experience tells us that every 'interaction' and 'relation' is double-valued, implies an alternative and hence requires a decision to be made and acted on, often in situations where the choices are equivalent or indeed incompatible. In fact, Merton (1959) has made ambivalence in this general sense into a sociological theory, arguing that social actors are embedded universally in networks of social incompatibilities. Though Merton's context is sociological, thus leading him to view ambivalence as inherent in social positions and not in the psychologies of people, nevertheless, his focus is still largely at the level of the individual actor. In contrast, Derrida offers an entirely new reading of ambivalence which goes beyond both the psychology and sociology of actors to the idea of the 'text'. The text — any discourse, whether political, social, philosophical, etc. — is the field of operation of deconstruction. Derrida's object in deconstruction is to reveal the ambivalences, or, more accurately, the self-contradictions and double binds, that lie latent in any text. Such a project has been nursed for some time by certain social theorists who view social action in terms of the metaphor of the 'interactional text' which has to be 'read' in all its 'variety and ambiguity' (Dawe 1978: 413). Derrida's work can be seen as a significant contribution to both the philosophy and methodology of this project.

Texts normally rest on the (usually unexamined) assumption that language is a means for the communication of thoughts. Consequently, thoughts take prime place and language is seen simply as a vehicle for the transmission of thought. Derrida calls this mental strategy 'logocentrism' since it centres human experience around the concept of an original 'logos' or presupposed metaphysical structure (e.g. mind, soul, reason, etc.) that validates and gives meaning to human activities. 'Logos' is a Greek word that encapsulates in a single idea 'the inward rational principle of verbal texts, the inward rational principle of human beings, and the inward rational principle of the natural universe' (Harland 1987: 146). Its more general meaning is 'the law', which serves to control and direct the extra-human world and thus provide the feeling of mastery over those forces of the unknown that continually besiege us. Logocentrism is thus a structure with a fixed centre or point of origin that also censors (i.e., to 'centre' is also to 'censor') the self-errant tendencies in the text. As Derrida (1978a: 278–293) points out, the centre not only orients, balances and organizes the structure, but above all it serves to limit excessive 'play' in the structure. In other words, logocentrism determines a centripetal form of organization with a single essential metaphysical centre which assures stability and therefore certitude.

Elias (1978) has argued that such logocentric tendencies pervade the literature of social science. In his study of the civilizing process, which was historically characterized by the imposition of stronger and more 'internalized' self-control within the individual, Elias has shown that the theories of knowledge which flowed from such self-control were 'concerned far more with the problems of the object of knowledge than with the subject of knowledge' (Elias 1978: 256). In sociology, this perspective is reflected in the traditional separation of the field of study into 'individual' and 'society' as self-contained entities. Elias illustrates this tendency in the works of Parsons (e.g., Parsons and Smelser 1957) who views 'social change' (i.e., process) as the malfunction of a 'normally stable state of social equilibrium' (Elias 1978: 308) and Merton (1959) who sees the social system as 'an ideal social state . . . in which there are no contradictions and tensions' and which is 'so counterposed to another in which these social phenomena, evaluated as "dysfunctional", exert a pressure toward "change" on a social structure normally free of tension and immutable' (Elias 1978: 308). The process of 'civilizing' is essentially one of 'cleaning up' and 'taming' but which is expressed in the 'semimetaphysical sense' of 'development' which itself is understood either as a 'mechanical necessity' or a 'teleological purpose' (Elias 1978: 223). Significantly, Elias argues that sociological concepts are themselves riddled with such 'civilizing' forces in which (often unconsciously) desired states of affairs are raised up over distasteful alternatives. The civilizing process is thus guarded against further, and possibly destructive, analysis by securing it in a metaphysical foundation which serves to 'hide' it from critical view. It is precisely this work of mystification that deconstruction aims to reveal. Its distinctiveness as process lies 'in the way it tries to avoid falling into the same (metaphysical) traps itself, even if this is to some extent unavoidable' (Wood 1987: 32). Deconstruction is therefore continually in danger of being consumed by the very problem it faces: how to critically open up a text 'without merely endorsing the wider framework to which its terms belong' (Wood 1987: 32). In order to prevent the possibility of logocentric incorporation, deconstruction employs a double movement of *overturning* and (what I shall call) *metaphorization*.

In overturning it is recognized that texts are structured around binary oppositions (e.g., good–bad, male–female) in which one of the terms dominates the other. As Derrida writes: '. . . we are not dealing with the peaceful co-existence of a *vis-à-vis*, but rather with a violent hierarchy. One of the two terms governs the other (axiologically, logically, etc.), or has the upper hand. To deconstruct the opposition, first of all, is to overturn the hierarchy at a given moment' (Derrida 1981a: 41). In itself, the phase of overturning is nothing new since it is a widely recognized *possibility* in all areas of social life, from politics to academic debate. It is implicit in Elias' critique of the metaphysical basis of the concept of 'civilization' as well as in the normatively-based interpretations of 'social system' that appear in the writings of Parsons, Merton and others. Derrida is careful to emphasize the potential trap of merely overturning the 'higher' term and replacing it with the 'lower' term, which then of course becomes the 'higher' and is thus itself ripe for overturning. This is merely another instance of structure, in which the opposing terms are kept separate and discrete: 'the hierarchy of dual oppositions always reestablishes itself' (Derrida 1981a: 42). It is therefore necessary to proceed immediately to the second movement of deconstruction — metaphorization — which is perhaps what makes deconstruction especially distinctive as a critical process. The point of this second stage is to keep process from degrading into structure. Derrida does this by reminding us that there is a perpetual double movement *within* the opposition so that the positively-valued term (e.g., 'civilization') is defined only by contrast to the negatively-valued second term (e.g., 'barbarism') which continually threatens the former's sovereignty. In fact, the relationship between the apparently opposing terms is really one of mutual definition in which the individual terms actually inhabit each other. In other words, the separate, individual terms give way 'to a process where opposites merge in a constant *undecidable* exchange of attributes' (Norris 1987: 35). It is this process of undecidability that underlies the movement of metaphorization with its mutual crossings and implications, making it a means of textual 'transportation' by which the speaker or writer is carried along — '*metaphorikos* still designating today, in what one calls "modern" Greek, that which concerns means of transportation' (Derrida 1987b: 6). Elias (1978) also recognizes the significance of undecidability and metaphorization when he critiques Parsons' manner of thinking about the relationship between the 'individual actor' and the 'social system' as being one of 'interpenetration'. In fact, as Elias argues, the process of interpenetration in Parsons' work is always subservient to the separate existences of the individual and the social system. This leads to the 'spatialization' of the social field in which, for example, the individual 'ego' is somehow 'inside' the human being and the 'society' somehow 'outside' it. While we may say that 'the human brain is situated within the skull and the heart within the rib cage . . . we can say clearly what is the container and what is contained, what is located within walls and what outside, and of what the dividing walls consist' (Elias 1978: 258). But such physical metaphors are completely inappropriate for the understanding of psycho-social processes since at 'this level there is nothing that resembles a container' (259) and therefore one cannot talk about the 'inside' or the 'outside' of a human being. 'One recalls that Goethe once expressed the idea that nature has neither core nor shell and that in her there is neither inside nor outside. This is true of human beings as well' (Elias 1978: 259). Elias clearly senses the central idea of deconstruction for, when he says that there is 'neither inside nor outside', he is saying that this particular binary opposition is really 'undecidable'. A more artful way of thinking about the problem of 'interpenetration' is required in order to reflect the complex, processual nature of social life and it is precisely this possibility that Derrida's work offers.

Writing

To grasp the general idea of the text, it is necessary to consider the operation by which texts come into existence — writing. Writing is the process by which human agents inscribe organization and order on their environments. In this sense, writing is a technology that is universal in the human world, dealing with such factors as 'ordering, listing, display, hierarchy of arrangement, edge and margin, sectioning, spacing, contrasts . . .' (McArthur 1986: 23). Writing is not concerned with the meaning and content of messages but, more fundamentally, with the structure and organization of representations. It is this latter feature that characterizes the idea of 'formalization' in bureaucratic organizations (Hall 1982) in which rules and regulations are written down in official documents. Writing in this sense was a necessary ingredient of administration and management from the earliest historic times as Goody (1977) points out: administrative functions dominate the use of writing in the ancient world, especially in the form of lists, formulae, recipes, prescriptions, etc. Goody even suggests that Western logic was dependent upon the development of writing: '. . . the setting down of speech . . . enabled man clearly to separate words; to manipulate their order and to develop syllogistic forms of reasoning . . .' (Goody, 1977: 11). Writing thus developed as a way of fixing the flux and flow of the world in spatial and temporal terms in what McArthur (1986) has called the 'taxonomic urge'.

Derrida (1976) begins with the assertion that the history of writing in the Western world shows it to have been always subordinate to speech. The spoken word is thought to be prior to the written word which is thus reduced to the status of a 'vehicle' for speech. Speech is viewed as the means by which the human mind expresses its thoughts. Speech becomes the privileged term and the real significance of writing is therefore suppressed. Derrida wants to overturn this logocentric conception of writing which sees language as a system of signs that represents ideas which are supposed to exist in the 'objective' world, independent of human intervention. For Derrida, there can be no metaphysical entities since his critical programme is utterly materialist and begins and ends with the physical world. His concept of writing is the physical action of inscribing marks or signs on a surface — a sheet of paper, the brain, the surface of the earth, etc. — and not a supposed logocentric origin beyond those marks. In developing this idea of writing, Derrida (1978a: 196–231) uses Freud's model of the Magic Writing Pad, a child's toy which possesses the novel feature of being able to self-erase any writing inscribed on its surface. The pad is constructed of an upper layer of transparent celluloid and a lower layer of translucent waxed paper. Writing is effected by pressing a stylus onto the celluloid surface which then causes the darker-coloured base to show through as writing on the lighter-coloured paper. The writing is thus not inscribed directly on the paper and it can be erased simply by breaking the contact between paper and base. But the waxed base still bears the impression of the stylus despite the writing being no longer visible on the surface. Freud compares the base to the unconscious mind, which 'remembers' what it does not consciously perceive, and the double surface (paper and celluloid) to the conscious mind, which receives and filters stimuli, but does not retain them. The physical basis of writing is further elaborated by Derrida when he compares the invisible traces of the stylus on the writing pad to the neurological pathways that external stimuli create when they impinge upon the nervous system. These pathways (traces, tracks) are literally incised or engraved (Derrida also uses the term 'graph', with its suggestion of 'groove', to refer to this latent aspect of the written sign) on the neurological system, thus facilitating the direction and flow of later stimuli. All writing for Derrida has this character.

Viewed in this way, writing shows how the human actor is materially involved in its world in a process of *reflection*. Writing is not a *direct* effect of the stylus' contact with the celluloid surface but is, instead, an *indirect* effect of the contact between the celluloid and the wax base; writing is thus a deferred impression of the wax base showing *up* rather than the stylus pressing *down* (Harland 1987: 143). Consciousness therefore comes on the rebound, so to speak, as the delayed effect of a purely unconscious, involuntary action; it is not a direct reflection on the outside world but a relationship made with what has already been inscribed. Extending the metaphor of the pathway into the world of modern transport, Derrida's analysis of writing would compel us to admit that it is the motorway that 'drives' (directs) us in our vehicles just as much as we think ourselves to be consciously in the driving seat. We are driven as we drive or, as Derrida would say, we are written as we write.

The operation of the delayed effect exemplified in the writing pad leads Derrida to propose that *later* ideas or experiences always take precedence over what was initially there; this delayed effect he calls 'supplementarity', i.e., adding something on at a later time. Traditionally, writing has been viewed as supplementing the spoken word, as simply communicating speech which is privileged as the direct voice of consciousness. But Derrida points out that 'supplement' also means that which is required to *complete* some deficiency in the present state of things. Seen thus, writing is no longer that which merely supplements oral communication; in fact, writing now has to be understood as the very condition of discourse in general, and without which communication is just not possible. Derrida's 'logic of supplementarity' surprises us by revealing a subservient term to be (unconsciously) dominant.

Now the concept of delay has a spatial as well as a temporal dimension and this is also brought out by Derrida in his analysis of the supplement, for one of the movements of supplementation is to delay by putting aside or placing in the margin (as well as postponing). The supplement is that which is made marginal to a controlling centre, such as we noted in the first overturning phase of deconstruction. But, as we have also noted, the marginal or inessential as supplement is actually the necessary and essential, as writing is to speech. This paradoxical feature of writing, in which a term is shown to be inhabited by its opposite, Derrida calls 'undecidability'. Freud (1957) drew attention to the presence of undecidability in the 'antithetical meanings' behind 'primal words'. In the earliest languages, opposites such as 'strong/weak', 'light/dark', 'big/small' were expressed by the same verbal roots. In Ancient Egyptian, *ken* represented 'strong' *and* 'weak'. In Latin, *altus* means 'high' *and* 'deep'; *sacer*, 'sacred' *and* 'accursed'. As these examples show, the essence of undecidability is the existence of contradictory meanings *within a single term*.

One of Derrida's (1981b: 61–171) best-known deconstructions is centred on the Ancient Greek term *pharmakon* as discussed by Plato in the *Phaedrus*. The word *pharmakon* is intrinsically undecidable since in ancient Greece it meant *both* remedy *and* poison; good *and* bad, at the same time. The 'problem' of the *pharmakon* is that it is the 'medium in which opposites are opposed' and in which one side insists on crossing over and contaminating (i.e., metaphorizing) the other. In the *Phaedrus*, writing is described as a *pharmakon* for while, on the one hand, it can facilitate the recording and transmission of knowledge, on the other hand, it depersonalizes human knowledge by taking it away from its oral tradition and therefore its authentic living source. But Derrida shows, by means of a subtly nuanced deconstruction, that the logocentric properties that Plato elevates (speech, memory, thought) in his campaign against the *pharmakon* of writing are undermined from the very start, because their philosophical defence has necessarily to use writing so that Plato's argument is pervaded by the same undecidability to which it objects. Writing turns out to be a necessary evil, full of strange tricks, but which Plato cannot do without. At best, he can only 'delay' its intrusion through the writerly trick of sup-plementarity. This point in Plato's argument is analyzed by Derrida in terms of the inside/outside polarity and thus enables us to connect Derrida's conception of writing with Elias' (1978) criticism of the inside/outside problem in social science discussed above. 'Apprehended as a blend and an impurity, the *pharmakon* also acts like an aggressor or a housebreaker, threatening some internal purity and security' (Derrida 1981b: 128). The purity of the inside can only be attained, says Derrida, if the outside is branded as a *supplement*, something inessential, even parasitical. The supplement is added in order to complete and compensate for a lack in what is thought to be complete. Yet, in order to cure the inside of the odious aspect of the *pharmakon*, it is necessary to keep the outside out. Derrida emphasizes how the outside as the unwanted supplement plays a necessary constituting role in the formation of the inside and, far from being a mere accessory, is thus a central feature of the inside. To illustrate this, Derrida uses examples from the human body whose innermost spaces — mouth, stomach, etc. — are actually pockets of externality folded in. An outside is thus seen to be the most intrinsic feature of a system, displacing the inside.

When Elias identifies the inside/outside problem as a major conceptual problem for social science, when he criticizes the 'container' metaphor of the human being with its spatial image of walls that include and exclude, when he recalls Goethe's insight that in nature there is 'neither inside nor outside', he is offering us a proto-deconstruction which leads logically to Derrida's more developed form of deconstruction. In fact, topographical spatialization is essential to the logocentric model which includes 'the whole history of the metaphor of structure . . . everything having to do with "the order of forms and sites", "the internal unity of an assemblage", a *construction* . . .' (Ulmer 1985: 11). Deconstruction disassembles the structured metaphors of logocentrism by revealing their intrinsic supplementarity and therefore their self-corrupting liabilities. The *pharmakon* is not just an 'ambivalent' term capable of various interpretations; it is a double-valued metaphor whose antithetical senses are always co-present in Plato's text, thus defeating any attempt to present a consistent, unilateral message. In other words, the *pharmakon* goes beyond the specific intentions of Plato because it is caught up in a play of forces that inheres within writing itself: '. . . the word *pharmakon* is caught in a chain of significations . . . (which) is not, simply, that of the intentions of an author who goes by the name of Plato' (Derrida 1981b: 129–130). Meaning spreads out in a process of *dissemination* like the dispersion of a drop of ink discharged into a glass of water. Derrida shows that *pharmakon* disseminates into even more remote and foreign contexts, though always returning to the problem of undecidability: it is closely related to *pharmakeus*, which means magician or sorcerer and thus, more generally, to the act of dissembling; it is linked with *pharmakos*, a scapegoat which was sacrificed in the Greek city-state as a symbolic purging of an invading evil; it also suggests the dye and perfume used as cosmetics by actors, a further example of dissimulation. In dissemination, the various terms of a text point away from themselves to other terms in a continuous, unstoppable movement so that writing appears to be in the grip of an autonomous, self-propelling force that lies beyond the intentions of the individual actor. This implacable movement of writing, which runs always beyond traditional metaphor, is therefore better called *metaphorization*, implying the act of being transported here and there in a vehicle that has no substance, by a driver whom one cannot see and to a destination that one can never know.

Derrida's concepts of deconstruction and writing rely for their effect on their denial of conceptual mastery and definition. If their movement were to be arrested, it would no longer be movement but just another immobilizing and immobilized circumscription. It is therefore necessary to develop a strategy of thought which reflects and preserves (but which does not 'capture') this process — hence the urge constantly at work in Derrida's project to express writing as a self-deferring process of 'difference'.

From Difference to 'Differance'

The concept of difference is fundamental to Derrida's view of process, including the activities of deconstruction and writing. His way of thinking difference is complex and subtle. But, for the moment, let us start with some very basic issues. Difference is roughly equivalent to the concept of 'information' in information theory where it appears as a *binary structure* based on the idea of division (Cooper 1987). The human world is constituted by such divisions, e.g., male–female, day–night, etc. There are two ways of thinking about division: (1) by emphasizing the two separate terms, or (2) by emphasizing the actual process of division itself. Step (1) is a definitive feature of logocentrism which, as we have seen, thinks in terms of hierarchized binary oppositions. Step (2) enables us to see that division is not just an act of separation but is also an undifferentiated state in which its terms are actually joined together, i.e., *division both separates and joins*. Paradoxically, it is the act of separation which creates the perception of something that is also whole or unitary. Division (i.e., difference) in this second sense is therefore like Derrida's concept of undecidability in which opposing terms inhabit each other. We now see that division is the sharing of a whole between two terms in a continuous *process* of differentiation or active alternation.

In order to dramatize the *processual* nature of difference as distinct from its meaning as a fixed presence (i.e., static difference), Derrida invents the term 'differance'. Differance embodies the two meanings of the French verb 'différer': to *defer*, or postpone, in time, and to *differ* in space. The very fact that these two meanings reside in 'différer' means that the differential nature of the word cannot be grasped as a singularity and that one of its meanings always has to be *deferred*. Derrida intends that differance should be understand as a continuous *absence*, as a force that is continually beyond our grasp and therefore never properly present: '*Differance* is neither a *word* nor a *concept*' (Derrida 1973: 130). In writing differance with an *a*, Derrida further emphasizes the absent force (i.e., non-presence) of writing, for in French the infractive *a* becomes apparent only in the written version of the word — when spoken it cannot be distinguished from the commonly accepted spelling, i.e., the two versions *defer* each other. Derrida always wants to bring out the active or processual character of difference and we can get some idea of this by returning to the example of the *pharmakon*. In terms of differance, the *pharmakon* does not simply include the two opposing meanings of 'poison' and 'remedy'; these are not just structurally different *from* each other; instead, they actively *defer* each other, the deferred term being postponed for the present, waiting for an opportunity to flow back to the medium from which it was severed. This latter point, especially, brings out the processual character of differance, for underlying the idea of *differance from* (i.e., static difference) is an originary force of 'sameness' (to be distinguished from static identity in which one thing is said to be the same as another) which works in a subterranean and unconscious way to bind differences together: 'In "differ-ance", alternative meanings are not the same to the extent of being identified in a single meaning; they are the same to the extent that a single force passes through them, crosses the boundary between them' (Harland 1987: 138). This moving 'sameness' is the process of metaphorization which underlies all the metaphors we use to give spatial and temporal stability to the undecidability of writing.

Differance, therefore, has to be understood as continuous movement, but it is not the movement of specific things. Writerly concepts such as spacing, contrast, organization are not physical properties of things; they are forms of differance and as such lack 'a specific locatability. This is also Elias' 'anti-container' argument in which he denies the locatability of 'inside' and 'outside'. It means, for example, that we cannot properly talk about objects or events as being 'in' the mind, for the mind 'contains' only differences. There is even a problem in talking about *the* mind since this gives the impression of a locatable place, a thing which contains other things. In fact, the mind, too, is difference. Differance thus destroys the idea of simple location and indeed the logic of identity which relies on locatability. But differance as undecidable movement which cannot be pinned down can at least be delayed or deferred, as we have noted, and it is this process of delaying that lies at the bottom of logocentrism. Logocentrism rests on a philosophy of 'presence', the idea that things and events are given to us as fully constituted experiences. The social sciences are replete with examples of presence — e.g., individual, society, organization, environment — whose unexamined 'naturalness' and 'obvious-ness' privileges them as 'essences' and thus puts them beyond critical analysis. Derrida reminds us that such 'presences' are actually the effects of differance, just as the 'presence' of the 'remedial' *pharmakon* depended on its com-plementary 'absence' of 'poison'. Logocentrism denies that presence originates in this way by positing it as a 'priority' that is 'held to be simple, intact, normal, pure, standard, self-identical, in order *then* to think in terms of derivation, complication, deterioration, accident, etc.' (Derrida 1977: 236). So ingrained is this procedure in our thinking that we 'naturally' start from the simple, normal, standard case and go on to consider other cases that can then be defined as 'less perfect' complications, derivations and deteriorations of the normal (Culler 1983). Logocentric presence is thus a form of covertly willed prior knowledge (i.e., 'presence' becomes 'pre-sense') which delays (and denies) differance by claiming to be a kind of 'perfect' foundation or origin from which the latter deviates. As we have seen, thought and speech occupy this role in relation to writing.

Presence is a form of thinking that goes from effect to cause — a track in the forest tells us of the presence (i.e., prior action) of some animal or person; the track is derived from, and therefore secondary to, the presence. At the same time, the presence represses the other traces of the track, the thousand other possibilities which are never realized as presence, which prompts Derrida to think 'track' as the metaphorization of writing: a road or path cut into the natural matter of the forest becomes a topography inscribed on the surface of the earth and which further re-inscribes writing and travel as traces of each other, thereby deconstructively transforming a specific effect into a more general cause: 'it is difficult to imagine that access to the possibility of a road-map is not at the same time access to writing' (Derrida 1976: 108). Presence is thus integral to repression ('pre-sent' is a writerly version of 'pre-ssion') and Derrida expresses this integrity in terms of the Magic Writing Pad: 'Writing is unthinkable without repression. The condition for writing is that there be neither a permanent contact nor an absolute break between strata: the vigilance and failure of censorship' (Derrida 1978a: 226). In other words, repression has that paradoxical structure of division in which separation and joining come together. This means that every presence is a form of censorship, albeit a necessary one — necessary not just for its own realization but for the emergence of differance and the trace. The human agent (as 'writer') thus re-presents in repression the excesses of writing that it censors; in this way, the agent both reproduces and is reproduced by the act of writing. The agent is in precisely the same position as Plato who, while condemning writing for its contaminating powers, was actually empowered by the very force he sought to deny.

Derrida clearly places the idea of the human agent at the centre of his analyses — all human action occurs within the matrix of writing and differance. Specifically, the concept of agency here is tied up with repression and censorship. Ideas *in* the mind, for example, do not exist: 'we are written only as we write, by the agency within us which always keeps watch over perception' (Derrida 1978a: 226). This 'agency' is the unconscious and automatic work of repression and censorship, a double-valued process which, as we have noted, denies that which gives it power. All this means that the subject is pervaded by the uncertainty and doubt intrinsic to differance and writing; indeed, that differance is incorporated into the human subject as its founding principle.

Differance as uncertainty and doubt is built into the very fabric of the agent as a social being: '. . . an agent living in a complex, heterogeneous world requires strong empathic capacities for acquiring the interests and motives of the members of his community. Rousseau and Freud have shown that the mechanisms that make social cooperation easy and natural are mechanisms that also internally divide a person. Precisely to the extent that a person can empathize with, and acquire the interests of the various members of society, to that extent he will be divided' (Rorty 1980: 910). Uncertainty, then, is not the mere 'absence' of certainty — the two terms *co-exist* as the result of the intrinsically divided logic of writing. Such effects of differance are therefore not 'outside' us, nor in our 'environments', since we have seen that we are actually 'inhabited' by writing and its contradictions. Among other things, this view of human agency destroys the idea that the subject is a more or less rational, self-contained unit — the latter is 'at best something to be hoped for (and) certainly cannot be presupposed' (Nehamas 1985: 182). Instead of being an accomplished fact — or, more specifically, a logocentric presence — the reality of the voluntaristic, rational agent is an approximation which is continually threatened from the inside by its own Doppelgänger in the form of writerly displacements, condensations and elisions, all of which evade cognition.

The paradox of human agency, in Derrida's analyses, lies in censoring that force — call it differance or undecidability — which gives the agent its power. Built into the actual process of agency, therefore, is an unconscious tendency to deny its own origins — the problem of 'presence' discussed above. In effect, this means that the agent *necessarily* suppresses the processes involved in its own 'becoming', its own history and causative processes, which emerge out of the conflict intrinsic to differance; indeed, if it were to grant proper recognition to its own differance, the agent would, like Hamlet's pithy and momentous enterprises, 'lose the name of action'. But the act of censoring is itself a product of differance and so cannot escape the latter's dissembling guile. What Derrida (1978a: 227) calls the 'punctual simplicity of the classical subject' that is capable of rational self-control, turns out, on further inspection, to be nothing more than an effect of differance. For example, Elias (1978) has shown that such self-control, while 'appearing in the consciousness of the individual as the result of his own free will' (p. 150), is, in fact, the product of increasing social differentiation which exerts itself through an automatic censoring process and is therefore quite definitely not under the individual agent's own control. Furthermore, this 'self-control' is continually subject to the vacillations of undecidability, for the more closely the ideal of self-control is approached and the stronger the habits that support it, then the more routinized and fixed actions become, leaving less room for adaptive self-control. Derrida's conception of agency is therefore more like a field of interacting forces dominated by differance: 'The subject of writing is a *system* of relations between strata: the (Magic) Pad, the psyche, society, the world. Within that scene, on that stage, the punctual simplicity of the classical subject is not to be found. In order to describe the structure, it is not enough to recall that one always writes for someone; and the oppositions sender–receiver, code–message, etc., remain extremely coarse instruments' (Derrida 1978a: 227). The subject here is written by a wider and looser community of terms than the logocentric functions we normally use to capture the supposed rationality of the 'classical subject'. If the agent appears only in a loose community of 'differantial' terms, it can perhaps be said to disappear when it sees itself as a specific, integumented presence. This, at least, is the position that Elias (1978) comes to after a meticulous analysis of the role of the human agent in sociological analysis. The history of human thought shows human agency to have been always interpreted in terms of the 'metaphysics of presence' (Derrida 1978a: 196–231). The scientific abandonment of the geocentric world-picture for the heliocentric view did not radically challenge the self-centredness of human thinking: 'Often this transition is presented simply as a revision and extension of knowledge about the movements of the stars' (Elias 1978: 254). More than new discoveries, more than a 'cumulative increase in knowledge about the objects of human reflection' (Elias 1978: 255), were needed to decentre the persistence of the metaphysics of presence at work in the geocentric perspective. 'What was needed above all was an increased capacity in men for self-detachment in thought. Scientific modes of thought cannot be developed and become generally accepted unless people renounce their primary, unreflecting, and spontaneous attempt to understand all experience in terms of its purpose and meaning for themselves' (Elias 1978: 255). A necessary component of such scientific decentring is the increased control over affects and the awareness of their influence in cognition and analysis. In the modern period, men have attained a certain stage of self-detachment but 'they are not yet able to detach themselves sufficiently from themselves to make their own self-detachment . . . the object of knowledge and scientific enquiry' (Elias 1978: 256). This is the precise point where the punctate, classical subject loses itself as the object of its own enquiry, for 'the detachment of the thinking subject from his objects in the act of cognitive thought . . . did not appear to those thinking about it at this stage as an act of distancing but as a distance actually present . . .' (Elias 1978: 256). The subject's self-detachment is viewed as an already accomplished fact, a magical instance of metaphysical presence which refuses to examine its own pedigree. In order to reclaim itself as active agency, the subject has to view itself *in the act of distancing*. In Derridean terms, this is exactly the function of deconstruction which shows agency to be an enigmatic process that denies the very thing that gives it life, oscillating forever between difference and differance.

Organizational Analysis

Writing, for Derrida, is primarily a form of control; its communicative function comes second to this. It is the control aspect of writing that makes it central to organizational analysis. According to Giddens (1985), formal organization finds its true nature in the formalization of the written word. Giddens quotes the time-table as 'one of the most significant of modern organizations' (Giddens 1985: 174): 'Thus, rather than the steam train, it is Bradshaw's directory . . . that epitomizes modern transportation' (Giddens 1985: 175). The first writing grew out of administrative contingencies in the ancient world where it recorded mainly business and statistical information. Derrida (1976) locates the emergence of formalized writing in the agrarian capitalism of the ancient world where it served to stabilize the hierarchical order of 'a class that writes or rather commands the scribes' (Derrida 1976: 86) in written balance accounts. Writing thus becomes inseparable from the division of labour in society and the inscription of solid foundations.

The specific connections between writing and the division of labour can be more clearly seen in Latour and Woolgar's (1979) study of scientific work in a biochemical laboratory. Basing their analysis on Derrida's conception of writing as a technique of 'inscription', Latour and Woolgar show how the entire social organization of the research activity revolves around the physical act of inscription carried out by the laboratory apparatus. Most of this apparatus functions as 'inscription devices' designed to transform material substances — a chemical, rats' brains, sections of muscle — into figures, graphs, diagrams, reports, which represent the 'writerly' end-products of the scientist's work. A significant feature of these inscribed end-products is that, once they become available, 'all the intermediary steps which made their production possible are forgotten' (p. 51). In other words, inscription is viewed not as a means of constructing the product but rather as a device for communicating the product's existence: 'Inscriptions are regarded as having a direct relationship to the "original substance". The intervening material activity and all aspects of what is often a prolonged and costly process are bracketed off in discussions about what the figure means. The process of writing articles about the substance thus takes the end diagram as the starting point' (Latour and Woolgar 1979: 51).

Scientific statements begin life as tentative and uncertain inscriptions. Eventually, the 'successful' inscriptions move beyond their materialist, graphic status and end up as 'ideas', 'theories' and 'reasons'. In this process, as Latour and Woolgar constantly remind us, the 'craft' basis of scientific production is forgotten or repressed: 'Our argument is not just that facts are socially constructed. We also wish to show that the process of construction involves the use of certain devices whereby all traces of production are made extremely difficult to detect' (p. 176). Two steps are apparently responsible for this mental sleight-of-hand: (1) *the splitting of the statement*, and (2) *its inversion* — a process which, significantly, reproduces the operations of the Magic Writing Pad used by Derrida to depict the micro-logic of writing.

In the first step, 'the statement becomes a split entity': (1) a set of words which represents a statement about an object, and (2) the object which is assumed to exist independently of the statement. Scientists *begin* with written statements.

Then there appear objects *and* statements about these objects. 'Before long, more and more reality is attributed to the object and less and less to the statement *about* the object. Consequently, an inversion takes place: the object becomes the reason why the statement was formulated in the first place. At the outset of stabilization, the object was the virtual image of the statement; subsequently, the statement becomes the mirror image of the reality "out there"' (pp. 176–177). In addition, the past also becomes inverted, for the object has been there all the time, just waiting for the scientist to come along and notice it.

Latour and Woolgar's analysis then shows how the social organization of the laboratory reflects the technical base of writing or, to be more precise, how the social division of labour repeats the actual operations of division intrinsic to the writing process, i.e., separation and inversion. Just as Derrida (1978a: 227) described the 'subject' of writing as a *system* of relations diffused among the different strata of Magic Writing Pad, psyche, society, and the world, so Latour and Woolgar show how the laboratory and its research environment are pervaded at every level by writing and its effects: separation and inversion not only organize the specific products of laboratory writing but research and ancillary workers are also subjected to the operations of division which *writing imposes on them as writers*, thus demonstrating Derrida's dictum that we are written as we write. Authority and position, group dynamics and structure, depend significantly on the power of researchers to construct credible accounts of the writing process, and the latter effectively means the suppression of the subjective and contingent in favour of the objective and the established in both the social and technical divisions of labour in the laboratory organization. By revealing the division of labour at work in the micro-logic of writing, Latour and Woolgar also show that 'formal organization' is a phenomenon to be explained and not to be taken routinely. 'Routine' approaches to the study of organization rely unreflectively on a conception of writing that represents an already constituted object from which the 'construction' function of writing is excluded. The object thus becomes a primary reference which can then be simply re-presented by a 'model' or a 'theory'. As we have seen, Latour and Woolgar's analysis reveals that the supposed 'primary reference' of representation is really a construction of the writing process and therefore comes *after* the latter and *not before* as the 'logic' of representation would have us believe.

The representational mode of analysis in organizational writing has been critiqued by Degot (1982). Degot singles out the concept of 'representation' as a key factor in the study of organizations, but places it in question in much the same way as Latour and Woolgar do. He argues that while it is generally assumed that orthodox organization theorists study organizations that are actually 'out there' in the real world, it can be shown that this often is not the case. The 'reality' of this literature is that the organization is a cultural object which is the product of a prior model. In effect, what the theorist sees is not the model as a representation of the organization but the organization as a representation of the model. Degot instances the systems model of Katz and Kahn (1966) to illustrate this point: '. . . the results produced present a relatively tautological structure: the organization is a system ruled by the system's laws: the variables identified in this system are created by laws whose form is such precisely because the organization is a system' (Degot 1982: 637). Similarly, the work of the Aston Group (e.g., Pugh, Hickson, Hinings and Turner 1969; Child 1972) relects not so much the real world of organizations, but rather the methods which come to represent those organizations. Psychological approaches to the study of the individual in the organization — whether based on behaviouristic learning theories or hierarchies of needs — are also afflicted with this paradox of representation. All these approaches are contaminated by a 'metaphysics' of representation which gives priority to an unexamined, taken-for-granted model or method which serves to 'represent' the organizational reality; they do not stop, therefore, to examine their own 'construction' practices: 'The construction of the object results from the application of a theory to the real world; the constructed object exists (has sense) only in relation to this theory . . .' (Degot 1982: 630).

A related issue (though not directly raised by Degot) concerns the nature of organizational analysis as an academic product of the university organization. Bourdieu and Passeron (1977) have argued that the role of the university is to *reproduce* the control structures of society and that its claim of academic freedom is therefore largely illusory. As a reproducer of control, the university cultivates a representational mode of research and teaching which, by definition, cannot be radically critical since it rests on logocentric norms of purity and rectitude. The key issue here is the status of writing (including representing) and how it is dealt with in the academic system. The function of the academic division of labour and its representational discourse is to police the effects of writing — undecidability, metaphorization — by maintaining the distinctions between disciplines and the order within them. It is this moral economy of good behaviour that is taught and reproduced in research rather than the quest for enlightenment and truth with which the university is traditionally associated: 'Naturally destined to serve the communication of laws and the order of the city transparently, a writing becomes the instrument of an abusive power, of a caste of "intellectuals" that is thus ensuring hegemony, whether its own or that of special interests . . .' (Derrida 1979: 124). Organizational analysis in the representational mode is therefore fated to reproduce in its discourse the very structures that give academic organization its communicative power and this is why one can describe systems theory as being tautological and criticize 'empirical' studies of organization for merely 'mimicking' their subject matter. As Latour and Woolgar's (1979) work suggests, a 'deconstruction' of the representational approach shows 'copy' and 'original' to be implicated in each other and therefore to be intrinsically inseparable.

Another version of this argument has been presented by Frug (1984) in a deconstruction of bureaucracy theories. Frug shows that the conceptions of bureaucracy used by organization theorists and scholars of corporate and administrative law are structured around the binary opposition of subjectivity/objectivity. Every effort is made by the theorists to secure a firm foundation for their conceptions by keeping subjectivity and objectivity separate from each other in order to objectify bureaucratic organization. Frug's criticisms thus repeat Elias' (1978) charge that social scientists are 'concerned far more with the problems of the object of knowledge than with the subject of knowledge' (p. 256) as well as Latour and Woolgar's (1979) demonstration that the 'object' of scientific research was the elimination of subjective and contingent factors in the development of knowledge and formal organization. Using Derrida's concepts of 'supplementarity' and 'undecidability', Frug shows that subjectivity/objectivity, like the double-term constituting Plato's *pharmakon*, continually threaten each other's separate identity and therefore must confound all attempts to make them serve as the firm foundation for a 'theory'. The 'theories' of bureaucracy theorists are essentially 'writings' and are therefore subject to the logic of division or differance that characterizes Derrida's conception of writing: they are motivated to hide their internal divisions in the interests of control and stable social order. These are big stakes because 'knowledge' by itself is not the key factor but the *status* of the theorists themselves in the hierarchy that reproduces itself (Bourdieu and Passeron 1977; Derrida 1979): knowledge and hierarchy 'supplement' each other. In short, the 'theories' explain and justify large-scale bureaucratic power. Frug argues that the theoretical justifications of bureaucratic organization have committed themselves to two tasks: (1) to defend bureaucracy against the fear of domination by showing that bureaucratic power is based on objectivity, i.e., 'neutrality' and 'pursuit of a common purpose'; since objectivity is 'neutral' and 'shared', subjective, personal values have to be treated as inconsistent with it: 'Objectivity is so important to the security of those threatened by the organizational structure that it must not be infected by its antithesis, subjectivity' (Frug 1984: 1286); (2) to show, *nevertheless*, that bureaucracy does enable personal freedom and self-expression by, for example, emphasizing the will of constituents to 'ensure that the bureaucracy does what they want it to do' or the freedom of officials to use their own knowledge and experience in their work; thus 'subjectivity in organizational life must be protected from the demands of objectivity' (Frug 1984: 1287). All the theories of bureaucratic legitimation 'share a common structure: they attempt to define, distinguish, and render mutually compatible the subjective and objective aspects of life. All the defences of bureaucracy have sought to avoid merging objectivity and subjectivity — uniting the demands of commonness and community with those of individuality and personal separateness — because to do so would be self-contradictory. Moreover, it has never been enough just to separate subjectivity and objectivity; each must be guaranteed a place within the bureaucratic structure' (Frug 1984: 1287). But because of the 'supplementary' relationship between subjectivity and objectivity, in which each term is necessary to, and yet at the same time threatens, the identity of the other, Frug is able to show that the theoretical project of separating and making them compatible is doomed to failure from the start.

Within organization theory, Frug identifies two major theoretical defences of bureaucracy: the formalist and expertise models. Based on the metaphor of the machine, the formalist model is defined in terms of its instrumental relationship to predetermined ends, its technical design, and its symbolic association with modern efficiency. In this model, bureaucracy is simply a machine for realizing its constituents' — citizens' or shareholders' — ends; it is 'based on the categories of instrumental rationality: it sharply distinguishes values and facts, ends and means, desire and performance. Values, ends, and desires — the subjective part of the human personality — are the attributes of the constituents who control the bureaucracy rather than the bureaucracy itself. The bureaucracy is "objective": it cannot exercise threatening discretion because it merely responds to constituents' commands. If the shareholders say, "Maximize profits" or the legislators say, "Eliminate dangerous health hazards", it does so. These directions are "formally realizable" — they impel the bureaucratic official to respond to a multitude of fact situations in a way determined by the directive itself' (Frug 1984: 1298–1299). By separating the objective and subjective in this way, the formalist model ensures the best of both worlds: the technical division of labour tuned to respond to constituents' needs with maximum efficiency which, at the same time, permits constituents to choose and pursue their own goals, totally free from bureaucratic impediment. At this point in the analysis, Frug shows that the formalist model can only work if it supplements objectivity with subjectivity: 'To be objective, the bureaucracy has to carry out the wishes of its constituents, but to do so it must refer to their general intentions ("maximize profits") or their specific commands ("fix prices"). Any application of (constituents') commands to specific situations requires the exercise of bureaucratic subjectivity — deciding what the words mean, what their purpose is, or how their meaning and their purpose can be made consistent with each other. Implementers cannot grasp other people's wishes in a way unmediated by their own consciousness' (Frug 1984: 1312–1313). The model assumes that the bureaucracy will work objectively to implement constituents' wishes but that it requires, as a necessary supplement, the exercise of discretion in order to reach these objectives. As Frug shows, this step destroys the objective emphasis of the model since the latter has no means of limiting the discretion once it is admitted: 'The idea of objectivity cannot by itself limit the discretion because bureaucratic objectivity includes within its meaning the need for bureaucratic subjectivity. Without limits, however, discretion threatens to become the exercise of arbitrary power. Paradoxically, the only apparent way to limit this discretion is through the discretion itself' (Frug 1984: 1313). In this way, the formalist model subverts its own basic premises: 'Bureaucratic organization loses its machinelike character and becomes one of the decision-makers — a decision-maker whose discretion the formalist model cannot defend' (Frug 1984: 1315). Hence, the model suffers the same fate as Plato's campaign against the *pharmakon* of writing, which turns out to be a necessary evil, full of strange tricks, but which Plato cannot do without.

The expertise model of bureaucratic organization was invented to compensate for the subjective deficiencies of the formalist model. The expertise model pictures the bureaucratic organization as a 'natural community' organized around a common purpose and which depends more on the psychology of its members than on the formal realizability of its rules. . . . People function within the bureaucracy with their whole personality and not just their rational, objective side. . . . As a consequence, organizational success depends on the creation of a successfully integrated organization personality, not on rationalist schemes to rid the organization of subjective discretion' (Frug 1984: 1319). Within the organization, the executive functions to lead, inspire and energize subordinates in the effective pursuit of their common purposes; the executive is an expert in group management and in the husbanding of human resources. Despite the priority given to subjectivity in the expertise model, it is recognized that experts' 'subjective' decisions are confined within objective boundaries; since these boundaries 'endanger the ability to exercise the necessary discretion, (they) must not assume the place of the rulelike, mechanistic restraints that made formalist bureaucracy undesirable and unworkable' (Frug 1984: 1331). Formalist objectivity must therefore be moderated by perfecting the 'discipline of professionalism', but, again paradoxically, the so-called objective qualities of professionalism which are assumed to exist somewhere outside the individual, are necessarily qualities that the expert himself helps to define: '. . . the objectivity of the expertise model can be defined only by its purported antithesis, subjectivity' (Frug 1984: 1331).

Frug's account of the vacillating relationship between subjectivity and objectivity in the formalist and expertise models illustrates the movement of Derrida's idea of differance as a 'doubled' term which cannot be grasped as a singularity and in which, therefore, one aspect of the 'double' always has to be *deferred*. This naturally creates problems for the theorist whose goal is to present a bureaucratic model based on sure foundations but, as Frug shows, a deft process of deception is maintained to protect the model's certainty. If, for example, theorists find that the concept of expertise is 'too manipulable to ensure objectivity, they can assume that the objectivity necessary to curb managerial power can be found elsewhere' (Frug 1984: 1379) — in the formalist model. But when they examine the formalist model, they see how unreliable it is as a standard for objectivity. Their normal reaction to this further denial of theoretical certitude is to assume that objectivity must be somewhere else. 'The same sort of deferral pervades the attempt to locate subjectivity somewhere: if it doesn't seem to be where one is looking, one can act as if it is safely lodged in another part of the system' (Frug 1984: 1379). Adding the models together — (Frug also discusses two other theories of bureaucracy — the 'judicial review' and 'market/pluralist' models — derived from administrative and corporate law) — enables theorists to defer endlessly the intrinsic intractability of the problem and so comfort themselves — for the time being. The deferral process is further explained by Frug in terms of Crozier's (1964) hypothesis that the reason for building bureaucracy is the evasion of face-to-face relationships which necessarily involve power and dependency. All Frug's models are themselves now to be seen as forms of evading the power problem by suggesting that relationships can be made unthreatening through some appropriate organizational arrangement. Mannheim's (1936) argument that 'the fundamental tendency of all bureaucratic thought is to turn all problems of politics into problems of administration' is cited as yet another version of this deferral process. The result of this step to moderate the problem of power is actually to disguise it as 'formal organization'; this merely 'conceals the exercise of personalized, human domination in the organizations within which we work and live' (Frug 1984: 1382).

Frug's deconstructive analysis of bureaucracy and the 'theories' which defend it can now be understood as expressions of the role of writing in human institutions. As we have seen, writing and the division of labour go hand in hand; social relationships reflect the micro-logic of the writing process. Intrinsic to this process is the necessity of control, and specifically the idea that division (the separation and inversion processes described by Latour and Woolgar 1979) *includes* the writer and his/her social world. Writers of every kind are compelled to write within the socio-technical structures that writing creates. Hence, formal organizations and the theories which represent them are necessarily implicated in the division of labour intrinsic to writing. Writing and its various movements — undecidability, supplementarity, differance — thus become central to the understanding of formal organization and its critical analysis.

The affinity between writing and the division of labour also marks the area of common concern between Derrida and Foucault, the subject of an earlier paper by Burrell (1988) in this series. Less concerned with the micro-logic of writing than Derrida, Foucault's (e.g., 1977) analyses of writing and the development of areas of professionalized, objective knowledge in modern institutions nevertheless complement and support Derrida's thesis that writing and the socio-technical division of labour are implicated in each other at all levels. Foucault refers to this synthesis as *knowledge-power*. The function of knowledge-power is to create and sustain a system of 'objective representations' based on separation and inversion (Latour and Woolgar 1979), i.e., the operation of division for Foucault is significantly bound up with the act of 'seeing' in which 'vision' is an intrinsic component of 'division' (Derrida has also analyzed this relationship: see Ulmer 1985: 32–36). The pursuit of visibility was advanced, as Foucault (1977) notes, through the introduction of the 'examination', a technique which combines the power of an 'observing hierarchy' with that of a 'normalizing judgement' in a 'network of writing' which captures and fixes its objects. Against this background of writing and visibility, Hoskin and Macve (1986) have traced the history and development of accounting out of the technology of the examination. Accounting is that branch of modern management which has capitalized on the two most obvious features of the visibility of writing — *instantaneity* and *distance*; in other words, writing enables information to be made available *at a glance* and in a *depersonalized* form (i.e., free from the possibility of contamination by undecidability and differance). Working within the general context of Derrida's and Foucault's work, Hoskin and Macve reveal accounting to be a product of the writing/division-of-labour synthesis centred on the universities: the 'examination, discipline and accounting are historically bound together as related ways of writing the world (in texts, institutional arrangements, ultimately in persons) into new configurations of power' (p. 107). These new ways of re-writing the social world date conceptually from antiquity, but their influence was limited until medieval times when a 'new knowledge élite appears, centred around the nascent universities' (p. 109). The new élite of clerks and masters produces 'a vast new range of pedagogic re-writings of texts, i.e., techniques which grid texts both externally and internally in the service of information-retrieval and knowledge-production' (p. 109).

The point of Hoskin and Macve's analysis is to reveal the power of accounting as 'grammatocentric organization' to create a specific form of knowledge (knowledge-power) which subjects individuals to a fixed and determinate visibility. As such, it is a specific example of a more general trend in modern society: the development of knowledge-power by means of professionalization. In fact, Hoskin and Macve characterize accountancy as a profession that is squarely founded on the knowledge-power of accounting technology. The implication here is that the professions are those groups in society that are accredited with the task of creating and maintaining the appropriate visibility or objectivity of social agents through such techniques as the examination. Writing is therefore viewed as performing the same function as Derrida noted in antiquity: the preservation of a hierarchical order of 'a class that writes or rather commands the scribes' (Derrida 1976: 86). Furthermore, this point is at least implicitly recognized in modern organization theory where 'complexity' and 'formalization' as definitive features of organization (and therefore the division of labour) are strongly associated with professionalization (Hall 1982). However, these studies lack the deconstructive cast that Derrida brings to the analysis of writing, and without this they are liable to give the impression that the formalized writing of the professional is firmly founded and therefore largely unproblematic. Frug's (1984) deconstruction of professional social science writing on bureaucracy shows that the firm foundations of 'theory' are continually deconstructed by the vacillating 'supplement' of writing which forces the theorist to continually defer theoretical certitude. Similarly, Samuel Weber's (1982) deconstruction of professionalism as social practice clearly shows that the professional's knowledge-power is also based on the deferral ruses noted by Frug (1984) in the writings of bureaucracy theorists and the techniques of separation and inversion identified by Latour and Woolgar (1979) in the construction of scientific knowledge. All this serves to remind us that professionalized knowledge in the modern world suffers from a preoccupation with what Elias (1978) has called, as we noted earlier, the 'object' of knowledge rather than its 'subject'. Derrida's work shows how this reversal can be realized through the recognition of 'writing' as the true subject of knowledge. Within the specific context of organizational analysis, as I have tried to show, this means that the 'writing of organization' must be overturned in favour of the 'organization of writing'.

References

Bourdieu, P., and J. Passeron
1977 *Reproduction in education, society and culture*. London: Sage.

Burrell, G.
1988 'Modernism, postmodernism and organizational analysis 2: The contribution of Michel Foucault'. *Organization Studies* 9/2: 221–235.

Child, J.
1972 'Organizational structure and strategies of control: a replication of the Aston study'. *Administrative Science Quarterly* 17/2: 163–177.

Cooper, R.
1987 'Information, communication and organization: a post-structural revision'. *Journal of Mind and Behavior* 8/3: 395–416.

Cooper, R., and G. Burrell
1988 'Modernism, postmodernism and organizational analysis: an introduction'. *Organization Studies* 9/1: 91–112.

Crozier, M.
1964 *The bureaucratic phenomenon*. London: Tavistock.

Culler, J.
1983 *On deconstruction*. London: Routledge and Kegan Paul.

Dawe, A.
1978 'Theories of social action' in *A history of sociological analysis*. T. Bottomore and R. Nisbet (eds.), 362–417. London: Heinemann.

Degot, V.
1982 'Le modèle de l'agent et le problème de la construction de l'objet dans les théories de l'entreprise'. *Social Science Information* 21/4–5: 627–664.

Derrida, J.
1973 *Speech and phenomena*. Evanston, IL: Northwestern University Press.

Derrida, J.
1976 *Of grammatology*. Baltimore: The Johns Hopkins University Press.

Derrida, J.
1977 'Limited Inc.' in *Glyph 2*. S. Weber and H. Sussman (eds.), 162–254. Baltimore: The Johns Hopkins University Press.

Derrida, J.
1978a *Writing and difference*. London: Routledge and Kegan Paul.

Derrida, J.
1978b 'The *retrait* of metaphor'. *Enclitic* 2/2: 5–34.

Derrida, J.
1979 'Scribble (writing-power)'. *Yale French Studies* 58: 117–147.

Derrida, J.
1981a *Positions*. Chicago: University of Chicago Press.

Derrida, J.
1981b *Dissemination*. London: Athlone Press.

Elias, N.
1978 *The civilizing process: the history of manners*. Oxford: Blackwell.

Elias, N.
1982 *The civilizing process: state formation and civilization*. Oxford: Blackwell.

Foucault, M.
1977 *Discipline and punish: the birth of the prison*. London: Allen Lane.

Freud, S.
1957   *Standard edition of the complete psychological works of Sigmund Freud*, vol. 11. London: Hogarth Press and Institute of Psycho-Analysis.

Frug, G. E.
1984   'The ideology of bureaucracy in American law'. *Harvard Law Review* 97/6: 1276–1388.

Giddens, A.
1985   *The nation-state and violence*. Cambridge: Polity Press.

Goody, J.
1977   *The domestication of the savage mind*. Cambridge: Cambridge University Press.

Hall, R. H.
1982   *Organizations: structure and process*. Englewood Cliffs, NJ: Prentice-Hall.

Harland, R.
1987   *Superstructuralism*. London: Methuen.

Hoskin, R. W., and R. H. Macve
1986   'Accounting and the examination: a genealogy of disciplinary power'. *Accounting, Organizations and Society* 11/2: 105–136.

Katz, D., and R. L. Kahn
1966   *The social psychology of organizations*. New York: Wiley.

Latour, B., and S. Woolgar
1979   *Laboratory life: the social construction of scientific facts*. Beverly Hills, Cal.: Sage.

Lyotard, J.-F.
1984   *The postmodern condition: a report on knowledge*. Manchester: Manchester University Press.

McArthur, T.
1986   *Worlds of reference: lexicography, learning and language from the clay tablet to the computer*. Cambridge: Cambridge University Press.

Mannheim, K.
1936   *Ideology and Utopia*. New York: Harcourt, Brace.

Merton, R. K.
1959   *Social theory and social structure*. Glencoe, IL.: The Free Press.

Nehamas, A.
1985   *Nietzsche: life as literature*. Cambridge, Mass.: Harvard University Press.

Norris, C.
1987   *Derrida*. London: Fontana Press.

Parsons, T., and N. J. Smelser
1957   *Economy and Society*. London: Routledge and Kegan Paul.

Pondy, L. R., and I. I. Mitroff
1979   'Beyond open system models of organization' in *Research in organizational behaviour*, Vol. 1. B. Staw (ed.), 3–39. Greenwich, CT.: JAI.

Pugh, D. S., D. J. Hickson, C. R. Hinings, and C. Turner
1969   'The context of organization structures'. *Administrative Science Quarterly* 14/1: 91–114.

Rorty, A.
1980   'Self-deception, akrasia and irrationality'. *Social Science Information* 19/6: 905–922.

Thompson, J. D.
1967   *Organizations in action*. New York: McGraw-Hill.

Ulmer, G.
1985   *Applied grammatology*. Baltimore: The Johns Hopkins University Press.

Weber, S.
1982   'The limits of professionalism'. *Oxford Literary Review* 5/1–2: 59–79.

Wood, D. C.
1987   'An introduction to Derrida' in *A radical philosophy reader*. R. Osborne and R. Edgeley (eds.), 18–42. London: Verso.

[25]

D. Harvey

Table 2.8   Contrast between Fordism and flexible accumulation according to Swyngedouw

Fordist production (based on economies of scale)	Just-in-time production (based on economies of scope)
A THE PRODUCTION PROCESS	
mass production of homogeneous goods	small batch production
uniformity and standardization	flexible and small batch production of a variety of product types
large buffer stocks and inventory	no stocks
testing quality ex-post (rejects and errors detected late)	quality control part of process (immediate detection of errors)
rejects are concealed in buffer stocks	immediate reject of defective parts
loss of production time because of long set-up times, defective parts, inventory bottlenecks, etc.	reduction of lost time, diminishing 'the porosity of the working day'
resource driven	demand driven
vertical and (in some cases) horizontal integration	(quasi-) vertical integration sub-contracting
cost reductions through wage control	learning-by-doing integrated in long-term planning
B LABOUR	
single task performance by worker	multiple tasks
payment per rate (based on job design criteria)	personal payment (detailed bonus system)
high degree of job specialization	elimination of job demarcation
no or only little on the job training	long on the job training
vertical labour organization	more horizontal labour organization
no learning experience	on the job learning

Table 2.8 cont.

Fordist production (based on economies of scale)	Just-in-time production (based on economies of scope)
emphasis on diminishing worker's responsibility (disciplining of labour force)	emphasis on worker's co-responsibility
no job security	high employment security for core workers (life-time employment). No job security and poor labour conditions for temporary workers

C SPACE

functional spatial specialization (centralization/decentralization)	spatial clustering and agglomeration
spatial division of labour	spatial integration
homogenization of regional labour markets (spatially segmented labour markets)	labour market diversification (in-place labour market segmentation)
world-wide sourcing of components and sub-contractors	spatial proximity of vertically quasi-integrated firms.

D STATE

regulation	deregulation/re-regulation
rigidity	flexibility
collective bargaining	division/individualization, local or firm-based negotiations
socialization of welfare (the welfare state)	privatization of collective needs and social security
international stability through multi-lateral agreements	international destabilization; increased geopolitical tensions
centralization	decentralization and sharpened interregional/intercity competition
the 'subsidy' state/city	the 'entrepreneurial' state/city
indirect intervention in markets through income and price policies	direct state intervention in markets through procurement

Table 2.8 cont.

Fordist production (based on economies of scale)	Just-in-time production (based on economies of scope)
national regional policies	'territorial' regional policies (third party form)
firm financed research and development	state financed research and development
industry-led innovation	state-led innovation

E IDEOLOGY

mass consumption of consumer durables: the consumption society	individualized consumption: 'yuppie'-culture
modernism	postmodernism
totality/structural reform	specificity/adaptation
socialization	individualization the 'spectacle' society

Source: Swyngedouw (1986)

[26]

D. Harvey

Flexible accumulation

Table 2.10   The losses in world stock markets, October 1987

Country	Per cent change from 1987 high point of share values
Australia	-29
Austria	-6
Belgium	-16
Canada	-25
Denmark	-11
France	-25
West Germany	-17
Hong Kong	-16
Ireland	-25
Italy	-23
Japan	-15
Malaysia	-29
Mexico	-30
Netherlands	-24
New Zealand	-22
Norway	-25
Singapore	-28
South Africa	-18
Spain	-12
Sweden	-15
Switzerland	-20
UK	-23
USA	-26

Source: *Financial Times*, 24 October 1987

[27]

G. Morgan

From Bureaucracies to Networks:
The Emergence of New Organizational Forms

Most of us are familiar with the bureaucratic organization that is specified in almost every detail and run in a tightly controlled way by the executive at the top. Many government organizations with their rigid departmental divisions and clearly defined roles and rules, mobilized through a hierarchical chain of command, provide obvious examples.

While this kind of organization once dominated many aspects of society, most bureaucracies are in the process of being reshaped along with the changing demands and challenges of the world around them. Sometimes the changes are quite marginal. Many organizations often resist fundamental change—because people, for one reason or another, wish to cling to a hierarchical model. But in some cases, significant transformations in organization can be achieved. The following pages explore some

of these changes, and how the bureaucratic approach to management is being challenged and replaced by newer forms of organization that are much more like networks than hierarchical structures. Conceptually, the range of organizational forms to be discussed can be represented by a continuum ranging from the rigid bureaucracy on the one hand (model 1) to the loosely coupled network, or organic form of organization (model 6), on the other. The aim of the discussion is twofold:

(a) to illustrate how a bureaucracy can, in principle, begin to transform itself over time from one form of organization into another (but probably not all the way from model 1 to models 5 and 6); and

(b) to contrast the principles that underpin organizations at different ends of the continuum.

EXHIBIT 27.1

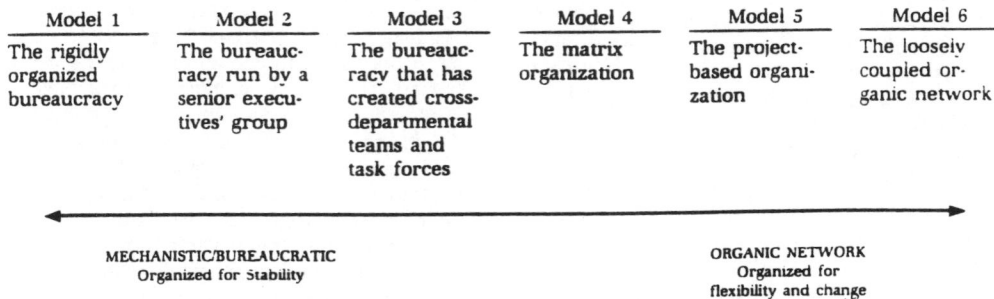

Model 1	Model 2	Model 3	Model 4	Model 5	Model 6
The rigidly organized bureaucracy	The bureaucracy run by a senior executives' group	The bureaucracy that has created cross-departmental teams and task forces	The matrix organization	The project-based organization	The loosely coupled organic network

MECHANISTIC/BUREAUCRATIC
Organized for stability

ORGANIC NETWORK
Organized for
flexibility and change

64

The purpose of the discussion is to provide a series of images and general principles against which you can identify the organizations with which you are familiar. A visual illustration of each model is presented in Exhibit 27.2.

Model 1

This is Weber's classical bureaucracy described in the opening paragraph (and in Resource 22). It represents the traditional organizational pyramid under the strict control of the chief executive. The organization has tried to codify all important operational principles, and is run in accordance with those principles. Meetings are viewed as a waste of time, and are rarely necessary, because almost every contingency is well understood: The organization is operating in an ultrastable environment.

Model 2

This organization is finding that the environment is generating novel problems, issues, and concerns on an ongoing basis. It is impossible to codify all appropriate responses. The chief executive has thus decided to create a "management team," comprising himself and the heads of principal departments, which meets on a weekly basis. This team makes all policy decisions, and settles the problems that cannot be handled through the organization's normal routines. Each department head exercises clearly defined authority in relation to his or her area of influence. Managerial styles vary from department to department, being shaped by the personality of the department head and the kind of task being performed. Some departments are highly authoritarian; others are more participative.

Model 3

This organization has found that the senior management team cannot handle all the issues that require an interdepartmental perspective, and has created a number of project teams and task forces involving staff at lower levels of the organization. The departmental structure and sense of organizational hierarchy, however, are very strong. The members of the teams and task forces tend to see their primary loyalty as being to their department head rather than to the team to which they belong. They realize that promotion is largely a departmental affair. They sit in team meetings as representatives of their department. They tend to give the "departmental line" on issues, and report back to their departmental head on what happens. When real problems arise, they are thus usually "delegated upward" for resolution by the senior management team. Team leaders feel that they have relatively little power, and find it difficult to develop commitment and momentum in relation to the activities that they're charged with managing. The organization *looks* as if it is moving toward a "matrix" or project-team structure, but in reality it operates like a loosely structured bureaucratic organization where information is passed up the hierarchy, and decisions down.

Model 4

This organization has decided to organize itself in a matrix form. Its special character rests in the fact that it has decided to give more or less equal priority to functional departments such as finance, administration, marketing, sales, production and R&D, and to various business or product areas. Thus people working in the various product or business teams that cut across the functional areas have to work with two perspectives in mind: functional and end product. This dual focus, under ideal conditions, allows the various operating teams to combine functional skills and resources with an orientation driven by the key tasks and challenges from the organization's environment—such as those relating to the need to fine-tune products for specific market segments or the needs of specific geographic areas.

EXHIBIT 27.2 Schematic illustrations of the six models

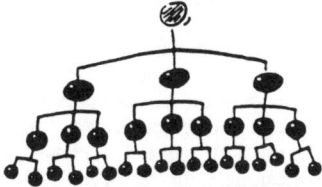

Model 1: The Rigid Bureaucracy

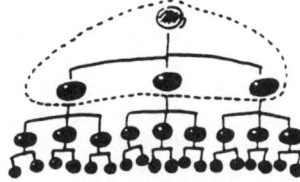

Model 2: The Bureaucracy with a senior "management" team.

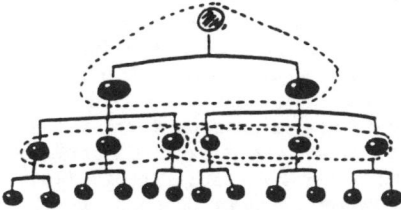

Model 3: The Bureaucracy with Project Teams and Task Forces.

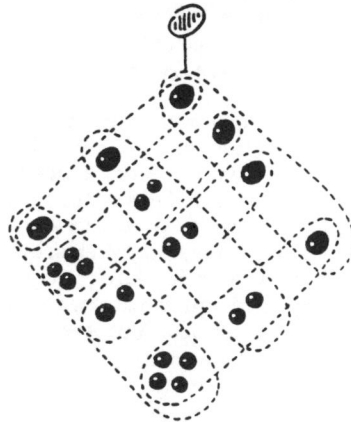

Model 4: The Matrix Organization

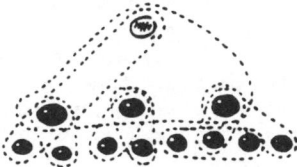

Model 5: The Project Organization

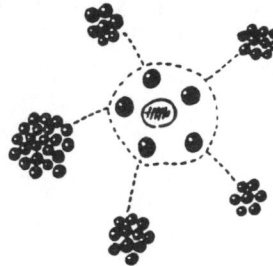

Model 6: The Loosely-coupled Organic Network

Model 5

This organization has decided to tackle most of its core activities through project teams. Notionally, there may be functional departments—but they only play a supporting role. Key specialist belong to teams, and make their main contributions through their team. The organization recognizes that its future lies in the dynamism and innovativeness of these teams, and tries to give them a free rein within the parameters and values that senior managers have used to define the strategic direction of the organization. The organization is much more like a network of interaction than a bureaucratic structure. The teams are powerful, exciting, and dynamic entities. Coordination is informal. There is frequent cross-fertilization of ideas, and a regular exchange of information, especially between team leaders and the senior management group. Much effort is devoted to creating shared appreciations and understandings of the nature and identity of the organization and its mission, but always within a context that encourages a learning-oriented approach. The organization is constantly trying to find and create the new initiatives, ideas, systems, and processes that will contribute to its success.

Model 6

This organization has decided to become, and stay, a loosely coupled network. Rather than employ large numbers of people, it has decided to operate in a subcontracting mode. It has a small core of staff who set a strategic direction and provide the operational support necessary to sustain the network, but it contracts other individuals and organizations to perform key operational activities. Its network at any given time operationalizes the "ideas" that the central group wishes to develop. For example, the organization may be in the fashion industry. It has created a name and image—"it's label"— but contracts out market surveys, product design, production, distribution, and so on. In the public eye, the firm has a clear identity. But in reality, it is a network of firms held together by the product of the day. It changes from month to month as different ideas and products come on line, and as the core organization experiments with different partners. The firm is really a system of firms—an open-ended system of ideas and activities, rather than an entity with a clear structure and definable boundary.

Models 1 through 6 are really different "species" of organizations. A firm beginning as model 1 may over time evolve into model 2, 3, perhaps even 4. And if it is prepared to engage in a major "revolution," it may develop the features of models 5 and 6. But in reality, the transformation process from one end of the continuum to the other is extremely difficult to make, and the required change is more than structural—it is cultural and political as well. The culture and politics of many organizations constrain the degree of change and transformation in which they can successfully engage, even though such change may be highly desirable for meeting the challenges and demands of the wider environment.

[28]

PUBLIC SERVICE AND THE FUTURE:
REFORMING BRITAIN'S BUREAUCRACIES
The Rt. Hon. William Waldegrave M.P.

I

CONSTITUTIONS: MONTICELLO AND THE OLD MANOR HOUSE

The owl of Minerva flies at dusk. When times are gloomy, people start writing clever new constitutions. Thank goodness, Britain's institutions have a low centre of gravity. They are not easily pushed over by the chattering classes. But it is time for those who want to preserve the British way of doing things to fight back. Let us remember one basic fact. There are only two constitutions (putting aside for a moment the admirable Icelanders) which have so far stood any significant test of time: the American, and the British. The others, though we wish them well, have so far only bobbed along on the following tide of a few decades of unparalleled prosperity. They are as yet untested by real challenge.

The American constitution is like a fine house of the age when it was written. The proportions and balance are near perfect. The rooms are adaptable to a large variety of uses unimagined by the architects. The house has mellowed and softened a little: but its strength is what it always was. The only weakness is perhaps that it is a little difficult to add to the design without spoiling it: but one should never underestimate it.

Britain's constitution is an older building. The shadow of a Norman arch here; a medieval foundation on solid rock down below; a Tudor hall there; some fine Georgian rooms and a somewhat overdone Victorian wing; some twentieth century modernisation, still looked at with suspicion but undeniably useful. The result can be seen in a hundred villages up and down the land - homes that have grown as if organically from the soil, and are the most desirable places in which to live in the world.

There is no question that such a rock-founded, slowly built, steadily improved constitution has served us, and is serving us, far better than anything anybody could sit down and design from scratch. But it needs constant attention. It is immensely adaptable - that is why it has survived - but the adaptations do not happen by themselves.

By far the oldest parts of the constitution are in fact its best features. There is a constitutional Darwinian principle at work which makes the shared survival for over a millennium of law, monarchy, and church not so accidental as the ignorant may believe. They work; they work better than the alternatives; they will continue. The savagery of the attack on members of the Royal Family for no reason other than the exploitation of the pain of an unhappy marriage has not affected our need for, and allegiance to, the Queen and her rightful heir one whit. In the end, it will be shown that it was those who tried to exercise their huge power for destruction so thoughtlessly and irresponsibly who over-reached themselves: their hubris will find its nemesis. It always does.

As happens often (ask any teacher in a school with a 1960s wing), it is the much newer bits of the edifice which need some work, and some new construction. We have not yet got the relationship between State and the citizen right in the provision and control of public services. The huge growth of these services, and the full extension of the franchise, are the great twentieth century constitutional innovations. If we do not get this crucial area into proper balance, great damage can be done to the State, which can lose its prestige by entangling itself in tasks for which it is ill-fitted, and to the citizen, who trusts the State to help him, and should not be disappointed.

After the Second World War a feeble, left-leaning consensus was established, when it appeared that there was no option for Conservatives other than to compete to be allowed to manage a public sector on the basis of plans mostly constructed by Labour. It was to be 'Tory men and Whig measures' all over again. This consensus was, however, deeply incompatible with underlying Conservative beliefs. Our trust in the 'little platoons', our knowledge, in the Prime Minister's fine phrase, of the need for 'an ear for history and an eye for place'[1], our suspicion of the compulsory application of ephemeral theory to people's individual lives, made us uneasy bedfellows for the enthusiasts for central planning and big government. The liaison could not last. It did not last. The Conservative nation stood up and shook itself free. And the result, to the astonishment of the pessimists, worked electorally beyond all expectations.

Not only have Conservative policies been endorsed at four successive elections but, on a whole range of issues (including all the key aspects of economic policy), neither the Labour nor the Liberal Democrat Party now advocates a reversion to the old position. Both grudgingly recognise that their long-held beliefs on income tax, for example, were not only unpopular amongst voters, but counter-productive in revenue raising terms as well. Labour has had to accept that the size of the state sector, although still too large, has been irreversibly reduced, both in housing and in the industrial and commercial sector. Even Labour's incestuous relationship with the trade unions will not lead them to advocate a return to the anarchic employment laws of the late 1970s.

As John Smith's speech at Bournemouth on 7th February this year finally proves, Labour have effectively thrown in the intellectual towel: they will attempt to compete for power on terms laid down by Conservatives [2]. In the long-term, it will leave them with no purpose, idealism, or future. In the short-term, it will make them sharp competitors with the Liberal Democrats for second place.

The intellectual revolution which underlay these changes goes back much further than is often recognised - above all to the crucial work by Tim Raison, David Howell, Geoffrey Howe, Geoffrey Rippon, Enoch Powell and others largely published by the CPC in the late 1960s. The practical implementation started, and then faltered, under Ted Heath. But no one can take the credit from Margaret Thatcher: it was her Government's reforms which fundamentally reshaped the nature and parameters of political debate in this country - not only in the short term, but for the foreseeable future.

An Uncompleted Revolution

There is, however, one crucial area in which the 'Thatcherite revolution' - to use a convenient, if imprecise, phrase - failed to have a decisive effect: large parts of the public services were left essentially unreformed. The reasons for this uncharacteristic lack of radicalism could be analysed at length. It would, for example, be naive to underestimate the political difficulties that are associated with even the most modest public service reforms. And very useful steps, such as the establishment of the Audit Commission and the Efficiency Unit in Whitehall, were taken. Nevertheless, it is surprising that, after ten years of radical Conservative government, our first truly fundamental health and education reforms were only beginning to move from theory into practice right at the end of the eighties.

Under John Major's leadership, however, the reform of our public services - and not solely health and education - has increased in momentum. The radicalism of these reforms has gone largely unnoticed: only a few of the more perceptive political commentators have seen their true significance [3]. Taken together, however, the reforms represent the emergence of a new, coherent, and extremely effective doctrine of the rôle of the public sector and its relationship to the citizen. In political terms, they incidentally represent an ambitious attempt to carry the political battle closer to the heartland of our opponents' traditional territory - to the public service issues which, electorally, Labour have always regarded as their trump card, and the issues of local and individual empowerment where the Liberals have, from time to time, sought to pitch their tents.

The early indications are that our opponents recognise the necessity to cede ground to us on these issues, even at the cost of dramatic shifts in their previous positions. The process was started, appropriately enough, by the present Labour Leader. In May 1991, in a speech to the Royal Institute of Public Administration, John Smith (then the Shadow Chancellor) indicated that Labour would no longer oppose the establishment of 'Next Steps' agencies - perhaps the key element in the Government's programme of civil service reform. Similarly, since the election, Labour have largely abandoned their previously forthright opposition to the creation of both Grant-Maintained (GM) schools and NHS Trusts [4]. Indeed, in a recent article, John Willman - the former general secretary of the Fabian Society - wrote that, far from being reversed, the principles of our NHS reforms should be applied throughout the public services [5].

What the effect on the morale of Labour activists who campaigned so vigorously behind, for example, Robin Cook's quite different health service policy at the election, will ultimately be is not for me to analyse. The important point is this. The centre-left's acceptance of our reforms is helping to build a remarkable new consensus on public service issues, but this time on a basis which largely derives from the Conservative Party (with valuable contributions from the old Social Democratic Party), and with which fundamental Conservative values and principles can be entirely comfortable - unlike the left-leaning consensus of the post-war years. For example, the Next Steps programme represents - in the view of one leading constitutional expert - the most fundamental and far-reaching reform of the Civil Service for 140 years [6]. It is not now a matter of Party controversy. Equally, the implementation of the Citizen's Charter in general, and market-testing in particular, are now matters of political argument and competition in terms of detail and of claims to greater competence in their administration [7] - just as once many Tories used to say that our claim to govern rested on greater competence in managing the post-war welfare state. There is still, however, a perception that we have not done enough to explain the coherence of our various reforms. I am, for example, conscious of Howard Davies' criticism that we have been reluctant to set out our overall approach [8]. I think the time is now ripe to attempt this, and I am grateful to the CPC for giving me this opportunity to do so.

II
THE NEED FOR REFORM

The problems that our reforms address were a product of the times in which the services in question were either created or extended - that is, the period shortly after the Second World War, when the belief in central planning was at its height. Such planning may have worked in wartime, when there was a single overriding national objective. We can now see, however, that it provided a poor model upon which to organise and deliver public services which should respond to people's individual needs.

The post-war Labour Government combined socialist theory with this alleged experience of wartime success and sought to control the 'commanding heights' of the economy by means of a top-down command structure. The same theory led them to exert an equally tight grip over the organisation and delivery of public services. Indeed, the structure of public services was virtually indistinguishable from that of the newly nationalised industries: public services were, quite inappropriately, given near monopolistic status and asked to fulfil the rôles of purchaser, provider and regulator of services at one and the same time. The contemporary view was that such a structure offered efficiency, via economies of scale and central planning which would end unnecessary duplication of provision; accountability, via upwards reporting to Parliament; and fairness, via rational processes of central resource allocation.

Today, with the benefit of both hindsight and modern management techniques, we can see that such attractions were illusory. Central planning and resource allocation were far *less* efficient than the pluralism of the market place, and soon became insensitive and remote; accountability only upwards and not directly to the user became more and more theoretical; 'fairness' became levelling down. Above all, the absence of either choice, the key to true accountability, or competition, the generator of quality and value, removed the dynamism and responsiveness necessary to drive big organisations. Saddled with their Forties-style structures, the public services all too often let standards slip and costs soar.

By a process that was, in retrospect, inevitable, it turned out that we had designed public services where the interests of the providers systematically outweighed those of the users, and which, driven only by the natural tendency of all provider organisations to claim that they can only do better with more money, contained an overwhelming dynamic

9

for increasing cost which was bound to end in conflict with reality. Many loyal public servants did good work within them - but the seeds of their own destruction were firmly embedded in the organisations' structures.

A New Vision of Public Service Provision

It took a long time for the underlying and all pervasive disquiet about the performance of the old-style public sector to translate itself into a serious programme of reform. Both the Labour and Conservative Parties should be willing to accept their share of the blame for this sorry state of affairs. Both, however, have long experienced apparently intractable difficulties in addressing the issue of public service reform. The Conservative Party, conscious that it had, initially, been seen as only lukewarm in its support of the NHS and the welfare state, has been understandably wary of proposing reforms that could be presented as attacks on the necessity of such public provision. The Labour Party, meanwhile, has been hamstrung by the closeness of its connections with the public sector trade unions. Moreover, it may be that, as Professor John Stewart has argued, the Left 'rested too long in the belief that because public services were needed, there was no need to consider criticism of the way in which they were delivered'[9].

A number of pressures, however, forced the issue finally to the top of the agenda. First, there was the increasing gap between available resources and the demands of the provider organisations - made most acutely manifest in health, but also elsewhere.

Second, the burst of high economic growth in the middle and late 1980s had a dramatic effect both on people's living standards and their expectations. These were largely met by a private sector able to deploy powerful new technologies of information and new theories of management - but not, however, by the public services. The gap between the performance of the two sectors - and the expectations that people had of them - needed to be narrowed.

Third, the increasingly apparent success of private enterprise tempted many people to believe in simplistic black and white distinctions between the attributes of the public and private sectors. In some respects, this view may have been self-fulfilling, by eroding morale amongst those working in the public sector, but it did at least increase the interest in transferring new management systems to the public sector from the private that would help public servants reach their full potential.

Fourth, the long and successful series of privatisations led to a growing belief that the best way of improving the quality of public services was simply to transfer them into private hands. This view was - of course - simplistic. The distinction between public and private ownership is only part of the story: private monopoly is not inherently any more efficient or responsive than public (though it may be easier to bring to an end). It is the distinction between monopoly and competition which is crucial. It was the challenge of introducing competition and choice into the public sector which was being missed.

Some of the language used in support of further privatisations may, ironically, have had the effect of making the extension of competition into the public services even more difficult than would otherwise have been the case. We did not find the right language to avoid the bogus accusations that if we were interested in competition we must only be interested in a few winners; or that if we wanted sharper comparisons of cost we were only interested in money. To us, it seemed obvious that, now as always, levelling *up* was better than levelling *down*, and that if you really care about helping those who need help, waste is criminal. We did not focus our language where, in reality, the focus of our concern is - on the user of the service - until the Citizen's Charter began to turn the national debate in the right direction before and after the election of 1992.

The Citizen's Charter: Outputs not Inputs

The almost exclusive emphasis on how much is, or could be, spent on a particular service compounded the problems caused by the traditional reluctance of the two main Parties - for their own, very different reasons - to advocate meaningful public service reforms. As a result, the political debate on these important issues has become peculiarly sterile. As Danny Finkelstein, of the Social Market Foundation, has observed, we have been reduced to a situation in which expenditure is used as an index of compassion [10]. It has to be said that Ministers can hardly lay all the blame at the feet of their Labour counterparts. For far too long, politicians on the Right - both in Britain and abroad - have regarded an increase in their Department's spending as an unqualified success, or an essential stepping-stone to greater things. Many have succumbed to the temptation to think solely in terms of inputs - at the expense of outputs, by which effectiveness would more sensibly be measured. It is not what you spend on a service that matters, but what you manage to buy.

As soon as you reassert the primacy of outputs, you begin to revolutionise the ways in which public services are organised and

11

delivered. You may perhaps also generate a more healthy and intelligent debate about the issues involved. Expenditure should no longer be seen as the only 'index of compassion'. The quality of spending should be analysed every bit as closely as its quantity - and never again should the electorate be presented with a false choice between low rates of taxation and high standards of service. What is needed is a third way, which manages to end the apparent paradox of people saying that they would pay more for better services but consistently voting against the tax-raising parties which promise to provide them. In reality, people feel that they are already paying enough towards the provision of public services. They believe, however, that they are entitled to more output from their input.

The situation is much the same elsewhere in Europe and in the United States. In those countries, as in Britain, more people are making demands upon the public services, and their expectations of quality are continuously on the increase. On the other hand, however, the number of taxpayers is static or falling and - inevitably in the current economic climate, but not just in the current economic climate - government expenditure needs to be tightly controlled. In these circumstances, there is an acute need to get what two influential American writers - David Osborne and Ted Gaebler - have described as 'more bang from the buck'.

Just as the United Kingdom set the pace on privatisation in the 1980s, so we are blazing a trail on public service reform in the 1990s. We are far from alone. Other countries have been working with us - sometimes following, sometimes leading. New Zealand has adapted some of our civil service reforms to meet its own requirements - and has gone further in some respects on health. Sweden, Norway and Finland have shown a strong interest in our health service reforms. France has published its own version of the Citizen's Charter and, in the United States, Osborne and Gaebler's book *Reinventing Government* [11] has taken Washington by storm and become one of President Clinton's themes. In Britain, however, we got there first - and in many respects we have gone much further: we are implementing at a national level many of the town and city level initiatives which *Reinventing Government* describes. Indeed, it is now fair to say that, following the introduction of the Citizen's Charter, Britain now has the most comprehensive public service reform programme of which I am aware.

III
THE HIERARCHY OF CHOICE

The materials out of which we are building the necessary new structure of public service consist of five key concepts. The first is the separation of the purchaser of a public service from the provider of that service, a doctrine first introduced to Government in 1971 by the late Lord Rothschild in relation to the procurement of applied research by Government Departments [12]; second and third are privatisation and the Next Steps programme, both developed by Lady Thatcher in the 1980s. The fourth is the extension of competition by market testing, and the fifth the introduction of the Citizen's Charter - both added by John Major. All of these fit with a coherent strategy for achieving better the proper purposes of a modern public sector. These concepts can be deployed in a hierarchy to test, first, whether the public sector should be involved in a function and, if it should, to show how public provision can be organised in such a way as to achieve fairness and accountability without losing creativity, responsiveness and sharpness in the avoidance of waste.

Reappraising the Rôle of Government

The first step in the hierarchy should involve nothing less than a fundamental reappraisal of the rôle of government itself. We should establish what the government really needs to do - and make sure that it does it and does no more. If we can identify functions that government no longer needs to discharge, we need to end its involvement. The implementation of this policy has helped to bring about a radical reduction in the size of the state sector. In 1979, as Stephen Dorrell recently reminded us [13], the Government was an oil producer, a car maker and a steel manufacturer - rôles for which it was clearly unsuited. In subsequent years, we have managed to reduce the state sector to a smaller - and much more sensible - size.

Our policy has been driven simply by a combination of scepticism and experience: a healthy scepticism about the capabilities of politicians and civil servants as managers, and a wealth of experience about the benefits of transferring businesses from the public to the private sector. We have learnt that where there are monopolies or oligopolies, instead of attempting to run industries, we can control them to the necessary degree much more effectively while restricting ourselves to their arm's-length regulation. This both avoids mixing up industrial investment with public spending decisions, and it also generates better management and frees Whitehall from the deadly embrace of privileged industrial lobbyists masquerading as 'sponsor' Departments. Even so, as Stephen Dorrell has pointed out, the public sector is still surprisingly large - even after almost fourteen years of Conservative Government. In addition to industries and services such as British Coal and British Rail, central government owns over £100 billion worth of tangible assets- and local government more than another £200 billion. This reminds us of the scale of the public sector which remains.

Much of it, of course, *should* remain. There are disciplined services such as the armed forces and police, which must always answer directly to the Crown. There are policy functions which are the essence of Government, such as financial, economic and foreign and security policy. There are social functions, such as the provision of health care, education and support for those who are in need, to which modern Conservatives judge there must be equal access for all at a satisfactory level.

There is a range of functions derived from the setting of sensible boundaries to the free market in land use planning, environmental control and consumer protection. There are some functions where the timescale of investment or the 'free rider' problem make it uneconomic for the market to provide goods which most people agree are needed, like science and some patronage of the arts. There is an always unquiet frontier between public and private in the area of support for industry and trade to match the alleged state interventions of trading rivals.

There is no doubt that the most radical of campaigners for minimal government must accept that a substantial public sector goes with modern democracy. That is why, after privatising all we should, we must have practical methods for preventing the remaining public sector reinfecting itself with the old ills of inefficiency, insensitivity, and waste - a disease that American writer Jonathan Rauch has dubbed 'demosclerosis' [14]. So we take the next steps in the hierarchy of choice, and introduce *competition* into the public sector, made real by the separation of the purchaser from the provider, by asking the immensely productive question: 'granted that we need to ensure this provision, *do we, the public sector, need to do the providing ourselves?*' From pursuing this question relentlessly comes the necessary injection of competition into the supply of goods and services by the public sector.

14

An Unprecedented Injection of Competition into the Public Sector

It is noticeable, however, that since 1979 we have had a rather mixed - and, on the whole, not particularly distinguished - record on the promotion of competition within the public sector in central government. Central government has often failed to practise what it has preached to others. For example, while we have encouraged local authorities to evolve from providers into enablers, and required them by law to put certain services out to tender, we have singularly failed to follow that example at the centre.

Our unwillingness to subject central government services to competition is all the more surprising given the evident success of compulsory competitive tendering (CCT) in both Labour and Conservative-controlled local authorities. They have found that CCT has helped to improve the efficiency and the effectiveness of a wide range of local authority services: indeed, the benefits have not been confined solely to the services that have actually been tendered [15]. These gains have, moreover, been experienced regardless of whether the work has been retained in-house or won by external contractors [16].

The success of CCT has been acknowledged by commentators at both ends of the British political spectrum. It is easy to confound poor Mo Mowlam, my shadow, with extensive quotations from left-of-centre observers and Labour local government leaders who have welcomed the application of competition to the provision of public services in this way [17]. Even *The Guardian* has criticised Labour's continuing opposition to CCT as 'a historical hang-up: a totem to please the unions' [18].

So the next stage is to introduce the customer/contractor, competitive tendering system to much of the work that is still done, and will continue to be done, by - or on behalf of - central government. The scope for progress is enormous: as a recent article in the *Financial Times* rightly observed, 'compared with local government, Whitehall is still in the competitive tendering stone age' [19]. In each of the last few years, central government work worth a mere £25 million has been tested against the market. In November, I was able to announce that, by September 1993, the value of our market testing programme should increase to around £1.5 billion - a fifty-fold rise. Even this, however, is not - in my opinion - anything like enough. With Government spending now measured in tens - indeed, in hundreds - of billions of pounds, the potential for further market testing, and further possible savings, is only too clear.

As with competitive tendering in local government however, the early stages of our market testing campaign have been the subject of vociferous criticism from the public sector trade unions. A number of wholly unconvincing arguments have been deployed, with equivalent lack of success, in an attempt to prolong the

15

monopolistic provision of public services. It has been suggested, for example, by one trade union leader that market testing, far from saving money, 'is costing the taxpayer a fortune' [20]. Wrong: there are, of course, certain costs associated with market testing that would not be incurred if competition did not take place. Those costs are, however, dwarfed by the savings that can be made through the market testing process. On past experience, it would not be unreasonable to hope for savings averaging around 25 per cent - even where the work is not actually contracted out, but continues to be performed by in-house providers. A second criticism is that the cards are stacked against the existing public sector providers. Wrong again: an in-house team actually starts with two large advantages over an external provider. First, it usually has no need to make the sort of profit for which a commercial organisation would be looking. Second, it will have invaluable experience of what the purchaser wants - and what the customers need. In these circumstances, public sector providers should have no cause for complaint about the fairness of the competition that they are being asked to face. A final desperate ploy is to allege that the European Acquired Rights Directive will stop the policy: it will not, any more than it has stopped the tens of thousands of private sector transfers of undertakings since 1977 when it was passed. All this is simply the usual noise you get, when a major new policy begins to affect powerful vested interests.

There is - I believe - little public support for the trade unions' campaign against market testing. Most people recognise that market testing is doing no more than applying to the public sector the sort of disciplines with which the private sector has always had to live. Indeed, less criticism is likely to come from the fact that market testing is taking place than from the fact that its introduction has been so long delayed.

People are not, I suspect, really interested in the identity of the provider of a service, but in the efficiency and effectiveness with which it is actually provided. Indeed, it is noticeable that, both here and overseas, even those on the Left are abandoning their long-held belief that public services should be provided only by public sector workers. In Britain, for example, Anna Coote - a research fellow at the Institute for Public Policy Research - has argued that, although the State should remain responsible for welfare provision, 'this need not imply that it must always be the provider' [21]. Similarly, in the United States, Mario Cuomo - the Democrat governor of New York - has recognised that: 'It is not the government's obligation to provide services, but to see that they are provided' [22].

16

Extending the Purchaser/Provider Split

The introduction of competition into public provision cannot, however, properly be done without one key organisational reform, namely the separation of purchaser from provider in the public sector. Those whose duty it is to spend public money on behalf of the citizen to buy public services must be quite free of pressure to provide work for whatever provider bureaucracy may happen historically to exist. They must get out into as wide a market as they can find (and help to create) - public and private - to buy on behalf of those they represent - sick people, children in school, people who want their dustbins emptied, people who want public transport. The bugbear of old-style public provision was the confusion of these two rôles, and the capture of the purchaser - the proxy for the citizen - by the self-interested provider. Only if the purchaser can compare competitive bids - competitive in quality and costs - from real alternative suppliers will he have a chance of escaping provider capture. Instead, there will be clear and healthy separation of responsibilities between government - which will act as the purchaser of services - and public and private contractors, who will be responsible for their actual provision.

In this way, the purchaser/provider split, most fully developed in the NHS, will gradually come to characterise the public services as a whole. As John Willman has written, this separation of responsibilities has three virtuous consequences [23]. First, it ends potential conflicts of interests and allows the purchaser - health authority, council, local education authority or whatever - to become the advocate of the consumer, rather than the defender of the producer. Second, it gives public purchasers a means of access to private sector resources and expertise; and, third, it forces both sides to define the nature of the service and the standards of quality which are to be provided.

The system of management by contract is introducing specific and enforceable standards of outputs into the public services - often for the first time. It is also, as Stephen Dorrell has said, helping to redefine the phrase 'mixed economy' [24]. In future, the distinction between public and private provision will dwindle in significance; what will really matter is that managers should have the freedom to choose between a number of competing service providers. That, I believe, will greatly increase both the efficiency and the effectiveness of public services, right across the board: it may also, I believe, do something to diminish and blur ancient English class distinctions embedded in a perceived difference between those who use 'private' or 'public' services.

17

The purchaser/provider division is an immensely powerful force for good in that it releases government to fight for the citizen, and frees it from having management as its main focus. It also forces government to be clear and open about what it requires from providers in the service contract it agrees with them. This is a gain for accountability and openness (I will return to this point) but above all it puts the public service back on the high moral ground, where the 'public service ethic' becomes again what it should be in the public mind - namely, an expression of the highest ideal of service on behalf of the common good, and not, as has sometimes seemed too much the case in the past, a self-interested doctrine, defensive of inadequate standards of provision.

Many providers will be in the private sector. Many others, however, will remain in the ownership of the public sector. Here too, however, management by contract and the purchaser/provider split is just as powerful. The principal mechanism for separating out these functions in the central government sector has been the Next Steps agency, described in the following section.

'Agencification': Improving Accountability

It was, I believe, Winston Churchill who said that short words were the best words - but that *old* short words were even better still. On that basis, 'agencification' fails on both counts. In this case, however, a long, new-fangled and essentially unattractive word hides a concept that is simplicity itself.

The process of agencification involves the separation of the Civil Service into a number of smaller, increasingly specialised units known as Next Steps agencies, which operate at arm's length from Whitehall. Each agency is set a number of specific performance targets, or outputs, in a service contract called a 'framework agreement'. The most suitable man or woman is recruited for the job of its chief executive - usually through open competition (which, in itself, is unusual by past civil service standards). They are then given the freedom to get on with the job - and rewarded according to their results.

The Next Steps system, introduced in the late 1980s, has already proved its worth - for both service users and providers alike. Managers have been freed from unnecessary Whitehall regulations and controls and, as a result, users have benefited from services that are more closely tailored to their individual needs. As Colin Hughes, of *The Independent*, has written: 'The devolution of executive responsibility means that decisions are being taken much closer to the customer'. Agencies, he added, 'represent, in fact, a real transfer of power away from central

18

government departments to staff further along the line' [25]. In this, they are part of the Government's campaign to devolve decision-taking nearer to users. NHS Trusts and Grant-Maintained schools show the extent to which we have been willing to reorder the organisation of service delivery in this way - devolving power down, closer to patients and parents, rather than up, towards Westminster and Whitehall.

The benefits of agencification are perhaps best demonstrated by the turn-around in the performance of two organisations which, in the past, seemed determined to drag the public services into disrepute. In years gone by, the delays that people experienced in obtaining passports and in booking driving tests appeared to demonstrate that public sector efficiency was something of a lost cause. Now, however, after only a few years of Next Steps status, both the Passport Agency and the DVLA have greatly improved their performance. The time taken to process passport application forms has been cut from an average of three and a half weeks to just seven days, and the average wait for driving tests has been more than halved. Indeed, the most recent figures show that agencies are meeting, or exceeding, three-quarters of the targets that have been set for their economy, efficiency and effectiveness [26].

A number of independent observers have now recognised the true radicalism of the Next Steps programme. Vernon Bogdanor has described the reforms as 'the most radical the Civil Service has seen since the Northcote-Trevelyan Report of 1853' [27]. Similarly, in Peter Hennessy's view, they represent 'the most profound change to the Civil Service this century'; their introduction was, he added, 'a long-delayed recognition that the nature of state provision had changed. Government departments before the Next Steps programme were essentially 1830s technology' [28]. What we must address next is the way in which, while modernising the technology, we can ensure that what was good in the old is protected. Two broad issues dominate: accountability, and the ethos of public service.

Accountability, the Citizen's Charter and the Spirit of Public Service

A smaller public sector, managed by open service agreement, with purchasers spending the citizen's money on the citizen's behalf, seeking and finding value for money, responsiveness to the user, innovation, and quality by means of competitive bids; fostering variety and plurality of suppliers; guarding against the old diseases of provider capture and top-down arrogance: this is how to deliver the true ideals of public service while avoiding the dangers we ran into in the forty years after the war.

19

But all these are means towards the end - revitalised public service. By bringing forward the Citizen's Charter, John Major put right into the forefront what we - and I think most people - mean by the true spirit of public service we are re-establishing. What the Citizen's Charter expresses - carried through into the individual Charters tailored to each service - are the standards which we should expect and the ideals which we should cherish in our public service.

First, we want to make a reality of the all-too-often theoretical concepts of accountability in the public service. The old myth of personal Ministerial responsibility for every action undertaken by each government Department was, in Herbert Morrison's words, 'The Minister is responsible for every stamp stuck on an envelope'; or, as Nye Bevan more colourfully had it, 'If a bed pan is dropped, the Minister will hear of it'. As Sir Robin Butler (the Head of the Home Civil Service) has said, this was not only a myth - it was a dangerous myth. In reality, no Minister can check the stamps and the bedpans. And if the Minister is responsible in theory, but not practice, who is actually responsible for the action in question? [29]. What we have done is to make clear the distinction between responsibility, which can be delegated, and accountability, which remains firmly with the Minister. The Minister is properly accountable for the policies he settles, and the service his Department purchases or for which it contracts; those who have agreed to provide services are quite properly responsible for their provision. Thus, far from impairing accountability, I believe that the purchaser/ provider separation, executive agencies, and management by contract have helped to make a reality of it. Clear targets are set, performance is monitored and published, and success or failure is rewarded or penalised. Agencies, in Sir Robin's view, represent 'a lastingly beneficial change in the management of the Civil Service' [30]. I would not dissent from that judgement; but the principle of clear devolution of management against agreed targets underlies the whole reform, from the NHS to the management of defence research.

Thus the first principle of the Charter is that explicit standards of service should not only be set, but published and then prominently displayed at the point of delivery. The purpose of this is to empower users, by providing them with the information they need to bring pressure to bear on the provider directly, or by bringing pressure to bear on the responsible purchaser, or, where possible, by introducing real choice so that the user can change to a better service. John Patten has spoken eloquently about this in his CPC lecture of 4th February 1993 [31].

Where possible, choice should be in the hands of the citizens directly, using the improved information, as it is in the hands of higher education students or, within the inevitable limits, of parents choosing schools. In health, the most sophisticated of the internal market systems increasingly makes the general practitioner the proxy purchaser for the citizen - and capitation payments to the GP make it worthwhile for him to seek to please his patients. The system genuinely devolves power right down. In other cases, where there is unavoidable monopoly, the customer's preference can only be set out in published targets after full consultation with him - and failure or success in delivery must be rewarded by the establishment of performance pay in the provider organisation and, where appropriate, effective pressure from above from the Government Department and below by independent and open inspectorates, with lay representation, which will together stand proxy for the citizen by means of establishing and then monitoring the service contract with the supplier. Rail franchising will be a useful new mechanism for bringing agreed standards directly to bear on providers of train services on behalf of passengers: it is likely to be far more effective than the old system of confrontational Departmental negotiation with a monolithic British Rail Board.

What is in every case essential is to provide full, accurate and up-to-date information about how public services are run, what they cost, and how well they perform. This policy of openness - which represents the second of the six Charter principles - is also an important part of our general campaign to bring about greater openness in government. Indeed, the proposed publication of league tables of local authority performance has been welcomed by the National Consumer Council as heralding a 'sea-change' in the amount of information that will be available to local taxpayers [32]. But it is probably the Parent's Charter that has provided the best example of the importance of, and the support for, publishing information of this kind - as well as the most characteristic protests from a defensive producer lobby. It is worth pausing for a moment to consider this example of a producer lobby in full cry: much more of it will be heard before we have succeeded in our reforms. Even those teaching unions which were prepared to tolerate the publication of educational 'outputs' appeared to believe that the figures needed expert adjustment before parents could be trusted to understand them: as *The Independent* observed, the providers of a service often have a vested interest in mystifying their clients [33]. Indeed, according to John Marks' Social Market Foundation booklet *Standards in Schools*, when ILEA first published comparisons of the exam results of its secondary schools, it issued only data that it had adjusted on socio- economic grounds. The authority 'gave no indication at all of the original results, of how much they had been adjusted, or even of how, in detail, these adjustments had been made' [34]. Yet, as John Marks added, the pupils concerned had to make their way in life on the basis of the grades that they had actually

21

achieved - not those that, after socio-economic adjustment, the experts
might want to attribute to them.

Having failed to convince the public that the release of unadjusted
data would be misleading to parents, the producer interest proceeded to
suggest that the exam league tables did nothing other than reinforce the
views that people already held. In the words of the NASUWT, 'they [the
league tables] do nothing but confirm the obvious, that children in the
gin-and-tonic belt do better than those from poorer areas' [35]. It is
difficult to know whether this remark is more objectionable for being so
patronising or for being so demonstrably wrong. It is offensive, as the
Prime Minister has said, to lower the expectations that you have of pupils
simply because of the background from which they come [36]. It is also
absurd to assume that there is a direct link between the affluence of a
particular area and the academic achievements of local schools. On the
contrary, there is a wealth of evidence to show that a school's performance is *not* directly dependent on any of a number of widely canvassed
variables, from the socio-economic background of its pupils to the level
of funding from the local education authority [37]. But even if it *was*,
would it not be vital for parents and Government to know it, and take the
necessary action? The argument for obfuscation beggars belief.

This leads me to the third of the six principles upon which the
Citizen's Charter is based: value for money. The Charter is not, and
should not become, an excuse for ratcheting up the level of expenditure
on the public services. It is, in Whitehall-speak, a 'resource neutral'
campaign: its aim is to ensure that we get better value from the enormous
amounts that are already devoted to the provision of public services.
Market testing and competitive tendering have already demonstrated
how we can improve the effectiveness of services without increasing
their cost. Education is only one of the services to have shown that we
are right to put the emphasis on outputs, as opposed to inputs, in this way.
Local government is another; the Community Charge, for all its faults,
did at least confirm, more clearly than ever before, that many of the
authorities with the worst services were also those setting the highest
local taxes in the country. The belief that there is an automatic link
between resources and results is rapidly losing support - not least on the
Left of the political spectrum [38].

The fourth principle of the Citizen's Charter emphasises the importance of regular and systematic consultation with service users. We want
to ensure that, wherever possible, their views about services, and their
priorities for improving them, are taken into account in the decision-
making process. There are, of course, limits to the scope of such a policy.
The level of social security benefits, for example, must remain the

responsibility of Government Ministers; claimants should, however, be consulted about the ways in which benefits can be paid. In some cases, this could actually help to reduce the cost of service provision. There would, for example, be little point in spending thousands of pounds on the refurbishment of certain benefit offices if, after consulting your customers, you found that they would actually prefer to have their claims processed by post or over the telephone instead.

The fifth Charter principle is accessibility. This is more than a requirement that name badges should be worn by all those who deal directly with the public - though the improvement that produces in the relationship between, for example, nurse and patient should not be underestimated. That, however, is only one symbol of the ideal of service we want to reinforce within the public sector. We want to lay to rest for ever the tendency for public services to be organised for the convenience of the providers - and anonymity is a powerful signal of provider remoteness and defensiveness. In practical terms, the renewed care for the user might mean the introduction of flexible opening hours, for example, or telephone inquiry points that direct callers quickly to someone who can be of help.

The sixth principle of the Charter concerns redress: we believe that, if things do go wrong, the service user should at least be entitled to a sincere apology or a satisfactory explanation. There are, however, cases when an apology or explanation is not enough. In some services, we have introduced new compensation schemes. In others, we are intending to introduce well-publicised and readily available complaints procedures. We are also, of course, looking to change attitudes so that complaints are not seen in a purely defensive light; they can frequently help to identify problems that need to be addressed. The fault will often be found to lie not with individual employees, but in the system which they help to operate.

The Public Service of the Future

These reforms will leave us with a smaller, less centralised and more customer-conscious public service. By the end of this decade, or at the start of the next, both at the centre and in local government, it is likely to consist of a comparatively small core, and a series of devolved delivery organisations - many of which will be as large as, or larger than, the core. At the centre, Next Steps agencies and the contracting out of services will generate this outcome; local government is already well on the way. As Howard Davies has said, our reforms, and the new management systems that they will introduce, amount to 'a revolution leaving few parts of the public sector untouched' [39].

23

IV
THE IDEALS OF PUBLIC SERVICE

The single uniting theme running through everything we are doing is the revitalisation of a public service of which we are proud, whether we work in it or use it. What I hope has become crystal clear is that there is no conflict between the reforms, replacing as they do the decayed structures of the old monolithic public service with the plurality of competing suppliers and accountable purchasers of the new. On the contrary, it was the overlaying of the ideals of service by the dreary growth of bureaucratism that depressed so many in the public sector itself.

The Charter challenges the public servant, certainly: but it challenges him or her to live up to the very ideals which in most cases made the public service his or her chosen career in the first place: the ideal of using the power of public money, without waste, on behalf of those who need it most (and not in defence of bureaucracy); the ideal of accounting, by spreading far and wide detailed information on the quality of what is provided, to citizens who are not just told to take it or leave it; the ideal of treating the public as the master, not the subject. These are the practical ideals, grafted on to unshaken, unchanging, unchallenged uncorruptibility and political impartiality, which can be liberated by the reforms. They are the new ethos of public service; but in reality they are simply the old ethos brought up to date, and writ large.

NOTES AND REFERENCES

1   'Conservatism in the 1990s: Our Common Purpose', speech to a meeting at the Carlton Club, 3rd February 1993 (to be published by the Carlton Club in association with the CPC).

2   Speech to the Labour Local Government Conference, Bournemouth, 7th February 1993.

3   Peter Riddell, writing in *The Times*, pointed out that: 'Most government initiatives are taken more seriously than they deserve. The Citizen's Charter has suffered the reverse fate' (26th November 1992). Similarly, following an announcement on market testing, *The Guardian* leader column stated that: 'For once Ministers yesterday understated the revolution that the Government has begun. William Waldegrave rightly referred to the hard slog that will be needed to change attitudes. But the infusion of competition into the monopoly which has gripped British public services is one of the biggest cultural changes in public administration since the Second World War' (2nd June 1992).

4   *The Times*, 26th September 1992.

5   *Fabian Review*, November 1992.

24

6   Vernon Bogdanor, writing in *The Guardian* (29th August 1992), described the Next Steps reforms as 'the most radical the Civil Service has seen since the Northcote-Trevelyan Report of 1853'.

7   For example, the Labour MP for York - Hugh Bayley - has frequently claimed that the city's Labour-controlled council was the first to introduce a form of Citizen's Charter.

8   *Fighting Leviathan.* Social Market Foundation, 1992, p.22.

9   *Meeting Needs in the 1990s,* IPPR/TUC, 1990, p.7.

10   *Fighting Leviathan,* p.8.

11   David Osborne and Ted Gaebler, *Reinventing Government,* 1992. It is noticeable that Labour have been so lacking in ideas that after the Democrats' victory in the US Presidential election - but not, you will note, before - Messrs Brown and Blair flew to America to find ideas that could be imported for the 'Clintonisation' of Labour. What they found would have surprised them: at the heart of the Democrats' domestic agenda was the very kind of public service reforms that they had been so keen to criticise in the run-up to last year's British general election. Indeed, Ted Gaebler - a major influence on President Clinton - has spoken particularly warmly of the Citizen's Charter, which Labour were initially so eager to dismiss.

12   *A Framework for Government Research and Development,* (Cmnd. 4814, November 1971).

13   'Redefining the Mixed Economy', speech to the Centre for Policy Studies, 23rd November 1992.

14   *National Journal,* 9th May 1992, p.1998.

15   See *Competitive Tendering for Local Authority Services,* Department of the Environment, February 1991.

16   As a *Financial Times* leader column stated: 'Contracting out local government services ... is now well established and widely accepted as a discipline for ensuring value for money. In most cases, the contract is awarded to the council workforce ... But even where the work stays in-house, the threat of losing it is persuasive in improving the efficiency and quality of services' (26th November 1992).

17   For example, Professor John Stewart - Head of the School of Public Policy at Birmingham University - has written that, 'because of CCT, local authorities and health authorities, in many cases for the first time, have had to specify what they wanted to see happen. It has been a laborious task. What is truly remarkable is that they had not done so: the councillors had organised services, but they had never specified what those services had to achieve' (*Meeting Needs in the 1990s,* p.8).

18   *The Guardian,* leader column, 2nd June 1992.

19   *Financial Times,* 26th November 1992.

25

20   Bill Brett, IPMS general secretary, quoted in *The Daily Telegraph*,
      26th November 1992.

21   *Meeting Needs in the 1990s*, p.22.

22   *The Sunday Times*, 10th January 1993.

23   See note 5 above.

24   See note 13 above.

25   *The Independent*, 2nd April 1992.

26   See *The Next Steps Agencies: Review 1992*, (Cm. 2111, December 1992).

27   *The Guardian*, 29th August 1992.

28   *FDA News*, January 1993.

29   *Public Service in a Changing World*, The Frank Stacey Memorial Lecture by
      Sir Robin Butler, 7th September 1992.

30   See note 29 above.

31   'The Home Front in a New Century', CPC lecture, 4th February 1993 (to be
      published shortly).

32   *The Independent*, 18th December 1992.

33   *The Independent*, leader column, 19th November 1992.

34   *Standards in Schools*, Social Market Foundation, 1991, p.40.

35   Quoted in the leader column of *The Independent*, 19th November 1992.

36   *The Next Phase of Conservatism*, Speech to the Adam Smith Institute, 16th
      June 1992 (subsequently published by the CPC).

37   *Standards in Schools*, p.14.

38   See, for example, Margaret Hodge, *Quality, Equality, Democracy*, Fabian
      Pamphlet, September 1991, p.2

39   *The Times*, 7th July 1992.

26

**Andersen Consulting has contributed to the
publication of this pamphlet
in the interest of
supporting public information and debate.**

[29]

Economics of Public Services

Public Choice and Public Sector Management

P. M. Jackson

Public sector economics and public sector management should complement one another more than they do. Public sector economists have not fully appreciated the issues of concern to public sector management, whilst those in public sector management have not had sufficient access to public sector economics. This article seeks to explore the relevance of public sector economics for public sector management. It emphasizes the importance of a strong theoretical foundation for management practice and the importance of the public choice perspective for an understanding of public policy and public sector decision-making.

The Role of Public Sector Economics

Public sector economics plays an important role in providing a firm foundation for the general principles of public sector management. Indeed, at a more general level it is economics which establishes most of the principles of general management. Public sector economics contributes to the design of fiscal institutions and the formulation of public policies. It lies at the centroid of the Trinity: theory, institutions and policy. This is insufficiently appreciated, especially by those who practise management. Lest this be regarded as an act of academic imperialism by economists, the balance should be immediately redressed by pointing out that economists have paid insufficient attention to the problems and issues of management. The theme of this essay is that a stronger symbiotic relationship between those involved in public sector economics and those concerned with the issues of public sector management would produce the synergy necessary to advance the quest for improved efficiency and effectiveness in the public sector.

By its very nature this essay must be idiosyncratic. Space does not allow consideration of the complete corpus of public sector economics. Many aspects must be ignored, in particular issues relating to macroeconomics will not play a significant part in the argument which follows. The essay also reflects the author's somewhat strident views on the state of management 'theory' with which many will disagree.

Academic research is by definition devoted to replacing legends with truth, and replacing myth with reality. However, there are some areas where myths are particularly tenacious and no more so than when it comes to 'management'.

The combination of theory with facts ensures that management by slogan is minimized. Whilst theory without facts might be regarded as sterile, practice without theory is usually blind. In this age of 'guruspeak', and the encapsulation of complex ideas into memorable and elegant epigrams, theory reminds us that quotable aphorisms do not have the general applicability often supposed and that such statements are, therefore, of little value to managers who face real problems. What public sector economics attempts to do is to get behind the slogans and aphorisms and to set out the essential elements which are necessary to design public sector organizations, establish management techniques, and formulate policy.

If management is about achieving an organization's objectives through efficient, effective, and morally acceptable processes, then economics has much to contribute to the formulation of management principles. Economists, however, have not been effective publicists of their trade. Moreover, some economists have failed to appreciate the limitations of their approach, especially when it comes to the implementation of their policy plans.

Too often, economists erect unnecessary barriers by publishing their research in an arcane and impenetrable language. They often write for other economists, forgetting that there are important issues, including public sector management, which might benefit from their approach to problem identification and problem-solving. Thus the social value of economics is reduced.

The methodology of economics is powerful in showing those areas where markets are a superior form of social organization and where

Professor P. M. Jackson is Director of the Public Sector Economics Research Centre at the University of Leicester.

there is, therefore, no role for government. Where, however, there is a role for government, public sector economics is useful in helping to identify that role and in defining the more important policy instruments which are both necessary and sufficient in achieving specific policy objectives. Public sector economics, however, is at its weakest when it is asked how public policies might be performed effectively. 'How' questions involve issues of implementation and the organizing principles of management, and, with few exceptions (for example Simon, Lindblom, Leibenstein and Williamson), economists have remained silent on these issues.

If the economist is to present useful prescriptions for social policy, and for public sector management, then more attention must be given to evolving methods that can be used not only to guide what the government's role might be, but also how that role might be played. More attention needs to be given to figuring out what rules might meet the ends of 'rough justice' and also 'rough efficiency', rather than complaining that the world is not organized in a way that will enable the implementation of the rigourous first-best rules of evaluation. If the economist is not sufficiently careful in matching up theory with context then the result can be a bias towards getting the right answer to the wrong question.

The Role of the Economist

What is the role of the public sector economist when it comes to discussing matters of public sector management? What are the areas of competence over which the economist might have some command, and, therefore, something useful to say? To answer these questions it is useful to have some idea of the subject matter of public sector economics.

Public sector economics brings together two branches of economics. These are *welfare economics*, with its emphasis upon efficiency theorems and issues of distributive justice, and *public finance* which is concerned with matters of tax incidence and the effects of taxation upon private sector behaviour. Welfare economics and public finance in combination provide powerful analytical tools when it comes to designing fiscal institutions and public policies.

Starting from the welfare economics proposition that market failure brings about a departure from the Pareto efficient resource allocations (i.e. essentially prices equal to marginal costs) of the first-best world of perfect competition, economists have designed policies to bring about improvements in efficiency. Thus, the catalogue of policies would include pollution taxes to correct the market failures of externalities; subsidies to ensure that certain public goods are adequately consumed; optimal taxes that minimize the deadweight losses or distortions caused by tax systems; and regulations which bring individual self-interest serving behaviour closer to collective objectives of the common good.

More recently, public sector economics has employed the analysis of welfare economics to understand public sector behaviour, rather than focusing solely upon private sector market failure. Critics of an active role for government, such as libertarians, have long pointed out that public sector failure is just as important as market failure. The public sector is essentially a monopolist which is divorced from the discipline of competitive market forces. This state of affairs can be a source of inefficiency within the public sector, unless fiscal institutions are designed in such a way that adequate systems of accountability and control ensure that the organizations of the public sector are managed efficiently.

Designing appropriate incentive and information structures for the management of public sector institutions is a new and challenging role for the economist. This is where the public sector economist and those involved in public sector management should work closely together. The application of the intellectual infrastructure of welfare economics to the problems of internal organization has in recent years brought forth a number of significant innovations which have changed the structure and the character of the public sector (see, for example, Leibenstein, 1987).

Efficient allocation of resources requires decisions to be well informed. The information revolution that has taken place in the public sector can be found in Whitehall, in local government and in the NHS. Whilst the revolution is in no sense complete, public sector decision-makers are now better informed than ever before. The Financial and Management Information (FMI) system introduced into central government departments during the 1980s enhances the abilities of public sector managers to allocate resources within the bureaucracy in a more efficient way. Not only is the probability of waste reduced, but there is a greater chance of scarce resources being allocated to priority areas which are more clearly articulated within the FMI system of devolved cost centres.

Similar management accounting/information systems have been introduced into local government and the National Health Service (NHS). The local management initiative for schools (LMS), through decentralized budgeting, aims to improve the allocation of educational resources; the health service reforms, which involve decentralized budgets for hospitals and general practitioners, seeks efficiency improvements in the allocation of resources for health care. Other services, such as police, fire and personal social services, are currently in the process of implementing financial management and value-for-money auditing systems.

Attempts are being made to introduce the benefits of the market mechanism into public sector decision-making. Thus, the notion of an 'internal market' is evolving for the NHS, and the contracting out of certain local authority services seeks to obtain the efficiency benefits of competitive tendering. Together with these policies to privatize more and more of the public sector, there is the need to design appropriate regulatory mechanisms to ensure that the interests of the clients of public sector services are being served.

These developments complement the more traditional approaches of public sector economists who designed such techniques as cost benefit analysis and policies based on marginal cost pricing. As the quest for improved efficiency advances, it is likely that greater use will be made of cost benefit and project appraisal techniques, and that the pricing of contracts will pay more attention to the pricing rules of economic analysis.

Pursuing Social Justice

Minimization of allocative and X-inefficiencies is only one string to the bow of the public sector economist. Economic analysis shows that it is possible to produce efficient market or pseudo-market allocations which are ethically unacceptable. Competitive markets are quite capable of producing efficient outcomes in which some individuals have insufficient resources to survive! The policy objectives of allocative and X-inefficiencies, therefore, need to be traded off against the objective of distributive justice. That trade-off needs to be identified and defined. How much efficiency is given up by pursuing an improvement in the distribution of welfare? The public sector economist is in a strong position to help articulate the dimensions of this policy problem. This is not to say that hard and fast guidelines, or measures of welfare gains compared to efficiency losses, are available. To suppose otherwise would be misleading. The economist is, however, in a strong position to force a number of issues into the decision frame such as, for example, to raise the question 'what are the distributive objectives of the policy?' Is the objective to pursue a utilitarian policy of the greatest good for the greatest number, or to maximize a weighted sum of each individual's welfare (if so which weights are to be used?) or is the objective to pursue a strategy of maximizing the welfare of the least well-off in society?

It should be immediately clear that simply by asking this series of questions the policy decision becomes both more complex and richer. Introduction of issues of distributive justice goes some way to counter the criticisms made by political scientists of the economist's rational model of decision-making. Of course economists have always recognized the importance of distributive justice and the efficiency/equity trade-off (Okun, 1975), and it was unfortunate that some political scientists, such as Self (1975), took the debate down a blind alley by failing to recognize that.

Political Economy

The role of the public sector economist in decision-making was usefully set out many years ago by Eckstein (1961, p.445): 'The economist must interpret the desires of the policy people whom he is serving and express them in analytical form as an objective function. He then seeks to maximize this function given the empirical relations in the economy and the institutional constraints that may be appropriate to the analysis. In this manner the economist can play the role of technician, of bringing technical equipment to bear upon policy problems with maximum effectiveness'. This statement is, however, subject to misinterpretation. It does not imply that the economist has a ready-made set of techniques which will automatically make decisions, thereby rendering decision-makers obsolete. The economist *qua* economist does not judge whether the objectives of the decision-maker are ethically acceptable. Rather, economic analysis helps the decision-maker to explore fully the implications of pursuing one set of policy objectives.

Some economists, such as Tinbergen (1956), minimize the role of the economist simply to that of providing data to the policy-maker. For example, the economist in his framework would determine the values of the instrumental variables required to hit a clearly specified set of policy targets. Experience has, however, shown that this approach is somewhat idealized. Policy targets are not sufficiently well defined and the economist has an important role to play in making them clearer. This can be done in the case of cost benefit analysis, for example, by varying the distributional weights in the objective function and thereby providing the decision-maker with information of the form, 'here is a menu of potential policy outcomes, choose from it'.

Serving up alternative menus or policy options is necessary, but not sufficient, for informed decision-making. There remains the issue of determining the criteria against which the policy options are to be ranked. Many economists have in the past shied away from that problem claiming that it is for others to come up with such criteria. As Schultze (1968) has pointed out such economists: 'serve only to rationalise what is being done and lose their potential as educators... [and] become "yes men" in the halls of political economy' (p.9).

If economists are to design efficient and effective policies, and if they are, as policy analysts, to assist in the evaluation of policies, then they require criteria founded in a logical framework. A minimum requirement is to be able to say whether or not a policy is acceptable on economic criteria. The changes that have taken place as part of the managerial revolution which has swept through the public sector over the past 10 years are superficially plausible as means of improving efficiency and enhancing performance. But have these changes been adequately designed? How should contracts be formulated; what principles should guide the choice of discount rate for cost benefit calculations; what choice of discount rate

16

for cost benefit calculations; what rules determine the costing of hospital specialities; how should the prices of public services be set; under what conditions will devolved budgeting improve efficiency? These and many more questions remain. The introduction of so many of the new methods of public sector management and decision-making are based on faith. Policy managers need policy analysts to provide them with the firm foundations of why they should do X rather than Y. For the public sector economist as policy analyst these firm foundations are to be found in economic theory.

The role of public sector economics is, therefore, to inform the debate about public policy and the design of fiscal institutions. This does not, however, just mean informing politicians, civil servants and public sector managers. It also includes the wider policy community, for example pressure groups. Public sector economics should help to raise the level of public debate which is essential for the operation of an effective democracy. James Maddison in *The Federalist Papers* (1790) recognized this when he argued that social statistics were vital to inform social legislation, a point which is confirmed by modern advocates of social policy indicators (see MacRae 1976; and MacRae and Wilde, 1979).

In Praise of Theory

Nothing is quite so practical as a good theory (Lewin, 1945). Theory in the social sciences, especially economic theory, is frequently attacked by practitioners because its function is so often misunderstood. Others, especially those outside of the discipline of economics, wrongly believe that there is an oversupply of competing theories and paradigms in economics. Economists suffer the butt of jokes such as, 'if you lay all of the economists in the world end to end you will never reach a conclusion'. The amount of disagreement amongst research economists, as compared to political economy commentators and scribblers, is much less than is often supposed. Indeed, that economists do not agree on policy prescriptions is a reflection of the complexity and uncertainty of the world in which we live and for which policy has to be designed. Policy rules are contingent upon a reality which unfolds with uncertainty. Other disciplines, even the hard sciences, have their controversies: what is the origin of the universe; what is the cause of cancer? Recently, forensic evidence provided to a court of law has been found wanting.

Do public policies promote the general welfare of citizens? Will policy X have an impact upon the welfare of a specific group of citizens? To answer these questions, and more, practitioners frequently adopt a set of policy indicators (for example educational attainment; mortality; economic indicators). But how robust are these indicators; what the causal relations between these statistics and individual well-being (welfare)? What

implicit social values do these indicators reflect? What is the set of causal links between public policies and individuals' welfare? These questions are often regarded as troublesome, by politicians and some career policy advisers whose interests lie in providing a quick fix to social problems. It is the role of theory to challenge and to question the adequacy of existing practice and to improve the quality of the arguments in the policy debate. Far from being impractical, theory is extremely practical and an appreciation of how to use theory in formulating policy arguments will lead to improved practice.

Economic theory's contribution to policy analysis and design is to provide an understanding of events and phenomena within the domain of public policy. Understanding and explanation of events is not, however, synonymous with prediction. Even when phenomena (consider, for example, earthquakes) are understood it is not always possible to predict when the phenomenon will next occur. Recently, chaos theory has taught that in complex systems small perturbations can build up to large events. Whilst an understanding of the processes and dynamics of a system is of importance for purposes of control and manipulation, it does not follow that the precise timing of events can be predicted. Instead, statements of future events must be made in probabilistic terms, i.e. if conditions X and Y prevail then there is a probability that Z will occur. An assessment of the probabilities informs managers and decision-makers. Thus, forecasts of economic and social events must not be regarded as having probabilities of unity assigned to them (i.e. complete certainty) instead the forecaster needs to inform the decision-maker of the probability (confidence) of the forecast being correct. The further a socioeconomic event lies into the future, the lower is the probability that its forecast will be accurate.

A useful theory must encompass the event which is to be explained: the event(s) should not contradict the theory. Furthermore, useful theories are those which are communicable to others. If an event can be incorporated into a theory then it means that the event (phenomenon) is understood. If it cannot be so incorporated then the event is not understood and the theory is not as general as might have been supposed. Policy interventions require an understanding of the events which lie in the policy domain: they require an understanding of the causal processes which gave rise to the event. Such understanding can only be the result of systematic research within a wider conceptual framework. This reduces the chances of futile and misdirected interventions which often result in catastrophic outcomes. There is nothing quite so practical as a good theory. Sound theory is a line of first defence against madmen and cranks. Policy managers need policy analysts and policy analysts need sound theory.

Theorists start from axioms, i.e. generally

agreed upon basic statements of the real world. A theorist seeks to find out if those propositions which are presented as policy statements are deducible from a set of these elementary axioms. Put another way - what does the world actually have to look like for the proposition to be true? It is at this point that the assumptions upon which a theory is predicated come in. Different assumptions in conjunction with the basic axioms produce different propositions.

The basic axioms used by the economist are that decision-makers are rational and that individuals are the best judge of their own welfare. This means nothing other than that either preference orderings are well defined, or that individuals have reasons for the choices that they make. Rationality also means that the choices which are made by individuals are logically consistent. Typical assumptions relate to whether or not the decision-maker is fully informed when making choices; whether decisions are made in a total system or a partial system at a single moment in time or inter-temporally; whether or not the future is known with certainty; and the extent to which market structures are perfectly competitive or monopolistic. To assume, as the public choice theorists do, that politicians and bureaucrats have preferences is an axiom. Making statements about the objective function of politicians and bureaucrats, i.e. that they are vote maximizers or budget maximizers, is to make assumptions. Different assumptions will generate different propositions (hypotheses) which might, if they are in a suitable form and if data are available, be tested (with a view to refutation) empirically. A theory provides a coherent framework within which the implications of different assumptions can be analysed.

The aim of theory is not to describe reality. It is to understand that reality. By necessity, abstraction from reality is required for understanding. Thus, the charge, often made by practitioners, that a theory is unreal is a weak criticism. Simon, Lindblom and Wildavsky have frequently taken economists to task for the strong form of rationality that they suppose economists to subscribe to. However, their alternative representation of rationality is a 'red herring'. Modern economic theory recognizes explicitly that rationality is bounded because the world is too complex and because the information requirements for decision-making over the complete choice set would make the whole exercise prohibitively costly. Of course, individuals statisfice because they do not have the wit to maximize. Such statements can be reformulated as an act of local maximization subject to the constraints of limited and costly means of computation. Individuals adopt routinized personal and organizational decision-making as long as these decisions produce acceptable (satisfactory) outcomes. However, individuals also engage in search behaviour: they look for new processes, systems and outcomes. There is

organizational learning and adaptation. The introduction of the FMI and systems of devolved resource allocation are attempts to generate more reliable information to expand the boundary of choice in the public sector. Search will continue as long as it is worthwhile to do so - provided the expected pay off exceeds search costs.

The axiom of methodological individualism frees the economist from making bizarre statements about collective decision-making. It asserts that individuals make decisions, not a mystical entity or a ghostly spirit of the collectivity. To assume otherwise takes the practitioner into the Hegelian mists where travellers end up lost forever to reason or science. The axiom of individual rationality does not imply a collective rationality. Indeed, one of the most powerful propositions which economists have to offer management theory is that of Arrow's impossibility theorem. Arrow demonstrated that starting from a reasonable set of statements about individual behaviour it is impossible to find a rule which will enable the aggregation of individual preferences into a collective preference that results in consistent collective choices. Arrow's analysis, along with that of Duncan Black's study of committee decision-making and Sen's general analysis of collective choice, forces managers, especially those in the public sector, to consider quite carefully how collective (committee) decisions should be made. What voting rules will produce allocative and ethically acceptable outcomes? (See Arrow, 1963; Black, 1958; and Sen, 1970.) These are issues which cannot be ignored, and theory, especially at a high level of abstraction, helps to clarify them.

The analysis of collective action using modern game theory, in addition to recognizing the aggregation problem outlined by Arrow, reveals that decisions which are rational from an individual's perspective often cease to be rational when considered in the context of collective interaction. There is a tyranny of small decisions which, when they are combined, produce adverse outcomes. This applies to market situations, as well as to bureaucratic decisions. The profit-maximizing behaviour of one factory owner which generates environmental pollution may be tolerable, but the collective outcome of many producers behaving in a similar way is not if it means destruction of the ozone layer. What is being described here is the familiar prisoner's dilemma problem (see Brown and Jackson, 1990, pp. 5-8). Again, theory at this level of abstraction is of practical importance. It throws into relief the need to consider carefully the circumstances under which individual behaviour should be regulated. This in turn forces questions about what form that regulation should take. The theory also challenges the libertarians who argue that institutions both in the public and the private sectors should be designed in such a way as to leave individuals free to make their own decisions.

Rights, Freedoms and Incentives

Public sector theorists cannot avoid abstract debates about individual's rights. Libertarians, such as Hayek, Friedman, or Nozick, constantly challenge the existence of the public sector on the grounds that public sector institutions and policy interventions infringe individual freedoms and liberties. Public sector managers should be familiar with the basis of such arguments.

Hayek and the radical subjectivists argue that it is insufficient to judge or evaluate policy, or indeed any event, solely in terms of outcomes or consequences. The means through which choices are made must also be evaluated - choice of an end is not the complete revelation of preference. When individuals choose a means they are expressing a preference. No-one would disagree that the evaluation of means is as important as the evaluation of outcomes. However, often Hayek *et al.* seem to argue that the means through which choices are made are more important. They evaluate social choice mechanisms with reference to the extent to which they are based on individual choices. If individual preferences are constrained or over-ridden, as in the case of regulated behaviour or bureaucratic decision-making, then the loss of individual freedom and liberty, which such means of decision-making entail, is regarded as being too great and alternative forms of social organization (especially *laissez-faire* markets) are sought.

Are the libertarians right to suggest that individual rights to freedom and liberty are of paramount importance? Most would agree that, wherever possible, it is best if individuals are given the freedom to determine their own destiny. That, however, is a right to a particular type of freedom or liberty, what Berlin (1958) called 'negative freedom', i.e. freedom from interference by others. However, there is another dimension to freedom which libertarians ignore and that is the right to 'positive freedom' - freedom to be able to do certain things: a right to have basic needs satisfied. A legitimate role for government, therefore, is to provide for positive freedom goods such as basic education and basic health. The decisions which remain are to determine the form in which that provision should be made, either by direct public provision or via the payment of income support and the level of provision.

Another dimension to positive freedom is that which is associated with citizenship rights. Such rights give individuals, as citizens, access to participate in the determination of the formation of laws. Some writers, such as de Tocqueville (1835), have argued that this is an essential part of human dignity (i.e. citizens direct themselves), and that such rights extend positive freedom. This love for the laws (what Montesquieu called *vertu*) is a public good - it is the basis of the civic humanist tradition of thought about republican rule.

Marshall (1964) set out to define citizenship rights in a comprehensive manner. Citizenship rights encompass civil rights (freedom of speech and equality before the law), political rights (universal suffrage) and social rights (guaranteed levels of health, education etc.). These rights move members of society towards an egalitarian social order. It is, however, an objective of libertarians to reduce these rights. Following Hayek, they argue that inequality is a requisite for economic development. Inequality is inevitable and acceptable. It generates the incentives required for progress through entrepreneurial actions.

Public policies have the potential to create incentive and disincentive effects. Theory, however, demonstrates that matters are seldom as clear cut as Hayekians would have us believe. It is insufficient to assert, as they do, that the extension of citizenship rights and positive freedoms reduce the potential for growth and development. these claims must be grounded in theory and that theory must be tested empirically.

Over the past 20 years public sector economists have done much to refine the analysis of the incentive effects of public policies. In particular, they have examined the impact of various forms of taxation upon the supply of hours of work, savings, investment and risk-taking. These magnitudes are important inputs to the process of economic growth and development. What this research agenda tends to conclude is that whilst taxes do distort private decision-making the disincentive effects are not as large as is often assumed. This means that improvements in welfare (income) distribution can be achieved without giving up too much economic efficiency or economic growth (see Atkinson and Stiglitz, 1980; and Brown and Jackson, 1990).

Are individuals always the best judge of their own welfare as methodological individualism asserts? Generally speaking, the answer is, yes they are. But individuals are not always adequately informed, nor do they have the technical skills to make decisions that will serve their best interests. Others have the competence and information to make decisions on their behalf. This is the 'principal-agent' relationship, in which the agent makes decisions on behalf of the principal and in the principal's interest. The doctor/patient and lawyer/client relationships are examples of principal and agent. For this relationship to be effective, the principal must 'trust' the agent. Trust is, however, a commodity which can be short in supply, so that once again there is a potential regulatory role for government to monitor and control some of the more significant principal-agent relationships.

Practical Theory

What insights do these examples of theoretical considerations provide for the practically minded public sector manager? Theory liberates us from slack and lazy thinking; from rhetoric and from aphorisms. It liberates us from those practitioners who, for their authority and legitimacy, appeal to 'judgement' gained from years of practical experience. Theory makes possible an orderly and coherent deepening of understanding. Without understanding, it is difficult to persuade others in the long term. The value of rhetoric only lasts as long as people can be fooled.

Theory imposes structure and pattern; it creates metaphors and *gestalts*. It helps us to order the facts of a complex reality: 'science is facts, just as houses are made of stone... but a pile of stones is not a house and a collection of facts is not necessarily science' (Poincare, 1903).

Theories, however, cannot account for or explain all phenomena. That which remains hidden from understanding constitutes the research agenda. Such understanding is not only hidden from the theorist, it is also hidden from those of practical affairs. Acknowledgement of our ignorance and acceptance of the complexity of the world would make for more humble and less extravagant policy. It would reduce the probability of creating in the future the great planning disasters of the past. This involves recognizing the boundary constraints of our theories, i.e. is the set of propositions true in all contexts and for all moments in time? Contingency theory forces us to recognise the probabilistic nature of the world in which policies are designed and implemented.

Public Choice and Bureaucratic Failure

The public choice perspective is now recognized as a distinct approach to the study of economic policy and public sector decision-making. Pioneered by the Nobel Prizewinning economist, James Buchanan, and his principal collaborator Gordon Tullock, public choice theory extends the standard welfare economics model of public sector economics and provides an economic analysis of politics, democracy and bureaucracy (see Mueller, 1989).

What is public choice theory? Buchanan's critique of the standard welfare economics approach to economic policy and discussions of the economic role of the state is that it uses theoretical constructs, such as a 'social welfare function', in an uncritical way. To say that policy-makers, when they are designing policies, aim to maximize a social welfare function is too abstract if the intention is to understand the policy-making process. Equally, arguments such as policy-makers are motivated to serve the 'public interest' are too vague. Public choice theorists seek to focus attention more narrowly on such questions as: whose interests are served by the policy, which interests dominate and why?

Rather than concentrating upon 'optimal policies', which by definition are those which maximize a social welfare function, subject to a number of restrictive contextual assumptions regarding the perfection of markets etc.,

Buchanan and his followers search for 'good decision rules'. This search for decision rules brings public sector economics closer to the interests of public sector management.

Buchanan argues that the welfare economics approach takes a naive view of the political process. It is straightforward to demonstrate why markets fail (see Brown and Jackson, 1990). This has been used to justify and legitimize government intervention, for example to correct externalities such as pollution, or to regulate monopolies. Such prescriptions are, however, made in the absence of any assumptions about the behaviour of politicians or bureaucrats. What Buchanan has done though the public choice framework is to demonstrate that there is not an *a priori* reason to suppose that governments will improve the allocative efficiency of markets through policy interventions. This is a powerful result which challenges much of the standard thinking about the desirability of public policy. If the efficiency losses of public sector interventions exceed the efficiency losses of market failure then why bother intervening?

Central to the public choice argument is the requirement that 'man' does not become a different species in the voting booth, or in a bureaucracy, or in a central bank compared to his behaviour in the market place. Individuals acting as politicians are assumed to behave in a way which will maximize their chances of election - this will influence the way in which they design policies. Bureaucrats are not administrative eunuchs, they have their own objective function which they seek to maximize (Niskanen, 1971; and Jackson, 1982), and central bankers do not blindly serve the objectives of monetary policy but instead have managerial interest (see Mayer, 1987).

Many political scientists object to the public choice approach to theorizing about political behaviour. Several reasons are given for this objection, especially that the assumptions are unrealistic. This does not, however, cut much ice. There are many different public choices each depending upon the initial assumptions used. The basic issue, however, is would, for example, a Marxist public choice theory come up with significantly different conclusions? What Buchanan *et al.* have done is to push open a door leaving a basic question to be answered: 'under what conditions will government policy interventions improve upon the allocative efficiency of the market?' It is this question which lies at the heart of the design of public sector institutions, and much of public sector management. Those who are not in sympathy with the public choice approach need to articulate their own framework, which will not only encompass that fundamental question, but which will also provide an answer to it.

If politics is the study of the resolution of the conflicts of interests of different pressure groups then a constitution must be found within which such resolutions can be achieved efficiently and effectively, such that each interest group will find it to their own long run advantage to accept the constitution's constraints. The search for a constitution, a set of decision rules and political constraints, is to be found in Buchanan's more recent work (Brennan and Buchanan, 1980).

When discussing the tax constituion for Leviathan, Brennan and Buchanan distinguish between the design of the fiscal constitution and the setting of tax rates within that constitution. The fiscal constitution is based upon the basic principles of taxation that a typical taxpayer would prefer, given the assumption that after the constitution has been set any government will seek to maximize tax revenues within the bounds set by the constitution. For Brennan and Buchanan, taxpayers will prefer narrow tax bases, rather than comprehensive bases, and progressive, rather than proportional, tax structures.

The public choice perspective and the attention given to the formulation of fiscal constitutions and decision rules has much to offer public sector management. A fiscal constitution could be extended to include the rules governing budget decision-making; the voting rules for choosing public policies that involve the preferences of future generations; and the organizational structure of central-local government relations. The economic analysis of bureaucracy, and its focus of attention upon non-market decision-making within hierarchies, is ripe for extension to incorporate the problems of designing internal markets and systems of performance measurement. 'Bureaucratic failure' is an expression of the fact that the internal organizational structure of public sector agencies, their incentive structures and their information systems, are inadequate to deliver public services efficiently and effectively. Poor performance and low value for money come about because of bureaucratic failures.

It would, however, be a false claim to suppose that public sector economics has an instant answer to these problems of bureaucratic failure. The current research agenda does, however, offer some hope that fresh insights will be provided for these problems. Attention is currently being given to the design of contracts; the design of internal incentive structures and the design of demand revelation systems (Laffont, 1988).

Conclusions

Public sector economics and public sector management share a common set of interests: the promotion of an efficient allocation of resources within the public sector, the minimization of bureaucratic failure, and the design of efficient and ethically acceptable fiscal institutions and policies.

Good management practice needs to be predicated upon sound theory, and public sector economics and public choice theory can provide public sector managers with the insights that will enable them to define their management problems more clearly.

To achieve the goal of improved public sector performance, the channels of communication between those who practice public sector management and those who study public sector economics need to be widened. A closer relationship between these two groups offers improvements in public sector efficiency and value for money.   ∎

References

Arrow, K. J. (1963), *Social Choice and Individual Values*. Yale University Press, New Haven.

Atkinson, A.B. and Stiglitz, J.E. (1980), *Lectures on Public Sector Economics*. McGraw Hill, London.

Berlin, I. (1958), *Two Concepts of Liberty*. Clarendon Press.

Black, D. (1958), *Theory of Committees and Elections*. Cambridge University Press, Cambridge.

Brennan, G. and Buchanan, J.M. (1980), *The Power to Tax: Analytical Foundations of a Fiscal Constitution*. Cambridge University Press, Cambridge.

Brown, C.V. and Jackson, P.M. (1990), *Public Sector Economics*, 4th Edition. Basil Blackwell, Oxford.

Eckstein, O. (1961), *Water Resource Development: The Economics of Project Evaluation*. Harvard University Press, Cambridge.

Jackson, P.M. (1982), *The Political Economy of Bureaucracy*. Philip Allen, Oxford.

Jackson, P.M. (1990), A survey of modern welfare economics. In J. Moroney: *Modern Economic Analysis*. Manchester University Press.

Laffont, J.J. (1988), *Fundamentals of Public Economics*. The MIT Press, London.

Leibenstein, H. (1987), *Inside the Firm: The Inefficiencies of Hierarchy*. Harvard University Press, Cambridge.

Lewin, K. (1945), The Research Centre for Group Dynamics at MIT. *Sociometry*, Vol. 8.

MacRae, D. (1976), *The Social Function of Social Science*. Yale University Press, New Haven.

MacRae, D. and J. Wilde (1979), *Policy Analysis for Policy Decisions*. Duxbury, North Scituate.

Marshall, T. H. (1964), *Class, Citizenship, and Social Development*. Doubleday, New York.

Mayer, T. (1987), The debate about monetarist policy. *Kredit and Kapital*, Vol. 20, pp. 281 - 302.

Mueller, D.C. (1989), *Public Choice*. Cambridge University Press, Cambridge.

Niskanen, W. (1971), *Bureaucracy and Representative Government*. Aldine-Atherton, Chicago.

Okun, A. (1975), *Equality and Efficiency*. Brookings Institution, Washington, D.C.

Poincare, J.H. (1903), *La Science et l'hypothese*. E. Flammarion, Paris.

Rawls, J. (1971), *A Theory of Justice*. Harvard University Press.

Schultze, C. (1968), *The Politics and Economics of Public Spending*. Brookings Institution, Washington, D.C.

Self, P. (1975), *Econocrats and the Policy Process*. Macmillan, London.

Sen, A.K. (1970), *Collective Choice and Social Welfare*. Oliver and Boyd, Edinburgh.

Tinbergen (1956), *Economic Policy: Principles and Design*. North Holland, Amsterdam.

de Tocqueville, A. (1835), *Democracy in America*. World Classics Edition, Oxford, 1965.

[30]

Michael Horsey | **Taking care of business: the public official as entrepreneur**

There is a feeling out there in the business community that most public servants are fat cats working within arcane systems incapable of producing results. The critics are many; the defenders few. "If only the public sector would organize itself and operate more like business," the argument goes, "many of the collective ills of the country would be resolved." While there may be some validity to the observation, the proponents of such a viewpoint are often pretty fat themselves and working with equally dated and quaint organizational infrastructure.

It is true that the public service working at its worst can be execrable. Process can dominate, with the result that there are no results at all. But business at its worst can plunge forward Rambo-like in pursuit of short-term and short-sighted goals. Battles are won and wars lost. It would seem that both the public and private sectors have been at their organizational and executional worst during these past few years of recession. However, it can be argued, private sector managers have been more successful in adjusting to the new realities.

The public sector, driven by its political leadership to tighten up and cinch its belt a few notches, has often moved in strange ways. Its managers have made decisions which appear to assume that once the unpleasantness of the recession was over, a return to the status quo was in order. Far too often government organization – denuded of bodies and stripped of various program elements – has a sickly look about it.

Of course, all is not sweetness and light in the private sector. One American commentator has suggested that "forced strategic planning" is what has been driving many businesses. As the recession took hold, and the basic uncompetitiveness of various business sectors was painfully revealed, there was a good deal of scrambling about to find answers. Advertising budgets were trimmed (perhaps to where they should have been in the first place but at the most inappropriate of times), middle management layers were stripped thin in the most arbitrary of fashions and all manner of bizarre moves taken to ensure survival. Forced it has been, but there is scant evidence of much true planning having taken place.

The author is deputy minister, Ministry of Tourism, Government of British Columbia.

CANADIAN PUBLIC ADMINISTRATION / ADMINISTRATION PUBLIQUE DU CANADA
VOLUME 29, NO. 4 (WINTER/HIVER 1986), PP. 681–685.

MICHAEL HORSEY

It turns out, as we are now only too fully aware, the recession masked very fundamental structural changes taking place in our economy. As Dr. Gordon Robertson, the highly respected former secretary to the federal cabinet has recently observed, "It is doubtful if there has been a time in our history when so many problems of major importance for the structure and character of business in Canada have thrust themselves upon us at one time."

The nature of the structural change is something that has been tackled by any number of futurists, economists and commentators. All sorts of theories about the future nature of the economy have been advanced in a cascade of popular books. Some of it, or course, is pure pap and simply provides a little "business psychiatry" for the depressed and disenchanted who seek solutions; solutions of any kind. Most of it centres on defining an appropriate role for business enterprise in an economy that is coming to rely more and more on the service sector. Interpreted variously as the development of an information society – wired together by computers and modems – or slick visions of a new age of manufacturing – where the essentially boring and repetitive process of making things becomes magically transformed under the influence of technology and human relations measures – advice and counsel is abundantly available. Insubstantial or not, there is plenty of debate raging in the private sector about the nature of business organization required for future success.

In the public sector it is quite another story. There are few witty or even superficially popular writings available. What does exist, voluminous and ponderous in nature, is long on rhetoric and short on solutions. The ills of public sector management are all too easily traced and documented. What other form of organization must comply to such rigid examination of its every move? For a sector that owns such a large chunk of the Gross National Product, there is surprisingly little real debate.

Business Week, Forbes, Fortune and our own *Financial Post* – to name just a few of the multitude – weekly hypothesize, intellectualize and report on activities within the private sector. Public sector comment is found in passing, or in cute little stories about how defence contractors have managed to charge government hundreds of dollars for screws which are otherwise readily available at your local hardware store for a few cents. Conversely, the public sector's activities are covered by earnest and sincere trade publications which, while doing the job, do not excite much passion outside their narrow audiences. Academia and management consulting professionals also produce material that addresses issues in the correct and proper manner which the disciplines behind those endeavours demand.

It is a pity that debate about public sector organization and activity does not abound in the business and general press. Without an abundance of spirited, easily understood pop material available many opportunities to explore creative solutions to problems are lost. It is relatively easy, fun even, to

THE PUBLIC OFFICIAL AS ENTREPRENEUR

find information about a proposed merger of major corporations in the most general of daily newspapers. Almost any manager who cares to, can follow every twist and turn of events in a hostile merger bid and so learn about tactics. The "shark repellent" manoeuvre (acquire a debt-ridden, over-priced company to dissuade an unwanted suitor) or the "scorched earth" ploy (start dismantling the object company thus rendering it valueless to the acquisitor) are as entertaining to read about as they are instructive. It is highly unusual to find anything intelligible written about the creation of new ministries or the consolidation of existing ones in any publication. As anyone who has experienced such ministerial activity will readily attest, there is a fair amount of pathos involved. More importantly, some of these unnoticed events have much greater impact on the economy than the most high profile of mergers.

So what can the public sector learn from all the sound and fury generated as the private sector regroups itself? Plenty, it would seem. The private sector is moving rapidly through a process which many observers feel will result in vastly different business organizations in a post-industrial future. As those organizations evolve, it will be vital that government make adjustments as well because, like it or not, the public sector will be braided firmly into the system. The private sector, if not already in large measure there, is moving toward increased flexibility and away from vertical hierarchies in organizing its affairs. The new economy of North America, with a heavy service sector influence, demands flexibility, featuring as it does so many small business units. Similarly, mega-business organizations, such as those found in the auto industry, are moving toward new and more nimble structures.

It is hardly a secret that the service sector in future will dominate the economy. Today, despite British Columbia's heavy reliance on its resource industries, about seven in ten workers draw a pay cheque from the service sector. During the past recession it has been the service sector that has seen employment growth and it is the service sector that will expand most dramatically through the end of the decade. With thousands of small business entrepreneurs, it has aptly been described as a "marketplace of midgets." Even the traditional industrial giant is changing significantly today. Industrial companies are busy "vertically disaggregating," as they say in the business schools. There is clear evidence that industrial corporations are more and more interested in forming coalitions to do what once might have been done by a single, vertically integrated business endeavour. In this circumstance, businesses rely on a network of companies to undertake manufacturing, marketing, distribution and other functions in a contractually bound coalition.

The network concept is tremendously appealing, not only to the private sector organization of the future but also to the public sector. Let's face it, the public sector is an unlikely candidate for further growth and, in fact, all signs point to some fairly aggressive "disaggregation" taking place. There

MICHAEL HORSEY

are two ways to view the inherent challenges of this situation. Public sector
managers can grumble about tight budgets and reduce service levels accordingly. Or they can critically analyze programs and help build networks
utilizing existing organizations to undertake various assignments that
previously may have been their sole responsibility. Better yet, they can take
a leadership role in making use of the immense resources of government to
develop creative solutions to assist in solving the vexations of living in such a
complex society. The willing partners are legion both within and outside
government. Inside, potential partners are all neatly lined up in divisions,
branches and departments. Outside, they are scattered in a vast array of
companies, associations and special interest organizations.

The disciplines required for an effective public servant in this environment are clearly entrepreneurial. The public sector manager must be a
"deal-maker," someone who wants to put something together in order to get
something done. The manager will have to have a solid understanding of
business structure and organization if he or she is to enter into any successful
business relationships with the increasingly flexible organizational structures encountered outside government. Similarly, that deal-maker mentality will have to dominate internal relationships in a fashion more reminiscent
of two developers trying to come to agreement on a project than two nation
states negotiating diplomatic exchanges. Contracts outlining roles, responsibilities and expected results should rule the day. Memoranda of understanding, frequently used inter- and intra-governmentally, should move over in
favour of more "deal-oriented" documentation.

Not only must public sector organization support managers so that they
can work in this entrepreneurial manner, but both managers and employees
must have a solid philosophical construct. Naturally, political leadership
will set an overall agenda based on its own set of philosophical principles.
But to the south of that, and somewhere north of specific and direct instruc-
tion to execute various elements of the political agenda, there is a real need
for some readily accessible guidelines. Decision-making for the public sector
manager will be easier if it can be directed by analysing problems and opportunities in the context of such a philosophical construct. It is better if
decisions can be made using quick reference points than having to jam bits
of paper up through a hierarchy before anything can happen.

It is not appropriate to detail the management structures which can allow
such flexibility. Different circumstances suggest different solutions. That is
a task which should flow logically from a strategic planning process. In the
British Columbia Ministry of Tourism two modest organizational models
have been developed to provide managers with deal-making capability. The
output, to date, has ranged from awful to exceptional.

Finally, any discussion of public servant as entrepreneur must deal with
the question of risk. In the private sector the formulas to determine risk are
reasonably well established. Certain financial criteria can be easily set.

THE PUBLIC OFFICIAL AS ENTREPRENEUR

Projects can be judged to have failed or succeeded based on these criteria. Often ultimate success or failure has somethng to do with what a friendly local banker feels about an individual, a project or where the economy is headed. Success is sweet; failure can mean considerable personal loss.

In the public sector a major component in any risk analysis relates to political considerations. The political process rightly sets the agenda and projects/policies must clearly conform to the dictates of that agenda. If, from time to time, the political criteria present a faster-moving target than a perfect world would produce, so be it. The public servant as entrepreneur will factor political risk into his or her activities and move forward. The public sector does not reward the success of its people as well as it should, but nor does it punish failure very well. However, risk must be identified and, more importantly, risk taken, if anything is to actually be done, if results are to be achieved. Otherwise, it will be said that public servants are fat cats working within arcane systems. And it will be true.

[31]

III COMPARATIVE OBSERVATIONS

ANALYSING INSTITUTIONAL CHANGE AND ADMINISTRATIVE TRANSFORMATION: A COMPARATIVE VIEW

THEO A. J. TOONEN

I INTRODUCTION

This contribution presents an effort to develop a public administration perspective on the ongoing process of institutional reform and transformation in Central and Eastern Europe. It is organized around three rather straightforward questions. The first refers to analytical issues. How should we study the subject at hand? We are dealing with a multi-dimensional and multi-level reform and transformation process. The Central and Eastern European experience has not yet generated any models and theories of its own which might drive the administrative analysis. The question is how one could arrive at a theoretically orientated perspective to explore adequately the ongoing, multifarious and turbulent administrative reform processes, without being unduly biased by 'western' presuppositions and preoccupations (section II).

The next question is: what may we learn from the developments? Which aspects of the administrative reform efforts merit attention from a comparative point of view, given the fact that the analyses so far, have been predominantly historical, economic and political in nature? What are striking features of the historical revolution in Central and Eastern Europe from the viewpoint of building a solid administrative system for guidance, evaluation and control in the public sector? Such a system, after all, is an indispensable cornerstone of the sustained development of the liberal market economies that serve as a guide for the ongoing reforms in Central and Eastern Europe (section III).

The observations in this paper refer predominantly to developments within the administrative systems of Poland, Hungary and the former Czechoslovakia as reflected in the country reports of the national experts represented in this volume. Empirical research and standardized data collection on the basis of an

Theo A. J. Toonen is Professor of Public Administration at the Rijksuniversiteit, Leiden, The Netherlands.

Public Administration Vol. 71 Spring/Summer 1993 (151–168)
© Basil Blackwell Ltd. 1993, 108 Cowley Road, Oxford OX4 1JF, UK and 238 Main Street, Cambridge, MA 02142, USA.

explicit public administration interest and a common theoretical framework are still rare. This analysis is part of an attempt to explore the topic of administrative reform in post-socialist countries and to formulate some issues and research questions from an administrative point of view. The third question is, therefore, whether we might be able to identify some needs, both in terms of research and of prescriptions for public sector reform that merit attention from a public administration perspective. Is there, on the basis of the material available, anything else that can be said other than the standard prescription that public sector management and training are still much needed in the aforesaid countries? (section IV)

II ASSESSING ADMINISTRATIVE REFORM IN POST-SOCIALIST COUNTRIES: ANALYTICAL PROBLEMS

Developments in Central and Eastern European countries are currently rather overwhelming and thus not easily categorized. The efforts to reform the administrative systems of the countries of the former Communist Bloc are dominated by an overall effort to 'privatize' state agencies, particularly in the industrial production sector. The current attention of scholars and researchers in the area of public administration is mainly focused on the question of how to 'reform' the respective administrative systems, which are mostly grouped together in one, undifferentiated category. A prescriptive bias dominates: how can we improve the system?

Rice (1992, p. 166) has presented an overview of what should be done to bring the public administrations of Eastern European countries into the post-socialist era. On the basis of several documents from Hungary, Poland, Romania and Bulgaria, he identifies five principles that are likely to guide Central and Eastern European societies in building their governments:

—the retreat from the discredited central government in favour of decentralization and privatization;
—the improvement of channels of communication between governments and their citizens in response to a demand for participation;
—the creation of a hospitable business environment and an adequate institutional infrastructure for a market economy;
—a concern for public welfare and social justice in terms of services and human rights;
—an efficient government administration at all levels within a setting of public review and internal and external accountability.

With this 'model' as the yardstick, Rice (1992, pp. 117–22) identifies a number of administrative needs and problems for public administration reform. To improve policy making, he primarily emphasizes the need to strengthen the capacity for economic projections and the development of strategies. The former central planning system was merely a bureaucratic device and not a system of

© Basil Blackwell Ltd. 1993.

forecasting in a market situation. Most basic statistical and other types of policy information are lacking or entirely missing.

Rice observes that the devolution of significant powers and responsibilities to sub-central governments has already advanced considerably, but that this radical shift also complicates the reform process in a number of ways. Questions about the desired central-local relationship have not been resolved, although formal pieces of legislation and local government reform offices have been established – Hungary and Poland in particular display strong activities in this field – but actual performance capacities at the local level are still far from clear. One of the problems is that, since the state enterprises formerly served as the main source of government revenue, a tax management and effective revenue-raising system, in the broadest sense, is largely absent.

Much in the same way, the various countries according to Rice (1992, p. 121) have so far largely ignored the need for civil service reform ' ... even though it is their civil servants who must implement planned reforms ... Governments have apparently not conceived of their employees as a bureaucracy-wide civil service'. They have yet to develop comprehensive reform strategies. He suggests that to this end central government change agents are necessary. Central government directorates should formulate and implement comprehensive action plans to overhaul the civil service by (1) transforming the bureaucratic culture and organizational structure, (2) introducing mechanisms to assure accountability, and (3) expanding training capacity.

Such prescriptions are not uncommon, but they also raise questions. In most Western European countries, the administrative modernization process over the past decade has taken the form of a rather incremental approach, but has seldom been a centrally steered innovation process (Hesse and Benz 1990; Dente and Kjellberg 1988). Available evidence seems to indicate that successful institutional development is usually best perceived as an evolutionary pragmatic political process using and blending the social and political forces and dynamics within the system.

Comprehensive plans have seldom resulted in the desired administrative reforms in Western administrations. Effective reform must largely come 'from within'. Former Eastern Germany is likely to remain the only example where the transition from 'socialist' to 'post-socialist' is being tried in a comprehensive, synoptical way on the basis of a complete 'management buy-out' and subsequent 'reorganization' of the system. All other countries will necessarily be required to make the transition in a more incremental, step by step way. It remains to be seen which societies, in the end, are or will feel themselves better off. But it is certainly true that, with massive help from elsewhere in the world, the starting point for Central and Eastern European countries will be to rebuild themselves with what they have.

Some will find this proposition difficult to accept. The primary task of an evolutionary-orientated approach to administrative reform is to provide a solid assessment of the actual existing situation, its deficiencies and its growth or

© Basil Blackwell Ltd. 1993.

154   THEO TOONEN

development potential. The development in the former socialist countries is, however, primarily defined in terms of a process of getting away from the previous situation instead of arriving at a desired state of affairs. The label 'post'-socialist, as such, indicates a preoccupation with what has been, without a perception of what should or will be. The future is left open.

For all three countries under observation here, a tendency is reported towards a degree of 'over-transformation' in terms of decentralization and massive streams of newly enacted legislation; distrust of the old regime and the rejection of both the 'old' central planning system and the former *cadres*, whatever their precise role, are identified with it. The people have a better idea of where they are coming from than where they are going to. Sometimes 'administrative reform' has become a goal in itself. Few people within the system – so far, but times may quickly be changing—will take the risk of 'defending' the previous situation, or show an interest that might be perceived as being associated with the Communist *ancient régime*.

The positive aspects of what was or is might, under the prevailing conditions, easily remain unarticulated. For the outsider looking at the situation, it is still very difficult to assess the precise nature and accuracy of the criticism and cynicism abundantly available with regard to both the past situation as well as the ongoing reform processes. The historically distinct character of the ongoing developments might imply that analysts have to concentrate on the innate characteristics of a transformation process which, from established Western theoretical perspectives – and their former 'Eastern' antipodes, are 'unknown'. These observations might easily be considered to be 'too romantic', 'too optimistic' or 'naive' for a strongly built and 'modern' public administration. As with developing non-western countries, however, one might envisage tendencies towards self-governance and self-administration of parts of the society outside the domains which we – i.e. 'western' analysts – would normally identify and recognize as government and administration 'proper'.

The ongoing reform processes can be studied from different administrative angles (cf. Toonen 1983; Kiser and Ostrom, 1982; Hood 1991). The economic orientation of both the reform efforts and the analysis stresses the need for building an efficient and responsive administrative system. With respect to the Polish case it is observed that the ultimate result of public administration reform is to achieve a pro-citizen mentality amongst the officials and a change for the better in society's attitude towards the administration. An interest in a more effective, responsive and responsible administration is the stated purpose of many western recommendations.

As time and developments progress, however, attention has shifted to complement a mere concern for economy and responsiveness with a concern for cooperation and rectitude in the public sector. Administrative scandals in Czechoslovakia as well as a growing critique of the Polish government have contributed to the awareness that the legitimation and acceptance of administrative systems rely not only on their effectiveness and efficiency in reaching goals,

© Basil Blackwell Ltd. 1993.

but also on the way in which goals are being reached and tasks are being accomplished. The achievement of a degree of joint decision making, fairness, reciprocity in public obligations and a proper discharge of duties in substantive and procedural terms, among the parties involved, are becoming increasingly important administrative concerns in the various reform processes.

The third angle which causes observers to worry and merits attention in an administrative analysis, is the robustness and sustainability of the reforms set in motion. Not enough attention is paid to the need to build administrative capacity to implement and follow through political and legislative initiatives. People are becoming frustrated by undelivered promises and are losing their faith in the process and the credibility of the operation in the longer term. Almost all observers, most explicit in Poland and Czechoslovakia, express their anxiety about the danger of stagnation of the reform process and a resultant fundamental political instability. There is a clear concern about the 'constitution' of the reform processes, not only in terms of its legal structure and containment, but more importantly in terms of the basic trust and feelings of reliability among the general population.

The different angles represent more or less distinct administrative value systems (Hood 1991). They also seem to refer to different worlds of action and administrative reform (Kiser and Ostrom 1982). The values of responsiveness, goal-orientation and effectiveness refer to the 'world of operational choice' and the management of day-to-day actions and decisions, within a given framework of rules and institutions. Issues of accountability, reciprocity, public obligation and procedural legitimation refer to the 'world of collective choice' and situations of joint decision making, policy formulation and implementation. The sustainability of the reforms, the question of reliability, trustworthiness and resilience of newly erected institutions refer to a concern about the soundness of the 'constitution' of the reform processes.

1 Multi-dimensional and multi-level problems

Every sound administrative system will have to satisfy the three different value complexes at more or less the same time. The different value systems and underlying questions apply not only to stable liberal democratic market economies, but to transitionary systems as well, as the various reports clearly indicate. The only difference is that in stable situations and institutionally well developed and established administrative systems the different functions and corresponding core values are usually served by more or less separate institutions and procedures. They are conventionally studied and evaluated accordingly by different theories and disciplines. To simplify: constitutional courts deal with constitutional issues, policy makers and legislatures deal with questions of collective decision making, and public managers, executives and civil servants deal with operational issues. Each type of issue requires more or less its own consideration, logic and approach. Constitutional questions are different and are therefore separated from operational management decisions.

© Basil Blackwell Ltd. 1993.

156   THEO TOONEN

The analytics of the ongoing transition process in Central and Eastern Europe are much more complicated than in more stable environments. The complexity and turbulence of the reforms are caused partly by the fact that, with respect to any concrete decision or development, almost all dimensions have to be considered at the same time. This often causes the different value systems to be in conflict and to overload any specific situation with analytically rather different considerations. Decisions on privatization, for example, serve in the Central and Eastern European countries different value systems at the same time. Privatization is defended for reasons of efficiency and economy. But privatization is also aimed at bringing about 'constitutional' changes in, for example, the economic or property rights structure. In the case of 're-privatization' or the restitution of private property to former owners, the 'constitutional' and 'operational' considerations are further complicated by questions of equity, fairness and rectitude.

On the other hand, efficient privatization at the operational level presupposes the existence of a market-like infrastructure (property rights, banking systems, public enforcement agencies, etc.) at the 'constitutional' level. The difference in meaning of privatization within the various perspectives, implies that western knowledge and expertise in the area are often not easily transferable. Where Western efforts to 'privatize' in say Britain are usually aimed at increasing the efficiency of the economy, privatization efforts in Central and Eastern Europe are largely aimed at constructing a market system. This strongly limits the lessons that British 'privatization' may hold for Central European countries. Other examples come easily to mind: many Western business firms and companies are interested in 'privatizing' firms or factories in one of the post-socialist countries precisely because these occupy a monopoly position. The 'hospitable' part of the business environment in the post-socialist countries, is 'constitutionally' just the opposite of what the privatization philosophy entails.

The confusion of the various dimensions and levels of analysis is also reflected in proposals to privatize public transport 'because the government can make no profit out of it'. Instrumental operational considerations often dominate constitutional questions. Constitutions, legal procedures and courts, on the other hand, are given a role in the operational management of the political process. This might be understandable in the short run, but the constitutional rule of written constitutions and independent courts might easily be evaded, if not threatened, when they are systematically drawn into solving policy and operational issues. Developments with respect to the role of the Revisional Chamber in the case of Hungary provide a case in point.

The reason that courts become easily involved in the world of operational action and collective choice has to do with their well-developed organizational and operational skills and capabilities. However, operational capacities within the system are sometimes easily overlooked because of veiling 'constitutional' contexts. The problem, for example, is not that people in the post-socialist countries do not know how to compete or how to deal with 'competitive and market-like situations'. They have always been competing: not for the favour

© Basil Blackwell Ltd. 1993.

of clients or citizens, but for suppliers of goods and services, their party bosses, government officials, etc. A desired capacity comes often in a different guise. Instead of writing off whole 'lost generations' in the respective countries, one may try to find ways to organize the institutional infrastructure and the relevant policy incentives away from hierarchy towards a responsiveness by which people can and will learn to apply their already existing competitive skills in the new (constitutional and policy) setting.

2 Framing and reframing

Whether we like it or not, the existing situation in Central and Eastern European countries requires an analytical capacity in which, in principle, it is possible to 'think the unthinkable' and, potentially, recognize 'the efficiency of inefficient approaches'. We need a sufficiently broad theoretical view and analytical framework. The topical issue in western public administration and organization and management sciences, i.e. to be able to (theoretically) frame and reframe the administrative problem at hand from various perspectives, is particularly relevant in the present case. 'Foreign models' and experiences are valuable and inspiring for the various countries, but cannot be applied directly and without modifications.

In Taras's opinion ' . . . it is better to fight against the causes of existing evil, than to search for a hypothetical good'. Indeed, we do not need a model to guide us in 'the search for a hypothetical good', but – apart from empirical evidence – an analytical and theoretical framework that allows us adequately to conceptualize the various dimensions of the complicated multi-level and multi-dimensional reform process at hand. The starting point of such a framework has to be that the market economy is only 'free' within a public and legal set of enforceable rights and constraints (Riker and Weimer 1992). Privatization presupposes a very elaborate and collectively maintained and publicly enforced 'economic constitution'. The success of introducing the mixed-market economy critically hinges upon the development of a reliable public infrastructure in terms of legal systems, regulatory agencies to safeguard competition, promotional agencies for economic and regional development and for scientific and technological development, as well as the exploration of potential markets for export and of the provision of some kind of basic welfare administration.

III ADMINISTRATIVE REFORM IN CENTRAL AND EASTERN EUROPE: COMPARATIVE OBSERVATIONS

From a comparative point of view, there is at least one point that cannot but surprise any Western European administrative observer when he looks behind the curtains of the formerly 'centrally planned' administrative systems of Central and Eastern Europe. Employment rates in public administration and particularly the segment identified as 'the civil service' are extremely difficult to compare. But the reported figures of, for example, Poland, with a total of 158,000 civil servants of which 53,000 are employed at national level and out of which about

© Basil Blackwell Ltd. 1993.

158   THEO TOONEN

10,000 work for the central ministries, are somewhat surprising for an outside observer. Rice (1992, p. 121) equally observes that compared to western standards, the central government civil services in Eastern Europe are surprisingly small, with staffing levels in government ministries ranging from 8,000 in Hungary, to 25,000 in Romania.

Lack of accurately defined comparative data means that it is hard to draw firm conclusions. Many services are conducted outside the 'proper' civil service. A surprise reaction is unavoidable, however, if one recollects that a relatively small country like the Netherlands has over 150,000 national civil servants without ever having had the ambition to be a centrally planned economy. Indeed it gives rise to the counter-intuitive thought that ' . . . rather than looking for ways to streamline these core civil services, the countries of Eastern Europe may need to consider strategies to expand and improve them (Rice 1992, p. 121).'

Experiences like these underline the fact that it would be difficult but very necessary and profitable to probe into the comparative facts and figures and the 'nuts and bolts' of comparative administrative systems and civil service reforms in Eastern European countries. Obviously the required retrenchment policies have to mean something else than the 'downsizing' of the civil service which is the main definition of reducing government intervention in western countries. If the figures are at all comparable, then, also from a comparative 'western' point of view, the charge of excessive outlays on public administration in terms of money and personnel are part of a misconception. In some cases public administration will have to grow instead of diminish.

It also means that one has to rethink the 'off hand' initial prescription that administrative modernization in Eastern Europe would imply the mere decentralization of administrative systems and the handing over of power from the central to the local authorities. Looking more closely at the situation in the different countries, one sometimes gets the impression that the real problem was that not only were there no local authorities, but, even worse, initially there was hardly any effective central power to hand over to them.

In one of the initial comparative assessments of administrative developments in Central and Eastern Europe, Hesse presents a somewhat gloomy overall analysis. The shared characteristic of the transformation process of these administrative systems is the development from a one-party rule to pluralist, multi-party systems with democratically elected and accountable governments; the principle of 'democratic centralism' is being abandoned in favour of the deconcentration and decentralization of political power under the rule of law; and it is universally accepted that administrative effectiveness, efficiency and flexibility need to be increased. According to Hesse (1991, p. 199)

> . . . the task of modernizing public administration goes much beyond . . . responsibilities in the majority of the industrialized countries of the Western hemisphere. The challenge with which public administration is faced is to redefine its role in society, or, more concretely, its relations with politics, the economy and the civil community . . . Administrative restructuring and reorganization must be pursued with the same vigour as political and economic reforms, and they require a similarly sustained effort.

© Basil Blackwell Ltd. 1993.

The situation varies, however, from country to country. There are no standard solutions.

1 Czechoslovakia

Czechoslovakia witnessed the quickest 'velvet revolution' of all countries, but in a way the two Republics are now lagging behind in modernizing their state structures. Despite the fact that much energy has been absorbed by trying to concentrate on resolving fundamental constitutional problems, one should not overlook another important explanation. The Communist regime in Czechoslovakia was amongst the most strict and conservative, particularly since it suppressed the '68 liberalization movement. They also stayed in power to the very last minute, until at the end of 1989, the regime gave way to a surprisingly swift take over.

Soon after the take over, several ministries were abolished in an effort to reduce central state control over the economy, but perhaps also to take away power from the federal government. New institutions were created for revitalizing the economy. Over the following year the entire federal state system has come under consideration. Federalization, or rather efforts in favour of its realization, had already led to a transfer of powers and responsibilities from the federal level to the Republics. Local government had already ceased to be part of the state administration. Discussions and ongoing constitutional and administrative reforms became burdened if not entirely stalled by the long-standing historical distinctions among Czechs and Slovaks and inherent centripetal tendencies.

The breaking up of Czechoslovakia may be understood as a classic case of the struggle between autonomy and influence or co-determination of the component parts of the state, in this case the Czech and the Slovak people. The striving for 'autonomy' by the Czech and particularly the Slovak Republic goes back a long time in history and has more often been dealt with, but not resolved, under the Communist regime by mere repression. The division of the territory by the Czechs and the Slovaks originates in the 1970s and the changes of November 1989 merely serve to expose them. More than a dissatisfaction with the old regime, the striving for autonomy, particularly by the Slovaks, seems to follow from a distrust of the centre over joint decision making; the central authority of the Federation has long been seen not as a centre of decision making but as being dominated by one of the two component parts, the Czechs. In addition, the Slovaks were more adversely affected, economically speaking, by the administrative transition. Their economy had faired relatively well under the Communist regime, being the regional centre of heavy steal (arms) industry.

The continued striving for 'autonomy' by both parties was caused less by a dislike of the *ancient regime*, than by the fact that the federal structures were invariably *not* perceived by at least one of the participants (the Slovaks), as just or fair with mutual administrative arrangements for joint decision making. This rift could be exploited by conservative forces aiming at strengthening their regionalized power bases.

The outside world might have tried to prevent the developments by giving

© Basil Blackwell Ltd. 1993.

160   THEO TOONEN

selective and 'velvet' support to those symbols, institutions, projects and persons representing the remaining world of collective choice. Perhaps President Havel might have been more effective in building joint decision-making structures, if at the operational level he had something more to offer than a relatively widespread trust in his personality and charisma.

The striving for 'autonomy', i.e. the separation of the Czech and Slovak Republics, might actually stabilize the situation and need not result in a total stagnation and conflict of the reform processes in the two Republics. Experiences in Spain and Belgium come to mind, where the granting of autonomy has stabilized the 'constitutional' situation, thus opening avenues for pragmatic joint policy making in the operational world of action, thus gradually contributing to efforts to talk from 'community to community' and to try to develop different and mutually acceptable forms of co-operation.

The process of (con)federalization, and eventually the breaking up of the Federation in January 1993, has complicated administrative reform efforts primarily because it absorbed most of the political energy. With all the attention concentrated on various constitutional issues at the federal and state level, the two Republics now both face the need to build their structures for joint decision making and effective operational management within their newly established states. Particular attention has to be paid to developing integrative institutional arrangements at the intermediary levels between the national and local levels of the two Republics. Operational administrative capacity to deal with the implementation of a stream of legislation seems required, with a view to enforcing agreed legislation, but also towards injecting realistic and feasibility considerations into an otherwise somewhat inflationary legislative process.

2 Poland

In Poland, the most notable developments are perhaps the (re)establishment of a system of democratic local government and the seemingly stagnating reform processes, due to institutionalized (should one say bureau-political?) rivalries and conflicts among the major institutional and political actors that comprise the national government. Both the functional and the territorial institutional differentiation entails a sharp break with the previous system of uniform, hierarchial and highly centralized state administration. This is true, despite the fact that, for example, centrally appointed governors of the (regional) *voivodships* still perform substantial supervisory functions.

At the national level, crumbling identification within the ranks of Solidarity has not been very favourable for designing and implementing a comprehensive plan for civil service reorganization. Nor has it been replaced by other integrative forces, although sometimes informal networks of civil servants are thought to be able to take over that role and act as an integrative force in a rather fragmented governmental system. It is questionable whether a strong presidency will be able to overcome the problems. From the outside, it sometimes seems as though the main problem is not so much the highly plural political game which is being played, but the lack of appropriate rules for the game of pluralistic

© Basil Blackwell Ltd. 1993.

politics. The game has to be played with inadequate constitutional, political and cultural rules for the game of consociational politics and joint decision making which is based upon accommodation and mutual adjustment.

In Poland it is equally observed that the conflict between 'autonomy' and 'co-determination' among rival political factions is resulting in stagnating reforms. Some maintain that one might even have to await the return of political stability in order to be able to make some progress. The ongoing difficulties do not start from scratch either, and need to be understood in the light of the reforms of the years of Communist rule. The difference with Czechoslovakia, in terms of our comparative framework, is that the difficulties originate at another level or institutional world of action. The inertia, paralysis, incompetence, bureaucratism, arrogance and corruption, as observed by country specialists, seem to originate less in the world of constitutional action and more in the world of collective choice. Although the problems may spill over into a constitutional crisis in terms of sustainability, trust and the break down of the system, the observed problems at the operational level of government seem to be particularly caused by problems at the level of joint decision making. It is noticeable that the once-held fundamental principles of legality, justice, and equality of opportunity are more and more questioned. Letowski therefore prescribes a basic code of administrative conduct, rules of a moral nature such as that the agency does not lie, does not prevaricate, keeps its promises, behaves honestly and decently. The values of the world of collective choice and joint decision making deserve attention owing to the lack of effective institutional arrangements to that end.

The problems of the actual legislative process, and the civil service or local government reorganization and decentralization exemplify the problems of joint decision making surrounding contemporary Polish administration. Within the institutionally and politically fragmented system the historical development has led to a situation in which the administrative hierarchy is missing and – more importantly – one in which little or no constitutional provision for conflict resolution and will formation has yet been developed. The great speed of legislation, the problem of the binding nature of 'ministerial law', the use of the legally wrong 'tools' for dealing with citizen affairs (instructions instead of statutes), the way in which 'emergency powers' are being demanded and the administrative battles between government, ministries, Parliament and President are all serious threats to the future development of the system.

At the same time the problems all sound familiar. The system of joint decision making in Poland displays in an extreme and enlarged form all the problems of ministerial collegial government which can also be found elsewhere. The Council of Ministers is obviously too weak to act as an integrating force, and the same is true for the President and Parliament which have not been able to tip the balance to either's advantage. Where a collegial ministerial and cabinet system already creates serious problems of interdepartmental co-ordination, this is *a fortiori* true for Polish government, where the informal culture and routines of consociational and consensual politics and administration have also had no time

© Basil Blackwell Ltd. 1993.

162 THEO TOONEN

to develop. In such a system the 'hands-on manager' who is politically pressed to undertake activities and 'solve problems' is almost forced to use whatever means are available within the existing situation. The goal starts to justify the means. Achieving results becomes more important than the way in which these results are achieved, which often leads to counter-productive outcomes.

The abuse of legal 'instruments' by goal-directed politicians, keen to score, is, in such a context, a familiar phenomenon in other administrative systems as well. In the operational world of action, the law is a binding act and therefore a vehicle for resolving problems of administrative uncertainty and incoherence. In such a system emergency powers may also provide a temporary solution, but are likely to be used instrumentally for too narrow and *ad hoc* purposes since they do not rest on a broader constitution which ensures the use of the special mandate for a broader purpose, thus eroding the 'instrument'. The desire for interministerial co-ordination or even a ministry for home affairs or the civil service centrally to direct the required reforms is predictable from a comparative perspective. From the experiences of other systems with collegial administration it is to be expected, though, that these will not do the job, since 'co-ordinating' ministers very often acquire the responsibility but seldom the power to co-ordinate their colleagues. The reason is simple: such a provision would erode the principle of collegial ministerial government since one of them would become the superior.

Experience with hierarchical non-consensual reforms – as in for example Thatcher's UK – suggests that a strong commitment from the Prime Minister is necessary to implement radical administrative reforms. The question is, however, whether such a centralized and non-consensual reform would fit in the rather diverse Polish political structure and culture and would generate enough support to last in the long run. In this case, outside instigation of a sustained but incremental and more consensual reform process could take the form of exerting external pressure on some strategic operational goals so as to force opponents into joint action. For a while an outside community like the EC could play the role of 'external coordinator', by generating pressures that indirectly and directly require goal-driven opponents to co-operate and co-ordinate their activities *vis à vis* the common (external) challenge. In the process, one might be able to generate sustainable, reliable and robust 'constitutional' routines, procedures and techniques for mutual problem solving.

Offering a perspective on future economic co-operation with the European Communities in exchange for the requirement to meet European financial and economic standards might provide such pressure and 'external co-ordination'. The promises of the European integration process have more often, and for several EC countries, turned out to be able to integrate and coordinate fragmented national decision making and foster effective informal co-ordination and mutual adjustment at administrative and political levels.

At the subnational level of the Polish administration, decisions are needed concerning proper relationships between various public and private actors. The regional government level has to be defined either as some kind of prefectorial

© Basil Blackwell Ltd. 1993.

system, which is responsible for the co-ordination of national executive functions in the region or as a territorial council which represents certain regional interests and may act as a partner in carrying out state functions as well. A mixed model – on the basis of comparative experience – would not be a bad solution for shaping complex Polish intergovernmental interests. But clarity about the role of regional government seems warranted.

The problems of local government seem to originate particularly in the operational world of action. Legislation has been issued. The problems reported indicate that a degree of politicization and 'confessionalization' of administration is frustrating its operations. From a comparative perspective it might be helpful to point to systems such as the Netherlands or Belgium and Italy where local-state-Catholic Church relationships were a prominent feature of the local government organization. Given the Catholic principle of 'subsidiarity', local authority in these systems usually means more than simply 'local government'. In the Catholic administrative doctrine a network of non-profit 'privatized' subsidiary organs may play an important role in carrying out local state functions. In that case a different concept of 'local *governance*' instead of 'local government' is called for. It has not prevented the development of strong local administrative systems in countries facing similar social features.

The politicization and party-political appointments in the local administration, again, exemplify a lack of trust in joint decision-making institutions and will not easily evaporate. Rather than criticizing the practice, one might consider the creation of institutionalized opportunities for political appointments in the higher ranks of the local administration while basing the award of these positions strictly on the grounds of merit.

3 Hungary

The most stable progress, so far, seems to have been made in Hungary, which has the longest history of market-orientated reform experiences. The legal foundations for a pluralist liberal democracy seem to have been laid. The most basic and also controversial change in Hungarian public administration concerns not so much the internal national government organization, but its relationship with the other levels of government. In 1990, the legal conditions for far-reaching regional and local autonomy and self-government were created as a reaction to the democratic centralism of Communist rule. Local and regional administration have been put under the control of elected councils. As elsewhere, the durability of reform of economy and public administration is threatened most by a stagnating economic development.

In Hungary, the administrative modernization and adaptation to a liberal market economy seem to be relatively well under way. The problems which are reported may be identified in terms of the 'operational world of action': the goal-directedness, the economy and the frugality of the system. A flood of legislation is being observed, to the extent that one may wonder about its effectiveness, suitability and enforcement. This is true, despite the fact that an equally abundant number of deconcentrated state services for supervising the implementation of national legislation has emerged in the region.

© Basil Blackwell Ltd. 1993.

The relative success of developments so far seems to be due to the fact that the Hungarians entered the modernization process at the end of the 1980s 'with their feet down running'. Again the roots of current developments are to be found in the past under the Communist regime. The 'Hungarian secret' seems to consist of three pre-existing conditions. First, already in the 1960s and 1970s, Hungarian government implemented a local government reform characterized by scale-enlargement and decentralization. A relatively strong local government system and the determined application of it is an important feature of the ongoing reform and modernization process. Secondly, even under the central planning of the *ancient regime*, Hungary used to be the regime most liberated from central planning, including as many liberal-economic elements as was politically possible. The Leninist-state and economic system was liberated to the utmost degree. Finally, Balázs observes that, just prior to the transformation, a new generation of bureaucratic 'mandarins' – technically well skilled and politically with a low profile – had risen to a position just below the top. When the established ministries were politically beheaded they were ready and able to take over, thus limiting the human resource problems which faced so many other administrative systems when faced with changes of regime. Thus a situation emerged, which is quite the opposite of Czechoslovakia, where leadership had to be brought in from the outside and was confronted with an administrative system which had not been reformed at all and needed to be fully 'reorganized'.

The 're-emergence of history' gives rise to all kinds of differential institutional logics and developments. It is this continuity, not the quick shift ('big bang') which has brought about what seems to be the relatively most stable ongoing reform process in the direction of a liberal market economy. The main problems in Hungary are being created by the decline of economic resources due to the economic stagnation following the transformations which revealed the gross inefficiencies – both economically, as well as in terms of human and environmental resources – of the previously 'centrally planned' economies. The trust of citizens in the transformation has been undermined by the fact that the reforms have not resulted in an immediate increase in welfare, but rather the contrary.

Also in other areas the arrangements for joint decision making and collective action among different administrative units are under pressure. Intergovernmental relations now seem to suffer from an initial tendency to move away and by-pass the county level which under the *ancient regime* performed many disputed intermediary tasks. This has left an institutional vacuum which is still not properly filled. In aspects of local government one may observe the tendency to feel the shortcomings of overstretched concepts of local 'autonomy' and a move back to stressing the need for developing adequate interrelationships among different planes of government.

The most fundamental problem the Hungarian administrative system seems to face, however, is the alienation of citizens and the lack of civic interest in participating in elections and other forms of collective choice procedures.

© Basil Blackwell Ltd. 1993.

Western nations may learn from the historical developments in Central and Eastern Europe that states do not easily lose the diffuse, general trust and confidence – regime legitimacy – of their citizens. Once it is lost, however, the impact is dramatic and it will be difficult to get it back. A regime shift is a necessary, but not sufficient measure. Regaining this trust primarily requires time.

IV ADMINISTRATIVE REFORM IN CENTRAL EUROPE: CONCLUSIONS

What conclusions may one draw from the previous analysis? One may want to take issue with the observation that ' . . . all the same, public administration across these (post-socialist) countries is more notable for similarities than differences both in its shortcomings and the stages of reform' (Rice 1992, p. 117). Administrative reform never starts from scratch. The analysis provided here suggests that there is no watershed or 'big bang' between the Communist and post-Communist era from the viewpoint of the recreation of an effective public administration system. The relative advantage (of Hungary) and dis-advantage (of Czechoslovakia) in terms of the ongoing reform process, are clearly rooted in events, preconditions and decisions sometimes dating far back into the history of Communist rule.

Given the magnitude of the changes and transformations at the end of the last decade, the degree of continuity and influence of the past comes as somewhat of a surprise. The ease with which countries seem to adapt to a capitalist mode of production so far seems to be determined as much by the historical circumstances during the Communist era as the decisions of the post-socialist reformers.

The common challenges which the different countries face entail at least the disentanglement of public administration and the civil service from party bu-reaucracy and membership. Whole sections of the administrative systems, previously responsible for the 'democratic centralism' of the centrally planned and controlled economy, are being eliminated, while, at the same time, new administrative capacities for economic market development have to be created. Planning and monitoring procedures need to be reorientated from the imperial categories of the internal 'central plan' towards external performance and public service delivery. Effective mechanisms for the protection of citizens against arbitrary or unlawful actions by administrators need to be installed.

In coping with these challenges, the systems have to deal with various puzzles. Removing civil servants closely connected with the previous Communist regime (as in Poland and Czechoslovakia) is prone to the accusation of politicizing public administration under a different label. Neither will the ideal of liberal democracy, based on the rule of law, feel comfortable in the company of a requirement that civil servants are not allowed to be members of a given political party, even if this is a Communist party in name.

Perhaps some new talents may be drawn into the civil service. Resources for attracting new people are scarce, not only in terms of pay, but also in terms of

© Basil Blackwell Ltd. 1993.

166   THEO TOONEN

all other kinds of incentives: prestige, image, infrastructure. This is not only because the private sector has so much more financial appeal. Just as important is that, again contrary to what one might have expected under Communist rule, the administration and its employees were treated as a necessary evil which would vanish when the state was transformed into Communist self-government. Quite different from what one might expect from a 'state-oriented system' of government, employees were already in low esteem before the changes, had the least protection by the state and were not respected by the citizens.

One has to find ways to restore pride and self-esteem in relation to working for and within the public sector. The existing rank and file members of the different civil service systems, which have been trained, recruited and socialized under a completely different set of bureaucratic and decision-making premises, will have to go through a time-consuming and difficult process of adaptation to the changing role of public administration in their societies.

In several cases, the danger sometimes seems to become more acute, that economic developments might not give the Central and Eastern European countries quite the time nor the incentives necessary for such infrastructural changes. There is little possibility of 'buying-off' frustrated interests. The redistribution issues which are inherent in any reform process have to be resolved in the present context of declining resources or, at best, in the short run, stabilizing resources. This often turns the reform efforts into a zero-sum or even negative-sum process. The call for strong political leadership to avoid chaos is, internally and externally, potentially dangerous. This is particularly true for the societies under consideration here. They have not yet had the time to develop a basic democratic, self-governing infrastructure. The same applies to a political culture and societal reflexes in which strong but checked and balanced leadership may develop.

The various countries sometimes seem to be half way through the reform, which results in situations in which the parties representing the conservative anti-reform interests may use the already introduced procedures and rules of democratic decision making to protect their interests and strengthen their vested positions. In one country – Hungary – an 'incomplete' constitutional structure seems to create fewer difficulties than in another country – Poland – where the 'flexibility' of the constitutional structure owing to lack of appropriate informal consociational devices contributes to stagnation and deterioration.

The retrenchment of state organization, i.e. denationalization, in favour of market organization has proceeded to a certain degree, but it is now generally considered to have slowed down considerably. Lack of (foreign) capital and investors is a frequently mentioned cause. Also, there is still much variation in the degree of state influence considered necessary or desirable. Furthermore, entrepreneurial skills to run complex, large-scale business organizations are almost completely lacking.

Stagnation of the reform processes and a corresponding destabilization of the

© Basil Blackwell Ltd. 1993.

political and social situation are explicitly expressed concerns particularly in the Polish and Czechoslovakian cases. The initial concern with respect to the developments behind the former 'iron curtain' was about the 'rationalization', 'decentralization', 'administrative modernization' and the 'upgrading' of system and personnel. This followed from an understandable, but in retrospect clear underestimation of the problems at hand. The main contemporary concern is, or rather, should be, that the current developments in the formerly socialist countries primarily ask for the capacity for stable and sustainable administrative development. Almost all country reports refer to, or reflect, a certain fear of social and political destabilization, stagnation of the reform efforts and a risk of escalating into potentially dramatic directions.

Instead of the design of a 'responsive and efficient system of governance and administration', the situation in the respective countries seems primarily to call for the constitution of a reliable, stable and adaptable system of self-governance, joint decision making and the corresponding forms of public management and administration. Some progress has been made and political prerogatives for developing an effective administrative system have been installed. The situation is far from stable, however.

On the basis of their comparative study of politics and society in Western Europe, Lane and Ersson (1991, p. 321) conclude that the degree of political instability is a function of the perceived (im)balance within these societies, which depends on the different social groups and interests in terms of subgroup autonomy on the one hand and the influence on national government on the other: 'Political stability in the long run perspective is related on the one hand to social cleavages and their conflict implications and on the other to the decision making system, in particular to the distribution of influence and autonomy between major groups within a society' (p. 322).

Lane and Ersson also observe that people and organizations in western societies demand both increased institutional and increased individual autonomy and that this demand is related to the perceived distribution of influence within centres for joint decision making. Citizens and organizations demand more autonomy when they experience government as unresponsive, inefficient, unfair or unreliable. When channels for co-determination and joint decision making do not work or are mistrusted, citizens ask for more autonomy.

When citizens feels that their activities in a certain field are no longer 'autonomous' they will try to influence government or other institutions for joint decision making in which they trust. If such an option is not available, this will easily result in a striving for autonomy regardless of the repercussions. Others that adopt a slightly different perspective of joint decision making will easily perceive this as an unproductive 'overtransformation'. This is basically what, in different forms, has been happening in all the countries under consideration here.

In cases where resources decline and the trust in public and other institutions for collective action is low on the basis of past experience, as is the case in

© Basil Blackwell Ltd. 1993.

168   THEO TOONEN

present day Central and Eastern Europe, the situation is unstable indeed. It is predictable that people will strive for individual and institutional autonomy, even if this autonomy is shrinking too. Granting a certain degree of institutional autonomy may contribute to the overall stability of the system. Stability does not require a 'strong centre'. The development of several viable, strong and trusted collective decision making centres with ample opportunity for co-governance by the respective social, political, economic and administrative interests might alleviate the pressure for 'autonomy' which is anxiously identified by the Polish, Hungarian and Czech researchers.

The collective distress and psychological stress of the individual citizens have been reported more than once as important constraints on possible reform measures. It is obviously something that needs to be taken very seriously. Indeed, there is much more to privatization than economics or legal instrumentality. More than to economics, political and administrative structures and processes, attention must be paid to the needs and fears of the citizens in the ongoing reform process. For more than one reason, it worries me, that as a western analyst I cannot easily get to grips with this problem.

REFERENCES

Dente, B. and F. Kjellberg. (eds.) 1988. *The dynamics of institutional change*, Beverly Hills: Sage.
Hesse, J.J. 1991. 'Administrative modernisation in Central and Eastern European countries', *Staatswissenschaft und Staatspraxis* 2, 2, 197–217.
Hesse, J.J. and A. Benz. 1990. *Die Modernisierung der Staatsorganisation*. Baden-Baden: Nomos.
Hood, Ch. 1991. 'Public management for all seasons?, *Public Administration* 69, 1, 319.
Kiser, L.L. and E. Ostrom. 1982. 'Three Worlds of action: a metatheoretical synthesis of institutional approaches', in: W. Ostrom (ed.). *Strategies of political inquiry*, Beverly Hills; Sage.
Lane, J. and S.O. Ersson. 1991. *Politics and society in Western Europe*. London/Beverly Hills.
Rice, M. 1992. 'Public administration in Post-Socialist Eastern Europe', *Public Administration Review* 52, 2, 116–25.
Riker, W.H. and D.L. Weimer. 'The economic and political liberalisation of socialism: the fundamental problem of property rights', *paper for the Social Philosophy and Policy Center, Bowling Green State University, Ohio*, April 1992.
Toonen, Th.A.J. 1983. 'Administrative plurality in a unitary state', *Policy and Politics* 11, 3, 247–71.

© Basil Blackwell Ltd. 1993.

Name Index